W9-BRE-154

Henry McBride Series in Modernism and Modernity

"It's going to take a lot of letters to tell you what a good nourishing galvanizing time I had over to your house."

Wilder and Stein photographed on 15–16 August 1937 by William or Mildred Rogers before he left for Zurich

The Letters of Gertrude Stein and Thornton Wilder

Edited by Edward Burns and Ulla E. Dydo

with William Rice

Yale University Press   New Haven & London

Copyright © 1996 by Yale University.
All rights reserved.
This book may not be reproduced, in whole or
in part, including illustrations, in any form
(beyond that copying permitted by Sections 107
and 108 of the U.S. Copyright Law and except
by reviewers for the public press), without
written permission from the publishers.

Designed by James J. Johnson and set in Electra
Roman type by Keystone Typesetting, Inc.,
Orwigsburg, Pennsylvania. Printed in the
United States of America by Edwards Brothers,
Inc., Ann Arbor, Michigan.

A catalogue record for this book is available
from the British Library.

The paper in this book meets the guidelines for
permanence and durability of the Committee
on Production Guidelines for Book Longevity of
the Council on Library Resources.

10 9 8 7 6 5 4 3 2 1

*Library of Congress Cataloging-in-Publication
Data*

Stein, Gertrude, 1874–1946.
    The letters of Gertrude Stein and
Thornton Wilder / edited by Edward M.
Burns and Ulla E. Dydo, with William Rice.
        p. cm.
    Includes bibliographical references (p.   )
and index.
    ISBN 0-300-06774-7 (cloth : alk. paper)

    1. Stein, Gertrude, 1874–1946—
Correspondence. 2. Women authors,
American—20th century—Correspondence.
3. Wilder, Thornton, 1897–1975—
Correspondence. 4. Dramatists, American—
20th century—Correspondence. I. Wilder,
Thornton, 1897–1975. II. Burns, Edward M.,
1944-   . III. Dydo, Ulla E., 1925–   .
IV. Rice, William, 1931–   V. Title.
PS3537.T323Z4974   1996
818'.5209—dc20
[B]   96-17169
                                                CIP

Contents

Illustrations

Acknowledgments

We gratefully acknowledge the permission of the Estate of Gertrude Stein, Calman A. Levin, Administrator, to publish Stein's letters and to quote from her published and unpublished work; the Estate of Thornton Wilder for permission to publish Wilder's letters and to quote from his published and unpublished work; the late Isabel Wilder for permission to publish her letters to Stein and to quote from Thornton Wilder's letters to his family.

In this edition are present innumerable writers, friends, colleagues, archivists near and far who gave generous help and interest. Their support is acknowledged in the list below. A few people became special enabling friends.

When Edward Burns completed *The Letters of Gertrude Stein and Carl Van Vechten*, a desirable next project became the correspondence of Stein and Wilder. Ulla Dydo, who interviewed Isabel Wilder, the sister of Thornton, for her own study of Stein, began reading her the letters of Stein and Wilder for comment and amplification. Soon her enthusiasm led her to support our proposal and give us unrestricted access to her own papers. Ulla Dydo saw her weekly from the mid-1980s until her death in 1995. To gain background, not available in printed and written sources, she read to her Wilder's notes, journals, and many sets of letters and taped her responses. Their discussions were reviewed by us to ascertain their accuracy. Isabel's comments, always trenchant and astute, inform our work throughout, even when they are not specifically quoted. Interpretations, unless they acknowledge other sources, are our own.

Donald Gallup, retired curator of the Yale Collection of American Literature at the Beinecke Rare Book and Manuscript Library at Yale University, advisor to the estate of Gertrude Stein, and, until the spring of 1995, literary executor of the estate of Thornton Wilder, is a lively presence in this volume. He welcomed our work, was pleased with Isabel Wilder's participation, and offered invaluable help, again and again tapping his own archive to answer questions.

The Wilder family, Amos Wilder, Thornton's brother, his wife, Catharine, his niece and nephew Catharine and A. Tappan Wilder, welcomed our work and gave us access to papers and information, never imposing restrictions.

Joan Chapman, who during World War II, with her mother and her stepfather, Paul Genin, lived near Stein and saw her regularly, gave us information about acquaintances they shared, about local affairs, administrators and friends still resident in Belley and Culoz, confirming dates and incidents documented in her own papers. Paul Genin, generous in his recollections of Stein, shared documents and reminiscences.

Robert A. Wilson, indefatigable bibliographer of Gertrude Stein, was a friendly and reliable source of information throughout our work. His skillfully revised edition, published in 1994, of his original bibliography of 1974 allowed us to verify details that might have otherwise gone unchecked.

Bruce Kellner, supportive colleague always ready with enthusiasm to answer questions, gave us access to his extensive records of Carl Van Vechten's photographs, letters, and friends.

Bill Rice has been a part of this project from the beginning. His contribution, not limited to the American lecture tour, included work on the transcriptions and research on personal, textual, and theatrical history. The annotations were drafted by us and coedited with him. Together, the three of us then put each letter and its notes through a further reading aloud and revision until we were satisfied that the pieces of the mosaic fitted together. Without this laborious triple process which evolved out of discussions and disagreements, this edition could not have been completed.

Throughout years of work, we have been generously assisted by Dr. Patricia Willis, curator of the Collection of American Literature, and the staff of the Beinecke Library including especially Stephen Jones, Lori Misura, Alfred Mueller, and Tim Young.

We acknowledge the following individuals and institutions for permission to quote material in their copyright or over which they have physical ownership:

The Bancroft Library, University of California, Berkeley, for Stein's letter to Wilder of 19 March 1935 (BANC MSS 72/191 No. 109).

The Poetry/Rare Books Collection, University Libraries, State University of New York at Buffalo, for Stein's letter to Charles D. Abbott, and the letters of Abbott and Mary Bernard to Stein.

Random House Papers, Rare Book and Manuscript Library, Columbia University.

Columbia University Press for excerpts from *The Letters of Gertrude Stein and Carl Van Vechten: 1913–1946*, ed. by Edward Burns ©1986.

The Harvard Theatre Collection, The Houghton Library, Harvard University.

The Houghton Library, Harvard University, for Stein's letter of December 1935 to Alexander Woollcott (BMS Am 1449 [1564]).

Garson Kanin and Marian Seldes for the letters of Ruth Gordon.

Bruce Kellner for letters of Prentiss Taylor and Alice Toklas.

Suzanne E. Knapp for letters of Alfred Lunt and Lynn Fontanne.

Library of Congress, Manuscript Division: The Benjamin W. Huebsch Papers and The Archibald MacLeish Papers.

Roderick S. Quiroz, Estate of Prentiss Taylor.

Donald R. Seawell, Executor of the Estate of Tallulah Bankhead.

The Harry Ransom Humanities Research Center, The University of Texas at Austin.

The University of Chicago Library.

The State Historical Society of Wisconsin for Wilder's letters to Alfred Lunt and Lynn Fontanne.

The Yale Collection of American Literature, Beinecke Rare Book and Manuscript Library, Yale University, for the letters of Gertrude Stein, Alice Toklas, Thornton Wilder, and other correspondents and texts cited in the text as YCAL.

The Yale University Press for excerpts from "Introduction" by Daniel-Henry Kahnweiler to Gertrude Stein's *Painted Lace And Other Pieces [1914–1957]* ©1955; and excerpts from *The Journals of Thornton Wilder: 1939–1961*, ed. by Donald Gallup ©1985.

We acknowledge the assistance of Galit Adani; Charles Andrews, Rush Learning Center, Birmingham-Southern College, Birmingham, Alabama; Jean Ashton, Director, Rare Book and Manuscript Library, Columbia University; Annette Axtmann; Melinda Barlow; John Barnett; Bibliothèque Nationale, Paris; Nora Beeson; Robert Bertholf, Curator, Poetry/Rare Books Collection, State University of New York at Buffalo; Birmingham Public Library, Southern History Department, Birmingham, Alabama; Alice L. Birney, American Literature Manuscript Historian, Library of Congress, Manuscript Division; Bill Brewington, Sherman Grinberg Film Libraries, Inc., Hollywood, California; Nancy L. Boothe, Director, Woodson Research Center, The Fondren Library, Rice University, Houston, Texas; Carol Cambell, Library Manager, *The Daily Oklahoman* and *The Sunday Oklahoman*, Oklahoma City, Oklahoma; Clark Center, Technical Archivist, W. S. Hoole Special Collections Library, University of Alabama at Tuscaloosa; François Chapon, Bibliothèque littéraire Jacques Doucet, Paris; Eric Concklin; Margaret Coope, President, The Woman's City Club of San Francisco; Anita Corfman; Olivier Corpet, Institut Mémoires de l'Edition Contemporaine, Paris; The Cosmopolitan Club, New York, archive committee: Miss Coxe, Mrs. Bernice L. Dickes, and Miss Evans; Judith Cousins, Research Curator, The Museum of Modern Art, New York; Sara D. Davis, Chairwoman, Department of English, University of Alabama at Tuscaloosa; Donald L. DeWitt, Curator, University Libraries, Western History Collections, University of Oklahoma at Norman; Gladys Ely; Vincent Faÿ; Charlotte Ford, Reference and Documents Librarian, Rush Learning Center, Birmingham-Southern College, Birmingham, Alabama; Robert Bartlett Haas; John Haggerty, Chairman, Department of English, University of Alabama at Birmingham; Bonnie Hartwick, Bancroft Library, University of California at Berkeley; James Hatch, Hatch Billops Collection, New York; Alumni Office, Hockaday School, Dallas, Texas; Archives Office, Indiana University at Bloomington; Eleanor M. Garvey, Acting Curator, Harvard Theatre Collection, The Houghton Library; Peter Gay; Kevin Joyce; Leon Katz; Jane Kramer; François Lachenal; Thomas McGonigle; Bill McPheron, Curator, English and American Literature, Stanford University Library; Joseph Margolis; Michael Molnar, Curator, The Freud Museum, London, England; Leslie A. Morris, Curator of Manuscripts, The Houghton Library, Harvard University; Eric L. Mundell, Head, Reference Services, Indiana Historical Society, Indianapolis, Indiana; Oklahoma Historical Society, Oklahoma City, Oklahoma; Oklahoma Publishing Company Library, Oklahoma City, Oklahoma; Courtney Page, Howard-Tilton Memorial Library, Tulane University, New Orleans, Louisiana; Lisa Palmer; Robert O. Paxton; Musée Picasso, Paris; the late Margaret Potter; Kieran Quinlan, English Department, University of Alabama at Birmingham; Archives Office, Rice University, Houston, Texas; William Roberts, Archivist, The Bancroft Library, University of California at Berkeley; Jaime Rodriguez, Rare Books and Manuscripts, Herbert Lehman International Affairs Collection, Columbia University; Mark Scroggins, Archivist, Dulaney-Browne Library, Oklahoma City University, Oklahoma City, Oklahoma; Tina Sixt, Department of Special Collections Intern, University Research Library, University of California at Los Angeles; the late Samuel Steward; Bernard Taverier; Archives Office, Texas South University, Houston, Texas; Office of Alumni Affairs and the Curator of Records, Tulane University, New Orleans, Louisiana; Archives Office, University of Montevallo, Montevallo, Alabama; University of Texas at Austin, Harry Ransom Humanities Research Center:

Linda Ashton, Cathy Henderson, Sally Leach, Thomas F. Staley; Philip H. Young, Library Director and Archivist, Krannert Memorial Library, University of Indianapolis; Elizabeth C. Wells, Special Collections Librarian, Samford University Library, Birmingham, Alabama; Patricia White, Archives Specialist, Department of Special Collections, Stanford University Library; William Paterson College of New Jersey: Assigned Research Time Committee, Career Development Committee, English Department, Sarah Byrd Askew Library Inter-Library Loan service; Brenda Wineapple; Martha E. Wright, Reference Librarian, Indiana State Library, Indianapolis, Indiana; Deborah Wythe, Archivist, The Brooklyn Museum, Brooklyn, New York.

Introduction

Gertrude Stein, aged sixty, and Thornton Wilder, thirty-seven, met for the first time in Chicago on 25 November 1934, when Stein delivered her lecture "What Is English Literature." She had returned to Chicago to lecture after a first flying visit to attend the opening performance on 7 November of the Chicago production of *Four Saints In Three Acts*, the opera she had written with Virgil Thomson. The opera was a society event with press coverage and publicity from which Chicago and she both benefited. Because Wilder had an early speaking engagement in Minneapolis the following morning, he did not attend the performance or the party that followed although he noted "Gertrude Stein opera" in his date book.

Stein was in America, after thirty years away in Paris, for a nationwide lecture tour following the success of *The Autobiography Of Alice B. Toklas*. Of the Chicago lecture Wilder wrote to Mabel Dodge Luhan, a friend who had in early years also been a friend of Stein, that it was the best he had ever heard. He was invited to most of the functions honoring Stein, for he was accepted in polite society, including that of Stein's hosts, as a social asset—Pulitzer Prize novelist, admired university lecturer, well-read guest always abreast of cultural and stage events at home and abroad.

Wilder was impressed by Stein and she liked him, as Alice Toklas, who watched over her, reported to Carl Van Vechten, Stein's friend and supporter since 1913, a few days after the lecture. Toklas must have understood instantly that he offered interest and devotion without demands and might be helpful without becoming burdensome. Stein was to recall their meeting in *Every-*

body's Autobiography: "We might have known him long ago" (201). Though they quickly became friends, Wilder and Stein did not know one another's work well before they met. Stein must have known his name but may not have read any book of Wilder. He knew little of her work until the American tour made her a public figure. By the time they met, he had read the *Autobiography* and had struggled unsuccessfully with the complete version of *The Making Of Americans*. He did not know the range of her early work and was not committed to modernism though he had read Proust and Joyce and since the midtwenties had known Hemingway and Fitzgerald, who regarded Stein as a master and admired Wilder. On trips to Europe, he had not seen her art collection, perhaps because he was not partial to Paris, perhaps because he had no deep sense of visual art. Once they were friends, however, he came close to Stein's later work on audience and identity, which struck a chord in his experience. In November 1934, Wilder was reading proofs for his new novel, *Heaven's My Destination*, the product of his own lecture tours following upon his own success, when he "crisscrossed America like a traveling textbook salesman," addressing audiences on literature and culture. He had already met what Stein faced now: publicity as part of fame. Within days of her lecture, President Robert Maynard Hutchins of the University of Chicago, probably prodded by Wilder, invited her to return in March for a special course with students selected for participation by Wilder.

Seven years earlier, in 1927, Thornton Wilder, at thirty, had won the Pulitzer Prize for his second novel, *The Bridge of San Luis Rey*. It had left him facing fame and fans in a bewilderment of inexperience. Like Stein's *Autobiography*, his book had made money and led to a demand for lectures. He had not foreseen that fame would make demands on his time. In order to free time for writing, he resigned from his teaching post at the Lawrenceville School in New Jersey and, in the belief that lecturing was less demanding than teaching, signed a five-year contract with the Lee Keedick Lecture Bureau for appearances throughout the United States. But lectures turned out to be strenuous work, with constant travel, social obligations, and no gain in time. However, the prize, continuing sales of *The Bridge*, teaching, and lecturing supported his family, a responsibility that Stein never faced. With the decline of his father from 1929 until his death in 1936 this obligation to the family grew more and more onerous. When, in *Everybody's Autobiography*, Stein said that fathers were depressing, she was thinking not only of her own father but also of Wilder's.

Wilder went to Chicago in April 1930 because Robert Maynard Hutchins, an Oberlin and Yale classmate and friend appointed in 1929 as president of the University of Chicago, had asked that he join him. He trusted him as advisor, and he saw in the brilliant prizewinner an asset for the university, which he was setting on a new course toward liberal education and learning from Great Books. He offered him a special lectureship, offensive to the professoriat because it implied that a writer could teach as well as a professor and that university credentials were less important than talent. In flight from publicity and lecturing, Wilder accepted the university's offer of economic stability, prestige, and lively students. Respected and popular as an instructor, he became one of the first in an American university to teach creative writing.

Unlike Wilder, who presented himself as writer, teacher, and lecturer, Stein thought of herself only as a writer. The closest she came to teaching was in the lectures and the Narration course at Chicago. How she impressed students can be heard in a letter of 4 March 1936 from the painter Gertrude Abercrombie, a member of the class, who spoke of having tried "to use my head as you said and to quit doing sloppy thinking, and so of course my drawing isn't so sloppy." Stein team-taught the Narration course with the young but experienced Wilder, her colleague, her stage manager—and her eager student.

By coincidence, then, Stein and Wilder, both best-selling authors, were in Chicago at the same time. Publicized by an autobiography and an opera, Stein was already a curiosity that many found more interesting for her personality than for her ideas. In coming to America she hoped to set the record straight about her work and herself. Unlike the young Wilder, who lectured about his work and a variety of literary and cultural topics for the general public, Stein spoke solely about her own work and her ideas. She wanted to make money because earning money from writing gave her "the feeling of being a real author," as she wrote to Bennett Cerf in October 1937. In thirty years of writing, she had earned only small sums from royalties while others made fortunes. By the 1930s, advancing age, the Depression, the country house, and her own Plain Edition drained her carefully husbanded income from investments and made the need to earn money more and more urgent.

A generation apart in age, dissimilar in literary interests, distant in background, Stein and Wilder met as the publicity sweeping over her in Chicago returned him to his own rise to fame. Yet they accommodated the experience in radically different ways. Wilder saw fame as a by-product of his book but unrelated to his art and tried, not very successfully, to disregard fame and continue writing in what privacy he could find. Stein, on the other hand, having quickly seen how what she called audience affected the writer's mind and art, proceeded to acknowledge it by studying it. Wilder was struck by her capacity to see, with clarity never blurred by vanity, the effects of audience and fame. The similarities of their situations and the differences in their responses must be understood if their twelve years of interaction in friendship, in work, and in the correspondence printed in this volume are to be understood.

Stein had always wanted to be lionized but she did not succeed until late, with a popular book in a style quite unlike what she was known for. Her long-time friend Henry McBride, the art critic, who knew how she craved fame, thought it was not good for geniuses. On 27 October 1933, he wrote her dryly that the *Autobiography* "was doomed to be a success" and would force him to give her up to an admiring audience. Wilder, on the other hand, had accomplished at thirty what she did at sixty; at thirty, Stein had just written her first, auto-biographical book, the novel *Q.E.D.*, not even published in her lifetime. She never again wrote an intimate confessional work but made the *Autobiography* a public book, deceptively impersonal.

She knew that the *Autobiography* was a success as soon as she finished it in November 1932. But even before publication she was made aware of the price of success when she experienced severe writer's block and lost her sense of who she was. She produced some occasional tales and a few abortive pieces about the *Autobiography* and problems arising from it, often confused and disjointed. By the summer of 1933, still in distress, she wrote *Blood On The Dining-Room Floor*, an odd murder mystery that appears to have absorbed displaced troubles of her own but to her was not real writing. She even composed a personal account of the writer's block in "And Now." It became a mere short text about the sad aftermath of the *Autobiography*. Its personal impulse, however, pointed the way to *Everybody's Autobiography*, which con-tinued the success story, starting upbeat, with the lecture tour, not downbeat, with the sadness of success.

Stein had always worked with conscious deliberation. She did not wait for the right mood or inspiration to produce words for her but cleared her mind of distracting associations and memory by centering it on the here and now. In a late, unpublished memoir written in 1972, when he finished *The-ophilus North*, Wilder described her meditating in a state of solitude, not loneliness, which allowed her to focus on the world outside rather than the self inside. In this state she could both talk and listen, participate and remain withdrawn. Stein relied on this state for writing, but she did not discuss it, theorize about it, or prescribe it for others. The writer's block cut her off from the world and so from her method of work. She became self-conscious and lost her assurance as an artist. She was unable to start a new major work. When she finally began a new book, in the autumn of 1933, it was a study already planned earlier and even discussed with her agent in the hope of another success. *Four In America* looked at what would have happened if George Washington had become not a general but a novelist, Henry James

not a novelist but a general, Ulysses S. Grant a religious leader, Wilbur Wright
a painter. She was thinking about American character, alternative vocations
for great minds, personality as determinant of greatness. Finished in the early
summer of 1934, when she was already planning the lectures for the tour, it
became an uneven assemblage of brilliant speculation and wavering rumina-
tion, constantly breaking out of the firm fourfold frame she had devised in the
hope of orderly composition, which all her writing habits refused. By October,
the prospect of lecturing once more dramatized her relation to the audience
and her uneasiness about who she was. In Wilder, winning author at thirty
and in 1935 still perplexed by his success, she met a living illustration of the
effect of fame, which allowed her to define its nature.

Wilder rose to stardom against a restrictive puritanical background that constantly denied the importance of the world even as it cultivated social conscience. Both his parents came from the deep moral commitments of American Protestantism. The first four Wilder children—by 1910, like the Steins,
they became five—suffered from the father's stern strictures while developing
deep bonds to their mother, whose devotion to her children compensated for
frustration in marriage. Wilder's grammar school teacher told his mother that
he was a gifted child whose talents she must foster. No one in the family was
ever allowed to forget this fact, a special privilege that became a burdensome
restriction.

On 4 May 1935, Stein sailed back to France. By June, Wilder was in
personal distress, which he attributed to overwork, and took a leave from the
University of Chicago. In the summer, he visited Stein at her country house in
Bilignin, in the Rhone Valley. Having with astonishing success managed fame
and publicity on the tour, she now returned to their effects in daily conversations with Wilder and, from the late summer through the fall, composed them
in a new book. *The Geographical History Of America Or The Relation Of
Human Nature To The Human Mind* echoes with talks between her and
Wilder, which she included in the text. She also wanted him to write commentaries on the book. In their exchanges and in her own ruminations she
developed two new sets of opposing terms, identity, which had to do with
history, memory, and self-interest in time, and entity, which had to do with
pure being, insight beyond personality, creation beyond time. Related to these
was her distinction between human nature, which refers to identity in time
and place, and the human mind, which refers to existing and creating.

Stein had observed Wilder in talk and in action—his attraction to personalities, his wish to please, his fear of being judged, a sense of duty that interfered with his art, his great restlessness. She came to call him community man
and company man. Elements of his behavior reappeared transmuted in her

novel *Ida*, a study of stardom with barely discernible cautionary features, in whose completion she tried to enlist his collaboration. He refused, but he is behind *Ida*, the *Geographical History*, the *Narration* lectures, and shorter pieces as a presence, though not as an identifiable model except in his portrait in the *Geographical History* and in the wordplay of the "T" section of "To Do: A Book Of Alphabets And Birthdays." He is prominent in *Everybody's Autobiography*. Stein never wrote stories of him such as he had written of George Brush, the blundering, comical hero of *Heaven's My Destination*. But she took him in hand and tried to teach him not to be obliging.

In 1965, nearly twenty years after Stein's death, Wilder, almost seventy, commented, with the true modesty of which he was capable, on her coaching, which he had learned but by which he had not learned to live: "I had the great privilege of being earnestly 'talked to' for scores of hours by Miss Stein. Unfortunately for me, I was already 36 when I first met her and began being influenced by her ideas, her principles.

"As far as I know she read only one of my books [*Heaven's My Destination*, which he sent her upon publication in January 1935]. She mentioned it only once—20 lines in a letter. Nevertheless, she took on the task of 'putting me right' as a writer. The works I wrote thereafter may not reflect her influence on the surface; it is all the greater for being internal" (*Writer's Digest*, September 1965, 37). How often her lessons return in his work from 1935 into late years says something about how deeply they impressed him in the face of his constant difficulties. He told Stein with pride that his address in Paris to a distinguished audience at the Institut de Coopération Intellectuelle of July 1937 rested entirely on her ideas. When at the Edinburgh Festival in 1955 the critics attacked *The Alcestiad*, he steeled himself in his journal, "Oh, it's to Gertrude that I owe this invulnerability to the evaluation of others!" (239).

Her freedom of imagination became for him a treasured touchstone. In notes on *The Eighth Day* written for Otto Klemperer, whom he deeply admired, he spoke of Stein as his Diotima. He thought her, like Ezra Pound, one of the great teachers and tried to pass on what she taught him. A skilled prose writer with a passion for exegesis and a sense of mission, he prepared introductions to her books, which for her became bridges into print. While he supported her efforts at publication, she held him to his vocation as a writer. Some members of his family frowned upon what they saw as Stein's use of Wilder for her own needs. Yet Wilder needed no protection from the satisfaction of supporting her work. If she seemed a threat to his family, it was because she asked that he give himself to his art and free himself from the ties that bind and that sing so eloquently in *Our Town*.

Without their friendship, the *Narration* lectures would not have come about, the *Geographical History* would have become a different book, the novel *Ida* might not have been written or Ida would have turned into a different personage, and *Doctor Faustus Lights The Lights* might not have become the play it did. And *Our Town*, Wilder's all-American play, in which you and I and all of us have acted in high school, would not have been written. *The Ides of March* of 1947, the year after the deaths of his mother and Stein, absorbs questions of identity and masterpieces that he had shared with her. How his later work would have differed without their meeting is beyond speculation. But his indebtedness to Stein carried through all his life.

It is to Wilder's care for Stein and for the literary heritage that we owe the deposit of her papers at what is now the Beinecke Rare Book and Manuscript Library at Yale University. The correspondence printed here shows how Wilder, anticipating war in 1937, urged upon Stein the need to preserve her papers in an American archive. Conferring in advance with the Yale Library Associates, he prepared the ground for their acceptance. At Yale her papers would be safe, would be part of the great collection his university was building, and would give Stein the sense of immortality for which she always hungered. His deposit of the manuscript of his novel *The Woman of Andros*, of his early one-act plays, and two typescripts that were gifts from Stein to him paved the way for Yale's acceptance, made clear that his own papers would go to the library of his alma mater, and symbolically joined him with Stein as his modernist mentor.

Related to Stein's deposit of her papers was the question of literary executorship. Stein considered appointing Wilder, who was young, energetic, conscientious, and well connected. But even as she discussed the prospect as a fact in *Everybody's Autobiography* (301), she wondered whether he was firm enough to withstand pressures or flattery; by 1946, his long silence far beyond the end of the war had pained her, casting a doubt on the friendship. In her last will, written just before she died, Stein appointed her old friend Carl Van Vechten to take charge of the publication of her unpublished work, always first in her mind. For years Van Vechten, in consultation with Donald Gallup, the curator of the Yale Collection of American Literature, also acted as de facto executor.

To anyone familiar with Stein's way with words, it is surprising that she should have considered collaborating with other writers, not only Wilder. In *Everybody's Autobiography* she speaks of having hoped to collaborate first with Sherwood Anderson and later with Lloyd Lewis on a history of General Grant and with Louis Bromfield on a detective story. Included in this correspondence is a document that suggests what collaboration meant to her. While she was grappling with the difficulties of *Ida*, in which she asked him to collaborate, Wilder took notes about the book. They are printed in Appendix VI. We at first thought they were his record of reading her work in progress, but they

turned out to be notes of conversations with Stein. Collaboration is insepara-
ble from conversation and commentary, words that appear separately in the
letters but are related.

In the late memoir cited earlier, Wilder describes Stein's gift for conversation as akin to that of Goethe, Samuel Johnson, or Coleridge, among other
writers. Great conversationalists, he says, never pass on warmed-up words of
wisdom but "see things for the first time in conversation." Such artists require
a participating partner, not merely a disciple. Stein said she had the ability to
talk and listen at the same time. Conversation as an activity of the mind can
generate writing.

Commentary—one thinks of Caesar, of Goethe's conversations with
Eckermann—preserves the liveliness of exchange, as Stein knew when she
asked Wilder for marginal notes on the *Geographical History*, though it became a one-voice introduction only. She may have hoped that commentary
would also enable readers to enter work that many found difficult. Exchanges
with Wilder lie behind much of her late work, just as shared questions of
writing animated her friendship with Sherwood Anderson, Lloyd Lewis, and
Louis Bromfield. Figures of conversation, whose unpredictable logic com-
poses much of daily life, also animate many of Stein's plays.

Collaboration, then, is less an effort to share writing than a function of
conversation that renews writing, keeping it supple, reflective, and lively. The
letters in this volume are not the wrought and polished exchanges of great
minds casting their ideas into perfected forms. Rather they offer a view into
the process that generates writing. They show minds groping for notions
rather than completing them. Often contexts of exchanges are assumed rather
than spelled out, or they appear in notes, letters to other friends, or ephemeral
papers beyond the correspondence. We have chosen to comment fully on
letters that do not reveal their contexts; on occasion, when texts appear to ask
for it, we editorialize.

Print, however complete and accurate the words, flattens and strips letters of
the touch of human beings talking and writing—voice, gesture, paper, ink,
letterhead, address, hand, speed, scrawl, lag. Not only what the letters say but
what they look like and how they are composed tell a great deal about the
writers. Wilder was as restless and irregular in letters as he was in all his habits,
his sense of himself, his work. He shaped his answers to what he saw as the
recipient's relation to himself. Passionately absorbed in literature, he often
quoted or echoed classics in letters, just as his work melded literary and
historical material with his own experience.

Perhaps relying on classics was a safe habit acquired in early years. Even
as a young boy he had to report on his progress to his distant father in China

and later to write home from boarding school and college—from age twelve until he started at Yale in his sophomore year, he was always at school and reached home in letters used to inform, please, and impress, always with an eye on the recipient. Quoting was safer than revealing his own feelings. After winning the Pulitzer Prize, he had the means to withdraw into solitude for writing but was often unable to sustain work. While away, however, he always sent letters home to his mother and sister Isabel, who read them aloud, sent them on to his brother Amos's family in Newton Center, Chicago, and later Cambridge, his sister Janet's in Amherst, and, while she was well, his sister Charlotte, and always they were returned home. One summer young Janet was made to type his letters home from his first trip to Rome in 1922–23. Hundreds of letters from him and other members of the family are thus preserved and will eventually become available. Written to the family rather than to individuals, however, these letters have a formulaic, impersonal quality. An example is his report of his visit to Freud in October 1935, which sounds rehearsed and reappears almost unchanged, as if mythologized, in letters to others and even in *The Eighth Day* of 1967.

On the other hand, letters that Stein received always extended thought processes that already engaged her. She always answered questions, and she liked news and gossip, but they never distracted her from her path. Here and there, as if in conversation, she drafted a response directly on a letter just read, transcribing it later into her answer. What she was writing and thinking determined her movements. In January 1935, from New England, she wrote to Wilder that she was doing a piece on "newspaper writing and detective story writing." Journalism and detective stories raised aspects of narrative, the topic chosen for the March course by Stein and Wilder because both had recently in writing grappled with narrative.

She attended systematically and regularly to composition, art, business, correspondence. Her letters are never intimately personal; only occasionally does she talk about ideas, and she never explains her work. One of the rare exceptions, printed here in Appendix IX, is an unpublished letter from 1940 to Robert Bartlett Haas, which responds at length to his questions about description. In general, however, her habit of writing the here and now of daily life carries over to the correspondence. Its interest builds as one learns to hear behind the low voice of her letters the voice of her work and of the contexts surrounding it. We have opened these second and third voices with full, sometimes speculative annotations to details inferred from but not spelled out in the letters.

Wilder enjoyed and cultivated friendships, but letter writing and even letters received often became heavy encumbrances. He destroyed or asked his sister to destroy certain personal letters while retaining others, some in a special letter box he kept on his desk. There is no clear pattern in what he chose to keep or destroy. And the alternatives were not simply retention or destruction. In early years, when copying was still widespread in America, he copied important poems, prose passages, reviews, casts of plays staged in the United States and Europe; he also in the early twenties transcribed letters sent and received into journals and letter books. The copying itself is not difficult to understand, but the copying of letters that were then retained or not retained raises new questions. Some originals of letters copied were retained, others destroyed. Among those copied are many from Stein. Perhaps copying was a way of incorporating their verbal and personal configurations into his mind. He never quotes from them in his work. Starting with the first copied letter of 10 September 1936, we identify all letters he transcribed and in notes discuss any problems arising from them.

In only one case does a series of copied letters make a systematic and comprehensible whole. Letters from Stein, Sibyl Colefax, Jed Harris, Ruth Gordon, Lynn Fontanne, and others, starting in the summer of 1937 and ending with a statement of his own of early 1938, document his personal history of the making and staging of *Our Town*. These letters, together with Appendix VII, for the first time show Wilder's struggle to write the play and, under pressures from the director and friends, to get it staged.

Most of Stein's letters look the same—regular lines of text from top to bottom, sometimes continuing on a second page, usually also filled. Few of her letters are long. She uses no abbreviations and rarely adds postscripts, emphases, or doodles. Often letters to different people of the same time use the same phrases or voice the same preoccupations. Yet she also makes choices about what to speak of to whom. In 1937, for example, she wrote again and again to Carl Van Vechten about her play *Daniel Webster*, once casually mentioned to Wilder. Such inclusions and omissions—they are never accidents—sometimes compose tiny subtexts that we spell out in our notes. Wilder, on the other hand, used nonverbal features to underscore feeling. He would add color for emphasis, enclose sections in boxes, underline, draw little flags, crosses, stars, and sign with his nickname Thornt or Thornie or with phrases for his special relation to Stein and Toklas. He was punctilious about good form. Never, when concluding a letter to Stein, did he omit a greeting to Toklas. When both of them, even in one letter, wrote to him, he included an answer to each in a letter to both. When each wrote on her own, each received an answer. The rituals of the Stein household were such that all family members, even the dogs, were included in salutations and closings. Sensitive to their shared homosexuality, Wilder basked in their friendship and acceptance

even as he remained the loner compensating for his alienation from the world
by paying obeisance to it.

The prelude to the letters of Stein and Wilder was Stein's celebrated American lecture tour, reviewed in the press, in *Everybody's Autobiography*, and in
letters and memoirs of friends. All the more amazing, its full details and the
extent of its labors remain almost unknown. William Rice has assembled in
Appendix I the most complete chronology and itinerary of the tour that it has
been possible to document. His introduction to the listing describes in detail
how the tour was planned, managed, mismanaged, publicized. He explains
why Stein set stringent limits on numbers admitted, manner of pay, and so
forth. The listing documents how hard Stein worked and shows her seeing the
whole country for the first time. In spite of details mismanaged, appearances
canceled, and bookings changed again and again, the tour turned into a
resounding success, one that surprised those who were close to it. Printed
along with the syllabus and reading list for the March 1935 Narration course in
Appendix I, the tour chronology is a context for the letters in this book and
indeed for the remainder of Stein's life.

Further contexts consist of published and unpublished material (Appendices II to V) that gives body to both sides of this correspondence: Wilder's
introduction to the University of Chicago production of Handel's *Xerxes* in
February 1935; his foreword to an exhibition in Chicago in 1935 of the painter
John Pratt, whom Stein met; Stein's exchange with Donald Vestal about her
marionette play "Identity," followed by Wilder's introduction to it, and Stein's
letter about her dog Basket to Alexander Woollcott.

The correspondence is not continuous from the November 1934 meeting
in Chicago until Stein's death on 27 July 1946. Short gaps are covered in the
notes. But sudden, large gaps require explanations. Stein's letters are steadier
in style and matter than Wilder's. She traveled little but regularly, moving
every spring and fall from Paris to the country and back; she took some short
trips for visits in France and went to England twice for lectures and performances. Yet these trips barely interrupted the orderly routine of her life.
Wilder, on the other hand, though he had a home in Hamden, Connecticut,
lived a less regular life. He traveled often, near and far, long and short, for
lectures, productions of plays, seclusion for writing, stays at the MacDowell
Colony, an endowed artists' workshop in Peterborough, New Hampshire,
visits to friends, cultural missions to foreign countries. His constant movements create discontinuity. As editors, we decided not only to identify such
gaps before continuing with the letters but to preserve the double biographical continuity we considered important for this volume by filling in what took
place in the lives when they diverged.

Appendix VII charts the complex course of events from October 1937 to the winter of 1938, from Wilder's writing of *Our Town* to the appearance in Europe of the producer-director Jed Harris, who wanted the play, to Wilder's early departure for New York and the play's eventual production.

We have included in Appendix VIII the first full staging history of *The Skin of Our Teeth*. The importance to Wilder of his new play, the personal drama of mounting a production with the best director and best actors possible, playing off one against the other against the background of World War II and his own imminent call to duty, makes of this story far more than an ordinary staging history. Included in this appendix is the revelation, occasioned by the relation of *The Skin of Our Teeth* to *Finnegans Wake*, of the link between *Our Town* and *The Making Of Americans*.

The most dramatic interruption, however, came in the second half of World War II, once Wilder was in the service. The letters stopped entirely. We bridge this gap for Wilder in our notes to Isabel Wilder's letter to Stein of 8 September 1944. Wilder wrote home and had some contact with friends in Allied countries but did not or could not send messages to Stein. In Appendix IX, Stein's life during the Vichy years receives new and full attention; it is now possible to document events of the second half of the war, in part as a result of new French archival collections and research into the Vichy years that make available information not known until now.

With the end of the war one would expect correspondence to resume, but it did not. On the evening of 3 July 1942, Stein had a vision of Wilder having returned to see Toklas and herself. The image was unfortunately to remain a dream. It was Isabel Wilder who finally wrote them of Wilder's wartime life. He himself sent a brief note in September 1944 after seeing the typescript of *Wars I Have Seen*, and no further letter until July 1945 and a letter of condolence to Toklas five months after Stein's death. The difficult conclusion of their relationship remained a source of pain for Stein and Toklas and of distress for Wilder.

Editorial Statement

This edition collects and prints completely the correspondence between Gertrude Stein and Thornton Wilder from 1934 to 1946. For the sake of completeness letters written to or from Alice Toklas and Isabel Wilder during those years are also included.

No edition of letters, including a facsimile edition, can reproduce all their physical qualities, paper, ink or pencil used, the flow of handwriting on the page. There can be no substitute for examining the actual letter. The most a printed edition can do is to preserve the words and indicate some of the physical features of the holograph original.

Transcriptions of these letters have been made from the originals in the Yale Collection of American Literature, and one letter from Stein to Wilder in the Bancroft Library of the University of California at Berkeley was transcribed from a photographic copy of the original. Wilder copied a number of Stein's letters into notebooks or onto loose leaves; the texts printed here accurately render his transcriptions. Their originals have not been found, except for the one of 15 September 1940. That letter is discussed in our full description of the copied letters in the note to their first appearance, Stein to Wilder, 10 September 1936. We have benefited from the transcriptions of Stein's letters prepared by Donald Gallup while curator of the Yale Collection of American Literature for use in the Yale library. Our departures from his texts and dates rely on new documentation.

Excerpts from these letters have been quoted by Stein and Wilder biographers. Wilder's letters to Stein of 23 September 1935, 7 October 1935, 14 October 1935, [June 1939], and [18 June 1939] are included, in part or in whole, in Donald Gallup's collection *The Flowers of Friendship: Letters Written to Gertrude Stein*.

In editing these letters, we have reproduced the texts as written, including slips of the pen and misspellings, which we have either corrected in brackets or identified in footnotes. We have used brackets for a word added to account for one missing, for a question mark where we have guessed at a word, and to add a first or last name for clarity. Wilder's own use of brackets has been indicated in footnotes to distinguish them from editorial insertions. Wilder's dots, used for pauses, not deletions or ellipses, are retained. Stein's characteristic "x" for "ex" at the beginning of a word has been retained. No attempt has been made to regularize grammar or punctuation. Evident typing errors in such letters as those of Isabel Wilder and Tallulah Bankhead are silently corrected.

Each letter begins with a heading indicating addressee and location. For letters that were forwarded, we give the final destination. Postcards and their images have been noted, telegrams reproduced in their unique forms. We have standardized the dates on the left and the addresses on the right. Postmarks as well as editorial assumptions about a date have been placed in brackets. Where the context warranted it, we have indicated the location of the postal cancellation. Salutations have been standardized to the left and closing signatures to the right. Material clearly written as a headnote is placed at the opening of the letter. All postscripts, wherever they appear in the letter, have been standardized below the closing.

We have made no distinction between stationery with a printed address and that with a handwritten one unless it is significant for the dating of the letter. We have noted when Stein used stationery with her circular motto, "ROSE IS A ROSE IS A ROSE IS A ROSE." We have also noted that Wilder, when traveling, often used his personal stationery imprinted 50 Deepwood Drive, New Haven or, later, Hamden, Connecticut. Titles of all Stein pieces and published volumes are capitalized throughout, following the system adopted by Stein and Toklas and by *A Stein Reader*.

Short Titles

Bibliographic references in the notes have been keyed either to the general bibliography or to the separate Stein and Wilder bibliographies. Full citations in the notes are not repeated in the bibliographies. Where we have not been able to determine the full citation for a newspaper article, we have listed the library where the article may be found. Birth and death dates, where known, appear in the index.

Throughout this edition, short reference tags indicate the location of cited materials. All uncited references are to the Yale Collection of American Literature (YCAL).

Bancroft	The Bancroft Library The University of California, Berkeley
Berg	The Henry W. and Albert A. Berg Collection The New York Public Library
Chicago	The Joseph Regenstein Library The University of Chicago Library
Columbia-Cerf	Bennett Cerf Collection Rare Book and Manuscript Library Columbia University Libraries
Columbia-R.H.	Random House Collection Rare Book and Manuscript Library Columbia University Libraries
Doucet	Bibliothèque littéraire Jacques Doucet Universités de Paris

Harvard-Houghton	The Houghton Rare Book and Manuscript Library Harvard University Library
Harvard-Theatre	The Theatre Collection Harvard University Library
Library of Congress M.D.	Library of Congress, Manuscript Division
NYPL-Lincoln Center	The Lincoln Center Library for the Performing Arts The New York Public Library
NYPL-Special Collections	Special Collections Department The New York Public Library
SHS-Wisconsin	State Historical Society of Wisconsin
Texas	Harry Ransom Humanities Research Center The University of Texas at Austin
YCAL	Collection of American Literature Beinecke Rare Book and Manuscript Library Yale University Library

The Letters of Gertrude Stein
and Thornton Wilder

1934

Toklas, Pépé, Stein, and Basket at Bilignin in May 1934. The photographs taken by
William G. and Mildred Rogers were used for publicity on the American lecture tour.

To Thornton Wilder, Chicago, Illinois

[postmark: 8 December 1934]

The Lowry
Fourth & Wabasha Streets
St. Paul, Minn[esota].

My dear Wilder,

Here we are[1] and I do want to tell you how charmingly you made our stay in Chicago completely delightful. Everything you did added so much to everything, and I am enormously looking forward to our always knowing each other, we had a nice time in Madison, the students were very nice and one of the professors[2] particularly so he has to do with the history of languages, then we had a marvellous flight in a tiny plane low over the snowed prairie, I am still all filled up with the xtraordinary symmetry of it, as a whole and in detail, well anyway I am awfully happy that we did get to be friends, Alice is writing to [Robert] Hutchins to give him our addresses,[3] because there was not a moment before and once more and always

Gtrde Stein.

1. Stein had left Chicago on Thursday, 6 December, for Madison, Wisconsin, where she gave lectures entitled "The History of English Literature as I Understand It" and "The Gradual Making of *The Making Of Americans*" at the university. On Friday she flew to St. Paul, Minnesota. For the itinerary of the lecture tour, see Appendix I.

2. Probably Robert C. Pooley, who was teaching a course on the history of the English language (letter from Eric Rothstein, 7 September 1988).

3. From the Hotel Lowry in St. Paul, on 9 December, Toklas sent to Robert Maynard Hutchins, president of the University of Chicago, a brief outline of their itinerary through the twenty-second of December (Chicago).

Thornton Wilder by Maude Hutchins during his early years at Chicago

1935

Party at the apartment of Charles and Elizabeth "Bobsy" Goodspeed in Chicago, 20 April 1935. Seated beneath a portrait by Bernard Boutet De Monvel of Mrs. Goodspeed leaning on a Chinese lacquered chest are (BACK) Stein, Fanny Butcher, Alice Roullier, and Alice Toklas; (FRONT) Mrs. Goodspeed, Richard Bokum, and Wilder.

To Thornton Wilder, Chicago, Illinois

[postmark: 9 January 1935]

Hotel Kimball
Springfield, Massachusetts.

My dear Thornton

       I have just rec'd the Heaven is my Destination[1] that you never told me was coming out, [Alexander] Woollcott[2] says it is not because of modesty but because of austerity that you did not tell me but anyway I have just read it and with a lot of pleasure, the thing has a great quality of balance I mean of inner balance,[3] and that keeps holding me all the way through and makes it all real, no matter what it does It is all held down by this curious quality of balance which makes it really self contained, I tell you I like it a lot and I like the way it begins again and does not begin, it is all interesting. I am awfully glad that we are seeing each other again, in March, and then perhaps you will come to see us in Bilignin and that would be so awfully nice, but first the book and then Chicago and it is all a pleasure[4]

Always

Gtrde.

1. For Christmas 1934 Stein inscribed copies of her *Portraits And Prayers* and *Four Saints In Three Acts* for Wilder (see Wilder to Stein, 15 January 1935). *Heaven's My Destination*, Wilder's gift to Stein, was published on 2 January 1935 in New York by Harper and Brothers (and in London by Longmans, Green two days earlier). Stein's copy, with Wilder's penciled inscription, "For Gertrude Stein / with the best of / Thornton Wilder / University of Chicago / January 1935," is in YCAL.

2. Alexander Woollcott, critic, radio personality, writer, and actor. Wilder had known Woollcott since the late 1920s. The first extant letter from Wilder to Woollcott (Harvard-Theatre) is dated Lawrenceville, New Jersey, 2 April 1928. Its tone suggests that they were already on intimate terms. Woollcott did not review either *The Cabala* or *The Bridge of San Luis Rey*, but the enormous success of these novels probably led to their first meeting. Stein met Woollcott at a luncheon given in her honor by her publisher, Bennett Cerf, on 25 October 1934, the day after she arrived in New York. It was probably in January during a brief stopover in New York on her way to New England that she and Woollcott discussed Wilder.

3. Stein is often concerned with balance, not only in writing but also in her perception of the

world around her. Later, in *The Geographical History Of America*, she speaks of balance in the landscape seen from the air.

    4. On 4 December 1934, Stein participated in the General Honors 100 course given by Robert Hutchins and Mortimer Adler. At a dinner party after the class, President Hutchins invited her back to teach a two-week seminar in March 1935. The invitation, which Stein accepted that evening, may have been discussed with Wilder. Subsequent letters (Chicago, YCAL) refer only to questions of itinerary and living arrangements.

———————————

To Gertrude Stein, Springfield, Massachusetts

15 Jan[uary] 1934 [i.e., 1935]   The best University
                                           [The University of Chicago
                                           Chicago, Illinois]

Dear Gertrude Stein:

            You can guess the lengths I go in order not to mention that I write books. While you were here wild horses couldn't have dragged from me an announcement that another book was coming out. I guess my attitude to them is just plain embarrassment. I know I'm not *sérieux* and I know now that apparently there is no way for me to make myself *sérieux*, so the best thing to do is just to talk of other things. But I am greatly pleased that you did find things to please you in them; and that fact I can put in my pipe and smoke when I'm tired.

    We're all very happy that you're coming back. The English Department and the President and Bobbsy [Goodspeed] have all brought to me the question as to where you would like to live. First I rush forward to offer you my apartment. I, very proud of my guests, would go over and live in the Quadrangle Club. My apartment is very small, but it has a very fine view of the Midway at seven in the morning. It has two very comfortable beds and two alcoves that are called the dinette and the kitchenette. Bobbsy says I may propose it to you, but that I had better say that the apartment building has no restaurant service and that you would have to engage some one to come in and cook for you. There is maid service, however, a Liverpool woman who talks to me about her family. (B B or the Birthplace of Bonnes.)[1] I am very fond of this apartment, but I would be even fonder of it, if I could lose it for a time to you two.

    The English Department says the girls dormitories do not have really comfortable suites, but that the new big stone Tudor men's dormitories have several suites just like mine at your disposal. The housekeeper would send your meals up to your rooms. Lots of good nourishing string beans and roast beef for growing boys.

The nearest hotel is the Windermere, and if you prefer hotel surroundings that is the best. It would seem to me to be really inconvenient to live at the
Blackstone or the Drake. To us South Chicagoans that seems a long ways off.
If you want your windows to look out upon the lake you could go a very little
beyond the Windermere and stay at the Shoreland. Both are immense ma-
sonry blocks, interior-decorated with flourishes, full of the fretful business
men's wives who slap playing-cards down from two until six. They are rude to
waiters and cranky to their children. I go to lunch there on purpose to watch
them and I enjoy it very much.

So there are your choices.

Franja Hutchins is still in the hospital.[2] The wound where the gland was
pierced in her armpit is still being drained and sores break out on her shoulder
and must be lanced with great pain. The illness is not supposed to be grave any
more; it is merely a matter of waiting. Like George Brush[3] I *know* that all
illness is psychogenic; I know why she's ill and how to cure it. Does Bob
[Hutchins] know? I watch him; as a cat watches a mouse-hole, but he never
lets on. Those two deep deep & wonderful girls are fighting it out.

Our School of Music is giving Handel's only comic opera *Xerxes* on the
two hundredth birthday of the composer. I am the stage-director.[4] Long rehearsals and very hard work. The famous Largo is the opening aria. All the
music is splendid and true. The baroque age was far more valuable than the
renaissance in every way except oil paintings. ¶ Tomorrow at eight o'clock I
shall lecture on the characterization of Helen in the Iliad. I have fallen in love
with one of the pupils and am talking with the tongues of men and of angels
this Quarter. High time, too. ¶ Aleck Woollcott will be here when you are and
I look forward to such goings-on.[5] ¶ Bobbsy and her Arts Club gave us a fine
thing last Sunday night. Stravinsky's[6] Octet for Wind Instruments was played
twice and the second time he conducted it himself and the grip on r[h]ythms
and relations was electrifying. ¶ My father is very ill (psychogenic) and my
brother Amos is in Florida very ill (psychogenic). ¶ I read in bed for an hour
every night. Last night I read Sainte-Beuve on Bossuet, Bourdaloue and Massillon. I was wrung with envy. I should have been a preacher. That's all; I
missed my train and there is no other. I am Fénelon. *Causons d'autre chose.*[7] ¶
Were you arrested by that lovely thing I stole from Nietzsche? You must do a
little harm to the man who mistreats you. To do him pure good is to humiliate
him, to efface him, to deny him a soul. A little correction of the Sermon on
the Mount.[8] It was Gene Tunney[9] who read a play of Shakespeare ten times in
search of a grain of talent. It was a great doctor of the Church who when he
was being tried for heresy replied: I haven't got up at five in the morning to
read the fathers for thirty years in order to have the ideas of the rest of the
world.[10] I'm a jackdaw and make my nests by depredation. ¶ Last week I heard

the Mass in B Minor twice.[11]—Miss Toklas, who did you and I once hear saying such shocking things about religion? Then what was it made the Mass in B. Minor; was it just Art? Well, it's all a bother to me; it's this week's bother.

Now it's midnight.

I think of you both with the greatest pleasure and affection.

Ever

Thornton

P.S. I now hear that the plan is to go to International House and that would be best of all; and I was crazy not to have thought of it first.

T

1. Maid service brings to Wilder's mind Stein's "B.B. Or The Birthplace Of Bonnes," a piece in her *Portraits And Prayers* that deals with the adventures of Stein's and Toklas' domestic help. Before leaving Chicago in December, Stein had inscribed copies of her books to be given as Christmas presents from herself and Bobsy Goodspeed. The inscriptions were collected and printed in the pamphlet *Chicago Inscriptions* (Chicago: Lakeside Press, 1934), which served as Goodspeed's Christmas card. Stein inscribed *Portraits And Prayers* to Wilder as follows:

> For Thornton,
> Bobsy says do whatever I like for him and whatever I like is all I like for him, and merry Christmas and a most Merry Christmas always from Bobsy and from me
> Gtde

Elizabeth Fuller Goodspeed, known to her friends as Bobsy, in a variety of spellings, was a well-known figure in Chicago's cultural life. She had studied at the Académie Julien in Paris and continued her studies at the Art Institute of Chicago after her marriage to Charles Barney Goodspeed, a member of a prominent Chicago family, leader of the Republican Party, and trustee of the University of Chicago. Bobsy Goodspeed served from 1932 to 1940 as the president of the Arts Club of Chicago. In the summer of 1934, she visited Stein at the country house in Bilignin, inviting her to lecture at the Arts Club; at the same time, through contacts with dealers whom Stein knew, she arranged exhibitions for Sir Francis Rose and Elie Lascaux. After her husband's death in 1947, she married Gilbert W. Chapman, the president of the Yale & Towne Locke Company, and moved to New York.

2. Mary Frances (Franja) Hutchins was the eldest of the three daughters of Robert and Maude Hutchins.

3. George Brush is the main character of *Heaven's My Destination*. In conversation with a pair of skeptical new friends in Oklahoma City in chapter 2, the naive Brush outlines his views on preventive medicine: "Sometimes I think I may get so discouraged that I may fall sick—or worse. Because that's all sickness is—discouragement. That's one of my theories, too. I have a theory that all sickness comes out of having lost hope about something. If they find out they're not as good as they thought they were—in business or in anything else—or if they've done wrong and can't undo it, then they gradually fall sick."

4. Under university auspices at Mandel Hall, Wilder, working with the artist John Pratt, directed the first Chicago performance of *Xerxes*, on 16 and 17 February 1935. The performances commemorated the 250th, not the 200th, birthday. See Appendix II for details of the performance and "Wilder Comments on 'Xerxes,' " his essay for the University of Chicago student newspaper.

5. In a letter to Harold Guinzburg of 1 March 1935, Woollcott gives his schedule in Chicago between 3 and 20 March. Item four of his nineteen-point list of "facts" reads, "Broadcast from Chicago Sunday-evening, March 10th. Later the same evening, Thornton Wilder, Gertrude Stein and I will be the guests of some undergraduate honor society for several hours of continuous discourse" (Kaufman and Hennessey, *Letters*, 144). The list concludes with items "17: April 1st, death of

Mr. Woollcott, as thousands cheer"; "18: April 2nd, dancing in the streets; half-holiday in all the schools, bank moratorium"; "19: Burial at sea April 3rd."

6. Igor Stravinsky was in the Midwest to conduct a series of all-Stravinsky concerts with the Chicago Symphony Orchestra. At Goodspeed's reception for him on 13 January 1935 at the Arts Club of Chicago, Eric de Lamarter, associate conductor of the orchestra, led an ensemble in the composer's *Octet for Wind Instruments* (1923). Stravinsky himself then conducted this piece as an encore (see *Musical Leader*, 2 February 1935, 7).

7. Hints to Stein suggest that Wilder feels the burden of his position as middleman between members of the Hutchins family, friends, colleagues, and children. Wilder also acted informally as advisor to Hutchins at the university, a position that necessitated discretion with colleagues and staff. With a certain self-pity, Wilder says that he cannot afford to come down with psychogenic illnesses as he must support his impecunious family.

Wilder's father, Amos Parker Wilder, had been coeditor of the *New Haven Journal-Courier* since 1915. By 1929 poor health had forced him to retire. Since that time, Wilder had been supporting the family. Also during that time, his older brother Amos fell ill, increasing pressures to which he could not yield. Because Wilder's father was a very religious man well known as a public speaker and his brother was a minister and theologian, references to sermons and oratory were far from neutral. In speaking of Bourdaloue, Massillon, Bossuet, and Fénelon, Wilder leads from dull, preacherly repetitiveness to Stein's view of repetition as insistence and variation, changing with each step.

In identifying himself with Fénelon, whose satiric novel *Télémarque* (1699) was an indictment of conservative French theologians in the court of Louis XIV, most notably his teacher Bossuet, Wilder may see a parallel with his own novel *Heaven's My Destination*, an indictment of cardboard dogmatists like his father and the fathers of his old classmates Henry Luce and Robert Hutchins: "Our fathers were very religious, very dogmatic Patriarchs. They preached and talked cant from morning til night— not because they were hypocritical but because they knew no other language . . . They thought they were 'spiritual'—damn it . . . they had no insight into the lives of others—least of all their families" (Wilder to Emily Foresman Tibby, 5 May 1967, YCAL).

8. Displaying his erudition to Stein, Wilder lists some sources of episodes in the novel. In chapter 11 of *Heaven's My Destination*, Brush and another new friend, both fresh out of jail, are driving to Kansas City when Brush has occasion to "turn the other cheek" in his own manner: "If you do pure good to a man that's harmed you that shames him too much. No man is so bad that you ought to shame him that way. Do you see? You ought to do just a little bit of bad in return, so he can keep his self-respect." Wilder is probably drawing from "On the Adder's Bite," in Nietzsche's *Thus Spoke Zarathustra*: "But if you have an enemy, do not requite him evil with good, for that would put him to shame. Rather prove that he did you some good. . . . A little revenge is more human than no revenge. And if punishment is not also a right and an honor for the transgressor, then I do not like your punishments either" (*Thus Spoke Zarathustra*, in *The Portable Nietzsche*, ed. and trans. Walter Kaufmann [New York: Viking Penguin, 1954], 179–81).

9. In chapter 5 of *Heaven's My Destination*, George Brush reads *King Lear* while shaving: "His teacher at college had once remarked that *King Lear* was the greatest work in English literature, and the Encyclopaedia Britannica seemed to be of the same opinion. Brush had read the play ten times without discovering a trace of talent in it, and was greatly worried about the matter. He persevered, however, and was engaged in committing the whole work to memory." The incident is based on an anecdote about Wilder's old friend the boxer Gene Tunney, who as a soldier in World War I was introduced to *The Winter's Tale*. When the play made no impression on him after a first reading, Tunney read it ten more times (see William Lyon Phelps, *Autobiography with Letters* [New York and London: Oxford Univ. Press, 1939], 792–99; Phelps, one of Wilder's professors at Yale, introduced Wilder to Tunney).

10. Wilder echoes this idea twice in *Heaven's My Destination*. In chapter 2, Margie McCoy remarks that Brush's ideas aren't the same as other people's. Brush replies, "I should think not. I didn't put myself through college for four years and go through a difficult religious conversion in order to have ideas like other people's." And in chapter 10, in answer to Judge Carberry's "Your ideas aren't the

same as most people's, are they?": "I didn't put myself through college for four years and go through a difficult religious conversion in order to have the same ideas as other people have."

11. Bach's *Mass in B Minor* was performed on the eighth, tenth, and eleventh of January by the Chicago Symphony Orchestra and the Apollo Musical Club as part of the celebration of the 250th anniversary of Bach's birth in 1685.

To Thornton Wilder, Chicago, Illinois

[postmark: 20 January 1935]   Hotel Kimball
                                                     Springfield, Massachusetts.[1]

My dear Thornton,

Thanks for all your thoughts for us and it is a delicate pleasure to have you be thinking for us. We are deep in New England, we have done everything in New England that is in this part of Massachusetts and in Connecticut that one can do, and it is strange but in a funny way it is the only strange part of America, but we will talk a lot about that when we wander about in March and I am looking forward a lot to our doing that,[2] we go back to New York next week for a few days then Richmond then North and then S[outh]. Carolina then Alabama then New Orleans St. Louis and back to you—all, and it will be all fun, I am getting more and more a feeling of what the feeling is and that too we will talk about a lot, and anyway it is nice in every way it is nice to be going to be seeing you again

Lots of love
Gtrde.

1. In Springfield, Massachusetts, Stein and Toklas saw one of their old "doughboy" friends, William Garland Rogers, known as "the Kiddie," and his wife, the poet Mildred Weston. Rogers at this time worked for the *Springfield Union*. For the Rogers memoirs about Stein, see Bibliography. For Stein's itinerary, see Appendix 1.

2. Preparatory to the classes she had agreed to teach at the University of Chicago in March, Stein was already thinking about narrative. Details of the lectures and conferences were arranged after Stein arrived in Chicago in late February 1935. Stein began working on the first lecture on 26 February, and by 28 February she wrote to Carl Van Vechten that two of the four lectures had been written and a reading list had been prepared (Appendix I). For details on the writing of the lectures, see Toklas to Van Vechten, 25 February [19]35, and Stein to Van Vechten, postmark 28 February 1935, in Burns, *Letters*, 1:397–98, 401–02.

To Thornton Wilder, Chicago, Illinois

[postmark: 23 January 1935]   Hotel Kimball
                                                               Springfield, Massachusetts.

My dear Thornton

         I am writing some little short things about newspaper writing and Detective story writing and I think of you, I am full of meditation about narrative and how it can be written and every solution is a solution and I think of you.[1] That is really what I want the course to be our course, just to find out how narratives should be written are written can be written may be written, it kind of worries me how they were written have been written worries me less but this other thing does worry me, quite a lot it worries me and sometimes I know and mostly I don't know and I think of you both ways I think of you,[2] I am now writing about American education, well anyway I do think of you, and it is nice to think of you, here in New England as well as elsewhere

Lots of love

Gtrde.

    1. Henry Staton of the Herald Tribune Syndicate had contracted through Bennett Cerf, Stein's publisher, a series of articles on the American scene. On 15 January (YCAL) Cerf reminded her that she would be writing for a wide readership and would have to "compromise sufficiently with that audience to insure that the majority of them will understand what you are saying." Six articles were published by the *New York Herald Tribune* and other papers between 3 March and 13 April under the titles "American Newspapers"; "The Capital And Capitals Of The United States," echoing her play *Capital Capitals* of 1923; "American Education And Colleges"; "American Crimes And How They Matter"; "American States And Cities And How They Differ From Each Other," echoing titles in her *Useful Knowledge* of 1928; "American Food And American Houses." Echoes of the newspaper pieces return in the lectures on *Narration*, especially the third. The newspaper articles are reprinted in Stein, *How Writing*, 73–105.
    2. The shared concern with narrative becomes part of their conversation and their work. It is interesting that Wilder, who made his reputation as a novelist, after this time turned to plays, perhaps as a result of exchanges with Stein. He returned to the novel in 1948, with the publication of *The Ides of March*, whose form he credited to Stein.

———

To Thornton Wilder, Chicago, Illinois

[postmark: 25 January 1935]   Hotel Kimball
                                                               Springfield, Massachusetts.

My dear Thornton,

         Have just had a letter from [Robert] Hutchins and it would appear that the International house is not for us, why not if not, but anyway it is not, so here we are back again and back to Thornton's flat at least we hope so, at least we hope we can, because there is a kitchenette and so one can do what one likes in a kitchenette and we may like to do a lot there at least Alice may but anyway it does seem ungracious to refuse and then to accept, but we do accept I do hope that it is still there to accept.[1] We met a lady yesterday in a snow-drift who says she does know you very well, at least the snow drift or drifts were afterward. Is it alright.

Address Algonquin Hotel, N[ew]. Y[ork]. 44 Street

Gtrde.

1. On 8 January 1935 Stein confirmed the lecture dates to Hutchins, and on the same date Hutchins confirmed that Stein was expected at the university on 1 March and that Wilder's apartment was available to her. Because the letters crossed in the mail, Stein did not learn of Wilder's offer until his letter of 15 January. Replying to Stein's letter of 23 January, Hutchins suggested alternatives to International House where they might stay. In her reply, received at Chicago on 4 February 1935, Stein indicated that she planned to accept Wilder's invitation (Hutchins to Stein, YCAL; Stein to Hutchins, Chicago).

To Gertrude Stein, New York, N.Y.
[TELEGRAM]

28 Jan[uary] 1935   Chicago, Ill[inois]

PROUD AND HAPPY THAT MYSELF AND THE APARTMENT CAN BE USEFUL TO YOU LETTER FOLLOWS DEVOTEDLY

THORNTON.

To Gertrude Stein, Charleston, South Carolina
[TELEGRAM]

13 Feb[ruary] 1935   Chicago, Ill[inois]

DON'T LET MY WORD CONSTITUTE UNJUSTIFIED PRESSURE BUT I RECOM-
MEND THE INVITATION OF BLACK MOUNTAIN COLLEGE A LIVE LITTLE EXPERI-
MENTAL COLLEGE THAT HAS LONG READ YOUR WORK BUT IF YOU ARE ECONO-
MIZING ENERGY DISREGARD THIS WIRE EXCEPT ITS LAST WORDS VIZ THAT I
SIMMER IN HAPPY ANTICIPATION

THORNTON.[1]

1. On 13 February, the rector of Black Mountain College, John Andrew Rice, telegraphed Stein in care of Josephine Pinckney, the poet and novelist, who had arranged her talk before the Poetry Society in Charleston, South Carolina:

IN A CONVERSATION WITH [T]HORNTON WILDER BEFORE CHRISTMAS HE TOLD ME OF THE PLEASURE WITH WHICH THE STUDENTS OF THE UNIVERSITY OF CHICAGO HAVE LISTENED TO YOU AND PROMISED THAT WHEN HE NEXT SAW YOU HE WOULD URGE YOU TO VISIT BLACK MOUNTAIN COLLEGE NEAR ASHEVILLE NCAR [i.e., North Carolina] STOP WE HAVE JUST LEARNED OF YOUR VISIT TO CHARLESTON AND SEND THIS INVITATION TO YOU TO COME TO BLACK MOUNTAIN STOP BLACK MOUNTAIN COLLEGE WAS FOUNDED A YEAR AND A HALF AGO BY A SMALL GROUP OF PEOPLE WHO WANTED TO TRY THE EXPERIMENT OF HAVING A COLLEGE OF LIBERAL ARTS IN WHICH ART SHOULD BE AT THE CENTER OF THINGS AND IN ORDER TO MAKE THIS CERTAIN BROUGHT TWO PEOPLE TO THIS COUNTRY FROM THE BAUHAUS STOP IF AGREEABLE WOULD LIKE TO GIVE A PUBLIC LECTURE SOMETIME WITHIN THE NEXT WEEK EXCEPT SATURDAY EVENING SIXTEENTH BUT MOST OF ALL WOULD LIKE THE OPPORTUNITY OF SITTING AND TALKING WITH YOU STOP YOU WILL FIND PEOPLE ADDICTED TO CONVERSATION AND NOT UNACQUAINTED WITH FOUR FAINTS [i.e., Saints] STOP SENDING BY SPECIAL DELIVERY PRINTED MATERIAL WHICH WILL GIVE YOU A CLEARER IDEA OF THE COLLEGE THAN IS POSSIBLE IN TELEGRAMS.

J A RICE RECTOR.

Black Mountain (1933–57) was a small experimental college of the fine and performing arts, inspired by the philosophy of John Dewey and the Bauhaus of Walter Gropius. Wilder had spent five days at Black Mountain College in March 1934, at the invitation of the composer John Evarts, brother of his Yale classmate Effingham Evarts ('19). In 1967 Evarts sent Wilder "Pages from a Journal: March 1934," a lively portrait of Wilder at Black Mountain (see Evarts to Isabel Wilder, 26 November 1967, YCAL). While at the college, Wilder gave a lecture entitled "The Relation of Literature and Life," read from his plays *The Happy Journey to Trenton and Camden* and *The Long Christmas Dinner* and held conferences with students about writing.

To Thornton Wilder, Chicago, Illinois

[postmark: 14 February 1935]

Villa Margherita
Charleston,
S[outh]. C[arolina].

My dearest Thornton

Why did we not hear about Black Mountain College before, it looks like a perfectly heavenly place and their account of themselves most amusing but now we are in Charleston and every moment we [are] taken, we could have gone from Chapel Hill which was already a place we liked immensely, but anyway every place left out is an inducement to come back and that is the way we are beginning to feel about it, I guess we are going to be awful lonesome in France, anyway that is the way we are beginning to feel about it. We get to Chicago around the 25 and I do want to talk everything over with you, now that the time is approaching I am getting a little nervous about just what I want to do, and now about our plans. Do you want us to go straight to your flat when we get to Chicago, your flat being of course our flat as we are arriving a few days before the first and what is the address of that flat so that we may have a trunk forwarded from New York, you will be getting a lot of mail for us which I hope is not being a bother. Our address in New Orleans is the Hotel Roosevelt, so will you let us know about all that there, we are still enjoying it all immensely, which is very nice of it

Lots of love and everybody loves you, and somebody just told us that a sister is just like you which must be nice for the sister

Love
Gtrde.

To Gertrude Stein and Alice Toklas, New Orleans, Louisiana

[16 February 1935]   [6020 Drexel Avenue
                                                          Chicago, Illinois]

Dear and splendid GERTRUDE dear and splendid ALICE

You're not to feel the slightest constraint. You move into your flat at the moment of arrival. It is at 6020 Drexel Ave, across the street from the University hospitals. If I'm not on the doorstep if I'm away teaching you walk into the office of the apartment building MIDWAY-DREXEL APARTMENTS and the attendant will take you upstairs. Your telephone is Midway 7030. For a time you will be inconvenienced by calls for me, but all you have to do is to tell them to reach me through the University.

And if it should turn out that there's anything about it that you don't like (the noise of the streetcars on Cottage Grove Avenue for instance don't hesitate; the International House guest suite is now free and the new management is jealous of my privilege in this matter).

I shall have moved over to the Visiting Preacher's Suite in Hitchcock Hall where I've lived for long stretches on two different occasions and where I'm perfectly at home.

I'm glad you're coming early. We are beginning to marshall the choice students for you. Aleck Woollcott is jubilant that he will be in town some of the time. He adores you, his own words.[1]

SO

Tonight and tomorrow night we give Xerxes.[2] Dress rehearsal last night until two. Every singer thinks the performance is about him; everybody in chorus and ballet and electrical switchboard thinks that the performance is about him. But I think it's about Handel whose endless musical invention puts me in an ecstacy. Eloquent strains follow one another and I get dizzy and am filled with a gaseous excitement of homage. I haven't done my directorial job very well, but let the chips fall where they may. ¶ Wednesday I was asked to Fanny Butcher's at 5:00 o'clock and found that at 4:30 she had been married. She looked very pretty and said she was very scared. She couldn't get over the awe-full character of the Marriage Service. I've always said it was one of the best written scenes in all drama. I wish I'd thought of it first. I shall never doubt that you had a hand in that wedding. There was Fanny hesitating and you clearly and encouragingly kept saying in front of them and us "Fanny's young man. . . . Fanny's young man" . . . . and so you helped her over. I had a letter from her this morning and she's as happy as can be.[3] ¶ I've been moving about in other people's lives too. The other night at 11:30 a former pupil of mine plunged into our apartment and wanted to borrow sixty dollars so that his girl could have an abortion. I could breathe into him my advice but I couldn't breathe into him my weltanschauung; so I promised him five hundred dollars for a wedding present. I talked to the girl, in the automobile in some whirling snow. She was afraid of her mother; she was afraid of seeing her life suddenly dwindle to a dingy little apartment with a squal[l]ing baby and a not very stable George. I held her hand and worked. Now they are married and the two families have surprisingly accepted it and are house hunting with them. It's true the story has scarcely begun; but with George Brush I feel that when you are in doubt about a matter you go back to first principles. It's better to have one's life wrecked over one's inadequacy to a First Principle, than to have it wrecked over one's assertive ego-centric wish. Yes, I'm a great Filahs'ter. ¶ The Hutchi are still away, but all well again, I hear. ¶ In my opinion Freud's *Totem and Tabu* is a tremendous book.[4] ¶ It's wonderful being rich again: I throw money around like it's drunken sailors. I actually bought two new pairs of shoes and two new suits at the same time, and every morning I look at them in dazed happiness and say which shall it be today the brown or the black.[5]

In my opinion dear Gertrude dear Alice, God (passez moi le mot) has been very good to me. He has not only let me have friends but He has let me realize it. The most beautiful thing in the world is the human human eye. Fortunately there are millions of them. And among the handsomest in the world are the two pair you're bringing to the joy and the strengthening of all who look at them.

So this foolish fellow draws to a close.

So devotedly

Honest Jack Wilder

1. On 12 January 1935 (YCAL), Woollcott wrote to Wilder, "I will be broadcasting from Chicago on the 10th and 17th of March and doing some lecturing in that vicinity during two weeks. . . . I'll be in Chicago enough of the time to do considerable rolling in the hay with you and Gertrude Stein" (see Wilder to Stein, 15 January 1935, n. 5).

2. For *Xerxes*, see Wilder to Stein, 15 January 1935, n. 4, and Appendix II.

3. Fanny Butcher, the literary editor of the *Chicago Tribune* and president of the Chicago P.E.N. Club, had visited Stein with the Chicago art dealer Alice Roullier in July 1931 (see Georges Maratier to Stein, 17 July 1931, YCAL). On 31 January 1935 she had written to Stein about her plan to marry Richard Drummond Bokum, an advertising executive, whom Stein had met at the Chicago premiere of *Four Saints In Three Acts* on 7 November 1934. Stein's inscription to Bokum in *The Autobiography Of Alice B. Toklas* is included in *Chicago Inscriptions*, as is Stein's dedication to Fanny Butcher.

4. *Totem and Taboo* (1913), one of Freud's studies in cultural anthropology, considers the primitive origins of religion and morality and the development of conscience to regulate the inclination to forbidden action. It is not clear what reading, writing, or lecturing led Wilder to *Totem and Taboo* or whether he had discussed Freud with Stein.

5. *Heaven's My Destination* was on the best-seller list in some cities. It was a selection of the Book-of-the-Month Club in America and of the English Book Society in England.

To Gertrude Stein and Alice Toklas, Chicago, Illinois

[10 March 1935]   [Hitchcock Hall
Sunday noon   The University of
                                                        Chicago
                                                        Chicago, Illinois]

Dear Gertrude dear Alice:

The meeting of Kappa Alpha is at the home of Mr. Samuel Gerson 1300 Hyde Park Blvd.[1]

South

	50
Midway	59
NORTH	

_____52nd St

HYDE PARK BOULEVARD   (really also
                                                        51st St. [)]

The meeting is at 6:30. I shall not be able to get there until 7:00 because the broadcasting lasts until 6:30. Aleck [Woollcott] will not come, hearing at the last moment that Prof. Allen was to start the subject on Succession in Poetry. Last night and all these days we have been vexing him about poetry.

His blind spot. His troubled failure to see what it's all about. I hope you will still feel like coming, but would understand etc. But for my instruction and pleasure and for theirs . . . .

Ever devotedly

Thornton

1. This letter with directions was presumably hand-delivered. Kappa Alpha was a national literary honor society. The University of Chicago chapter, seven students and seven faculty members, met regularly for dinner and discussion. Stein had attended a meeting of the society on 24 February, the evening of her arrival in Chicago. At that meeting, Robert Morss Lovett, a member of the English Department, presided. The meeting on 10 March was in the home of Noel B. Gerson, a graduate student, with Philip S. Allen, a member of the German Department presiding (letter from Richard L. Popp, University of Chicago Library, 20 June 1991; see Wilder to Stein, 16 February 1935, n. 1; see also Toklas to Van Vechten, 25 February 1935, in Burns, *Letters*, 1:397–98).

To Thornton Wilder
6020 Drexel Avenue
Chicago, Illinois
[MS Bancroft]

[postmark: 19 March 1935]   The Miss Hockaday School for Girls
                                                                              Dallas, Texas

My dear Thornton,

Here we are, we had a wonderful day down, bumping over the Mississippi river and the spring green, it would have been nice if you could have gone on with us and not left us at the airport, it was an awful nice two weeks, it could not have been a nicer, and now we think pleasantly and regretfully of your inhabiting our apartment, and we will talk all about that at Bilignin. Texas is rather nice and the population very good to look at, Let her do what she wants in Texas, is what one woman said of me and I thought that was rather nice, let her do what she likes, in Texas. I think they want [Alexander] Wo[o]l[l]cott to come to Texas do you think he would come, it is a nice place and so wealthy just pleasantly and definitely wealthy, and you do eat well, and such vegetables and such cream, and such curious looking land, and we like it all, but not like our home in Chicago, best of love to you and lots and lots of it,

Gertrude

To Gertrude Stein, Pasadena, California
[TELEGRAM]

2 Apr[il] 1935   Chicago, Ill[inois]

PLEASE FORGIVE DELAY IN ANSWERING HAD AN ODD LITTLE UNIMPORTANT
NERVOUS BREAKDOWN PERFECTLY RECOVERED WE ARE ALL REMEMBERING THE
GREATNESS OF YOUR VISIT LOVE TO BOTH
THORNTON[1]

1. See Wilder to Stein, 6 April 1935, for his account of the "unimportant nervous breakdown."

To Thornton Wilder, Chicago, Illinois

[postmark: 2 April 1935]   Hotel Vista Del Arroyo
                                                             And Bungalows
                                                             Pasadena, California

My dear Thornton,

Just had your wire, I am so sorry that you were not well and
so glad you are and now you must come over and be quiet with us in Bilignin
and get all rested, and always have your lunch every day and not work more
than the hours in any day and be a good boy about it all, and if you cannot take
it easy take it as easy as you can, we were so happy with you in Chicago, it is
really what I liked best, it was so fruitful and so just right, and everything
pleased us from the refrigerator the kitchenette and the snow to everything
else. Here we are in Hollywood, I have not gone on the lots and eaten in the
green room but last night we did accept an invitation to meet the big directors
and Charlie Chaplin, and it was a curious xperience,[1] in Bilignin we will talk
it all over but I am hoping that we will see you again before that, we probably
will break our trip to New York at Chicago and spend the night with Bobsy
[Goodspeed] and I am hoping that you will still be there and we will see you
again but at any rate surely and entirely at Bilignin, we both love you so much,
and please be all well and we will be all happy, lots and lots of love from us
both
                              Always
                              Gtrde.

1. On the evening of 1 April 1935, Carl Van Vechten's friend Lillian May Ehrman of Hollywood gave a party in Stein's honor. According to the society editor of Hollywood's *Citizen News* for
10 April 1935, the guests included Charles Chaplin, Dashiell Hammett, Anita Loos, John Emerson,
Lillian Hellman, Paulette Goddard, and Rouben Mamoulian. The party is described in *Everbody's*

Autobiography (4–5). It also appears in *A Play Called Not And Now*, and in Toklas' *What Is Remembered*, 151–52.

To Gertrude Stein and Alice Toklas, Del Monte, California

6 April 1935   Hotel Abraham Lincoln
Fifth Street at Capitol Avenue
Springfield, Illinois

Dear Gertrude, dear Alice,

It wasn't much, but it was strange. Suddenly one noon in a Greek restaurant on 63rd Street where I go for lunch, I meaninglessly fainted twice. I promptly felt wonderfully well, except that at the end of any conversation or interview that lasted more than an hour I found myself trembling.

With that commonsense-sense which is the bottom-nature of a poet I took these events to be a Nature's Warning.[1]

And went for a long week-end at Galena, Illinois.[2] Wherever we are now, we your children, we carry your ideas about with us, finding a thousand corroborations in the life around us to those ideas as far as we are able to grasp them, that we call Recognition, Daily Life, Talking and Listening, Vitality and Sensitivity, and so many others. But Galena has above these a special reference to yourself and you know what that is.

From Galena, a town under a glass bell, very beautiful, I went back much restored. But so taken with the idea of a trip that this week I have come down to Springfield.

"Friendly as a hotel bedroom in a town where you know no one."

Next week I think I shall try Crawfordsville Indiana. The week-end after that will include three performances of the Passion Music according to Matthew[3] and then I shall go home to New Haven.

All my children are well. Bob Ardrey,[4] the dramatist, is sick with deferred hope, Peggy Barnes[5] not yet having made up her mind on the play contest that should bring him four hundred dollars and the New York managers still withholding their word. John Pratt,[6] the artist, has just delivered to Alice Rouillier[7] ten more painting[s] on glass that show him at his best. One of them called *Lorenzo the Magnificent's Giraffe*, shows a group of nuns admiring the animals, some of them on a second story gallery carressing his nose. Robert Davis,[8] the philosopher, rereads each lecture in the new volume[9] eight times deriving more and more illuminations and scarcely daring to move on to the next lecture lest the bright light of the first be somehow lost while the new begins. Really, Gertrude, that was the listener, that was the fiery incitement that lecture-writer must have divined; if ever your mind should think of an Eckermann[10] there is one waiting,—one that for all my love and grateful receptivity makes me ashamed of my inadequacy to pure abstract thinking.

The University Press committee[11] is solemnly sitting on your lectures, but I have a private word that they are pleased and proud. All I want now is that they hurry.

My ice box when I returned was full, Alice, of equipment, especially the most delicious white butter—I found a number of works of fiction on the shelves which I assume I may enjoy and disperse. If you have errands for me to do, rejoice me with the commission.

As an hour has gone by and I have begun to tremble I shall now take my leave and write you again under the SIGN of a more POSSIBLE RECOGNITION. Outside the window the automobile horns of Springfield sound like the bleating of friendly lambs in a meadow and the first electric signs of evening conduce to tranquil thoughts.

I thank you with all my heart for the beautiful concern in your letter.

> Devotedly
> Thornton

SAMPLE[12]
This is an
example of
words written
in this con-
dition

1. These details about the odd "unimportant nervous breakdown" identified in the telegram of 2 April return in a letter postmarked 17 April 1935 (YCAL) to his sister Charlotte Wilder in New York: "Did you hear I fainted and hung under the shadow of a nervous breakdown. It was wonderful. All due to unrequited love for Gertrude Stein."

2. During academic quarters, Wilder often spent weekends away from Chicago looking for the solitude he desired. According to his date book (YCAL), from Friday, 29 March, until 31 March or 1 April, Wilder was in Galena, Illinois, where Ulysses Grant in 1860 worked as a clerk in his father's leather goods business. Wilder knew of Stein's interest in Grant and of her conversations in November 1934 and March 1935 with Lloyd Lewis, the writer and journalist for the *Chicago Daily News*, with whom she shared an interest in Grant and to whom she lent *Four In America*, her study of Grant, Wilbur Wright, Henry James, and George Washington. Lewis returned the typescript to Carl Van Vechten on 5 April (see Gallup, *Flowers*, 297). Wilder apparently did not read the typescript until early September 1935. (See also Stein to Wilder [early September 1935], n. 2, and Wilder to Stein [early September 1935]. Although he did not collaborate with Stein, Lewis's study of Grant, *Captain Sam Grant*, was published posthumously in 1950.

3. Frederick Stock led the Chicago Symphony Orchestra, with the Apollo Club and the Chicago Symphony Choir, in Bach's *Passion According to Saint Matthew* on 18 and 19 April.

4. Robert Ardrey, playwright and anthropologist, had been a member of Wilder's creative writing class at the University of Chicago in 1930 and remained a protégé for some years afterward. In 1935 Ardrey submitted "House on Fire," a play about Polish family life in Chicago, for the Charles

Sergel Award in Drama at the University of Chicago. Wilder informed Ardrey on 21 May (Chicago) that the four-hundred-dollar prize would be divided between himself and another contestant. Wilder worked hard to get the play produced in New York, arranging a meeting for Ardrey with Jed Harris, who asked for revisions but, as he was wont to do with many people's calls, refused Ardrey's once the rewriting was completed. Under the title *Star Spangled* the play opened in New York under Arthur Hopkins's direction at the Golden Theatre on 10 March 1936 and ran for twenty-three performances.

5. Margaret (Peggy) Ayer Barnes was a Chicago-born playwright and novelist who in 1935 served as the judge for the Charles Sergel Award in Drama. Barnes's dramatization of Edith Wharton's *The Age of Innocence* was produced in New York in 1928. With Edward Sheldon she wrote the plays *Jenny*, produced in 1929, and *Dishonored Lady*, produced in 1930. Her novel *Years of Grace* won the Pulitzer Prize in 1931.

6. Wilder contributed a foreword to the catalogue of an exhibition of Pratt's watercolors at the Increase Robinson Gallery in Chicago from 23 September to 14 October 1935. See Appendix III.

7. Alice Roullier, whose name Wilder misspells, was a Chicago art dealer. From 1918 to 1941 she chaired the exhibition committee of the Arts Club of Chicago.

8. Robert Frederick Davis graduated from the University of Chicago in 1935. He was interested in philosophy and metaphysics and was encouraged by his professors to go abroad for a year's study. He had also met Stein, who considered him extraordinary. He came from a large family who could not support advanced training. Wilder spoke to his parents and arranged for a stipend from his own funds. With Davis, he went to Europe, visited Stein, and proceeded to Vienna, where Davis learned German and continued his study of philosophy.

9. *Lectures In America* was published by Random House on 14 March 1935. On 20 March Stein wrote to Carl Van Vechten that she had received copies (see Burns, *Letters*, 1:416–17)

10. *Conversations with Eckermann*, (1823–1832) is the record of Goethe's conversations with a young admirer, Johann Peter Eckermann. Wilder read, reread, and annotated his copy of *Conversations with Eckermann* throughout his life. Isabel Wilder writes,

> From childhood Thornton was a hero worshipper (and advised the young to go out and become the same). . . The essay "Goethe and World Literature" is his *hommage* to Goethe, companion from his sixteenth year when he heard our mother read (she attended German classes at the university [University of California, Berkeley] so that she could "keep up" with her children):
>   *Kennst du das Land wo die Zitronen blüh'n?*
> The cadence and glow of that poem caught and held his imagination. Open on his bedside table the day he died was a heavily annotated copy of a German edition of the *Conversations with Eckermann* (Wilder, *American Characteristics*, xiv).

Although Wilder proposes Robert Davis as Stein's Eckermann, it is clear that Wilder's relationship with Stein had reached the point where he understood her needs and had committed himself to fulfilling them. His introductions to *Narration* and later the *Geographical History* established an intermediary relationship between her and her audience that was profitable to both.

11. Wilder recommended to the University of Chicago Press on 11 March that they publish Stein's lectures on narration. The director of the press, Dean Gordon J. Laing, circulated the manuscript among members of the publications committee and the board of publications. Among those who reported on the manuscript was Robert Morss Lovett, who did not concur with Wilder's recommendation but felt that the lectures "may be properly published as a part of literary history. Gertrude Stein is a fact, as Dadaism is a fact, and records of both ought to be preserved" (Lovett to Press, 5 April 1935, Chicago). Others took a far more negative view of the project. On 19 April the publications committee approved the publication of the lectures provided Wilder added an introduction to "bring home the significance of the book" (copy, Chicago) (see Wilder to Stein and Toklas, 26 May 1935).

12. Marginal note next to the paragraph beginning "As an hour has gone by. . . ."

To Thornton Wilder, Chicago, Illinois

[postmark: 12 April 1935]

Hotel Mark Hopkins
Nob Hill
San Francisco [California]

My dearest Thornton,

It was nice hearing from you again and so much has happened and now we are to pass one night and a piece of a day in Chicago, we get there next Saturday at about three spend the night at Bobsie [Goodspeed]'s and leave the next afternoon for New York and during that time we must be together,[1] and please plan to get to Bilignin very soon after because there we will rest you up, we really truly will, we sail on the Champlain the 4 of May and after ten days in Paris we are off to Bilignin and you too very soon oh yes very very soon and all the rest when we meet in Chicago, I love Chicago and I guess I liked the two weeks there in your apartment and with all your family[2] the best of everything, and I think I tell everybody so so much so that Alice tells me not to because it is not polite to the others but it is true and we did have a most awfully good time there, and in return you will come to Bilignin and have an awfully good time there, so much love to you Thornton

Always
Gtrde.

1. On 20 April, during Stein's stopover in Chicago on her way back to New York, Wilder saw her at a dinner party given by Goodspeed.

2. "Family" refers to Wilder's friends in Chicago, not to the Wilder family. Stein met only Wilder's sister Isabel, who stopped in Chicago in March 1935 on a book promotion tour through the Midwest for her second novel, *Heart, Be Still* (1934).

To Thornton Wilder, Chicago, Illinois

[postmark: 25 April 1935]

Hotel Algonquin
59 to 65 West Forty-fourth
Street
New York [New York]

My dear Thornton,

Here we are and shopping and then we leave on the 4 by the Champlain and we are sad most sad because we loved it, we really truly loved it, we loved it all and this summer we will tell each other about it each other includes you and you will be there. I am inclosing a letter from the Bread loaf, I think it looks promising for [Robert W.] Stallman,[1] I hope it works out alright, perhaps we will be seeing you here, let us know, Carl [Van Vechten][2] is mad to photograph you, and we hold out hopes, lots and lots and lots of love and it was so nice seeing you,

Gtrde.

27 rue de Fleurus—Paris
Bilignin, par Belley, Ain.

1. Robert Wooster Stallman was one of Stein's students in Chicago. Stein wrote a recommendation for him to the Bread Loaf School and the Writers' Conference, Middlebury College, Vermont. Wilder provided Stallman, who owing to illness was unable to work, with a monthly stipend paid anonymously through the university. Stallman later became professor of English at the University of Connecticut at Storrs. He was a specialist in Stephen Crane and Henry James. His book *The Houses that James Built and Other Literary Studies* (East Lansing: Michigan State Univ. Press, 1964), was dedicated to Wilder:

> TO THORNTON WILDER
> In token appreciation for his sponsorship of an apprentice
> poet and critic: 1934–1935
> *We go to gain a little patch of ground*
> *That hath in it no profit but the name.*
> —Hamlet: IV, iv, 18–19

Stallman acknowledges his debt to Wilder in "To Thornton Wilder: A Note in Gratitude," in *Four Quarters, Thornton Wilder Number,* La Salle College, Philadelphia, 16: 4 (May 1967): 28–29.

2. Van Vechten, critic and novelist, turned in 1932 from writing to photography. His work documents major figures in the arts, the Harlem Renaissance, and cultural events. Van Vechten did not photograph Wilder until 1948, as Mr. Antrobus in *The Skin of Our Teeth* at the Westport (Connecticut) Playhouse. Although both were devoted to Stein, they did not become friends.

To Gertrude Stein and Alice Toklas, New York, N.Y.

Breakfast among the bishops[1]   Century Club
4 May 1935   7 West Forty-Third Street
                                           New York [New York]

Dear Gertrude—Alice[2]

When people go away on boats we always say: Now have a good rest in the ocean air. But how can I say that to you two, who find a daily restorative in the exercise of your gifts and who have been exercising your gifts to such an extent that you seem to be even twice as well as when you came over.

So all I can wish you—along with these *nectarines—is that you find, right and left, people as appreciative as me, on whom Alice may exercise her gifts of graciousness and thoughtfulness and on whom Gertrude can turn the detonations of her ideas and her eyes.

Because appreciative I certainly am, appreciative I certainly am.
Your slow-thinking but quick-loving
                    Thornton
*"Charles" assures me there are no nectarines, so I send what I can.[3]
Anything but a book, I said to myself.
                    T.

    1. "Breakfast among the bishops" describes breakfast at the Century Association, 7 West 43d Street in New York. Members of the association were senior men of distinction. Wilder was sponsored for membership at an unusually young age, in January 1930, as a result of his early fame as an author.
    2. Wilder wrote the names Gertrude and Alice in the form of a circle, perhaps in imitation of the circular rose motto that appeared on Stein's stationery.
    3. Wilder was in New York on Friday, 3 May, for a farewell dinner with Stein and Toklas the night before they sailed. His note was sent to the boat with a basket of fruit by Maison Charles, which regularly sent gifts for departing passengers to boats.

To Gertrude Stein and Alice Toklas, Bilignin, France

26 May 1935   50 Deepwood Drive
                                               New Haven [Connecticut]

                                               Sailing from Montreal June 28
                                               American Express Co. Paris
                                               July 6—

Dear Twain:
            Your letters arriving this morning were a great pleasure.[1] I'm going through such a spiritless interim, marking time. Cleaning my desk, reading without plan, conversing with the family, occasional trips to New York (amid uneasy defeatist New Yorkers who practically burst into tears if you say a natural simple word to them). I feel like a cad to be going abroad: here my women-folk are standing by, attending the protracted exasperating unlovable death of my father. I pass through the house having come—in their eyes— from a brightly lighted gay life in Chicago en route to a life of pleasure and glamor in Europe. No, they don't indict me for criminal non-participation, nor are they swamped with self-pity; but—
            Non parliamo più, ma guarda e passa.
    The proofs of the lectures with the introduction will be sent you soon.[2] The introduction is simpler than I first planned, is no intellectual treat, but I hope is redolent of happy admiration and persuasive tact. If the Press wants it to come out very promptly I assume that you will let me and two other enthusiasts (Ev Bouria[,] possessed by the god) read the proofs: scrupulously

observing the punctuation, since la verité se cache dans les nuances. The director of The University of Chicago Press is Dean Laing, retiring head of the Humanities Division, an authority on Roman law and a dry wit, pleasantly weary and cynical.[3]

I am going straight to Paris arriving about July 6.[4] [Robert] Davis gets off at Plymouth and goes to visit his ancestral Scotland. I have no time to visit my ancestral lands, for I have just figured out that my sixty-four great-grandparents' great-grandparents were distributed as follows:

New England English: 36
Scotch (Hebridean; Isle of Skye and Ila): 18
Polish-German: Nitsky, Nietsche, Nitchie, 2
Jew: (Captain Nehemiah Marks of London and Derby, Conn. 1746–1800)
    4
Dutch (Josue Slydel m. Elzbet Jannsen, Nieu Amsterdam, 1780) 2
French (The Riverains of Montreal, from a marchand-bourgeois of Tours)
    2.

There's the battlefield of my mind and pardon the digression.[5]
so
While Dr. Davis is listening to his atavisms I shall be looking around Paris with the faint malaise that capital always gives me. I shall go to the Petit Palais and educate my eyes on the four Giorgiones.[6] I shall try to get a little work done in my hotel room.

[Four hours later.[7]

Curses. Execrations. Begonias, Eschatological Acrocoraunia.

My brother Amos was to have been married in September. I unfortunately would not be able to be there and usher in striped trousers and a camellia. The fiancée arrived for lunch today and announced that they were advancing the date of the marriage. Suppose they got married about the Fourth of July, *then* could I postpone my sailing and usher?[8]

I played the Languid. I'm not well, no,—I certainly hope I can be at the wedding, but I'm really not well. I have funny moods. I have to withdraw when there are large groups of people, etc.

What fetishes there are about us. This notion that one must be present at weddings and funerals.

Gr—r—r—r.

If I have to postpone my sailing, I'll put on such a performance of a death's-head at the ceremony as will never be forgotten.

Think nothing of it; I'll find a way.]

But even if I do arrive on your doorstep about July 18th that will be much later than I had first suggested, and may inconvenience you.

So do remember that I can go perfectly well to the hotel at Belley where you used to live.[9] You never have to be concerned about such matters as housing with me. I don't notice places as *having any relation to me.* I want to look at you both often and hear you talk to me; I want to be with you, and that can be arranged in a great many ways.

Half my time is spent in persuading people that I only see life as energy—affections and ideas and glances—and that things don't speak to me. People give me presents! Imagine! What does one do with a present? I begin to see that I am one of the most non-daily life Americans that ever walked. I live in two suitcases and a brief-case. Similarly Gertrude with TIME. When I have looked at a thing I have, as far as I am able, possessed it. Duration can do very little to reinforce that.

So there's another digression to explain that I rejoice in every inch of me that I shall be seeing you again, but that the *how* and the *how long* is not at the heart of the matter.

Bobsy sent a sheaf of photographs of that evening. Fine.[10] ¶ You will be glad to know that Liberty Magazine has tried to solve the problem of Journalism and the time-sense. They wrestled and wrestled and then evolved the following slogan: Read LIBERTY—The NEWS BEFORE IT HAPPENS—READ LIBERTY.[11] ¶ Gertrude in all seriousness, music is only for adolescents? Do I have to make my peace with that thought? ¶ Do you know Robert Frost's poem about the girl whose life was changed before her father called her Maple?[12] ¶ Alice, when we take that house in Washington Square, having first all got terribly rich off the syndicates, my sister Isabel says that she'll lend us the thing she loves best in the world, an entire dinner service of early Victorian milk-glass, with a parade of old ruby goblets to go with it and a milk-glass statuary for a center piece. Our guests will be pâmés [swoon].[13] I can see you up in your sewing room surveying the Park while I solemnly walk Basket around for his constitutional. I'm quite serious about it all and have been cudgelling my brains about how to get rich. I've just been offered some rôles on the stage (sic). I'd come home every evening at eleven-thirty, dizzy with applause and we'd all have oysters and champagne until my excitement abated, Gertrude in the meantime having written some detective stories that solved both our problem of riches and her problem of how the corpse could be rendered interesting. ¶ Other people when they have nothing more to say, draw to a close; but I prefer to run on and on.

At all events I shall write you again and again (with and without RECOGNITION)[14] before I arrive in person bursting with happy ecspectancy [i.e., expectancy].

Your devoted
Thornton

1. Stein's first letters following her return to France have not survived. In the Italian following the first paragraph Wilder appears to be misquoting Dante, *Inferno*, Canto III, line 51: "non ragioniam di lor, ma guarda e passa." ("let us not talk of them, but look and pass." tr. Allen Mandelbaum).

2. A memorandum from Dean Gordon J. Laing to a Miss Alexander at the University of Chicago Press on 21 May (copy, Chicago) informed her that Wilder had returned the typescript of *Narration* with his introduction. With the text now ready for the compositor, Dean Laing reminded Alexander to "give the copyreaders very definite instructions to waive Press style and use only the punctuation now in the manuscript. As you doubtless know the paucity of punctuation marks is one of the notable features of Miss Stein's work." Neither Stein's manuscript for the lectures on narration nor the typescript used to set the printed edition survives. In a notebook bought in America she drafted an outline of each of the four lectures. By 28 February she wrote to Carl Van Vechten that she had completed two (Burns, *Letters*, 1:401–02). In the same notebook she later entered notes for other texts. An extant typescript of *Narration* in YCAL contains some author's changes that appear in the printed text, some that do not, and a few indications of where Stein, perhaps during delivery, incorporated examples from her writings.

3. Gordon Jennings Laing taught Latin at the University of Chicago from 1899 to 1935 and was general editor of the University of Chicago Press from 1909 to 1940.

4. Wilder sailed on 28 June from Montreal to Le Havre aboard the RMS *Ascania*.

5. In the Wilder Archives at YCAL is a detailed family tree as well as a biography of his maternal great-grandfather (see Arthur Channing Downs, Jr., *The Architecture and Life of the Hon. Thornton MacNess Niven (1806–1895)* [Goshen, N.Y.: Orange County Community of Museums and Galleries, 1971]).

6. The summer exhibition at the Petit Palais that year was *L'Art Italien de Cimabue à Tiepolo*. Organized by Raymond Escholier, the exhibition contained more than twenty-two hundred works on loan from more than twelve countries. Among others, four paintings by Giorgione were on view: *La Tempête, Judith, Portrait de Jeune Homme*, and *Le Concert Champêtre*.

7. Wilder brackets the section from "Four hours later" to "Think nothing of it; I'll find a way," marking it as an aside.

8. Amos Niven Wilder married Catharine Kerlin on 26 June 1935 at her parents' house in Moorestown, New Jersey.

9. From 1924 until 1929, when Stein and Toklas acquired a lease on a house in Bilignin, a village near Belley, they stayed at the Hotel Pernollet in Belley, which they had discovered on the way to Nice in 1923.

10. Presumably photographs taken at Goodspeed's farewell party for Stein in Chicago on 20 April.

11. *Liberty Magazine*, founded in 1924 by the McCormick-Patterson press syndicate, was purchased by Bernarr Macfadden in 1931. With *Collier's* and the *Saturday Evening Post*, it was among the most popular five-cent weeklies. *Liberty* dated its issues a week in advance—hence Wilder's observation. Stein discusses the problem in *Narration*, 35–37: "Newspapers want to do something, they want to tell what is happening as if it were just then happening. They want to write that happening as if it was happening on the day the newspapers are read that is not as if the thing was happening on the day the newspaper is read a little that all the same but as if the writing were being written as it is read, that is what they mean by hot off the press, but yet after all there is an interval generally six hours or so but always an interval, and that interval they try to bridge by head lines, and do they succeed, not very well I guess not very well because it is not possible to tell in the way they have to tell a thing that is told as a reality, all this has an awful lot to do with the writing of history" (35).

12. A reading of Frost's poem "Maple" suggests that Wilder meant "because" rather than "before" to describe the girl whose life was changed by her name. Frost's poem may have come to Wilder's mind because on 2 May he had taken a walk with the poet in New Haven (date book, YCAL). Wilder and Frost were friends, and one of Wilder's college themes from 1919 was an appreciation of Frost's poetry (YCAL).

13. After their bon voyage dinner on 3 May, Stein, Toklas, and Wilder went for a last stroll, this time in Washington Square. Wilder, fantasizing, suggested that they might take a house there together when they all became rich. Isabel Wilder notes that she assembled her Victorian milk-glass dinner service a piece at a time.

14. "Recognition" occurs in the fourth lecture in Stein's *Narration*. Considering the difference between spoken and written language, she writes, "When you write this is of course recognition there is the recognition that you recognize what you write as you write, while as you talk there is of course some recognition but really is there any real recognition of what you talk as you talk. I myself think not, and therefore naturally not you do not write as you talk, because as you write you recognize what you write as you write and as you talk you do not recognize what you talk as you talk. There really is no real reason why you should since after all you are not your audience as you talk nobody is not really as anybody talks that is just talks" (53–54).

Alice Toklas: To Thornton Wilder, New Haven, Connecticut

7th June 1935   Bilignin par Belley
                                                                Ain

Dear Thornton—

Because we want you to know at once that the 18th [July] is perfect and that we expect you of course to try the house. We are so proud of the running hot water in the bath room and we've a nice cook and we'd mind terribly if you thought the hotel at Belley could compensate with its greater conveniences for the missing view—nightingales and american coffee. So you'll try us please and we would think it the perfect test of humour for the future if you were to prefer Belley caf[e] to pace Bilignin. And now about Washington Square and the Victorian dinner set and the red glass ware and the center piece to match the dinner set. My heart stopped with envy of your sister Isabelle's possession when I read about them—but last night when G[ertrude]. said "you write to tell Thornton about the 18th (we go to market solemnly once a week—Saturday today—and G. is never ready early enough—every thing is sold by the time we get there) and don't forget to say we accept his sister's offer of the glass ware when we settle at least for the winters there—I don't think it would be so expensive." I was breathless then and still am. I forgot to say G. added "We have plenty of furniture." So perhaps we will all be in Washington Square yet—of course it's the hope of my declining years—it's the last thing I'll want for myself. Please tell your sister how many happy thoughts her generosity provides—and if we do realise a Wash. Sq. domicile I'll wash them myself[.] Perhaps you'd have some idea if there is a story or two free at what price and would that happily include your Midway frigo—bath & heating—you see how desperately I want it. I'd be loving you for the dream alone—if there weren't so many other reasons

always yours
Alice

To Thornton Wilder, New Haven, Connecticut

[postmark: 8 June 1935]   Bilignin par Belley
                                                            Ain

My dear Thornton,

   Yes you shall and will stay where you like as you like as long as you like and wherever you like, but I think at your date at any of your dates we will be free and so glad to see you, there has not been much sunshine so far, there are nightingales and it is pretty and by the time you come there will be sunshine and so please us and please everybody, yes certainly correct the lectures if you will be so kind that is the proofs I want awfully to see the introduction in print not having seen it otherwise so do whatever you want to do about it,[1] I have almost begun my new work, not really but almost, it remains the geographical history of America with the sub title the relation of human nature to the human mind, which of course allows me anything and is once more to be the history of the Universe that is our universe,[2] I feel that necessity coming over me again, it is a necessity, but I am hesitating to begin but begin it will, and go on it will at least it will, their wills a bouquet, that was always a favorite work of mine, of mine, and some day you will have them play it in Chicago,[3] you see I am beginning, and it will be nice seeing you and we liked your grandparents,[4] it is not a confusion, although it might have been if it so completely had not, so any date you set will do, really and truly do, because Alice and I love you very much and Basket and Pepe will too,[5] in part you might say they already do, too
                                  always
                                  Gtrde.[6]

   1. See Wilder to Stein and Toklas, 26 May 1935.
   2. *The Geographical History Of America Or The Relation Of Human Nature To The Human Mind* occupied Stein throughout the summer and was completed by the end of September (see Stein to Wilder, 20 September 1935).
   3. Stein's play *A Bouquet. Their Wills* is also an opera libretto and concerns property and status that lead to marriages and families and in turn necessitate wills. The bouquet of the title is a funeral bouquet that is also a memorial portrait. The piece comes up because Stein plays on the word *will* throughout this letter. Written in the summer of 1928, the play was published in *Operas And Plays* in 1932.
   4. An allusion to Wilder's list of ancestors in his letter of 26 May.
   5. Basket was Stein's white poodle, acquired in early 1929. Pépé, a Chihuahua, was bred by the painter Francis Picabia and given to Stein and Toklas in June 1932 to replace Byron, who lived less than a year. The dogs were treated as family members and entered Stein's writing.
   6. The letter of 7 June from Toklas was probably included with this letter.

To Alice Toklas and Gertrude Stein, Bilignin, France

9 July 1935   American Express Company
                                                       Rue Scribe, Paris
                                                       Or
                                                       Hotel Buckingham
                                                       43 rue des Mathurins
                                                       Paris VIII

Dear Alice dear Gertrude dear Twain:[1]

There's really nothing to write about. The voyage was as foreseen, the arrival was as foreseen, and my present days are as foreseen. The Unforseen begins at Bilignin on the 24th. The Good, the Beautiful, and the Wise alone are unpredictable. Have I an idea there or haven't I? No matter; at present I am reposing on the feather-bed of what my imagination had prepared for me: this tiny pink and white room, the cafe-au-lait in the morning and the automobile klaxons under my window. The majority of French women still wear black and have very fine eyes; the majority of French men still have the beginnings or the whole of pomposity, but reserve one feature, eyes or mouth, to express wit and disillusion. I have been two days without speaking to a soul, practically. The benefits accrue. Twice a day with my meals I have half a carafe of wine and get drunk. For an hour I drift through a metabolic paradise, thinking strange things. I don't suppose it does me any harm, for I am raging with good health, but I am disturbed at finding a happiness in chemistry alone.

The show of Italian paintings is wonderful; yes, wonderful beyond foresight. Glory succeeds glory; as though it were some prodigious baseball game where each player comes to the bat, swings and knocks the ball into the remotest fields and runs home. Some players I never heard of, like Cossa and Tura come trotting back as unwinded as Raphael and Bronzino. For once in a gallery I did not fall to "composing" the features of my fellow-visitors.

It's as though I had never seen Botticelli before.

My principle gratitude goes to an angel in blue high up in one corner of a Piero della Francesca, slate-blue with a violet girdle. I never saw such beauty in my life. I've *heard* it but I never saw it before.[2]

I underwent things last night, too. Ludmilla Pitoëff was appearing in an unimportant play. I never paid money to intrude on such simple suffering before. (I almost said: I never *caused* such simple suffering, so direct was it.) I walked all the way to the Place St. Germain and back.[3]

But to Business:

I have the Publisher's Dummy of the Lectures on Narration. In a letter I am forwarding to you Mr. Bean the manager of the University Press says that budgetary troubles have prevented their printing the work until Fall. Proof follows very soon. The contract is here in my things and goes down to you tomorrow. I told them, long ago, that I was a little afraid of going ahead without your express permission, but that I would read the proofs, conclude the business and perhaps suffer your scoldings later. Mr. Bean decided not to use my tentative intermediacy, I see, though you[r] letters since then have accorded me the rights. I don't know whether you will like the plan of bringing out a special signed edition as well as a regular edition. If you do accept such a procedure will you write me a word and I will cable to him Plans Approved, adding to the cable only that there is no justification for me signing the *de luxe* edition also. I want to sign my name below yours on any page in the world that implies my affection and indebtedness but I will not be shown as pretending to share in the radience of those lectures which bear in every word, ma foi, the mark of one hand.[4] Mr. Bean's notions of publishing decorum do not rise above the level of a collector of Christopher Morley.[5]

Robert Davis, that grave yet turbulent soul that accompanies me on my journies has gone off to Stonehenge and Glastonbury and to Scotland. All the way over he read *Process and Reality*[6] and *The Making of Americans*.[7] Behind that princely reserve there rage three hero-worships, Freud, Whitehead and Gertrude Stein.[8] On board a distinguished Yale history professor happened to say that he thought Whitehead wrote unclearly; slowly and surely Davis stirred himself and the Professor is wary to this day of venturing outside his province. I too have been taking lessons in Metaphysics, yes, ma'am, and I do not allow myself to gaze long at the comic aspects of myself with my little picture-book mind trying solemnly to grasp all the factors involved in Whitehead's description of an Occasion of Experience, I mean: a Prehension. I had to draw a diagram: there it is: there's the stream of consciousness flowing by like a river, Alice, from the Country at the left marked "Antecent Occasions" to the Country at the extreme right, Gertrude, marked "Passes into Objective Immortality i.e. The Past," there from above enters the Object ("provided by Creativity—passive until Creativity gives it this activating potentiality,["] my friends, to START OFF this occasion.) There it all is, on that journey from left to right, from Re-enactment to Anticipation, under the teleology of the Universe.[9] In return for these illuminations I teach Davis the German language.

A radiogram arrived to me on the boat that gave me a stirring satisfaction. It was from Ruth Gordon the best actress in America.[10] At my urging on my long varied unstanchable persuasion she had set aside her troubled lassitude, her forebodings before her own self-criticism and had gone to Westport Connecticut to open the season in the best of the summer theatres playing Mrs. Pinchwife in Wycherly's *The Country Wife*. The radiogram reads: *Personal triumph Times rave notices gratitude love Ruth*. The performance must have been the soul of wit and slyness and drollery. She sketched out for me some of the business she had planned and I brought her all the accounts I could find of Ada Rehan in the part.[11] *Gratitude.* The minute the word has been said it becomes unnecessary, but what a minute it is.

Up Ruth climbs, through many a disadvantage, but within five years she will have effaced Lynne Fontanne and her two best friends Kit Cornell and Helen Hayes. I keep whispering to her *Rejane, Rejane, Ada Rehan.*[12] ¶ I keep putting things in my books and a few years later they start happening in my life. There I am as Uncle Pio; there is Ruth, even down to her wonderful little five-year old boy.[13] What does my diagram say? "The Past is immanent in the Present (1) as a Previous occasion to be re-enacted (2) as an Object to be prehended by the Present."[14]

Tomorrow I go back to take up the drawings of the old masters.[15] I shall lose my wits.

Dear Alice, dear Gertrude, Bilignin never had a more devoted visitor than is, and will be

Your friend
Thornton

1. This letter has a number of misspellings transcribed as Wilder wrote them: "principle," "radience," "Antecent," And "Wycherly."

2. The exhibition *L'Art Italien de Cimabue à Tiepolo* (see Wilder to Stein, 26 May 1935, n. 6) included Botticelli's *The Birth of Venus.* The catalogue lists four paintings by Piero della Francesca. Wilder is probably referring to the polyptych *Madonna and Child with Four Saints; The Annunciation* (no. 367 in the catalogue, listed as *Vierge et l'enfant*). The uppermost part of this polyptych is a panel, *The Annunciation,* with the archangel Gabriel as Wilder describes him.

3. The husband-wife team of Russian-born actor/managers Ludmilla Pitoëff and Georges Pitoëff with their own Pitoëff Company performed Chekhov, Ibsen, Shaw, Maeterlinck, Leonid Andriev, Tolstoy, Bjørnstjerne Bjørnson, and Oskar Schlemmer, among others, in Geneva, 1915–22, and in Paris, 1919–39. Wilder had been impressed early by the Pitoëffs. In a letter of 20 May 1923 to the theatrical producer Brock Pemberton, he commented on their production of *Six Characters in Search of an Author* and noted, "Little modest Pitoëff and his white-washed barn now constitute one of the great theatres of the world" (Wilder Letter-Book 1923, letter XVIII, YCAL). The "unimportant play" Wilder saw was Henri de Ghéon's *La Complainte de Pranzini et de Thérèse de Lisieux.*

4. Donald Bean wrote to Wilder on 19 June (copy, Chicago) about the contract for the book and the bindings for the different printings. *Narration* was published on 10 December 1935 in an edition of 872 copies at $2.50. On 17 December 1935 a deluxe slipcased edition of 120 numbered copies, signed by Stein and Wilder, was also published. Only one hundred copies of the limited edition were for sale, at $10 (full bibliographic information is given in Wilson, *Stein,* A 25a and b, p. 35). Stein eventually inscribed the dummy to Carl Van Vechten: "For Papa Woojums/and every blank page in it is filled full of love for you/Baby Woojums" (YCAL). Woojums was an affectionate name that Van Vechten gave to some friends (for a discussion of this name and its origins, see Burns, *Letters,* 1:255, n. 2).

5. Christopher Morley was a prolific American novelist, newspaper columnist, and writer on book collecting and selling. Wilder likens Donald Bean to the charming but lightweight Morley.

6. *Process and Reality: An Essay in Cosmology* by Alfred North Whitehead, based on his Gifford Lectures at the University of Edinburgh in the winter of 1927–28.

7. Davis and Wilder were reading the abridged version of *The Making Of Americans* published by Harcourt Brace in 1934.

8. Stein and Toklas met Alfred North Whitehead in July 1914 and spent a weekend with him

and his family. As a result of the declaration of war, they stayed on with them for eleven weeks, returning to Paris on 19 October 1914 (see Gallup, *Flowers*, 100, and Burns, *Letters*, 1:28–31). In *The Autobiography Of Alice B. Toklas*, Stein has Toklas say of Stein, Picasso, and Whitehead, "Only three times in
my life have I met a genius and each time a bell within me rang." Davis, following his own interests,
changes the three to Freud, Whitehead, and Stein. Davis would have had the opportunity to hear
Whitehead in person in 1933 when Whitehead delivered two lectures, "Nature Lifeless" and "Nature
Alive," at the University of Chicago. They were published in 1934 by the University of Chicago Press.

     9. In a notebook from 1935 marked "Ascania," after the ship on which he traveled to Europe
(YCAL), Wilder diagrams the ideas of Whitehead that he describes in this letter in words.

     10. Ruth Gordon, the stage and screen actress, met Wilder in 1930, through either Alexander
Woollcott or the playwright Edward Sheldon. Their friendship was immediate and lasting. Gordon
always considered Mrs. Pinchwife in Wycherley's *The Country Wife* one of her most successful roles.
In 1954 she would create the role of Dolly Levi in *The Matchmaker*, Wilder's rewritten version of *The
Merchant of Yonkers*.

     11. Ada Rehan came to America from Ireland and made her theatrical debut in Newark, New
Jersey, at the age of six. She triumphed as Peggy Thrift in *The Country Girl*, Augustin Daly's adaptation
of David Garrick's version of *The Country Wife*, with Daly's company in 1883 and again in 1898. We do
not know precisely what Rehan material Wilder sent to Gordon.

     12. Lynn Fontanne (the addition of "e" in *Lynne* was a common error), Katharine Cornell, and
Helen Hayes were leading American actresses. Réjane, born Gabrielle Réju, was a much-loved
ornament of Parisian boulevard comedy and the first French Nora of Ibsen's *A Doll's House*.

     13. In Wilder's *The Bridge of San Luis Rey*, Uncle Pio is described as Camila Perichole's adviser:
"Only one person knew for certain that the Perichole was a great performer and that was her tutor,
Uncle Pio." He later received permission from the dying actress to take her son, Don Jaime, to Lima.
"I shall teach him all that a gentleman should know—fencing and Latin and music," Uncle Pio says.
The passage reflects the relationship between Wilder, Ruth Gordon, and Gordon's son by Jed Harris.

     14. Wilder refers to the diagrams he made in the "Ascania" notebook while reading Whitehead's
Process and Reality.

     15. The drawings were in the exhibition *L'Art Italien de Cimabue à Tiepolo* at the Petit Palais.

To Thornton Wilder, Paris, France

10 July 1935[1]   Bilignin par Belley
                                                                    Ain

My dear Thornton,

     We are as happy as happy can be that you always are on
our side of the sea and that you will be here soon, is [Robert] Davis coming
with you and we will call for you at Tenay and bring you back in triumph but
there is plenty of time to arrange about that.[2] I am pleased next to going to be
seeing you soon with the book, it is a beautiful page the proportions the
printing and everything just right so will you tell Mr. Bean so, and how pleased
I am, the signatures will be yours and mine I like the way you sign your name I
would like there to be two ffs in it because you make ffs so beautifully but
anyway Thornton Wilder is quite pretty enough, and Thornton Wilder is to be
signed with me or there is to be no signature, so tell Mr. Bean so, the only

thing I have done is to take out two paragraphs in the contract the ones 5 and 6 which since they are lectures might later if any body wanted to make trouble might be a bother, as the subject well is as you might say any subject,[3] I am working a lot on the relation of human nature to the human mind and in it you come in, as which well that is for you to see.[4] Alice makes fun of me, but I think it is pretty good and I like to be made fun of if it is alright that there is none no relation between human nature and the human mind, my it will be fun having you here it makes us happier than we can say

Always

Gtrde.

1. The date, supplied by Wilder, may be the date of receipt or of the postmark; no envelope has survived.

2. Tenay, a railway stop between Lyons and Geneva. On 17 July Stein suggests that Wilder will arrive at Culoz. However, Wilder's date book (YCAL) indicates that Stein met Davis and him at Aix-les-Bains.

3. A sample colophon page for signatures came with the dummy of *Narration*. Stein alludes to the way Wilder shaped the two *ffs* in *Pitoëff* in his letter of 9 July 1935.

4. Wilder first enters the *Geographical History* in "The Portrait of Thornton Wilder" (71–73), written before his arrival in Bilignin on 23 July. His name turns up again when Stein considers the nature of relations: "Jo Alsop is he a relation./René Crevel was./Thornton Wilder is" (97). Stein had met the journalist Joseph Alsop in America; René Crevel appears in the past tense because he committed suicide in the night of 17–18 June 1935. Wilder is also in one of the many short plays incorporated in the *Geographical History* (100–01). His presence can be felt from page 180 to 216, where Stein recreates her long conversations with him and Davis and their exchanges about music, masterpieces, and Shakespeare. She returns to Wilder near the end of the book: "Anybody knows how easy it is for anything written to be real. Not when it is almost anything but when it is anything oh yes and to some something is real and to some nothing is real that is written but writing can make anybody cry. Yes indeed yes. It is so difficult to have anything to do with master-pieces."

"Yes Thornton" (240).

To Gertrude Stein and Alice Toklas, Bilignin, France

16 July 1935

American Express Co
11 Rue Scribe
or
Hotel Buckingham
43 rue des Mathurins
Paris VIII

Dear Deux:

The cable and the contracts have gone off.

It'll turn my head ("Mr. Wilder, you must be terribly careful that you don't get *spoiled* in life" literary hostesses are always telling me among the potted palms) but I'll sign my names.[1]

Not a gunshot on Bastille Day.

Winged Victory, very fine.

Mansards and the tug boats on the Seine and the bookshelves on the quais and women in musty black carrying sticks of bread have a delirious charm for everybody except me.

[Robert] Davis crossed over from London a week early.[2] Deeply moved by the countryside of Devon and Somersetshire, the streams of Glastonberry [i.e., Glastonbury] and dawnwalks to Stonehenge, but oppressed by London, and averse from the journey to SCOTLAND. Custodian Wilder exhibits Paris, including a night among the joints of Montmartre. Finally with successive drinks I almost lost him to a poule at the Bal Tabarin; my loud and high-minded No must still be echoing among those fly-speckled mirrors. I get a shy and grateful thanks the next morning. Very complicated thinking behind all that.

We go to Fontainebleau for three days. Long walks in the woods and elevated reading. May I come and see you a little before the 24th? My first plan was to come three days then he to follow for the next three days, then Innsbruck. The plan still holds. But if there are signs that the stream of sex-consciousness that for a Chicagoan's eyes hangs over Paris continues to stir up a turgid adolescence I may have to bring him down with me. All this is no disparagement of his rare, locked-up wisdom and passionate dedication to ideas.

I've begun working, may God give me lights.

I can no longer conceal from you two that I love you and am looking forward like a madman to gazing into your beautiful eyes. At the heart of love lies the consciousness of the fleetness of time. If I had only known your [i.e., you] four and six years ago when I strayed about this town looking in windows.

devotedly

Thornton

1. "Literary hostesses" may be an indirect reference to Lady Sibyl Colefax, who maintained a salon in London. Wilder had met her after winning his first Pulitzer Prize in 1928. He lunched with her on 14 July and hoped to interest her in publishing Stein's work in England. He did not know at the time that Stein already knew Lady Colefax. According to Isabel Wilder, "Thornton considered her a railroad station. She had a career which was to make people meet. She worked hard at that career, prepared for meeting people, read, got ready. Others laughed at her, but Thornton saw her as a kind of professional at what she was doing" (interview, 25 August 1988).

2. Davis had planned to join Wilder in Paris on 20 July but arrived on the thirteenth.

To Thornton Wilder, Paris, France

17 July 1935[1]   Bilignin par Belley
                                                   Ain

My dear Thornton,

        The train leaves Paris at 7:30 and gets to Culoz some-
where around 3 and that is where we are all to be but when are you coming or
would you rather take a night train, and is [Robert] Davis coming too, it will
be wonderfully delightful to have you, Alice is sad that the garden does no one
credit but there is nothing but sunshine which we like but other things do not
not undiluted, but anyway the country is very lovely and we will like everything we do like which is everything, when you will be here. There has been
another literary white hope for us Jay Laughlin and he says may he see you
and speak to you in Salzburg, and I said probably yes,[2] but anyway Belley that
is Bilignin, *Culoz* and then here, let us know when we are to get you at Culoz,
if you want the night train it suits us just as well anything suits us that brings
you, I like the page of printing more and more it is very beautiful[3]

                                    Gtrde.

    1. The date, supplied by Wilder, may be the date of receipt or of the postmark; no envelope has
survived.

    2. James Laughlin IV, later founder of New Directions, visited Stein on his way to Salzburg. A
year earlier, in the summer of 1934, he had been introduced to Stein by Bernard Faÿ and had worked
on publicity for her lecture tour. Stein had met Faÿ in 1924 through René Crevel when Faÿ was a
young professor at the University of Clermont-Ferrand. In 1932 he was elected to the chair of American civilization at the Collège de France.

    3. The printed page in the dummy of *Narration* (see Wilder to Stein, 9 July 1935, n. 4).

To Thornton Wilder, Paris, France
[TELEGRAM]

[postmark: 18 July 1935]   [Bilignin par Belley
                                                   Ain, France]

    YOU AND [Robert] DAVIS COME AS SOON AS YOU WANT LET ME KNOW WHEN
LOVE=[1]

                   GERTRUDE

    1. Wilder had originally planned to leave for Bilignin on 18 July, Davis joining him on the
twenty-first to stay until the twenty-fourth. Wilder and Davis in fact took the night train on Monday,
22 July, for Aix-les-Bains, where they met Stein the following day (date book, YCAL). During the ten-day
visit, Stein, Wilder, and Davis talked at length on long walks. Their conversations are transmuted into
Stein's *Geographical History*. On 27 July, Stein, Wilder, Toklas, and presumably Robert Davis drove to

Geneva, perhaps to purchase tickets for the men's trip to Zurich and Innsbruck. They also visited the castle of Chillon on Lake Geneva, sending a postcard to Carl Van Vechten (Burns, *Letters*, 2:438). That afternoon they saw Hilda Doolittle (H. D.) and Winifred Bryher in Vevey, but there is no record of how the meeting was arranged. Stein had known them since the midtwenties and had contributed to early issues of *Close-Up*, a magazine devoted to film, which Kenneth Macpherson edited with his wife, Bryher, from 1927 to 1933. Wilder had met H. D. in London in the summer of 1928. His arrival there was heralded not only because of the Pulitzer Prize he had won for *The Bridge of San Luis Rey* but also because of his planned walking tour of Europe with the boxer Gene Tunney. From H. D.'s first letter to Wilder of [?] August 1928 through his letter to her of 2 October 1935, Hellenism is the thread that carries through the correspondence: H. D.'s autobiographical novel *Hedylus* (1928), set in the third century B.C. on the island of Samos; Wilder's not-yet-finished novel *The Woman of Andros*; H. D.'s *Hyppolitus Temporizes* of 1927.

Doolittle would write Wilder in January 1931, after *The Woman of Andros* was published, and recall their conversations of 1928. Doolittle's letter of 29 July 1935 refers to a conversation they must have had during this visit about productions of Greek plays in America and the possibility of her translation of Euripides' *Ion* being staged. Wilder, in his reply of 2 October, gave her a detailed account of Greek theater in America from before World War I to 1935.

Wilder's meeting with Doolittle, an analysand of Freud in 1933–34, raises the possibility that it was she who arranged or helped to arrange Wilder's meeting with Freud. In her letter of 29 July, H. D. referred Wilder to friends in Vienna who were close to the psychoanalytic movement and gave him two introductions. One of these was to Frau Dr. Eugenie Schwarzwald; the other may have been to Dr. Alice Modern. However, there is no mention of Wilder or any of the friends named by Doolittle in Freud's letters to Doolittle. Modern was helpful in finding rooms for Robert Davis in Vienna (see Wilder to Stein, 23 September, n. 4). But who finally arranged Wilder's meeting with Freud remains a matter of speculation.

To Thornton Wilder, ?Innsbruck, Austria

[?2 August 1935][1] Bilignin par Belley
 Ain

How we do miss the Rover boys[2] after we got home we were so sad we thought we would have to light a fire to cheer us but then we took to talking about all their sweet and pleasant ways, the Rover boys and that soothed us. The Thornton lapped-spoiled little Mex[3] asks plaintively where is that lap do you remember when a congressman after the war spoke of the french women ruined niggers,[4] well that's Pepe, but really and truly we did enjoy every minute of you and only want you to do it again, I haven't begun to work yet but I will and then I'll tell you about it, I will like telling you about it and now bless you both

Always
Gtrde.

1. A page or two may be missing from this letter because there is no salutation. (See Wilder to Stein, 10 August 1935.) Presumably it was written after Stein and Toklas returned from driving Wilder

and Davis on 2 August to Geneva, where they took the train for Zurich. By Saturday, 3 August, they were in Innsbruck (date book, YCAL).

2. The Rover boys were heroes of a popular series of adventure stories written by Edward Stratemeyer under the pseudonym Arthur Winfield.

3. See Stein to Wilder, 8 June 1935, n. 5; *Everybody's Autobiography*, 48–49; Camfield, *Picabia*, 244 and n. 4.

4. Southern congressmen had angrily complained that allowing black soldiers to fraternize openly with European women would only encourage them to challenge segregation when they returned home.

To Gertrude Stein and Alice Toklas, Bilignin, France

6 Aug[ust] 1935

12:15 p.m. in a tiny room in
The Albergo Italia, the last
room vacant in the overcrowded
summer station:
Cortina d'Ampezzo.
The very fine dolomites are
pointing up to the sky on all
sides of the valley

Dear Friends:

The train from Geneva to Zurich was all right, but the train from Zurich to Innsbruck was terrible; we stood packed like sardines for hours, knee deep in teetering piles of luggage. In Zurich we passed the night in a deliriously expensive hotel. I knew no better.

There was a lot of rain in Innsbruck; no snow on the mountains. My Aunt Charlotte[1] appeared and for Bob [Davis]'s benefit I drew her out on the International Committee work of the Y.W.C.A. and the secondary committee work at the League, yes, all about agricultural planning, pest-fighting, the sale of opium, the traffic in women, and we got so mixed up about the SOCIAL CONSCIENCE that we almost came back to Bilignin to iron it out.

German language lessons went apace. Peter Vischer's statue of King Arthur.[2]

We bought leder-hosen and complete rig and will soon send you a photo-postal, illustrating the unquenchable flight (to from) identity which is the masquerade. Robert looks like something that grew up among the mushrooms of the Sch[w]arzwald but I resemble strangely an American of academic tendency who went into a shop to buy a costume.

The ride in a neat plate-glassed electric train from Dobbiaco to Cortina was very impressive. The vertical granite turrets go on for miles and miles. On how stupendous a scale Nature knows how to be boring; tears came to the eyes at the extent of the imposture:

ODE TO NATURE

"..... .... !
"...... .... ?
"... ...."

... . !

I have bought a copy of my hero Goldoni's comedies[3] and am rivetting my mind to the problem of how the HUMAN MIND hides and reveals itself in comedy. I like to think that such an enquiry never before was pursued in Room 15 of the Albergo Italia.

These days my more "consecutive" travelling companion and I have had many a tussle over that SUBJECT-MATTER which has become the gadfly in our minds, the hornet in our ear.

This is not the letter to include our tentative little *lumières*. This is just a note to say that our minds and hearts turn back all the time and that we miss you in the most recognizably human-nature way.

What? What? you won't allow me to build, (I mean ratify) a construction of an extra-human interference into the tedium and nullity of so great a part of the world's converse,—when I see so rich and beautiful and lovable a privilege approach me as that visit constituted?

Well, the rival interpretations of experience are at war within me and I shall accept the decision that will be presumably arrived at in my eightieth year. For the present I rejoice in the word GRATITUDE however metaphysically impure it may be.

Give Baskit [i.e., Basket] and Pepe all my best. I guess it's Pepe that is my particular favorite, though that is no disparagement to the beautiful white mage-malgré-lui.

My thoughts return all the time to the great book as beautiful in its elegant tracery as it is in its tremendous ideas.

So, dear and wonderful friends, thanks for a thousand gracious things. My cup runneth over.

devotedly
Thornton, "Honest Jack Wilder."

1. Charlotte Tappan Lewis Niven, the younger sister of Wilder's mother, was an activist who liked people and had a strong social conscience. She organized student hostels, then worked for the International Committee of the YWCA in Florence and in London. She was a presence in the lives of Wilder and his siblings, who saw her regularly when they went to Europe. Also present at the dinner with Aunt Charlotte, according to Wilder's date book, was a Mrs. Blake, the wife of a Scotch Presbyterian minister in Florence who became devoted to Aunt Charlotte, thought of her as a member of her family, and maintained a lifelong, deep friendship with her.

2. Peter Vischer's statue of King Arthur, commissioned by the emperor Maximilian, is now in the Hofkirche in Innsbruck.

3. Carlo Goldoni abandoned the improvisational tradition of commedia dell'arte to create a series of realistic comedies of aristocratic, bourgeois, and working-class manners. Many of the most popular were written in Venetian dialect.

To Alice Toklas and Gertrude Stein, Bilignin, France

10 August 1935   Hotel Arlbergerhof
                                                               Innsbruck [Austria]

                                                               Yes, practically from the above
                                                               hotel, though it happens to be
                                                               from the Hotel Continental,
                                                               Meran; but both are clean and
                                                               brave and willing and
                                                               attractive and Austria is the
                                                               most lovable country in the
                                                               world, even when it's under
                                                               Italian rule.

[*]Dear Alice:[1]

Today after some blood-warming tilts with a party-appointed bureaucracy (I had to go to the Post Office-Dogana at 6:30 p.m. to see a Signor Payèr whose official office hours were from 11:00—12:00 a.m.—meridian) I obtained the sweater of sweaters. I rushed over to the hotel and put it on, and it's just FINE. It's fine in every way, in fit, in color, in looks and in texture, and I'm the happiest fellow in the world. The weave at the girdle and the trellice-weave on the torso and the expert workmanship around the V at the neck made it a sweater such as there is no other.

I bow down and thank you a thousand times for this beautiful practical thing made with your own hands and worn always with a proud happy sense of its giver.

Well, the Rover Boys was to Cortina d'Ampezzo for three days. Walks and meals and reading and writing and a conversation that began last November and has been going on ever since like a 12-volume novel.[2]

And wherever the Rover Boys go little things happen, as in those Saints Legends (sic parva licuit componere magnis)[3] wild flowers spring up under the feet of the Good.

We sit one night in a café drinking. Four very beautiful gals are playing salon-music. We respectfully ask them if they play anything by Mozart. They get so excited they don't know what to do. They are on the faculty of the Conservatory at Milan. One of them files upstairs for the music and presently in full open café—above the hubbub of vulgar *pescecani* [sharks] trying like mad to be eleganti and mondains, they play for us a trio for violin, cello and piano by Mozart, casting such sheep's eyes at us the while as would melt a dolomite. Then they must play for us a potporri from Thanhaüser [i.e., *Tannhäuser*], then the Lieb[e]stod; and then come and have drinks and talk in such a twitter of music and youth and good looks as you never saw. Wherever we go—I am speaking as Saint to Saint—wildflowers spring up under our feet. [Continuéd firmly on Page 3][*]

[**]Letter to Miss G. Stein. Delete on the Punctured Line.

. . . .

Dear Gertrude:

Your letter was waiting for me and made me very happy. My mother once pointed out (you've gotta be immaculate to permit yourself certain jests) that there was a lot of air[e]dale in me. She noticed that dog-like I liked to ride by the window in our automobile my tongue hung out to catch the breeze and that in a house I liked to roam about the rooms until I found somebody and then settle down with a detonation of relaxed bones. Well, also I have the dog-complex of needing to be told that I am liked, and your letter bucked me up in my canine doubt and forlornless[ness]. And by the time you affirmed it again at the end of the letter I was in a perfect jelly of self-pity and tragico-comic humility; like a red-eyed St. Bernard. Yes Pepé and I understand one another with an appalling complicity.

My farce-comedy is shaping up in my mind; I hope it continues. Your comic opera for Virgil Thomson is a great proposal and I love it sight unseen.[4] And just the thing to refresh yourself with after the stern tussels [i.e., tussles] of the Geography.[**]

[*]Dr. [Robert] Davis, Rover Boy B, fell ill at Cortina d'Ampezzo. Fact is, he's always ill. At the age of three his nose was broken by a baseball bat and ever since one septum has been faulty; he wheezes away, employing ten handkerchiefs a day, and I shall have to remember this trip as one long asthmatic catarrhal sniffle. In addition he gets every sort of ear-ache, growing-pain, infantile colic, and heart attack and influenza. Naturally I like it; it constitutes a perpetual allusion to my own invariable health, and it calls into play my bossy hen-life bedside manner. Well, Rover Boy B collapsed into twelve superimposed maladies, like Geo[rge]. Brush in Chapter XIII; and instead of walk-

ing heroically from Cortina to Bo[t]zen to Meran, we took a train back to Bighearted Austria. And there with Aspirin and Antipholgystin and laxatives-oh-my-god and hot whisky we pulled the trembling soul out of the gates of death. The recovery was almost as sudden as the collapse. So today we bussed down to Meran over a prodigious mountain pass, far higher than the Brenner.

As I told you in my last, I don't see Eye to Eye with the rest of the world on this matter of Nature. Nature doesn't speak to me. No'm'm. I can take it or leave it. On the previous trip I saw seventy dolomites. Each was different; but I feel that from now on I could MAKE A DOLOMITE, and from the moment that I feel that I could do it, too, a thing loses interest. In fact I grew so startled at my own complacency about Nature that I bought a little book called Emerson's Essays on Nature. Well, Emerson feels just the opposite from me and ex-presses himself with so revolting a coyness that I feel absolutely corroborated in my opinion.

But Nature can be nice. This Minit under my window a cataract is making a noise that no manipulation of sandpaper could quite reproduce, and to that voice I shall lyrically fall asleep. The mountains around here are pretty fine, though I can't imagine how they passed their time previous to the inven-tion of the camera.

We shall be here until Monday noon. Then Tuesday again at Innsbruck. Then three days in Mieders in the Stubai—that [is] where I shall write one farce, one mystery-play and one play about ghosts. Then off to Salzburg, where we shall be Poste Restante, if not Poste Dormante. There in Salzburg— (but Gertrude mustn't know that I said so—) all that is most adolescent in Beethoven and all that is most adolescent in Toscanini and all that is most adolescent in me will s'amalgament in the Leonore Overture and in the close of Fidelio. But more of that when I get there.

In the meantime cut your roses in the morning simply garlanded with my thanks and my appreciation and my affection, dear Alice
Ever thine
Thorny.[*]

[**]Concl'd from the bottom of PAGE TWO, as it were, man and boy, ergo—

I'm still obstinately trying to find a sally-port whereby the Human Nature may be permitted an irruption into the Human Mind. I keep saying to myself: Othello, Othello.

Anyway that's all so complicated that every now and then my poor head feels like a hot box on a railroad train where the wheels have turned around too long without lubrication.

   While I was a[t] Bilignin I had both provocation and lubrication, the best in the world. Now I have to lubricate myself: I buy these cheap reprints of the classics every day—have just read Voltaire's Zadig and Goethe's Tasso. I don't happen to be crazy about either of them, but they are what they are. Goldoni's Locandiera and Nestroy's Der Zerrissene are far finer, and Goldoni's Quattro Rusteghi must be better yet, but I can make nothing of the Venetian dialect, and had to give up.[5]

   The fact is I'm a little cranky from travelling, from not being in one place more than two days at a time, from seeing striking views and having them (the views) wring my admiration from me before I'm ready to give it; from having to speak and think in French German and Italian and English (every now and then I have amnesia and can't remember one word in any). That's all me; but my travelling-companion is a constant pleasure and every now and then we fall into conversations where each of us surpasses ourself and a sort of mystery takes place. All I need just now is WORK and if we can find that farmhouse outside Salzburg I shall work half-the-day and swim and walk and listen to music the other half.==. Again all my love and devotion

                    Thornt.[**]

   1. Wilder begins by writing to Toklas. Halfway down his second page, he begins a separate letter to Stein, filling the rest of the page. On his page 3, with "Dr. Davis, Rover Boy B," he returns to the letter to Toklas, finished at the top of his page 4. The letter to Stein takes up the remainder of page 4, from "As I told you in my last" to "camera." Wilder's text is printed here in its original sequence. To facilitate a continuous reading of each of the intertwined letters, a single asterisk [*] indicates the beginning and ending of portions written to Toklas, and two asterisks [**] indicate the beginning and ending of portions written to Stein.
   2. The continuing conversation, whose echoes can later be heard in the Geographical History.
   3. Virgil, Eclogue 1, "sic parvis componere magna" [Thus it is common to compare small things to great]. Wilder compares himself to Virgil. Heightened perception, such as Virgil experienced upon going to Rome, gives great meaning to even the smallest event of this summer in Austria. The spirit of Virgil had dominated Wilder's first novel, The Cabala (1926), and returns often in his work.
   4. The references may concern details on missing pages of the letter of ?2 August or matters talked about in conversations between Wilder and Stein. Wilder's "farce-comedy" appears to anticipate his Merchant of Yonkers, completed in 1938; if so, it was germinating two years earlier than has been known. The play was Wilder's transformation of Nestroy's Einen Jux will er sich machen [He Will Go on a Spree] (1842), in turn based on A Day Well Spent, John Oxenford's comedy of 1835. Wilder later revised his play as The Matchmaker (1954), eventually recast as the musical Hello, Dolly! (1964). Stein's comic opera is Byron A Play.
   5. Wilder comments on books casually picked up for travel reading. Neither Zadig, or Destiny. An Oriental Tale nor Torquato Tasso were as useful to him for giving shape to his own ideas as the plays of Goldoni and Nestroy.

To Gertrude Stein and Alice Toklas, Bilignin, France

17 Aug[ust]. 1935[1]   Until Sept[ember] 15th
                                                        Poste Restante,
                                                        Salzburg, Austria

Dear Friends
                    This is just a mezzanine-note between letters to enclose the
picture.[2]

Also under separate cover I enclose the spooky story that decides there
are no spooks after all.[3] I liked the picturesque local color and have stolen
some of the specific details into my voracious notebooks.

¶ Our characters have gone to pieces here. Did we hunger and thirst
after knowledge and the lyrical life of ideas, once? Did we love simple customs and manners? Did we judge human beings by the speaking Something
in their eyes?

That's all over now.

We are worldly and vulgar. We only bow to celebrities; money flies from
our pockets like sand; we take a bilious pleasure in picking faults in perfection
itself. We have become a part of the snobbish-dilettante-mélomane Intelligen-
tsia. *N'en parlons plus.*

Kit Cornell is here. She loves you and hopes on the way home to drive
down from Geneva and call on you.[4] [What a splendid girl, as true-blue in
daily life as she is hesitant in art. (Confidentialissimo).] Had a long and tear-
prompting talk with Fritz Kreisler last night—of his boyhood in Vienna, of a
virtuoso's life in hotels, of the humiliations he was put to in his visits to allied
countries during the War.[5]

Last night I heard Toscanini conduct Verdi's (aetat. 80) "Falstaff." So
glorious a work that all the time a great gaseous balloon filled my chest,—so
bouyant [i.e., buoyant], so youthful, so inventive in the loquacious witty subtle
orchestra.[6]

Before long, solemnly, I hope quietly, I shall DIE of benefits and beauties.
With folded hands I shall turn my face to the wall and DIE. And the crown and
garland of this unsustainable happiness is the energy-strength and the energy-
goodness that lives in you two.

                    Expiring and loving
                    Thornton

    1. The first part of this letter, up to "N'en parlons plus," was written on 17 August, the second part
on 18 August.
    2. Wilder enclosed a snapshot of himself and Davis in lederhosen (see Wilder to Stein, 6 August
1935). Stein responded to the photograph in the letter marked "Arrived 26 August 1935."
    3. This section must refer to a book or story Stein may have lent Wilder, perhaps in view of his

intention to write a ghost story. It must have been more than a few pages as it is returned under separate cover.

4. Carl Van Vechten introduced Stein to Cornell in New York on 28 January 1935 (see Burns, *Letters*, 1:376–83). On 20 August [1935] (YCAL), Cornell wrote to Stein from Salzburg that she had just seen Wilder, "and he was full of telling things you had said" (in Gallup, *Flowers*, 266, this letter is incorrectly dated 1933). Because she was to sail from Nice on 13 September, she suggested stopping at Bilignin on her way, but she apparently changed her plans. Wilder had adapted a contemporary French play, *Le Viol de Lucrèce* by André Obey, for Katharine Cornell in 1932, and they had been friends ever since.

5. Fritz Kreisler had difficulties not only in Allied countries before the United States entered the war, but also in America, even though he was married to an American woman. With the outbreak of World War I, as anti-German sentiment swept the still-neutral United States, his American concert appearances were widely condemned.

6. Wilder and Cornell heard Arturo Toscanini and the Vienna Philharmonic on the evening of 17 August in Verdi's *Falstaff*. After the performance they had supper with the Fritz Kreislers, the singer Emanuel List, and several other guests.

To Thornton Wilder, Salzburg, Austria

18 Aug[ust].[1935][1]   Bilignin par Belley
                                                               Ain

My dear Thornton,

The proofs have come and Alice and I each seized a copy to read your introduction and she got through first and I said shut up till I finish and then we were both very moved, it is wonderfully right and is such fine and simple writing and ends up so much so in the last sentence. It makes me very happy and the book is going to be very beautiful and thank you Thornie oh so much. There was a use in being a little boy if his name was Thornie.[2] I always like ie better than y. We have been enjoying your letters so much and let us have more of as much of the same as the same. We are correcting the proofs and will send them corrected with your ms. to correct and send on day after to-morrow. Bob [Davis]'s letter solidified that is made it get solid in page III page III of his letter and I liked it that is solidness and it all gets into the ms.[3] you and your nature Thornton and Bob and his solid, don't go bragging about that nature business when you replace it by mine, is nature too for adolescents, but what is romance, well perhaps well anyway, I have been going on quite a lot and it will go to you also in a few days, I get well do I get have I gotten any nearer to what master-pieces are, one should not embrace m[aster]. p[ieces]. oh no, Alice says it is clearer but oh my, I go around and around and around it, what is it, what master pieces are. And we loved the story of Bob's resustications [i.e., resuscitations], I am a great believer in symptoms, I think they are the safety valve of the timid, Bob and me, you and Alice Thornton don't need them you are not weak nor meek, oh no, well anyway we love you so always

Gtrde.

Inclosed what the Giraud Jouffroys found to amuse you.[4]

1. "Aug. 18," entered on this letter by Wilder, may be the date of receipt or of the postmark.

2. The last sentence of Wilder's "Introduction" to *Narration* reads as follows: "These lectures in their method and in their content are brilliant examples of the breadth and movement and energy that the perspective of time will reveal to have been our characteristic" (vii). Stein plays with a sentence that returns in various forms several times in the *Geographical History*: "What is the use of being a little boy if you are going to grow up to be a man" (58). Here she applies it to Wilder.

3. In saying that "it all gets into the ms." Stein means that in the *Geographical History* she is constructing a conversation among herself, Wilder, and Davis about nature and romance. In this conversation she also comments on a letter from Davis in which he speaks as a philosopher about her work (see Wilder to Toklas about the illness of Davis, 10 August 1935; Stein to Wilder, 10 July 1935, n. 5, about Wilder and Davis in the *Geographical History*; and Davis to Stein [Hotel Arlbergerhof stationery, n.d.], YCAL).

4. The enclosure has not remained with the letter (see also Wilder to Stein, 20 August 1935). It may have been a newspaper clipping from Madame Marthe Giraud, a friend of Stein who summered in Ceyzérieux, about twelve kilometers from Belley. The Jouffroys may be her daughter Christiane and her husband.

To Gertrude Stein and Alice Toklas, Bilignin, France

20 Aug[ust] 1935   Poste Restante,
                                                       Salzburg [Austria]

                                                       about 11:00 at night, in a
                                                       pretty flower-box at
                                                       13 Bergheimerstrasse in the
                                                       care of Fräulein Schöndorfer

Dear Friends-reading-proof:

                       My proofs[1] came today too and I have just read the lectures all through again and understood more that [i.e., than] I understood before, and that makes me happy in addition to the happiness in reading the places I already understood. (There! everything I write is influenced by Gertrude's style, but I can't swing the serpentine phrases correctly and that makes me mad.) There are still little pockets in the IIIrd and the IVth that I don't understand, but I will. I am very proud that you were not displeased with my preface, and hope some day to write very well indeed about Gertrude and about all of us. ¶ I saw Bobsy [Goodspeed] several times and we gallivanted

about town. You can imagine Bobsy in a High Festival Town. She even went
to [Felix] Weingartner's course in How to be an Orchestra Conductor. I went
with her. When she returns to Chicago Mary Garden is to give her singing
lessons (sic).[2] ¶ Today I had Sybil Colefax to lunch and we told her about
Gertrude, repeating ourselves with increasing emphasis, and she was very
arrested. As Bob [Davis] said: she asked all the right questions. We see her
again Thursday and then I shall go into that other matter with her. I shall lend
her my proofs and my London publisher is to see that she gets a *Making of
Americans* and the *Lectures.*

Thursday our Immersion begins:

Thurs. 11:00 a.m. Toscanini & the Vienna Philharmonic
"   7:30-12:00 p.m. Reinhardt's "Faust"
Frid[ay] Don Giovanni (Bruno Walter)
Sat[urday] Fidelio (Toscanini & Lotte Lehmann)
Mon[day] Falstaff again (Toscanini)
Tues[day] Rosenkavalier (Lotte Lehmann)
Fri[day]. Nozze de Figaro. (Weingartner)
Sunday Faust again.[3]

Next day 3:45 p.m.

Today I received your proofs and will send them on to America (after
comparing them with the proof-reading notes I made) with every safeguard
known to the Postal system.

Hasn't it been fun?—the "bothers," then the writing, then the lectures,
then us disturbed and aroused [i.e., aroused] listeners, then the promise of
the goodlooking book.

Oh, what a dignified word "fun" is.

Dear twain, I always have fun when I'm with you.

I sincerely hope that I appear to you in a funny light.

Thank you very much.

¶ 4 I went to the Goldene Rose and my host told me that both Mr. Laflins
[i.e., Laughlins] had gone.

¶ 3 Robert Locke-Hume-Davis held a constipation for five days, and was
frivolous about it. I came near pushing him off a bridge into the Salzbach, and
going with pleased relief on my way. There's a limit to which people con-
sciously or unconsciously can tease me.

¶ 2¼ Travelling is over and in our pleasant rooms an equable routine has
been established. The morning and afternoon hours roll by. They roll by,
sunlight on the floor. My pipe is in my mouth. I read a little, walk up and
down a little, eat peaches. Silly little bloodless letters arrive in piles from

America, so remote, so nullanvoid. High school girls want autographs, sewing-circles want lectures; my juicy peaches stain their pages.

In the next room Robert plays over and over again the gramophone records, the newly-discovered god of music compresses his chest with a kind of anguish. He turns on the Brandenburg concerto in order to suffer terribly.

I drift toward my farce, but in no hurry.

¶ O: I've read Faust twice in the last month. Quelque chose, but I don't think it belongs on Our List. There is a slightly vulgar "display" tone to it, Mephistopheles and all that. The devil should be approached reverently, *ma foi*.

Please thank the Giraudes-Geoffroys[4] warmly for the very amusing clipping with its *éloge de l'inconduite* [in praise of misconduct]. John Calvin Wilder would like to point out to the writer that it's not only in respectable homes that people are burned to cinders. Ever since the 18th Century the French have been giggling nervously at the thought of sin. The great age had none of that; silly old Voltaire began it, I think.

so, having spoken disparagingly of Goethe and Voltaire I shall disappear in a cloud of megalomania and begging your pardon for my bavardage I shall remind you again that I am your devoted and spoiled friend
Thornie-berry.

1. For *Narration*.
2. Felix Weingartner, Austrian conductor and composer. Mary Garden, the American soprano, whom Goodspeed would have known from Garden's long association with the Chicago Opera Company (1910–31).
3. The Salzburg Festival ran from 27 July to 1 September. On Thursday, 22 August, Toscanini conducted an orchestral program including works by Handel, Mendelssohn, Debussy, Wagner, and Verdi. After the performance, Wilder and Davis lunched with Lady Colefax at the Oesterreicher Hof, where she was staying (see also Wilder to Stein, 16 July 1935, n. 1).
4. Wilder anglicized the spelling of Jouffroy (see Stein to Wilder, 18 August 1935, n. 4).

To Thornton Wilder and Robert Davis, Salzburg, Austria

arrived 26 August 1935[1]   Bilignin par Belley
                                                            Ain

My dears

We are so pleased with the lovely photo,[2] Alice is troubled about that band over your chest, I thought Bob did not have it but closer xamination shows him having it, is it a baldric over the broad chest to perhaps hold the broad arrows that match the hat, Bob too discreetly does not show his feather but the shameless Thornie shows it all, we are engulfed in the French army, our peaceful barns are filled with french recruits doing their 21 one days, to-day I met a most drunken one and he said Madame couldn't you make it that the 15 days would be over. It does complicate time.[3] Katharine Cornell writes that you were in wonderful form, the Air[e]dale completely xcited,[4] and we know all about that, we were kind of upset by the advent of our 28 in the barn, and so we went to Artemare[5] last night to cheer up, kind remembrances from the inn-keeper. Did the ms.[6] come alright and are you happy, we are and we will all be happy together again by and by,

Always
Gtrde.

1. Wilder's notation of the date he received this letter.
2. Wilder and Davis in lederhosen (see Wilder to Stein, 6 August 1935).
3. Stein was asked to billet twenty-eight soldiers in her barn during a large French army training exercise in the area (see Stein to Van Vechten, 29 August 1935, in Burns, *Letters*, 2:442–43).
4. Cornell to Stein, 20 August [1935], YCAL. See Wilder to Stein, 17 August 1935, n. 4.
5. Artemare is a small town about seventeen kilometers north of Belley, on the road from Virieu-le-Grand to Culoz. Chez Bérard was one of their favorite restaurants in the region.
6. The next section of the *Geographical History*.

To Thornton Wilder, Salzburg, Austria

[postmark: 29 August 1935]   Bilignin par Belley
                                                        Ain

My dear Thornton,

Carl [Van Vechten] has sent the Four In America and I'll be sending it along in a few days, I have just been looking at it, and it has spots that are on the way. It was written the year before I thought of going to America, two years ago now. The book goes on,[1] I think it gets clearer about m. p. master-pieces, I think it does and then I lose it or I think I lose it, anyway I will be sending you what has been done pretty soon. A man by the name of Donald Vestal in Chicago do you know anything about him who does marionettes wants me to do a marionette [play] for him, he talked to me one day on the street and now he has a government marionette job, it might be fun to do a marionette of a dog and identity.[2] I don't suppose time and master-pieces could come in but money and romanticism might, I do wish you were both here, it has been raining most dreadfully but now it isn't, we are hoping to see Katharine Cornell next week, and lots of love to you both from us all,

Gtrde.

1. The next installment of the *Geographical History*.

2. Donald Vestal, a puppeteer, had introduced himself to Stein on Michigan Avenue in Chicago on 30 November 1934. Stein acknowledged the meeting and expressed interest in his work. On 13 August 1935 (YCAL) Vestal, who was working with the Works Progress Administration, reminded her of the meeting and asked if she might be willing to write a play for marionettes. See Appendix IV.

To Gertrude Stein and Alice Toklas, Bilignin, France

30 Aug[ust]. 1935   13 Bergheimerstrasse
11:00 a.m. and very sunny.   Salzburg [Austria]
                                                     Bei Fräulein Schöndorfer.

Dear Friends:

Every day when I present my passport at the Poste Restante my heart stops beating while the great slow-witted oafs turn over the WA—WI letters; I hope to see them stop at one of those pink slips that says that Wilder Thornton must go to Window 13 and receive a package or registered letter; and that package will be some more of the Geography of America.

I don't tell you that to hurry you, but just to remind that the happiest anticipation lives in me, etc.

My days have become more tranquil. Not only has the nightly attendance at masterpieces become more intermittent, but the excellence of their performance has been relaxed. Last night *The Marriage of Figaro* was downright bad.[1]

Something happened to me and like all purely Outside things, being only a Happening, it was not interesting.[2] [Max] Reinhardt and Frau Reinhardt invited me to midnight supper at their castle[3] to meet the Thomas Mann's and Reinhardt took the occasion to offer me the directorship of a large School of the Theatre he expects to establish in Los Angeles. I told him I would think it over; but in four minutes I had already thought it over and since then also I have been thinking of other things.

[Robert] Davis has bought himself a bicycle and spends the middle of every day in distant roads and woods, reading Locke on the Human Understanding. Apparently sometimes Locke does well for a page or two at a time, but then falls into error.[4] Davis writes long harsh comments in the margin in which the initials G.S. and A.N.W. and S.F. appear,[5] like beacons that light up the shoals where the ship lost control.

                    Two day[s] later:
                    7:30 a.m. in the Railway Station

I am an early riser and every morning I get up early and walk down to the railway station to have a pre-breakfast. I like all railway stations and esp[ecially]. Austrian ones. Even Sunday morning at 5:00 it was crowded; Mass was being served in the II class waiting-room; throngs were singing folksongs in 4 parts in the III class restaurant and dozens of families including babes in arms were starting for a day in the mountains. Well, I have paid you the tenuous compliment of writing you a letter when I have nothing to say: the important thing is that I am

Your devoted friend
Thornton

1. See Wilder to Stein, 20 August 1935, n. 3.

2. Wilder uses terminology from the *Geographical History* about the Salzburg Festival.

3. The supper took place after the performance of *Faust*, part I, on Thursday, 22 August. It was Wilder's first meeting with Thomas Mann. He had met Reinhardt briefly in 1923 through Rudolph Kommer, Reinhardt's American agent, whom Wilder already knew. In a letter to his mother of 16 May 1923 (Letterbook 1923, YCAL), Wilder recounts the meeting.

4. Davis, a student of Kant and Hegel, was unlikely to have been in sympathy with the father of British empiricism.

5. See Wilder to Stein, 9 July 1935, n. 7.

To Thornton Wilder, Salzburg, Austria

[early September 1935]   Bilignin par Belley
                                                        Ain

My dear Thornton,

I do like my editor he does write a nice crusty letter but I do not quite make out one name Donald what, so that I can write to him and tell him I like him, and do hope that they will publish more of me in the future,[1] we are sending you the 4 in America,[2] I think you will perhaps find the Washington best, it was all written 4 years ago when I was first wondering about identity, as the result of writing the Flowers of Friendship, and meditating resultantly about Shakespeare's sonnets,[3] there is quite a good deal more of the Geography written and some of it helps along quite a bit I think but Alice has been drowned in domestic complications[4] which now are soothed we are once more back to a china boy and very shortly now it will be ready for you, I can't tell you how happy it makes me your feeling about it like you do, I will be writing again very soon love to you both

Gtrde.

We had an awful scare we thought Pepe had been stolen out of the car but not at all he had just been forgotten and left miserably at home with the china boy, grand reunion.

1. Donald Bean, manager of the Publications Department of the University of Chicago Press, wrote to Stein on 23 August 1935 about the cancellation of clauses in the standard author's contract that Stein had requested and that he was willing to waive (copy, Chicago).

2. This undated letter was probably written a few days after Stein to Wilder postmarked 29 August 1935, in which Stein refers to the receipt of *Four In America* from Carl Van Vechten. Wilder acknowledges the typescript in an undated postcard that follows.

3. Stein's *Before The Flowers Of Friendship Faded Friendship Faded* began in the summer of 1930 as a translation of *Enfances*, a sequence of poems by Georges Hugnet that evolved into what Stein called a "reflection" of Hugnet's work, a sequence of Stein poems in their own right, no longer a literal translation. Stein and Hugnet had planned to publish their work jointly in a single volume. When Stein, who considered her poems equal to Hugnet's, demanded equal billing for her name and his on the cover and title page, a quarrel erupted that terminated a warm friendship. The results of the quarrel are described in Stein's "reportage" piece, "Left To Right," of January 1931. Later they published their versions separately. Stein devised the title for her own publication in her Plain Edition.

This experience forced Stein to think about the nature of authorial identity. In the fourth lecture of *Narration*, she defines translation as writing that is "carrying out an idea already existing" and distinguishes it from original [writing of] "recognition as the words are forming" (51–52). To her, translation was not true writing of an artist's own perception but writing the emotion of another to order, which led to a softening of the language. She illustrated this distinction by pointing to the difference between Shakespeare's plays and his sonnets. She considered the plays original compositions in his own voice and the sonnets writing done to the order of a patron that fell back on the language conventions of the time. She discusses the distinction in the Henry James section of *Four In America*. Once Stein had written the successful *Autobiography Of Alice B. Toklas* to satisfy the demands of a real or imagined audience, this distinction became central to her worries about the effects of fame. She felt she had abandoned her true voice as an artist and had instead undertaken "audience writing" to satisfy her need for personal success. In the *Geographical History Of America*, the worry about having sold out for popularity and success leads her to distinguish human nature, tied to personality, from the human mind, independent of personality and capable of artistic creation. It also leads to the further distinction of identity and entity.

4. The "domestic complications" are recounted in *Everybody's Autobiography*, 159–61.

To Gertrude Stein and Alice Toklas, Bilignin, France
[Postcard: Unser Volkskanzler Adolf Hitler
am Königssee-Obersee]

[early September 1935][1]   [Berchtesgaden, Austria]

Dear Twain:

Salzburg is only 20 miles from the German border and came up to this beautiful *trop beau* lake for a few hours. This is the home of our dear leader. I never see that splendid symbol the swastika without seeing where it could be planted to advantage.

I am all happy and grateful about Grant; scarcely understand a word of Wilbur Wright; and still have the other two to read—read slowly and aloud. It all reminds me that I love reading. I am happy and well and smittenly devoted to you, my friends.

Ever thine
Thornton

1. This postcard was mailed in an envelope that has not survived.

To Thornton Wilder and Robert Davis, Vienna, Austria

[postmark: 20 September 1935][1]   Bilignin par Belley
                                                                     Ain

My dears,

   The Geography is finished, it did not come to an end, but I stopped,[2] Alice has typed it and I am correcting it and you will have it in a week or so, and Thornton what is Mr Donald Beans' name is it Bean and did you get the letter of his I sent you and will you send it back so that I may have his proper address,[3] Basket has been full of sheep's jiggers [i.e., chiggers] and removing them has been a job and Pepe only had one or two he wished it might have been more because Basket had so much of all our attention, the Abdys have been and left,[4] and we are settling down again and lots of love

Gtrde.

1. The letter was addressed to Wilder in Salzburg and forwarded to him at the American Express office in Vienna, where it arrived on 23 September.

2. The last line of the *Geographical History* reads, "I am not sure that is not the end."

3. See Stein to Wilder, early September 1935, n. 1.

4. Sir Robert ("Bertie") Abdy and Lady Diana Bridgeman, his second wife, lived in Saint Germain-en-Laye. Stein became friends with them in the early thirties. Sir Robert was a charming man of cultivated traditional taste, a would-be artist who became a collector and dealer. In *Everybody's Autobiography* (208–300) Stein says that it was he who gave her the idea of writing *The Autobiography Of Alice B. Toklas* when in fact the suggestion had been made by many friends and publishers. Stein cleverly attributed it to Sir Robert, a man of rank more interested in a traditional narrative of a distinguished subject than in modernist literary experiments. In her account Sir Robert is paired with Sir Francis Rose, her other titled friend at the time, and, like Sir Robert, English. The Abdys' visit to Bilignin in 1935, after the billeting of French soldiers as described to Wilder on 26 August [1935], appears to be the first of a series of visits.

To Gertrude Stein and Alice Toklas, Bilignin, France

23 Sept[ember] 1935   American Express Company
                                                   Kärtnerring 14
                                                   Vienna I

Dear Friends:

I cast myself out into the open seas of friendship and hope to be supported and understood. so: there are long long stretches of the *Four in America* where I don't understand a word. Almost none of Wilbur Wright after the first beautiful statements about the actor and the painter. And to my pain, almost none of the figure of speech whereby George Washington was a novelist. The movement of the poetical opening—the autumnal mood—*that* I got and then I was lost. The Grant I followed best of all and it is full of beauties— on religion and war and America, though even that slips away from me in the last quarter. The first part of Henry James was the clearest of all, because there I could follow the ideas from my memory of your expressing them in other places. So that degree to which I can express my happiness and confidence in the whole of the work, is bound up with my mortification and my rueful apology of my inadequacy to so much of it.[1]

Anyway it's no news to you that I am a slow-poke plodder in so many ways, still stuck in the literal XIXth Century; but very proud every time I feel I have made more progress and have been given more and more flashes of insight into the endlessly fascinating individual expression which is Gertrude's style. Unless you want the MS back soon I shall keep it near me and get deeper and deeper into it.

Still I haven't settled down.[2] A morning work-routine began in Salzburg after the Festival closed, but it wasn't clear-cut enough. And now in Vienna such floodgates of Viennese hospitality open up that concentration is impossible. Not only something Mediterranean flows through the air of this town, but something oriental as well. The endless café-sitting, the headwaiters who are indifferent as to whether one has ordered or not, the relaxed idea of time. A journalist said to me; "You know, no one does any work here." Oh, yes, some do. Golly, what hard work Freud did. And the high level of acting and the precision in theatrical production shows that someone works, but apart from those two activities everybody merely works hard at avoiding work. They put a determined will into café-sitting.

That's not my tempo. So I'm going out Thursday to stay at that hotel forty five minutes away. There I'll take my walks and read my Grillparzer[3] and write my plays.

Robert [Davis]'s plans likewise are being held up. "Nobody's in town." I give him drastic German lessons, and see that he gets to know more and more

people. There are signs that the Psychoanalytical Institute has only two interests: to make practicing analysts, and to analyze patients. The courses he wants
on the Components of the Ego, and so on, are only open to advanced students
who have been through an analysis. An analysis takes a year and a thousand
dollars and during it the patient is not allowed to read about psychoanalysis.
The patient must sit in cafés and meditate with a mixture of glee and pain on
the great gobs of strange material that have been dug up out of his mind
during the recent sessions. As far as Robert can see there is only one good
psychoanalyst in the world and only one that has any glimpse into the more
abstract possibilities in the material. Robert had an interview with a Great
Man who is supposed to be the philosopher of the movement, and for three
quarters of an hour he was fed such childish thinking invested in a horrid
manner,—you know; gimlet-eye Svengali "I can see *right* through you" stuff.[1]

But it's a fascinating town. It has the eleven great Breughels in it. And an
impoverished Graf Czernin has just loaned his Vermeer to the Kunsthisto-
rische Gallerie here—a wonderful thing.[5]

So again *la vita commincia domani* [life starts tomorrow]. I'll write you
next week when I'll feel that I have my feet finally squarely on a road. And feet
is here no metaphor—walking is bound up with any existing I am permitted
to do.

All my best, best, best from your
devoted
Thornton

1. See Stein to Wilder, 29 August 1935. The conceit of *Four In America* is that these four brilliant
Americans could have become successful at anything and were not locked into their historical roles by
destiny. In the order printed, she considers Grant as a religious leader, Wilbur Wright as a painter,
Henry James as a general, and George Washington as a novelist. The section of George Washington
subtitled "Scenery And George Washington," written in the fall of 1931, was only later incorporated
into *Four In America*.

2. Wilder arrived in Vienna on 17 September.

3. Franz Grillparzer (misspelled by Wilder), as director of the court archives in Vienna, had
access to historical material that he used in his plays. His main concern was to illustrate the relationship between events and people and to show how the past influences and directs present action. A
disciple of Schiller and Lope de Vega, Grillparzer was an important influence on Wilder.

4. Davis did not realize that the Vienna Training Institute (what Wilder calls the "Psychoanalytical Institute") was, by 1935, a three-year program to train future psychoanalysts and to advance
psychoanalytical theory. The program required analysis as well as theoretical and practical training
(see Uwe Henrik Peters, *Anna Freud: A Life Dedicated to Children* [New York: Schocken, 1985], 67–
69).

5. An exhibition of paintings owned by Count Czernin was held at the Kunsthistorisches Museum in Vienna. The painting by Jan Vermeer is *An Artist in His Studio*.

To Thornton Wilder, Vienna, Austria

[postmark: 25 September 1935]   Bilignin par Belley
                                                 Ain

My dear Thornton,

          I am afraid you did not get the letters I sent to the home address you gave me in Salzburg because you never sent me back the letter of Donald Bean is it of the Chicago Press and did not tell me if that is really his name, he wrote me such a nice crusty letter and I have an answer to it written but could not quite make out his name. Will you send me his name and address even if the letter of his I sent you is lost. The Geography is finished and I will send it to you next week, I think you will like the autobiography parts,[1] and I am sorry that Bob [Robert Davis]'s adventures in psychical analysis seem not so happy, he has to get it in and out of his system, but as it is completely based on human and animal nature it is not at all interesting. There is no knowledge in human nature, some day I will have a try at a description of all the writing in the world that is not interesting, it is an interesting subject, the qualities it has the certain thickness and stickiness anything has that is not interesting, well more of that very much later. I am interested in what you say of the 4 [*Four In America*]. It has in it the fallow of the essays and the Geography, perhaps in Paris we will go over [it] together. We are here until the 15th of October and perhaps later if the weather continues good, and we do like to hear from you and so much love

Gertrude and Alice[2]

    Pepe stept [i.e., stepped] on a piece of something and is a distinguished invalid.

    1. On page 180 of the *Geographical History*, Stein begins a section of "autobiographies" with the heading, "To Thornton and Bob Davis an autobiography." These autobiographies continue until page 199. They can be read as records and echoes of the conversations Stein had with Wilder and Davis at Bilignin. The *Geographical History* continues Stein's struggle with questions of authorial voice and methods of composing. These issues also occupy her in *Four In America*, the lectures in *Narration*, and the lecture "What Are Masterpieces."

    2. Both signatures are Stein's.

To Gertrude Stein and Alice Toklas, Bilignin, France

[27 September 1935]
Friday morning

Hotel Bristol the minute
before going up to my new
house on the hill.
[Vienna, Austria][1]

Dear Twain:

I don't dare write you. I'm afraid.

I'm humbly apologetic for having so long neglected your request to send you DONALD BEAN's name, though when I wrote you the other day I was perfectly clear about the fact that that name was to be in the letter.

But also, after consideration of his enclosed letter, it seemed to me that you would not be wanting it back, and I'm afraid I destroyed it.

Do forgive me. It seemed to me that even his discussion of the cancelled clauses was in such general terms that the letter did not require saving. Alice, intercede for me, too. I hope I haven't made anything difficult for you.

So here's the address

DONALD BEAN

University of Chicago Press

5750 Ellis Ave

CHICAGO

Illinois

Today at one o'clock, my new life begins.

On a hilltop—nobody near. Long walks through woods stretching on every side of the hotel, with great prospects of the city in the distance with St. Stephen's tower, the Danube winding about the plains that stretch toward Hungary[.]

And the hours falling like leaves.

At last I shall hear myself and when the inner monologue gets too loud I can go into town.

And then in all that silence and solitude, I shall be reading the 4 [*Four In America*] again and next week the book on which I've already had such glorious preparation and help.[2]

Ever completely

devoted

Thornton

1. In his date book Wilder indicates that he moved to the Schlosshotel in Kobenzl on 27 September.

2. The *Geographical History*.

To Thornton Wilder, Vienna, Austria

[postmark: 1 October 1935]   Bilignin par Belley
                                                                Ain

My dear Thornton,

I am sending you the ms. to-day, I guess it goes on all right, and the portrait of Bob [Robert Davis] is pretty good, and keep them both the ms. until we meet in Paris[1] and you come with everything to say and comedies[2] and lots of love, and thanks for the belated address but belating it did no harm, and here we are with so many grapes and so much wine, quantities but just a little sour, which only goes to show how mistaken even master-pieces can be, do let us know that [the] ms. gets there alright and lots of love from us all to you both

Gtrde.

1. Addressed to Wilder in care of American Express, Vienna, the letter and typescript of the *Geographical History* were forwarded to him at the Schlosshotel Kobenzl. The "portrait" of Robert Davis may refer to pages 208–09. Wilder returned the typescript of *Four In America* when he saw Stein in Paris.

2. Stein looks forward to talking with Wilder about his projects when they meet again in Paris. In the "Ascania" notebook (YCAL), under the heading "Projects for Plays," Wilder lists numerous plays, some with brief comments. In his letter to Stein of 6 August he speaks of his preoccupation with comedy, connecting it with the "Human Mind." Wilder commonly made lists of projects planned or accomplished. On his list is "8. The Merchant of Yonkers (first convinced of it night of Nov. 17. St. Lucia)." Wilder apparently titled or worked on the play in 1935. The parenthetical note after the title, however, is a personal reminder, made at a later date. Wilder was in St. Lucia in November 1936, but when the note was added to the title is not known. Although he may have worked on other ideas between July and November 1935, what is preserved in the "Ascania" notebook is an early draft of *The Merchant of Yonkers*. Also in the "Ascania" notebook are other titles, for example, "Our Village," conceivably a precursor of *Our Town*, and "The Top of the World," an early title for what became *The Ides of March*.

To Gertrude Stein, Bilignin, France
[TELEGRAM]

[postmark: 7 October 1935]   Wien [Vienna, Austria]
Urgent

SPLENDID BEAUTIFUL FASCINATING DEVOTEDLY
THORNTON

To Gertrude Stein and Alice Toklas, Bilignin, France

7 October [1935]   At the Hotel Schloss Cobenzl
on Monday October 7   [Vienna, Austria]
at 2:06 p.m. overlooking Vienna
and the Danube

Dear ONES:

What a book![1] I mean What a book! I've been living for a month
with ever-increasing intensity on the conceptions of Human Nature and the
Human Mind, and on the relations of Masterpieces to their apparent subject-
matter. Those things, yes and identity, have become cell and marrow in me
and now at last I have more about them. And it's all absorbing and fascinating
and intoxicatingly gay, even when it's terribly in earnest.

Here's riches. Here's fun. It's fine.

Don't be mad at me if I say again there are stretches I don't understand. This time it doesn't seem important that I don't understand, because
there's so much that I do understand and love and laugh at and feed on.
Gertrude, Alice, what a grand book. What an airplane ride, what a quilting-
party, what a spelling-bee. I hope you two are as happy about it as it's possible
to be.

And how jubilantly naughty of Gertrude to sail in and smash half the accepted ideas of the world and to make such havoc so gaily—Volume One, Play
Three, Page Nine. And then to shake her head over the fact that the important
literary thinking is being done by herself. Gertrude's incorrigable [i.e., incorri-
gible]. True, of course, but the Truth's scarcely the thing one offers to the
timid asthmatic regurgitating critical world. Where's poor furrowed-brow T.S.
Eliot now?[2] I ask you? I love it. I'm proud that I'm a U. S.'er. And every time
my own name appears in it I'm pâmé [overcome] with pleasure. Aristotle
Davis [i.e., Robert Davis] likewise trembled like a leaf all day after he knew
that he was addressed in it. He hasn't had a chance to read it yet; I told him
The Autobiography would slay him. Oh what proud and lucky boys we are.
Gertrude, Alice, how can we be adequate to such plenteous over-heaping
goodwill.

Anyway, lissen. There's something else I'm excited about, too.

Something's happened to me. I'm crazy about America and I want to go
home. I'm going to leave here in about three weeks. If you're still in Bilignin
can I stop off at poor vexèd Geneva and come and see you at Bilignin, or by
then—about Oct[ober] 30—will you be in Paris again?

I've got so much to ask, I've got so much to say.

Yes, I'm crazy about America. And you did that to me, too.

Vienna buildings are fine, I kneel to the Baroque. But I meet people and people. A wan cultivated charm, with messes of vulgarian curiosity about all the wrong things. There isn't much left to the great Viennese air but little rodent-minded curiosity about who you know, and how much you paid, and what authors are slipping now, and who's next.

I never knew I was an author before, but in this town I'm continually told that I'm an author and that's terrible.

My country tis of thee. I always knew I loved it, but I never knew I loved it like this. Every Childs' restaurant, every shoe-blacking parlor. I don't feel as though I ever had to leave it [word?]. After this I'll be content to look at picture-books of Spain and Greece. I was born into the best country in the world. Gertrude told me so.

Robert [Davis] is very well installed.[3] He has at an incredibly cheap price a fine room with breakfast and lunch; a landlady who adores him so (a Professor's widow) that she gives him daily interminable German lessons and wants to give them twice a day. Robert is completely seduced by Vienna, even to that dreadful custom of sitting hours a day in cafés. Sitting. Not for me. He's signed up at the University for some courses in philosophy. And is weaning away from the Psychoanalytic Institute (Yes, Gertrude—you began it—all you had to say was three words: "What of it?"). The only thing he lacks is a circle of superior friends, so I'll stick around a little longer and peer about for a foundation-group. I'll hate to leave him, wonderful little prince that he is, but I'll get in return the wild singing air of the U.S.A. Oh, my god, the first snow in New York!

so—I've got too [i.e., two] bonfires in my being—one: your great big book that's as big as an alp and yet as homely as a walk in the village; and my return to my country. And my two excitements send a thousand messages to one another. MORE SOON: for the present I knock my forehead on the ground and rejoice that I am

Your friend
Thornton

1. The *Geographical History*.

2. Stein flies in the face of conventional order and critical form by refusing titles and subtitles in numerical or alphabetical sequence. Wilder's references here may come from the *Geographical History*, 201–11, in which he sees her pitting herself as the inventive American against the stodgy critical establishment epitomized by T. S. Eliot.

3. Davis was renting a room from a Frau Wollitz. In a letter to Stein (n.d., YCAL), written perhaps after Wilder had left for Salzburg and then Paris, Davis says that he has learned German, has made a few good friends, and is sharing with friends passages he copied from Wilder's typescript of the *Geographical History*.

To Gertrude Stein and Alice Toklas, Bilignin, France

14 Oct[ober] 1935   American Exp[ress]. Co.
a beautiful autumn afternoon.   Kärtnerring 14.
                                                         WIEN I [Austria]

Dear Friends:[1]

So I shall see the Rue de Fleurus at last and my friends in it.
And the pictures around them.

I still don't know when. I beg you not to change your plans one jot—
because I can come to you in either place perfectly well. I still haven't the
faintest notion when I'm leaving here. There's so much in town here that
vexes me, the kind assiduities of authors, playwrights and stage directors—
such phone-calls, such When can I talk to you about New York, and Perhaps
you can tell me which are the best literary agents. Such meetings in café-
houses. The way strangers call up and ask for an appointment is the limit. And
even if I were hard as nails about putting them off what can I do, if at social
gatherings every body wants to make an engagement for a good long talk,
freighted with self-interest.

Excuse all this self-pity.

There are compensations. Prof Freud was told that I had expressed (under pressure, but certainly true) a wish to see him, and he asked me to go
yesterday at 4:15 to his villa in Grinzing. I was all alone with him for an hour
and a half, and it was fine. He's seventy nine. He talked of many things: "I
don't do anything any more.... loss of interest... satiety... impotence." "The
poet we call Shakespeare was the Earl of Oxford... the sonnets are addressed
to Wriothesley who was about to marry Oxford's daughter when Oxford fell in
love with him himself." "I could not read your latest book... I threw it away.
Why should you treat of an American fanatic; that cannot be treated poet-
ically." "My sister-in-law admires your *Cabala* the most; I do not think so."
(One of the characters makes a slighting reference to Freud in it!) "I am no
seeker after God. I come of an unbroken line of infidel Jews. My father was a
Voltairean. My mother was pious, and until 8 I was pious—but one day my
father took me out for a walk in the Prater—I can remember it perfectly and
explained to me that there was no way that we could no [i.e., know] there was
a God; that it didn't do any good to trouble one's head about such; but to live
and do one's duty among one's fellow-men." "But I like gods" and he pointed
to handsome cases and cases full of images—Greek, Chinese, African, Egyptian—hundreds of images! "No, my work did not require any particular intellectual gifts—many people could have done it—the quality I had was courage.
I was alone, and every discovery I made required courage. Yes, the courage to
publish it, but first the courage to think it, to think along that line." "Just these

last weeks I have found a *Formulierung* [formulated a new definition] for religion." He stated it and I said I had gathered it already from the close of *Totem and Tabu*. "Yes," he said, "it is there, but it is not expressed. Hitherto I have said that religion is an illusion; now I say it has a truth—it has an historical truth. Religion is the recapitulation and the solution of the problems of one's first four years that have been covered over by an amnesia." "No, I am as unmusical as I am unphilosophic." "My daughter Anna will be so sorry to have missed you. You can come again? She is older than you—you do not have to be afraid. She is a sensible reasonable girl. You are not afraid of women? She is a sensible—no nonsense about her. Are you married, may I ask?"!!!

Really a beautiful old man.

What a lucky boy am I. My cup runneth over.

For my own help and for the pleasure of it I have begun a vast apparatus of pencilled glosses on the margin of your MS; but I shall erase it all before you can see it.[2] That's the way I close in on it and really digest. And the more I see, the more I see. 'Küss' die Hand.

Robert [Davis]'s German goes on like wild fire. He has started at the University. He is reading the book, slowly, intensely and devotedly. I hope he'll write you about it; but his awe of you and his distrust in himself have awful battles.

I have the courage to write, anyway—even if it's such shifty, disorganized letters as these last. The trouble with me is that I can't be soul-happy outside of my belovèd U.S.A. and that's a fact. So I think I'm sailing from [Le] Havre or Southhampton on Nov[ember]. 2. But first I'll have five days in Paris and every day I'm going to pay a call on two of my most loved Americans in the world. Oh, say can you see what I mean. So again Küss die Hand, Küsse die Hände

Thornton

1. A shortened version of this letter is printed in Gallup, *Flowers*, 306–07. Wilder met with Freud twice at his villa in Grinzing, a wine village (*Heurigen*) in the countryside north of Vienna. The first meeting took place on 13 October and is mentioned by Ernest Jones in his biography, but Jones offers no source for his information: "On October 13 there was a pleasant visit from Thornton Wilder of Chicago, the well-known author of *The Bridge of San Luis Rey*" (see *The Life and Work of Sigmund Freud* [New York: Basic Books, 1953–57], 3:199). A second meeting took place at 6 P.M. on 25 October (date book, YCAL). There is no indication here or in other letters as to how the meetings were arranged.

Wilder's "latest" book was *Heaven's My Destination*. In *The Cabala* there are two references to Freud. In the chapter "Astrée-Luce and the Cardinal," the narrator visits the cardinal and remarks, "A pile of volumes lay on the table beside him: *Appearance and Reality*, Spengler, *The Golden Bough*, *Ulysses*, Proust, Freud." An earlier reference is perhaps what Freud is commenting on. In the "Marcantonio" chapter, the cardinal has expressed a desire to see the narrator:

I found him in the first of the two small rooms that had been set aside for him at the Villa. He was writing a letter, standing up to it at one of those high desks known to the clerks of Dickens and the illuminators of the Middle Ages. I was later to receive many of those famous letters, never more nor less than four pages long, never falling short of their amazing suavity, never very witty nor vivid yet never untouched from beginning to end by the quality of their composer's mind. Whether he declined an invitation or suggested a reading of Freud's book on Leonardo, or gave suggestions on the feeding of rabbits, always from the first sentence he foresaw his last and always like a movement from Mozart's chamber music the whole unit lay under one spirit and the perfection of details played handmaid to the perfection of the form. He seated me in a chair that suffered all the light that was in the room, treating himself to a fine shadow.

2. See Stein to Wilder, 22 October 1935, n. 1. The typescript with Wilder's penciled glosses cannot be located and may have been lost.

To Thornton Wilder, Vienna, Austria

[postmark: 22 October 1935]   27 rue de Fleurus
                                                               [Paris]

My dear Thornton,

       Here we are just come and just settling in, we cannot offer you a bed but we can board and welcome and we are xpecting you to accept the same, we were awfully pleased with your letter about Freud there is so much to say oh so much, and please do not erase one of the marginal notes I want to see them all,[1] and do let us know just how soon you are going to be with us at 27 rue de Fleurus, dear Thornton, love from us all

               Gtrde.

1. On 15 October, Stein wrote to Carl Van Vechten, "Thornton Wilder is here he is quite mad about the new book of Human mind and human nature, and we have talked it over so much that we all think it would be an amusing thing if he added a running commentary of our xplicating conversations, he is leaving here soon and you will be seeing each other and he will be seeing Bennett [Cerf], and I hope you do like the idea" (Burns, *Letters*, 2:449).

To Gertrude Stein and Alice Toklas, Paris, France

26 Oct[ober] 1935   Vienna [Austria]

Dear Friends:

       I am leaving today for the home journey I shall spend a few days in Salzburg in order to see it under snow for once. I think I shall be in Paris Wednesday; maybe I shall be a day late—I sail on the Britannic—boat train from Paris on Nov[ember]. 6.

Wonderful new vistas from your book all the time.
Am surrounded by the disorder of my higgledy-piggledy packing.
                    Devotedly
                    Thornton

To Gertrude Stein and Alice Toklas, Paris, France

22 November 1935   50 Deepwood Drive
                                          New Haven, Conn[ecticut]

Dear Twain:

I came back to discover my father very ill indeed. While I was on the ocean he had a major operation and now we call on tiptoe through ranks of nurses. There's nothing anybody can do, so I invent activities to distract the girls who have been under tension for three years over this matter.

A week ago today I called on Bennett Cerf with the MS and with my rewritten Invitation to the Reader.[1] On the boat I reread the work for the fourth—or fifth? time and proudly acquired new lights on it and estimated the regions in which I have no lights. My confidence and relish in the former deepens all the time (and now when I'm working on *Grant* again the pleasure of reference from one work to the other is especially great), but my dejection before the latter is deeper.

Mr. Cerf and partner were waiting eagerly to see the text and I left it with them. I begged them to call in some other heads to read it, too, suggesting Edmund Wilson who is in Russia however—all year on a Guggenheim Foundation. Can you think [of] anyone else who has written of you with particular understanding, from New York and environs. I want to assemble as many rejoicers as possible; and I want Mr. Cerf to have his ballet of secretaries transcribe as many copies as possible. I only saw Mr. Cerf for a short time but I don't think "an emergence from identity" ever occurred to him, and as I said in my Invitation, that book is valuable in proportion as one had asked oneself its questions previously. I wish [Robert] Davis that other great "rejoicer" in it, could have his own copy to turn over and over in his immured existence. *I have the Four in America* to grow into. Gertrude! what high and exhilarating goings-on that contains! I'm crazy to share my adventures with it and speculatively ransack New Haven for a companion in enthusiasm.

Anyway all is safe; time and energy will discover its friends. Only I'm more impatient than you are. Yes, I'm "full of impatience in my middle living."

I gotta go now.

¶ The ship's crossing was the only disappointing one I ever made. I had to gallant my two pretty young charges, from deck-chair to meals to smoking-room to dance floor to deck games etc, and so was prevented from knowing all the two hundred other passengers. ¶ I read several miles of Balzac, all about money and fixed ideas and duchesses in the power of pawnbrokers. ¶ Kit Cornell has been playing Juliet here and I had some fine times with her.[2] She is full of regret not to have been able to come to Bilignin. ¶ Isabel sends her love. I could a tale unfold rê papa's illness. ¶ More soon. I have jitters and musn't write letters until I can hold a thread of thought for more than a minute at a time.

> Ever
> Devotedly—to your dear fine
> selves—
> Thornton

1. Wilder arrived in New York on 14 November and the next afternoon delivered to Cerf and Donald Klopfer at Random House the typescript of the *Geographical History*. Perhaps when Stein and Wilder met in Paris she suggested that he write an introduction.

2. Cornell's season in 1935–36 began on 10 October 1935 with a revival of her own production of *Romeo and Juliet* staged by Guthrie McClintic. Wilder saw the play in New Haven on 18 and 20 November. In the cast were Maurice Evans as Romeo, Ralph Richardson as Mercutio, Cornell as Juliet, and Florence Reed as the Nurse.

To Thornton Wilder, New Haven, Connecticut

[postmark: 23 November 1935]   [27 rue de Fleurus
                                                 Paris]

My dearest Thornton,

There you are and here we are and we wish we were where you are or you were where we are, anything like that is completely beautiful, incidentally Othmar[1] is outdoing himself, a ham soufflé that is a dream, but we have to call a halt to avoid increasing weight, he is very devoted and talks as if he were ours for life which is pleasant for every one concerned, and now Thornton you did not weaken, about doing your half of our book, Carl [Van Vechten] is mad about it as an idea, and very enthusiastic about the book, he read it through in one sitting having intended only to look at it and that always does touch an author, so please please Thornton do not weaken.[2] I had a nice letter from [Edward] Aswell, who was in the Atlantic and is now at Harpers, asking what he could do for me and what I could do for him, you know him do you not,[3] and everybody says what a dear you are, Daisy [Fellowes] and Nathalie [Barney], and Romaine [Brooks],[4] Romaine is much looking forward to see you in New York, she left yesterday, and please send me the volume of one act plays which I only heard about the night you left[5] and please ask your sister to send her Wilder novels,[6] they would give us pleasure, and please please please do not weaken about your half of the book, it is to me as if it were only lopsided if it did not have that gracious and decorative half, perhaps we will speak before the English Club at Oxford perhaps[7] but the important now is your half, Thornton, please lots of love from us all including Pepe and Othmar and Basket, who has a sweet character

Gtrde & Alice.

1. Othmar Baumgartner, Stein's Viennese cook.

2. In a letter postmarked 1 November 1935, Stein wrote Carl Van Vechten that she was sending him a typescript of the *Geographical History*: "I am sending you the ms. Relation of human nature to the human mind, it is all finished now, and I am not showing it to Bennett [Cerf] yet so don't say anything about it just read it and let me know how you like it." Van Vechten replied enthusiastically, "I think the idea of T[hornton] W[ilder] doing a running commentary in connection with the book is an INSPIRED one and I can't wait to see it all in PRINT" (Burns, *Letters*, 2:453–55).

3. Edward Aswell, as assistant editor of the *Atlantic Monthly* in 1933, edited *The Autobiography Of Alice B. Toklas* for serial publication. He told Stein on 30 October 1935 (YCAL) that he had transferred to Harper Brothers as general books editor and asked her for names of talented writers or work of her own. She later submitted her two lectures "What Are Masterpieces" and "An American And France," which were rejected. She also recommended Wendell Wilcox's work (see Stein to Wilder, 11 December 1935, n. 11).

4. Daisy Fellowes was an English journalist, author, and editor of *Harper's Bazaar*. Natalie Clifford Barney and Romaine Goddard Brooks had a long-lasting lesbian relationship. Barney, born in Dayton, Ohio, settled in France in 1899 and maintained a salon frequented by leading French writers, artists, and intellectuals. She published poetry, drama, fiction, and essays, primarily in French. Brooks was an American painter born in Europe who lived most of her adult life in Europe.

5. Wilder sent Stein an inscribed copy of his *The Long Christmas Dinner and Other Plays* (1931). The book, which is in YCAL, has a penciled inscription: "For Gertrude and Alice/with Christmas greetings of/Thornton/1935/Please only read 1, 3, and the last." The plays Wilder recommends are *The Long Christmas Dinner*, *Pullman Car Hiawatha*, and *The Happy Journey to Trenton and Camden*.

6. Isabel Wilder, a graduate of the Yale School of Fine Arts ('28, Yale Drama School), had recently published two novels: *Mother and Four* (1933) and *Heart, Be Still* (1934). A third novel, *Let Winter Go*, was published in 1937.

7. Stein had for the first time spoken at Cambridge and Oxford on 4 and 7 June 1926, when she gave the lecture *Composition As Explanation*. The plans here tentatively mentioned were realized in February 1936 (for full details, see Stein to Wilder, 25 January 1936, n. 2).

To Thornton Wilder, New Haven, Connecticut

[postmark: 11 December 1935]   [27 rue de Fleurus
                                                                    Paris]

My dearest Thornton,
                        This will be for Christmas and it would have been a
Christmas all together if you had been here or we had been there but anyway
we are all together in every which a way anyway. You will be pleased I think,
they are starting a franco American something which has to do with mutual
translating and appreciating of books, and we were all convoked chez Daisy
[Fellowes], academicians, [André] Maurois great ladies Louis Bromfield and
me and the Plon editions and Daisy presided[1] and she had Thornton's book
on the table as an xample of what we were to appreciate and Maurois said he
had liked it immensely and thought it perfectly translatable[2] and everybody
said charming things about the absent so you see Daisy has not forgotten the
wild Wilder boy, you will also be amused that in a topical song so Mme
Clermont-Tonnerre told me at the Alcazar d'Ete they made fun of me nicely,
so my home town is taking me on, America is my country but a Paris is my
home-town I guess,[3] its weather is frightful but otherwise all is well, we are all
pretty well where you left us, I have not heard anything from Bennett Cerf and
I am not sure about what is to happen, on the other hand [Alfred] Harcourt
sent me a clipping about the new book for which I was interviewed by the
Herald Tribune,[4] I also gave a lecture about the new book, entitled what are
master-pieces and why are there so few of them, I gave it to students English
speaking here, very well received Alice will send it along in due time,[5] which
she says is very due, and I think if the Wilder austerity permits it would be nice
if you would go and see Harcourt sometime, I am telling him that I want you
to see him because he has been so good to me in spite of the fact that he does
not know what it is all about it but that he will when you are through with him,
I think if the other thing does not look promising it would not be uninteresting
to try Harcourt although really I am not sure I do not like Chicago University
press best, I like their ways,[6] Alice having been impressed by possibilities of
revolution, has been typing all my inedits to send to Carl [Van Vechten] for
safe keeping[7] and so she has been completely covered up with ms. but the
most of that is over and as soon as she breathes again she will start on a copy for
Bob [Robert Davis], I am writing to him very shortly but I have been helping
correct and it has been a job all of which has to be xplained to the lit[erary].
xecutor,[8] I had a charming letter from [Alexander] Woollcott, and I have
written him his lovely letter about Basket[9] they both sleep peacefully and send
their love to Uncle Wilder, poor Pepe[10] had a hard day before yesterday, we
took him to see his future wives and present sisters the Nina twins chez

Picabia, how he suffered it was terrible, he kicked and screamed, and tried to swallow the head of the littlest one and he would not look and he just suffered and suffered, intolerable he said that those little things called themselves dogs, and made out that he was bigger, as soon as he got home he played lovingly with Basket and Basket kept telling him how little and how adorable he was and now he has almost forgotten the most awful day of his life. I had a nice letter too from [Wendell] Wilcox, he is a nice fellow, have you seen his new novel,[11] I guess that's all xcept all our love which is all yours and the best of merry Christmases

Always
Gtrde and Alice.

1. Stein agreed to serve on the Comité Littéraire Franco-Américain proposed by Librairie Plon. In a letter to Stein on 3 December 1935 (YCAL), Librairie Plon wrote of plans for the committee, sent a list of people contacted with an indication of who had accepted, and indicated that the first meeting would be held at the home of Daisy Fellowes in Neuilly on Friday, 6 December 1935. The committee's purpose outlined to Stein by Plon was to make known in France important American writers and in America, through translation, French writers. Among those who had agreed to serve on the committee were Paul Claudel, Julien Green, Edmond Jaloux, André Maurois, Paul Morand, Gabriel Marcel, Louis Gillet, and Maurice Martin du Gard. Other "personalities" were Princesse Edmond de Polignac, Comtesse Jean de Pange, and Mme Jagerschmidt. Louis Bromfield, the American writer who lived with his wife, Mary, in Senlis outside of Paris, is not on the typed list; his name was probably a late addition. Stein may also have suggested Bobsy Goodspeed, Elizabeth Cutter Morrow, and Edward Wassermann (later Waterman).

A draft of a letter to an unknown recipient, written on the verso of Bennett Cerf's letter to Stein of 28 February 1936 (YCAL), indicates that she had second thoughts about the committee. "It is with great regret that I find myself unable longer to continue a member of the Committee—and I have already informed the Librairie Plon of my withdrawal.　Always very sincerely Gtde Stein."

2. Probably *Heaven's My Destination*.

3. Stein met the Duchesse de Clermont-Tonnerre, born Elisabeth de Gramont, through Natalie Barney. The duchess was a friend of Marcel Proust, who borrowed some of her characteristics for his Duchesse de Guermantes. Under her maiden name, the duchess wrote several popular histories of nineteenth-century French life as well as family and personal memoirs that included descriptions of Stein. She also wrote two of the earliest studies of Proust, *Robert de Montesquiou et Marcel Proust* (Paris: Flammarion, 1925) and *Marcel Proust* (Paris: Flammarion, 1948). In 1930 Stein wrote a portrait of her, which the duchess warmly acknowledged. What song the duchess might have heard in the Alcazar d'Eté, the open-air music hall off the Champs Elysées, has not been determined, but by 1935 Stein had become enough of a popular public figure to be referred to in songs and films. Two films from 1935, for example, mention Stein: R.K.O. studio's *Top Hat*, starring Fred Astaire and Ginger Rogers, and Paramount's *The Man on the Flying Trapeze*, starring W. C. Fields.

4. The interview with Stein about the *Geographical History* was published on 2 December 1935, 2, in the European edition of the *New York Herald Tribune*. Similar advance publicity was also written by Janet Flanner for her "Paris Letter" in *The New Yorker* on 15 February 1936, 51. (The "Paris Letter" is reprinted in Flanner's *Paris Was Yesterday: 1925–1939*, ed. Irving Drutman [New York: Viking, 1972], 157.)

5. We do not know where Stein lectured in Paris. "To students English speaking here" may refer to the American Students' Club, 107 Boulevard Raspail (see Stein to Wilder, 19 December 1935, n. 2).

6. Disturbed by Bennett Cerf's silence since his letter of 15 November acknowledging delivery of the manuscript, Stein considered submitting it to other publishers, including Harcourt, Brace, who had published *The Autobiography Of Alice B. Toklas* and the abridged version of *The Making Of Americans*.

7. Since 1931, France had been going through a period of political and economic unrest. Governments, none lasting more than a few months, were unable to stabilize the country. Revolution seemed a real possibility, and Italy's war in Ethiopia helped fuel a sense of insecurity. Stein therefore sent Van Vechten typescripts of all of her unpublished writings, which Van Vechten later presented to YCAL.

8. We know of only two wills that Stein made: one in 1928, not preserved, and her last will, dated 23 July 1946, a few days before her death. In that will she gave Carl Van Vechten the responsibility for her unpublished work. However, in *Everybody's Autobiography* (1937) she writes of plans not executed in any known will: "Then I worry about Thornton I have made him my literary executor will he get weak and let any one he admires and believes in some, he does in me but that is not the same thing of course not, well anyway here and now it is said that he is not to let his left hand know what his right hand is doing and his left hand does lead him where he is led. I am not leading him I am confiding in him and that is what we did in going up and down the hills near Bilignin and he loved Pépé because as he said Pépé passed and existed from one caress to another" (301).

9. Woollcott wrote Stein on 8 October 1935 (YCAL) that he was assembling material for a "fond monograph," to be called "The Brotherhood of the French Poodle," with stories of various owners and their dogs. On 25 November he wrote that he was counting on her piece. Stein's reply is an undated letter of late December about Basket (Harvard-Theatre). See Appendix V.

10. The Chihuahua.

11. Wendell Wilcox was a graduate of the University of Chicago (1929) who first read Stein's work in 1926. He attended her lecture in November 1934 and was one of those invited to her lectures at the University of Chicago in March 1935. Wilcox was one of a small group of young writers that Wilder was encouraging. Stein unsuccessfully submitted a novel by Wilcox to Harcourt, Brace, Random House, and Harpers. Whether Wilcox's only published novel, *Everything Is Quite All Right* (1945), is the one Stein submitted is not clear. Stein's letters to Wilcox, edited by Philip Galanes, were published in *The Paris Review, One Hundredth Issue*, as "Gertrude Stein: Letters to a Friend" (Summer/Fall 1986): 359–78.

To Gertrude Stein and Alice Toklas, Paris, France

14 Dec[ember]. 1935   50 Deepwood Drive
                                                           New Haven[,] Conn.

Dear Twain:

I sit waiting for word from Mr. Cerf and wishing I had the MS back in my own hands.

In fact all I do is wait. Grant didn't wait, I know; but I gotta. My father with the tenacious physique of an exemplary life amazes the doctors and nurses by surviving strokes and convulsions and paralyses.

I've reread all the plays of Nestroy and almost all the *Lundis* of Sainte-Beuve—which is perfect reading for waiting.

Christmas comes ominously on and Isabel has filled a whole room with tissue paper and red ribbons.

Walter Winchell, the key-whole reporter and Aretino of our time, says that Sylvia Sidney is changing her mind about Bennett Cerf and that he is commuting with Hollywood in order to retain her favor. Walter Winchell walks the tight-rope over an abyss of libel cases and is always cautious and never wrong; so perhaps Mr. Cerf hasn't time to write letters.[1]

So here I am, cranky and unfit to write letters.

The only enlivening thing I have to tell you is that a research-worker at Yale has been experimenting and has taught dogs *to pay for their meals*. So dog nature has stolen some more territory from human nature, to the mortification of us all.

We're all so *indignant* about England's Ethiopian plan yesterday.[2] Booh!

So, you see, I have nothing to write you, and merely write to show you that I think of you a lot and to keep testimonials of my affection crossing the ocean.

Affectionately

Thornton

1. Walter Winchell in 1935 was writing his gossip column about theater for the *Daily Mirror*. He also produced a syndicated radio program. Wilder compares Winchell to Pietro Aretino, the sixteenth-century Italian satirist whose attacks on his powerful contemporaries earned him the nickname Scourge of Princes.

Cerf's silence about the submission of the *Geographical History* is explained by his domestic problems. Sylvia Sidney was planning to leave and divorce Cerf. Delays in mail service raised Stein's anxiety that Cerf had rejected the book. He would write her on 17 December 1935 explaining his plans for publication.

2. Border clashes between Italy, through its African colony Somaliland, and Ethiopia were common throughout 1935. In October 1935, Italy invaded Ethiopia. By December a peace settlement called the Hoare-Laval plan, which awarded Italy 220,000 square miles of Ethiopian territory, met with public outcry.

To Thornton Wilder, New York, New York

[postmark: 19 December 1935]   [27 rue de Fleurus
                                                       Paris]

My dear Thornton,

        Well perhaps you did sell me, you can't most generally always tell, I wrote to her and said you so sweetly always tell one lady about another that she spent the summer telling me about her and her about me, well not so crudely but I gently let it drop, and I will tell you all about it when it happens,[1] Alice typed the lecture I did here but I am making it more for merrie England and so I will wait a bit before sending it on[2] nothing from [Bennett] Cerf,[3] but I have just heard that his marriage is going to pieces and perhaps that is that, in a few days I will write to him and ask him, and tell him to see you again if you will and give it back to you, we want anybody who does it to be enthusiastic, the little lecture about it has aroused so much interest that Dalli[4] sends me a book and signs himself my affectionate friend, I wish you were here we do miss you a lot Thornton and once more merry Christmas

Gtrde and Alice.

1. Stein enclosed an undated letter from Lady Sibyl Colefax telling her of Wilder singing Stein's praises to her in Salzburg. Colefax, who had met Stein through Méraud Guiness Guevara in Paris, hoped to see Stein again at Christmas in Paris.

2. Stein sent Wilder typescripts of "What Are Masterpieces" and "An American And France," which Wilder deposited in YCAL in 1937. At the top of the typescript of "What Are Masterpieces," Stein had written, "The first part first is pages given here and the whole to be given in Oxford Feb 11." The first six and a half pages of this typescript appear to have been typed at the same time (in the printed text, from the beginning of the essay through the end of the paragraph beginning, "I do not know whether," 89). The remainder of the lecture is typed on a lighter ribbon. Stein's note may allude to this distinction (see Stein to Wilder, 11 December 1935, n. 5).

3. Stein had not yet received Cerf's letter of 17 December.

4. Salvador Dali, the Spanish artist, may have given Stein a copy of his book *Conquest of the Irrational* (New York: Julien Levy, 1935).

To Thornton Wilder, New Haven, Connecticut

[postmark: 22 December 1935]   [27 rue de Fleurus
                                                                     Paris]

My dear Thornton,

I am inclosing two letters about the ms. one from Carl [Van Vechten] and one from Mark Lutz and a nice one from Donald Vestal which will amuse you, and dear dear Thornton will you as a nice Christmas present from me go and see Carl, 150 West 55 Street, I do want you to talk to him about what to do about the ms., it does look as if Bennett Cerf did not like his portraits or something and I think there ought to be perhaps something done, so will you dear will you oh will you go and see Carl, he says in his last Thornton Wilder hasn't been near me I hoped he would walk right in with all the news,[1] so will you that is our own dear Thornton, will you go and be a happy Christmas and a glad new year and go and see Carl, I am asking Bennett to return to you the ms. and talk to you about it,[2] my lecture for Oxford is almost done and I will be sending it, and poor Daisy [Fellowes] is ill, she got an infectious grippe and she has been in bed with a terrible fever, and still is, and it makes a lot of difference, and Paris is almost as cold as America, and Donald Bean has written another nice crusty letter and we xpect the lovely books any minute, and I will give one with both our signatures to Daisy, for Christmas,[3] Pepe says it's so cold he won't walk and if he is not carried he will be dragged and so we went out to St Germain into the woods and that he said was not so bad, and Lady Colefax is coming next Saturday and we all including Othmar and Pepe and Basket, dear forgiving Basket do oh do so wish that you were here, and lots of love oh so much love and a happy happy new year to you and all the Wilders, papa and mama and all the young Wilders.

Gtrde.

1. Van Vechten's letter may be [? November 1935] in Burns, *Letters*, 2:454–55. Mark Lutz was a friend of Van Vechten who had met Stein and helped arrange for her visit to Richmond; his letter is not in YCAL. The letter from Donald Vestal in YCAL that discusses the marionette play, "Identity: A Play," may be the one dated 12 November 1935. Wilder returned the enclosures with his letter to Stein of 25 January 1936. On 9 December [1935], Van Vechten again complained, "Thornton Wilder hasn't been near me. I hoped he would stalk right in with all the news" (Burns, *Letters*, 2:463–64).

2. Stein, anxious to have the *Geographical History* published, assumed that Cerf's silence since 15 November was a rejection (see Stein to Wilder, 11 December 1935, n. 6, and 9 January 1936, n. 3).

3. Bean wrote to Stein on 6 December 1935 (copy, Chicago) that ten copies of *Narration*, five from the trade edition and five deluxe copies, were being sent to her: "Please accept them with our congratulations and our very special appreciation of your participation in the printing process, which made that experience so pleasant, and relatively expeditious, in spite of your distance from us."

To Thornton Wilder, New York, New York

[postmark: 10:45   [27 rue de Fleurus
25 December 1935]   Paris]

My dear Thornton,

Just had your telegram of greetings and your book and our books[1] and now a nice message to you from Daisy [Fellowes],[2] she has been very ill so ill she cannot write but she sent over her daughter to give me to send you this message dictated to her daughter and to me a little bird that sings in a jeweled box which you will see and listen to soon we hope, and first your book of plays, I liked best the queens of France[3] you did not say to like that one best but I think and not because it is France but because it is you that it is a perfect jewel, I think as nearly perfect as a thing can be, you won't mind my liking that best, I liked the others but that one has all the qualities of perfection that we know a master-piece has, really I am quite mad about it, it has local color but it completely transcends its local color, and our books are so satisfactory, so deliciously satisfactory, had a letter asking about french reviews for it, which we will answer after consultation with Mme Clermont-Tonnerre, I gave a copy to Daisy and she was pleased the one with both our signatures and everybody even Othmar thinks the books beautiful, well we are very happy and merry Christmas Alice is fixing her creche, Basket a little uneasy thinking we are going traveling, watches Pepe deep under two covers sleeps and we all say happy new year to you happy happy new year to you

Always

Gtrde.

1. The books referred to here are Wilder's *The Long Christmas Dinner and Other Plays* (1931) and author's copies of Stein's *Narration*, one of which Stein inscribed for Daisy Fellowes. Wilder's telegram has not survived.

2. Enclosed with this letter was a card announcing a lecture on Jeanne d'Arc by Daisy Fellowes as part of a series, "Les Grandes Conférences des Ambassadeurs," on 17 December. On the back of the card is a message to Wilder, "Daisy rather wind blown will be better soon sending best wishes."

3. *Queens of France*, the second play in the book, takes place in New Orleans in 1869. Cahusac, a confidence man, convinces a succession of women that they are the legitimate heirs to the French throne. Each pays Cahusac to continue the research on her claim and the play ends with a stage direction: *"The reed curtain is parted and a Negro boy pushes in a wheel chair containing a woman of some hundred years of age. She is wrapped in shawls, like a mummy, and wears a scarf about her head, and green spectacles on her nose. The mummy extends a hand which* M. Cahusac *kisses devotedly, murmuring, 'Your Royal Highness' "* (see Stein to Wilder, 23 November 1935, n. 5).

To Thornton Wilder, New York, New York
[Rose motto]

[postmark: 17:30   27 rue de Fleurus
25 December 1935]   [Paris]

My dear Thornton,

Every day a letter to you and it is a pleasure to me and I guess a pleasure to you, I am afraid Bennett Cerf is in a mess, too bad he was made to be happy and if you are made to be happy it does not come easy not to be. I have just written them to right away send you the ms. and so if you don't get it will you call them up, and after you have it why do what you like with it, having showed it to them I have no further publishing obligations,[1] just had a charming telegram from [Alexander] Woollcott, he sort of replaces Mildred Aldrich in our life a necessary thing to have in one's life,[2] Basket and Pepe had a Christmas dinner, much appreciated, Pepe slept through the lighted creche but Basket was sweetly sentimental, Alice says that is because Pepe is more honest, well anyway we love you a lot and may it be a glad new year, and we do love you a lot,

Gtrde and Alice.

1. Anxious at not having heard from Cerf since November, Stein assumed that Random House did not want to publish the book and instructed first Donald Klopfer and then Cerf to return the

typescript to Wilder (see undated letters to Klopfer and Cerf, Columbia-R.H.; see also Stein to Wilder, 11 December 1935, n. 6; Wilder to Stein, 14 December 1935, n. 1; Stein to Wilder, 19 December 1935, n. 3; Stein to Wilder, 22 December 1935, n. 2).

2. Woollcott's Christmas telegram (YCAL) may have led Stein to recall her friend Mildred Aldrich, the American writer who lived in France for many years, until her death in 1928. Woollcott and Aldrich, who had known each other, shared a common love of France while retaining strong American characteristics. Both had "served" in World War I. Woollcott's experiences as a soldier are recorded in his *The Command Is Forward: Tales of the A.E.F. Battlefields As They Appeared in The Stars and Stripes* (1919). Aldrich wrote five books, including *A Hilltop on the Marne* (1915), which brought the realities of the war home to Americans. Stein and Toklas were devoted to Aldrich, frequently visited her on weekends, and late in her life helped organize an annuity fund for her. Stein wrote two portraits of her, "Mildred Aldrich Saturday" and "Mildred's Thoughts," and frequently mentioned her in other writing over the years.

"We bought leder-hosen and complete rig and will soon send you a photopostal illustrating the unquenchable flight (to from) identity which is the masquerade."

Wilder and Robert Davis in studio photograph, Innsbruck, Austria, August 1935

1936

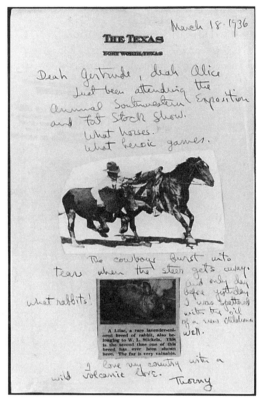

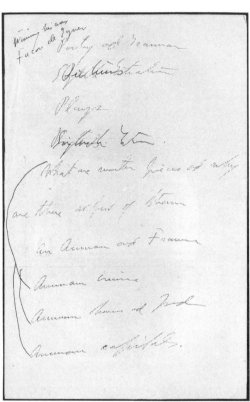

"But I enjoy the travel. The endless hotel rooms; the endless Pullman berths." (Wilder on 14 March)

On the verso of Wilder's letter of 18 March, Stein plays with titles of lectures and essays for a collection.

To Thornton Wilder, New Haven, Connecticut

[postmark: 4 January 1936]   [27 rue de Fleurus
                                               Paris]

My dear Thornton,
                    Just had a charming letter from Bob Davis, full of pleasant
words and solid thoughts, we will be sending him his copy soon,[1] Alice is
almost at the end of the unpublished which are being sent to Carl [Van
Vechten] in case of a revolution here, but the revolution here seems to be very
tranquil, the left is dying and the right is flying the french flag so we may go on
peacefully with the third republic Any news from [Bennett] Cerf yet and how
are you, we seem very full of seeing each other, and I guess I won't settle down
to anything until we get back from England. We are staying with Lord Berners
and they say he has a beautiful home near Oxford so that will be nice.[2] Poor
Pepe had a miserable time yesterday evening, the Picabia puppies came to
dinner and Pepe was oh so miserable and then they quickly attacked Basket
and then Pepe's identity disap[p]eared, he had none and he literally during
the night vomited bile, a yellow foam the first time in his life, I did not know it
was so literal ne te fait pas de bile mamma [don't let it bother you] as the
soldiers used to say at the end of their letters,[3] now he and Basket are biting
and embracing and identity has come back, it is awful to give up identity if
there are no master-pieces, awful, I do hope you are well and reasonably
happy, indeed even more happy than reasonable and I wish you were here,
Daisy [Fellowes] is still quite ill, she seems to have had some kind of intestinal
[word?], lots and lots of love from us all
                    Gtrde—Alice.

1. After two weeks in the Austrian Alps, Davis wrote Stein details of his life in Vienna and his new
friends (undated, YCAL). Stein had promised to send him a typescript of the *Geographical History*.
    2. See Stein to Wilder, 23 November 1935, n. 7, and Berners to Stein, 6 January 1936, in Gallup,
Flowers, 312. See Stein to Wilder [postmark: 25 January 1936], n. 2.

3. There are numerous letters in YCAL from soldier godsons whom Stein and Toklas "adopted" when they worked for the American Fund for French Wounded (March 1917 to June 1919). For a printed sample, see the letters of Abel Leglaye in Gallup, *Flowers*, 124, 127–28.

To Thornton Wilder, New Haven, Connecticut

[postmark: 9 January 1936]   [27 rue de Fleurus
                                                                                      Paris]

My dear Thornton,
                    Are you all well and happy and enjoying the same, we do hope so, the Hutchins sent us a very pretty angel, really a very elegant angel colored by the little girl, there is a lot of elegance to the angel, Lady Colefax turned up, we talked about you and about England, she is going to arrange that we see the Chinese show all by ourselves,[1] and other things, and she was sweet and pleasant, I wrote to Bob Davis but have not heard from him.[2] I finally heard from Bennett Cerf, [he] does not say much about the book and suggests printing it in the fall, I suggested that there should be lots of preparation for it, and in any case he should see you, which I hope by this time he has,[3] Daisy [Fellowes] is still very ill, she seems not to get better, we see her daughters and they give us the news, I think she would appreciate hearing from you, address 19 rue St. James Neuilly, Seine, Paris we do miss you awfully and I do hope everything is alright with you,
                                        Always
                                        Gtrde.

1. An international exhibition of Chinese art was held in London at the Royal Academy of Arts from 28 November 1935 to 7 March 1936. More than three thousand works were exhibited.
2. Stein's letters to Davis have not been located.
3. The delay in receiving Cerf's letter of 17 December (YCAL) raised Stein's anxiety about his reaction to the *Geographical History*. Cerf says little about the book but does comment on a description of himself and his uncle, Herbert Wise (80–82): "Needless to say, Herbert and I were both vitally interested in the chapter that you devoted to us in your new book. I am afraid that Herbert comes off as a much better person in this chapter than I do, but maybe I do not quite understand what you are saying about me. I still remember the day in your room at the Algonquin when you put your hand on my shoulder and said, in a rather pitying voice, 'Bennett, you're a very sweet boy, but you're dumb!'" Cerf also argues that because the University of Chicago Press is publishing *Narration* "[I]t will be a great mistake to bring out this new book during the coming season. I think it should be launched in the Fall so that you have one new book for each publishing season of 1936. Do you not agree with this?" Cerf apologizes for his long silence by explaining that the "amusing tale" of his hectic married life to a famous "moving picture star" is too long a story to write, and that it will have to wait until he comes to Paris in the spring.
    In her reply (?January 1936, Columbia-R.H.), Stein expresses relief at having news from Cerf but is upset that he fails to comment on the *Geographical History*: "Tell me what you do feel about the

book." "[T]here seems to be something about it that gets under people's skins, which makes me very happy." She agrees with his timing of publication but hopes that "it should be fairly well prepared in advance and it was about that that I wanted you to get together with Thornton Wilder."

To Thornton Wilder, Greensboro, North Carolina

[postmark: 25 January 1936]   [27 rue de Fleurus
                                                                          Paris]

My dear Thornton,

Not a word from you for ever so long are you lost in the wilds of our own dear native land, are you perhaps in the blizzard or in Chicago or just in New Haven. How can our imagination fix you if we do not know where you are.[1] We are here, and on the 9 we go to England, I am now doing two lectures in Oxford, the second one to the french club, An American and France, and I have gotten the romance thing much clearer, I will send it to you very soon, and then too I am going to Cambridge also to the English Club and so we are looking forward to an amusing time, we are teaing with Lady Colefax she has been very nice about hotels and everything for us,[2] and I guess even with England in mourning but by that time the new king will be in full activity we will have a good time,[3] I wish you were here. Bennett Cerf has been writing very nice letters about the book, and by this time everything is all arranged, he is to be here in the spring to talk further, the Narrative book[4] seems to be making a nice stir, I do not know how it is selling but even Nathalie Barney who never reads a book has read it twice so there is hope, they are celebrating me here on March 2 at the Amis de 1914[5] and it would be nice if you were here for that, but you are not alas you are not. Othmar the austrian is gone, he got drunk and then he got drunker and then he suddenly put in an announcement in the Herald looking for a job and when we fired him he said it was an enemy had done that thing an Austrian lady who wanted to marry him, so we parted in tears but we did part, he has been succeeded by a Norwegian intellectual, come over soon and see her, otherwise family life is peaceful, the Norwegian intellectual just appeared at the door and the animals barked, Othmar when he is very drunk came in very sentimentally and said, je vous en prie madame, laissez moi seule une fois seule avec le[s] chiens [I beg you, madame, leave me alone for once with the dogs], so I withdrew, Basket withdrew, Pepe barked terribly and tried to bite him, otherwise as I say family life is peaceable, we have had a really cheerful winter and the only thing we miss is you. Daisy Fellowes is a little better but far from well yet, very

far from well, we have seen her once and she asked after you but we had no news, alas no news, and if you are in Chicago remember us to them all, and our best to the Hutchins, and everybody and lots and lots of love
Gtrde.

1. This letter was forwarded to Wilder in care of Professor L. B. Hurley of the Woman's College of the University of North Carolina in Greensboro, where Wilder was lecturing.

2. Stein and Toklas flew from Paris to London on 8 February for two nights before taking a train to Oxford on 10 February. Stein delivered "An American And France" before the Anglo-French Society on 11 February and the next evening "What Are Masterpieces And Why Are There So Few Of Them" before the English Club of Oxford. On 21 February she repeated "What Are Masterpieces" before the Cambridge English Club. Between lectures Stein and Toklas were the guests of Lord Berners at his home, Faringdon House, in Berkshire and then of Sir Robert and Lady Abdy at their home in Callington, Cornwall. They flew back to Paris on 25 February. "An American And France" is an expanded version of a lecture, "An American And Paris," that Stein delivered before English-speaking students in Paris in December 1935 (see Stein to Wilder [11 December], n. 5, [19 December 1935], n. 2, and [4 January 1936], n. 2; see also Lady Colefax to Stein, n.d. 1936; Rosamund Frere to Stein, 17 January and 30 January 1936; Comte A. de Biéville to Stein, 25 January 1936; and C. Lombardi Barber to Stein, 3 February 1936, YCAL).

3. King George V died on 20 January, and Edward VIII acceded to the throne on 22 January.

4. *Narration.*

5. A letter from Stein to Natalie Barney of 3 December 1935 (Doucet) makes clear that Stein was a member of this group and occasionally attended meetings. The idea of its founders was to provide a forum for artists to meet and discuss their art in an atmosphere that recalled the calm before "la catastrophe de 1914." Weekly meetings were held and speeches about writers being honored were often satirical. In her letter to Barney, Stein comments, "You know I did not ever get introduced when I spoke." Neither the Bibliothèque littéraire Jacques Doucet nor the Bibliothèque Nationale has a bulletin about the reception of Stein.

To Gertrude Stein and Alice Toklas, Paris, France

25 Jan[uary] 1936   50 Deepwood Drive
                                                     New Haven, Conn[ecticut].

Dear Friends:
        Please forgive me for being silent so long.
        I've been in the intertia [i.e., inertia] of the between-engagements; between returning from Europe and going off on the Tour; an interim not long enough to be a good in itself, and yet too long to be an energetic preparation. And the whole thing's been colored by the invalidism downtown.[1]
        I went to Mr. Cerf and borrowed back the MS and reread it with all the old pleasure and always with new pleasures. As with *Four in America* which I am always sharing with chosen friends, I made enthusiastic converts. I was on the point of taking it to Mr. Harcourt when your and Mr. Cerf's word arranged

the fact that Random House would bring it out in the Fall. I received a note
from Mr. Cerf saying that he wanted it back right away to start work on the
format.[2] He will make another beautiful-looking book of it.

I would especially like to see a list of all your works opposite the Title
page, under categories. Like:

Narratives

Three Lives
The Making of Americans
Lucy Church Amiably 1931
As a Wife has a Cow
The Autobiography of A.B.T. 1933

Poetry and Portraiture

Tender Buttons
Useful Knowledge 1928
Portraits and Prayers
Before the Flowers 1931

. . . .

Theatre

Operas and Plays
Three Saints in Four Acts

. . . .

ESSAYS:

On Literary Creation

Explanation as Description
An Acquaintance with Description 1929
How to Write 1932
Narration

On Science

Phenomena (??)

On Philosophy and the Human Mind

Four in America
The Geographical History of America[3]

[Naturally, this is humble and tentative. Whenever I start making lists I
get led on.]

I can't wait until "They" come to see your work as being many sides of a
central intention.

Aleck [Woollcott] said he got a wonderful letter from you about Basket.
Apparently it's to be the chief ornament of his next book. It's a secret still, but

he's thinking of going abroad for a few weeks next month, one of the aims being to have a talk with you. He went off the air in January because his sponsors objected to his discussing "controversial subjects"—i.e. polysyllabic snarls at Hitler and Mussolini. Aleck for a time saw himself as a blazing tribune of the people under tyranny, but is now enjoying his leisure and is wearing the Toga more nonchalantly.[4]

> (Cont'd at 6:45 in the Periodical Room of the Pub Library. The Wilders are always making appointments to meet one another in public places, then getting some detail of the appointment wrong. Here I wait.)

Two weeks ago—three, I mean—I went down to Philadelphia to see the opening of *Ethan Frome*. I no longer get much real pleasure from going to a play, but I get more and more from hanging around theatres. This was like a great week end party, only it was at the Hotel Ritz. Kit Cornell; Guthrie [McClintic], her husband, who staged it; Pauline Lord; Ruth Gordon; and others. Every night the performance and after it talk until three and four. The play has since opened in New York to great success. Ruth is very fine indeed, and this performance brings her up one more peg to the position that in five years will efface all the others. She's Mrs Fiske. She's Réjane. And she's the person in America I want you to meet most, and she's eager to meet you.[5] [Kit was there on vacation between Juliet and Joan; which begins rehearsals this week.][6]

Bob Davis was beside himself with pleasure at your letter.

I gather from his letters to me that he is [in] alternation between dark dejections as to whether he can "think" at all, and ecstacies at sudden illuminations.

I leave for Boston tomorrow to call on my brother and new sister-in-law and to see Harvard Philosophy Dept (Prof. Hocking) about a fellowship for Bob Davis.[7]

Alice, we are in deep snow. You should see my coral-cum-saffron sweater gleaming through my unbuttonable Tyrolian jacket in grey and green—you see that against a snow drift.

I don't know whether you're letter-filers, but I return the letters you sent me about the Marionette Play and about the book. Awful nice, they are.[8]

I apologize for misinforming you. The experimental station has trained chimpanzees NOT DOGS to buy their own meals. Not only that. The monkeys are given red chips for a banana, white for a drink of water and yellow for mush and so on. And a chimp who loves bananas will hoard his red chips for a big feast.

When Pavloff called to see them all the chimps spat on him. They copied it from the gardner in the grounds, but they saved up their new acquisition for Pavloff. He wears cutaway and striped trousers wherever he goes and he was very angry. "This is not science" he cried, "this is charlatanism."

Very sorry about Mrs Fellowes. I shall write her at once. And now that my lethargy is leaving me at the approach of the trip I shall write my MDs more often. (The Journal to Stella.)[9]

The whole Human Nature—Human Mind thing has fastened on me like a vise: sometimes I resist it and sometimes I accept it and sometimes I am exhilarated by it. Slowly it circulates through all the arterial system of my notions and assimilates all the new material that comes along.

More soon.

I think of you all the time with proud and devoted affection.

Yours

Thornton

1. At the University of Chicago Wilder taught two quarters per year. What should have been time for writing was instead filled with lecture engagements to raise money to support his family. "Invalidism" probably refers to his father's illness.

2. Wilder returned the typescript to Cerf on 20 January 1936 but retained his notes to work on his introduction (Wilder to Cerf, 20 January 1936, Columbia-R H.). In his reply, Cerf invited Wilder to lunch when he was next in New York and explained that when they had last met he was "a little distracted by personal affairs" (copy, Cerf to Wilder, 27 January 1936, Columbia-R.H.). See Stein to Wilder, 11 December 1935, n. 6.

3. Wilder's idea was not used by Random House either opposite the title page or on the dust jacket. He was probably making the list from memory, shortening or twisting some of the titles, i.e., *Four Saints In Three Acts* and *Composition As Explanation*. Under "On Science," Wilder's "Phenomena" is Stein's "Natural Phenomena."

4. The undated letter from Stein was not used in Woollcott's printed text and is therefore included here as Appendix V (see also Stein's second letter to Wilder, 25 December 1935, n. 2). Woollcott's program, "The Town Crier," was not sponsored until 1934, when it was picked up by the Cream of Wheat Corporation. From his radio debut on station WOR in New York in September 1929, he had been used to speaking his mind, and in 1933, when he moved to CBS, its chairman, William S. Paley, sustained the broadcasts without a sponsor. By 1935 isolationism was particularly strong in the Midwest, and he was warned by his sponsors that his remarks about Hitler and Mussolini were endangering sales among Germans and Italians. Woollcott persisted in speaking his mind; he was informed on 22 November 1935 that the Cream of Wheat Corporation was canceling his program as of 29 December. In a letter to Paul Harper, whose agency represented his sponsor, Woollcott wrote that he would not cease from taking "pot shots" at Hitler and Mussolini, "or, for that matter, at any other bully, lyncher or jingo whose head happened to come within shooting distance" (see Kaufman and Hennessey, *Letters*, 152–55).

5. *Ethan Frome*, by Owen and Donald Davis, had been suggested by Lowell Barrington's earlier dramatization of Edith Wharton's novel. The play opened in Philadelphia at the Garrick Theatre on 6 January 1936 and in New York at the National Theatre on 21 January 1936, where it ran for 120 performances. Max Gordon's production was staged by Guthrie McClintic and had scenery and costumes by Jo Mielziner. In addition to Ruth Gordon as Mattie Silver, the cast included Raymond Massey as Ethan Frome and Pauline Lord as Zenobia Frome.

6. Cornell began her season of 1935–36 at the Martin Beck Theatre, New York, by reviving *Romeo and Juliet* for fifteen performances on 23 December 1935. In this production, Maurice Evans played Romeo and Ralph Richardson played Mercutio. Cornell played the starring role in George Bernard Shaw's *Saint Joan*, which opened on 9 March 1936 and ran for eighty-nine performances.

Maurice Evans played the role of the Dauphin and Brian Aherne the role of the Earl of Warwick. Both plays were staged by Guthrie McClintic and had settings by Jo Mielziner.

7. The letters from Robert Davis to Wilder have not survived. In his letter to Stein [? February 1936] Wilder reports some success in soliciting Prof. William Ernest Hocking's help to get Davis into Harvard. Hocking's letters to Wilder are not in YCAL, and it has not been possible to determine what steps Hocking undertook.

8. See Stein to Wilder, 22 December 1935, n. 1, and Appendix IV.

9. This is the first time Wilder addresses Stein and Toklas as his MD[s], connecting himself and the women with Swift and the *Journal to Stella*; on 2 March 1939, he refers to himself as "Presto." The journal is a collection of letters addressed between 1710 and 1713 to the young Esther Johnson, whom Swift had installed at Sir William Temple's Moor Park estate with Rebecca Dingley as chaperone. Swift's letters, intended for Stella, whom he admired and courted, were addressed to the two women as M[y] D[ears] or to Mrs. Dingley as Dd or D[earest] D[ingley]. That Wilder relies on literary games with coded parallels, wordplay, and the persona of Swift is not in itself surprising. However, he almost certainly did not know that Stein and Toklas in intimate love exchanges had long used Swift's "little language." D.D. and Y[our]. D. often appear in private marginal notes that were not included in the texts Toklas typed. Only occasionally did they enter Stein pieces, to be typed and printed, as for example in "A Sonatina Followed By Another. Dedicated By Request To D.D." of 1921. Of course, Wilder's MD might also suggest medical doctor, given Stein's medical training. Wilder could not have read in print any of the pieces that included the prattling little language. "A Sonatina" was not yet printed. What he had seen in print—*Geography And Plays*, *Portraits And Prayers*, *The Making Of Americans*, *Lucy Church Amiably*, and later works, which never use this language—had no coded initials. The little language appears even in the early notebooks for *The Making Of Americans* and returns throughout the years, into the thirties and perhaps beyond. Only when Wilder carried manuscripts to New Haven in late 1937/early 1938 could he have seen the code, but by this time he had already used Swift in letters. Neither Stein nor Toklas in their letters ever took note of his references to Swift. Other letters in which Wilder uses this code are 27 September 1936, 15 November 1937, 23 April 1938, and 2 March 1939.

Donald C. Gallup in *Pigeons on the Granite* describes how upset Toklas was when she realized that some of the private love notes had ended up at Yale. She asked that they be destroyed but at last reluctantly permitted their preservation (155–56).

To Gertrude Stein and Alice Toklas, Paris, France

[? February 1936]   [50 Deepwood Drive
                                                      Hamden, Connecticut]

Dear Gertrude; dear Alicia:

Just a word to enclose these letters for your file.[1]

No news here.

All excited about my trip: a week from tomorrow I shall [be] in Georgia where they propose to make their flour meal and meat.[2]

Calling on my brother just outside of Boston I found myself in a circle of theologues and I gave them the doctrine of public-speaking without recognition and the interference of the audience. The better of them of them [*sic*] clutched their heads with recognition of its truth; they begged for mercy. I told them you had once said that if a person through writing gets the habit of recognition it is possible to extend it somewhat into the spoken word. (Is that all right?)

I didn't dare tell them that masterpieces dispense even with recognition.[3]

This is only a covering-letter and now squeaks to a close.
Tout mon coeur
T. N.

P.S. Oh, yes, I have very encouraging letters from Prof. Hocking of Harvard as to Bob Davis getting a fellowship there for next year.[4]
P.S. II Tomorrow night I shall be seeing the new Chaplin picture under Alec [Woollcott]'s care.[5]

Thornton (sans identité)
Wilder

1. This refers to letters that Stein sent to Wilder (see Stein to Wilder, 22 December 1935, n. 1). His letter of 25 January 1936 suggests that he is returning the letters, but he does not seem to have done so until this letter.

2. Wilder echoes a sentence from a proclamation of Gov. Eugene Talmadge of Georgia in 1935 that Stein may have seen on billboards, "Let's Make Our Flour Meal and Meat in Georgia" (see the *Atlanta Journal*, 3 March 1935, p. 6).

3. *The Autobiography Of Alice B. Toklas*, published in 1933, made Stein a public personality, as did her American lecture tour. Stein was very clear that composition should not be guided by the need for recognition. She had always excluded audience from the meditative process that was part of her compositional method. In fact, she struggled in the last decade of her life to recapture the intensity of pure writing that characterized the first thirty years of her writing life. She articulates these anxieties in the Henry James section of *Four In America*, in *Narration*, in the *Geographical History*, and in the lectures "What Are Masterpieces" and "An American And France." The themes of recognition and audience are central to this correspondence and to their relationship. Wilder may have read excerpts from Stein's "What Are Masterpieces" to his brother, Amos, Norris Professor of New Testament at the Andover Newton Theological School, and some of his colleagues (see Wilder to Stein, 20 February 1936).

4. See Wilder to Stein, 25 January 1936, n. 1.

5. Charles Chaplin's *Modern Times* opened at the Rivoli Theatre, New York, on 5 February 1936. The film, written, produced, and directed by Chaplin, starred himself as a worker and Paulette Goddard as Gamine.

To Thornton Wilder, Aurora-on-Cayuga, New York[1]

[postmark: 7 February 1936]   [27 rue de Fleurus
                                                              Paris]

My dearest Thornton,

We never did think that we would see that nice nervous hand-writing again and we did not know how to bear up but here it is twice, and twice is better the [i.e., than] once, I love your list under categories, I love lists and I love categories, if you won't make marginal notes you will do that but I still wish that you would make marginal notes. I just read over the Four in America I like it, yes I do, and perhaps if the Chicago University Press is contented with the sale of Narration, they might do that, in that way [?moving] the inedit might be edited and that would make me happy, they look so fair and real in print, not quite so excellent as in the original, but more actual.[2] We fly to London Sunday, I am sending you the second lecture you did not say but did you get the first yes you did.[3] I saw Daisy [Fellowes] yesterday, we spoke of you, she poor darling is not any too well yet, but she knows your one act plays, she says she owns everything you have ever written, I said that you would were writing, she said she knew you would. I have written to [Alexander] Woollcott again telling him how pleased I was that he was coming[4] and perhaps you could come too after the lecturing is over and Bob [Davis] too and there are new ones who want to know you here, lots of new ones, some quite funny ones, and all the old ones want you again, will see Lady Colefax in London I've had a continuous correspondence, I just wrote a postal to Bob [Davis] and told him that we will write after England we are going to be in the lap of luxury chez Lord Berners they say the most luxurious Victorian home in England Oh if we could only be there to enjoy it together, well Thorny you will come back to us or we will go to you, is not there also Washington Square and the tea-set,

lots of love

Gtrde.

and Alice says the red glasses to go with it and that it is a complete dinner set.[5]

1. This letter was forwarded to Wilder from Hamden to Wells College, where he was lecturing.

2. See Wilder to Stein and Toklas, 25 January 1936. The University of Chicago Press published no further Stein books after *Narration*. *Four In America*, with an introduction by Wilder, was published by Yale University Press in 1947. From 1950 to 1958, it also printed eight volumes of her unpublished writing, the "inédit."

3. Stein had sent Wilder a typescript of "What Are Masterpieces" and now sent "An American And France." Both were first published in *What Are Masterpieces* (1940).

4. Immediately following Wilder's letter of 25 January announcing that Woollcott would likely be in Europe in a few weeks, Stein had written Woollcott of the pleasure they would have in "showing each other Paris." From London Woollcott set 30 March as the date of his arrival in Paris (see Gallup, *Flowers*, 314). Stein invited him to lunch on 30 March and proposed a tea party for Wednesday, 1 April. On the verso of his letter, Stein played with a guest list for the party. Among those listed were Colette, Ambroise Vollard, Max Jacob, Henri Sauguet, Natalie Barney, Bernard Faÿ, Mary and Louis Bromfield, Picabia, de Chirico, Julien Green, Marie Louise Bousquet, and the Duchesse de Clermont-Tonnerre. Woollcott confirmed the luncheon and the tea party in a letter to Stein from London on 23 March and again when he arrived in Paris on Sunday, 29 March (Stein, undated letters to Woollcott in Harvard-Theatre; Woollcott to Stein in YCAL).

5. See Wilder to Stein, 26 May 1935, n. 13.

To Gertrude Stein and Alice B. Toklas, Paris, France

20 Feb[ruary]. 1936

On Tour, on tour
Wells College,
Aurora-on-Cayuga,
New York
In the visiting Preacher's Suite, as usual

Dear Wuns:

What an ignoble life. How nervous and artificial the congenialities before and after the lecture. And what nonsense I utter. The judicious grieve, and it's no consolation to perceive that there are very few judicious about. *Causons d'autres choses* [Let's change the subject].

Yes, I wish I could cross with [Alexander] Woollcott, and come tearing across the courtyard of 27 rue de Fleurus, shouting "How are yuh, how are yuh?" And I wish I could overhear you in England where you will be giving a lecture that *is* a lecture, migod. The first one you sent me I have practically memorized and can be heard retelling it (with those persuasive parentheses). The new one with the latest *lumières* on Romance I await eagerly.[1]

I hope the Chicago University Press will feel able to do *Four in America*. Publishers have a feeling that no two works by the same author should reach the public without a judicious interval between them. Hence Mr. Cerf's postponement of *The Geographical History* until the Fall, and on the same principle I suppose the University Press would delay *Four in America* until a year from this Spring. I'm only a poor bespectacled academic, but I think I see erroneous "sales-psychology" tactics everywhere: yes, I think I could write better advertisements and plan better campaigns and estimate "purchasing-strength" more accurately than those office-people. But so far I merely sit congratulating myself in the warm bath of my unexpended gifts.

Let's see, what news:

Charlie Chaplin's picture is not so good as its predecessors. It doesn't *sing out* as purely; but there are great passages. ¶ Kit Cornell has a smashing success on the road with *St. Joan*, no masterpiece. ¶ Ruth Gordon's *Ethan Frome* is in for a good run, but she, poor wight, is as usual deep in woes.

Her wonderful vivid little seven-year old son was taken by his nurse to see Ruth act. Naturally he fell into conversation with his neighbors. At the conclusion of the play a lady sitting beside him told him to tell his mother that she was a very great actress indeed. Little Jones (Jones Harris=son of Ruth Gordon née Jones and Jed Harris, the bat out of Hell) didn't mention the message for several days, but finally reported: "Mama, a lady that sat next to me in the theatre told me to tell you that I was a very great actor." There in a nut-shell is the purgatory of Ruth's past with Jed and her future with Jones. ¶ In these endless trains and hotel rooms, I have been much consoled by reading in succession the plays of Jean Giraudoux.[2] ¶ Everywhere unprecedented cold. Atlanta said: Bring your golf-clubs and I arrived in a sleet-storm that increased to a whirlwind of ice and snow. The South was in such a consternation at its weather that it turned on all its furnaces full blast. The heat of Summer is terrible; the steam-heat of Winter is worse. ¶ My father continues to linger in the expensive luxury of a *bravura* hospital. At such terms the whole Wilder family could be giddily fulfilling their every wish: Amos could be following Albert Schweitzer about, as amanuensis and disciple; Charlotte could be living at Santa Fé writing her long secret books; Isabel could be dressing herself at Lanvin's and I could be arranging the house in Washington Square for your immanent [i.e., imminent] arrival. (Janet—Janet would not change a jot in her mode of life. She would still be looking through microscopes at the eggs of may-flies.) ¶ How predictable it was that Bob Davis, all alone in Vienna finally, should be tortured by alternations of ecstatic self-confidence and hellish self-doubt. Thank God I was not endowed at birth with the Philosophic Question. I admire it; I respect it; but am glad that I was not Called to sit forever on the hot stove of Consciousness Conscious of Self-Consciousness. Goethe *aetat* 77 wrote a flippant epigram explaining why he had been able to do so much work: *Ich hab' nie uber das Denken gedacht* [I've never thought about thinking]. I guess that's going too far.

Well, I had no business writing you a letter from such an uncongenial state of mind as this (dumped off a train at 6:00 a.m. this morning at 5 below zero and catapulted into the timorous hospitalities of a girls' college) but your letter was waiting for me here and the Joy of You set me at once to answering you, willy-nilly. Wait until I am hit by the first sunbeams of Texas and the Rio Grande: then I'll write for fair.

Love to you both, lots of it.

Ever
Thornton

1. Even in 1934, when writing the lectures she was to give in America, Stein spoke of the creative process. "The Gradual Making Of *The Making Of Americans*" stresses that the novel and the process of writing it are not "historical." It is not a copy of actual American history—events, people, places— but is created freely within her. Stein implies that to create a truly American work the artist need not be in America but must be free to delve into the creative mind. She in part responds to pressure upon expatriates in the early 1930s to prove that they were true Americans by returning home.

"An American And France," the last piece of 1935 or the first of 1936, extends this preoccupation to the distinction of romantic and historical. True creative work is romantic, for it is the product of foreignness or the total freedom to be creative. Such work has nothing to do with writing about or living in America. Romance refers to work of artists removed from the society to which they belong and which has bred them into a state of creative freedom, unhampered by time, memory, or the claims of verisimilitude. Historical, on the other hand, characterizes the relation of artists to their own civilization, which includes the sense of time and identity. England and English literature, familiar to Americans as elements of historical continuity, represent the tradition to which they belong. Spain or

France, to which they do not belong, offers them freedom to create. America is her country, Stein says, but Paris, which makes no claims upon her, is her home town, where she lives and enjoys the freedom to write. Stein sent "An American And France" to Wilder on 7 February 1936, having (apparently) already sent him "What Are Masterpieces" (both are in *What Are Masterpieces*).

2. Jean Giraudoux's published plays at this time included *Siegfried* (1928), *Amphitryon 38* (1929), *Judith* (1931), *Intermezzo* (1933), *Tessa* (1934), and *La guerre de Troie n'aura pas lieu* (1935). Wilder was an early admirer of Giraudoux and would meet him in Chicago in June (see Wilder to Stein, 25 June 1936, n. 6).

To Thornton Wilder, Chicago, Illinois

[postmark 6 March 1936]
[27 rue de Fleurus
Paris]

My dear Thornton,

When we came back here you were, I wish you had really and truly been here, we do we always do, had a letter from [Alexander] Woollcott to-day, he is in England but says he will come here in April,[1] perhaps you will too, we are kind of home-sick for England, we did have an awfully good time there, they made a nice fuss about us, and it was soft and gay and we liked it, and the discussions after were pretty good, at Cambridge very good, not so good as Chicago but good and I liked it. Here we are back home and I have begun a play,[2] I was pleased that in England they were interested in the possibilities of my plays, not that anything is yet happening but they are interested, and I am always pleased when they are interested, there are three young men who are making a film out of some early Geography and Plays plays, they think they can make it commercial, that would be nice, this is in America,[3] and Paris is full of pictures, Alice says never again to any picture but any way Paris is full of pictures, so many things to tell you why are you not here to be told them, I am entirely of your advice that there should not be too long between drinks, it was what the Governor of N[orth]. C[arolina]. said to the Governor of S[outh]. C[arolina]. but no editor can see it that way, it is a mistake they have to have it early and often to get used to it, but they are as they are and they certainly do not change, I do hope Chicago which being less in intention of commerce may see it that way, no news from Bob Davis I will write to him soon, and [Wendell] Wilcox wrote a rather despairing letter,[4] anybody I suppose is despairing and if they are not well then they will be, that is the way it is, but it is a cheerful life all the same, I guess we did well not to tour America this year, my it does sound cold and hot, not that it has not been cold here without the hot because it has, Pepe the other day slept 26 hours out of the 24, he said what is the use, Basket goes out with me and comes home and sneezes, Pepe and Alice cuddle each other to keep warm, and in England well one house was warm, that is a pretty good average, write soon and often the sight of your hand-writing is a pleasure

Gtrde.

1. Woollcott to Stein, 4 March 1936 (YCAL).

2. Stein had begun work on her play *Listen To Me*. In England, she had discussed productions and new musical settings of her works with Lord Berners and the Abdys, and immediately upon her return to Paris she sent Lord Berners a copy of her *Operas And Plays* (see Lord Berners to Stein, 1 March 1936, YCAL).

3. The three young men were Harry Dunham, a student at Princeton University, in Europe to study photography and cinematography; the composer and writer Paul Bowles; and the painter Maurice Grosser, who had written the scenario for *Four Saints In Three Acts*. Dunham had approached Stein with a project to film *What Happened. A Play* (1913) and *Ladies Voices* (1916). The scenario was prepared by Grosser, and the music was to be by Bowles. Stein and Dunham signed a contract witnessed by Toklas on 12 April 1936. For two years Dunham unsuccessfully struggled to raise money to make the film (see Stein to Van Vechten, 25 February 1936, in Burns, *Letters*, 2:483–84).

4. In an undated letter (YCAL), Wilcox discussed his writing problems.

To Gertrude Stein and Alice B. Toklas, Paris, France

14 March 1936

The Hotel Tulsa
Tulsa, Oklahoma
Friendly Atmosphere
i.e. a convention of the
Mystic Shriners.

Dear Twain:

So you enjoyed England.

I wish I could have heard "Identity" at Cambridge. The ideas surrounding Identity are now lodged in me, deeper and deeper—old slow-digester Wilder.

Yes, and I spent three days in Salt Lake City and now I understand that page.[1]

I should be more ashamed at how nullenvoyd my lectures are. I'm going to try and get out of that contract to do one season more.

But I enjoy the travel. The endless hotel rooms; the endless Pullman berths; the endless shaking hands with the English teaching staffs of schools and college; the endless sitting at dinner by hostesses.

I saw the Hutchins in Chicago. Bob is in great shape; Maude isn't well; the Baby's wonderful.[2] Franja has grown up and is a Big subtle girl.

A week from today I shall be back in 6020 Drexel. The Year's vacation will be over. I reverently leave a blank space for thoughts.

Every now and then on the trip you spy a nice person. In a few minutes a splendid young couple (young, that is they have two prize children 9 and 11) are calling for me to have dinner and then put me on the train. I spied'em among hundreds.[3]

I've seen an oil well, and an old Creek Indian—from that tribe the American transported from Louisiana with such graft and blood. In Salt Lake City a granddaughter of Brigham Young told me a set of appalling stories of grandfather. In Hollywood Walt Disney showed me five of his masterpieces that I happened to have missed and I danced at the Trocadero. At Tucson I dined at a tuberculosis sanatarium and wearied a few patients back to life. The Rover Boy.

The newspapers over here read very threatening about your peace of mind over there. This time you won't be able to endure the Stew of Human Nature and you'll be in Chicago. Is that possible. In Chicago I saw Bobsie [Goodspeed] and Alice Rouiller (Fanny [Butcher] was sick and couldn't be there) and they all send you such love.

The phone's rung. I'm called for.

> more soon
> devotedly yours
> Thornton

1. As Wilder makes clear, he enjoyed the travel that lecturing permitted him, but he was disturbed by the toll it took on his writing. Wilder, using Stein's term *Identity*, is probably referring to the passage in "What Are Masterpieces" in which Stein talks about time and identity (see Stein, *What Are Masterpieces*, 92–93).

2. The youngest daughter of the Hutchinses, Joanna Blessing.

3. We have been unable to identify the couple.

To Gertrude Stein and Alice Toklas, Paris, France

18 March 1936   The Texas
                                                           Fort Worth, Texas

Deah Gertrude, deah Alice

Just been attending the Annual Southwestern Exposition and Fat Stock Show.

What horses.

What heroic games.

The cowboys burst into tears when the steer gets away.

What rabbits![1]

And only day before yesterday I was spattered with the oil of a new Oklahoma well.

I love my country with a wild volcanic love.

Thorny[2]

1. After "heroic games," Wilder attached a newspaper photograph of a cowboy roping a steer, and after "rabbits" a newspaper photograph with the following printed legend: "A Lilac, a rare lavender-colored breed of rabbit, also belonging to W. L. Stickels. This is the second time one of this breed has ever been shown here. The fur is very valuable."

2. On the verso of this letter, Stein listed the titles of some of her lectures and journalism.

Winning his way
Façon de Gagner
Poetry and Grammar
English Literature revised to Pictures
Plays
English Literature revised to British Literature
What are master pieces and why are there so few of them
An American and France
American crimes [i.e., American Crimes And How They Matter]
American homes and food [i.e., American Food And American Houses]
American capitals [i.e., American States And Cities And How They Differ From Each Other]

"Winning His Way" was a long, unpublished narrative poem about reasons for writing poetry. If "Façon de Gagner" is a loose translation of this title, then it becomes a comment on lecturing and journalism as a way of making a living, something she and Wilder shared. Stein may be responding to Wilder's letter of 14 March.

This list is a draft for the contents of the planned Bodley Head volume of lectures, which was not published (see Burns, *Letters*, 2:493–94). Lines drawn along the margin suggest that Stein was planning a chronological listing.

To Thornton Wilder, Chicago, Illinois

[postmark: 25 March 1936]   27 rue de Fleurus (VI)
Paris

Dear Thornton in dear Chicago and looking out where we looked out, we are giving a tea-party on April fools' day for [Alexander] Woollcott, would that you could be here, it would mean everything to us if you were. Listen Thornton, did you ever get the second lecture I sent you about romanticism,[1] and now since we have been home I have been working like anything, I have just finished one play about Sweet William and his Lillian[2] it is called Listen to me, I was worried lest it have too much meaning but Alice says not, says it's nice, and now I have started another which is to be my best and is called Not and now, and I do think it is to be my best it has commenced like a best anyhow, and we once more have a chinaman, the whites don't seem to do in this climate anymore, he is a nice chinaman and his name is Am, I get not so home-sick for America but home-sick for traveling in America I like like you like everything about the traveling, Alice says it is the kitchenette of the Drexel that she likes, and please give it her love and might it be that one and not this one, we sometimes wonder as life gets more and more xpensive whether we will go over and earn more over there, well I don't know, I wonder, I some-times think that I never do again and then I remember that traveling, and you can't travel at least there would not be the same sense of traveling without earning, I am working so hard now that I am in a gentle fog, a pleasant spring fog, it came upon me just after England. I even pick up stray Egyptians and mixed Spaniards[3] Picasso is working on poetry, they now that is the frenchmen say his Spanish poems are fine, but he is having a most successful show of his pre-poet pictures and he has kind of decided that this is that, Picabia is having a good show too,[4] Paris is very pleasantly deep in everything, it buys up all the trunks and suit cases but otherwise does not worry,[5] will write to Bob [Davis] as soon as I come out of the fog I sent him the lectures did he get them lots and lots and lots of love

Gtrde and Alice

1. Stein's "An American And France."

2. Sir Robert and Lady Diana Abdy (see Stein to Wilder, 20 September 1935, n. 4).

3. On the verso of Woollcott's letter of 18 March 1936, Stein makes a list of people she intends to invite to the tea. It includes "the Egyptian" and several Spanish names.

4. On 31 October 1935, Wilder had lunch and then dinner with Stein, after which they went to Picasso's home for a reading of his poetry. Picasso had begun to write in April of that year. His writings from this period were published in *Cahiers d'art* 10, nos. 7–10 (1936): 90–102. This issue of *Cahiers d'art* also includes André Breton's essay "Picasso poète" and "La Literatura de Picasso," by Jaime Sabartés. Picasso's complete writings are in *Picasso écrits* (see Bibliography). Picasso exhibited twenty-eight oils and gouaches of 1931–32 and 1934–35 at the Paul Rosenberg Gallery, Paris, from 3 to 31 March. Picabia exhibited in February at the Galerie Jeanne Bucher in Paris.

5. Stein acknowledges, though she plays down, the fears of rising German militarism and an-other French-German conflict.

To Thornton Wilder, Chicago, Illinois

[postmark: 2 April 1936]

Plain Edition
27 rue de Fleurus (VI)
Paris

My dearest Thornton

Everybody was here but you everybody, we had Alexander [Woollcott] for three days and we had a good time and I think a good time was enjoyed by all, we had no steers and horses but we had everything else that makes a good rodeo and we had Basket clean, we look at him reproachfully now and say the Woollcott is wearing off. As Alexander came of a Monday Basket had to be washed Saturday and as it was raining I said it is cruelty to animals but you are not going out into a dirty Paris and have that beautiful white turned to grey, and we kept him in and he was beautiful and he was proud only he could have done with less, lots of xciting things are happening, the french translation of the lectures are made half by Mme Clermont-Tonnerre with her introduction to her three and half by Bernard Fay with his introduction to his three, she was firm about that and Bernard Fay talked very successfully about Heaven is my Destination at one of his lectures and we are hoping that the N[ouvelle]. R[evue]. F[rançaise]. will be interested in it, everybody liked the bits he translated at his lecture, and then there is an offer for an English edition of the lectures,[1] and we are getting that ready now, and then there is the possibility of Picabia and myself doing my new play Listen to me as a gorgeous spectacle, don't say anything but this is a perhaps and we are most xcited.[2] And now that you are in dear Chicago is the University Press pleased with our book and do they want to do the four in America. *Alice says we must not frighten them* I ask to hear so that I may take the ms. along for proof-reading, *Alice says we must not frighten them* I love to read proof, don't you, never will that pleasure pall, Alexander took quite a fancy to Dolly Wilde,[3] but then she did think that he was the only American who wrote English like an Englishman and I said Dolly Dolly, and she said but I have read every word he has written, then when she met him she said very regretfully but he is very American, oh Thornie Thornie why are you not here to talk and hear, well anyway we love you lots and lots,

Gtrde

1. The translation of *Lectures In America* by Bernard Faÿ and the Duchesse de Clermont-Tonnerre was never published. The *Nouvelle Revue Française* did not print Faÿ's lecture, but the *Revue de Paris* 4 (July–August, 1937) published an essay by him, "L'Ecole de L'Infortune ou La Nouvelle Génération Littéraire aux Etats-Unis" (644–65), which may have been part of his Collège de France lecture. In it he discussed in detail Thomas Wolfe, William Faulkner, and Margaret Mitchell, but not Wilder.

2. In her letter of 2 April 1936 to Carl Van Vechten (see Wilder to Stein, 18 March 1936, n. 1),

Stein discusses at length the planned Bodley Head edition of *Lectures In America* and the planned collaboration with Picabia on a production of *Listen To Me.*

   3. Alice Toklas, in a letter to Natalie Barney, recalls that Stein and she met Dorothy (Dolly) Ierne Wilde, the only child of Oscar Wilde's brother, Sir William Wilde, in 1916 when she was serving with an Anglo-American ambulance unit in France. Barney published Toklas' letter in a memorial volume for Dolly Wilde, one of her lovers (see bibliography).

To Gertrude Stein and Alice Toklas, Paris, France

[12 April 1936]   6020 Drexel [Avenue
Easter Day   Chicago, Illinois]

                                                                   (Easter, as my teaching
                                                                   notes on Dante inform me
                                                                   —and where would I be
                                                                   without them?—is
                                                                   determined by
                                                                   ascertaining the first
                                                                   Friday on which the moon
                                                                   is in opposition to the
                                                                   sun after the sun enters
                                                                   the Sign of the Ram.
                                                                   Thank you very much
                                                                   You're very welcome.)

Dear Alice.

          The kitchenette is as perfect as ever and returns your kind message. It says you were the most skilful, charming, tasteful and considerate fellow-worker it ever had, and (like its present ludicrously inept owner) it wishes you back as soon as possible.

Dear Gertrude:

          Indeed I did get that additional lecture about Narration and its price is above rubies.[1] Unfortunately I left it in New Haven when I last touched at home in the middle of the Lecture Tour; but I shall be able to pick it up soon enough, hélas, when I return there at my father's demise.

Dear Alice:

          I just can't tell you how beautiful the Midway is these early mornings.
          Add together suggestions of

(1) The prospects at Versailles and St. Germain.
(2) English lawns with their churches in the distance
(3) Something of the American prairie.

Liebe Beide, liebe Zwey [Dear both, dear two]:

Let me see.
Oh, yes.

I called up Bennett Cerf Saturday and got him, begging him to let me see the MS again. I didn't dare tell you before that his office had recalled it (the last time I had it) before I had had time to make my transcript beyond the 12th page. And Saturday (a whole holiday for me) I had sat down and written a lot more of that reader-enjoy-this-with-me foreword of mine and much better. Now it begins where it ought to begin:
    "This book grew out of Miss Stein's meditations on literary masterpieces. Why are there so few of them? What is it that makes them survive . . . . ." etc.
    Then to:
    "It seemed to her that the distinguishing mark of a masterpiece lay,—not in its . . . nor its . . . . nor its . . . . but in its possession of a certain relation to the sense of identity and to time."
    And then to:
    "In order to approach these relations more closely, she has made a distinction between Human Nature and the Human Mind" etc. etc.
    Then:
    "Then Miss Stein asked what is the principle [i.e., principal] activity of the Human Mind, and the answer was: it writes."
    And then:
    "What geographical conditions are most favorable to the development of the Human Mind?"
    And so we arrive at the U.S.A.
    That's the right *order,* isn't it.
    Then I can go into my number about

(1) Metaphysical Metaphors.
(2) The spirit of play
(3) and so on.

I am resolved that my pleasure shall be contagious.
    And at present I'm eager to have one more wrestling bout with the Detective Stories about Pigeons; and with Money and Romance.[2]
    And oh, Kinder, I can't tell how some of those Other Ideas have been fermenting in me. Wherever I turn my eyes I see illustrations: audience,

human nature, human mind . . . . . . listening . . . . About *listening:* oh that's incorporated in my Inner Language forever.

And:

If I didn't have my Friends, and these idea-excitements, I'd be a very dejected boy; because some of the former rewards of life have lost their savor. Yes, classes, for instance. I no longer hear what I say. And Going Places.—All that.

I get a lot of pleasure from seeing my little Ardent-Zoologist sister.[3] I can only pry her away from her ten-hour experiments once a week (metabolic changes in *daphne* under cruelly prearranged conditions) but then we polka off to a dinner and a show.

      . . .   . . .

I went over to the Chicago U. Press long ago to read the clippings re Narration and to sound them about *Four in America.* Nothing doing now, but I think all will be well after *The Geographical History* finds its friends.

       . . . .

[Robert] Ardrey is back from New York, unhurt by the treatment of his play in New York and all bent upon another,—about Casey Jones, the perfect locomotive engineer.[4]

Robert Stallman, has just returned from the funeral of his mother in Milwaukee; she had been 7 years insane. On the train, forsooth [i.e., forsooth], he must needs compose a sonnet on his emotions. The sestet was a prayer beginning "Oh, Christ!" I no longer look for any improvement from him. He has a job teaching in a Junior High School which he carries on while working toward a graduate degree.[5]

You remember the *traveller?* He sent me a MS of his accounts of Central Asia, which he expected to send to Nat[ional]. Geographic and Sat[urday]. Even[ing]. Post. (Probably they had both come back rejected already.) I wrote him they were full of labored facetiousness and dated slang. He wrote me back an indignant and even impudent letter saying that there lay his fresh quality and that his sense of humor was his best quality. N'en parlons plus [Enough].

You remember the *Communists?*

I meet 'em on the walk. Grinning sheepish Communists at best. They adore your memory and are very nice fellows.

Do you remember *Winston Ashley?* The Arkansas turgid highbrow. He is the undergraduates most "famous" author. To be famous for literature on a campus almost invariably ruins an undergrad. They become as Olympian as Romain Rolland, and strike dreamy poses in public places. They wear capes and mutter to themselves as they go up & down stairs. I am to read the novel next week.

Do you remember Gertrude Abercrombie, the painter with the thin

sharp face and the disheveled hair and Wendel[1] Wilcox the too-perfect story-
writer? They are coming here for a home-made spaghetti dinner Wednesday
night. Forgive me, but I can't like them. "At most I have no tears" and golly
what they ask is tears.

Do you remember the *grocer?* I find 2 stories waiting for me, less interesting than the long troubled introspective letters that accompany them.

Na, ja, I've so deflated my élan by writing you this catalogue of aspiring-
despairing adolescents that I can't collect myself to say a ringing goodbye to
you.[6]

I wish I were running across your courtyard in the rue de Fleurus, arous-
ing a storm of barking and kissing you both loudly and asking you 1000
questions.

More soon.

devotedly

Thornton

1. Presumably Stein's lecture "An American And France," not one of the *Narration* lectures.
2. The draft of his introduction to Stein's *Geographical History.* From page 120 on, she discusses
detective stories about writing, including a humorous one about pigeons, as well as money and
romance.
3. Wilder's youngest sister, Janet, was working for her doctorate in biology at the University of
Chicago.
4. Ardrey's play *Star Spangled* had closed after twenty-three performances (see Wilder to Stein,
6 April 1935, n. 4). His next play, *Casey Jones*, would not be produced until February 1938 (see Wilder
to Stein, 27 March 1938, n. 10).
5. See Stein to Wilder, 25 April 1935, n. 1.
6. Wilder here recalls people whom Stein met during her stays in Chicago in 1934 and 1935. The
"traveller" and the "grocer" have not been identified.

To Thornton Wilder, Chicago, Illinois

[postmark: 26 April 1936]   Plain Edition
                                                   27 rue de Fleurus (VI)
                                                   Paris

My dearest Thornton,

We were glad to have your letter and to know that even
if you are not enthusiastic and not happy you are still quite enthusiastic and
quite happy still if you are not too perhaps you will come over this summer
and there is nothing in the world we would like better then your coming over
this summer. I am interested in the new version of the preface, the more it
partakes of the character of a commentary the more I will be pleased, couldn't

you commentarize it at intervals all through, I have always wanted it done that way and perhaps you will yet. I don't know but I cannot help thinking that it would be lots of fun that way and I do want that way but after all it is your way whichever way it is and I want it your way. Mme Clermont-Tonnerre has translated 3 of the lectures beautifully and the xamples she has done awfully well into french, the grammar and poetry comes out very wonderfully and its xamples but then she is awfully intelligent and sensitive, some day you must know her well, Daisy [Fellowes] has not come back yet, they say she is much better but not yet ready for Paris, they are projecting doing the Four Saints here and in London, it would be wonderful if they did, they think that everybody being awfully bored with everything an operette negre about Saint Therese of Avila would just please them, if it is done it is to be done in June and July[1] and we might be together for that well anyway think about coming over and seeing us again, we leave on Thursday if weather and Chinaman permit, we are back to Chinamen only just now we have not got one, but anyway everybody sends you their love and make it a commentary, from my childhood with Caesar I always hoped to be a commentary, do Thornton well anyway, it will be nice having it this autumn and I am patient about the four [*Four In America*].[2] Mme Clermont-Tonnerre is going to do a piece of the 4 into french[3] and so much love, they elect to-day here in Paris but everybody is completely and entirely indifferent

love

Gtrde and Alice.

1. The idea of a production of *Four Saints In Three Acts* in Paris and London may have been suggested to Stein by her friend the art dealer Pierre Colle (see Colle to Stein, 21 May 1936, YCAL). Stein discussed the idea with the composer Lord Berners during her visit to England in February. He reported to Stein on 27 April 1936 (YCAL) his unsuccessful attempt to interest the producer Charles Cochran in the project but suggested that word of a Paris production of *Four Saints* "might stimulate him." Lord Berners also wrote that he would try to speak with the American producer Gilbert Miller when in London. Stein wrote to a number of people enlisting their support. In reply to a letter from her, Edward James, a well-known supporter of the arts, excused his active participation in the project because of his health. He did, however, suggest names of possible supporters for the project (James to Stein, 23 April 1936, YCAL). Efforts to produce *Four Saints* were unsuccessful. The first staged production in Paris would not be mounted until June 1952 (see Toklas letters in *Staying on Alone*, 254–59).

2. See Stein to Wilder [7 February 1936].

3. No translation by the Duchesse de Clermont-Tonnerre was published, but copies are in YCAL.

To Thornton Wilder, Chicago, Illinois

[postmark: ?11 May 1936]   Bilignin par
                                                                Belley, Ain.

Our dearest Thornton,

Here we are in Bilignin par Belley Ain and we would so like Thornton to be here too, and to walk and to talk and to dig in the garden, don't think we made you dig in the garden enough last time, but now we are doing all the planting ourselves, and they look quite comfortable everything we have put in and may it go on, but you know a farmer's life is a hard hard life. The puppies are so happy and so are we, it is nice after a very xciting winter to cultivate the garden. The Chicago Press sent us the clippings, the only good ones xcept Fanny [Butcher]'s were from the South but the South were awfully good, and now a young fellow from Los Angeles sends me another with a nice letter hoping that I will like the same, it's funny that the South seems to have more sense of literature than the North, the North does seem to think it has to be funny the South does not take the obligation of being funny quite so solemnly,[1] I had a nice letter from Bennett [Cerf] they are very much looking forward to the book and you, I hope it is commentaries and lots of them, I think it will be a lovely book, he says they want to make a lovely book of it and I guess they will, he is coming over in June perhaps you will see him before that.[2] After having passed through all the nationalities in the way of domestics we have now a french boy named Gabriel and he just is that and gives us much pleasure but perhaps you will come and have that pleasure too, Belley has taken on elections with much more xcitement than Paris, lots of funny stories but too long to tell, everybody remembers you and sends you love but we and Pepe and Basket of course most, Pepe has never barked so much in his life since he has been here, he says it's wonderful, the first chicken was preserved from them with an effort, yesterday, dear Thornton how we miss you and how and where and what is Bob Davis just now lots love

                                    Gtrde.

1. The *Narration* file of the University of Chicago Press includes no copy of a letter sent to Stein with reviews. Fanny Butcher reviewed both *Narration* and *Lectures In America* in the *Chicago Tribune*, 11 December 1935 (YCAL). Who sent the clippings from Los Angeles is not known. For a listing of reviews of *Narration*, see White, *A Reference Guide*.

2. No such letter to Stein has been found in YCAL, Columbia-Cerf, or Columbia-R.H.

To Gertrude Stein and Alice Toklas, Bilignin, France

25 June 1936   Yes, 6020 Drexel Ave
                                                      Chicago [Illinois]

Carissime sorelle [Dearest sisters]:
    Please forgive me my sad discreditable silence.

My brusqueness in this making my apologies doesn't mean that I'm not truly contrite; it merely means that I don't like discussing my everpresent shabby irresponsibility, and that I want to hurry on and talk of happier things.

Yesterday, for instance, Gertrude Abercrombie and Wendell Wilcox and I went down to see the people who are preparing your puppet-play.[1] I gave them a lecture on Human Nature and the Human Mind and Identity (even I) and they have returned to the work with even more zest. The musical score is very skillful and droll and written with that dazzling virtuosity in the new dissonances and new rhythms that all these young composers seem to have in equal measure. It requires the finger-technique of [Vladimir] Horowitz to play any one bar of it. He has made some glorified Offenbach couplets out of the capacities and incapacities of dogs, and the uninterestingness of human nature is affirmed very amusingly amid scandalized polytonality from the piano. Old sour-faced Wilder holds that the whole group is a hot-bed of sensibilità-senza-vitalità, but Wilder's grudging about everything to do with puppetts [i.e., puppets], Stravinsky-epigoni, and such things. The première is to be at a big convention—three days long—of Marionette- theatres, and the remaining evenings are to be devoted to Macbeth, Faust and Aristophanes'—The Birds or The Clouds. The funny thing about it, for me, is that Miss Stein's play is to be subsidized by the same federal expenditures that she has been rebuking lately in The Saturday Evening Post.[2] Mr. Vestal's Human Nature is an egg-shaped Brancusi abstract and his Human Mind is a baroque Aubrey Beardsley fée [fairy];—I told him to reverse them; I hope I was right.

The last month of cynical inertia combined with feverish activity on nonessentials at least had one good result. I resigned from the University. Suddenly I saw it all quite clearly and completely. It takes effect September first, and until then I'm patient—impatient.

First I shall go to Hollywood for six weeks and make the money to pay for my father's long illness. I hope I'll be allowed to do The Casting Away of Mrs Lecks & Mrs Aleshine. Last month I turned down The Garden of Allah for Marlene Dietrich and Captains Courageous for Freddie Bartholomew. The Money we refuse no moth nor rust can corrupt. It lies in our imagination glowing goldenly to be boasted about.[3]

The Summer Quarter enrollment is 15% bigger than ever before. The prestige of our university grows and grows. Bob Hutchins just received the highest degree that Harvard has to offer—in its Tercentenary Celebration, too.[4] The Greatest Greek Scholar in the World has just joined the faculty from Germany.[5] And we have acquired three astronomers all under 38 of ineffable distinction that makes our Observatory the pilgrimage place of the world. oo—oo—oo.

Had lunch with Jean Giraudoux last Friday. One of the few authors on the planet who could stir up any hero-worship in me. I had no notion that he was in this part of the world and had just finished four of his novels.[6]

Imagine.

Alice, isn't it a pity I have to leave this place just as I've found a solution for the running-of-the-daily-life. I love the apartment more every day. Getting up in the morning in the presence of my Midway and going to bed at night are daily miracles; I now know what to do when I'm in no mood to eat at the Quad[rangle] Club or any public place; the piano is back; one of John Pratt's drollest pictures is on the wall. Will I ever have as happy a set-up again? Yes, I know it: I shall become rich; oriental butlers will pad about my house bringing me telegrams on silver platters, but I shall never be as happy as this again. [But at least I shall not be delivering shameful repulsive lectures, full of imitation-ideas and cheap judgments. Too [[i.e, To]] be free of *that* will be wonderful, too.][7]

And for a time I don't want to see any human being. I am temporarily revolted at the How-do-you-do's of life; of being asked Wasn't Katharine Cornell wonderful last night in S[ain]t Joan; of being asked what I think of thissa-and-thatta; of asking after the health of absent relatives; of hearing people say that Bob Hutchins has good ideas but is tactless; of hearing people say that any party is better than the Democratic; of agreeing that things look very bad in Europe. I shall go to the American desert, Tucson, Arizona, among the dear opinionless cacti.

Oh, dear Gertrude, how right you are. Without tears I say it human nature is not interesting only Robinson Crusoe is interesting.[8]

Tomorrow I shall send you a cablegram to tell you that for all my being the residue of devils—of stultitia and accidia—I love you very much and that my silences don't mean anything except that I am a poor wind-blown wretch who can only gather himself together to do the chores that are right in front of his nose and lets lapse for a time the good and prized things—among which I count you chief.

Tender confidences to Pepe and manly shake-paws to Basket.

love
Thornton

1. For details on Donald Vestal's marionette play *Identity: A Play*, see Appendix IV.
2. Wilder refers to "Money," the first of Stein's five pieces on the subject, which had appeared on

13 June 1936 in the *Saturday Evening Post* (the pieces are collected in Haas, *How Writing*, 106–12). In it, Stein speaks of governments feeling free to spend money they have not earned: "Now if there was some arrangement made that when one lot voted to spend money, that they would have to wait a long time, and another lot have to vote, before they vote again to have that money, in short, if there was any way to make a government handle money the way a father of a family has to handle money if there only was. The natural feeling of a father of a family is that when anybody asks him for money he says no" (107).

3. None of these projects materialized (see Wilder to Stein, 14 August and 27 September 1936). This was not the first time that Wilder, in need of money, had agreed to write for Hollywood. In 1933, he had worked with the writers Leonard Praskins and Paul Green on *We Live Again*, an adaptation of Tolstoy's *Resurrection* that starred Anna Sten and Fredric March; however, final credit for the screenwriting went to Praskins, Preston Sturges, and Maxwell Anderson. In 1934 he wrote a screenplay, "Joan of Arc," for Katharine Hepburn that was shelved (copy in YCAL).

4. Hutchins received an honorary doctor of laws degree at the closing exercises of Harvard University's three hundredth year.

5. Werner Jaeger was professor of Greek and ancient philosophy at the University of Chicago from 1936 until 1939, when he left to teach at Harvard University. The three astronomers were S. Chandrasekhar, Bengt Strömgen, and G. P. Kuiper.

6. Jean Giraudoux arrived in New York on 25 March and a few days later began a trip that took him through the Caribbean, Central America, Mexico, Texas, and California. On his way back to New York he spent three days, 15 to 17 June, in Chicago, where Wilder met him probably under the auspices of the university. Which of Giraudoux's novels Wilder had read at this time has not been determined (see Wilder to Stein, 20 February 1936, n. 2).

7. Wilder's brackets.

8. In the last paragraph of *The Autobiography Of Alice B. Toklas* Stein writes, "About six weeks ago Gertrude Stein said, it does not look to me as if you were ever going to write that autobiography. You know what I am going to do, I am going to write it for you. I am going to write it as simply as Defoe did the autobiography of Robinson Crusoe. And she has and this is it." References to *Robinson Crusoe* appear in a number of Stein's works in the following decade. This refers to Wilder going out into the wilderness and leaving "gossip of human nature" behind.

To Thornton Wilder, Chicago, Illinois

[postmark: 29 June 1936]   Bilignin par Belley
                                                             Ain

My dear Thornton,

It was a nice telegram[1] but we hoped that it would say that you follow, well even a letter is something but we could do with seeing you again yes we could. Bennett Cerf has just been with us and he says as soon as they have the ms. he will go to print, he is also going to do an anthology of all our high spots in the Modern Library next spring,[2] and that makes me very happy, I got so much to tell you filled with telling you, won't you come, everybody wants you won't you come lots of love from us all

Gtrde.

1. Wilder's telegram, mentioned in his letter of 25 June, has not survived.

2. During a visit that Cerf and the sculptor Jo Davidson made to Bilignin, Cerf appears to have discussed a number of projects with Stein: the publication of the *Geographical History*; an anthology that would eventually appear in July 1946 as *Selected Writings Of Gertrude Stein*, edited by Carl Van Vechten; and a volume of autobiography discussing the American lecture tour and her return to France—Stein's *Everybody's Autobiography*. As the next letter indicates, Stein began work on the new autobiography as soon as Cerf left.

To Thornton Wilder, Chicago, Illinois

[postmark: 8 July 1936]   Bilignin par Belley
                                                                   Ain

My dearest Thornton,

Yes we are xcited, and you are funny, Alice and I laughed a lot, I am pleased on the whole that you are giving up the U[niversity]. [of] C[hicago]. for a bit, and going to Hollywood, I wish we could be there together, it would be fun, listen Thornton, couldn't they do the Autobiography of Alice B. Toklas at Hollywood, that might make a lovely film, I do not know what makes lovely films but that might and they could shoot the background here and in Paris and we could be taken in Hollywood including the puppies Basket and Pepe and we would have enough money to make a leisurely trip across the continent and the Mississippi valley taking on a college boy for the more difficult driving and then we could have an installation in Washington Square and go to and fro for ever. Do you think there is anything in it, I am not just perfectly sure there isn't, and I have done a new chapter bringing Picasso up to date and it's pretty good.[1] I'd love you to put us on the Hollywood map, but don't think about it twice only perhaps there is something in it. All that about money was to clear my mind about that chapter, romanticism and money and I finally got it right, in a last one, which perhaps they will not buy beginning with it is funny about money. And then going on about man and animals ending with but the thing no animal can do is count, and the thing no animal can know is money and so as long as the earth turns around there will be men on it and they will count and they will count money. [T]he queen was in the parlor eating bread and honey the king was in his counting house counting out his money, counting is funny.[2] And then it goes on I think I am getting it clear and then I have to do more about romanticism, as they are going to have a revolution in France I may find out more about that, well anyway, I hope Detroit is a success, I love to be a success, and I love to have all of them be a success along of me, I like that, oh how I do like that, and you do not mention it but I guess you have sent the ms. to Random House by now, they are going to do a volume of selected selections in the Modern Library next spring, putting in all the things of mine that make a volume, if you have any suggestions will you, but perhaps oh certainly perhaps we will see you before then. France is sad, hardly xcited just a little lifeless and sad and the weather is rotten but we love you oh how we love you all of us

Gtrde.

1. At the end of the first chapter of *Everybody's Autobiography*, Stein devotes several pages to Picasso's recent exhibition and his poetry (see Stein to Wilder, 25 March 1936).

2. In this letter Stein responds directly to Wilder's letter of 25 June. She quotes almost verbatim from "All About Money," written for the *Saturday Evening Post*. After echoing "Sing a Song of Sixpence," she continues,

> That is the way it is and the only trouble comes when they count money without counting it as money.
> Counting is funny. (*How Writing*, 110)

She is concerned that perhaps the *Post* will not publish this piece because it is even more critical of New Deal policies than the earlier pieces. She reflects here on how money loses its reality: "It is funny, if you buy anything well it may cost four dollars and fifty-five cents or four hundred and eighty-nine dollars or any other sum, but when government votes money it is always even money. One or five or fifteen or twenty-five or thirty-six more or less. The minute it gets to be billions it does not make any difference" (*How Writing*, 110). Animals and money also appear in *A Play Called Not And Now* of this year.

To Thornton Wilder, Chicago, Illinois

[postmark: 27 July 1936]   Bilignin par Belley,
                                                          Ain.

My dearest Thornton

Donald Vestal has just written me how wonderfully sweetly and brilliantly you wrote the introduction and sent it to him in the midst of everything, not forgetting anything, it seems to have gone off very well, he has not yet sent me the introduction, he was too xcited about the success of Identity, and too grateful to you and to everything to do that yet, but I am writing him to remind him.[1] With us we are kind of upset by the Spanish revolution, we know the terrain so well and everything in it so well and the Spanish violent ways so well that we kind of feel ourselves there, I never really forget it, here the rain raineth every day[2] and but there is always a moment when I can go out for a walk and condole with the farmers, they need a lot of condoling which always ends up "si nous avons un peu de beau temps nous avons bien besoin,["] [oh, how we need some good weather] in spite of all this we have had a pleasant summer and are still having the same, we have an electric stove and Alice is going religiously through all the cakes in the Austrian cook-book and then I have solemnly to decide the good and bad quality of the new one, being conservative I always like the one we had better but that is not the right answer, because Alice always [likes] the last baby best, how we wish you were here to decide with us, my it rains, and lots of love and I do hope your mother is very well and everything as you wish it, lots and lots of love.

Gtrde

They sent me the proofs of the relations to correct,[3] but not your introduction, I would like to see the final form, perhaps the next one will be commentaries, had a charming note from [Alexander] Wo[o]l[l]cott, he said you were a lovely flower girl at the wedding, and perhaps we would have you as [word?] for ours.[4]

G.

1. Vestal wrote to Stein on 13 July 1936 (YCAL) that Wilder's "preface" arrived the morning of the performance and thus was not available for distribution. Wilder had been unable to finish the text in time because of the death of his father on 2 July. For "Introduction to Miss Stein's Puppet Play," see Appendix IV.

2. Stein echoes the Clown's closing song in *Twelfth Night*.

3. The *Geographical History*.

4. Wilder assisted at the wedding of Frode Jensen, a Dane whose medical studies Woollcott sponsored. In his letter to Stein of 10 July (YCAL), Woollcott reported on the wedding and proposed to Stein, "If you and I are ever married, we must have him [i.e., Thornton] for the flower-girl." Stein replied, "Yes with enthusiasm I do accept the offer of your hand and heart and when we get married it would be fun to do it we will have Thornton as a flower girl, Bennett [Cerf] and Donald [Klopfer] as pages" (n.d., Harvard-Theatre).

To Gertrude Stein and Alice Toklas, Bilignin, France

About 14 Aug[ust]. 1936

6020 Drexel Ave[nue]
Chicago [Illinois]
until Sept. 10, 1936

Carine sorelle delle belle occhi [Dear sisters with the beautiful eyes]:

How—all in all—are you?

Just today I read aloud to a caller—it must be the tenth time I've done it—the lecture on *An American and France*. Miss Stein is simply radiant with health-giving ideas and when I read her I become all luminous and gay and I send her a great big hug.

Did I tell you that my revered papa died? Yes. . . . . . . Yes. . . . . .
All of us five children were back.

[[SPACE HERE RESERVED

FOR

THOUGHTS[1]

Before long I must be leaving this apartment, this town, this work. Of course I'm glad: I'm revolted by the things I hear myself saying on platforms. But I'm pretty sorry, too. I've got to go out in the world and roam about as an Unattached.

A telegram from Hollywood asks if I won't go to M.G.M. (Metro-Goldwyn-Mayer) for more than six weeks, please, and I made a face and telegraphed okay, until Dec. 4.[2]

It'll be either:

> Kipling's Captains Courageous for Freddie Bartholomew, or
> Pride and Prejudice for Norma Shearer, or
> A Benjamin Franklin for Charles Laughton

And I don't want to do it. Not for that long, anyway. I hate that Southern California sunlight.

Then January and February my last lecture-tour.

So I'm not a free man until March.

Then I'll go to Tucson, Arizona, rent three rooms over a drug-store and spend a Spring.

You know: in a foolish, undiscriminating way, I've been very happy these last few months. I don't know why. I just am. I love my friends; I love my pupils; I love what I read; I—dammit—love my thoughts. I love the taste of oranges.

And yet all my friends, except yourselves—are not at all happy. Things aren't at all as they should be chez Hutchins. No, m'm. Nor chez Ruth Gordon.[3] And [Alexander] Woollcott on his last trip obviously found me tedious and exasperating, which certainly must indicate something wrong in HIM.

And lookit SPAIN and lookit England.

Apparently nothing can cast me down.

Maybe my subconscious has heard that I'm not going to teach any more.

Maybe it's the sunlight and the swims.

Maybe it's your ideas working in me.

Maybe it's because I'm almost forty, and that's my natural age.

Far be it from me to send you a copy of the Preface. Somewhere some-

one is coming who will write of you adequately. In the meantime I love trying
to do what I can, and I hope the words are persuasive.

Sat[urday]. morning.

Just got a letter from Isabel

In Paragraph 8 . . . . "I feel better than I can remember. And I'm happy,
too. Perhaps everything is too good to last."

And in ¶ 12 . . . . "Mother is simply fine. I am so happy about that. She
looks well, she sleeps solidly at night, she's full of interest and energy. . . . . . .
She bought in my absence several new dresses and a lovely new hat."

Can it be . . . . ? See what I mean?

The house of mourning.

Alice is laughing. I think that's downright heartless of her.

Anyway, I've absolved you from the duty of writing me a tender letter of
condolence.

The University:

We're getting the great Greek man in the world—Dr. Jäger of Berlin.

We're getting three new astronomical—physicist—mathematicians
that make us the pilgrimage-place of that world. The constellations are thrilled
about it.

Dr. Weiss had discovered something about the transmission of energy
along the nerves that upsets all previous theories.

Dr. Bailey has found out something about tumors of the cerebellum that
reduces them to the level of tonsils.[4]

And yet Bob H[utchins]. writes from Ipswich the litany of his antago-
nists. There he sits in that house in a ferment of HUMAN NATURE at its most
predatory. You know what I mean. I long to put a number of things into
this letter, but I don't dare. It would be DISLOYAL. A Nineteenth Century
word.

No wonder that to my astonishment Bob has been carrying on a correspondence with me this summer. Hell, what business have Bob and I corresponding? The poor fellow doesn't know it; but he longs for fresh air and
unsultry talk.[5]

Just as I'm leaving I'm learning to know such awfully nice people on the
faculty. Must I spend my days henceforth among the Bourgeoisie and among
artists? Ugh.

My, just to think of you too is a pleasure.

I wish I was there. Alice, I'd help you with the garden. I can hear your
matutinal shears under my window. And Gertrude could cuff and trounce my
poor laggard head all she pleased.

Anyway I'm with you in spirit, as my three dozen letters of condolence say. And I'm your third dog—

> devoted, wide-eyed
> Air[e]dale Thornton

The only thing that makes me cranky is that I've lost my fountain-pen again. If that happens once more I'm going into business. For years my cousin Alex Walker has been trying to make me give up writing sugary novels and go into the importation of ponjee-silk with him.[6] And I will too. Freud says that one only loses things for which one has a secret resentment. And I disperse fountain-pens like confetti.

1. Amos Parker Wilder died on 2 July. Two large single brackets, one red and one blue, precede the three lines.
2. The telegram has not survived (see Wilder to Stein, 25 June 1936).
3. Wilder refers to their marital problems and to Ruth Gordon's relationship with Jed Harris.
4. Werner Jaeger (see Wilder to Stein, 25 June 1936, n. 6). Paul Weiss and Percival Bailey taught at the University of Chicago.
5. Throughout his tenure at Chicago, the educational reforms of Hutchins faced stiff resistance. Wilder served as a sounding board and gave advice on strategies and appointments. See Hutchins to Wilder from Ipswich, Massachusetts, 7, 11, 19 August 1936 (YCAL).
6. Alexander Walker, a cousin of Wilder's mother, went into the silk business in China as a young man, becoming a millionaire with a successful silk import firm of his own in New York. In an interview, Isabel Wilder characterized him as the prototype "noisy businessman," aggressive even when he acted the part of the perfect gentleman.

To Thornton Wilder, Chicago, Illinois
[Transcribed by Wilder—1][1]

[Two letters from Gertrude Stein, both rec'd Chicago September 10, 1936]

> Bilignin par Belley
> Ain

My dear Thornton

During the war Alice used to say that filleuls answer letters so quickly and here I am doing the same. . . . . I understand about Hutchins, he does belong just a little too much to Tom Brown at Rugby and Tom Brown at Oxford,[2] they die young and if they do not they do not. Let us hope that he will not. A great many things happen but mostly it happens that we like it so much here and would only like it more if you were here too. Pepe is going on the stage. Lord Berners has written the music for a ballet based on the play They must be wedded to their wife, and it is most amusing and it is going on in February at the Sadler Wells theatre, and there has to be a dog and it is going to be Pepe. Alice told him about it and he munched his (dear?) paw in his xcitement and there he is a distinguished invalid under my best waist-coat, he is going to be played by the littlest girl but Berners is afraid he will look more like a greyhound than Pepe but everybody all the same will know it is Pepe.[3] Then there is Spain, at first we were so worried about everything we hear there but now we seem to forget and just read it in the papers. Is there no way of changing [My proposed movie-subject] Benjamin Franklin into Pablo Picasso and Alice B. Toklas if I do not make money there I may be driven to do a cigarette advertisement they have just asked me, we will like to travel around and not lecture, can't Hollywood do something about it, someone once dreamed of doing the Gentle Lena there but I never did quite see that; but they [? Mrs. Shuman] seemed to think so,[4] perhaps you will come to London to hear the ballet, oh well come over anyway, I smile all the time that is not quite as much as usual because we are liking being here so much; more than usual I think, but I have been writing some of it I think will please you, the DAiguys and Madame [Pruolest] have been leading the usual active French life of 84 years old;[5] they ask after you frequently, and then lately they the young people have been giving 'surprise parties' and they ask us all it is very pretty in the [?] chateaux, and they dance all night, come over and we will have one here in your honor; the girls and [i.e., are] pretty and they dance nicely; Alice says it will be awfully cute to have a surprise party for Thornton in Belley; come along and so much love

Gtde.

1. From his incoming correspondence between September 1936 and November 1937 and between January and September 1940, Wilder selected and transcribed a number of letters from Gertrude Stein and other correspondents. When these transcriptions, which exist in the formats described below, were made is not clear; all but a few of the letters were addressed to him. Of the transcribed Stein letters, only one holograph letter is in the Wilder Archives at Yale.

Wilder's transcriptions indicate his difficulty in deciphering Stein's handwriting; we have left his approximations as they stand. Where he tried to guess at a word and used an undefined squiggle, we have used [?word]. We have avoided editorial insertions—the brackets and misspellings are Wilder's. In our notes we have supplied and corrected names where the context of the letter and our knowledge of Stein's activities lead to that conclusion.

Wilder's motivation for transcribing these letters may have varied. Lady Colefax's letter of 23 September 1940 requesting that Wilder circulate it to friends in New York is the only one providing a clear motivation for copying.

This is not the first time that Wilder transcribed letters. From May to December 1923 and from January to November 1925, he kept letter books in which he transcribed his outgoing correspondence and occasionally letters received. Scattered throughout his papers are copies or drafts of other letters. Such efforts, in the days when correspondence was by hand, are understandable. The transcriptions of 1936–37 and 1940, however, are part of a far more complex pattern.

The bulk of the transcriptions under *d* below, of thirty-seven letters to Wilder, including one cable to Lady Colefax and one letter to Stein, were transcribed with care for their chronological order. Read in sequence, as Wilder no doubt intended, they become not a series of random transcriptions, but a carefully constructed letter-history of the preproduction history of *Our Town*. They also record cautionary advice about Jed Harris.

The transcriptions are in the following formats:

a. Two letters from Stein, "both rec'd Chicago September 10, 1936" are transcribed on leaves 174–75 of Wilder's 1924–25 letter diary.

b. Four letters from Stein: 17 May 1937; an undated letter; 2 May 1937; 9 June 1937, are transcribed on leaves 130–31 of a notebook for an early draft of *The Merchant of Yonkers* and an early draft of "Alcestis," his play *The Alcestiad*.

c. Four letters from Stein: postmark 10 October 1936, rec'd Oct 16; 26 October 1936; 20 January 1937; 8 March 1937, are transcribed on a series of loose sheets of a single ledger numbered 195 (blank) to 200. The letters are transcribed in chronological order, and Wilder has given each letter an arabic number. In addition, these pages include Wilder's transcriptions of letters and telegrams from Ruth Gordon to Wilder and Woollcott, 9 September 1936; Gordon to Wilder, London, 26 October 1936; Lady Sibyl Colefax in New York, circa January 21, 1937; as well as transcriptions of poems by Maude Hutchins dated 15 March 1937. The numbered leaves were not used in the order of their numbers.

d. Thirty-seven letters and postcards transcribed on sixteen hand-numbered pages of an unsewn folio from 18 July to 11 November 1937. Wilder transcribed the letters in chronological order, giving all but one a roman numeral. At some point in the transcription process, additional letters were inserted into the chronological order. Wilder then changed the roman numerals and inserted directions to the arabic numbered page for the inserted letter. Except for one telegram and one letter, the letters in this folio are all addressed to Wilder. The letters are as follows: I. Stein, Bilignin, July 18, 1937; II. Stein, July 25; III. Ruth Gordon, from Neshobe Island, Lake Bomoseen, Vermont, August 18 [1937]; IV. Stein, postcard, August 25, 1937; V. Stein, August 28, 1937; VI. Lady Colefax, Schloss Wasserleonburg, Kärnten, Austria, postmark September 3, 1937; VII. Stein, postcard, Aix-les-Bains, September 7, 1937; VIII. Stein, postcard, September 7, 1937; IX. Sibyl Colefax, at the house of the Berensons in Florence, September 10, 1937; X. Sibyl Colefax, "a few days later"; XI. Stein, postmark 13 September 1937, XII. Stein, postcard, September 17, 1937; XIII. Stein, postcard, postmark Bilignin, September 22, 1937; XIV. Stein, "illegible P.M., a few days later"; XV. Sibyl Colefax, Kent, postmark, September 26, 1937; XVI. Sibyl Colefax, Dorchester, October 3, 1937; XVII. Stein, Bilignin, postmark October 4, 1937; XVIII. Sibyl Colefax, London, postmark October 5, 1937; XIX. Stein, postcard, postmark Bilignin, October 5, 1937 (this letter is followed by a transcription of a letter to Stein from her niece, Gertrude Kempner); XX. Sibyl Colefax, Leicester, October 10, 1937; XXI. Sibyl Colefax, London, October 14, 1937; XXII. Jed Harris, cable from New York, October 14, 1937; XXIII. Stein, Belley, October 16, 1937; XXIV. Ruth Gordon, cable, Detroit, Michigan, October 18, 1937; XXV. Sibyl Colefax, postmark London, October 21, 1937; XXVA. Lynn Fontanne, National Theatre, Washington, D.C., October 21, 1937; XXVI. Jed Harris, cable, London October 22, 1937; XXVII. Stein, Bilignin letterhead but postmarked Aix-les-Bains, October 22, 1937; XXVIII. Jed Harris, cable, London, October 25, 1937; XXIX. Lady Colefax, postmarked London October 25, 1937; XXX. Stein, postcard, postmarked Belley, October 26, 1937; XXXI. Jed Harris, telegram, London October 28, 1937; XXXII. Stein, Paris, November 3, 1937; XXXIII. Jed Harris, cable, Southampton, England, November 3, 1937; XXXIV. Jed Harris to Lady Colefax, New York, November 8, 1937; [unnumbered letter—XXXV] Stein, Paris, November 11, 1937.

e. In the same format as above, two letters from Lady Sibyl Colefax: 1 January 1940 and 23 September 1940, the latter to be transcribed and sent to Alexander Woollcott, Alice Duer Miller, Beatrice Kaufman, and Mrs. Murray Crane. A letter from Stein, postmarked from Bilignin, September 15, is the only one of the transcribed Stein letters for which there is an original in YCAL.

2. The enormously popular *Tom Brown's Schooldays* (1857) and its sequel *Tom Brown at Oxford* (1861) by Thomas Hughes described the life of an English schoolboy at Rugby under its headmaster,

Dr. Thomas Arnold. Stein may be playing on Hutchins as a progressive teacher-administrator like Arnold and at the same time as a schoolboy type like Tom Brown.

3. Stein and Lord Berners had discussed collaboration when she stayed with him in England. By 1 March (YCAL), acknowledging receipt of *Operas And Plays*, Lord Berners wrote, "I think They Must. Be Wedded. To Their Wife. looks very suitable for music." On 18 July (YCAL) he wrote Stein referring to sketches for the music for their ballet with chorus, *A Wedding Bouquet*: "I hope you will like the music, there is a fugue, a waltz, a tango and a very moving adagio on the theme 'Josephine will leave.'" From 21 to 25 or 26 August he visited Stein and they discussed the ballet.

4. Lillian May Ehrman, not Shuman, the socialite friend of Carl Van Vechten who entertained Stein in Hollywood, asked for the right to sell "The Gentle Lena," the third story of *Three Lives*, to a film studio and suggested that her brother, Ivan Kahn, a Hollywood agent, handle the matter. Nothing came of this project (see Stein to Wilder, 2 April 1935, n. 1). Ehrman wrote to Stein on 27 July 1935 (YCAL).

5. In addition to working on *Everybody's Autobiography*, Stein wrote two compositions before leaving Bilignin for Paris in November, "What Does She See When She Shuts Her Eyes" and "The Autobiography Of Rose." Both deal with life in the country and bring in Madame Pierlot (Wilder's transcription is "Pruolest") and her family, her son Baron Raymond (Bob) d'Aiguy, his wife, the Baroness May d'Aiguy, and their only child, Rose. Stein met the family, who lived in the Château de Béon, not far from Belley, sometime between 1924 and 1927. They became friends, and Stein often brought visitors to meet them. Rose d'Aiguy is the Rose of Stein's *The World Is Round*.

To Thornton Wilder, Chicago, Illinois
[Transcribed by Wilder—2]

rec'd Chicago   Bilignin par Belley
10 Sept[ember] 1936   Ain

My dear Thornton,

        I just read in this morning's paper that Wodehouse says that they give him $104 000 for doing nothing at Hollywood they keep him there but they do not use what they ask him to do,[1] now that would just suit us fine, we want a payed which is à la mode here now, and of course we are not valuable like he is, but for considerable less would we write dialogue and titles that they do not want to use, not at all do we insist that they use our works printed or unprinted not at all, we just want to run around and do nothing and be payed largely for it, that is as everything they do not want, it is a pleasant xtravagance and we are just pining for pleasant xtravagance, so keep your eyes and ears open, if they want us we will come, we would love to be payed largely and we are kind of tired of just staying here beside it is coming too high to live in Europe like that, we are nutting in the woods and then Alice makes cakes of the nuts, which is a pleasant life too, but a vacance payé[2] and it might be with you dear Thornton and lots of love

                Gtde.

1. Stein had probably read in the *New York Herald Tribune* that P. G. Wodehouse had signed a contract to write scenarios for Metro-Goldwyn-Mayer. Referring to his experience in Hollywood five years earlier, Wodehouse is quoted: "I was engaged at this big salary [$104,000] to write stories for the screen, but apparently they had the greatest difficulty in finding me anything to do. Twice during the year, they brought me completed scenarios of other people's stories and asked me to do some dialogue. I found that fifteen or sixteen other people had already had a hand in these stories and the dialogue was adequate" (Paris edition, 29 August 1936, 2).

2. Earlier that year, the Popular Front government of Léon Blum had introduced paid vacations in France.

To Gertrude Stein and Alice Toklas, Bilignin, France

27 Sept[ember] 1936   50 Deepwood Drive
                                                   New Haven, Conn[ecticut].

Dear Gertraclice:
or as Swift used to say
Dear MDs.[1]
    There is to be no Hollywood call, due to [Irving] Thalberg's death.[2]
    so
    I'm sailing on October 8th for the Virgin Islands, there to spend all October and November writing gay plays [3]
    It's very beautiful, very temperate, and very cheap, and it's under the[4]
    Maybe Aleck Woollcott, the mirror of friendship, will go there with me, just for the ride.
    I am still going about with my wicked feeling that the world is a very delightful place to live in. Full of treasurable people, splendid books to read and wonderful pieces of music have been written down. Yesterday I went to the music store and asked them to play for me the records of Beethoven's Kreutzer Sonata that had been made by Jehudi Menuhin, and his little sister Hephzibah. And I remembered that they came from San Francisco Bay region as we all did.[5] Most of the people I know are biting the insides of their cheers with worried thoughts but when I write to my MDs I know that they too are not afraid to come out boldly into the open and affirm that there are wonderful things in the world. It is a pleasure.
    Tonight I read aloud to ten people who had come to dinner the dazzling paragraph in A Long Gay Book about what one feels as one grows older. It is very exact writing and I read it very slowly and they too marvelled at it.[6]
    I have been reading aloud to my mother a droll and noble and touching little book translated from the Chinese. It is an account by a small provincial

magistrate of the Boxer Rebellion, of the flight of the Empress Dowager from the Forbidden City and the reëstablishment. It is full of loft utterances at the point of death, of absurd anxiety over etiquette, and of long intimate conversations with the "Old Buddha." And yet it is a slight little book and I am afraid that even sending it to MD will put it in such a mandatory light that the bloom of its modest charm will be rubbed off, but I shall send it just the same.[7]

Aleck [Woollcott] is making a big conspicuous radio address on *Why I shall vote for Roosevelt*[.] We all wish you were here to help[.][8]

Keep me green in your memories, for I am

your devoted
Thornton

1. See Wilder to Stein, 25 January 1936, n. 9.
2. Thalberg, executive production manager at Metro-Goldwyn-Mayer, died on 13 September. As a result, the projects, including those proposed for his wife, the actress Norma Shearer, were postponed.
3. Among the projects Wilder was working on was *The Merchant of Yonkers*.
4. After the word "the," in blue and red pencils, Wilder drew an American flag.
5. Yehudi (also spelled Jehudi) Menuhin and his sisters Hephzibah and Yaltah, Stein, Toklas, and Wilder all spent their early years in the San Francisco Bay region. Menuhin and his sister Hephzibah had recorded Beethoven's *Sonata in A*, Opus 47, the "Kreutzer" sonata, in 1934.
6. An undated typed sheet in the Wilder Archives contains a section from Stein's *A Long Gay Book*, pages 25–26, beginning, "Being a young one and an older one and a middle aged one . . ." and ending, "They are then completely old ones and not any one is knowing everything of that thing." This passage, much like an entry in a commonplace book, was one of Wilder's favorites.
7. Wilder sent Stein the book by Wu Yung, *The Flight of an Empress* (New Haven: Yale University Press, 1936) (see Stein to Wilder, postmark 26 October 1936).
8. In the margin beside this paragraph, Wilder has drawn another American flag in blue and red pencils. The text of the broadcast is not listed in bibliographies of Woollcott, although it may be in the archives of CBS.

To Thornton Wilder, New Haven, Connecticut
[Transcribed by Wilder][1]

[postmark: 10 October 1936]   Bilignin par Belley
(rec'd Oct 16.)   Ain

My dear Thornton,
Of all sad words of tongue or pen, the saddest are these it might have been, it is sad, [rê the fact that Hollywood did not call this year] it would have been so nice to see the money nice and almost necessary but nice and necessary are not what is, nor what will be, that is not [?heaven] what makes them all so sad, they are all sad because everybody wants to be a father and being a father is depressing, and having a father is depressing and every-

body has a father just now only the English, they have no father and so they are all cheerful—even France is suffering from a father, that is the reason I would vote for Landon, I do not think he would be a father, Hutchins would oh dear yes Hutchins would,[2] otherwise it is as it was, Alice has gotten a lot of ms. cookbooks, from Mme Giraud from several generation[s], and they are all wonderful reading, one beautiful cake made of nothing but cream and flour, [ ] croquante, and another [?brochette] which says no butter no flour no this no that and [no ?word should ?word,] but I spoil them she will send them to you sometime, next Thursday I am giving my first french lecture to students up in the mts, it will seem funny hearing it in french, the thoughts are American well I suppose the french will be too.[3] You are always going somewhere, we almost wanted to go somewhere too, it might be the Virgin Islands, but I guess it will only be Paris, and it is cold and there are lots of nuts and we collect les trompette[s] de la mort a beautiful black tulip of a mushroom and we love you very much and we would like to do something about it, when shall we meet again and so much love

Gtde.

1. This letter is on a loose sheet torn from a notebook, numbered 198 in the upper left corner and numbered in a circle, in pencil. 2. On the page it follows a transcription of a telegram numbered 1 from Ruth Gordon to Alexander Woollcott and Wilder that Wilder quotes to Stein on 30 October 1936. Where Wilder uses a squiggle to approximate a word in his brackets, we have added [?word] instead.

2. This letter and sections of *Everybody's Autobiography* are similar. Stein echoes Wilder's letter of 14 August 1936, about his father's death (132). She goes on to Bennett Cerf's father. She originally wrote, "Bennett Cerf had a father but he was not much of a father." Cerf, whose father was living, revised her sentence to "Bennett Cerf has a father but he is more than a father and Bennett himself is more a brother and a nephew or a great nephew than a father, that is the reason we like him and like him as a publisher" (133). Stein then develops the father concept further by relating it to a negative definition of political leaders: "There is too much fathering going on just now and there is no doubt about it fathers are depressing. Everybody nowadays is a father, there is father Mussolini and father Hitler and father Roosevelt and father Stalin and father Lewis and father Blum and father Franco is just commencing now and there are ever so many more ready to be one. Fathers are depressing. England is the only country now that has not got one and so they are more cheerful there than anywhere. It is a long time now that they have not had any fathering and so their cheerfulness is increasing" (133).

Alf M. Landon, governor of Kansas (1933–37), was the unsuccessful Republican candidate for president in the election of 1936.

3. We have only partial information about Stein's lecture, "La France Est Mon Chez-Moi," a translation of "An American And France," delivered twice in Grenoble. The first time she spoke to law and medical students at the university. The second time, on 3 November, she spoke under the auspices of Le Centre de Documentation Interallié de la Délégation Régionale à l'Information at the Salle de Réunion, introduced by the young writer René Tavernier. In her reply to the *Atlantic Monthly*'s letter agreeing to publish her composition "Butter Will Melt," Stein indicated that she had read the piece at her recent talk (see excerpt from Stein letter in the *Atlantic Monthly* 159, 2 [February 1937]: xvi).

To Thornton Wilder, New Haven, Connecticut
[Transcribed by Wilder]¹

[postmark: 26 October 1936]   [Bilignin par Belley,
                                                                Ain]

My dear Thornton,

         Our book² has just come and I am just pleased with the introduction and my only trouble is that there are not enough commentaries I love commentaries and I love your commentaries and I would like a whole book of your commentaries please Thornton won't you sometime for Christmas or for Thanksgiving make me a whole book of commentaries, we had a Thanksgiving lunch yesterday, turkey mince pie celery and just as American as possible and all for the Daiguys and Madame Pierlot and we talked a lot about you and wished you were here, we all wished you were here, they may only have been polite but we were in deadly earnest, and then the Chinese book³ came [The Flight of an Empress: Yale Press] and Alice and I are both loving it, you know we always [?took] on the old empress very much and it brings her very near, and one likes her near if not too near. We are still here and the sun is shining and we are gardening but they all tell us it will rain soon and then we go. The text of our book kind of made me home-sick for the flat lands, I dream of wandering around them in a Ford car and you with us and when we got tired of driving a nice young Universitarian would come along for the pleasure, it would be nice, and perhaps with [?prosperity] somebody will pay us enough just so we can have the pleasure, we live in hope, it would be fun though wouldn't it almost more than Washington Square, but New York's [?prosperity] might run to both, well anyway things are as calm as they can be here which is not too calm, I am writing the narrative book which we talked about that last night,⁴ it goes slowly and simply perhaps too simply, I always want to be commonplace perhaps I have managed it this time well anywhere there is nothing commonplace about our love for you Thornton and always
                              Gtde.

    1. This letter is transcribed by Wilder on loose ledger sheets (see Stein to Wilder, letter 1, received 10 September 1936, n. 1-c).
    2. The *Geographical History* had been published on 19 October.
    3. See Wilder to Stein, 27 September 1936, n. 7.
    4. In *Everybody's Autobiography* Stein recalls Wilder's last evening in Paris, 5 November 1935: "But Thornton and I liked walking around even so, and we walked around the last evening, he was going away to America the next day and I walked home with him and he walked home with me and we talked about writing and telling anything and I said I had done things I had really written poetry and I had really written sentences and paragraphs but I said I had not simply told anything and I wanted to do that thing must do it. It would simply say what was happening which is what is narration, and I must do it as I knew it was what I had to do. Yes said Thornton.
    "And now I almost think I have the first autobiography was not that, it was a description and a creation of something that having happened was in a way happening not again but as it had been

which is history which is newspaper which is illustration but is not a simple narrative of what is happening not as if it had happened not as if it is happening but as if it is existing simply that thing. And now in this book I have done it if I have done it" (302–03).

To Gertrude Stein and Alice Toklas, Bilignin, France

30 Oct[ober]. 1936

Bluebeard's Castle Hotel
Charlotte Amalia
St. Thomas
Virgin Islands
West Indies.

Box 361
St. Thomas, V.I.

Care Tuttedue [Dear Two-of-you]:
Our daily rain is falling, terrible but brief. The oleanders and hibiscus writhe; the palms are in an agony; the ten million lizards are scandalized; the negroes rush to the porticos and cackle. Then it's all over under a very fine rain-bow; the sun comes out hotly; the harbor sparkles and I go for a long long walk.

It's all a great success. The only drawbacks are: that between 11:00 and 4:00 it's a little too hot for climbing; that for all the cocktail-parties dinners and army-post gregariousness there's no one to talk to; that there's no music.

But there's solitude. Wonderful. Since I met you I'm very sheepish about my thoughts, but anyway I enjoy them, and a whole lot of them have come out from their holes. A lot of them were fathered and mothered on the hills of Belley.[1]

The Geographical History came out Oct[ober] 19, but I haven't heard a word about its reception yet. I'm forever cured of the notion that reception of a book—short of five hundred years—is interesting; but I hope this one is cordial enough to encourage Random House or the Chicago Press to bring out *Four in America* next Spring.

I'm dying to know what you've been working on lately. And I'm dying to come over and see you. As I see it now I shall be Feb[ruary]. and March: Lecture Tour
June and July: MacDowell Colony.[2]
August (half of it): Aleck Woollcott's island.[3]
Then I think settled in Berkeley, California. A big library and long walks. But I may be able to come and see you then, continuing on to try and

work for a while at Antibes or Ville-franche. Anyway I pine for you. Alice, do you need a handy-man for the garden? I can chop wood; tetten-up the hay; make a good potato-hill. I can do everything except kill chickens.

Ruth Gordon, the best actress and the finest girl in America, has just made a roaring success in London in Wycherl[e]y's *The Country Wife*, and will be repeating it in New York on November 25th. The long tragico-ludicrous climb from the Butterick-patterns girl of Wollaston, Mass[achusetts], is at an end. It's Rejane. Did I ever tell you that life? all the tears split wide-open with laughs. As she set off on the boat she telegraphed: "Here I go off tomorrow on Queen Mary leading with my left my chin out to play Country Wife at Old Vic October six opening New York November sixteen [The run in London has been prolonged] Make out of town plan for that night. Edith Evans doing Mrs Fidgett what will I be doing. All I can think of is Fielding sitting in the green room drinking hard opening night of his play and as Garrick passed by Fielding said drearily What are they hissing now? Address Claridge Love Dick Whittington."[4]

Success is a bauble, but it's lovely to see courage and merit rewarded.

Oh, Alice and Gertrude within five years may we all be living in New York, the greatest city in the world: Aleck and Ned Sheldon and the Hutchi and Ruth and you and I. That'll be something saved from the moil. Soon after Hutch [Robert Hutchins] will be in the White House and we can all go down and rock the nation. Think it over.

Yes. I'm crazy to see Mme Giraud's cook-books. The food's no good here: the hotel's run by a Georgian-Russian, Major Sterossebsky.[5] I gently asked him the other day what the Russian for a knout was. He said it was a KNUT and why? I remembered Gertrude's lesson on the Russians, and how true. However one can make up for the bad food by the good liquors. Mango cocktails and papaya punch and the true the true pirates' old rum.

Now I'm going for my walk: up to Drake's Seat. Within a few steps you can see both the Atlantic and the Caribbean and fifty-six islands including Porto Rico seventy miles away. In the channels to the East Sir Francis Drake outwitted some great pirates. Here Columbus came on his second voyage.

Gandhi's autobiography "The Story of my Experiments with Truth"—two big volumes bound in the Khadi-cloth which he taught the Indians to make towards their economic independence—is a very interesting book. Also Alain's *Histoire de mes Penseés*.[6]

I know how to begin a letter, but I don't know how to end one except by saying that I love you more than tunkantell.

                    your
                    Thornton

1. A reference to the discussions of Stein and Wilder on walks in the hills of Belley in July 1935. Their walks and conversations became part of the *Geographical History*, and Stein recalls them in *Everybody's Autobiography*: "I am not leading him [i.e., Wilder] I am confiding in him and that is what we did in going up and down the hills near Bilignin and he loved Pépé because as he said Pépé passed and existed from one caress to another" (301).

2. Under the sponsorship of Edith J. Isaacs, editor and publisher of *Theatre Arts*, Wilder was accepted for residence at the MacDowell Colony for the first time in the summer of 1924. Wilder was a colonist for many years and actively supported the colony.

3. Woollcott and a group of nine friends, including members of the Algonquin Round Table, purchased Neshobe Island, Lake Bomoseen, Vermont, in 1923. Woollcott considered Lake Bomoseen one of the most beautiful spots in the world, and what began as a summer residence soon evolved for him into stays of at least six months of the year. Wilder was a regular visitor.

4. According to Ruth Gordon, at a party that she and Wilder attended in New York, she learned that Lawrence Langner intended to produce and direct Wycherley's comedy *The Country Wife* at his Westport Country Playhouse. Although she had never read the play and had no idea which role was suitable for her, she convinced Langner to cast her in it without even knowing what role was suitable. She was an immediate hit beginning with her first performance on 1 July 1935. More than a year later, on 6 October 1936, Gordon recreated her role at the Old Vic Theatre, London, in a production presented by Helen Hayes in association with Gilbert Miller. In addition to Gordon in the role of Margery Pinchwife, the London cast included Edith Evans as Lady Fidget. The New York production, at the Henry Miller Theatre, delayed until 1 December 1936, ran for eighty-nine performances, Lady Fidget was played by Irene Browne (see Gordon, *My Side*, 330–33, 373–81; Gordon reprints a letter from Wilder on 373–75). With some minor changes, Wilder is quoting from a telegram that Gordon sent to him and Woollcott on Neshobe Island on 9 September 1936 (the telegram is included in the transcriptions described in Stein to Wilder, first letter received, 10 September 1936, n. 1-c).

5. Wilder may be giving an approximation of the name.

6. Gandhi's autobiography was published in English in 1927–29. Alain is the pseudonym of Emile-Auguste Chartier, a French philosopher and moralist who taught at the Lycée Henri IV in Paris. His *Histoire des mes pensées* was published in 1936 by NRF—Gallimard.

To Gertrude Stein and Alice Toklas, Paris, France

20 Dec[ember]. 1936   The Century Association
                                                             7 West Forty-Third Street
                                                             New York [New York]

A
Dear G, and very dear, too:
                       Christmas is almost here, celebrating, as your friend Prof[.] Whitehead said "The greatest acceleration that ever took place in the teleology of the universe"—(no, he didn't say it, but it can be strictly deduced from *The Adventures of an Idea*) [i.e., *Adventures of Ideas*]. And the season gives me another pretext to say, on a background of bells, that *I love you*. Yes, and I've been thinking about you so often and gratefully that if it's possible, if my lawyer permits me, I'm coming over to see you in April or May,

when my lecture-tour is over. Some small Cunarder, or *The American Banker* will deposit me at Le Havre, wild with anticipation to look into your beautiful faces and to see hurled upon the carpet the tumultuous store of all that we have to say to one another.

You can't deny it: you're angels. I mark with a white stone the day when you *schwebten durch meinem Zimmer* [floated through my room], whisking away so many foolish notions and allowing me the healthful privilege of loving you.

I came back from the West Indies a new fellow, remade by solitude, by the long straight lines of the sea, and with my notebooks full of projects.[1] I went for five days to père and mère Hutchins at Berea College among the shy semi-royal mountaineers of Kentucky;[2] in Cincinnati I got to know Dr. Gustav Eckstein whom you would and will love, and saw the twenty-five canaries that he has been observing for years and about whom he writes in a way that reminds one of Homer, mighty emotions in mortal breasts;[3] then I went to Chicago.

How beautiful on the mountain are the feet of those that bring tidings of joy.[4] On my last evening in Chicago I had supper at the Hutchins. A telegram lay on the table saying that the Rockefeller Foundation had just voted six hundred thousand dollars a year for five years to the University, one, because it had born the brunt of a conspicuous attempt to restrict academic freedom and so served as precedent and bulwark for similar attacks against smaller institutions, and, two, because of the brilliant reforms in higher education advocated by its president.[5] Beautiful on the mountain. . . . .

Bobsy [Goodspeed] was down with a cold, brought on by her months of eight-hours-a-day labor in reconstructing the new Arts Club; but she was pretty, loquacious and wide-awake. Fanny [Butcher] and her Dick [Richard Drummond Bokum]—*quorum magna fuisti*—are deeply and tranquilly happy.[6] The Hutchins new baby—Joanna Blessing—at sixteen months is a glorious little affair, tirelessly toddling all day the whole house over.

Aleck [Woollcott] has taken a new apartment,[7] where in a generous dressing-gown, before an enormous ever-renewed cup of coffee, he sits, receiving the world, tossing commands to a corps of secretaries, stewards and ministers.

He gives dinners. They are prepared *de longue main* [with elaborate care], "the elements so mixed in them, that we may stand and say to all the world, 'this was a dinner.'" Some meditate sonnets; some meditate dinners. I am going to one tonight: 7:30 at the Hapsburg. Gerald Murphy—Scott Fitzg' [Fitzgerald] and Ernest H'ing's [Hemingway's] idolized Gerald;[8] John Gielgud, whose *Hamlet* had 120 standees last night;[9] Ruth Gordon whose divine foolings as *The Country Wife* made twelve-thousand dollars last week (forgive these gauges of achievement; but, a-hem, they are among the elements of the dinner-party); and Thornton, that taciturn little abbe of the Ritz system.

Then Monday to New Haven, to my little, pretty, apparently fragile but in reality strungle[10] on gold-wire, my gentle garden-making, sock-mending, French translating, my—Gentlemen! my mother. And my sister, Isabel. And Amos and his Katherine who is presenting us with a Wilder-baby in February.[11] And independent self-tormenting home-fleeing Charlotte. Janet remains in Chicago, engrossed in discovering which of the four methods for determining the oxygen-content of water is the best.

But you are in my Christmas wherever you are, and I send you all my love and my thoughts of a meeting before long.

devotedly

Thornton

1. Wilder sailed for the West Indies on the S.S. *Nerissa* on 8 October and returned on the same ship on 29 November.

2. The Reverend William J. Hutchins and Anna Hutchins, father and mother of Robert. The father was president of Berea College in Kentucky from 1919 to 1939. Founded in 1855, it was the first college to promptly admit black students following the Civil War. Like other Oberlin College students, Wilder spent the summer of 1917 at Berea. His father considered it a toughening experience.

3. Gustav Eckstein was a professor of physiology at the medical school of the University of Cincinnati. Woollcott was fascinated by his book *Canary* (1936), which explored his empathy with his birds. A warm friendship developed between them. Woollcott may have arranged for Wilder to meet Eckstein in Cincinnati, knowing he would not be able to attend Woollcott's dinner for Eckstein on 10 December in New York (see Woollcott to Wilder, 20 and 25 November 1936, Harvard-Houghton).

4. Isaiah 52:7.

5. The General Education Board on 17 December voted an award to the University of Chicago. The board, a philanthropy founded by John D. Rockefeller, Sr., in 1903 to aid education, was associated with other Rockefeller philanthropies and often confused with the Rockefeller Foundation. In response to our inquiry, Darwin H. Stapleton, director of the Rockefeller Archive Center, wrote, "[T]he GEB's rationale for the grant is not that recorded by Wilder, but Wilder's comments could easily reflect the comments made by Hutchins, who may have discerned a deeper meaning for the GEB's support. Moreover, the grant was made for the support of the School of Medicine and its clinics, rather than the University of Chicago as a whole" (22 June 1992).

6. Bobsy Goodspeed was president of the Arts Club of Chicago from 1932 to 1940. Transferred from the North to the South Tower of the Wrigley Building on North Michigan Avenue, the new Arts Club rooms and galleries opened on 9 December 1936. Wilder adapts the words of Aeneas to Dido about his role in the Trojan War (*Aeneid*, II, 6) to convey how large a part he played in bringing Butcher and Bokum together.

7. Woollcott moved from East 52d Street to 10 Gracie Square.

8. Gerald Murphy was the scion of a wealthy family, a painter, and the model for Dick Diver in F. Scott Fitzgerald's *Tender Is the Night*.

9. John Gielgud played Hamlet in a production staged by Guthrie McClintic with settings and costumes designed by Jo Mielziner. Judith Anderson played Queen Gertrude and Lillian Gish played Ophelia. The production opened in New York at the Empire Theatre on 8 October and ran for 132 performances.

10. Clearly "strungle."

11. Catharine Dix Wilder was born on 31 January 1937.

The studio at 27 Rue de Fleurus before the move to 5 Rue Christine. On the walls are paintings by Picasso, Gris, Cézanne, Picabia, and many by Francis Rose. The needlepoint chairs by Toklas after designs by Picasso are in front of the fireplace.

1937

"It's called 'Our Town' and its third act is based on your ideas as on great pillars."
(13 September 1937)

Wilder as the Stage Manager in an unidentified production

To Gertrude Stein and Alice Toklas, Paris, France

[?7–9 January 1937][1]

The Copley Plaza
Boston [Massachusetts]

Blest pair of sirens, pledges of Heav'n's joy,

This morning I walked along Beacon Street hunting for breakfast and I found a First Edition of *Geography and Plays*. A very smart bookshop had filled its windows with the first appearances of famous poems. There was "Marco Bozzaris" and "the shot heard round the world" and "You got to git up early ef you want to (something) good" and there in a *folio* periodical, signed "submitted" was the first printing of "Sweet Alice, Ben Bolt."[2] And there, with the appropriate lines from the "Autobiography" was the first appearance of "Rose is a rose."[3]

It's brightened my days a thing Boston cannot do in itself.

Roosevelt's a very great man.

¶ Ruth Gordon's The Country Wife is in its sixth week and has climbed to the weekly gross of $14,000.

¶ Last year Sybil Colefax lost the husband she adored; and Argyll House, one of the most beautiful 18th Century houses in London;[4] and had a grave operation. So last June Aleck Woollcott told her that five anonymous friends were giving her a Christmas present: a month in New York, all paid, from her doorstep to her doorstep,—a suite in the Waldorf-Astoria Tower; a maid; a car and chauffeur; a secretary. And such a series of engagements and attentions. It sustained her through her operation and she arrives next Wednesday. Kind of Americanish, I think.[5]

¶ I'm deep in my play, but not so confident about it.[6]

¶ I was consulted by a half-baked culturo-anaemical zaney named Pierce or Pearson who is preparing for the Oxford University Press and [i.e., a] vast textbook tome of Readings from American Literature (vast? It has room to

include the whole of The Scarlet Letter.) Of Gertrude he is reprinting the
speech at The Choate School and some of the Tender Buttons. (Of Henry
James he is including "Crapey [i.e., Crapy] Cornelia" and of Ernest Hemingway, the last chapter of *Farewell to Arms*, the last chapter ohmygod.) I tried to
persuade him to use *Look east and not west* and the fearful and wonderful
paragraph from *The Long Gay Book* on what it feels like to be growing older;
but I soon discovered that he was incapable of hearing what was being said to
him. He had merely asked me there to admire his conversation and to receive
his delicate advertisements as to what a bad author I was.[7]

¶ Yes, yes, I hope to come over in the Spring and bring you back to
America. You will spend the Summer at the MacDowell Colony in a studio
deep in a New Hampshire pine wood, with an occasional fox looking in the
door. In the Fall we shall go to Taos New Mexico and rent one of Mabel
Luhan's adobe houses. Two or three nights a week we will go up to the Big
House for dinner, otherwise we will let that glorious valley and the sun and the
air, dustless-powdered-topaz clear up every "humour" in our bodies. Think it
over, dear friends, friends above rubies, above diamonds.[8]

More soon.

Thy

Thornton

1. According to his date book, Wilder was in Boston on 7–9 January 1937.

2. Wilder refers to "Marco Bozzaris," a poem on the Greek struggle for freedom by Fitz-Greene
Halleck, published in 1825; Emerson's "Concord Hymn," written for the commemoration of a monu-
ment to the Minutemen and published in 1837; two lines misquoted from James Russell Lowell's *The
Biglow Papers*, first series, published in 1848, "An' you've gut to git up airly / Ef you want to take in
God"; and "Ben Bolt," a popular ballad by Thomas Dunn English, published in the *New York Mirror*
in 1843. The ballad began, "Oh! don't you remember sweet Alice, Ben Bolt? / Sweet Alice, whose hair
was so brown." "Ben Bolt" was set to music more than twenty-six times, and its popularity was revived
when it was introduced into George du Maurier's novel *Trilby* (1894).

3. In *The Autobiography Of Alice B. Toklas* Stein writes, "Speaking of the device of rose is a rose
is a rose is a rose, it was I who found it in one of Gertrude Stein's manuscripts and insisted upon
putting it as a device on the letter paper, on the table linen and anywhere that she would permit that I
would put it. I am very pleased with myself for having done so" (169). The line makes its first
appearance in "Sacred Emily." The poem, a portrait of Madame Matisse, was written in 1913 and
published in December 1922 in *Geography And Plays* (187).

4. Sir Arthur Colefax, who was knighted for his war service in 1920, was a barrister. He and Lady
Colefax were married in July 1901 and in 1920 moved to Argyll House, 211 Kings Road, Chelsea. After
Sir Arthur's death in February 1936, Lady Colefax was forced to sell their home and move to 19 Lord
North Street. Lady Colefax worked as a professional decorator with the firm of Dolly Mann before
founding, in 1933, Sybil Colefax Limited. In 1938 John Fowler became her partner in the firm of
Colefax and Fowler (see Colefax to Wilder, 27 April 1936, on the death of her husband; 25 October
1936, on leaving Argyll House, YCAL).

5. In a letter of 14 May 1936, Woollcott invited Lady Colefax to New York (see Kaufman and
Hennessey, *Letters*, 165–67, 175–76). She stayed in America from mid-January until early February. A
typed accounting of expenses is in the Woollcott Collection (Harvard-Theatre).

6. Probably *The Merchant of Yonkers*.

7. Norman Holmes Pearson, a graduate of Yale ('32), was pursuing graduate studies there and working with William Rose Benét on the two-volume *Oxford Anthology of American Literature* (New York: Oxford University Press, 1938). The final selections differ from what Wilder reports here. Hawthorne is represented by a selection from chapter 10 of *The Scarlet Letter*, a selection from *The House of the Seven Gables*, and three short stories. Stein is represented by "How Writing Is Written," a talk given at the Choate School, Wallingford, Connecticut, on 12 January 1935, first printed in the *Choate Literary Magazine* 21, 2 (February 1935): 5–14; "The Life Of Juan Gris. The Life And Death Of Juan Gris," and a paragraph from *A Long Gay Book*, titled at Wilder's suggestion, "When They Are A Little Older" (see Wilder to Stein, 27 September 1936, n. 6). Which text by Stein Wilder meant by "*Look east and not west*" is not clear. Henry James is represented by the essay "The Art of Fiction," the short story "Crapy Cornelia," and selections from *The American Scene, The Wings of the Dove,* and *The Golden Bowl.* Hemingway is represented by the short story "The Undefeated." Wilder himself is represented by a selection from *The Woman of Andros.* Wilder wrote Pearson on 25 January 1937 (YCAL) enclosing the paragraph from *A Long Gay Book*, made clear his objections to some of Pearson's proposals and asked him to reconsider the last chapter of *A Farewell to Arms.* "It seems to me," Wilder wrote, "to be from the worst level of Hemingway; and the clinical discomfort depicted can only be borne when one has traversed the whole arc of the story." Wilder thought "Crapy Cornelia" did "little justice to the greatness of Henry James." For the fragment from *The Woman of Andros*, he suggested the titles, "The Hopes and Dejections of Paganism" or "Long Thoughts by the Aegean." The editors used "Aegean Moods" and made some minor alterations in Stein's "How Writing Is Written."

Stein prepared the Choate talk at the suggestion of James Laughlin, who considered her other lectures too difficult for preparatory school students. The talk, for which there is no manuscript or typescript, was stenographically recorded and probably adjusted by Dudley Fitts, the English teacher, for printing in the *Choate Literary Magazine.*

Wilder's characterization of Pearson represents a personal dislike that did not change over the years, although their shared concern for the Yale Collection of American Literature often brought them into contact.

8. Stein's working style would have precluded an environment like the MacDowell Colony. Wilder may have known that Stein had repeatedly refused during the 1934–35 lecture tour to meet Mabel Dodge Luhan, whom she had known since 1910. Wilder first came to know her when she wrote to him on 6 April [1929] (YCAL), asking him to come to Taos, where she had gone to live in 1917 with her third husband, the painter Maurice Sterne, and now lived with her fourth husband, the Taos Pueblo Indian Antonio Luhan:

> Certainly one should wait for an auspicious mood or something to write a letter like this one so that it will carry through & effect the difficult conviction it is intended to stir & clinch. But I'm not waiting for anything. I read The Bridge last week & Cabala today and what I want to say without preambles or arrangements is: won't you come out here to Taos and do something about these people? Yes—I see that looks very sudden. It is. But if you knew how I've been looking for someone to come who can *get it* before it's too late. One might think I'd be discouraged in such attempts as this for I did it once before. I wrote in the same way to Lawrence before I even knew him, because he is so sensitive to animals & flowers & things & he came—& it didn't happen right because he was too subjective.

Wilder did not immediately visit her, but in subsequent visits to the Southwest he did. Luhan was responsible for attracting a number of writers and painters to Taos. As early as 1923, she was renting a house on her property: "For Rent: From August first attractive five room furnished adobe house near Taos Pueblo. Communicate Mabel Sterne Luhan, Taos, New Mexico" (*The New Republic,* 4 July 1923, back cover).

To Thornton Wilder, New Haven, Connecticut
[Transcribed by Wilder]

[postmark: 20 January 1937][1]   [27 rue de Fleurus]
                                                                 Paris

My dear Thornton,

         We are awfully pleased cannot tell you how pleased but you know how pleased that you are coming over this spring, that will be lots of fun, we know some new people and we will give a party for you and it will be all delicious and after that well not MacDowell and not Mabel, no [??Ma] no not at all, we have happy [??plans?], I am thinking of being appointed by some foundation to visit all the countries of the world particularly funny ones, to meditate upon the outcroppings of creative activity,[2] all we need is the rich foundation to endow us, some people say that they exist, we live in hope, but actually it will probably be just Paris and Bilignin which is after all not so bad, and I am awfully pleased with the Atlantic Monthly[3] [??taken?] its foolish to be so but it is a pleasure, and I was delighted with the first edition of Geography and Plays, and its company, only you could have found it in such perfect company, dear dear Thornton I can't tell you how we are looking forward to seeing you again, I always remember our last night in Paris, I am still going on trying simple narrative,[4] once in a while not so bad, am interested in your play we will compare plays, I have two I would like to show you[5] and I am now doing one which was to have been about the Civil War and has become one about Daniel Webster,[6] Alice likes it, well anyway we will talk and we will, we will talk when you get here and you will get here, and that will be nice, pleased about Lady Col[e]fax , it is a nice idea and give them all our love but most and always to you now and always

                        Gtde.

     1. This letter is transcribed on a loose sheet from a ledger stamped 196 (see Stein to Wilder, letter 1, received 10 September 1936, n. 1-c).

     2. The phrase "Creative Activity" in relation to foundation support for artists may echo her "Genuine Creative Ability," a piece of 1929. Stein had written a letter of reference for Bravig Imbs in support of his application to the Guggenheim Foundation and, in the piece, plays with the notion of evidence of creative ability, stressed by the foundation.

     3. In late September or early October, Stein sent the *Atlantic Monthly* two short compositions: "Butter Will Melt," which tells of the life of her cook, Trac, an Annamite from French Indo-China, and "What Does She See When She Shuts Her Eyes." On 26 October 1936 (YCAL), Ellery Sedgwick, the editor, accepted "Butter Will Melt" for the issue of February 1937. Stein's delighted response (n.d., marked received November 1936, YCAL) was published in the "Contributors' Column" (xvi) of the February issue. The transcription is faulty and creates the mistaken impression that "Butter Will Melt," rather than "What Does She See When She Shuts Her Eyes: A Novel," was read at a Stein lecture at the University of Grenoble. The portion of the letter printed (a sentence was also dropped) should have read, "I am pleased that you like *Butter will melt*. One does do a quite perfect thing once in a while. I hope that you will gradually like the novel, it does translate so well into French. It was read at a talk I gave the other day to some french law and medical students in the mountains near here, and

it went well. I [?was ?am] interested in their interest in William James, they wanted to know more and more about him. He is the one American that means a lot to french students and he meant so much to me and I like it." Acceptance by the *Atlantic Monthly* meant a great deal to Stein. Its associations with Henry James and William Dean Howells gave her the sense of becoming an American classic. Although the magazine had printed excerpts from *The Autobiography Of Alice B. Toklas*, this was their first acceptance of a piece Stein considered her "real" writing. The February issue probably also gave her pleasure because it included an autobiographical piece by the Spanish bullfighter Juan Belmonte, about whom she had written in "I Must Try To Write The History Of Belmonte" (1916), and an essay by Bertrand Russell, whom Stein had known in England in 1902–03. For a partial history of Stein's relationship with the magazine through 1933, see Donald C. Gallup, "Gertrude Stein and *The Atlantic*."

    4. The "simple narrative" may be *Everybody's Autobiography*.

    5. Stein's *Listen To Me* and *A Play Called Not And Now*.

    6. *Daniel Webster. Eighteen In America: A Play* is made up of historical figures and people Stein knew who do not overlap in chronological time. Four of the principal characters are also in *Four In America*: Ulysses Grant, George Washington, Henry James, and Wilbur Wright. The play was published in December 1937 in *New Directions in Prose and Poetry 1937* (Norfolk, Conn.: New Directions, [162–88]); see also Stein, *Reflection*, 95–117.

To Gertrude Stein and Alice Toklas, Paris, France

25 Feb[ruary] 1937   Tucson[,] Arizona[1]

Dear Friends:

        We are as our air and light and earth are, "as one of your own poets hath said."[2]

    And of those things this place has my favorite them.

    So, having three days free between lectures at Iowa City and Pasadena I have stopped here. Even in mid-Kansas I started looking out the train-window for the first tumble-weed—those filigree balls that the graziers hate, but which are rolled by the wind for hundreds of miles and are the signature of New Mexico and Arizona. And now I'm here with the best sun and air and earth in the country.

    Three weeks ago I had five days on the Florida coast.

    Two weeks ago I had three days at Charleston. My first time there, and *just as you said* they began alluding to the Civil War within ten minutes of the introduction.

    During the lecture at Rollins College, Florida, I was illustrating a modest point of mine ("to the poet the world is every moment at a state of crisis") by giving that 'ladder of argumentation' whereby you 'explain' "a rose is a rose. . . . ." (as always: it slayed 'em; it laid 'em low) and during Questions and Answers someone asked me How does one go about understanding Miss

Stein's work. Well, I did a Portrait. Con amore. And afterwards I found out that my old friend Mrs John W. Alexander was there, at whose house Gertrude read her first lecture in America (is that right?) and she was tremendously pleased and so was I and so was the audience.[3]

Then I had three days in Chicago. Lord, a whole afternoon would be all too short for the things I fancy myself analyzing about the Presidential Mansion. Apparently everything is much better than it's been for a long while. Both look finely. What's more, the Rockefeller gift is doing wonders ($600,000 a year for five years—count it!). But. But. I think that at last Bob [Hutchins] is on to it. I don't know quite what I mean, but I think that Bob begins—as Henry James would say—to watch it. Now the second baby's ill. Again the whole staff of servants has been dismissed. Oh, if I were right beside you I'd go into it; I'd throw some rope-ladders into the air and then try and climb them. So subtle is it; so deep is it. That must wait.

Bob Davis is fine. He's deep in the courses on Symbolic Logic. The Vienna School of Logical Positivism has moved over to Chicago; Bob H[utchins]. doesn't like it, but at least it's close difficult thinking which is more than the Philosophy department had before with its post-John Dewey fumes. Mortimer Adler is still there, but the Hutchi never mention him to me, never. No, ma'am, he's at the house at the same little tabouret suppers that I get; he's there the evenings before and after me, but he's never mentioned.[4] *Pensez-y.* So, Bob Davis is following [Rudolf] Carnap's courses whose motto is: the snow is white, if—and only if—the snow is white.[5] Did I tell you that Bob Davis left a Madame Butterfly behind him in Vienna? Yes, I get long letters from both her and her baleful mother asking me when he will return to marry the girl. (Note: there are no men-folk in her family.) She's a very nice girl a number of years older than he is, a musicologist and well able to sing *Un bel di vedremo.*

Fanny [Butcher] has not been well. Bobsy and Barney [Goodspeed] are a hundred miles from where I sit this minute.[6] I'm going to ask them to dinner with me Sunday noon at Phoenix. The Arts Club had a show of Van Dongen,[7] hideous and cheap, and a show of Duchamps, glorious. I was riddled and pâmé by *Le roi et la reine entourés de nus vites.*[8]

In New York Aleck [Woollcott] was fine. On the air again with 8,000,000 listeners (sic) but seldom good there.[9] Kit [Cornell] is having a considerable success with a play that some don't like.[10] Ruth [Gordon] has been made 10 years younger (i.e. 30) by her great success and is adored by all her adorers.[11] Jed [Harris] is mulling plans: "Uncle Vanja" in London with Charles Laughton, Cedric Hardwicke, Ruth Gordon and Lillian Gish—*folie de grandeur.*[12]

❡ I am an uncle—Katherine Dix Wilder.[13] ❡ Isabel's beau is getting seriouser—we may lose her! ❡ But the only real thing in my life is that on April first I shall be free. Not a class, not a lecture—and as I feel this minute—not a conversation for three or four years. (Except with you, of course.) And the projects for plays, and fragments of them, are running down my forearm like ants. On this trip I'm looking for a place to live. Not Tucson, wonderful as it is, (it's midnight, but I'm going out in a minute to get some beer up a Mexican side-street.) Maybe San Francisco bay. The new hunch is that maybe it'll be Zurich. If so I shall ask if I can come and see you in Bilignin in late-August. Otherwise it will be a visit this April. I hope. I hope. I can't be sure yet.

I love you very much and live and die

Your friend

Thornton

POST—breakfast—SCRIPTA

Coffee tastes wonderful in this air. And hot-cakes, oo—oo. Just took a walk out among the cacti and rattlesnakes and crumbling yellow soil. Credo in unum deum omnipotentem. . . . . .

¶ You'll like the following.

When I set out on a tour my manager gives me a carefully-typed schedule. On it appears the item:

March 8 Monday Los Angeles, California

AUSPICES: Los Angeles Ebell Club

CORRESPONDENT: Mrs. W.C. Warmington

(address, etc)

SUBJECT: "The Relations between Literature and Life."

AUDITORIUM: Ebell Clubhouse 4400 Wilshire Blvd.

HOUR: 2:15 p.m.

HOTEL: Los Angeles-Biltmore.

NOTE: The contract stipulates that inasmuch as some of their members have already heard Mr. Wilder deliver "The Relations between Literature and Life" they trust he will give them an entirely new lecture.

The fact is that the mental atmosphere of Southern California is so idiotic that wherever you touch it, out springs an illustrative anecdote. The Silly Sector.

¶ At present one of the most interesting things in the world to me is what's going on at the *Comédie Française*: that superb roll-call of guest-*régisseurs* blowing new life into the repertoire. God willing, you and I will soon be sitting charmed before Baty's staging of *Le Chandelier* and Jouvet's *L'Illusion Comique*.[14]

My life-long I've been ecs[ta]tically praising performances which circumstance prevents my attending.

¶ Had tea with Mrs. Longworth. *Genre* Ethel Barrymore, but much sharper. *Roucoulement* [cooing] voice, willowy entrances and exits; did a minute's brilliant imitation of Cousin Eleanor's radio-manner. *Au fond* [In effect] gave that air that Sibyl Colefax and all true widows have, that *Su[t]tée* [long-suffering] air, that life is really over and that what is left is a senseless show from which one extracts little ephemeral distractions. She talked of Pauline, but even one's children don't equal one's husband. My idolized Saint-Simon would have said of her:

"Elle avait été belle de sa jeunesse et en conservait des restes jusqu' à la fin de sa vie. Elle avait dans la perfection les usages du monde et plaçait des mots, avec une justesse qui frappait, avec un point de malice qui ne blessait pas mais qui faisait des envieux. Ses manières marquaient sa haute naissance, mais sans l'afficher. D'ailleurs un grand bon sens et un coeur solide. Après la mort du Senateur elle s'égarait un peu parmi les idoles du marché, conduisant un colonne dans les quotidiens qui parlait politique et mondanités et qui faisait tort à ses qualitiés supérieures."[15]

¶ Georges Simenon's *La Tête d'un Homme* is so far (page 125) a very good mystery story; but his *"Le Pendu de Saint-Pholien*["] is not worth the paper it's printed on. I also liked *La Nuit du Carrefour*.[16]

Alice, if it turns out to be next late-Summer that I go abroad; and if you invite me to Bilignin, I hereby promise to weed gardens, cut hay, play gramophone records, hold knitting-wool, soothe dogs, skirmish the countryside for rare pâtés and rare *chevaliers*:[17] I long to give visible representation to my devotion and gratitude. And to this Deed of Bondage, I sign my name.

Your indentured slave

Thornton

1. This letter is written on stationery from the Copley Plaza Hotel in Boston and the Century Club in New York. At the time he wrote it, Wilder was staying at the Santa Rita Hotel in Tucson.

2. Wilder is echoing the second sentence of Stein's "An American And France": "After all anybody is as their land and air is" (see *What Are Masterpieces*, 62).

3. Wilder left New York on 4 February for Florida to lecture at Rollins College, in Winter Park, Florida, on 12 February and in Charleston on 17 February. From Charleston, he traveled to Chicago and then on to Tucson.

Wilder knew Mrs. John W. Alexander, the widow of a well-known portrait painter, because of her connection with the MacDowell Colony. "Plays And What They Are" was Stein's first lecture in America before an invited audience at Alexander's home in New York on 30 October 1934. An informal prelude to her first public lecture on 1 November before a group of friends of the Museum of Modern Art, the evening had been arranged by Prentiss Taylor, a lithographer and friend of Carl Van Vechten. Looking back, Taylor recalled, "Carl had telephoned me rather early one Saturday morning to ask if I knew of a drama group that would be suitable for the lecture on Plays. I said I didn't but that I'd ask my friend Mrs. Alexander, widow of the painter. Mrs. A said she would be willing if I would take care of all the arrangements" (Taylor to Bruce Kellner, 29 April 1980, quoted in letter received 30 July 1992).

In reply to a condolence letter from Taylor, in which he also offered Alexander's sympathy on the news of Stein's death, Toklas replied, "Gertrude Stein never forgot her extraordinary kindness in opening her home to a stranger—and permitting her to learn how to read a lecture before a New York audience—for Gertrude Stein was frightfully nervous—as you could easily see. She thought it so extraordinarily kind of Mrs. Alexander and you—and then she asked us later to lunch with her surrounded by all of her treasures—which we hadn't appreciated the night of the lecture" (Toklas to Taylor, 4 November 1946, quoted in letter received from Bruce Kellner, 30 July 1992).

4. The appointment of Mortimer Adler to the Philosophy Department was the first major skirmish that Robert Hutchins faced after his appointment as president of the University of Chicago. Members of the department, schooled in pragmatism and John Dewey's progressive philosophy and educational theory, saw in Adler and Hutchins's other appointments a radical shift toward Aristotelian methodology and a scholastic approach to the Western tradition. The Chicago Fight, as it came to be called, was an acrimonious battle (see Ashmore, *Unseasonable Truths*, chap. 16).

5. Rudolph Carnap, professor at the University of Chicago from 1936 to 1952, was one of the founders of logical positivism or logical empiricism. Wilder is paraphrasing an exchange between Carnap and the Polish logician Alfred Tarski, who, when asked to state the truth-condition for a simple statement of fact, such as, "This table is black," replied, " 'This table is black' is true if and only if this table is black."

6. The Goodspeeds were at Castle Hot Springs, Arizona.

7. Wilder may be referring to an informal, undocumented hanging of Van Dongen's paintings.

8. Marcel Duchamp's first one-man exhibition was held at the Arts Club of Chicago from 5 to 27 February 1937. The catalogue for the exhibition of nine works had a preface by Julien Levy. The correct title of the work Wilder cites is *Le Roi et la Reine Traversés par des Nus Vites* (April 1912)

9. Woollcott had returned to the radio on "The Granger Program" (see Wilder to Stein, 25 January 1936, n. 4).

10. Cornell played the role of Oparre, a Malay princess married to Nathaniel McQueston, a New England sailor, in Maxwell Anderson's *The Wingless Victory*, his version of the *Medea* by Euripides. The play, produced by Cornell, staged by Guthrie McClintic, and with sets by Jo Mielziner, opened in New York at the Empire Theatre on 23 December 1936 and ran for 110 performances.

11. Gordon was playing in *The Country Wife*.

12. None of these projects was realized. Harris had produced and directed a production of Chekhov's *Uncle Vanya* with Lillian Gish as Helena in New York in 1930.

13. See Wilder to Stein, 20 December 1936, n. 11.

14. Gaston Baty staged Alfred de Musset's *Le Chandelier*, which opened on 16 December 1936. Louis Jouvet staged Corneille's *L'Illusion*, which opened on 15 February 1937.

15. Alice Roosevelt Longworth was the daughter of President Theodore Roosevelt and first cousin to Eleanor Roosevelt. Her husband, Nicholas Longworth, was a member of the House of Representatives from 1903 and its speaker from 1925 until his death in 1931. Their only daughter was Pauline Longworth. The following translation cannot render the affectation of Wilder's description, perhaps modeled on Saint Simon: "She had been beautiful in her youth and retained traces of beauty until the end of her life. She had perfected worldly manners and spoke most effectively, with enviable pointedness that did not hurt. Her manners showed but did not show off her social position. For the rest, lots of good sense and a solid heart. After the death of her Congressman husband, she circulated for a while in society and wrote a column for a daily paper about politics and society, which did not represent her real qualities."

16. These three novels are part of Georges Simenon's Inspector Maigret series.

17. *Omble chevalier*, a fish found in the deep lakes and rivers of Switzerland and the Savoy region of France. The Lac du Bourget, not far from Belley, is noted for this fish.

To Thornton Wilder, New Haven, Connecticut
[Transcribed by Wilder][1]

[postmark: 8 March 1937]

[Stationery: stamped with a
rose encircled by A ROSE IS A
ROSE etc and
27 Rue de Fleurus.]

I am awfully pleased to hear about Bob Davis, we did like him

Dear dear Thornton,

[?word] be it April and August we are all for As, it will be welcome, it would be nice if you were here in time for the premiere of our English ballet, Berners has done the decor as well as the music and it sounds lovely,[2] it is coming on the end of March, it would be nice if you were there, well anyway we love you a lot, and then there is a possibility that they will do my not of Adam and Eve called Listen to me in french, Pràhó to do the decor, if they did I would have something to do with the staging and I would love to have you help, I think you would have lots of ideas, I am not sure I will have any, and then you could help turn it into french.[3] And then I am writing a rather nice play about Daniel Webster, Alice thinks it is the best yet, and I would like you to look at that[4] and we would like well of course we would like Thornton for any purpose, and that purpose is just having him; they are going to make Pepe['s] ears go three ways, just as they do in the masque of him,[5] I kind of feel it is not necessary to write any more because you are going to be here Dear Thornton, yes, say we all, and how

Gtde.

1. This letter, responding to Wilder's of 25 February, is transcribed on a loose leaf from a ledger stamped 197 and numbered 7 in pencil by Wilder. The brackets throughout the letter are Wilder's (see Stein to Wilder, received 10 September 1936 (1), n. 1-c).

2. Lord Berners wrote Stein of the ballet's progress in a letter of 9 February and an undated letter later in the month (YCAL). A *Wedding Bouquet* had its first performance on 27 April 1937 at Sadlers' Wells Theatre, London. The decor and costumes by Lord Berners were executed under the supervision of William Chappell.

3. A more likely reading of "not of Adam and Eve" may be "*play* of Adam and Eve"; "Pràho" is probably Picabia. Stein, the art dealer Pierre Colle, and Picabia hoped to mount a production of Stein's *Listen To Me* in conjunction with the Exposition Internationale des Arts et des Techniques dans la Vie Moderne opening in May 1937. Nothing came of this plan. Stein almost never indicates sources of her meditative process. In a number of letters, however, she has given hints about *Listen To Me*, a play begun either in England in February 1936 or shortly after she returned to Paris from her lectures at Oxford and Cambridge. For the characters of Sweet William and his Lillian, Stein draws on Sir Robert and Lady Diana Abdy and Adam and Eve. In a letter to Carl Van Vechten, postmarked 25 March 1936, Stein writes, "I tried to make it [i.e., *Listen To Me*] like my memories of the Kirafly brothers and the Lion tamer" (see Burns, *Letters*, 2:491–93). To Bennett Cerf she writes in an undated letter of March 1936, "I have just finished a play, I think it pretty good, it is called Listen to Me. I had an idea of making an old fashioned thing like [Francis] Wilson used to do in the Lion Tamer" (Columbia-R.H.).

4. See Stein to Wilder, 20 January 1937, n. 6.
5. In *A Wedding Bouquet*, Stein's dog Pepe was danced by Joyce Farron.

To Thornton Wilder, New Haven, Connecticut
[Postcard: Birthplace of Marechal Joffre at Rivesaltes, April 1917]

[postmark: 19 March 1937]   [27 rue de Fleurus
                                                             Paris]

My dear Thornton,
            The ballet is going on Sadlers Wells Theater April 27,
London and Pepe is having a bigger and bigger part he is doing a classic dance
with pointes et entrechats and all that and he is to be in a white gauze tutu and
a wreath, and we are all xcited, and Fred[erick] Ashton and Constant Lambert
are to dance,[1] will you be there and lots of love
            Gtrde.

1. Lord Berners wrote Stein on 17 March (YCAL), "I have done a lot of work with Frederick
Ashton and Constant Lambert and the ballet part seems to be working out very well." Stein seems to
have assumed that they were both dancing in the ballet. In fact, Ashton was the choreographer and
Lambert the musical director.

To Gertrude Stein and Alice Toklas, Paris, France

26 March 1937   The Graduates Club
and oh, the difference unto me   New Haven, Connecticut

Dear Friends:
            No news, just groaning and waiting until my freedom arrives on
April first. Just got back from the State of Maine and just starting out for the
State of Indiana. (In Maine I took a bus from Portland to Brunswick so I could
see better: a darlin' state.[1] Then I took a train from Brunswick to Boston so as
to see that chaplet, that garland of stations that Richardson flung for the
Boston Maine Railroad.)[2]
            I forget where I last wrote you from. I guess I told you how idiotic, as
usual, Southern California was; how I told Oakland listeners that all three of
us used to walk miles to draw books from their public library, and what a rosy

three: Isadora [Duncan] and Gertrude and I; how grandiose and farflung the bridges are across San Francisco bay; how securely [Mount] Shasta rises from its snowy skirts and long fields of jack-pine;[3] did I tell you I was at Albuquerque [New Mexico] for two days and a half and saw much of Mabel and Tony [Luhan]? Mabel delicately but firmly showed me that I was under displeasure for not choosing Taos as my workshop in the years to come. But I pretended not to notice that I was being disciplined. I like them as much as ever, and have become very fond of Tony, who I think distinguishes me slightly from among the other nervous culture-crammed pale-faces that haunt the house.

Yes, I wish I could come and see the Ballet and help think up ways to project the play. What fun it would be to sit beside you and suggest things.

I've been reading *Lucy Church Amiably* and though I often fall among briars, I get a lot of pleasure, and there are long passages where I do "get the movement" and rise and stride about the room with exhilaration, *Küss die Hand*.[4]

The family's fine. Ma loves having two chillun in the house; she darns my socks; listens avidly to all radio news-reports, detective stories and serial dramas. I lie on my stomach on the floor playing solitaire and listen to the concerts (today, was the Brahms' *Requiem* and half of the *St Matthew Passion* and the whole of the Bach cantata *Christus lag in Todesbanden*—what's America coming to?)

It's about decided. I shall spend eight or nine months in Zurich next year. I'm in no doubt about my country and countrymen being the best there are, but I got to get away from them for a while. Oh, oh, isn't conversation *awful?* The worst about my being a visiting lecturer is that everybody lectures to me. For a month and a half I've been harangued by people. And now I see it all through the terminology Gertrude put into my hand: *listen* I must though I don't want to, and what do I hear but people *repeating* themselves, and pathetically asserting their *identity* and remorselessly disclosing themselves as *resembling* one another.

So black and blue from conversation, during April and May I shall spend in my study on Deepwood Drive and June and July I shall spend in my studio in Peterborough (as Mme de Sévigné said "*Quelle belle chose qu'une feuille qui chante!*" [How beautiful—a leaf that sings!].

Isabel's in love and is to be married I suppose pretty soon. She's in a pitiable state and hangs about hoping I'll tease her. She finished a light novel that may run serially in one of the woman's glazed-paper magazines and make her an heiress.[5] Their [i.e., They're] all going up Sunday to see my niece christened.[6]

(Now I gotta hurry home or I'll be late for supper. As Lucy Church Amiably says—now that I'm a successful author nobody treats me with consideration anymore and I'm scolded as though I were an unemployed half-wit in the family.)⁷

    Thy bound-hand-and-foot-to you
           Thornton

script on last page:

P.S.

    Just think.

    Bob Ardrey—that student of mine at Chicago—who had a play on in New York year before last, has just won a Guggenheim scholarship, and has just finished his 3rd play which he says is even 10 times better than the other two, and I believe him and it is probably very good indeed.

    He's the next American playwright.

    If he takes his scholarship abroad I want you to talk to him loud and clear.

    He had already graduated when you were in Chicago, but he went to the lectures and several of the conferences and was thunderstruck and transported.⁸

           T.

P.S. II

    I'm so delighted by tonight's news from Spain I don't know what to do. Perhaps all that boo-I'm-Frankenstein stuff is breaking up.⁹

           T.

1. Wilder gave a lecture entitled "The Relation between Literature and Life" at Bowdoin College in Brunswick, Maine, on 24 March.

2. Beginning in 1881, Henry Hobson Richardson began designing train stations, first for the Boston and Albany Railroad (not the Boston Maine Railroad) and then for several other New England railroads, including the Old Colony Railroad and the New London and Norwich Railroad. Wilder may have thought of a popular song of the nineties, "Ridin' Down from Bangor on the Boston Maine."

3. In *The Autobiography Of Alice B. Toklas*, Stein writes of knowing the Duncan family during her childhood in Oakland, California. Wilder also writes of San Francisco Bay connections in Wilder to Stein, 27 September 1936.

4. *Lucy Church Amiably*, written in the summer of 1927 in Belley and published in January 1930 as the first volume in Stein's Plain Edition of her own work, is a pastoral romance. With no plot or chronological narrative it places a series of androgynous figures in the space of the landscape and the geography of verbal composition. They undertake no significant actions but get up, sit down, walk around, and engage in conversation. The figures move in the landscape as the words move in space. Wilder comments on learning to follow the movement of words of which Stein may have spoken. He compliments either Stein or the figure of Lucy Church with a formal German greeting.

5. Isabel Wilder did not marry. Her third novel, *Let Winter Go*, published in September 1937, is about the lives of four people in a New England university town.

6. Wilder's niece, Catharine Dix Wilder, was born on 31 January 1937, and christened on 28 March.

7. Wilder echoes a passage in *Lucy Church Amiably*: "A genius says that when he is not successful he is treated with consideration like a genius but when he is successful and has been as rich as successful he is treated like anybody by his family" ([9]–10).

8. See Wilder to Stein, 12 April 1936, n. 4.

9. Spanish Loyalist forces attacked the Falangists at Pozo Blanco in an effort to stop their march toward the mercury mines (needed for TNT) at Almadén. The Loyalists' display of air supremacy in this attack led some people to believe that Franco's forces (Hitler's creation) were not invincible.

To Thornton Wilder, New Haven, Connecticut
[Transcribed by Wilder][1]
[Rose motto]

[postmark: 2 May 1937]

[27 rue de Fleurus
Paris]

My dear Thornton

Here we are having come back from a wonderfully good time in London saw Ruth Gordon and we talked of you and Lady Col[e]fax but by that time I was pretty well xhausted with all the xcitement it did go well I wish you might have been there and I think a lot about the stage all the time, I want to do a play or have them do one of my plays like a play, it would be lots of fun,[2] I think a lot about you, Thornton, sometimes you are a puzzle to me but then I do know what a puzzle is if it is a puzzle, I wonder how you will like the Autobiography, I sometimes think I have at last done narrative, Bennett tells me he is passing it over to you[3] and I wish you would come I think you need it and it would be lots of fun all our love

Gtde.

1. See Stein to Wilder, received 10 September 1936 (1), n. 1-b.

2. Stein is not only reporting on her interest in the stage but also hoping to enlist Wilder's interest in productions of her plays. She began writing plays as early as 1913, but none was professionally produced until *Yes Is For A Very Young Man* on 13 March 1946, a few months before her death. Wilder, on the other hand, had for years been involved with the theater, known producers, actors, and reviewers, and was now thinking about his new plays with a view to their production, as is obvious from his many references to Woollcott, Gordon, Reinhardt, Cornell, and others. Stein at this point not only needed Wilder's interest but may have wanted to tap his connections.

3. Cerf cabled Stein on 31 March 1937 (YCAL) acknowledging receipt of part of *Everybody's Autobiography*; he expressed his delight and pressed her to finish it. On 2 April 1937 (YCAL) he again wrote Stein and mentioned seeing Wilder in Boston. Stein assumed that Cerf would be sending the incomplete typescript to Wilder, but Cerf was waiting to hear from the *Atlantic Monthly* about printing a portion of the book. Not until 21 June (YCAL) did Cerf write Stein that Van Vechten had seen the book and Wilder would soon be getting it.

To Gertrude Stein and Alice Toklas, Paris, France

3 May 1937   Century Club
                                              7 West Forty-Third Street
                                              New York [New York]

Dear Friends:

I wonder whether you're back from England yet. I wonder whether it went off fine and you're very pleased; whether you're packing up for Bilignin. I wish I were with you; everything over here, except my work, is a weariness to me. The misanthropy I brought back with me from my lecture-tour is still with me. Almost all conversation I receive and return with inward groanings. Therefore with redoubled excitement do I climb upstairs to my study and add new passages to my comedy which is almost done and which I think is very good. Play No II is all planned; Play No III is all planned and half-written.[1]

Today I came down to New York to deliver for a second time a talk on the MacDowell Colony to a group collected for the Colony's Endowment Drive. Ladies "open their houses" for these things and we colonists make veiled pleas for money. As I "use" the Colony and very gladly, it's only right I do this, but it's a soiling saddening business.[2]

¶

You remember that Beacon Street bookshop where I got the copy of *Geography and Plays?* Well, they wrote the other day that they had a copy of the Paris edition of *The Making of Americans* and did I want it? Oh, did I? And I've been reading like a wild man ever since and now I've been drawing up charts of the different kinds of human beings, and I love it. Oh, it's a wonderful book, and the index of subjects that I've been constructing in the fly-leaves is a guide to such treasures that if any anthologist ever approaches me again on quotations from Gertrude's work, I shan't only heap him with *What it feels like to grow older* from the *Long Gay Book* but with a heap of excerptible jewels.[3]

¶

Had dinner with Aleck [Woollcott] tonight. So much to tell, and so much burden to share that I must wait until I see you.—He's fine. His radio talks are collecting millions of listeners; but the consciousness of the audience is making vast inroads into his mind and endangering many of the things we love most.

¶

Did I tell you I had retranslated (i.e. revised the translations of) *A Doll's House* and that Jed Harris will put it on this summer at the festival season at

the Central City Opera House above Denver, Colorado, and bring it into
New York in the Fall? Ruth Gordon will play Norah and be wonderful in it.[4]

¶

Spring is coming on, and my daily walks among our suburban woods and
lakes are glorious.

Birds and everything.

Flowers, as it were.

Turtles on the ends of logs.

Warmth on one's back.

Spring, practically.

Alice, I brought home a *Streletzia* [i.e., Strelitzia] to give my Ma. Do
[you] know it? It cost two dollars, but I told her it cost seventy-five cents and
even then she turned pale.

We are being driven mad by a woodpecker which for the third year
mistakes some tin-ware on our chimney for worm-rich wood. It tattoos away
all day, and we go out and throw stones and shriek at it. Isn't that a delicious
trouble to have?

¶

So you see I have no news. The only things that are happening are
happening in my plays.

I keep thinking of meeting you at the station of Aix-les-bains, and gazing
at your dear selves again, and walking with you and the dogs along the paths
under your terrace and everywhere.

Devotedly, devotedly

Thornton

P.S.

I sent to you with a letter of introduction, Charlie Lederer. He is a good
friend of mine, but the very apple of Aleck's eye. He is the nephew of Marion
Davies and astonishingly repeats her Botticelli-esque oval. But he is very
famous in Hollywood for his enormous practical jokes and impertinences. I
think you will be delighted some afternoon by his (to me—dazzling) non-
chalance. He was delighted that I wrote a Hollywood writer of the WORST
DESCRIPTION. The half was not told you.[5]

T.

1. Wilder's habit was to number his works in progress with roman numerals, but the reference to
a play by a number often changes. Here, the "comedy which is almost done" is *The Merchant of
Yonkers*, Play II is *Our Town*, and Play III is probably the unfinished play "Homage to P. G. Wodehouse."

2. From 1924 on, Wilder had spent part of many summers at the MacDowell Colony. Such
ceremonial assignments as he describes here came with his growing success.

3. During the summer of 1935, Wilder and Robert Davis were reading the abridged version of
The Making Of Americans, which had been published by Harcourt Brace in 1934 (see Wilder to Stein,

9 July 1935, n. 7). Four years earlier Wilder had tried to read the complete *Making Of Americans* and wrote to Alexander Woollcott,

> I suppose you've read the Alice B. Toklas. Well, Gertrude Stein is a fine big serene girl, is she? beyond prejudice,—beyond being touched by the world's good or bad opinion? THEN: why does she never mention that she or Miss Toklas are Jewesses? And why in the bundle of pages which were all that I could endure of that 1000 page work ("the first great book written in the future") "The Making of Americans" does she not mention that the family she is analyzing in such detail is a Jewish family. And why in fabricating a fictitious name for her family does she contrive one that only faintly might be Jewish.
>
> It's Henry Adams' wife, again. It's possible to make books of a certain fascination if you scrupulously leave out the essential. (16 September 1933, Harvard-Theatre)

4. During the run of *The Country Wife* in New York, Ruth Gordon persuaded Jed Harris to mount a production of Ibsen's *A Doll's House* for her. In an interview she said, "I had had the part vaguely in mind, but when I reread the play last season I was sure I must do it next—provided Jed Harris would direct it. He wasn't enthusiastic; still, he said he would read it on his way to Europe. He hadn't been gone more than two days when he sent me a radiogram. He was crazy about the play—only he wanted a new acting version. So he got Thornton Wilder to do it" (*New York Herald Tribune*, 13 March 1938, sec. VI, 1–2). *A Doll's House* opened at the Central City Opera House in Central City, Colorado, on 17 July 1937 and ran for 24 performances. Gordon played the role of Nora Helmer, and in that production Walter Slezak was Thorwald Helmer, Dennis King played Doctor Rank, and Sam Jaffe played Nils Krogstad. A tour of the production, with cast changes, began on 11 October at the Royal Theatre in Toronto. Paul Lukas was engaged to play Doctor Rank, and Dennis King moved to play the role of Thorwald Helmer. The tour took the cast to Detroit, Madison, Chicago, Minneapolis/St. Paul, and Cincinnati before it opened in New York at the Morosco Theatre on 27 December 1937 and ran for 144 performances. Jed Harris produced and staged the production, Donald Oenslager did the settings and costumes, and Gordon's "Tarantelle" dance was choreographed by Martha Graham. The chronology established by this and subsequent letters is at variance with Garson Kanin's article "Ruth and Thornton and 'Our Town' " in the *New York Times*, 9 January 1989, 17.

5. The letter of introduction has not survived. Lederer's mother, Reine Douras, was the sister of Marion Davies. In 1927, at the age of seventeen, he played the role of the Express Boy in Chaplin's *City Lights*. The sequence was cut from the final print, but it remained vivid in Chaplin's memory (see Robinson, *Chaplin*, 403). After a brief career as a journalist, Lederer turned to screenwriting. He eventually went on to direct and to produce films and plays.

To Thornton Wilder, New Haven, Connecticut
[Transcribed by Wilder]

[?15–16 May 1937][1]   [Bilignin par Belley
                                                                        Ain]

My dear Thornton,

        Here we are, why why are you a community man, I puzzle about that a lot and Alice says give it up but why are you a community man,[2] well anyway we wish you were here, although we are glad that the plays are getting on, I had to give [sic] Daniel Webster for while, everything was so exciting and Lord Berners was here, I can't remember did I tell you all about London well anyway there was all about London, I like a play to be played, it is [so? as?] pleasantly as pleasant of it to be on the stage, I wish you were going to be here in June, Freddy Ashton who did 4 Saints and who did the Wedding Bouquet is to be here and you would have a good time together,[3] but we could have a good time together, you come in lots in Everybody's Auto, do you like it, tell me because I must know and very soon also[?] tell me and oh we do wish you would come over over here, well anyway Gerald Berners bought [brought] a lot of [notices?] of The Wedding Bouquet and now we are sleepy all four of us so sleepy and so loving

Gtde.

1. Although this letter is transcribed after Stein's letter postmarked 17 May 1937, internal evidence suggests that it was written on either 15 or 16 May in response to Wilder's letter of 3 May and following the visit of Lord Berners. Wilder identifies the first letter as being Stein's and the following three with "Ditto" (see Stein to Wilder, received, 10 September 1936 (1), n. 1-b).

2. Stein is reacting to Wilder's complaints in his letter of 3 May about the effect on his writing of his lecture tours and his ceremonial obligations to the MacDowell Colony. To supplement his income and support his family while he was teaching at the University of Chicago he had often added a burdensome lecture load.

3. Frederick Ashton, who choreographed *A Wedding Bouquet*, Robert Helpmann, who danced the role of the Bridegroom, and William Chappell, who danced the role of John and executed the decors and costumes, visited Stein in July on their way to Austria (see Burns, *Letters*, 2:557).

To Thornton Wilder, New Haven, Connecticut
[Transcribed by Wilder]

[postmark: 17 May 1937]   Bilignin, France

My dear Thornton,

Having just written to you I kind of feel like writing to you again, you are a puzzle to me and if I could solve that puzzle I could solve the puzzle of America [answering?] that America is a puzzle yes yes as Virgil would say, listen perhaps I will do a novel about you and call it Ida about you or about Mrs Simpson, I think it is time for me to write a novel, now Mrs Simpson is not a puzzle to me but you are, but I can see that she might be a puzzle to me, so perhaps I could write that novel, come, Thornton, come, I could do it so much better with you to make commentaries but now that the Autobiography is done I must do it, I have begun, Ida, a novel,[1] do come, well anyway Alice and I [*sic*] gardening to-day and we feel a lot more cheerful oh so loving,

Gtde.

1. Stein uses similar phrasing in a letter to Robert Bartlett Haas, postmarked on the same day: "[I]n a kind of way novels are still a puzzle to me" (YCAL). *Ida A Novel* preoccupied Stein in various versions until June 1940. Wallis Warfield Simpson, whose romance with King Edward VIII elevated her to a publicity icon in the eyes of the media, no doubt played a role in Stein's meditations on the narrative. This connection was picked up by Bennett Cerf and others as a means of selling the novel. Of far greater importance, however, is Stein's effort to understand how to write narrative.

The poet bpNichol, in an essay, "When the Time Came," minutely examines the opening of the novel to show that "tho she was whimsical & had a highly developed sense of play, the whimsy & the play were part of an over-all & continuous strategy of engagement with some of the central issues of any writer's writing: the role of the I; the relationship of the role of the I to the function of narrative time; the whole issue of narrative time in general" (Neuman and Nadel, *Gertrude Stein and the Making of Literature*, 194–209). The effort to understand Wilder's personality, the "puzzle of puzzles," which may in itself be an echo of Whitman (*Song of Myself* #26), may have been absorbed into the character of Ida. Twinning, which plays a part in many Stein texts, here may be referring to Wilder, whose twin brother died at birth. The restlessness of Ida, which is a theme of the novel, may in part have been drawn from Wilder's experiences. Stein at first asked Wilder to make commentaries on the novel, in the manner they had discussed for the *Geographical History*. By July, as Stein struggled with the narrative, she proposed that they collaborate. The prospect made him uneasy.

To Gertrude Stein and Alice Toklas, Bilignin, France

30 May 1937   The Graduates Club
                                                       New Haven, Connecticut

Dear Friends.

Not only am I coming to Bilignin; but I'm coming sooner than I had expected; and my boat-passage is being paid for by the Carnegie Foundation.

I've been waiting for the Last Confirmation before I wrote you. Still that hasn't come but Dr. Keppler seems to take it as settled and I guess Foundation heads know how to hedge when there are Things Still Unsettled about; so I can assume it to be a fact.[1]

I sail from New York on the De Grasse July 3rd.

To attend the *Entretiens* in Paris, July 20th—under the Institut de Coopération Intellectuelle of the League of Nations. Paul Valéry's *agenda* are sort of hit or miss—the impoverishment of vocabularies in modern languages; the decay of syntax (let's revive the subjunctive, everybody); the inability of the moderns to understand long sentences; what radio-listening is doing to literary forms. And so on.

I'll cross those bridges when I get to them.

So August first I'm coming to see you.
Can I?

I'm going to stay at the hotel in Bellay [i.e., Belley] and write farces all morning. The rest of the day I'm going to haunt you, *invitus invitam?*[2]

———

Lord, it's all I can think about. I'm so excited.

I want to read everything Gertrude's written. . . . . I'm so much more ready to than before. . . . I've digested so much of the previous matter and made such progress.

And I want to show myself like an eager intoxicated pupil, show how the Ideas have trellised all thru my mind. I want More.

But most of all, I simply love you both and want to look at you. Tout court, I want to look at you.

———

There's only one thing that's a little disappointing about this. And that is missing July at Peterboro'. I shall be there all June, but the advantages of that place lie in duration.

June and July in that deep pine-wood is what I need most of all. I have an Arabian Night play-subject that's a house-afire, and I could only grasp it and devour it in the Green Isolation up there.[3]

———

But I've been working.

The other night I had six friends in and read them some of my new stuff and they laughed until they hurt themselves. And so did I. I never dreamt that it was as funny as that.[4]

———

Still Bennett [Cerf] doesn't send me the new autobiography. He says he must wait for it, or a copy of it, to come back from The Atlantic Monthly.

———

The Roaring Girl—Ruth Gordon is back. I talked to her on the phone and she said she'd seen you but only for a minute; but that she adored the ballet and had never seen an audience show such enthusiasm.[5]

———

———

Do start mentioning my name to the neighbors, so that things can pick up smartly at once.

And to the dogs.

And Alice, choose the part of the garden that's to be assigned to me.

Is there anything you want brought over to you?

with love

Thornton

1. Wilder replaced Frederick Paul Keppel, president of the Carnegie Corporation (1923–41), as the American delegate to the League of Nations' Institut International de Coopération Intellectuelle, 2nd Paris Conference, 20–24 July. The subject was the future of literature.

2. If you are willing.

3. He may refer to "The Hell of the Vizier Kabâar," a play about Haroun al-Raschid, an eighth-century caliph of Baghdad, on whom the caliph in the *Arabian Nights* is in part based. An incomplete manuscript of twenty pages is in the Wilder Archives in YCAL.

4. In a letter to Alexander Woollcott [31 May 1937, Harvard-Theatre], Wilder identifies them as friends from New Haven: Mr. and Mrs. Carl Rollins, Mr. and Mrs. Norman Donaldson, and Mr. and Mrs. Sidney Withington. Wilder writes, "The comedy I wrote you about [i.e., *The Merchant of Yonkers*] has suddenly gone stale on me. I think behind the clouds, it's probably as good as ever.

"I had invited some friends in to hear a reading the other night. At the last moment, I couldn't read that play, and instead read the First Acts of Play No # 3 and Play # 5—namely 'Our Town' and 'Homage to P. G. Wodehouse.'"

5. Gordon had seen A *Wedding Bouquet*.

To Thornton Wilder, New Haven, Connecticut
[Transcribed by Wilder][1]

[postmark: 9 June 1937]   Bilignin par Belley,
                                                  Ain, France

We are as happy as happy can be that it is going to be we three, nobody else is to be here then and you are to have your room and nobody will know of your xistence until lunch time and you can sit in any part of the garden you like and even Pepe will be taught to respect the solitude of a maker of dramas and you will stay and stay and we will all be happy every day, and it's lovely, and so much to say and so much love from all of us and I am awfully happy that plays are going on I like plays not so much to see as to know |??hear| and any way we do love you all of us all the time and the happy first of August and we call for you where, anywhere and so much love all of us
                    Gtde.

1. See Stein to Wilder, 10 September 1936, rec'd (1), n. 10b.

To Gertrude Stein and Alice Toklas, Bilignin, France

22 June 1937   The MacDowell Colony
                                             Peterborough, New Hampshire

Dear Gertralicitude; dear Algertrudicé:

I have something thundering to tell you, but I'm going to wait until the end of the week. A great healthful forest fire has been raging in my head all week; but this isn't a letter about that tho' I am entirely full up with it. I'll just

give you a hint: I've been r–ding the full, the glorious, the Paris edition of The
M–g of A–ns [i.e., *The Making Of Americans*]. I'm on page 867, bombs are
bursting in air. I'm full of angry feeling about anyone who reads the abbreviated edition, but I'm also full of delirious being at the showers of light and
wisdom, but I'm not going to write you about it until I've finished with David
Hersland's being a living one. [Who said they had no constructive imagination? Alice, Gertrude, who said that? There are such lightning-flashes into a
boy's growing mind that only constructive imagination, and the highest, could
ever have told.]

Such glories.

I kiss on both cheeks the great-hearted captain who made that terrible
journey and found that continent, and both cheeks of the constant untiring
crew that stood by the captain.

I long to see you. And it'll be very soon.

I leave New York a week from Saturday on the De Grasse; report to the
Institut in Paris; retire to a little hotel in Fontainebleau and draw up a memorandum on M. Paul Valéry's agenda and prepare my remarks. It's all a little
alarming for a provincial little intellectual (the stenographic report of our conversations is being published by the League of Nations),[1] but hell,—I hope my
life will be a succession of alarms, y'know what I am, one terror after another
and a laugh in every box. The minute it's over I hop a train for Aix-les-Bains.

Yes, you must have been very surprised to see Thornton getting very
upstage and touch-me-not as to whether he was staying in the house or not.
My God, he began to refer portentously to his work.

Well, I've never referred to my work before and I never will again.

That was just a mask.

A mask to cover a funny New England Trait: that I'm no house-guest; up
from my childhood rises the feeling that I'm in the way, that I'm treading on
people's toes; that I'm not free to rise up and take my dawn-walks (Don't
misunderstand that=that's DAWN); that no one can continue liking me for ten
hours at a stretch,——a whole series of oddities that all the Wilder children
possess and that our Ma has even worse than we have.

But if you like I'll try and relax and stay with you.

But, Lord, don't let it constrain you: let there be anyone else in the house
you like; signal to me any hour of the day or night.

However I can't write you much of a letter, because I'm so full of the next
letter I want to write.

[The worst thing about being in this colony is that now Mr. Robinson's
dead there's no one to talk to.[2] It's awful. Fifteen writers and painters and
composers and no one to talk to, just now when I want terribly to talk to
someone about Gertrude and the book.

However, last night I gathered three poetesses and a sculptress around me and read them passages—culled from the elaborate index I've made in the fly-leaves.[3]

And when I read the definitions of the two fundamental types of being, one woman gave a cry like she'd been transfixed. She'd been looking for that all her life.]

At Salzburg I'm to hear again, and twice, and under Toscanini, Verdi's Falstaff. Oh, oh, a tumult of wit and skill and worthy of Shakespeare, and written at the age of eighty. Here I am tip-toe-ing into adolescence at forty, so there's hope for me. Say there's hope for me; swear it on the Bible.

Now, it's five o'clock and I must leave my stoodio (you should hear the hermit-thrushes as evening comes on) and I must go up to the Hall and have supper amid my fellow-pensioners, and after supper I make them play anagrams so as to discourage cultured conversation; I shoo all the hens around a table and then there's grim silence for two hours.

More soon; but early and late
lots of love
Thornton

1. The proceedings of the conference, presided over by Paul Valéry, were published in *Le Destin prochain des lettres*, Bulletin no. 8 of the Institut International de Coopération Intellectuelle (Paris, 1938). Wilder's remarks at the sessions "Langage et Milieu" and "L'Écrivain: sa situation matérielle et morale dans le monde moderne" appear on pages 30–32 and 80–81. His paper on the state of letters in the United States is on pages 267–70.

2. Wilder met Edwin Arlington Robinson, a long-time resident of the MacDowell Colony, during his first stay in 1924. He admired him and enjoyed conversations and walks with him.

3. Wilder's copy of the complete *Making Of Americans* was not in his library at the time of his death (see also Wilder to Stein, 24 June 1937).

To Gertrude Stein, Bilignin, France
[TELEGRAM]

[24 June 1937][1]
[postmark, Belley: 25 June 1937]

[The MacDowell Colony]
Peterbor[ough] N[ew] Hamp]shire]

JUST FINISHED LONGER MAKING AMERICANS WONDERFUL GLORIOUS LOVE
THORNTON

1. This telegram, received in Belley on the twenty-fifth, was probably sent on the twenty-fourth.

To Gertrude Stein and Alice Toklas, Bilignin, France

24 June 1937   The Veltin Studio,
                                                The MacDowell Colony
                                                Peterborough, New Hampshire.

Dear Friends:

Now I have finished the book. It is a very great book. Everybody should read it and go to school to it and learn to see and hear by it and go to sleep in it and wake up in it. And some day every body will. What a wonderful thing it would be to live to be a hundred and so watch that book slowly and certainly entering into everybody's mind.

It is entirely a different book from the shortened version. I greatly admired that, but in an entirely different way and less. No one should be allowed to read that. I remember thinking that the story of Redfern and Miss Charles and Miss Downer and Martha was unclear and an upsetting departure into a different rhythm (movement as you call it), but in this version it's not only right, but it's wonderful.

The greater part of the book I read rivetted, my tongue hanging out, and every now and then I would jump up and cry aloud. Almost all of it is powerful and long stretches are beautiful, the few very few places where it is less than powerful are the places I know so well from the conferences at the University of Chicago and that I call "striking matches"—inviting an idea, provoking an idea that is not ready to come. But Thornton way off in a New Hampshire log-cabin is not marking any drastic disparagement: "striking matches" goes on in Don Quixote, Rabelais, and War and Peace, and they too, are what they are.

The fifty pages where Alfred Hersland refuses to become a whole one— and where I groaned in sympathy—are not among these intermissions, for the author turns aside and flings terrible and wonderful descriptions of similar or allied beings and are among the greatest pages in the book.

Yes, I read it with the same breathless absorption with which I last read both parts of Don Quixote. Then too, I made lists, appendices, notes, a whole apparatus. And the absorption was not troubled by the fact that for long stretches at a time I was not understanding it all. Even the primary distinction between Dependent Independents and Independent Dependents is not constantly clear to me; it comes and goes and sometimes it comes with terrific impact and sometimes I'm all upset and distressed and lose it.

But Lord! how well I know that I'm a slow digester. How many of Gertrude's ideas have taken a whole year to flower in me; but when they come they come to stay and they grow and cover whole hillsides and reproduce their kind.

And how wonderful it is to see in this book the first appearances of later ideas and later books. There's the doctrine of the audience approaching on pages 430, 485 and 666. There's recognition on page 486. There's an important light on G. Stein's use of the word "description" on page 744. And how inevitable, one can see, is coming the necessity of writing in another way—the way that was to break through suddenly in the middle of a Long Gay Book.[1]

Already in these three weeks I have been so sharpened in my listening, using as best I can the "grammar" that has been put into my hands that I feel like a new being. And I look forward to a year, two years, from now when the descriptions will have circulated all through me and when I shall similarly be understanding so much better the Portraits and Prayers and The Geography of America[.]

So I send to the two stout-hearted beings who did all that for me, for us, all my love and obligation and look forward to being with them.

Ever your
Thornton

1. "A Long Gay Book," written by Stein between spring 1908 and summer 1912, was not published until 1932 in the Plain Edition volume G.M.P.: Matisse Picasso And Gertrude Stein With Two Shorter Stories. According to Leon Katz, "The first entry to what I take to be the Long Gay Book is in the third entry of a notebook that dates between June and December of 1908 It reads: 'Short note for long book, a history of everybody.' Seems sufficient to guarantee that it's a note for LGB. . . . [I]t's got to be that LGB was already being written during the early stages of The Making of Americans, to be precise, during the writing of the first chapter of the novel, or before the writing of published page 149 (which ends the 'Mr. and Mrs. Hersland' chapter. . . . Further proof: a few pages further on in the same notebook, this entry: 'Bring out strongly in both books the difference between follower and leader, between individual egotists and school.' The only two books she could have been working on were MA and LGB" (letter, received 16 February 1993).

During an impasse in the writing of the Alfred Hersland chapter of The Making Of Americans, Stein announces, "[S]ometime I am going to write a book and it will be a very long one and it will be all full up, completely filled up with pairs of them twos of them, sometimes threes and fours and fives but mostly with twos of them, twos of men, of women, of women and men, of men and women" (549). This book became "A Long Gay Book" and in its first part Stein's themes parallel those of The Making Of Americans. She uses friends, relatives, college classmates, and members of her Paris circle as subjects for her probing analysis of the basic elements of personality. But gradually, she moves on to devise a language describing the act of composition itself. This struggle becomes a significant theme in much of Stein's writing.

To Gertrude Stein and Alice Toklas, Bilignin, France

10th [July 1937]   Approaching Cobh
Sat[urday] noon.   à bord, le De Grasse

Dear Mirours of freindship:[1]

A pleasant fretful idiotic crossing.

Exploring all the nullity of conversation: the conversation-stupifying; the conversation pseudo-intimate; the conversation equal-to-equal-we-agree; the conversation badinage-I-hate-you.

Read two very good books: *L'histoire des mes pensées* of Alain and Mencken's *The American Language*.[2]

Made chemical tests on myself drinking Pernods.

Tried tests on people rê Dependent-Independent, Independent-Dependent. Becoming very clever at it. A wonderful key to unlock "listening."

Already in France: in smoking room asked for coffee: the cups brought us still retained the lipstick on the rims left by the previous drinkers. Lady with me sends them back to be washed, with violent moral indignation; steward apologizes with mock-consternation, but doesn't give a damn. On a Cunarder the steward would have thrown himself into the sea, all Britain having been wounded through him.

Samuel Insull is on board: the 300 million dollar bankrupt. Great apoplectic rages against the servants over a delayed grape-fruit. Napoleon on St. Helena.[3]

Later in Paris
[13 July 1937]

Am at Hotel Buckingham again 43 rue des Mathurins; (sort of behind the Madeleine)

My "meetings" begin a week from today.

Not a sole knows I'm in town exc. a few people off the ship with whom I celebrate the Quatorze tomorrow.[4]

I think of you all the time and can't wait for these extra things to be over. Is it most convenient for you that I come by Aix-les-Bains; or have you some other suggestion?

Yours for ever
Thornton

1. The misspellings are Wilder's affectation.

2. Alain was the pseudonym of the French philosopher Emile-August Chartier, whose *Histoire de mes pensées* was published by N.R.F., Gallimard, in Paris in 1936. H. L. Mencken's *The American Language: An Inquiry into the Development of English in the United States* was published in 1919. The fourth edition appeared in 1936.

3. Samuel Insull, at one time private secretary to Thomas A. Edison, controlled various utility companies. Three of his largest companies went into receivership in 1932; he was indicted, avoided arrest for two years, and was tried and acquitted in 1935.

4. In a letter to his family on 8 July 1937 (YCAL), Wilder mentions various people on the ship known to the family. On board, too, were two friends of Alexander Woollcott, Elizabeth Duval and Terry Lewis. According to his date book, Wilder celebrated the Quatorze Juillet with them.

To Gertrude Stein and Alice Toklas, Bilignin, France

16 July 1937   Hotel Buckingham
                                                43 rue des Mathurins
                                                [Paris, France]

DEAR ONES:

What is it? Do they mix perfume with the street cleaners' disinfectant? My nostrils keep trembling like a rabbit's all day.

———

I go to a theatre every night to improve my French. And all day I sit in on the Sessions at the Institute where I hear
   Chinese French
   Roumanian French
   Brazilian French
      etc.
Next week they want me to do my stuff in French, but I guess I won't. I'll lean on the translator.

———

Georges Duhamel has been added to the list of delegates. He wrote the ugliest travel book that has ever been written about the U.S.A. There's a fight I shall enjoy. And if he hits below the belt, I shall have to draw on certain responses I have all ready.[1]

———

The exposition!!![2]
When a Frenchman thinks of the two words COQUET and GALA the gods suddenly strike him with madness.

———

There are two darlin' American girls who are driving South, and I asked them to stop in [to] ask you for a cup of tea, but they're terrified of you.
I took them about town the night of Bastille Day to see the dancing in the streets. My, they're nice and they love you sight-unseen, but they have the hearts of field-mice when it comes to calling on you.[3]

———

I enclose a clipping which I think will give my dear San Francisco girls a lot of pleasure.[4]
Pleasure! That's what I live for! My watchword! and I'm hurrying down to get it from your eyes as soon as I can.
                         affectionately
                         Thornton
POST-SCRIPTUM The ***Venus de Milo is a very good statue and I agree with Baedecker that it should have three asterisks.
                         T. N. W.

1. Georges Duhamel of the Académie française was one of thirteen writers who participated in the conference. His *Scènes de la vie future* (Paris: Mercure de France), a satire on American life, won the Grand Prix de l'Académie française in 1930.

2. Forty-four nations participated in the Paris Exposition of 1937, officially titled Exposition Internationale des Arts et des Techniques dans la Vie Moderne. The exhibition opened in May and by the time it closed in November, more than thirty-one million people had visited it. The Palais de Chaillot and the buildings of Les Musées d'Art Moderne (now known as the Palais de Tokyo and the Musée d'Art Moderne de la Ville de Paris) are several buildings that remain today.

3. Elizabeth Duval and Terry Lewis.

4. The clipping has not remained with the letter.

To Thornton Wilder, Paris, France
[Transcribed by Wilder][1]

[postmark: 18 July 1937]   [Bilignin par Belley
                                                                             Ain]

Dearest Thornton,

        will you but you would never say no to me but will you really will you, ever since my earliest days when I read Erckman Chatrian's l'Ami Fritz in what language I do not know I have loved the word collaborate and I always always wanted to and now will you oh Thornton will you will you collaborate on Ida the Novel,[2] we must do it together not now like you did the commentaries the other [facsimile. . . . . . ?] but really and really and truly just like Erckman and Chatrian,[3] a really truly novel is too much for me all alone we must do it together, how we will talk about it and talk about it oh dear it will be wonderful to collaborate at last, you would not say no Thornton and worse still you would not do no, just think how we could do Ida a novel together and what a theme, and please tell Sybil Colefax that if she is en route while you are here it would be such a pleasure to have her stop with us on the way, xplaining of course that it is rough and rude a common bathroom and no maids or luxuries, but plenty of fresh air food and us, I am writing this at the mystic moment when little Thornton is sitting [serenely?] at the conference-table just about to speak 11:30 of Monday morning, god bless our little Thornton and make him stout of heart and loving is his nature god bless him all of us

Gtde.

Give our love to Marie Louise Bousquet[4]

1. See Stein to Wilder, rec'd (1), 10 September 1936, n. 1-d.

2. From May until December 1937, Stein struggled with the first version of *Ida A Novel*. In her papers at YCAL there are three, possibly four, drafts of this first version. Stein wrote at least two more before she completed the novel in June 1940 (see Stein to Wilder, 17 May 1937).

3. Emile Erckmann and Alexandre Chatrian achieved fame as joint authors of novels and plays.

They began their collaboration in 1847 and had their first success with their novel *L'Illustre Docteur* in 1859.

4. Wilder was introduced by Lady Colefax to Marie-Louise Bousquet, a Parisian hostess and at one time Paris editor of *Harper's Bazaar*.

To Gertrude Stein and Alice Toklas, Bilignin, France

[?18 July 1937]　　　　　　　　　　　　　　　Hotel Buckingham
Sunday Morning　　　　　　　　　　　　　34 [i.e., 43] rue des Mathurins
　　　　　　　　　　　　　　　　　　　　　　[Paris]

Dear Friends:

All the ten people I know in Paris have left Paris, so I'm a little lonely and cranky and shall write a letter.

The two American girls have rented a car and gone South.[1] The lady I sat at table with on the boat has gone to Holland. Sibyl Colefax has gone with some worldlings to visit some worldlings in the country. Last night I hardly slept a wink and at four-thirty could be found sitting up in bed reading *A Long Gay Book*. I never have been able to sleep well in the great city of Paris anyway—I who sleep perfectly everywhere else in the world.

I've seen a lot of paintings. The new Palais des Arts; the Petit Palais—so proud to see that Gertrude is on the Comité d' Action and has all those pictures there;[2] the El Greco show;[3] and the Maitres Populaires show from Grenoble.[4]

The insomnia last night was partly do [i.e., due] to the impertinent champagne of Giraudoux's *Electre*, a lot of adorable pirouetting under the great vaults of the fearful story. As one critic said of Sophocles' treatment of the same subject: a mixture of matricide and high spirits.[5]

Yesterday I took out one of my American girls and Madame Bousquet and gave them a delicious and expensive luncheon at Lucas'. When Mme Bousquet knew I knew you she opened her not exactly inert arms and gave me a big kiss. (Lord! seems like I spend a great deal of my time meditatively brushing lip-stick off my cheeks). I liked her very much.

Very interesting thing happened:

Two of the personages that have some bearing on *Ida: A Novel* almost collided.

Conversation in a taxi:

Sibyl: Now I have something very embarrassing to lay before you. The couple at Bessalogne ((my guess as to this name)) has asked us to come and stay with them.

Thornton ?

Sibyl. I can't imagine how they knew. I don't suppose there are four people in all London whom I told that I was to be seeing you in Salzburg. But they seem to have heard of it some way. She writes ". . . and we should like it very much if you bring Mr. Thornton Wilder with you."

Thornton ?

Sibyl Why, the Windsors.

Thornton !!!!!

Sibyl But I really don't recommend it, unless for curiosity etc you would like to. On the way down to Italy I shall arrange to stop over for lunch. It represents many *gênes* [embarrassments] of all kinds. . . . . friends whom I perfectly adore, but who have made one foolish mistake after another. . . . . They don't really speak our language. . . and I can't say I really recommend it, but since the invitation was sent I merely pass it on to you.

—

Wasn't that a funny thing?

Banquet de Tantale; banquet barmécide.[6]

—

Tomorrow at 10:30 I shall be sitting at the conference table.[7] Shall I be called on soon? I have about six little speeches all ready, depending on which direction the discussion takes.

Oh, and I've stolen from Gertrude's ideas with both hands. Yes, defense of the American's right to remake himself a language from the fabric of the English language, with a diagram of the difference between the American and English minds. All Gertrude. And in answer to Paul Valery's question as to how the masterpieces of the future will be paid for in an age when there are no patrons, no élite and so on, I rush in with a garbled account of the doctrine that there never has been any relation between the moment of creation and the element of audience and I deduce some of the practical implications. Gertrude's inadequate but adoring little *beau page, chevalier errant*, and missioner. I feel like some brand-new Chinese convert, ardent but immature, who tears about Nanking mixing up his lessons pêle-mêle and saying that a Christian must turn his back on his family, expect the end of the world any minute, and must lose no opportunity to provoke his own martyrdom.

I wish I were safe and sound in Bilignin, that's what I wish.

Or sitting of a morning on a terrasse in Belley waiting for a car to come hurtling by, containing two busy shoppers that I love.

Or that we three were ensconced therein roaming the countryside searching for chevalier-fish, or for rural ancestral pâtés.

That's what I wish.

Love

Thornton

1. Elizabeth Duval and Terry Lewis.

2. The Musée d'Art Moderne de la Ville de Paris and the Musée Nationale d'Art Moderne were constructed as part of the exposition of 1937. The Petit Palais housed the Musée des Beaux-Arts de la Ville de Paris in addition to providing space for temporary exhibitions. As part of the exposition, the City of Paris organized an exhibition, *Les Maîtres de l'Art Indépendant, 1895–1937*, at the Petit Palais. Raymond Escholier, conservator of the museum, invited Stein on 18 January 1937 (YCAL) to become a member of the organizing committee. Stein accepted and attended the first meeting on 20 January. The archives of the Petit Palais indicate that she attended subsequent meetings and participated in discussions about which artists and works should be included in the exhibition. Stein lent two works by Picabia, two works by Juan Gris, and one by Matisse to the exhibition, which was to have lasted from June until October but was extended through December.

Of the thirty-two works by Picasso in the exhibition, Stein lent eleven. In addition, two small chairs and a footstool with needlepoint by Toklas after designs of Picasso were lent. The signed receipt of delivery (3 May 1937, YCAL) differs slightly from the catalogue listing of works lent by Stein.

3. The Gazette des Beaux-Arts organized an El Greco exhibition that opened in their gallery in June 1937. More than fifty works were exhibited, including nine from the royal collection of the king of Roumania that had never been publicly shown.

4. An exhibition entitled *Les Maîtres Populaires de la Réalité*, organized by the Musée de Grenoble, was held at the Salle Royale in Paris from June to September. Among the artists were Henri Rousseau, Louis Vivin, André Bauchant, Maurice Utrillo, and Camille Bombois. Different versions of this exhibition were later seen at the Kunsthaus in Zurich and the Museum of Modern Art in New York.

5. Jean Giraudoux's *Electre* opened at the Théâtre de l'Athénée-Louis Jouvet on 13 May 1937. Louis Jouvet played the role of Le Mendiant and also directed the play. Wilder attended a performance of the play on 15 July with Lady Colefax and her traveling companion, Violet Leconfield (Wilder to family, 16 July 1937, YCAL).

6. Lady Colefax met Wallis Warfield Simpson in the summer of 1935. A year later, she gave a dinner for the Prince of Wales and Simpson at her home, Argyll House. The prince responded by inviting her to dinner at St. James' Palace. Lady Colefax's intimacy with King Edward VIII and Simpson is detailed in many of her letters to Wilder (see also chapter 6, "Means and Ends," in McLeod, *A Passion for Friendship*). After their wedding, on 3 June 1937, the Duke and Duchess of Windsor spent their honeymoon at Schloss Wasserleonburg, near Villach in the Austrian Alps, a castle rented from Lady Colefax's friend Peggy Ward, a former business associate, now Countess Munster. In almost identical language, Wilder repeated this conversation to his family in a letter of 19 July 1937 (YCAL). Wilder comments ironically how tantalizing it is to have been invited to a banquet by the Windsors, already deprived of station and title like the Barmecides.

7. This part of the letter may have been written on Monday, 19 July, because the conference began on Tuesday, 20 July.

To Gertrude Stein and Alice Toklas, Bilignin, France

[?20 July 1937]   [Hotel Buckingham
                                                                   43 rue des Mathurins
                                                                   Paris, France]

Dear Friends:

In Gertrude's prayer for my success Gertrude spelled God with a small letter but He was not offended: He did what she asked.[1]

This morning was one of those French Ouvertures Solennelles. We had a Ministre, and Herriot and the Bibliotheque.² Lots of "amitiés" and lots of "culture française" and lots of wit.

This afternoon real work began and within an hour a secretary whispered in my ear: "Le Président (Paul Valéry) espère que vous prendrez la parole après M. de Madariaga."

It was on languages and the peculiar phenomenon in American English. So I took the floor, made a defence of the American language, and against all the rules of the conference I was applauded.

But now let me tell you: it was all Gertrude's. Yes, there was the divergence of the American nature from the English; the nomad American with his so difference [i.e., different] sense of time, and his long struggle to reshape the language to suit his nature. When I came to the formula: ["]An Englishman hopes that tomorrow will be like today, if but only a little better; but an American, even a happy one, hopes that tomorrow will be quite different from today," Mr. Gilbert Murray and Mr. M. E. Forster [i.e., E. M.] laughed delightedly and M. Valéry turned with pleased amusement to his right and his left.³

So I kiss the hands of my dear inspiratrix and thank her for the thousandth time for her help.

———

As to a collaboration, Lord knows there is no length to which I would not go to be beside, to watch and to be stimulated by such a collaborator; but all the time I should be feeling: oh, when will she find out how inadequate I am.

I should love to, if I felt within me, deep within me, in those realms beyond persuasion and reassurance, that I could, could *produce* and *share* and add good things alongside her good things.

I certainly don't say *no* yet I tremble to say *yes*.

So I am thinking about it all the time.⁴

All my loving best

Thornton

1. See Stein to Wilder, postmarked 18 July 1937.

2. In the printed record of the conference, *Le Destin Prochain des Lettres*, the "Discours Officiels" are printed on pages 203–16. Among the speakers were François de Tessan, Sous-Secrétaire d'Etat aux affaires étrangères, and Edouard Herriot, Président du Conseil d'Administration de l'Institut International de Coopération Intellectuelle. Whom Wilder means by "Bibliotheque" is not clear; possibly Julien Cain, director of the Bibliothèque Nationale, made a brief speech of welcome.

3. Paul Valéry, president of the Permanent Committee of Arts and Letters of the League of Nations, chaired the meeting. In the first session, "Langage et Milieu," Wilder spoke directly after remarks by Salvador de Madariaga (for Wilder's contributions to the conference, see *Le Destin Prochain des Lettres* in Wilder bibliography). Gilbert Murray, formerly professor of Greek philosophy at Oxford University, was president of the Commission Internationale de Coopération Intellectuelle. E. M. Forster was one of the invited writers.

4. Wilder did not collaborate with Stein on *Ida A Novel*, but they talked about it in both Bilignin

and Paris. Perhaps before he left Paris in November, Wilder put down what had transpired in conversations with Stein. The pages are in YCAL (see Appendix VI; see also Stein to Wilder [17 May 1937], n. 1, and Stein to Wilder [18 July 1937], n. 1).

To Thornton Wilder, Paris, France
[Transcribed by Wilder][1]

[postmark 25 July 1937]   [Bilignin par Belley
                                                            Ain]

My dearest Thornton,

        Oh no no nice god could mind a small g they know that a small g is natural,[2] and now day by day you are coming near and any day almost any day here we will be and collaborating, oh happy day, how are you coming, where are you coming, when are you coming let us know and all four of us will be there and so happy to see Thornton so much to say but will have to tell then

                        Gtde.

    1. See Stein to Wilder, rec'd (1), 10 September 1936, n. 1-d.
    2. This letter responds to Wilder's letter of [?20 July]. See Wilder to Stein [?25 July 1937], n. 1.

To Gertrude Stein and Alice Toklas, Bilignin, France

[?25 July 1937]   [Hotel Buckingham
                                                            43 rue des Mathurins
                                                            Paris, France]

Dear Friends:

        god willing I shall be with you soon and I am looking forward to it with a wild bound.[1]

        But first a funny thing must take place that looks almost like treachery.

        You remember those two nice girls. Well, one of 'em—a high-paid high-speed girl in Radio-programs—came over after a nervous breakdown from overwork. Kinda convalescent. And there were fine talks on the boat, and I guess I talked to her more earnestly about work and LIFE than she'd been talked to for a long time.

        And like always I'm a great weakling about saying good bye. So I said I'd meet them again, on the 30th. They've driven a car to Sa[i]nte-Maxime-sur-mer, but must be back in Paris by the 2nd of August. So I said I'd meet them on the 30th in Aix-les-Bains.

I felt in my bones it was TREACHERY to be so near you and yet not with you. But I didn't see what else I could do. So all the 30th I shall be walking up and down Mt Revard with Terry Lewis and Eliz[abeth]. Duval. Then the morning of the 31st I shall say goodbye to them as they drive back to Paris; and Pepe and Basquet and their protectrices can come to Aix-les-Bains and please take lunch with me. I shall be at that same hotel facing the station on the Station Square. Is that treachery? I hope not.[2]

With fiery anticipation

Thornton

1. The game of the lowercase g begins in Stein's letter of 18 July, is commented upon by Wilder in his letter of [?20 July], and again by Stein in her letter of 25 July.

2. Stein invited Lewis and Duval to a lunch at Bilignin before they left for Paris (see Lewis to Stein, on board *Europa*, 7 August [1937 YCAL]).

To Gertrude Stein and Alice Toklas, Bilignin, France

17 Aug[ust] 1937   Carlton Elite Hotel
                                                 Zurich [Switzerland]

                                     ". . . and Zurich is my
                                     hometown."

Dear One and One:

Though I took my leave of you many years ago, the grief is as fresh as though it were yesterday.

Much has happened since, however.

I traversed a level country, Switzerland, with so few elevations that certainly it would have taken the name Netherlands had it not already been adopted elsewhere.

As soon as the train got into the *deutschesprachgebiet* I decided to recall and extend my German by going into the *Wagonrestaurant* entir[e]ly covered by signs that read *Non sputare nella carozza* and had a White HORSE WISHKY. So, thoroughly Germanised, I went back to my place.[1]

When I arrived in Zurich I was surprised to find that it had no more mountains about it than the rest of Switzerland; but that it did have a darling lake and was crossed by dozens of streams full of swans.

In fact, it's a lovely town. Like Munich—though they're both big cities—it's so quiet that it's like a city under snow. The store windows are square, handsome and everything on display is hideous beyond words—the women's clothes, the florists' bouquets, the paintings, the shoes, everything. So I knew it was the town for me. A town without Art and a town without Taste, Oh City of my Adoption, here I pitch my tent.

The streets have been manicured with chamois and pumice. The directions for traffic are so clear and ingenious and radiant that it would take a whole letter to describe them. The citizens—especially the girls—are all homely, but there are signs that they like one another and are ready to like me.

There are some old leaning-gabled, polychromed-balconied streets. I went up one of them inhaling Grimm's Märchen and came up against

MARY'S GOOD FRIENDS' BAR: OVERSEAS ENTRANCE with a BODEGA CATA-LANA next door to it.[2]

The food's awful, but I guess all food's awful when you come away from Bilignin.

Tomorrow I go on to Salzburg.

I've bought a hat, so never mind the other.

Perhaps my glasses are in the breast-pocket of one of my other suits. I suddenly thought of that. They're at the station.

It's going to take a lot of letters to tell you what a good nourishing galvanizing time I had over to your house, so I'll just touch on the subject lightly now.

Tell the Rogerses[3] that they're in my prayers.

I miss you and go for long thought-walks about you.

Love

Thorny

1. Entering the German-speaking region of Switzerland, Wilder practices his language skill by going to the dining car, reading the Italian sign, "Do not spit in the car," and ordering a White Horse Whiskey, written in his imitation gothic script.

2. Wilder boxed each of the capitalized phrases in this line. Mary's Bar, behind St. Peter's Church in the old town of Zurich, was an arty bar friendly to Americans.

3. Anticipating a trip to France, Rogers ("the Kiddie") wrote to Stein that he wanted to return to the places they had seen together when they first met in World War I: "[T]here's only one thing I really want. And that is to go back to Arles and Orange and Les Baux with Gertrude Stein and Alice B. Toklas and Mrs. Kiddie" (n.d., probably May 1937, YCAL). Rogers and his wife arrived in Bilignin on 15 August; Wilder had been there since 31 July. On 16 August William and Mildred Rogers, Stein, and Toklas drove Wilder to Geneva and after a few days in Bilignin made a three-day tour of Provence.

To Thornton Wilder, Salzburg, Austria
[Transcribed by Wilder][1]
[Postcard]

[postmark: 25 August 1937]   [Bilignin par Belley
                                                               Ain]

Here we are all sitting around and missing you, we had a lovely trip in
Provence remembering everything and ending up at the Pyramide[2] where we
missed you some more and a lot of it. I have been meditating a lot even so, and
a little is more nearly there than it was, when do you get back to Zurich, you(r)
(?word) (vests) the non-recommended ones, since at the Hotel Pernollet for a
night and a meal, and the (Bryinte)[3] was all xcited about it, almost as much so
as at an accident, otherwise well naturally there is no otherwise tell us about it,
and when do you get back to Zurich you seem nearer there which is a comfort
and lots of love always

                              Gtde.

    1. See Stein to Wilder, rec'd (1), 10 September 1936, n. 1-d.
    2. The Restaurant de la Pyramide in Vienne, not far from Lyons, opened in 1922. Chez Point, as
it was often referred to after its owner, was for more than thirty years one of the great restaurants in
France.
    3. In this postcard Wilder had difficulty deciphering Stein's handwriting. The vest is mentioned
in subsequent letters.

To Gertrude Stein and Alice Toklas, Bilignin, France

26 Aug[ust] 1937   Poste Restante
                                                              Salzburg [Austria]

Dear Endeared Dears:

           So at last I decided to buy some stationery and resume
correspondence.

    I've changed unrecognizably.

    For the worse.

    I've decided to live entirely for pleasure.

    Yes.

    Never try to think again. Never try to write again. Just pleasure.

    The other night after a performance of *Falstaff*, wonderful, too, I went as
one must, to the Mirabell Bar.[1] Went into the Casino and gambled a little,
cosi cosà, then sat drinking and talking with friends until the Bar closed. No
one wanted to go home; so we went, as all true Dedicated Drinkers must after

curfew, to the IIIrd Class waiting-room at the Railway Station, and there we sat until eight in the morning. The party was slightly mixed. It consisted of Erich Maria Remarque, the author of "All Quiet on the Western Front," and Carl Zuckmayer, author of Der Hauptmann von Köpernick, an elegant play; and a wonderful German Archbishop—incognito and in *civil*—on obligatory vacation; and Frau Tal, my German publisher; and a Swedish streetwalker. Just us. At 4:45 every morning Mass is read in the Station for the line workers, and the Host was solemnly carried among the outstretched legs of us dogs, no disrespect to Pépé.

Pleasure comes in all shapes and sizes and it's now what I live for. For instance: there are two polychrome baroque archangels on the altar of the Peterskirche in poses of flight and ecstacy that no human body could ever assume, and as far as I'm concerned they're my definition of ART. For instance: the meals in Austria are deplorable, deplorable, but the Sacher-torte and the cup of chocolate that goes with it at the Café Tomaselli (founded 1704— Mozart as a child, played with the little Tomasellis and no doubt lingered about when the cakes came out of the oven)—pleasure, that's what they are, pleasure, and that's what I live for.

After the close of the Festival on the 31st I'm going to linger in town a week.

Do you think I will ever regain my Former Viewpoint?

Anyway New or Old I count you among my Pleasures, and that's what I live for.

> Your
> Thornton

1. Wilder attended the performance of Verdi's *Falstaff* on 23 August with Lucy Tal, the wife of his German publisher. This experience is mentioned in letters of 24 August to Mrs. Murray W. Crane (YCAL), 26 August to his family (YCAL), and 29 August to Alexander Woollcott (Harvard-Theatre).

To Thornton Wilder, Zurich, Switzerland
[Transcribed by Wilder][1]

[postmark: 28 August 1937]   [Bilignin par Belley
                                                           Ain]

My dear Thornton,

The Kiddies have been and gone, the sentimental voyage was a perfect success and now once more I am left to Woodward and to Ida,[2] and here we are always here we are, it is getting vaguer and vaguer but a little fuller and now I have the proofs of Everybody's (sic) to correct,[3] and then you will be back in Zurich and I will be plein for collaboration, Gray's Elegy is good, I do not know quite just why just now I feel that way about it but I do, I wish you had been with us on the sentimental (sic) that would have been nice. We have been meeting a lot of feminist french (?) rather cunning wish you were here for their party tomorrow,[4] we love you a lot and we are fearfully proud of the clean path made by Thornton, lots and lots of love

Gtde.

Have decided to spend the winnings on a new jack for the car the one we had trouble [?gutter] so much and it would seem right that the winnings should go to that[5]

Gtde.

1. See Stein to Wilder, rec'd (1), 10 September 1936, n. 1-d.
2. Woodward, one of the men in Ida's life, appears in chapters 5 and 6 of part 1.
3. Belle Becker of Random House wrote Stein on 5 August 1937 that she was sending the galleys for correction. The corrected galleys were received by Cerf on 15 September, and *Everybody's Autobiography* was published on 2 December 1937.
4. In a letter to Stein [?3 August 1938] (YCAL), W. G. Rogers recounts some of the things they did together in August 1937 and mentions, "We also went to Chambéry, and to Mme Machard's the go-getting feminist, and to top it all off we went to the midi Friday, Saturday, and Sunday." Stein attended a meeting of La Femme Nouvelle at Aix-les-Bains in mid-September (see Stein to Wilder, 17 September 1937). On Saturday, 20 November, Wilder had lunch at Stein's with the Duchesse de Clermont-Tonnerre and Louise Weiss, a leading advocate of women's rights and founder of La Femme Nouvelle. We have not located any correspondence between Stein and Weiss (see Stein to Wilder, 14 November 1937).
5. Stein and Wilder had gambled at the casino at Aix-les-Bains. An admission card is in the Wilder Archives at YCAL.

To Gertrude Stein and Alice Toklas, Bilignin, France

[?31 August 1937]   [? Salzburg, Austria]

DEARS:

This "Lefty"—is a rich man (went to school with me in S[outhern]. California in 1912!) who is now the world's authority on Horace Walpole and is preparing an immense definitive edition of the Letters that supercedes the Paget-Toynbees'. He owns scores of 'em; has built a Strawberry Hill Printing Press in his back yard, and is a fine fellow. I modestly accept your thanks for the decoding of his holograph.

I wrote you yesterday so all that I'll add is that I'm still happy.

devotedly
Thornton[1]

1. Wilder's note to Stein follows a handwritten letter to him of 24 August 1937 by Wilmarth S. "Lefty" Lewis (Yale '18), chairman of the Yale Library Associates. The letter, on Library Associates' stationery, was written from his home in Farmington, Connecticut. In June Wilder had given the Yale library the autographed manuscripts of the first and second versions of *The Woman of Andros* (see *New York Times*, 17 June 1937, 16) and deposited in the library manuscripts of "Notes of a Roman Student" (*The Cabala*), *The Bridge of San Luis Rey*, *The Queens of France*, *The Happy Journey to Trenton and Camden*, and *The Long Christmas Dinner*. Knowing that Stein was concerned for the safety of her manuscripts, Wilder may have sought assurances that the Yale library would accept her papers before proposing the idea to her. Perhaps as an incentive, he deposited three typescripts that Stein had sent him—*Four In America*, "An American And France," and "What Are Masterpieces"—in the library (see Wilder to Andrew Keogh, 14 June 1937, YCAL). During his visit in July, Wilder discussed the proposed gift with Stein and, with her agreement, wrote Lewis on 5 August. His letter is a reply to that "postal":

Dear Thornton,

On getting back from the Old Country this morning (where I found masses of H[orace] W[alpole]'s MSS. your very welcome postal of May 5 was peeping shyly out from the pile of mail. I am writing again in the panoply of this note paper to assure you that we shall receive with open arms Miss Stein's MSS. (I don't mean to be voluptuous). You need not wait to hear from the good Gilbert about this to extend to Miss Stein Yale's ecstatically eager attitude in the matter. If these Mss should come there would be waltzing in the Aldis Collection, where one of the more sought-after waltzers is The Woman of Andros. Have I made it quite clear: Yale would be honored & flattered to be the recipient of these all-important treasures. And I think you may truthfully say to Miss Stein that no other place in the U.S.A. has so rich a store already of American Literature or is more actively interested in supplementing it with the MSS of outstanding contemporary authors. Bless you for proposing it to her!

Please adjust your mind *now* to a day, at least, here when you come back. I think you'd like it, & we'd love to have you.

Yours,
Lefty.

Wilder had met Lewis when he entered the Thacher School in Ojai, California, in 1912. Wilder's older brother, Amos, already at Oberlin College by that time, had roomed with Lewis, who took a brotherly interest in Thornton. They renewed their friendship at Yale in 1917. When Lewis began the Yale Edition of Horace Walpole's correspondence, Wilder was invited to become a member of the advisory board. The "good Gilbert" was Gilbert McCoy Troxell, curator of the Yale Collection of American Literature and a college friend of Wilder's. The Aldis Collection, given to the Yale library in 1911 by Owen F. Aldis of the class of 1874, consisted of some six thousand books of first and important editions of American belles lettres.

To Gertrude Stein and Alice Toklas, Bilignin, France

3 Sept[ember] 1937   American Express Co. Zurich
                                                —
                                                Innsbruck [Austria]

Dear Kinder:

Nothing in the world is so sweet and clean as an Austrian hotel or an Austrian face—outside Vienna.

The mountains are so great and there are so many of them and they all know about music, which cannot be said of the Pyrénées, nor of Mount Shasta.

As soon as Sibyl [Colefax] arrived in Salzburg things began to move twice as fast. Great cars were sent to take us to great houses. The torches in the courtyard at Kammer that was built to welcome Charles V were lighted to welcome us.[1] (I gave your love to the von Hoffmansthal's chauffeur, and to the von Hoffmansthals and all their faces lit up.)[2]

Then Sibyl went South to see the W—nd—rs and [Bernard] Berenson[3] and I came here to collect myself for three days before going to my new home-town.

[Frederick] Prokosch was in Salzburg—very upset about the confusion in letters and telegrams. He is as nice and nicer than I thought. A few of my reservations remain.[4]

———

Part of my time at Zurich will be spent up in the mountains at Sils-Maria. I must face the fact that I shall be very lonely, but there at the least, in terrifying loneliness, Nietzsche sent out his Zarathustra into the world,—the time-bomb that took fifty years to explode and then what havoc.[5]

My loneliness will only increase my burning you-wards with my

love
Thornton

1. Schloss Kammer was a fashionable lakeside resort just outside of Salzburg on the Attersee.

2. Presumably a reference to Raimund von Hofmannsthal, younger son of the Austrian dramatist Hugo von Hofmannsthal. There is no indication that Stein knew the family.

3. See Wilder to Stein [?18 July 1937], n. 6.

4. In *Voices, A Memoir*, Prokosch writes that at Wilder's invitation he visited Stein in Bilignin in August (92–96). Prokosch had met Stein a few years earlier when he and a friend, John Lineaweaver, were in Paris (16–22). Prokosch, like Wilder, was born in Madison, Wisconsin. He came to know the Wilders, however, when his father was a professor at Yale in the early 1930s and he was working on his doctorate. Wilder was on the committee that awarded Prokosch's novel *The Seven Who Fled* the Harper Prize in 1937. Nothing in the extant Stein/Wilder/Prokosch correspondence explains the "confusion in letters and telegrams."

5. The Engadine valley in the Grisons canton of Switzerland extends for sixty miles from the Austrian border to the steep descent of the Maloja Pass toward Chiavenna and Lake Como in Italy. At an altitude of eighteen hundred meters, the valley is famous for its scenery, climate, and resorts, with elegant St. Moritz, rustic Pontresina, quiet Sils-Maria, and Sils Baselgia on Lake Sils. On the peninsula Chastè is the famous boulder inscribed to Nietzsche with his own words from "The Other Dancing Song" in part 3 of *Thus Spoke Zarathustra* (1883): "O man, take care, / What does the deep midnight declare? / I was asleep— / From a deep dream I woke and swear: / The world is deep, / Deeper than day had been aware. / Deep is its woe; / Joy—deeper yet than agony."

To Gertrude Stein and Alice Toklas, Bilignin, France

4 Sept[ember] 1937   Still at
                                                      Innsbruck [Austria]

Dear Friends:

Enclosèd are some political treatises that may interest you. They were given me by Mrs Crane to enlarge my views.[1] Read and destroy, or just destroy. The Kiplinger Letters are supposed to be Hot Stuff—thousands of Big Business Men pore over them as Matins.

I (late as usual) am deep in the politics of 44 B.C., and am reading a very good and frightening book called *Der Kampf um Caesar's Erbe* by Ferdinand Mainzer.[2] I can't wait for Augustus to finish his cruelties, get Marc Antony out of the way, and begin his long and glorious reign. My interest in 1937 will begin in 1977, if someone has written it up well.

Austria's a very lovely place.

love

Honest Jack ("Ivory Tower")

Wilder

Postum Scriptum: No one, no one can address an envelope as well as I can. Postmen get dizzy as they view such coöperation and consideration.

1. Josephine Boardman (Mrs. Murray W.) Crane was a well-known supporter of the arts. Beginning in the 1920s, writers, artists, and musicians lectured and performed at her New York home. Wilder met her in 1929, when he was invited to a Sabbatical Club dinner—a group of seven women who invited seven men in arts and letters for dinner and conversation at the Colony Club. Thereafter, Wilder attended several Sabbatical Club dinners as well as lectures and concerts in Crane's home on Fifth Avenue. As a founding member of the Museum of Modern Art, Crane helped organize Stein's first public lecture in America, for members of the museum at the Colony Club on 1 November 1934. Stein delivered her lecture "Pictures."

2. This book, given to Wilder by Josephine Crane, narrates the destruction of the Roman empire during the last days of the Republic from the death of Julius Caesar to the crowning of his heir, Augustus. This work became part of the accumulated background information woven into *The Ides of March*. Although Wilder uses the German title of the book published by E. P. Tal in Vienna in 1934, he may have read the book in the Eden and Cedar Paul translation, *Caesar's Mantle: The End of the Roman Republic* (New York: Viking, 1936).

To Thornton Wilder, Zurich, Switzerland
[Transcribed by Wilder][1]
[Postcard]

[postmark: 7 September 1937]   [Bilignin par Belley
                                                                     Ain]

My dearest Thornton,

[Helen Berkhead? Tallulah Bankhead] is marrying it
was nice when we saw in the papers hearing all about her[2] and Alice has just
had a charming letter from Isabel[3] and all evening she was crowing over ice
cream recipes and telling me how lovely America is and now the Kiddies are
gone[4] and now Sam Steward who wrote Angels on the Bough is coming[5] and
enjoy yourself but not too much, remember Satan still finds mischief for idle
hands to do,[6] and beside what would become of Ida and I am brimming with
ideas, nothing [practical?] yet but quite xcitable oh and you left a vest here
Alice says a lovely one we are keeping it against your return but no [spectacles]
Alice says that Louise[7] offers the vest to each new guest as a choice morsel but
here it is yet [?]

Gtde.

1. Wilder's transcription of the date may be an error. The context, the departure of the Rogers on
27 August and the arrival of Steward on 3 September, suggests that this card was written before
7 September (see Stein to Wilder, rec'd (1), 10 September 1936, n. 1-d).

2. Wilder first transcribed "Helen Berkhead," then, perhaps when he understood the context,
added the name Tallulah Bankhead. Bankhead married the actor John Emery at her family home in
Jasper, Alabama, on 31 August. Bankhead's notoriety and the fact that her father, William B. Bankhead, was Speaker of the House of Representatives no doubt made the story of her marriage "news."
Letters from Carl Van Vechten during the 1920s briefly mention Bankhead to Stein in connection
with her work on the London stage. Stein may have read that Bankhead was to open in November as
Cleopatra in Shakespeare's *Antony and Cleopatra* with Van Vechten's wife, Fania Marinoff, in the role
of Charmian (see Burns, *Letters*, 2:568–80). Wilder may have mentioned her in discussing the New
York theater scene. Bankhead created the role of Lily Sabina in Wilder's *The Skin of Our Teeth* in 1942
(see Appendix VIII).

3. This letter from Isabel Wilder has not been located.

4. William G. Rogers and his wife, Mildred.

5. Samuel Steward began corresponding with Stein in 1933, when he wrote her about the death
of Clarence E. Andrews, a professor of English at Ohio State University with whom Stein had had a
correspondence in the 1920s. Andrews had introduced Steward to Stein's work. During Stein's tour,
Steward tried unsuccessfully to arrange a lecture at Carroll College in Helena, Montana, where he
was then teaching. Stein was enthusiastic about his novel *Angels on the Bough* (1936) and had been
looking forward to meeting him. Stein's letters to Steward are collected in *Dear Sammy*. Steward's first
meeting with Stein took place when he arrived in Bilignin on Friday, 3 September.

6. The Reverend Isaac Watts, *Divine and Moral Songs for Children*, no. 20, "Against Idleness
and Mischief": For Satan finds some mischief still, / For idle hands to do.

7. Their housekeeper.

To Thornton Wilder, Zurich, Switzerland
[Transcribed by Wilder]
[Postcard]

[postmark: 7 September 1937][1]   [Aix-les-Bains
                                                          France]

My dear Thornton,

      I am delighted about the Yale Lib it will be lots of fun,[2] we have been having a young fellow here Sam Steward, he is the one who wrote Angels on the Bough and is a college professor we like him and he goes to Zurich on the way to Cherbourg, college professors do do these things and he is taking the vest to you and all our love, will you leave word for him at the American Express Co that you want to see him, he will not interrupt your solitude much because he has to be in Cherbourg the 15 but he will tell you again how much we love you and we do.

G.

    1. This card may have been written after Stein and Toklas had driven Steward to the train. For transcription information, see Stein to Wilder, received 10 September 1936 (1), n. 1-d.

    2. This seemingly offhand remark is the first written reference to the proposal to deposit Stein's papers in the Yale library. A formal response was dictated by Stein to Wilder in Paris on 23 November 1937 and delivered by Wilder to Andrew Keogh, Yale University librarian, on 2 February 1938 (see Gallup, "The Gertrude Stein Collection," [21]).

To Gertrude Stein and Alice Toklas, Bilignin, France

9 Sept[ember] 1937   American Express Co
                                                         Zürich [Switzerland]

Dear Girls:

      It's decided at last: I like Zürich.

    Hm-hm.

    The suspense is over.

    There was some wavering.

    Zürich lost ground every time I saw a swan and there are a lot of them with red crosses on their chests and the word Helvetia.

    Zürich regained it when I saw a sign that read:

ALKOHOLFREIES SELECT Bar.[1]

    Zürich lost ground when I found that for American tourists they tuck the sheets into the mattress. Hotelkeeping should not aspire to Perfection. I like exotic inconveniences.

Zürich regained it when I ate a divine Italian Ravioli, heard some wonderful Austrian music and saw a breathtaking show of the drawings of Delacroix.[2]

Alice, I have no girl in this port and am not likely to have. The only good looking Swiss girl in the world is now in New Haven. Looks to me like they drove her out.

Even if their faces are almost pretty, their figures are bad and their lack of any sense of dress shipwrecks their slight advantages. The other day I saw a slightly pretty girl; but she was taking on weight about the middle, so this is what she wore (a white picquet [i.e., *piqué*] jacket over a dark-blue skirt, mind you:)

E.D. depinxit

Ce qui est faire valoir ce qui justement devrait être tu.[3]

Although/Because I haven't scarcely spoken a word to a human being for over a week, I like Zürich and am very happy here.

This morning I received your word about Sam Steward and joyously left a note for him at the American Exp[ress]. telling him where he could find me[.]

(Did I tell you?)

(Am I repeating myself?) that

I received a long letter from Sibyl [Colefax] at Wasserleonburg—from which I send you a glittering letterhead.[4] She said she talked with them from lunchtime until 2:15 in the morning; that they are completely happy: that he is abounding in vitality of mind; that between lunch and tea they joined the haymakers in the valley and that he took a scythe and cut the best swathe of them all.

I also got a letter from the Roaring Girl of Wollaston, Mass[achusetts], the best living actress, Ruth Gordon[.][5] We were all wrong. The play was a very great success. A long road tour begins in Rochester this week and will not go into New York until Xmas and that I shall draw translator's royalties for the liveliest and most natural text ever made of Ibsen. Our error arose from the fact that the first night audiences (and notably Lucius Beebe) was drunk. . . . . . "and in the Dr. Rank scene in the Second Act at least four people fell out of their chairs onto the floor; but I just acted along and took no notice of anything."

You say that Steward is bringing "the rest."[6]

Does that mean some more material about "Ida." I'm all ready. I keep thinking a lot about her. And especially at Salzburg where the world was composed of people who know in their bones what pure Ida-ness is and hopefully—hopelessly struggle along to attain it. Salzburg is a Walpurgisnacht of Celebrities.

But I just about despair of finding out what our Ida did, despair just in proportion as I close in more and more happily on what Ida was.

And I'm more and more thinking about Money, and what fun it is to think about Money, and how the world now bristles for me with illustrations about it.

But as for "plot" about Ida, I'm stuck, like a mule in a bog.

so

you can imagine how I'm waiting for what Steward brings.

ALICE! Honest, did I leave a vest, a dark blue one?

Isn't that awful!

Y'see, dear, I have nothing to wear. I'm the worst-dressed man outside Asia.

The pants of my brown suit have no cuffs. (They were cut off by a mending tailor in Paris.)

The coat of my grey suit is stained with acid or soup or liquor or something irremoveable.

And:

The vest of my blue suit is missing.

I was on the point of going to a Zürich tailor to see if he could match me one. However I won't really need it until it gets colder; but I'm hoping Louise can be persuaded to part with it by November.

I can't read the name correctly of the girls whose marriage was so interesting—Helen Berkhead, some such name. Somebody I know, too?

I enclose a good review that Isabel's novel got in the New York Herald-Tribune. Isn't that nice?[7]

The "interest" of her private life has broken up, nothing doing, pretty hard hit. I telegraphed her to come over, both ma and her to come over, but apparently not now. Janet, the biologist-wunderkind is spending September with them.

Next Monday or Tuesday I'm going to Sils-Maria, viâ Chur and St. Moritz. And the first week in November I'm going for a short time to Ascona. Isn't Europe *little!*

What'ya readin'?

I wish you were here and I could take you out to those ravioli and those Delacroix. Wouldn't it be funny, Gertrude, if I got to be able to see Art, after all? Anyway those Delacroixs get me and I certainly used to hate him as a painter. And in the gallery there are three Juan Gris that look like the most high tense elegance I ever saw.[8]

Now I'm going out for a long walk by the Lake. It is 9:16 p.m. and I've had no supper nor wanted any.

As for me I like what I have; and if the cap fits you put it on, because it's your friendship I am alluding to.

Lovi

Thorni

Züri

Schweizi

1. Zurich regained ground in Wilder's mind by the contradiction of "alcoholfrei," i.e., non-alcoholic, and "Bar." The Select Bar served coffee, soft drinks, and light meals at reasonable prices but no alcoholic beverages.

2. Almost three hundred drawings were in an exhibition, *Zeichnungen franzöischer Meister von David zu Millet,* at the Kunsthaus in Zurich from 18 June to 12 September 1937. Delacroix was represented by twenty drawings.

3. At this point in the letter, Wilder has sketched the young woman. Next to the sketch he writes "E.D. depinxit"—a joking reference to himself as Delacroix—and adds in bad French the equivalent of "You are what you wear."

4. Wilder transcribed this letter, postmarked 3 September, for his records (see Stein to Wilder, received 10 September 1936 (1), n. 1-d). He sent Stein the letterhead with the "Coat of Arms of England . . . Schloss Wasserleönburg." The original letter has not been located.

5. Wilder also transcribed Gordon's letter of 18 August 1937. Gordon was vacationing with Woollcott on Neshobe Island, Lake Bomoseen, Vermont, before resuming performances of Ibsen's *A Doll's House* (see Wilder to Stein, 3 May 1937, n. 5; for transcription information, see Stein to Wilder, received 10 September 1936 [1], n. 1-d).

6. Wilder misreads "vest" for "rest."

7. A review of Isabel Wilder's third novel, *Let Winter Go,* was published in *New York Herald Tribune Books,* 29 August 1937, 9.

8. What Wilder means by "gallery" is unclear. Douglas Cooper's *Catalogue raisonné* (1977) of the paintings by Juan Gris lists only one picture, *The Viola* (March 1920, Cooper # 331), as belonging to the Kunsthaus, Zurich, at this time. Other paintings by Gris may have been on loan to the museum.

To Thornton Wilder, Zurich, Switzerland
[Transcribed by Wilder]

[postmark: 13 September 1937]   Bilignin par Belley
                                                               Ain

My dear Thornton

You have seen Sam by this time[1] and found there was no rest only a vest but soon there will be I xpect to get quieted down now, and Alice had already proudly found the review of Isabel's book[2] I do hope they come over I would like to meet your mother, and Billy Haas is touched to the heart by your letter and says they gave a play of yours The Christmas Dinner at the University of California and it was a great success and he wants to answer your letter but is timid but I will tell him yes he does not sound timid but you never can tell[3] and I was delighted with Yale's enthusiasm, there is only one thing that worries me, I am giving or I am depositing these ms which is it if I should get poor later on and need to sell them can I or do I. You see I speak as one not able to earn but who likes to spend money to one being able to earn and who does not like to spend money, the Buffalo University has been writing to have me give them a ms. but I have not payed (sic) any too much attention to them but I would like them to be safe, and Yale does sound safe, you know what I mean, of course probably no one later on would want to buy them that is the most probable, well anyway I am awfully touched with "Lefty's" enthusiasm and in Paris we will go over everything golly it will be nice seeing you again lots of love

Gtde

I have been thinking about it a lot more and I think this would be it deposit the things there and during my lifetime if I need to I have the right to sell and in the event of my death they will automatically come into complete possession of everything there and also we will include in the deposit all the letters the Picasso Matisse Juan Gris Hemingway Mildred Aldrich well anything you want to include how about his oh literary xecutor and we will go all over everything together in Paris, there are daily themes and Fortnightly at Radclyffe still there and plenty of odds and ends beside the ms. It seems to me that this is not too ungenerous, naturally they do not pay the living the way they pay the dead, that is I suppose they do not really know which of the living are going to be dead or not dead, I was thinking a little gloomily (? yes) of Mr. Walpole, but I do think this proposition is fair, please tell me tell me truly,[4] have just had a letter from Francis Rose,[5] Pekin seems to be placid under Japan and they all cheerful that it is not [?word] you never can tell where you are going to live next I threaten Alice with Japan, perhaps we will go I would love to [? 2 words] you wouldn't it be as [?word] as Zurich, they probably have American bars

Gtde.

1. For transcription information, see Stein to Wilder, received 10 September 1936 (1), n. 1-d. Wilder collected Stein's card of 7 September the morning of Thursday, 9 September, from American Express and immediately left a note for Steward: "I've just heard from Gertrude Stein this minute that you are soon to be in Zurich. I am at the Carleton-Elite hotel and would be delighted to see you at any time. I know scarcely anyone in town and will be free anytime so do not hesitate to call" (n.d., Thursday morning, YCAL). Steward arrived in Zurich the same day and arranged to see Wilder and return his vest on the evening of the tenth. Steward wrote Stein from Paris on 15 September that he and Wilder had "talked like madmen for two days" because Wilder "hadn't talked to anyone in English for ten" (YCAL).

2. See Wilder to Stein, 9 September 1937, n. 7.

3. Billy Haas is Robert Bartlett Haas, a student at the University of California at Berkeley in 1935. After hearing her lecture there, Haas began corresponding with Stein, asking detailed questions about her work. Replying to Haas on 31 August 1937, Stein urged him to write Wilder with his questions about her work and gave him Wilder's Zurich address (see Stein to Haas, 13 September 1937, YCAL).

4. Wilder and Stein continued the discussion of the gift/deposit to the Yale library in Paris in November (see Wilder to Stein, 22 September 1937, n. 1, and Stein to Wilder [16 December 1937], n. 3). Stein had been contacted by Charles D. Abbott, director of the University of Buffalo libraries, in the late spring or early summer with a request for a donation to the Lockwood Memorial Library's collection of materials on modern poetry. When he received no reply to his first letter (which has not been located), Abbott wrote again on 12 August 1937, requesting "examples of your manuscripts—not 'fair-copies,' but the genuine work-sheets, whether they be pencilled, written in ink, or typescript." By contributing, Abbott wrote, Stein would be "aiding in the foundation of a collection which will be of inestimable service to the scholars of the future, and to the poetic activity of later generations, and without your collaboration, the collection cannot win through to the perfection which it contemplates" (YCAL). It is possible that Bernard Faÿ, who on 2 October 1936 gave a lecture at Buffalo entitled "Gertrude Stein as a Poet," helped to stimulate interest in her manuscripts. "Because I am in the country," Stein replied in a letter postmarked 10 September 1937, "and all my ms. are in Paris, when I am there I will send you something just what I do not know." She asked that he remind her "sometime in November." A second letter to Abbott, probably written in January 1938, before the move to the rue Cristine, informed him of her change of address and suggested they meet should he come to Paris. The requested gift never developed beyond these letters (Stein to Abbot, SUNY-Buffalo). On 3 October 1939, Mary Barnard, curator of the Poetry Collection at the Lockwood Memorial Library, wrote Stein, "In Mr. Abbott's absence, I am taking up the correspondence which he began some time ago, and which lapsed when he was unable to see you in Paris. He regrets the delays which made the meeting impossible, and hopes that another time he may be more fortunate in his plans." Barnard continued that the collection had developed and included printed works and manuscripts "from almost all the important English and American poets": "There are a few important exceptions, covered by the 'almost,' of which Gertrude Stein is one. We hope very much that you are still in sympathy with the purposes of the collection, and that you will be good enough to supply the lack, which is most serious" (YCAL). Having made the decision to deposit her manuscripts at Yale, Stein did not make a contribution to the University of Buffalo collection. We have not located Stein's reply to Mary Barnard.

5. Undated letter from Rose to Stein (YCAL).

To Gertrude Stein and Alice Toklas, Bilignin, France

13 Sept[ember] 1937   American Express Co.
Monday   Zurich [Switzerland]

Dear Friends:

If I said anything against Zürich I take it back.

I walk out into a new region every day and all of them restful. One day it's the old town covered with dedicatory tablets to Zwingli and the Reformation troubles; another it's to a park a little ways up the Lake from which you can see mountains, mighty mountains deep blue and dazzling white, very far away. And sometimes to the Zoo—don't you love wild animals?

The fact is I'm happy. I'm the happiest fella in your acquaintance. I spring up mornings with a bound and I go off to sleep nights with all-but-prayerful content.

I'm so happy I'm not even afraid of being happy. Now isn't that a funny thing?

I can no longer conceal from you that I'm writing the most beautiful little play you can imagine. Every morning bring[s] an hour's increment to it and that's all, but I've finished two acts already. It's a little play with all the big subjects in it; and it's a big play with all the little things of life lovingly impressed into it. And when I finish it next Friday, there's another coming around the corner. Lope de Vega wrote three plays a week in his thirties and four plays a week in his forties and so I let these come as they like.

This play is an immersion, immersion into a New Hampshire town. It's called "Our Town" and its third act is based on your ideas, as on great pillars, and whether you know it or not, until further notice, you're in a deep-knit collaboration already.[1]

[Samuel] Steward was here two days and a half and he's a fine fella and it was a pleasure. And one of the finest things about it was to learn that at your house he had written down twenty-five closely-written pages of Gertrude's talk—Ah-ah-ah—added to mine and [Robert] Davis's and I hope a good many more.[2]

I keep postponing going up to Sils Maria or rather Sils-Basc[lgia] (the sunny side), but I think I'll go day after tomorrow.

A thousand thanks for the vest. Now I can go out to tea at Thomas Mann's without the psychological impediment of being unpresentable to servants.[3]

love
Thornton

1. This letter is a powerful acknowledgment of Wilder's debt and devotion to Stein. Even before writing the third act, he says that his play rests on *The Making Of Americans*, whose impact he has recently received from the unabridged version and extended in conversations with her. The power of her ideas and her personality freed him from his uneasy preoccupation with himself and his problems of writing to concentrate on his work. "Deep-knit collaboration" not only speaks of the debt of *Our Town* but also refers back to Stein's suggestion that he collaborate on her novel *Ida*. Well aware of the fact that Wilder offered her subject matter for *Ida*, Stein observed his restless travails in the service of propriety and publicity as he traveled from Bilignin to Salzburg to meet Sibyl Colefax and other figures in the world of stars—Reinhardt, Remarque, von Hoffmannsthal, Toscanini. Stein observed his behavior, flattered him, chastened him and made her new novel of the configurations of that world. A complex interaction was already taking place.

Stein and Wilder played elaborate parts in a staged relationship. Wilder, well connected, successful, and expert at popularizing ideas, helped to introduce Stein to resistant American readers in books that might not have been published without his intervention: the *Narration* lectures, the *Geographical History Of America*, and, after her death, *Four In America*. Wilder in turn gained greatly from Stein's friendship and from the power of her mind to free him from excessive constraints.

Except for this letter, unpublished until now, neither Wilder nor Stein made public statements about the debt each owed the other. Critics and reviewers did not see the connection; no two works are more dissimilar in plot, detail, characterization, and language than *The Making Of Americans*, rolling along inexorably in huge, incremental epic waves with its great population of personalities and relations, and *Our Town*, in its small, homey, and often sentimental New England setting with its astonishingly accurate portrayal of daily life. The play's clean lines and its powerful local sense conceal the stark, curtainless principles of its abstract conception. To reader or spectator, the two works appear to come from utterly different worlds.

Wilder's borrowings are never obvious or mechanical. No details, names, phrases, elements of plot or character carry over. Wilder was an expert translator or popularizer of large ideas. His Stage Manager transposes Stein's universals to the tiny setting of *Our Town*, where they become visible on the empty stage, reduced in scope. Not all spectators feel comfortable with them in the tiny town of Grovers Corners, the houses of Doc Gibb and Charles Webb, the drugstore, Main Street, or even the cemetery. To many, Wilder's stage cannot contain the great movements of Stein's ideas.

Julian Sawyer, a Stein critic of cunning detective intelligence, in the *Saturday Review of Literature* for 17 April 1943 pointed out the kinship between *Our Town* and *The Making Of Americans*. He identified close parallels in detail, from act I as setting out "the daily life," to act II as "Love and Marriage," and act III as "Death," the three parallel to Stein's history of a family. Both works rely on marriage of two families; both eliminate scenery, stage sets, descriptions of settings. Sawyer sees Stein's history "culminating in death and thus flattening life and death into a synonymy which . . . makes for her 'complete description' of social immortality." However, he describes *Our Town* disparagingly as a "misapplied adaptation" of the novel.

The daily life as the material for work and the source of perception is a central theme in Wilder's play. However, whereas Stein's daily life is a continuous source of unexpected verbal ideas and compositional surprise, Wilder sets the daily life, in meticulous sequence of exquisitely chosen detail, into a day-by-day, week-by-week plot. The charm of the unexpected is sacrificed to the charming recognition of the expected.

Our Town does share the structure of *The Making Of Americans* but their worlds are utterly unalike. Wilder's intelligent conception of universals is always problematic for a director because the tight daily life narrows access to the great world that Stein opens with sweeping natural ease, even when she irritates us with her large pen's slips. As Alice Toklas commented on Wilder's perception of Stein in her letter of 14 December 1948 to Carl Van Vechten, "Wilder considers Baby's work important because of her philosophy, her metaphysics, not her aesthetic" (YCAL).

2. Steward's papers are in the library of the University of California at Berkeley. We have been unable to locate any notes that Robert Davis may have made of his conversations with Stein. Wilder may have used notes to write his introductions to *Narration* and the *Geographical History Of America* but these do not seem to have survived. See Appendix VI for his notes on conversations with Stein on her novel *Ida*.

3. Wilder met Mann in the summer of 1935 through Max Reinhardt (see Wilder to Stein, 30 August 1935).

To Thornton Wilder, Zurich, Switzerland
[Transcribed by Wilder]
[Postcard]

[postmark: 17 September 1937]   [Bilignin par Belley
                                                                  Ain]

My dearest Thornton,

Hurrah for the Play Marathon, I'm betting on you Glory be, and Alice has just found Isabel's photo in the books,[1] she heads her adwriter's books books, and we were at a meeting La Nouvelle Femme at Aix[2] at the theatre in the Casino and I showed Alice the lovely mirrored doors through which we went and the lovely orangeade which we drank but I did not show her the lovely table at which we played because alas there was no Thornton and we could not pass those lovely mirrored doors without Thornton, god bless Thornton, I'm glad you liked Sam Steward, some day you can perhaps get him out like you were at Lawrenceville he is [? drowned] at Loyola³ but perhaps Rops⁴ will get him a job in a lycée here and then he will have time to write I think he will do something really good sometime, we love you so Thornton we do we do

always
Gtde.

1. For transcription information, see Stein to Wilder, received 10 September 1936 (1), n. 1-d. A photograph of Isabel Wilder appeared in reviews of *Let Winter Go* and in some ads for the book.

2. La Femme Nouvelle, an organization advocating changes in French laws affecting women, was founded by Louise Weiss. Stein and Toklas may have met Weiss earlier in the summer (see Stein to Wilder, 28 August 1937, n. 4). Wilder would meet her at a lunch at Stein's on 20 November (see Stein to Wilder, 14 November 1937). Stein and Wilder had gambled in the casino at Aix-les-Bains on 31 July.

3. From 1921 to 1928, with one year off to pursue a master's degree at Princeton University, Wilder taught at the Lawrenceville School in Lawrenceville, New Jersey. Steward at this time was teaching at Loyola University in Chicago.

4. Henri Daniel-Rops was a teacher and a prolific writer, primarily on Catholic subjects. He was born Henri Petiot but chose his pseudonym in part because he admired Félicien Rops, the Belgian-French artist. He taught in Paris, but his country home was in Rothonod, a tiny village one kilometer from Belley. The earliest extant letter from Daniel-Rops to Stein is from November 1936 (YCAL). This may mean that they met the previous summer, perhaps through the Baroness Pierlot. He was one of the neighbors whom Stein often introduced to visiting friends. Steward had expressed interest in returning to France, and Stein enlisted Daniel-Rops to find him a job teaching English. Nothing came of the project (see Stein to Steward, postmarked 25 September 1937, in Steward, *Dear Sammy*, 132–33).

To Gertrude Stein and Alice Toklas, Bilignin, France
[Postcard: Pontresina mit Julierkette]

18 Sept[ember] 1937   Pontresina [Switzerland]

Dear Gertrude and dear Alice:

Walked over here from St Moritz this morning, bursting with grateful feelings. I've just had my 22nd birthday and I feel 18. Will pine-trees smell as good at 40, and autumn crocuses look as pleasant; and snow covered peaks be so light?

Tonight I'm at Sils-[Baselgia], and for five nights. Just one long round of pleasures.¹

I kinda take back what I said about mountains two years ago. They're all right in their way, I think; but not in Wordsworth's way. That's all I meant.²

When you look at the paths remember me and sometimes betweentimes.

y[ou]r. loving gardener
Thornton

1. See Wilder to Stein, 3 September 1937, n. 5.
2. See Wilder to Stein and Toklas, 6 and 10 August 1935.

To Thornton Wilder, Zurich, Switzerland
[Transcribed by Wilder]
[Postcard]

[postmark: 22 September 1937]   [Bilignin par Belley
                                                            Ain]

Dearest of collaborators,

                   Ida has started pretty nearly nearly started, there are
going to be one or some from every state perhaps every country [?county] and
they well they are not to get to Bay Shore and they are not to know about Ida
but they are going to leave where they are, two from Utah have been very
good, but the rest well anyway, did you use to say shame shame fie for shame
everybody knows your name well it is going to be the other way[1] and did you
leave a pair of shoes, if not it was the Kiddies or it was Sammy but you are the
nearest so we ask you first[2] lots of love
                   Gtde

1. This may be an indication that Stein had started another draft of the first version of *Ida A
Novel*, begun in May 1937. In the published novel, geographical names play an important role in
indicating Ida's wanderings.
2. The shoes were Frederick Ashton's ballet slippers (see Stein to Wilder, 22 October 1937).

To Thornton Wilder, Zurich, Switzerland
[Transcribed by Wilder][1]

[illegible P.M. a few days later]

Dearest Thorni,

                   Now that you are walking around how about walking to
Geneva and we meeting you there and you coming here for a bit and bringing
your plays and reading them to us in the evening before the wood fire, and me
telling the sad story of Ida it has been going a little and taking the weeds out of
the garden and filling the massifs with dead leaves, and opening our walnuts,
how about it, and I am not telling you how much I love you because you are to

leichtsinnig pas un gars sérieux and Mme Giraud asks after her 'flirt' and says he has her heart perhaps it is mutual perhaps and how about it[2]
Gtde.

1. This transcription marked "DITTO" directly follows the transcription of Stein's card of 22 September. In this text Stein responds to Wilder's card of 18 September.

2. Wilder's date book indicates that he and Stein and Toklas had lunch with Mme Giraud and Mme Geoffrey and her daughter on 4 August. Assuming Wilder's transcription to be fairly accurate, Stein suggests that he is "too irresponsible, not a serious young man (*garçon*)."

To Gertrude Stein and Alice Toklas, Bilignin, France

22 Sept[ember] 1937   Sils-Baselgia [Switzerland]

Dear Ones:
        Glorious place.
The great ghost of Nietzsche.[1]
Coronet of peaks and an emerald to sapphire lake.
        Last night no sleep, but an influx of ideas that make my little play the most beautiful one you can imagine.[2]
Back in Zurich tomorrow.
Will write you a Literary Executor letter—all will be arranged fine.[3]
I insist on knowing whether you love me—this shilly—shally—ing about the bush has got to stop—
        Anyway, rebuffed and unrequited, I love you more than Tunkantell.
                Your
                Thornton

1. See Wilder to Stein, 3 September 1937, n. 5
2. *Our Town.*
3. See Stein to Wilder, 13 September 1937, n. 4.

To Alice Toklas, Bilignin, France

[late September 1937]   American Express Co.
                                       ZURICH [Switzerland]

Dear Alice:
        Will you give further evidence of your angelic origin and do me a favor?
Take as long as you like to [do] it and don't let it be a bore to you.

It's like this:

My lawyer I. Dwight Dana is an awfully nice shy very New England young man, very capable and amid his brilliant practice of millionaire estates and railroad corporations, I think he is endlessly amused with that minuscule client, myself, to him exotic and slightly mad.

Now Dwight has a nice stout pleasant wife, Anna English Dana—all these names are *Bourbon* and *Montesquieu* in New Haven.

I wrote Dwight a Florid Letter from Paris and I added: tell Mrs Dana that I had lunch with Mme Chanel and dinner at Mlle Schiaparelli's and that the news I bring her from the Front is that they're wearing beads, nothin' but beads this year.[1]

Apparently that wasn't what she wanted. He writes:

"By the way, Anna is more interested in recipes, so don't forget her if you run across any that an Irish-American cook might be able to cope with."

Alice-Angelica, could you copy out two, Any Two, that might interest her?[2]

If you think for a minute what our New Haven bourgeoisie must be like, you can imagine what excitement it would cause especially when she knows it comes from The Autobiographer-malgré-elle.

I don't dare add a word about myself, because the report is monotonously the same: I'm the happiest fellow in your whole circle of acquaintance. Gertrude doesn't have to vex herself any longer as to why I'm a Community Man because I'm not and it agrees with me like a house-afire.[3]

[Alice, come nearer: I want to whisper.

When I was in Sils the phone rang. A call from Zürich.

It was Bob Davis's repulsed Mme Butterfly who has been pursuing him about Europe like a demented being.

Could she come down and see me?

No, I'd have dinner with her in Zürich two nights later.

So I took her to the smartest place in town. Gave her a cocktail, and venison, and *Neufchatel*.

I knew there was nothing like a little mondanité to take a girl's mind off her troubles.

And at last: a narrative: oo, so undignified, and tragi-comic, and mortifying.

Fiction wouldn't *want* to touch it.

Such hiding in his room. Such taking him apparently to Italy, but really to Austria. Such money trouble at borders.

Don Juan Davis had been living in trigamy all Summer. And guess what his defense was under her anguished reproach?

"Well: Goethe did."

To say that to a "German"!

As Gertrude says: ["]The world's full of plots. Your life's full of plots; my life's full of plots. Plots aren't interesting any more."[4]

Love, dear Alice,
Thornton

1. We have no documentation for these meetings.
2. We have not located the letters to Mrs. Dana.
3. See Stein to Wilder [2 May and ?15–16 May 1937].
4. Wilder does not close the bracket. See Wilder to Stein, 20 October 1937. Wilder's two French words in this letter refer to the autobiographer in spite of herself and to a "little worldliness."

To Thornton Wilder, Zurich, Switzerland
[Transcribed by Wilder]

[postmark: 4 October 1937]

Bilignin [par Belley Ain]

My dear Thornton,

Where oh where are you, we feel that we are responsible to your family for their wandering boy and where is he tonight, oh where, answer, where, we miss you, yes, we do, we vendanged yesterday with the Pierlots cutting grapes all day,[1] and now the Picabias are here and he made a lovely painting of Basket for me,[2] and let me see what else well really nothing else, Ida was getting along quite nicely, and Carl [Van Vechten] wrote that Fania [Marinoff Van Vechten] is to do Charmian for Tallulah Bankhead and Virgil Thomson the music,[3] and so from Tallulah having been a stranger she is now quite in the family, I also found her in an English detective story, where somebody is told not to think they were like that, so once you know you do know,[4] Picabia is full of dark Spanish thoughts, otherwise we are cheerful Americans.

Gtde.

1. Madame Pierlot and her family, the d'Aiguys, had a house surrounded by vineyards in Cerveyrieu, a small town four kilometers from Béon, just outside of Artemare. Stein often went to the vendange, the grape harvest (see Stein to Van Vechten [? October 1938], in Burns, *Letters*, 2:613). For transcription information, see Stein to Wilder, received 10 September 1936 (1), n. 1-d.
2. We have not been able to find any information about this painting.
3. Wilder's brackets in this letter. Van Vechten had written Stein on 21 September the details of the production of *Antony and Cleopatra* (Burns, *Letters*, 2:568–69). Directed by Reginald Bach, it opened at the Mansfield Theatre in New York on 10 November and closed after five performances. Bankhead's new husband, John Emery, was singled out as the only member of the cast who understood how to read Shakespeare's poetic lines.
4. We have been unable to identify this detective story.

To Gertrude Stein and Alice Toklas, Bilignin, France

4 Oct[ober] 1937   American Express Co[.]
                                                             Zürich [Switzerland]

Dear Friends:

        I always forget to ask you whether you like clippings and en-
closures. Some people hate 'em. Until further notice I shall enclose divers
curiosa that reach me. Burn them.[1]

    Day follows day.

    I'm getting homesick. Without poignance, but homesick.

    I say to myself, the most beautiful thing in the world is the first snowfall at
about 7:00 p.m. on Madison Avenue.

    Oh, New York. Wonderful.

    I have to speak in the Great Aula of the University of Zürich on Novem-
ber 17th.[2] So I think about the 20th I'll come to Paris for a week to interview
Austrian butlers for you. Then London for a week. Then, not yet having lost
my return-ticket, home.

    In the meantime I maintain my solitude—dreaming and yet dramatic—
as though I were balancing a glass of water on my head.

    Ever[y]day—rather: over-night—my play grows four inches—Play No #2.[3]

    It's too late. I dare not turn aside now, not even for Ida. Besides, she
obstinately refuses to give up the secret of her "action." There she is: glorious
as "description" and like Aristotle's god: the mover—unmoved.

    Perhaps her description is all her narration.

    Perhaps just as poetry now gives way to prose; so narration gives way to
description.

    My play No #1 is as far as the stage has gone toward "mere" description. A
New Hampshire town: its daily life; its living; its dead; its weather; its geology;
its sociology; its *mores* as seen by an archeologist a thousand years from now, its
birth and death statistics; and how Mrs Gibbs ironed Dr. Gibbs' shirts—all in
one great curve: quod erat demonstrandum.

    A nice letter from [Robert B.] Haas, but he asks me a pack of questions I
can't answer.

    When is your work poetry and when is it prose? I think I *know*: but I can't
explain how.[4]

—
—

    And then when I get in America after having contemplated the eyes of
my adorable ma and my adorable sister,[5] what'll I do then?

    Go and tease Ruthie [Gordon] after her performances.[6] Go and ask the
Hutchi [Robert and Maude Hutchins] what they're thinking about. And then

go to Mexico City for three months and write 3 more plays. Oh, death where is thy sting? Only a happy man is in a position to say that.

More anon.

love

Thornton

1. The enclosures have not remained with the letter.

2. The Lesezirkel Hottingen of Zurich (1882–1941) fulfilled a broad cultural mission, beginning as a readers' subscription club to major journals, expanding to a membership library, a social and cultural club, and a prestigious sponsor of lectures by speakers from many fields and countries, usually offered at the large auditorium of the University of Zurich. Wilder, young, successful, and fluent in languages, was a desirable speaker in Europe, as he already was in America. (See Conrad Ulrich, *Der Lesezirkel Hottingen*.)

3. *The Merchant of Yonkers*. Play #1 is *Our Town*.

4. The Haas' letter to Wilder has not been located and Haas confirmed he did not keep carbons (Haas to Dydo, 19 August 1993). Wilder's reply from Chicago is dated 10 December 1937 (YCAL):

Dear Mr. Haas:

Please forgive my delay in answering your letter. There were many reasons, but I'm afraid one of the reasons lay in the psychological obstacle—that I foresaw I would be unable to answer most of your questions, and so postponed your disappointment in finding it out.

For instance:

(1) The effect of Three Lives on its contemporary world is only to be gathered from the books it was found, some time afterwards, to have influenced,—notably Sherwood Anderson's and most of the literature on the negro, notably Carl Van Vechten['s] "Nigger Heaven."

(2) The change in the middle of A Long Gay Book.

Over and over I tell Gertrude that I cannot understand the poems or prose in that style; but she always forgets my declaration and starts talking about that material as tho' I were one of the initiated. And you are doing the same. If I cannot understand the second manner, how could I explain the reasons that led to it! All I can do is to refer you again to the passage about it in the Lectures.

(3) Which is poetry and which is prose. Here I go even more gingerly than you. In a burst of presumption (partly based on things I have heard her say, but which I may have interpreted wrongly) I should catalogue the works you name as follows:

An acquaintance with description: literary criticism

The Plays	Most of them poetry—all except the "witty" ones like Woman's Voices [i.e., *Ladies' Voices*].
Is Dead	Solving the problem of Narration—Prose. (She now has a feeling that prose is the "great form," superior to Poetry. We were talking about Julius Caesar's life-time regret at not having been a good poet: she implied that he was better than that; that the Commentaries are about the greatest prose ever was, and that constituted a superiority. [)]

Geographical History

Literary Criticism—with interpolated lyrics. (This is my timorous guess.)

Lucy Church Amiably

Prose. I asked her what place it had in her attack on the problem of narrative and she said: None at all. It was description.

Re James, Whitehead, Dewey;—I wouldn't know about that earlier academic background of her thinking, tho' I overheard her once discussing them with Bob Davis. My feeling is that in [William] James (whom she refers to with great personal and some intellectual indebtedness) you might find many important basic sources, always realizing that for the most part the journey of her mind has swung far away from systematic philosophy and gone an extremely individual course of its own.

—

When I arrived in N. Y. two weeks ago I brought to [i.e., two] large valises full of her MSS which she is donating to the Yale Univ. Library. There are several "layers" of parts of The Making of Americans; there is A Long Gay Book; Tender Buttons, etc. There also are her daily themes at Radclyffe, with red-ink comments by her instructor, William Vaughan Moody! These MSS could be seen by "serious enquirrers."

All best wishes to you on your work.

I always stand willing to help, but as this letter show[s] so little fitted to help.

Sincerely yours
Thornton Wilder

5. Isabel Wilder, who continued to live with her mother after her father's death.
6. Wilder is anticipating the New York opening of his adaptation of Ibsen's *A Doll's House* (see Wilder to Stein, 3 May 1937, n. 5).

———

To Thornton Wilder, Zurich, Switzerland
[Transcribed by Wilder]
[Postcard: Picture of Hotel de Ville, Tarascon]

[postmark: 5 October 1937]   Bilignin [par Belley Ain]

So glad that it is only lonesome,[1] we were a little worried that perhaps all was not well, and in Paris all together we love to have you wherever we have you, and we always have you, yes, we always,

lots of love,
Gtde.

1. Stein is responding to Wilder's letter of 4 October, in which he speaks of his seclusion and solitude. For transcription information, see Stein to Wilder, received 10 September 1936 (1), n. 1-d.

———

To Gertrude Stein and Alice Toklas, Bilignin, France

[9 October 1937]   Amexco
Sat[urday]. a.m.   [American Express Co.]
                                                   Zurich [Switzerland]

Dear Ones:

At 3:30 today I shall be going through the St. Gotthard's Tunnel.[1] It takes half an hour. There will be lights on in the train to discourage kissing.

—

I promised you a long letter on the Yale Library matter.

But it all boils down to this:

To be sure, you can deposit the material there with a possibility of withdrawal for sale.

I think it'd be nice if you gave them outright ONE MORSEL as earnest of more to come and as thank offering for their stewardship of the rest.

My, you'll feel fine when all that material is there, where rust cannot a. . . . . what does the Bible say? . . . . nor thieves break in to steal.

And since Buffalo wants something I'd give it to them, too. . . . . say, one of those recent stories.

Anyway we'll have fine long talks about it in Paris.[2]

(Please Turn Over. It Gets Better).

I'm sailing from Southhampton on Dec[ember] 11. So I can stay longer in the two capitals than I thought.

Sibyl Colefax is coming over to Paris to steal two of your Paris days: so you'd better go over to London with me and steal two of her London days.

———

My play, golly![3]

———

I have a grippe-y cold coming on. Alice will understand me when I diagnose it as 80% boredom at this girl's confession-miseries rê Bob Davis.[4]

3% pretext for a week on Lago di Maggiore.

17% walking about the wet streets and eternal rains of Zurich.

———

Sam Steward's letters have a courtly elegance about them, haven't they? The last of the elegants.[5]

———

Oh, I forgot to tell you about my new talent, skill, consolation and devotion. I've taught myself to Read even Difficult Music in silence. So all I do now is read the Masses of Palestrina up page, down page. Wonderful, wonderful.[6]

LOVE.

THORNTON

1. Wilder was on his way to spend a week in Ascona.

2. The Bible passage from Matthew 6:20–21 reads, "But lay up for yourselves treasures in heaven, where neither moth nor rust doth corrupt, and where thieves do not break through nor steal: / For where your treasure is, there will your heart be also." For Buffalo, see Stein to Wilder, 13 September 1937, n. 4.

3. Our Town.

4. See Wilder to Toklas [late September 1937].

5. Steward's letters to Wilder have not been located.

6. Wilder's interest in Palestrina goes back to his college days in Oberlin. In an unpublished

Oberlin essay, written at Christmas 1916 and tentatively titled "The Boy Sebastian," he describes reading Palestrina Masses.

To Gertrude Stein and Alice Toklas, Bilignin, France

15 Oct[ober]. 1937   Monte Verità
                                                              Ascona [Switzerland]

Dear Friends,

I couldn't prize solitude so much did I not vary it from time to time with adroitly calculated trips here-a and there-a.

So having caught a grippe-y cold I passed from the wet skies and pavements of Zürich through the St. Gotthard Tunnel and found myself under Italian sunshine.

The sun,—oh, what a feature.

But there were other novelties.

This hotel was founded many years ago—as its pretentious name implies—to house cults,—isms and—ologies. A Dutch baron of vast wealth, still here and eating in our dining-room. But he also built the hotel to house his picture collection, and all the public rooms and the bedrooms are full of paintings. Picasso, Delacroix, Courbet, Matisse, Marées, Dali, and a host of Chinese paintings. At breakfast I insist on sitting under a Juan Gris *Harlekin* that is—as you say—a perfection. Really, it's a wonderful picture.[1]

Lago Maggiore is down the hill. I refuse to cross the border into Italy— about two miles away—but that's very hypocritical of me, because, the houses, streets, churches, villages are all purely Italian and I get the pleasure without the name. Yes, I still hold that fascism is a greater insult to the human mind than communism is, tho' communism also is no picnic. My father was an unconscious fascist—he wanted to be wise for other people willy-nilly, so my political notions flow from that.

My plays flower and stretch themselves every day, and I enjoy it; but I long for my Paris visit to begin. I want to *look at you,* and then home. My unit for contemplating the future is about three months: I don't know what will— or should—follow after that.

¶ Monday I'm back at Zurich for my last deep plunge into work and then holiday and some roaring evenings with you—whom I adore.

Adoringly
Thornton

1. The Dutch-born Baron Eduard von der Heydt built a hotel in Ascona in 1926 and displayed his important collection of pictures there. In 1956 the collection was given to the state museum in Wuppertal, Germany (from 1961 on named the Von Der Heydt Museum). From Wilder's description, it is not clear which work by Gris he means. Von der Heydt owned two works by Gris: *Pierrot with Guitar* (1922) (Cooper # 386, now in Wuppertal) and the *Head of Harlequin* (1924) (Cooper # 476, now in a private collection).

Ascona had a long history as a haven for Europe's spiritual and intellectual rebels. For a history of Ascona during the first two decades of the twentieth century, see Martin Green, *Mountain of Truth*.

To Thornton Wilder, Zurich, Switzerland
[Transcribed by Wilder]

[postmark: 16 October 1937]   [Bilignin par] Belley
                                                                     [Ain]

Dearest Thornton,
            As I gardened in the garden I thought how nice it was that you had made it all clean outside and I said to Alice didn't he do it beautifully and Alice said he did. Alice also said that now the Picabia's are gone the first Sunday and any day might be Sunday by and by she would write and send the recipes, she quite knows which one[1] and she will also write to Isabel who wrote her such a nice letter[2] and please tell Thornton and Thornton have you by any chance on your person and could be parted from it a map of these United States I kind of need it to make Ida go on, she is going on some, but a map would help, and here there are none. I said somewhere where there are germans there would be more likely to be one but Alice did not like that, and I am very pleased about our going to get our ms. in order and of course they can have lots of them, I think we ought to make it quite legal for them that they will be the owners of everything not sold, of course probably nothing will be sold, and do you think it a good idea to give them the letters too and would they want it, well it is still rather nice[3] so we are here but when you are there we'll be there we love you very much
                                        Gtde.

1. See Wilder to Toklas [late September 1937], n. 2. For transcription information, see Stein to Wilder, received 10 September 1936 (1), n. 1-d.
2. The reply to Isabel Wilder's letter mentioned in Stein to Wilder [7 September 1937] has not been located.
3. See Stein to Wilder [13 September 1937], n. 4.

To Gertrude Stein and Alice Toklas, Bilignin, France

20 Oct[ober] 1937   Am[erican]. Ex[press]. Co.
                                                    Zurich [Switzerland]

                                                    Now really settled down no more
                                                    trips, at Hotel Belvoir,
                                                    Ruschlikon. Alice, in this
                                                    little town Brahms wrote a part
                                                    of the German Requiem. Perhaps
                                                    he wrote the part: How lovely
                                                    are thy dwelling-courts, oh
                                                    Lord of Hosts, a tune that
                                                    would create a soul beneath the
                                                    ribs of death, as our older
                                                    brother Shakespeare said.[1]

Dear Friends:

The best bookstore in Zürich is sending you a map of the greatest country in the world. Love it dearly. Someday we'll drive all over it together pointing out BEAUTIES to left and right. There is only one part of it I do not like and that is greater Los Angeles, but all the rest I love more than Tunkantell, "twill be my theme in glory, to tell the old old story."[2]

I feel all funny and ants-in-my-. . . . . . . shirt to think that IDA is leaning on that glorious map and going on. If I see light on Ida, the light on Ida that I've been groping for two-and-a-half months I shall become very obstreperous and wish to share it with you. Did you see in the paper that [Alf] Landon is trying to take the Republican Party away from Woodward? He won't be able to, no, ma'am. Woodward holds what he has, and so easily that there's no struggle.[3]

Not only has [Robert] Davis's Innamorata Abandanata arrived in town and stayed in town to tell her story, but now Davis's Travelling Companion—abandanato—arrived in town also. This new one writes quite good stories.

But ever since the Doctrine of Audience, I'm strong enough to stand alone. Yes, and ever since Nietzsche at Sils-Maria I'm a cold-hearted Beggar.

Confession-stories and Pity-my-sad-lot stories don't move me no more.[4]

I'm five miles away from town. That's me.

Ruth [Gordon]-the-best-actress-in-America is doing sensational business in my "adaptation" of A Doll's House. Toronto and now Detroit. In fact I'll quote a cable from her filling out the elisions

Detroit Oct 18
Darling Notices here [and] Toronto absolute sensation.
Eighteen curtain calls [at] Toronto. [They] cheer here.
Mailing notices you are triumphant Deepest love=Ruth[5]

She don't know the half of it yet.

I'm now galloping through Play No #2 and will be on Play No #3 very soon. My present one's a comedy and I'm hilarious all the time. The next one's very serious and there'll be no giggles from Room 10 in November.[6]

Are you having sunlight, too, dears?

I love the sun. Y'know what I mean?

Oh, dear, is it possible that my dear Sibyl Colefax has no sense of humor? I wrote her a letter in the style of St. Paul and I don't think she enjoyed it at all. It was very very very funny and in it I revived St. Paul's low opinion of women. ["Remember always all the councils with which I have counselled thee; be not puffed up, nor large in thine own conceit, but forgetful of thyself as befitteth a woman. I long to come unto thee with many groanings in the night-watches, if so be I can first visit the church of Lutetia and behold with mine own eyes the works of our sisters in the Lord, Gertruda and Aliciola.] And so on.

Oh, dear, I hate to *waste* a fancy.[7]

¶ Now I'm going to walk into town along the heights above the lake—under yellowing autumn trees, kicking the chestnut burrs before me, and I'm going to enjoy it very much. And in town I'm going to buy some more Palestrina Masses and read them, eating a kilogram of Italian grapes on a certain bench in the shadow of the University, my whole dinner, and I'm going to enjoy all that very much; but my chief enjoyment is FREINDSHIP,[8] and that's what I ask of you

                    Thy
                    Thornton

P.S. Remember Terry Lewis? She's got something the matter with her. Maybe T.B.!!

                    T.

1. The text of part IV of the *German Requiem* comes from Psalms 84, 1, 2, and 4. The lines "And took in strains that might create a soul / Under the ribs of Death" are from Milton's "A Mask" ("Comus"), not from Shakespeare.

2. A line from the hymn "I Love to Tell the Story."

3. Alfred "Alf" Landon, titular head of the Republican Party since his unsuccessful presidential campaign in 1936, was dissatisfied with the direction of the Republican National Committee headed by John Hamilton. Wilder may be connecting Hamilton with the character Woodward in Stein's *Ida A Novel*. Stein had met Hamilton in 1934 through the Goodspeeds. From 1932 to 1940, Hamilton was a member of the Republican National Committee and served as its chairman from 1936 to 1940. He was in Europe with the Goodspeeds in May and June 1937 when they made a brief visit to Stein in Bilignin (see Hamilton to Stein, 16 November 1937, YCAL).

4. See Wilder to Toklas [late September 1937]. According to his date book, Wilder met Davis and the man with whom he was traveling in Paris on 25 July.

5. Wilder transcribed this telegram (see Stein to Wilder, received 10 September 1936, n. 1-d).

6. Here Play # 2 is probably *The Merchant of Yonkers* and Play # 3 *Our Town*.

7. Lady Colefax had returned from a visit in Paris with the Duke and Duchess of Windsor when

she received Wilder's letter. In response to our inquiry, Richard Goldstone, who controls access to the letters from Wilder to Lady Colefax, deposited by him in the Fales Collection at the New York University Library, replied that no such letter appeared to be in the collection (letter to Dydo, 6 March 1992 [i.e., 1993]). Colefax's reply, from Brooksby Hall, Leicester, is, in Wilder's transcription, dated 10 October: "In London I picked up certain Pauline words. I never did much hold with Paul and found him rather obscure!!" Although Wilder does not close the quotation marks, his imitation of Paul written to Lady Colefax probably ends after "befitteth a woman." The style continues when he speaks to Stein and Toklas. (For information on Wilder's transcription of Lady Colefax's letter, see Stein to Wilder, received 10 October 1936 (1), n. 1-d).

    8. "FREINDSHIP" here is an intentional misspelling; "gallopping," earlier, may or may not be.

To Thornton Wilder, Zurich, Switzerland
[Transcribed by Wilder]

[postmark: Aix-les-Bains   Bilignin par Belley
22 October 1937]   Ain

My dearest Thornton,

               Thanks for the map, the big one was not right but on the back some little ones with the straight lines of the states and they are inspiring they are so good for Ida, it is lovely weather and I wish we were seeing you in Geneva, but anyway very soon in Paris, and there is so much to tell, everybody hopes that it might have been their shoes that were left because then Thornton would come to Springfield or Chicago to deliver them but now we think they are Freddy Ashton's shoes[1] and perhaps you will deliver them to him in London Town, it's lovely weather just lovely, and crack nuts with the hammer of an evening and burn wood and wish Thornton were here, thanks again so much for the map and everything and everything and lots of love we are trying a little late to teach Pepe not to bark, he begs pardon but he barks

    lots of love and lots

               Gtde.

    1. See Stein to Wilder [22 September 1937]. For transcription information, see Stein to Wilder, received 10 October 1936 (1), n. 1-d.

To Thornton Wilder, Zurich, Switzerland
[Transcribed by Wilder]
[Postcard: Picture of Abbaye d'Hautecombe]

[postmark: 26 October 1937]   [Bilignin par] Belley
                                               [Ain]

Dear Thornton

getting ready to go and so getting ready to see you, yes Ida
needs helping she goes on but any kind thought is more than welcome,[1] Mme
[Goudet?] gave me a new vest and there is to be a new hat to go with it,[2] and I
am digging up the dahlias and I guess that's all till then we think your thoughts
are gay

Gtde.

You will read us the comedy.[3]

1. Stein is responding to Wilder's comments on *Ida A Novel* in his letter of 20 October. For transcription information, see Stein to Wilder, received 10 September 1936 (1), n. 1-d.
2. Perhaps Wilder's misreading of Madame Sylvia Godet in Talissieu.
3. *The Merchant of Yonkers.*

To Gertrude Stein and Alice Toklas, Paris, France
[Postcard: Baden Thermalkurort]

28 Oct[ober] 1937   [Zurich, Switzerland]
In the Post office Thursday night

Dear Friends:

Saturday night I'm going to Paris for four nights on very urgent
business. Is there any chance of your arriving there before Wednesday night.
I'll be at the Hotel Buckingham Rue des Mathurins.

Jed Harris telephoned from London for 20 minutes (!!) the other night.
And maybe my "Our Town" will go in New York for the Xmas season. Imagine. The terribly official "reading" will take place in Paris.

And for excitement's sake, guess who may act the long lanky New England Talkative Stage-Manager in it (who as in the Chinese theatre hovers
about the action, picking his teeth, handing the actors their properties and
commenting drily to the audience)—Sinclair Lewis. He's been plaguing Jed
for a long time to let him act.

Let's all act.

Think it over. In the meantime I dream you may be in Paris by the 4th.[1]
>   love ever
>   Thornton

1. See Appendix VII, "Wilder, Jed Harris and *Our Town.*"

To Thornton Wilder, Paris, France
[Transcribed by Wilder]

[3 November 1937][1]   27 rue de Fleurus
Wednesday   [Paris]

My dearest Thornton,

We did have a good time last evening [dinner at La Pérouse and saw De Musset-Baty's Les Caprices de Marianne][2] and Alice is looking forward to tomorrow [Dinner at Lucas' and seeing Giraudoux-Jouvet's Electre] and on Friday you lunch with us and then we go off to the museums, the conservator of the Petit Palais, M. Escholier a charming man wants us to meet him at 2:30 there and he will show us everything including if you like the finest Rembrandt etchings in existence, we forgot to talk about the ms for Yale, but we will on Thursday, I have an idea for rewriting Ida, lots of love,
>   Gtde.

1. Wilder either wrote the date he received the letter or mistranscribed the word "tomorrow." For transcription information, see Stein to Wilder, received 10 September 1936 (1), n. 1-d. The words in brackets are Wilder's.

2. A revival of Jean-Victor Pellerin's *Cris des coeurs* and Alfred de Musset's *Les Caprices de Marianne*, directed by Gaston Baty, opened at the Théâtre Montparnasse on 30 October.

To Gertrude Stein and Alice Toklas, Paris, France

[?4 November 1937]   Hotel Chambord
                                                     123, Avenue des Champs Elysées
                                                     [Paris][1]

Dear Angelicals, and Thrones:

In Paris everything takes three times longer than anywhere else. Nobody's *there.* So I'm deep in phone-calls and vague foggy efforts to reach people, etc.

However, it's a darlin' city, and packed with French people, and I love'm.

—

Because of these Parisian obstacles to getting anything done I spent all yesterday stark alone.

I had a good mind to come and encumbre you; but I remembered that your house was full of workmen and that you weren't free.

—

So I read and reread IDA.

And often with bewitched delight; and sometimes in the dark—oh, yes, confident for *her*; but in the dark, for me.

But my incomprehensions are an old story.

I'm proud of being a slow-digester, a struggler-de-bonne-volonté and a ruminator.

Oh, Ida.

—

The play is again at nine.[2]

I'll be on the doorstep again at 7:30.

I'm afraid Louis Jouvet continues to be *souffrant* [ill] and will not appear, but Giraudoux's mixture of *Matricide and Mignonnettes* is still there and Sophocles continue[s] to revolve in his grave.

love
Thornton

1. Letterhead of the hotel of Jed Harris. Wilder was at the Hotel Buckingham.
2. Wilder was taking Stein and Toklas to Giraudoux's *Electre*, which he had already seen in July. See Wilder to Stein [?18 July 1937], n. 5.

———

To Thornton Wilder, Zurich, Switzerland
[Transcribed by Wilder]
[Rose Motto][1]

11 Nov[ember]. [1937]   27 rue de Fleurus
                                                [Paris]

My dearest Thornton,

Are you back in peaceful Zürich yet,[2] we are so looking forward to you again, the ms and notes for Making of Americans are all packed in a leather suitcase, and all the rest will go into an officer's canteen that we have left over from the war, and I hope all that will not be too much for you, the Rops want so much to meet you and it is arranged for Tuesday the 23 for dinner, and Picabia is having his vernissage Friday the 19 evening[3] so you will dine here then probably with them if that suits you, and there is lots xciting, Ida gently progressing but just now not so much there pictures and a new young man [Toulouse-L. age 20, Orleans][4] and something else [commission to do a book about Picasso][5] but all that when we meet, Bob Davis wrote a long and pleasant letter[6] but is he here, and Sammy Stewart sent wonderful gadgets,[7] love,

Gtde.

1. For transcription information, see Stein to Wilder, received 10 September 1936 (1), n. 1-d. The words in brackets are Wilder's.

2. On 6 November Wilder left Paris for London, where he visited Lady Colefax and discussed his meeting with Harris. He also read *Our Town* before an invited group of friends, including representatives of his English publisher, Longmans Green (see Michel Saint-Denis to Wilder, 23 July 1938, YCAL). Wilder returned to Zurich to organize his affairs and was back in Paris on 18 November.

3. An exhibition, *Francis Picabia, peintures Dada, paysages récentes*, was held at the Galerie de Beaune from 19 November to 2 December 1937.

4. The poet Max Jacob had introduced Stein to the young painter Roger Toulouse.

5. Raymond Escholier, curator of the Petit Palais and editor at Librairie Floury, suggested that Stein write a book on Picasso. She wrote in French and revised with Toklas, Escholier helping to polish the French version and adding the footnotes. Toklas prepared an English translation not from the published French text but from Stein's original draft before it was worked on by Escholier. Stein's *Picasso* was published in France in March 1938, in England in October 1938, and in the United States in February 1939.

6. Undated letter from Davis (YCAL).

7. From Chicago, Steward had sent Stein and Toklas a number of kitchen gadgets (see Steward, *Dear Sammy*, 134). Stewart is Wilder's misspelling.

To Thornton Wilder, Zurich, Switzerland

[postmark: 14 November 1937]   27 rue de Fleurus
                                                                 [Paris]

My dear Thornton,

Your telegram[1] just came sure change Saturday evening if you like but not Saturday lunch, Madame Weiss[2] and Madame Clermont-Tonnerre are coming early to meet you, Saturday at one, so Saturday one o'clock, Elmer Harden[3] is dining with you and us here Friday night, Picabia vernissage after and Tuesday night the Rops everything else is a moveable feast, and you will be it lots of love

Gtde.

So we will go with you Thursday is [i.e., if] this is all straight, we love you

Gtde and Alice.

1. The telegram has not been located. This letter confirms and expands the appointments that Stein mentions in her previous letter.

2. See Stein to Wilder 28 August 1937, n. 4, and 17 September 1937, n. 2.

3. Elmer Harden was an American soldier from Medford, Massachusetts, who settled permanently in Paris after World War I and became a friend of Stein.

To Gertrude Stein and Alice Toklas, Paris, France

15 Nov[ember] 1937   Carlton Elite Hotel
Monday morning   Zurich [Switzerland]

Dearest Kinder:

As I cabled you I've got to reserve Saturday night after all. I found a pile of mail waiting for me, and have to jostle around the Paris engagements to get everything in.

But I also found that if I leave here Thursday morning at 5:36 a.m. I can get to Paris at about 3:00 p.m. And so Thursday evening is full and clear.

So, that night you come out to dine with me (I beg your pardons; I didn't mean that to sound bossy. I meant: please accept my invitation to . . . . . .) and go to a play. There is no sign yet of the revival of Giraudoux's Guerre de Troie n'aura pas lieu; but there's Cocteau's Chevaliers de la Table Ronde; Claudel's L'Echange; and Baty's Madame Bovary.[1]

And I can read all the new Ida

And the new Picasso. . .

And I can go to the Louvre.

And can I look into the Canteen or is it all sealed?[2]

and it'll be grand and fine.

So Presto is saving for MD—(?? Swift, Stella and Mrs. Dingley—)[3]

Thursday, Friday and Tuesday evenings. Saturday lunch. And Tuesday lunch you're lunching with me, too.

Isn't it awful to see such pleasures regimented as tho' they were business appointments.

The sun's shining on Zürich

love

Thornton

1. Jean Giraudoux's *La guerre de Troie n'aura pas lieu* had been presented for the first time on 21 November 1935 at the Théâtre de l'Athénée-Louis Jouvet. Jouvet directed and played the role of Hector. The play ran for 255 performances but had not been revived. Cocteau's play was being performed at the Théâtre de l'Oeuvre and Claudel's play by the Pitoëffs at their theater. Gaston Baty's adaptation of Flaubert's *Madame Bovary* closed on 29 October.

2. See Stein to Wilder, 11 November 1937.
3. See Wilder to Stein, 25 January 1936, n. 9.

To Thornton Wilder, Paris, France

[postmark: 17 November 1937]   Gertrude Stein
                                                                 27 rue de Fleurus
                                                                 Paris

My dearest Thornton,

        Let's just dine and not go to the theatre we have so much to tell we are moving, we are going from rue de Fleurus to the rue Christine most xciting,[1] you can see we are in no state for a theatre so call for us and we will eat and talk

love

Gtrde.

    1. In a letter to Bobsy Goodspeed of 16 December 1937 Stein writes, "It happened like this, this summer we had been vaguely talking about moving because the kitchen and things aren't modern enough for a modern french servant and that complicates life too much but nothing would have happened of course not if the landlord's son had not married and wanted this place for himself, we might have said no but we were really half glad and on the same day within two hours we found the apartment of our dreams on the rue Christine, 17 century home with big rooms and it was all signed next day" (YCAL). It was through Méraud Guinness Guevara, wife of the painter Alvaro Guevara, that Stein found the apartment. Mme Guevara, who lived in the rue Dauphine, was herself looking to move and knew of apartments in the neighborhood. When Stein came to see her that afternoon, she immediately took Stein to see the apartment on the rue Christine (see Burns, *Letters*, 2:578–79).

To Gertrude Stein and Alice Toklas, Paris, France

24 November 1937[1]   Cherbourg [France]
Wednesday 11:20 a.m.

                                      I travel in order to sit in
                                                                 hotel-rooms writing letters.

Dear Friends:

        A radiant day.

        A radiant boy. The crisis is over. After I left you I slept all night. On the train I fell asleep twenty-times. I fell asleep in the afternoon in Cherbourg. I slept all night. And now I'm as *gaillard* [vigorous] as the harbor outside. The sunlight and the cloud-life of France were never more beautiful than they are at this moment. Wasn't there a painter Boudin, or something like that, who recorded, signed and sealed forever these blue-gray skies, promontories and sunny waves. Anyway Corot did it before he fell among the willow-trees.

Anyway, I'm getting great satisfaction from the landscape, like Alice, with my back to it. I've read forty pages of *La Chartreuse de Parme*, enjoying those continual sharp nips that Stendhal takes at France in order to glorify Italy. I think Mme de Clermont-Tonnerre ought to follow her lecture with another on WHY THE FRENCH DO NOT AND DO LIKE FRANCE. I've also read several masses by Palestrina, but it's not in the rue de Fleurus, alas, that I can find companionship in such pleasures.[2]

I can't get on to the boat until six. But I expect to enjoy it all mightily.

All my devoted best, and as always, thanks for a thousand good things.

> Your
> Thornton

1. Wilder dated this letter 24 November 1937, Wednesday 11:20 A.M. The dating may be an error caused by fatigue. If his account is correct, the letter would have to have been written on Thursday, 25 November. On Tuesday, 23 November, Wilder had dinner with Stein and the Daniel-Rops and then took the night train to Cherbourg. He spent Wednesday the twenty-fourth in Cherbourg before leaving for the United States on Thursday, 25 November.

2. An allusion to Stein's professed lack of interest in music.

To Gertrude Stein and Alice Toklas, Paris, France

6 Dec[ember] 1937   50 Deepwood Drive
New Haven[,] Conn[ecticut].

Dear One and One:

All that like art please raise their hands.[1]

You see I never really finished that play.

But I arrived in New York to find daily announcements in the papers of the new actors engaged for it, and so on.

So Jed [Harris] met me on the dock and whisked me off to a cottage he had engaged on Long Island, imprisoned me there and commanded me to write.

All day he's off at the office interviewing ingénues and I sit in a lot of chintz and butlers and expensive gramophones ("contented plays from contented authors") writing.[2]

It was very clever of Jed so to harness my ineradicable sense of obligation and the play's getting better every day.[3] A very great, much-loved actor has been engaged for the principal role.[4] Doll's House has been winning delirious favor in the Middle West. Lloyd Lewis is bewitched by it.[5]

Just wrote a letter to the Kiddies explaining all this, telling them that I have a present from you to them, and that when I am at last *enlarged* I shall give it to them.[6]

I snap open the dailies every morning looking for the reviews of Everybody's Autobiography.[7]

I'm well, fat & joyous.

I stipulated from Jed that every other day I should be allowed to come into Town. I had a talk with Terry Lewis last night and she is having lunch with me today.[8] She is overworking like mad, but she has at least cut down on the private life. Liz [Duval] will be back next week from her philanthropies in Kentucky and will go into her bookshop.

Mme Bousquet has found a lecture manager, but was too late for any lectures this year; has build up a good ground work for a tour next year if she wishes to return here to fulfil it.

She is living at Mme Helena Rubenstein's a lady who takes pleasure in insulting her in devious ways, enjoying the house guest who is superior to herself but who has the bad sense to be poor.

My family is fine; but Isabel is fretful & bored.

Soon you will be moving. Oh, dear, I forget whether it is 5 or 6 rue Christine.

I long for these plays to be <u>on</u> so that I can steal away to Quebec and make more.

Alicia—Isabel was screaming with pleasure over the pastry-dessert book.

I kiss you resoundingly and am your
bound-hand-and feet
Thornton

1. Wilder had cleverly written the salutation in colored pencils.
2. Wilder was staying in a cottage on a property in Old Brookville, Long Island, rented by Rosamond Pinchot, who was having an affair with Jed Harris. With Wilder on the property, Harris could visit her and her children without raising problems with her estranged husband.
3. Harris saw the publicity value in letting it be known that Wilder was in seclusion. A headline in the *New York World-Telegram* read, "Wilder Locked Up Till He Finishes That Play of His. But Jed Harris Lets Him Out To Tell About It" (7 December 1937, 26).
4. Frank Craven was engaged to play the Stage Manager.
5. As part of its pre–New York tour, the production of *A Doll's House* opened at the Shubert Grand Opera House in Chicago on 29 November 1937. Lloyd Lewis reviewed the production for the *Chicago Daily News* (30 November, NYPL-Lincoln Center).
6. Wilder's letters to William and Mildred Rogers have not been located. In an undated letter to Stein (YCAL), Rogers wrote that they had a card and a letter from Wilder, "including the promise to send us what you entrusted him with."

7. The publication date for *Everybody's Autobiography* was 2 December.

8. See Wilder to Stein, 16 and 18 July 1937.

To Thornton Wilder, New Haven, Connecticut
[Rose motto]

[postmark: 8 December 1937]   27 rue de Fleurus
                                                             [Paris]

My dearest Thornton,

We are waiting waiting waiting for all about the play,[1]
the play is the thing well anyway, the house is getting painted and electrified
and plumbified and kitchenified and when we are not too busy we are there
every day and it will be lovely really and truly it will and all ready for Thornton
to come back,[2] it will be heavenly in the spring, and I have finished with my
french Picasso, not so bad, Alice is struggling to reduce tenses grammar
spelling and genders into some kind of order,[3] would that you were here, you
love to struggle, dear Thornton we do miss you, and the scenes are all right I
hope, and I have just corrected the proofs for the English edition[4] and more
and more over I think I have a scheme for Ida which will pull it together, it
came out of our last talk together the one about the difference between
Making of Americans and Freud, I have an idea I have not yet had time to put
it in order it is just commencing but in a couple of days I xpect to begin and
then later we will send it to you, dear Thornton have a good time and accept
anything anybody wants to give you, and we give you lots of love you bet

Gtrde and Alice
and family.[5]

1. *Our Town.*

2. According to his date book, on the afternoon of 19 November Wilder had gone with Stein to
see the new apartment at 5 rue Christine.

3. The date assigned in section "D" of the Haas-Gallup Catalogue for *Picasso* in French is 1938.
This letter and that of 16 December make clear that her manuscript, first mentioned to Wilder on
11 November, was completed in 1937. In January 1938, Stein wrote an "Epilogue" discussing the return
of her pictures from an exhibition at the Petit Palais. (See Wilder to Stein [?18 July 1937], n. 2, and
Stein to Wilder, 11 November 1937, n. 5.)

4. *Everybody's Autobiography*, published by William Heinemann in 1938.

5. Both signatures are Stein's.

To Gertrude Stein and Alice Toklas, Paris, France

[?early December 1937]   The Century Association
                                                           7 West Forty-Third Street
                                                           New York [New York]

A MERRY

CHRISTMAS

To

ALGERTRUDICÉ

from

their loving nephew

Thornton[1]

Yes, dear friends, and a host of affectionate thoughts to you.

Busy, busy, I am . . . . . interviewing types chosen for this and that . . . . and altering here and there a sentence . . . but not so busy that I'm not reminded all the time of you and remembering so many good times with you and promising myself more.

Remember your wandering boy as wishing he were speeding up Raspail and hurrying across the court and ringing the bell, and hushing the dog and asking you a thousand questions.

devotedly

affectionately

Yours

Thornty

1. The Christmas salutation is in colored crayons.

To Thornton Wilder, New Haven, Connecticut
[Rose motto]

[postmark: 16 December 1937]   27 rue de Fleurus
                                                           Paris

                                                           5 rue Christine 6 arr.
                                                           15 Janvier[1]

My dearest Thornton,

          The parti-colored letter came and Merry Christmas and Happy New Year and send us still 27 rue de Fleurus a cable that the play went beautifully, we are waiting for that, Bennett [Cerf] seems content with

the beginning of the reception of Everybody's [*Autobiography*][2] and Daisy
Fellowes is giving a party for it, a sort of franco American celebration, and
Mme Clermont-Tonnerre talked charmingly about the delights of America
and of France, so that went very well and aren't you homesick for Paris and us,
well you ought to be and the french book written by me is finished and next
week it goes to the editor,[3] a very xciting moment, and you seem faithless
Thornton you never said a word about my ms. did they get over safely are they
in Yale,[4] oh faithless Thornton, and [Paul] Valery did his initial talk at the
College de France on the relation of Poet to his audience,[5] well anyway we
love you oh so much, and are praying for your success and happy happy days
Gtrde & Alice.

1. Stein has crossed out the rue de Fleurus address and added the new address with the date of
their move.

2. Cerf to Stein, 7 December 1937 (YCAL).

3. Stein's *Picasso*.

4. On 23 November, Stein and Wilder collaborated on a letter to Andrew Keogh, librarian of
Yale University. Stein gave to the library the manuscript of "A Long Gay Book" and deposited other
manuscripts as "a loan for safe-keeping, available to such persons as may wish to study them." She
indicated her intention to forward other manuscripts and correspondence "in the near future." She
concluded by stating, "In the event of my demise all of this material becomes automatically your
property" (see Wilder to Stein [9 October 1937]). For the text of Stein's letter to Keogh, see Donald C.
Gallup, "The Gertrude Stein Collection." Because of production pressures of *Our Town* and the
suicide of Rosamond Pinchot in the early morning of 24 January 1938, Wilder did not mail the letter
until 2 February 1938.

5. Valéry's inaugural lecture at the Collège de France, "Première Leçon du Cours de Poétique,"
was given on 10 December 1937. Stein attended the lecture with Bernard Faÿ, who held the chair in
American civilization at the college.

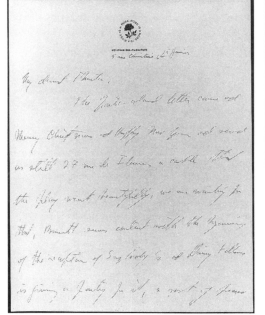

Characteristically undated, this letter announcing the move to Rue Christine for 15 January 1938 was mailed on 16 December 1937. Chatting about friends and events, Stein completely fills the pages as she so often filled her notebooks to the end of the last page.

1938

PICASSO

CHAPITRE PREMIER

La peinture au XIXᵉ siècle, en France, était faite entièrement par les Français. A l'étranger, la peinture n'existait pas. Au XXᵉ siècle la peinture est faite en France, mais par les Espagnols.

Le XIXᵉ siècle exige la présence du modèle. Au XXᵉ siècle, il ne faut jamais regarder le modèle.

Je me rappelle, comme s'il datait d'hier, ce passé de 1904 à 1908, quand les gens s'essayaient à comprendre chez nous les dessins de Picasso.

La première et la plus étonnante des choses à dire sur ces dessins, c'est qu'il les faisait merveilleusement, comme avec un modèle et sans jamais en avoir. Maintenant les jeunes ne se servent pas de modèle. Tout change, mais non sans raison.

Le jeune Picasso arrive à Paris, à dix-neuf ans, en octobre 1900[1], dans un milieu de peintres qui avaient

1. Picasso arrivé à Paris en octobre 1900, y retrouve ses compatriotes Sunyer, Nonells, Canals.

Stein's study of Picasso, written in French in 1937, underwent revisions by the author and Toklas. The French edition was published by Librairie Floury in March 1938 and Stein's own English translation by Batsford, London, in October 1938.

To Thornton Wilder, New Haven, Connecticut
[Rose motto]

[postmark: 6 January 1938]   27 rue de Fleurus
                                                               [Paris]

My dear Thornton,
      Where oh where is that cable telling all about how the
play went, what happened, we say it to each other every morning, why no
word from Thornton about the play, what is the matter with Thornton, is there
anything from Thornton and there is not even an echo that answers nein,
quick let us know,[1] we are deep in moving so deep that cold as it is we go on
just the same, the pictures are almost all washed now, and what happens next
well everything, tell us what happened to you and be quick about it and lots of
love now and always
               Gtde.

   1. Stein assumes that *Our Town* has already opened.

To Gertrude Stein and Alice Toklas, Paris, France

12 Jan[uary] 1938   Century Club
think of it   7 West Forty-Third Street
                                                             New York [New York]

Dear Ones:
      Yes, faithless is what I am.
      And even this spurt of fidelity is due to the fact that I have a sore throat
and refuse to go to rehearsal and refuse to rewrite a certain scene in Act Two.

My only defense is that I have been faithless to everybody equally. I went to New Haven Christmas eve but by Christmas day at six o'clock I was back in New York *at work*. And similarly on New Year's day.

But that's not all.

Between work, there are fights.

As you predicted Jed [Harris] got the notion that he had written the play and was still writing it.

As long as his suggestions for alterations are on the structure they are often very good; but once they apply to the words they are always bad and sometimes atrocious.

There have been some white-hot flaring fights. At present we are in a lull of reconcilement.

———

The play opens a week from Sat[urday] (Jan 22) in Princeton, New Jersey, for one night; then goes to Boston for two weeks; then enters New York.

Even with Jed's sentences in it—which I hope gradually to *abrade* away—it is a very good play. The cast is fine.[1]

———

But that's not all:

Morning's—Jed's first phone calls don't start before noon, nor cease until 3: A.M—mornings I['m] hurriedly but joyously finishing up Play No #2 for [Max] Reinhardt in California.[2]

———

Yesterday, on a long-established promise I went down and gave (in two senses) a lecture at Haverford College.

Leslie Hotson had long discovered more new data about Wm Shakespeare than any human being.

I told him if he discovered anything more about Him I'd come and lecture.

And sure enough Leslie did. He found out all about the man whom Shakespeare made the executor of his will: how close in among his circle of friends were the conspirators of the Guy Fawkes plot; and a lot of things.

Leslie's now going back to work for 1½ years on the archives and he thinks he's hot on the identity of "Mr. W.H."—not a peer.[3]

———

"Doll's House" is fine, but it's not going very well. Balcony is alway[s] sold out; but the rich people downstairs seem to shrink from the name of Ibsen.[4]

———

Be patient with me a little longer. The hurly burly will soon be over.

You wouldn't know me and I don't know myself, but translated tho' I am I know that I love you more than tongue can tell.

Ever

Thy

Thornton

1. The first performance of *Our Town* was at the McCarter Theatre in Princeton, New Jersey, on 22 January 1938. The next morning the cast left for Boston, where the play opened at the Wilbur Theatre on 25 January. Before going to Princeton for the opening performance, Wilder wrote and sealed a statement about the production:

The Following Elements in the Production of
"Our Town" are likely to harm and perhaps
shipwreck its effectiveness

See Appendix VII.

2. *The Merchant of Yonkers.*

3. Wilder's lecture was entitled "The Novelist versus the Dramatist." At the top of Hotson's letter of 10 October 1937 (YCAL), Isabel Wilder wrote, "Explained you were abroad until Christmas. But I guess you'll just have to come across after these 7 years of promising." Wilder had known Hotson since the 1920s and was fascinated by his research. The information Hotson found in the Public Record Office about Shakespeare's friends, especially Thomas Russell, the overseer of his will, is presented in his *I, William Shakespeare, do appoint Thomas Russell, Esquire* (New York: Oxford Univ. Press, 1938). His identification of William Hatcliffe as the "Mr. W. H." of Shakespeare's sonnets is argued in his *Mr. W. H.* (New York: Alfred A. Knopf, 1964).

4. *A Doll's House* opened at the Morosco Theatre, New York, on 27 December 1937; it moved to the Broadhurst Theatre on 10 January 1938. The production closed on 30 April 1938 after 144 performances.

To Gertrude Stein and Alice Toklas, Paris, France

1 Feb[ruary]. 1938   The Graduates Club
                                                          New Haven, Connecticut

Dear Friends:

All I can do is still throw myself on your mercy.

The theatre's a furnace.

It's been one long fight to preserve me [i.e., my] text from the interpolations of Jed Harris, and I've only won 50% of the time.

We opened in Princeton.

Then we opened in Boston.

Now we open Friday night in New York.

The play no longer moves or even interests me; now all I want out of it is money.

Money so that I can feel justified in going off to Arizona and write some more,—reconstruct the mode of life I had at Zürich.

The play may be a failure.

The newspapers in Boston were not much more than luke-warm.

But in every audience there are a few people who are extremely enthusiastic.

It's hard for me to realize that I've been back in this country 8 weeks and all that time bent over this one little work. That's undignified.[1]

I think your new address is 5 rue Christine but I'm not sure, and until I'm sure I'd better continue writing you to 27 rue de Fleurus.

So here I am still writing you the flurried letters of a crazy man; but when I get to Arizona, I'll be myself again. The whole blame of my state rests at Jed Harris's door. I don't *enjoy* contemplating or getting excited about any work of my own.

However, even when I'm *not myself* I love you and send you my love as ever.

Your

Thornton

1. The Boston reviews of *Our Town* were tepid and, on the second night, Harris posted the closing notice. By the midweek matinee, the audiences were sparse. Alexander Woollcott, who had brought the *New York Times* critic Brooks Atkinson to Boston to see the play, convinced Harris to cancel the second week in Boston and move the play directly to New York. Because of the Boston notices, the Shubert Organization would not risk giving Harris a theater. However, the Henry Miller was scheduled to be free for three weeks, and *Our Town* opened there on 4 February.

Harris had understood that Woollcott's enthusiasm and Atkinson's opportunity to reflect on the play before writing a New York review would be important. Although Woollcott was no longer writing drama criticism, he did discuss *Our Town* on his national radio program. In addition to his daily review on 5 February, Atkinson wrote a Sunday piece on the play on 13 February. Later, Eleanor Roosevelt in her "My Day" column wrote, "When I went to see 'Our Town' I was moved and depressed beyond words. It is more interesting and more original [than Katharine Dayton's *Save Me the Waltz*] and I am glad I saw it, but I did not have a pleasant evening" (*New York Daily News*, 5 February 1938). Answering Roosevelt in a column on 13 March 1938, Atkinson wrote, "Far from being depressed, I came away from the theatre exalted by the bravery, kindliness and goodness of American people. In the deepest sense of the word, *Our Town* is a religious play" (see Atkinson, *Broadway Scrapbook* "Our Town," 85–88, and "Mrs. Roosevelt on *Our Town*," 89–92).

Woollcott responded to Mrs. Roosevelt as follows:

And now, as your senior and better in dramatic criticism, let me make a word of comment on your progress as a play-goer. The late Charles Frohman used to say that sometimes it wasn't the play that failed, but the public. I gather from your diary that when you went to see *Our Town* you were not at your best. I am afraid you didn't give what I could conscientiously call a good performance. If, at that gentle masterpiece, you were "depressed beyond words," it must have been on some evening when you would not have been spiritually equal to reading, let us say, Gray's *Elegy*.

So now this is what you must do. You must eat some lettuce, read a little Charles Lamb, take a nap and go to see *Our Town* again. After that, kindly report to me at once and oblige. (Quoted in

Alexander Woollcott: The Man Who Came to Dinner, Edwin P. Hoyt [New York: Abelard-Schuman, 1968], 306–07.)

To Gertrude Stein and Alice Toklas, Paris, France

14 Feb[ruary] 1938   50 Deepwood Drive
                                                    New Haven, Conn[ecticut].

Dear Friends:
        Today I called up the Kiddies to ask them two things:
        (1) What was your street number Rue Christine.
        I had wobbled between 3 and 6 and it turns out to be 5.

        (2) Whether I could stop & see them Feb[ruary] 25 when I pass thru on my way West. Will your ears burn?

        I enclose an essay (sic) I wrote on my play.
        Gertrude, does it make you squirm when you see us children reducing your doctrines to baby-talk?
        They may not be your ideas; but according to my lights, that['s] what I think they are.[1]

        Today I took down the first batch of the MSS to the Yale library. I know the delay has been shameful but I *could* no other.
        On the ones I took down I had pasted neat labels

MEXICO:
a play
ACT IV

Like that.[2]
        And I took the whole of "How to Write" "Three Lives" "Lucy Church Amiably" and "Operas & Plays." And scores of smaller works. The Librarians were ecstatic. I'll make a lot more trips when I come back from New York Friday.

        Oh, oh, oh, I can't wait to get away to the West—hot sunlight, desert air, (I've had a long lingering cold), long walks among the tumbleweeds and rattlesnake nests.

And when I get there away from this Bedlam I shall again encumber you
with long letters.

All my love

Thornton

1. "A Preface for *Our Town*" was published in the *New York Times*, Sunday, 13 February 1938, sec.
10, 1. The "Preface" is in Wilder's *American Characteristics*, 100–03 (cited as unpublished). See
Appendix VII.

2. Wilder pasted a 1½-×-2¾″ label on the letter similar to the labels on the manuscript *cahiers* of
Stein's work (see Stein to Wilder [16 December 1937], n. 4).

To Gertrude Stein and Alice Toklas, Paris, France

[?20–24 February 1938]   [50 Deepwood Drive
                                                         New Haven, Connecticut]

Dear Ones:

Not a letter, dears, just a "mezzanine note." Bad cold has got into
every joint and I'm a mess of grouchiness inertia and longing for Arizona &
solitude[.]

All morning I've been aiding librarians by pasting labels on the cahiers:
The work; a day's
sun; Camelia's
in Perpignan etc

Will we see them
again, etc.
I can feel the beauty

Tourty and Tourtebattre

Come sister[1]

like that. Saturday I go up to Springfield and see the Kiddies.

Your new house sounds lovely.

Oh, oh,—I wish I could a long Tale unfold: Jed Harris. You diagnosed
him to a T.

Got my first letter from a person who *loathes* the play. That always
solidifies things. I always remember O[scar]. Wilde's remark to a hisser from
the galleries: Yes, but what are we two against so many?

love & more soon

Thornton

1. Wilder placed each of these titles in a box to suggest his labels on Stein's manuscript *cahiers*. He plays with titles and phrases from Stein's work of 1917–19, beginning with "The Work" (1917), a title that includes the two poems "A day's sun" and "Camelias in Perginnang," perhaps a misspelling of Perpignan. "Will We See Them Again" and "I Can Feel The Beauty" are included in the same *cahier*. "Tourty Or Tourtebattre. A Story Of The Great War" is a piece from 1919. "Come sister" is not a Stein title or line.

To Thornton Wilder, New Haven, Connecticut
[Rose motto]

[? March 1938]   5 rue Christine.
                                                    [Paris]

My dearest Thornton

How we wish you were here, there are the banks of the Seine more banks than ever, come Thornton come, and we saw the photos of the play and we liked them in Life,[1] out at the Bromfields,[2] and Alice said that they said there was no scenery and there are all those props, but we did like it, and it goes on, and we wish you were here, we would like to tell you about something else but there is only our apartment and our quarter, we even have our municipal counciller and xchange calls, we are full of projects, an opera,[3] a ballet,[4] a cinema,[5] and you will do the novel yet yes we will,[6] you know Thornton I find so many on the quays and I read them all and I begin to really know what a novel is, come Thornton come and I'll tell you and do you like the Picasso[7] and do you like everything, Sammy [Steward] wrote charmingly about you[8] and lots of love

Gtrde and Alice

1. The *Life* essay was titled "Plays Without Scenery Give New York Theatre-Goers A New Dramatic Thrill" and illustrated with photographs not only from *Our Town*, but also from *Father Malachy's Miracle*, *The Cradle Will Rock*, and the Mercury Theatre production of *Julius Caesar*. A *New Yorker* cartoon of three ladies at a box office with one asking, "Does this play have scenery?" was also reproduced. See *Life*, 4, 9 (28 February 1938), 27–29.

2. On Sundays Stein and Toklas often visited Louis and Mary Bromfield, who lived in an old vicarage with an extensive garden, in Senlis (Oise), some twenty-five miles north of Paris.

3. On his way to Rome for a vacation, Lord Berners visited Stein in Paris and discussed a new joint project—an opera on the Faust theme, which became Stein's *Doctor Faustus Lights The Lights*.

4. Ever since the London premiere of *A Wedding Bouquet* in April 1937, Stein had been urging friends and acquaintances to arrange for an American production. Lord Berners, who had earlier worked with George Balanchine, wrote to him and to Leonide Massine. Bobsy Goodspeed also had been speaking to Massine and reported in mid-February that Massine would see Stein in Paris (see Berners to Stein, undated letter [?1938], YCAL, and Goodspeed to Stein in Gallup, *Flowers*, 325–26, and 14 February 1938, YCAL).

5. This may refer to a project between Stein and the French writer Germaine de Perdiguier to do a film about Picasso.

6. Stein still hoped Wilder would collaborate on *Ida A Novel*.

7. The French *Picasso* was published in March 1938, followed by the English edition in October of that year and the American edition in February 1939. "Picasso et Gertrude Stein," an article by Germaine de Perdiguier to help promote the book in France, appeared in *Sud Magazine*, June–July 1938, 19.

8. Steward to Stein, 13 March 1938 (YCAL).

To Gertrude Stein and Alice Toklas, Paris, France

27 March 1938   General Delivery,
                                                                 Tucson[,] Arizona[1]

Dear Friends:

Oh, the unjustified reproaches! I can call witnesses to prove that all those weeks you alluded often to moving but that you never once mentioned the number of your residence in the Rue Christine.

I hope the concierge however duly forwarded my mail from Rue de Fleurus.

I have just moved in, too.

A tiny apartment, nice, but nowhere near as nice as 2060 Drexel, Chicago.

And through the window come the desert air and the Arizona sunlight, wonderful things.

Through the walls come my neighbor's radios and my neighbor's quarrels—and reconciliations.

The desert's wonderful. I just returned from spending the day at a ranch sixty miles away,—between 20 and 30 thousand acres, the cows browsing among the cacti and rattlesnakes. I climbed the nearest hill and looked out over a tremendous prospect of mountains, plain, clouds and mesquite.[2]

You may remember that I was left cold by the Tyrolian Alps. Not so, by the Desert. *Explique qui peut* [Explain it if you can].

Play No #2 draws to an end and soon I shall be taking it to [Max] Reinhardt in Hollywood.[3]

I worry about you in Europe but I put my trust in Georges Maratier's knowing when to warn you and telling you what to do.[4]

Every day brings its new ugly news from Europe.

Egon Friedell threw himself out of a window.[5]

—Freud, age 82, calming his family, while the troopers ransacked his house.

I had some good talks with Alice Roullier in Chicago. She is fine.[6] Bobsy [Goodspeed] was away in Arizona, a hundred miles from here. The Hutchins are well, but the new baby is now the one in the family that is having constant ups-and-downs in health. Bob is losing heart about his post. Fanny [Butcher] looked bonny. Mortimer Adler made exaggerated overtures of friendship to me—exaggerated because I like him already, but not *that* much. I almost burst out: No, no, I can see by the shape of your head that you are an arguer; you can make black white, and white black,—no, no, I don't argue.[7]

———

Under your aegis I bought a Trolloppe [i.e., Trollope] and read it: The Belton Estate. Very good.

———

I enclose a clipping about the Yale gift.[8] Soon I must come over and bring back the next instalment. My mother sent it to me so I don't know what date or paper it is—looks like the New Haven Evening Register.

———

In New York I had lunch with Mabel [Dodge Luhan]. She is now being analyzed by Dr. [A. A.] Brill.

———

Isabel sails for London about April 15 to stay a month or two with the Dan Thompsons of the Courtauld Institute.[9] I hope she will go over to Paris and see you before you leave. She needs a rest and change very much; that "heart" trouble slow a-healing.

———

Bob Ardrey (do you remember, you liked him, pupil at the U[niversity]. of C[hicago]. who wrote plays) had two plays on Broadway since January. Neither lasted very long, but he had a call from Goldwyn to write in the movies—20 weeks at $1000 a week. He is in town here now *en route* to his job which he cannot begin until his Guggenheim expires on April first.[10]

———

A thousand apologies for such a dull letter, but apart from baking sun-light, long walks and hard work I have no news.

But even at my dullest, I'm still

with love

Yours

Thornton

1. Wilder left New York on 1 March, stopped off in Chicago until 7 March and arrived in Tucson on 8 March. He moved into an apartment at 732 North Sixth Avenue on 16 March.
2. The J-6 Cattle Company, a ranch in Benson, Arizona, owned by Jack Speiden.
3. *The Merchant of Yonkers.*

4. Georges Maratier first appears with the painters Pavel Tchelitchew, Kristians Tonny, Eugene Berman, the writers Georges Hugnet, Bravig Imbs, the composer Virgil Thomson, and the pianist Allan Tanner as a member of Stein's *seconde famille* of young friends and followers. He worked with Hugnet on the publication in his Editions de la Montagne of *Morceau Choisis de la Fabrication des Américains*, a selection, in French translation by Hugnet with help from Stein, from *The Making Of Americans*. Whether he worked as a friend or had a financial interest in the publishing venture is not clear. In June 1929, upon publication, Maratier discovered and reported to Stein that Hugnet had removed some twenty copies from the stock, which Maratier felt he was using improperly to promote himself.

The son of landowners familiar with French bureaucracy, Maratier was not an artist making a career but a trustworthy friend who from 1930 on, when Stein spent long summers in the country, gave her practical assistance in many forms. He helped her obtain the country house by submitting for promotion and transfer the name of the officer who occupied it. He also assisted with the car, with transfer of money, hiring and work permits of servants, supplies of wine, and the sale and purchase of paintings. Stein also appointed him her agent for publications in France. Her portrait of him, "G. Maratier," was written in 1929. Wilder, like many friends, was concerned for her because of the political unrest in Europe. W. G. Rogers, for example, advised her to put provisions in the car in case she and Toklas had to leave Paris on a moment's notice (Rogers to Stein, 15 March [1938] YCAL).

5. Friedell's three-volume *A Cultural History of the Modern Age* (1928–31) was published in English by Alfred A. Knopf in 1930–32. Friedell, an actor in Reinhardt's company, was well known in cabaret circles in Vienna. The German edition was dedicated to Reinhardt, the English edition to George Bernard Shaw.

6. Wilder saw Roullier in her gallery the afternoon of 2 March.

7. Wilder dined at the home of Robert Hutchins with Adler and the Goodspeeds on 3 March. He is remembering Stein's comment to Adler during a heated argument the evening of 27 November 1934. In a letter to the columnist Elsa Maxwell, Bobsy Goodspeed remembered the evening: "They [Stein, Robert Hutchins, and Mortimer Adler] were all three arguing about the writers of the 19th Century in England, and the argument soon turned to the real meaning of 'ideas,' and, naturally, from that moment on, grew into a great altercation, Gertrude marching up and down the room with her hands thrust into the pockets of her little woolen vest which she always wore. After a long dialectical dissertation on the part of the professor [Adler], Gertrude went over to him and pointed to his forehead, saying, 'I knew you would say just that kind of thing. Look at your forehead, it is narrow, narrow. With your dialectics, you could *prove anything* to me, but, of course, you would be *wrong*'" (copy, Goodspeed to Maxwell, 22 December 1941, YCAL). This confrontation is commented on by Stein in *Everybody's Autobiography*, 206–07, 212–13; by Toklas in *What Is Remembered*, 147–49; and by Adler in *Philosopher at Large: An Intellectual Autobiography*, 138–40.

8. The clipping has not remained with the letter.

9. Daniel Thompson briefly taught in the Art Department at Yale, then received a research appointment at the Courtauld Institute in London. Isabel Wilder was friendly with him and his wife, and they shared an interest in cooking.

10. Ardrey's *How To Get Tough About It* opened at the Martin Beck Theatre, New York, on 8 February 1938 and closed after twenty-three performances. The play was produced and staged by Guthrie McClintic. Ardrey's *Casey Jones* was presented by the Group Theatre, staged by Elia Kazan, at the Fulton Theatre, New York, on 19 February and closed after twenty-five performances. Ardrey comments on this experience in "A Preface to the Plays: Including Certain Personal Reflections," in his *Plays of Three Decades* (see also Wilder to Stein, 6 April 1935, n. 4).

To Thornton Wilder, Tucson, Arizona
[Rose motto]

[postmark: 9 April 1938]   5 rue Christine.
                                                           [Paris]

My dearest Thornton,

It is nice to get a letter that sounds like you that is you and sounds like you both and we forgive you everything and we will just go on doing some of the same. I do wish you were coming here, there is as much sunshine as there is in Arizona and not as near neighbors, we don't seem to pine for Bilignin at all of course we will go but this is really country air sunshine and space right here, do come and see it Thornton do, and what is happening to us well everything as usual, work, a new painter Darna[1] is his name and he comes from Corsica, and he is religious and of course there is a fair amount of xcitement, and Pepe and Basket and I go out on the Boulevard St. Michel and hear them sing as yet it is just singing and running so perhaps it will just begin and end with that[2] otherwise it is very lovely never has been such a nice spring and the life on the quays is a great occupation for all of us and you will partake of it yes you will, in the meanwhile we are looking forward to Isabel tell her to be sure and come she will like Paris, any Wilder has to come to it sometime,[3] we will not be leaving until the end of May we love our new house so so there will be time, golly Bob Ardrey, well give him my love, and thanks for the clippings. Francis Rose sent me a postal card of the sacred room and do come and get some more and do come and always do come lots of love[4]

Gtrde et al.

1. We have been unable to discover any information about this painter.
2. On 8 April the Fédération socialiste de la Seine demonstrated in support of Léon Blum against the Senate, which forced the evacuation of the Luxembourg Gardens. The demonstrators then marched along the Boulevard St. Michel chanting and singing (*Humanité*, 8 April 1938, 1).
3. Isabel Wilder did not go to Paris.
4. Rose sent a card of the Rare Book Room, Sterling Memorial Library, Yale University. He had been there to see her manuscripts (postmarked 2 March 1938, YCAL). Stein uses this occasion to suggest that Wilder visit and return with more. Before Stein met Rose in 1930 or early 1931, at the home of the painter Alvaro Guevara and his wife Méraud, she had already acquired some of his paintings. She continued collecting them, although she knew that Rose was a charming, unreliable liar. She remained friends with him, and he illustrated *The World Is Round, The Gertrude Stein First Reader, The Alice B. Toklas Cook Book*, and designed Stein's headstone in Père Lachaise Cemetery in Paris. Through Stein he obtained commissions for paintings in the country houses of Louis Bromfield, Sir Robert Abdy, and others. Portraits of Stein and Toklas are at YCAL, and a gouache purchased by Wilder is now at the National Portrait Gallery (see Wilder to Stein, 31 May 1939, n. 3).

To Gertrude Stein and Alice Toklas, Paris, France

23 April 1938   For one and a half weeks more:
                                                    General Delivery,
                                                    Tucson, Ariz[ona].

Dear *Engelstoff* [Angelstuff];
                          Yes, I'm longing to see you installed in your new
home, and the dogs out on their sun-walk and the pictures in the niches and in
the long gallery.

But I can't come this summer.

I think I can come in the early Fall, though it may still be in your Bilignin
days. Anyway, North or South, you're still Presto's adored MDs and the object of many long affectionate thoughts and partners in many imagined conversations.[1]

Just last night I was in a company of alert young people and was asked
"What Gertrude Stein was like"; and I did my portrait, and my sheaf of stories,
and my paraphrase of some of the "ideas" and I was so happy doing it and they
were so happy hearing it.

One of the reasons I must come over in the Fall is to ask Gertrude to
expand for me that phrase, which I may have got all wrong, that a "dramatist hears what the audience hears" and in what sense, he has his own "recognition" untroubled by that audience's hearing.[2] Oh, what fun it is to be
cudgelled by Gertrude, to be enlightened, and slapped, and warmed, and
crushed, and slain, and brought alive by Gertrude. As the ladies of the invaded
island in *L'ile des Pengouins* cried: "When do the atrocities begin?"

No news here.

Wonderful piercing hot days.

The cactus is in flower, Alice,—beautiful.

I make many of my own meals, primitive, but good. Alice, I wish I could
introduce you to the Oregon Blue Ribbon Prize Loganberry Juice. Lucullus
would have given his right hand for it.

Monday night I read my new play to a circle of friends on a nearby ranch.
Some of it's very funny—sly deep deep records of "human nature" getting itself into frightful predicaments. Max Reinhardt wrote that he was very pleased
with the first two acts I sent him and as soon as I can I'll be in Hollywood
showing him the rest.

Ruth Gordon's run in A Doll's House closes tonight. She has by far ex-
ceeded the world's record in the part: 240 almost consecutive performances.[3]

I wonder what Gertrude's working on mostly. Brentano's is sending me
the Picasso the moment it comes in. Is IDA A NOVEL still the chief work on the
desk. I long to hear that Gertrude has begun the "BILIGNIN HISTORY OF ENGLISH
AND AMERICAN LITERATURE OR WHY THERE IS SO MUCH AND SO LITTLE OF IT."

CHAPTER ONE: IT IS EASIER TO BE A POET WHEN THE WORDS ARE NEW.

CHAPTER TWO: WHY THE ELIZABETHAN WORDS WERE LIVELY

CHAPTER THREE: YOU AND I KNOW AS MUCH PSYCHOLOGY AS SHAKESPEARE, WHAT ELSE DID HE HAVE THEN

CHAPTER FOUR: HOW FIELDING ALMOST MISSED HIS MASTERPIECE

CHAPTER FIVE: JANE AUSTEN WAS NOT ANXIOUS

CHAPTER FIVE: THACKERAY-DICKENS AND TROLLOPE or the HARE AND THE TORTOISE.

CHAPTER FIVE: THE MAKING OF AMERICAN AUTHORS OR ISLAND PEOPLE CANNOT ROAM.

CHAPTER SIX: THE CHURCH LIBRARY AT AIX-LES-BAINS AND THAT'S ALL THERE IS ABOUT IT.

There's great danger of my trying to go on with it, and that must not be; but I hate to think of all that happy excitement joggling about inside me—topsy-turvy and only half-understood but very exciting.

Well, well, well, I've got to come over soon and be scolded again.

In the meantime all my love to you and to Basquet and Pépé.

Ever thine
Thornty

1. See Wilder to Stein, 25 January 1936, n. 9.

2. Wilder, working on *The Merchant of Yonkers*, may have been uneasy about reshaping of the material inspired by Nestroy and Molière. Afraid of losing his sense of his own voice, he appeals to Stein as his conscience for writing. See "Henry James" in *Four In America*, "Plays" in *Lectures In America*, and lecture four in *Narration*.

3. Wilder is counting the road tour and the New York performances. The New York run of *A Doll's House* was extended an extra week. The original plan had been to take the production to London, but Harris changed his plans: "A spokesman for the management of *A Doll's House* disclosed that instead of taking the production to London immediately, Jed Harris has decided last night to present it for a two week engagement at the Forrest Theatre, Philadelphia, beginning May 2" (undated, uncredited press release, NYPL-Lincoln Center).

To Thornton Wilder, New Haven, Connecticut

[postmark: 11 May 1938] 5 rue Christine
[Paris]

My dearest Thornton

Ida has become an opera, and it is a beauty, really is, an opera about Faust, I am dying to show it to you, I have the first act done, and I am now working on the second one, an opera with arias and duets and quartets and quintets and solos and choruses [Lord] Berners is going to do the music and I am as xcited as can be, some day she will be a novel too, she is getting ready for that, but as an opera she is a wonder,[1] wait, and you were awfully sweet Thornton about Bobchen Haas, you have made his path easy for him, he writes and and writes about it,[2] and oh Thornton can't you change your mind and come to Bilignin, but anyway 5 rue Christine is so beautiful, a Rumanian said the other day that Brancusi was so beautiful, he was a Rumanian, and Alice said rue Christine was so beautiful she was a Christinienne and she is and we are and you will be too, so much is happening so much so much please come and hear and tell please please

Gtrde.

1. "Ida has become an opera" sounds simple but is in fact ambiguous. Stein did little work on the novel from November to December 1937 while she wrote *Picasso* in French and in English. Work on the new apartment at 5 rue Christine continued longer than anticipated, and they did not move in until late January 1938. Stein had just settled in when Lord Berners visited in March and an opera on the Faust theme was agreed upon as their next joint project. When he returned to Paris in April, Stein had almost finished the first act of *Doctor Faustus Lights The Lights*. Back in England, he wrote to her, "Please send me the first act of Doctor Faustus. I was very thrilled by what you showed me and read to me" (28 April 1937, YCAL). Although Stein's letters to Berners have not been located, his to Stein allow us to follow the libretto's development. Regarding how "Ida has become an opera" *A Stein Reader* comments, "We can only speculate about the mysterious process of transmutation that must have taken place to start *Faustus*, for Stein said nothing about it. Ida does not become Faustus, but she undergoes a change and is transformed, the traditional Marguerite becoming Marguerite Ida and Helena Annabel, a protean figure from a charmed, demonic world who summons Faustus as Faustus summons Mephisto" (595).

2. See Haas to Stein, 25 April and 3 May 1938 (YCAL), Stein to Wilder, 13 September 1937, n. 3, and Wilder to Stein, 4 October 1937, n. 4.

To Gertrude Stein and Alice Toklas, Bilignin, France

7 June 1938   The Graduates Club
                                         One Hundred Fifty-Five Elm Street
                                         New Haven, Connecticut

Dear Ones:

Perhaps rue Christine is so delightful that you have delayed going down to Bilignin; but I'll assume that you're there and send this fat envelope with two mighty interesting enclosures.[1]

There's no news in my life. On the 15th I leave for Los Angeles to rewrite and rehearse my new play under [Max] Reinhardt. I've been reading it to groups of friends and they laugh the whole way through. High time.[2]

Isabel is in England, getting a big change after that long harrowing sentimental error of last year. She's going to Paris for a few days, maybe she's been there already in time to see you. Maybe she'll hurry back here and go to California with me as my secretary, and gradually elbow into the organization and become Reinhardt's lieutenant. (Isabel has been trained as technical theatre worker,—knows the electrical business and everything).[3] Reinhardt's plans are alarmingly vast: *Faust* outdoors in one arena; *The Blue Bird* in the Hollywood Bowl; and my *The Merchant of Yonkers* in a small theatre.[4]

Isn't the enclosed inventory a fine piece of librarian's work? Since Gertrude presented her MSS to the library many American authors have followed suit and the collection will become the great source reservoir for Americ[an]. Lit[erature]. in the first half of the 20th Century, *telle quelle*.

And, Alice, you'll burst into tears, dear, when you read the ballade about the street cars of San Francisco, and Gertrude will have to forward it to her brother.

I dream of coming abroad in the early Fall. Maybe Alec Woollcott will cross with me. I want some more ideas in my head: I've chawed all the previous ones that Gertrude gave me so thoroughly and regurgitated them so often for friends and interviewers that I need a new array before I can go out in public.

Are you all well?

And the dogs?

And Madame Giraud and la baronne?[5]

Are you driving carefully around the further side of the Lake?

Are you honking devastatingly in front of the bread, butter and vegetable shops?

Are the paths in great need of attention?

Oh, dear, I wish I were there instead of in this New Haven that I never did and never shall like.

But near or far, or late or soon I send you, as ever,

all my love

Thornton

1. One enclosure, preserved in typescript copy in the Yale Archives, is a list of the works deposited at the Yale library. The second enclosure, the "ballade about the street cars of San Francisco," has not remained with the letter. Gertrude Stein's eldest brother, Michael, worked with his father at the Omnibus Cable Company and later became a branch manager for the Market Street Railway Company in San Francisco.

2. *The Merchant of Yonkers.*

3. Isabel Wilder took her degree at the Yale School of Drama in 1928, under George Pierce Baker.

4. In 1934, Reinhardt settled permanently in California. For the California Festival in Los Angeles he had planned an ambitious program, but the funds did not become available and the only production he mounted was Goethe's *Faust* (Part One). It was presented at the Pilgrimage Outdoor Theatre in Los Angeles from 23 August to 17 September and at the Civic Auditorium in San Francisco from 26 September to 1 October. Among the projects planned but not produced were Maurice

Maeterlinck's *The Blue Bird*, Eugene O'Neill's *Strange Interlude*, Johann Strauss's *Die Fledermaus*, and Pedro Calderón de la Barca's *The Great Theatre of the World*.

5. Madame Giraud and the Baroness Pierlot, Stein's neighbors in the Bugey, the region around Belley.

To Thornton Wilder, Hollywood, California

[postmark: ?27 June 1938]   Bilignin par Belley
                                                             Ain

My dear Thornton,

It is a magnificent list, and I am proud it sounds like more even than when we did it, and it will be nice seeing you at 5 rue Christine which is almost as nice as here but here is wonderfully nice and we are sounding the horn in front of all the shops as we were, and the sun shines as it did and everything is as it was and we would like to add you, and that is true, my Doctor Faustus is done, the opera that I did for Lord Berners,[1] perhaps [Max] Reinhardt would like to do my Faust, it has some interesting theology, and now once more I am going to do the novel Ida, I am beginning all over again just as if it never had been done,[2] and we are so sorry to miss Isabel and I hope it will be all very well, and I don't know where Basket was but he has just come back, and Pepe says please remember me to Thornton and Alice is very well and we all want you and lots of love

Gtrde.

1. Lord Berners had received act I of *Dr. Faustus* by 17 May (YCAL), but because he was orchestrating *Cupid and Psyche*, a ballet score, he did not begin work on the opera. In late May or early June he received the second act and requested some changes, among them the following: "I think that perhaps in the first act the sentences ought to be a little longer at the opening." He also suggested that, "from a musical point of view," the opera should start off with an aria, which Stein wrote. Prior to a proposed visit to Bilignin in September, Lord Berners inquired about act III, which had not yet reached him. Although Stein would make further changes in the text at his request, the libretto was finished by late June 1938.

2. Stein had in fact picked up the Ida story a month earlier. In a letter of 9 May 1938, Page Cooper wrote her requesting a contribution for a volume to be called A *Boudoir Companion*. Stein immediately wrote "Ida," a brief sketch that stands as an independent work but draws on the first version of *Ida A Novel*. Cooper acknowledged receiving the typescript on 29 May. The completion of the opera, and the ease with which she had picked up the Ida material after a hiatus of almost six months perhaps gave her the impetus to return to the novel. The evolution and history of *Ida A Novel*, *Doctor Faustus Lights The Lights*, and "Ida" are discussed by Shirley Neuman in " 'Would a viper have stung her if she had only had one name?': *Doctor Faustus Lights the Lights*," in Neuman and Nadel, eds., *Gertrude Stein*, 168–93.

To Gertrude Stein and Alice Toklas, Bilignin, France

10 August 1938   Villa Carlotta,
                                                        5959 Franklin Ave.
                                                        Hollywood, Calif[ornia].

Dear Ones:

"Hope deferred maketh the heart sick"—The Bible.[1]

Here I've been all summer waiting, and now it looks as though the thing I've been waiting for won't take place until mid-September.[2]

I might have been in New Hampshire. Or in Maine. Or possibly abroad, and in Belley.

[Max] Reinhardt has had many difficulties and overcame them. At last he got 100,000 dollars and is putting on *Faust*. I go to rehearsals every night from 9—1. They can't rehearse by day, because the carpenters are building the Faust-stadt—the scenery being a whole village before your eyes.

I still hate Hollywood, doubly hateful in hot weather.

But I drown my troubles in working; play No #3 is progressing.[3] And in spite of the angry sun I take long walks into these powdery rock-less hills.

Isabel was here for a while, but has gone home to solitary Mama.

Isabel loved it here.

We went for two weeks to Taos and Santa Fe. I got laryngitis—or rather an alkali dust variant, and had to leave Taos.[4]

One of the greatest experiences of my life was seeing the great Corn Dance at the Pueblo Santo Domingo. All day they call on rain and growth, in complex formations, in withdrawn concentration, oo-oo.

¶ You're right, Gertrude, as always·

I'm no community man.[5]

¶ Sam Stewart told me you had talked to him about Wordsworth and Coleridge. I told him I was starving and begged him to send me the lines; which he did. Thanks, again.[6]

Alice, angel, have you a copy of Gertrude's *Dr Faustus?* First, I long to read it myself, and then I want to show it to the Herr Professor.

Did you ever get such a lifeless letter from me before? I am bursting with health and yet wasting away in a slow decline.

I have just enough strength to send you

my devoted love

Thornton

1. Proverbs 13:12.

2. *The Merchant of Yonkers* was not produced until December 1938 in New York.

3. Wilder was still working on *The Merchant of Yonkers*, but the reference here to Play #3 is probably to the first sketches he was making for the play that would become *The Alcestiad*.

4. After her trip to Europe, Isabel Wilder joined her brother in Hollywood on 3 July. One plan

was that she would work in Reinhardt's school, but inadequate funding and administrative difficulties led her to reconsider. Wilder had hoped that Reinhardt would produce *The Merchant of Yonkers* by the end of August. When it became apparent that the production would be postponed, he and his sister left on 20 July to visit Mabel Luhan in Taos, New Mexico. The Wilders arrived in the middle of a domestic drama orchestrated by Luhan. Convinced that the lagging inspiration of Robinson Jeffers needed bolstering, she encouraged an affair that precipitated a suicide attempt by Una Jeffers. The woman Luhan chose was Hildegarde Nathan, another house guest and a friend of the Wilders from New Haven. Nathan was a violinist who was recovering from a disrupted marriage. Curtailing their stay, the Wilders left for Santa Fe. From there on 7 August Wilder returned to Hollywood and his sister returned to New Haven (see Bennett, *The Stone Mason*; Zaller, *The Cliffs of Solitude*; Rudnick, *Mabel Dodge Luhan*).

     5. See Stein to Wilder [? May 1937], n. 2.

     6. For Stein's letter to Steward, see *Dear Sammy*, 136–137. Wilder's letter to Steward is dated 29 July 1938 (YCAL). Wilder misspells Steward's name.

To Thornton Wilder, Hollywood, California

[postmark: ?25 August 1938]   Bilignin par Belley
                                                        Ain

My dearest Thornton,

               I was just going to write you a most reproachful letter telling you that North East and South they say they hear from Thornton but never a word to Belley,[1] and here it is, I wish you had been here this summer it was one just to your taste, nobody in the house and the most delightful neighbors, the Daniel Rops have been here, he is a writer and she is his wife and we think them the nicest french couple we have ever known and they took us day before yesterday up to Chambotte and Mont Revard[2] and in between right on the top of everything she driving and it was lovely and I did not mind it a bit and we had a heavenly time, and Alice told how you walked down, and then there are the Leyrises, a young french writer married to an English wife, he nice but dullish but she the most charming English girl we have ever met, her name is Betty and she and you would have gotten along wonderfully, and alas all this time you are not here, they have a home just on the rise of the Col du Chat a fortified farm,[3] well some day, dear Thornton some day he'll wander back again, and now about Faust, here it is and I think a wonderful play, and please get somebody to play it cinema stage but somewhere, it is our old friend Ida but I think completely created, and I think it would be very popular, I judge from the people who love it,[4] dear Thornton sweet Thornton nice Thornton, come back to us soon, love from us all
                        Gtrde.
I am working a lot but I'll tell you about that some other time.

1. Samuel Steward and W. G. Rogers were among Stein's correspondents who sent news of Wilder.

2. Stein, Toklas, and the Daniel-Rops probably went for lunch to La Chambotte, a village above the Lac de Bourget, opposite the Abbey of Hautecombe. Mont Revard is on the southeast side of the lake. See Stein to Wilder, postmarked 17 September 1937, n. 4.

3. Pierre Leyris, the French writer and translator, and his wife, Elizabeth, met Stein when she stopped to help them with their car. They were living in the village of Champrovent (Pierre Leyris to Burns, 10 June 1986).

4. Stein enclosed a typescript of *Doctor Faustus Lights The Lights*. For her revisions of *Ida A Novel*, see Stein to Wilder [?27 June 1938].

To Gertrude Stein and Alice Toklas, Bilignin, France

23 Sept[ember] 1938   Century Club
                                                         7 West Forty-Third Street
                                                         New York [New York]

Dear Apprentice Angels:
                    Don't blame Miss Dorothy Ulrich on me.[1]

I didn't send her to me, either.

She's a mighty persistent girl.

Girls, what do you think? I'm playing the leading rôle in my play—six nights a week and two matinees.

Wouldn't that freeze you?

Every night my insides turn white—all that memorization to sustain—it's like walking a tight-rope of danger.

I'm only doing it for 2 weeks while Frank Craven gets a rest.[2]

[Max] Reinhardt is coming to New York to stage Play No #2 in November.[3]

I had to leave Calif[ornia]. for this job so hurriedly that I missed receiving the *Dr Faustus*, but it'll follow me here soon. Crazy to see it.[4]

Oh, New York.

Alice—that Commissioner Moses has taken Gov't money and all those unemployed and built a Babylon of parks, terraces, highways and hanging gardens. There's a great allée along Riverside Drive over-hanging the Hudson-six o'clock at night it's the most beautiful soft hushed yet grandiose stroll in the world.

Gertrude dear, "have you ever noticed that the great wars come a hundred years apart"?

                    Who loves you best?
                    Your devoted boy
                    Thornton

1. Dorothy Livingston Ulrich (later Troubetskoy) was a student at the University of Chicago and attended Stein's seminar there in March 1935. Having asked whether she might visit, she and her mother stayed in Belley for one week in August. See bibliography for her articles on Stein and Wilder.

2. *Our Town* was nearing the end of its New York run, and perhaps Harris felt he would generate publicity by replacing the leading actor with the author. Wilder arrived in New York on 8 September and rehearsed with the company stage manager, Edward Goodnow. By this time he and Harris were barely on speaking terms and were still arguing about changes Harris had made in the script (see Wilder to Stein, 12 January 1938, n. 1); however, the Coward-McCann edition of 1938 prints the text as Wilder intended it. Harris closed the play on 26 November after 336 performances and then took it on a national tour.

Reviewing Wilder's performance, Lewis Nicholas wrote in the *New York Times*, "For an acting debut the 'Our Town' role is to all intents and purposes a twentieth century Hamlet: commentator, stage manager, scene shifter, director and bit player. Being a lecturer of some renown and having been at one time a schoolmaster, Mr. Wilder has, as they say, stage presence. Starting slowly, and apparently with an eye on the missing Craven performance, he warmed up as the evening went along, and by the final curtain was jaunty. No ball of fire, perhaps, but on the other hand, the ball of fire didn't chase him around the stage.

"The performance, on the whole, was not unlike Mr. Craven's. Gone was Mr. C.'s pipe—and pretty important that is—and not yet come was an Equity senior's ability to be casual before an audience. At the start members of the audience at the back couldn't hear all of it, but during a hiatus Mr. Wilder had a talk with either his conscience or Jed Harris and after that gone was silence from the rear rows. Also, and this occasionally happens in debuts, Mr. Wilder had a bit of trouble with his lines; putting words out of place and then going back to set them straight" (16 September 1938, 17).

3. *The Merchant of Yonkers* was first performed at the Colonial Theatre in Boston on 12 December 1938; the New York engagement opened at the Guild Theatre on 28 December 1938.

4. It is not clear whether Wilder received the typescript. It is not among his papers at YCAL.

To Gertrude Stein, Paris, France
[TELEGRAM]

24 December [1938]   New Haven, Conn[ecticut]

LOVING THOUGHTS AND GREETINGS

THORNTON

1939

Stein with Basket in a photograph by William G. or Mildred Rogers, Bilignin, May 1934

To Gertrude Stein and Alice Toklas, Paris, France

2 March 1939
a Thursday

Hotel Andrew Johnson
Knoxville, Tenn[essee].

Returning from Mexico to
50 Deepwood Drive
New Haven, Conn[ecticut].

Dear Friends:

My affairs have gone badly. I guess that's why Presto hasn't written to his MDS.[1]

May Presto never live to write a despondent letter to his MDS.

Suffice to say that that play which had taken from July to December to get produced, was damned by the critics and withdrawn.[2]

The first play, though doing good business, was likewise withdrawn by Jed Harris in a paroxysm of spite against the leading actor and against me. Gertrude told me when she saw Jed Harris that I should have trouble with him, and there's been an unbroken succession of skullduggeries.[3]

I went to Mexico, hoping to find a pseudo-Rüs[c]hlikon[4] where I could walk and work, and I found Mexico was a magnificent tortured country and no place where a body could work.

So I'm easing gradually homeward.

I stopped a week at San Antonio—everybody likes San Antonio,—and a week at Corpus Christi, and now I'm going for a few days to Washington.

I'm well, but fretful.

There's nothing like a little failure to give one an attack of audience,—of audience-in-the-head,—but I'm recovering, and I expect that Audience will have soon retired into that vague limbo where it lives and which is none of my business.[5]

I heard of the death of Basket and send my fellow-grief to you. Not only did I love Basket for his snowy self, but I am indebted [to] him to the end of my life for the many things he taught Gertrude—some of which were permitted to take their place in the grammar of my mind.[6]

I hope the alert and dancing Peppino is well and a joy and instruction daily.

All the Wilders are well, particularly Ma, who's entered whole new fields of well-being, but Isabel is fruitful, too, and has gone to live in New York for a month under the impression that "life is passing her by."

I have retired, bruised and discredited, from the practice of prophecy, so I cannot inform you as to whether there will be a war or not, but every alarm abroad gives me a new fit of concern about you.

—Alec [Woollcott] is in bloom, and talking, entertaining, and writing hard. He has a piece now in every number of the Atlantic Monthly and they're very readable.

Bob Davis is married and has a baby.

I met the Whiteheads in the lobby of the theatre in Boston where my play was being tried out (to two weeks of crowded laughing houses). They're darling people.[7]

Freud (look at that chain of association, will you) sent me his nephew to find an editorial or academic job for.[8] Also, your M. Rops sent me a Viennese exile. I've done what I could. The irons are in the fire. Addresses, letters of recommendation, etc. etc., but it's hard going.[9]

I'm delighted that your Picasso book is getting such a good reception over here.[10] I wonder what you're on now. I long to have some good long drives with you treasures, and I need all my ideas tightened, scolded and renewed. I dream of coming over in the late Spring. Keep out of harm's way because you are the adored of your devoted

Thornton

1. See Wilder to Stein, 25 January 1936, n. 9.

2. *The Merchant of Yonkers*, directed by Max Reinhardt, previewed in Boston at the Colonial Theatre on 12 December 1938 and opened in New York at the Guild Theatre on 28 December. It closed after thirty-nine performances. Alexander Woollcott summarized for Stein the condition of Wilder and his play: "The ineffable Wilder has just gone through what would be to a more normally constituted person the harrowing experience of having had his second play turned into a good deal of a bore by unfortunate casting and heavy handed direction. He thought he was writing an adaptation from the Viennese but all unbenownst to him his good American ancestry took possession of him and what he really wrote was a pure Charles Hoyt farce of the 1885 vintage. If this had been given to any American stock company prior to 1900, it would have presented no problem and they would have put it on the following Monday with great success. Under Reinhardt's hand it all went faintly Launcelot Gobbo. Or so it seemed to me when I watched the tryout in Boston last week. Now it will come to New York and I suspect be trampled upon" (Gallup, *Flowers*, 333–34).

3. Although Wilder recognized the genius of Harris as a director, he found it increasingly difficult to deal with him. In order to keep *Our Town* going during the summer of 1938, Harris requested a reduction of 50 percent in Wilder's royalty. The negotiations over the reduction became acrimonious, Harris at first refusing the Dramatists Guild's compromise. Wilder telegraphed him on

12 July 1938: "YOU SO RESENT THE DRAMATISTS GUILDS EFFORT TO BE FAIR THAT YOU THREATEN TO
CLOSE THE PLAY NOW UNLESS A HUNDRED DOLLAR DIFFERENCE IN THE MINIMUM IS ESTABLISHED STOP
UGLY CHEAP SHRILL BLACKMAILING METHODS THE CONSTERNATION OF EVERYONE WHO HAS TRIED TO
SPEAK UP FOR YOU" (see copies to Harris, J. Dwight Dana, 9 July 1938, and Wilder, 12 July 1938, YCAL).
After the play closed in New York on 26 November 1938, the original company started on a national
tour that began in Philadelphia and took them to Washington, Baltimore, Pittsburgh, Cleveland,
Detroit, and Chicago. The plan was to have a long run in Chicago, but Harris, realizing that Frank
Craven was earning more money than he, posted a closing notice. Wilder traveled to Chicago to
persuade him to keep the production going, but Harris ended the tour on 11 February in Chicago.
After a hiatus, Harris presented *Our Town* at the Biltmore Theatre, Los Angeles, beginning 10 April
1939, and then at the Curran Theatre, San Francisco, beginning 24 April. In his autobiography and in
interviews, Harris remembers the history of *Our Town* differently (see bibliography and "3 Recall
Exciting Birth of 'Our Town,'" in *New York Times*, 27 November 1969, 55; Coley, "*Our Town*"
Remembered, 9; *Variety*, 22 March 1939).

4. See Wilder to Stein, 20 October 1937.

5. Wilder is echoing conversations with Stein. When Stein first met Wilder, she was already
formulating, out of her experiences with *The Autobiography* and the lecture tour, her concern with
audience and fame. Stein used Wilder as a foil to develop her ideas about audience, human nature
and the human mind, and the dangers of fame. Their conversations were used in the *Geographical
History* (see Wilder to Stein, [? February 1936], n. 3).

6. Except for a Christmas telegram, Wilder had not written to Stein since 23 September 1938,
and Stein had not written him since [?25 August 1938]. Nothing in the preserved letters suggests
missing correspondence. Basket, Stein's white poodle, died in late November 1938. Wilder may be
remembering such lines as "I am I because my little dog knows me" (*Geographical History*, 107) and
"She says that listening to the rhythm of his water drinking made her recognize the difference between
sentences and paragraphs, that paragraphs are emotional and that sentences are not" (*The Autobiography*, 305). (See Stein to Van Vechten [25 November 1938], in Burns, *Letters*, 2:616–17; see also Mme
Marthe Giraud to Stein, 3 December [1938], YCAL.)

7. Alfred North and Evelyn Whitehead (see Wilder to Stein, 9 July 1935, n. 8).

8. Freud had written Wilder on 10 October 1938 (YCAL) asking him to take a "kind interest" in
his niece's husband, Dr. Ernst Waldinger.

9. Daniel-Rops had asked Wilder's aid for the Austrian teacher and critic Frederick (Fritz)
Lehner and his wife. They had been imprisoned after the anschluss of 13 March 1938 and, when
released, made their way to England and then to America (Daniel-Rops to Stein, undated note, YCAL).

10. Stein's *Picasso* was published in the United States on 6 February 1939 by Charles Scribner's
Sons because of a disagreement between Random House and Stein's English publisher, B. T. Batsford. In 1938 Cerf had admitted to Stein that Random House "acted with all the speed and dexterity of
a senile hippopotamus" in failing to acquire the rights to her *Picasso* (24 August, YCAL). (See Burns,
Letters [26 July 1938], 2:600–01).

To Gertrude Stein and Alice Toklas, Bilignin, France

31 May 1939   Hotel Buckingham
                                                                     43 rue des Mathurins
                                                                     Anjou 81-62

Dear Angel Visitants:
                        Gay worldly fascinating time in London.[1]
        All kinds of encounters.
        Two Toscanini concerts the Heavens parting.[2]

Went alone to Bath for an afternoon and night. "Here lived Mrs Piozzi." "Here lived Jane Austen." "Here died Beau Nash."

Better than the Alps.

Saturday I leave this hotel—address henceforth: American Express Co[mpany]; Rue Scribe—for five days in Fontainebleau.

Read [Marcel] Jouhandeau's *Chroniques Maritales*. Goose-flesh at the prodigious disorder of that woman; but mighty interesting. Also read his *Jardin de Cordoue* (lavender-water) and his *Pincengrains* (mixed).

I bought the Sir Francis Rose of you two sitting with the dogs.[3] Also I almost bought a beautiful little Juan Gris at £ 50 but thought in time of my starving wives and children.

Sir Robert Abdy sent me the *Reflexions* which I have kept, assuming that you want them in Yale, but I shall return them to him, if they are his.[4]

Had an hour with M. Peyret-Chappuis whom I could never like in a hundred years, a rare attitude for me. The pear-shaped head of Louis XVI does not help matters either.[5]

My, I'm crazy.

I can't discover what day of the week it is.

Last night I rushed over to the Comédie-Francaise to see *Asmodée*, was ushered late to my seat, and having got the day wrong sat all through the double-bill that you and I saw together, the Molière-Marivaux.[6]

Good for my French, but I wish I were a little more sensible.

Vast envelopes of mail forwarded from America by Isabel. Boring boring mail. Little far distant voices wanting things.

On the 16th I'm going back to London: week-end at Mells chez Lady Horner aetat 82—the house that Jack Horner pulled out as a plum.[7] Also conferences with Michel St. Denis again.[8]

In London at Stefan Zweig's[9] I met Mrs Desmond Flower, wife of the head of Cassel's publishing house. She comes from Ashland, Ohio and is interested in children's books. She wants very much to see The World is Round. Surely, they sent you the customary extra proofs and we can forward them to her.[10]

May I come and see you Saturday June 24th and stay until Tuesday or Wednesday?

I hope you are both roaringly well as this finds me.

Now I am going to the Galleries Lafayette, on command, to buy some gloves, size eight, red, grey and black, for Marion Mill Preminger, the serpent of the Danube.[11]

But the important burden of this letter is that it brings you my
L O V E
Thorntonberry

1. On 6 May, Wilder sailed on the *Britannic* for two months in England and France. He returned on the *Ile de France* on 29 June.

2. Toscanini conducted the Beethoven symphonies, overtures, and *Missa Solemnis* with the BBC Symphony Orchestra during May. We have found no record of which concerts Wilder attended.

3. *Bilignin Interior with Gertrude Stein and Alice B. Toklas*, National Portrait Gallery, Smithsonian Institution, Washington, D.C., gift of Isabel Wilder (Accession # NPG. 91. 175). The gouache is 19⅜ × 25½ inches and is signed and inscribed in ink in the lower left: "Francis Rose, August 1938/ Gertrude Stein Miss Toklas/Basket & Pepe at Billignan." The gallery acquired from Robert Bartlett Haas a second Rose gouache, of Stein and Toklas in the salon of 5 rue Christine (Accession # NPG 88.161). The gouache is 28 × 23 inches and is signed in the lower right: "Gertrude Stein/and Alice Toklas/Francis Rose/ 12-1939." An inscription to Haas, the original purchaser, is written on the support verso at the top center. Stein first purchased works by Rose in late 1929 or early 1930. According to the *Autobiography*, she did not meet him until a tea given by the Chilean painter Alvaro Guevara and his wife, Méraud, in 1930 or 1931, by which time Stein had bought more than thirty works by Rose (see the *Autobiography*, 283–84, 308).

4. "Reflexions" was one name for Stein's "Stanzas In Meditation," a book-length sequence of poems written and typed in the early summer of 1932. In *The Autobiography Of Alice B. Toklas*, Stein writes, "The last thing that she has finished, Stanzas of Meditation, and which I am now typewriting, she considers her real achievement of the commonplace" (276). "Now" refers to the typing, in late October or early November 1932, of a substantially altered manuscript text, which is also the one printed in volume 6 of the posthumous work (1956) and the one submitted to *Poetry*. The only copy of the original typescript was deposited by Stein with Carl Van Vechten.

By mid-1936, perhaps as a sign of friendship for Stein, who had included the Abdys in *Listen To Me*, Sir Robert Abdy proposed to print a deluxe edition of "Stanzas In Meditation." In *Everybody's Autobiography* Stein wrote, "[H]e has tried four different printers already but printing like everything is something of which there is more bad than good of that he is perfectly certain" (300). By 1939 he had lost money and had to give up the project. How Stein may have asked him to return the typescript through Wilder is not clear. Lady Diana Abdy wrote her on 30 May, "Bertie has at last reluctantly parted with the manuscript" (YCAL).

5. Charles de Peyret-Chappuis, French playwright, author of *Frénésie* (1938) and *Feu Monsieur Pic*, which was being performed in Paris. Why Wilder met with him is not clear. In 1938 Katharine Cornell and Guthrie McClintic had purchased the rights to *Frénésie*, which had opened in Paris at the Théâtre Charles de Rochefort on 3 February 1938 and was printed in *La Petite Illustration* on 26 March. Stein translated the first three pages of the printed text and then abandoned the project. McClintic wrote Stein on 30 April 1938 (YCAL) asking to meet her, but nothing suggests it was more than a social visit. She may have abandoned *Frénésie* to concentrate on *Doctor Faustus Lights The Lights*. McClintic never mounted a production of the play.

Marie-Louise Bousquet, writing to congratulate Wilder on winning the Pulitzer Prize, also told him about Stein's efforts to become involved in the *Frénésie* project: " 'Our' Gertrude Stein (to amuse you!) was chasing after the author of 'Frénésie' and wanted him to collaborate with her. The latter refused, so she managed to meet McClintic, then had a meeting with Depret-Chapuy [i.e., Peyret-Chappuis] and told him that she is the only one who could translate his play into English. If she translated it, in good English, and if she did not add anything of her own, then I think the translation might be good, but . . . but . . ." (Bousquet's ellipses, 11 May 1938, YCAL). Bousquet concluded by saying that she hoped to arrange for him to write a ballet for the Ballet Russes, for which Christian Bérard would do the décor and costumes. Nothing came of this idea.

6. This part of the letter was written on 1 June. On the evening of 31 May, Wilder saw a double bill of Molière's *L'amour médecin* and Marivaux's *Le jeu de l'amour et du hasard*. François Mauriac's *Asmodée* was given its first performance at the Comédie Française on 22 November 1937 and revived in 1939. In November 1937 Stein and Wilder attended the theater on several occasions, but these plays are not named.

7. Wilder was invited to accompany Lady Colefax to Mells Manor, the home of the Horner

family near the village of Frome, where the Horner family had lived for three hundred years. The estate was the "plum" given to the original Jack Horner by Henry VIII at the dissolution of the monasteries. Lady Horner was a well-known hostess with an interest in the arts.

8. While vacationing in England in July 1938, Ruth Gordon gave Michel Saint-Denis a copy of *Our Town*. In a letter Gordon brought back to America, Saint-Denis wrote, "I have the same feeling as I had when I met André Obey for the first time: to be faced with something new and perfectly true and authentic" (Saint-Denis to Wilder, 23 July 1938, YCAL). Saint-Denis, a director, began his theatrical career in 1920 when he joined his uncle Jacques Copeau in his Théâtre du Vieux-Colombier. In 1930, he and other members of the Copeau Theatre founded La Compagnie des Quinze. He came to England in 1935 to direct John Gielgud in André Obey's *Noah*, decided to remain, and founded the London Theatre School (1935–39), modeled on Copeau's ideas.

In a letter to Wilder of 17 August 1938 (YCAL), Saint-Denis expressed his interest in a production of *Our Town* with John Gielgud as the Stage Manager since Gielgud's brother Val had seen the play in New York and recommended it. Saint-Denis anticipated that Jed Harris would create difficulties, and because Harris would not permit a London production he did not direct, Saint-Denis suggested that André Obey prepare a French adaptation. Wilder had adapted Obey's *Le Viol de Lucrèce* for Katharine Cornell in 1932 (see Saint-Denis to Harold Freedman, 26 August, and to Wilder, 13 October 1938 and 7 March 1939, YCAL). Saint-Denis was eventually given the rights for one year ending 1 March 1940, and Wilder met with him in London to discuss the production. Saint-Denis outlined his plans in a letter of 19 July 1939 (YCAL)—his production of Chekhov's *The Cherry Orchard* was scheduled for October 1939, and after that he would begin work on *Our Town*. "I feel more and more," he wrote to Wilder, "that we ought to do our utmost to start a significant theatre here with your play." The outbreak of World War II put an end to Saint-Denis's plans.

Our Town was not presented in a professional production in London until after the war, and then in a production directed by Jed Harris. Gielgud never acted in *Our Town*; he did, however, perform the role of Caesar in James Kilty's adaptation of Wilder's *The Ides of March* at the Haymarket Theatre, London, in 1963.

9. Zweig fled his native Austria for England in October 1933. He came to America in 1940 and briefly settled in New Haven to be close to his friend Richard Beer-Hoffmann and work on a study of Amerigo Vespucci. Zweig and his wife, Elizabeth, committed suicide in Petrópolis, Brazil, on 23 February 1942.

10. Desmond Flower held various executive positions at Cassell and Company, Ltd., from 1931 to 1971. There is no correspondence from him or his wife, Margaret Cameron Cross, in YCAL. John McCullough, an editor at William R. Scott Publishers, wrote Stein on 2 August 1938 (Columbia-R.H.), asking if she would write a children's book for their new juvenile list. Stein must have replied immediately, for she wrote Carl Van Vechten on 15 August that she was starting the book, to be called *The World Is Round*. Stein finished it by early October and sent Van Vechten a typescript, which he acknowledged with his usual enthusiasm on 23 October (see Burns, *Letters*, 2:603–04, 614). *The World Is Round*, with illustrations by Clement Hurd, was published on 15 September 1939.

11. Marion Mill Preminger was born in Hungary and studied acting in Vienna. When Wilder met her in 1935, she was the wife of Otto Preminger, then an assistant to Max Reinhardt and beginning to make his reputation directing at the Josefstadt Theatre. After a brief theatrical career, she became known as an international hostess and a devoted supporter of Albert Schweitzer, whom she regularly visited in Lambaréné from 1950 to 1965. She traveled the world speaking and raising money for Schweitzer and enlisted Wilder in her efforts. Although Wilder resented her relentless pursuit of him as a means of entering the literary establishment, he remained a friend until her death in 1971 (see Preminger in bibliography).

To Gertrude Stein and Alice Toklas, Bilignin, France

6 June 1939   Fontainebleau [France]

Dear Herzenskinder [Children of my heart]:
                    Saturday I ran off here: not even a forwarding address.
Won't rejoin my mail until Wednesday.

It's wonderful hot. I walked 10 miles yesterday through this endless forest.

¶ Like a ninny I postponed looking up return boats and now I see that in
order to rejoin my first rehearsal on July 10th and have a few days with my
family first I must sail on the Ile de France on the 29th. That puts forward all
my schedule. Tomorrow I'm going to telephone you and ask whether you can
see me earlier—perhaps even this coming Saturday. Remember if it's inconvenient I can always install myself in the hotel in town, famous in song and story.

I had lunch with Sir Francis [Rose] on Sat'day (at Chez Marius). And
tomorrow night midnight supper with Louis Jouvet.[1]

What do you think? Mrs Fellowes forgot her date with me. Cela m'apprendra, m'apprendra [That'll teach me]. Whenever I stray out of my natural territory Circumstance manages to give me a warning blow: I'm always
pleased when the blow is merely a slight amused rap on the knuckles because
sometimes Circumstance gives terrific disproportionate bludgeonings. Cela
m'apprendra.

                              L O V E
                              Thornty.

    1. Wilder had known of Jouvet since at least 1913, when the French actor first joined Copeau's
Théâtre du Vieux-Colombier. Between the two world wars he became one of the best-known actor-
directors in France, in part because of his association with the plays of Jean Giraudoux. Marie-Louise
Bousquet had arranged a meeting between Wilder and Jouvet to discuss a French production of *Our
Town*.

To Gertrude Stein and Alice Toklas, Bilignin, France

[15 June 1939][1]   [Hotel Buckingham
Thursday evening   43 rue des Mathurins
10:37 Bilignin time.   Paris]

Dear Friends:
                    After visits like ours I long to know what you, what they, did after
I left.

Whenever I finish a good book I at once turn back and begin it again, and
so I wish I could with the visit, and so I wish I could know *what happened next.*

I stood for a long while in the corridor of the train looking at Le Bugey,[2] and then I returned to my place and read *Everybody's Autobiography* until dinner time (Seconde Service 8: p.m.) Better than ever. Better than ever.

(This afternoon I met Marie Laurencin, and she spoke of how displeased she was with passages in the Autob[iography]. of A[lice]. B. T[oklas]: "but," I said, "what beautiful things you said to explain your displeasure. . . . all that about a painter being unable to see his past, etc." And then she looked very pleased to think that her displeasure had been turned to such good profit, and we became very good friends.)[3]

This morning I did the shopping that would help me look less like an absent-minded American brought up so stringently that he was not accustomed to nice things, and yet so neatly that he was not driven into a passion, or even an observation, of nice things; I have been assembling the disguise, the fancy-dress that I must wear at Mells. I enjoy mascarades, but not those in which one must disguise one's-self *in order to be recognized.*

Then I went to Mr. Schoop's and he took me to the luncheon of the American Business Men's Club, and they begged me to address them next Thursday and I said no. It's only in the last few years that I've learned how to say no and now I say it all the time just to hear that lovely dental and that sliding vowel. It was hard to refuse Mr. Schoop anything, though, because I hadn't seen that kind of American for two months, so I accepted for a cocktail-party instead.[4]

See enclosed the letter that was waiting for me at the Am[erican] Ex [press] Co[mpany]. Isn't that fine? I didn't think as highly of George Dillon as that.[5]

Also an enclosure for Alice. Alice has opened my eyes, has opened my mouth, to a new and wonderful world. But Lordy, that last lunch was something that I'll never see again; it was the flag hung at its highest point.[6]

All the flags were flying high all the time, dear friends, and I shall be recalling and re-grati-fying it all for years to come: all those fine drives and fine pictures and fine talks.[7]

I shall report to you soon from England, and always with lots of love

Thornton

1. Wilder visited Stein from June 10 to 14.
2. The region around Belley.
3. Although Laurencin objected to what Stein had written about her in *The Autobiography Of Alice B. Toklas*, she did not contribute to the *Testimony Against Gertrude Stein*, a pamphlet issued as a supplement to *transition* number 23 (February 1935). The pamphlet contained an introduction by Eugene Jolas and passages from *The Autobiography Of Alice B. Toklas* with refutations by Henri Matisse, Maria Jolas, Tristan Tzara, Georges Braque, and André Salmon. In *Everybody's Autobiography*, Stein recounts a meeting with Laurencin at the home of Marie-Louise Bousquet: "I knew that Marie had not been pleased that I had spoken of all of them and of the old days but then I knew

painters were like that so when we met there at Marie Louise's salon we embraced as we had always done and then she told me just how she felt about everything that I had done and this is what she said.

"She said of course no painter could be pleased the past of a painter was not a past because a painter lived in what he saw and he could not see his past and if his past was not his past then it was nobody's past and so nobody could say what that past was" (34). Laurencin and Stein continued to be friends. In 1946, she painted *Portrait of Basket II*, which is now in YCAL.

4. Max Shoop, whose name Wilder misspelled, was an American lawyer in Paris. Wilder accepted an invitation for cocktails on Friday, 23 June (see Shoop to Stein, 21 June 1939, YCAL).

5. Just before leaving for Europe in May, Wilder wrote to George Dillon, editor of *Poetry*, asking that his name be removed from its associate committee because he no longer lived in Chicago. Wilder mentioned his trip to Europe and a planned visit to Stein. Dillon replied on 2 June, "Having been one of her [Stein's] enthusiastic admirers ever since I was old enough to read The Dial, I would take a particularly deep pleasure in publishing something of hers during my editorship." On 16 June, Wilder wrote to Dillon, "Day before yesterday Gertrude Stein was saying to me do you suppose there is any paper in Amurrica [i.e., America] that would be willing to publish parts of my two hundred stanzas in meditation and I said I've got an idea I'll send it to George Dillon at Poetry and at least he'll have to make the decision of accepting or refusing it.

"So I'm bringing them home with me and you shall receive them soon after I land, July 5th. They're in the style of Gertrude's that I 'don't understand' but I can get the movement of them just as algebra gives the situation of computations without the specific numbers, so these stanzas give the movement of lyric feeling without the words. I think you'll be the first to look at them."

Stein herself also would take action to insure publication. On 2 July (YCAL) she wrote to Ellen Alix Du Poy that "Thornton is going to try to get Poetry to do my 200 Stanzas of Meditation, perhaps you can help. Thornton has them with him over there." To Du Poy's excitement about the stanzas Stein responded on 18 August (YCAL) with the hope that Dillon might publish not only a selection but the complete book of "Stanzas." Du Poy, a journalist and novelist who had lived in Paris and helped Stein plan her Plain Edition, had returned to Chicago and her affiliation with the *Chicago Daily Tribune*. Stein wrote her in care of *Poetry*, where she had an informal connection.

When Wilder sent Dillon the typescript of "Stanzas In Meditation" is not clear. In an undated letter to Dillon, probably written in the fall of 1939, Wilder acknowledged Dillon's selection of stanzas and wrote, "I'm fully empowered to give the permission. In fact, Gertrude will be very pleased." Wilder backed away, however, from Dillon's suggestion that he write a note to present the poems: "As to the Note to accompany them. The reason I don't feel I can do it is *au fond* that I don't really understand them. I've already been to the bat with two prefaces for her, and am often approached as an expert and gradually I feel more and more hypocritical. I often told G. that I don't understand her extreme style, but she forgets that I've said so and starts talking to me about some of it as tho' I were an initiate.

"Couldn't you get Wendell Wilcox there in Chicago to do you a note? He understands her." Wilder concluded, "I'm very glad you're doing this; the verses tho' 'unintelligible' to me, nevertheless have that air of unmistakable authority." A selection from "Stanzas In Meditation" was printed in *Poetry* 55, 5 (February 1940): 229–35. "A Note on Stein and Abstraction," by Wendell Wilcox (254–57) was also included. Perhaps by coincidence, the same issue printed two poems by John V. Healy (236–37), one of Wilder's Chicago pupils. (Wilder's letters to Dillon and copies of Dillon's correspondence are in the University of Chicago library.)

6. The enclosure for Toklas has not remained with the letter.

7. During his stay in Bilignin, Stein, Toklas, and Wilder visited the exhibition *Les Chefs d'oeuvre du Musée du Prado* at the Musée d'Art et d'Histoire in Geneva.

To Gertrude Stein and Alice Toklas, Bilignin, France

[18 June 1939]
Sunday Morning
10:30 a.m.

The Manor House, Mells,
Frome.
Tel.: Mells 24.

Dear Girls:

It is raining and Somersetshire is polishing up its profound greens.

A little inadequate American is being permitted to see, in a pure state, The English Week-end.

I keep saying to myself, "relax, boy, relax."

It's all perfect.

I can see Henry James on his knees before it.

But the ease of it, their ease, the ripple that does service for conversation, the being willing to accept this courtesy-deep emotion-hidden interchange as the social sufficiency is hard to understand. I have to keep, strange to say, the memory of the War before me. The tablets in the beautiful church at the very door of the house are my bridge into our table-talk. I cling to the days of the War when agony lived here. Lady Horner's daughter, beautiful and composed, was married to [Henry Herbert] Asquith's oldest son, dead in the War.[1] Brothers, cousins, nephews, died in the War. Gardeners, farmers, delivery boys, died in the War. If they could read my thoughts, as with great kindness, they talk to me of the strawberries this year, or the village doctor who was very good last week in a performance of *The Mikado*, wouldn't they be surprised to read in capital letters: You lived through the War.

Two days later—London.

Well, well.

What do you suppose happened?

That Sunday I fell in love with everybody in the house.

The Wilderishness vanished.

That strange phenomenon LOVE that pops up in the strangest places, that hurdles the most obstinate barriers, that refuses the most pressing invitations; there it was.

It popped up again yesterday, too, at Max Beerbohm's.[2] And Sunday night at dusk there it was, as for a few minutes our car stopped in the roadway before Stonehenge.

And here it is, as usual, on my shoulder as I write to you. I pass to him the pen and we both sign this letter.

LOVE
Thornton

1. Raymond Asquith enlisted at the outbreak of World War I and was killed in May 1916. At the time of his marriage to Katharine Horner in 1907, daughter of Sir John and Lady Horner, his father was the chancellor of the exchequer and in 1917, prime minister (see MacKenzie in bibliography).

2. Wilder had met the Beerbohms through Lady Colefax in 1928. Leaving their home in Italy in the autumn of 1938, they moved into Abinger Manor Cottage in Surrey as guests of Sidney and Violet Schiff in January 1939. A translator of Proust, Schiff wrote under the pen name of Stephen Hudson. Wilder and his sister Isabel were devoted friends of Beerbohm.

To Gertrude Stein and Alice Toklas, Bilignin, France

[24 June 1939]

Room 49
Hot[el]. Buck[ingham].
43 r[ue]. d[es]. Math[urins].
Par[is]. Fran[ce].
Wor[ld].

Dear s raeD.

My journey's drawing to an end.

Yesterday I went to Miss Barney's Vendredi.[1] Very brilliant. Dr. Mardrus.[2]

I had to leave early to go to Mr. Schoop's cocktail party for me.[3] Very brilliant. Walter Lippmann.[4] Valentina Schley [i.e., Schlee].[5] Etc.

Tuesday night I am giving a dinner chez Marius[6]—Adrienne Monnier, Sylvia Beach[7] and the German photographer named Freund.[8] Wish you were there. Very brilliant.

In London I had an hour with Freud and his daughter.[9] Oh, I love him. As always the occasion flowered into characterizing anecdote but it takes all my face and hands to tell it correctly so I'll save it until our next visit.

I'm beginning to think New-England-Summer. Oh, Lordy, uphill downhill Connecticut, Massachusetts, New Hampshire, Maine. I hear you. I see you. Hold everything, baby, I'm coming.

I've found Marion Mill's memorandum rê gloves: it's an 8 all right.[10] Hand in hand Marion and I stroll along, but you can guess whose hand's in whose'.

I do not enclose the enclosed fan-letter in order to, —— well, you read it and see why I enclose it.[11]

I'll be glad, man and boy, when I'm on that boat. My trip is over and these days are but postscrip[t]s and untucked corners.

Tonight I'm going to see Ludmilla Pitoëff in Camille.[12]

Last night I heard Berlioz's Les Troyens.[13]

MORE SOON

L O V E

THORNT

Champion envelope addresser in the wide WORLD.

1. Natalie Barney's "at home" was on Fridays.

2. Dr. Joseph Charles Mardrus, French doctor, writer, and orientalist who translated *Arabian Nights: A Thousand and One Nights* (1898–1904) as well as the Koran (1926). He and his wife, Lucie Delarue-Mardrus, also a writer, were long-time friends of Natalie Barney.

3. See Wilder to Stein [?15 June 1939], n. 4.

4. American editor and writer.

5. Valentina, the fashion designer.

6. A restaurant near Place d'Alma.

7. Adrienne Monnier, of La Maison des Amis des Livres, which opened in 1915, and Sylvia Beach, of Shakespeare and Company, which opened in 1919, both played a crucial role in the intellectual life of Paris between the two world wars. Their bookshops were important meeting places, and their support helped ease the life of struggling writers. Beach was the first publisher of Joyce's *Ulysses* (February 1922). Wilder met them in 1921 during a visit to Paris.

8. Gisèle Freund, the photographer.

9. Precisely when this meeting took place is in doubt. There is no record in *The Diary of Sigmund Freud: 1929–1939* of a meeting in June 1939 with Wilder, but not every meeting is listed. Wilder lost his first 1939 date book and only began a second one on 26 June. Wilder first met Freud in 1935 (see Wilder to Stein, 14 October 1935).

10. See Wilder to Stein, 31 May 1939.

11. We have not located the letter.

12. Ludmilla Pitoëff played Marguerite Gautier in *La Dame aux Camélias*, by Alexander Dumas fils, in a production directed by Georges Pitoëff which opened in the Théâtre des Mathurins on 19 June.

13. Wilder attended a performance of the complete *Les Troyens* by Hector Berlioz at the Paris Opera on 23 June.

To Gertrude Stein and Alice Toklas, Bilignin, France
[Postcard: Tapestry. Scene of lordly life.
France about 1500. Musée de Cluny]

[postmark: ?28 June 1939][1]   [Paris, France]
Wed[nesday] aft[ernoon].

Dear Ones

Just had lunch with the Harry Luces—he editor of Time, Fortune & Life—she, beautiful, enormously informed etc. John Hamilton and I have talked of you to her so much that she wants to see you. She may phone some day from Aix[-les-Bains], asking when they can come to tea. I hope you don't mind; I think you would find them greatly interesting.—Tendres amitiés and au revoirs.

Ever thine,
Thornton.

1. This postcard was probably written the day before Wilder returned to the United States. The postmark is illegible; the number "24," which is legible, is clearly an hour stamp, not a date. The Luces and Hamilton arrived in France in late June and visited Stein in July. Wilder and Luce had known each

other since they were students in the China Inland Mission School in Chefoo, and later as classmates at Yale, graduating in the class of 1920. (See Stein to Wilder, postmark 4 July 1939, n. 3; Wilder to Stein, 20 October 1937, n. 3; and Boothe to Stein, 16 August 1939, in Gallup, *Flowers*, 341–43.)

To Thornton Wilder, Cohasset, Massachusetts

[postmark: 4 July 1939]
                                              Pavillon de l'Ermitage[1]
                                              Chavoires
                                              (Lac D'Annecy)
                                              H[au]te-Savoie [France]

Dearest Thornton

        Here we are without Thornton, alas and alas and the sun is shining and we have eaten, Sammy [Steward] wrote and told me what a beautiful time you gave him, but that you did not think much of his novel,[2] and [Henry] Luce has calmed the french fears[3] and we would like to see them tell them they can telephone 168 Belley and we would be delighted, everything else is calm, Madame Giraud is here, too, we are all here, only Thornton lacks, let me see what else, working a little, the boite de nuit liked the operette apparently your corrections were just right,[4] give our love to our dear native land, it is the 4 of July and love to you always and always
                Gtrde.

Il paraît que vous adorez être admiré alors!![5]

With as much affection and more courage
                Alice

    1. The restaurant in Chavoires, above the Lake of Annecy, was well known for its regional cooking.

    2. Steward arrived in Paris on 23 June. On 30 June (YCAL), he wrote Stein of Wilder's reaction to his "Chicago" novel, first mentioned to Stein in Steward's letter of 23 January 1939 (YCAL). In it he quoted Wendell Wilcox: "[A] novel like that had to be either sentimental or tragic or comic and this wasn't any of the three and therefore it was not good." The novel was not published.

    3. Coincident with Henry Luce's arrival in France in late June 1939, the Syndicat de la Presse Parisienne announced that it was bringing a five-million-franc damage suit against Luce for an article that appeared in *Time*, 8 May 1939. The article commented on the decree law of the French government against foreign propaganda in the French press and claimed "The Paris press has long been the sewer system of world journalism. Few are the Parisian newsmen who cannot be bought and rare is the newspaper unwilling to be 'subsidized.' Not only does the French Government, which always maintains a secret fund, pass out generous pay checks to writers and editors, but foreign Governments also contribute. During the Ethiopian crisis of 1935 the Italian Government bought a few editorial pages. The way some prominent Paris newspapers have handled their German 'news' recently suggests that slush funds from the Third Reich are also being passed around. In pot & kettle fashion, Leftist editors have cried that the Rightist press lived on funds from Germany and Italy, while Rightest editors

pictured the Leftist press getting gold from Moscow" (21). Luce, editor and publisher of *Time*, claimed that he had not read the article before it appeared in his magazine and issued a letter of apology on 2 July (*New York Times*, 3 July 1939, 2).

4. Agnes Capri, a singer with a following among French intellectuals, planned to open her own *boîte de nuit*, night club, in the rue Sainte-Anne on 21 September 1939 and contracted Stein for a text that might be set to music. Stein at first suggested either Virgil Thomson's setting of eight poems by Georges Hugnet, *Le Berceau de Gertrude Stein*, or the Stein-Thomson *Film: Deux soeurs qui sont pas soeurs* (see Stein to Thomson, postmark 28 May 1939, YCAL). Capri, however, wanted a new work, and so in June Stein wrote "Les Superstitions," a series of monologues for four characters: L'Araignée (the spider), Le Coucou (the cuckoo), Le Poisson Rouge (the gold fish), and Les Nains (the dwarfs). The *cahier* contains Stein's text with some minor revisions by her and a copy by Wilder of her text with his corrections of her French. Before preparing a typescript, Toklas went over Wilder's text to make the French more idiomatic.

Capri acknowledged receipt of the typescript on 26 June. In a later, undated letter, she reported that Georges Auric would compose the music if Stein would make some changes. Perhaps because of the outbreak of World War II in September 1939, the project was never realized. There are no typescripts of the French text in YCAL (Capri to Stein, n.d., YCAL).

Laid into the *cahier* are two sheets of four-by-five-inch notepaper. On the first Stein writes, "What is important is that you are one of the rare writers in America who is not haunted by the spoken word. You write the written word and the written word speaks, the spoken word written never speaks." The second reads, "melifluis [was] brilliant a [certain] real magnificence ad [really funny], really funny because it makes you suddenly [giggle] laugh. [funnily] (bracketed phrases are crossed out).

"Had enough of what they make us do, [?tired] of crisis sunset of woman the [?at] Victor Hugo understood [?words]." The intent of these two notes and when they were written are not clear. The first may have been written to Wilder when she gave him the *cahier* and asked him to read and correct her French manuscript. The second note may relate to the inscribed copy of Wilder's *The Merchant of Yonkers*, which he gave her during this visit and is now in YCAL.

Stein prepared an English translation of "Les Superstitions" in 1940, "[H]oping someone might do something with it and that would be fun" (Stein to Sir Francis Rose, 16 March 1940, Katz transcript, YCAL). Receipt of the piece is also acknowledged in a letter from Cecil Beaton: "Many thanks for Superstitions which is delightful. I will let you know if and when I have an opportunity to do anything with it" (n.d., YCAL). Lacking focus for continuing *Ida A Novel* in its third version, Stein incorporated "Superstitions" (122–28) and "My Life With Dogs" (96–106) with connecting material to complete the novel.

5. Madame Giraud writes, "you seem to love being admired!"

To Thornton Wilder, Stockbridge, Massachusetts

[postmark: 28 July 1939]   [Bilignin par Belley
                                                                   Ain, France]

My dear Thornton,

   The Kiddies say they are going to see you act very soon and we wish we were going to too.[1] The Yale Library has been most cordial in thanking,[2] and here is a letter some one I do not know inclosed for you,[3] and then we saw a lot of the Luces and we did like them, we had a very good time together, and some day not too far away we will talk and talk and talk about it, and Sammy [Steward] has been here, very sweet, and very useful, now he has gone to Algeria,[4] otherwise it rains, but we do not really seem to mind it, we washed Basket yesterday, he is sweet, and everybody loves you and we do lots and lots

Gtrde and Alice.[5]

1. Rogers wrote Stein in late June and early July about Wilder playing the Stage Manager in *Our Town*. Rogers and his wife attended a performance at the Berkshire Playhouse in Stockbridge, Massachusetts, during the week of 14 August (Rogers, n.d., YCAL).

2. Bernhard Knollenberg acknowledged on 15 July (YCAL) the deposit of the typescript of *Everybody's Autobiography* and the manuscript notebook of an early version of *The Making Of Americans*, which Stein had sent through Wilder.

3. Stein enclosed a note to Wilder, dated 26 June, from Grace (Mrs. Joseph) Sprague asking for his address so that she might get in touch with him. In the note she reminded him that "it has been many years since I danced with you at Lawrenceville."

4. Steward arrived in Bilignin on Saturday, 15 July 1939, and stayed at least a week before leaving for Marseille and then Algeria. He returned to Bilignin on 14 August (see Steward to Stein in YCAL: 10 July [Paris], 25 July [Marseille], 7 August [Algiers], and postmark 12 August [Marseille]).

5. Both signatures are Stein's.

To Gertrude Stein and Alice Toklas, Bilignin, France

[20 August 1939]   The Graduates Club
                                    One Hundred Fifty-Five Elm Street
                                    New Haven, Connecticut

Dear Friends:

Here at last is a whole day without a duty or a worry or an assignment in it.

Sunday.

Yesterday I played two performances at Stockbridge and tomorrow I begin rehearsals at New Hope, Pennsylvania but today I'm in New Haven, and care-free, and with time to write you and to ask your forgiveness for the silence.[1]

Last week I saw the Kiddies. I went to a tea at their house in Springfield and they sat an hour with me after the performance in Stockbridge.[2] I looked for the things you suggested I look for, and though I may be obtuse, I thought things were going well. He's back on that novel that he's been on for years; and she (even he doesn't know this) is finishing a play; she says soon she will have to call him in on it to help her. I thought they were—in glances and joking parentheses—idyllically bird-like happy towards one another. They had a lot of friends in to tea whom they seemed to like very much; I did, too; but it was cruelly hot. Springfield is a furnace. My memory of the Summer will be hot damp heat; an agony of wet forehead and shirts sticking to one's back.

Bobsy [Goodspeed] and Alice Rouiller I saw both on Cape Cod and at Stockbridge. Bobsy has decorated her Cape Cod house in a droll loony Victorian way, of pinks toward magenta and shell landscapes under glass bells and bow ribbons on the legs of chairs—which is good fun.[3] Her hair is greyer, but she is as pretty and sure of herself as ever. Alice is resting up on her visit from a trying year, I take it, trying to make two ends meet. I especially love Alice.

So I've been acting all Summer. I will have played it in four different theatres with four entirely different casts. It's been very successful. In places we've broken house records; chairs in the aisles; ovations; weepings. Being present at these repetitions I get to know the play pretty well and I find a lot to wince at in addition to some fine wincing at the actors' renderings, but I hope I've learned a lot that can go into future plays.

One of my absorptions and consolations during these occupied and hot six weeks has been James Joyce's new novel, digging out its buried keys and resolving that unbroken chain of erudite puzzles and finally coming on lots of wit, and lots of beautiful things has been my midnight recuperation. A lot of thanks to him. My, the critics have been silly about that book, esp[ecially]. in England, and especially the small-fry disciples that weave about him in Paris.[4]

I sent back François D'Aiguy's article. In his accompanying letter he alternately longed for its publication and trembled before the fact that someone might see it. So the latter won.[5]

Yes, you know me, I thought that Sammy Stewart's novel was a big mistake. You know me.[6]

As soon as my present chores are over, Sept[ember] 2, I'm going to recline at home for a bit and then retire to the solitudes of New York or Washington and put down some more plays.

I still hug the notion that there'll be no war, but every day I look at the newspaper and am a little shaken, but I still follow Gertrude and say there'll be no more.

Forgive, Angel-presences, my foolish self-gazing silence, and love me to[o] as much as I love you.

Ever y[ou]r

Thornton

1. Wilder performed the role of the Stage Manager in *Our Town* at four summer theaters, three of them in Massachusetts: the Bass Rocks Theatre in Cohasset the week of 17 July, the Cape Playhouse in Dennis the week of 31 July, the Berkshire Playhouse, Stockbridge, the week of 14 August, and also at the Bucks County Playhouse in New Hope, Pennsylvania, from 28 August to 2 September. In New Hope, Martha Scott repeated the role of Emily Webb from the Broadway production.

2. Wilder went to Springfield, Massachusetts, on 15 August to do a radio interview. Later that

afternoon he had tea with them before returning to Stockbridge for the evening performance, which they attended (see Rogers to Stein [? August 1939], YCAL).

3. The house, Weeping Willows, was in Osterville, Massachusetts. They attended a performance at the Berkshire Playhouse. Wilder misspells Roullier and Steward.

4. Joyce was featured on the cover of *Time*, 8 May 1939, following the publication of *Finnegans Wake* in England and America on 4 May 1939. Wilder, who had been reading Joyce since his college years, met Joyce at Sylvia Beach's bookshop, Shakespeare and Company, in 1921 (see Wilder to Bill Bissell, 1923 Letter Book, letter 53, 20 August 1923). Wilder's fascination with *Finnegans Wake* continued until the end of his life, and he filled several hundred notebook pages with his research.

5. What the article is and whether it was published have not been determined. While Wilder was with Stein in June, he also visited Madame Pierlot and the d'Aiguys in Béon. François d'Aiguy and Wilder discussed an article by Claudel or by d'Aiguy about Claudel. (See Rogers to Stein, n.d., 1939.)

6. See Stein to Wilder [4 July 1939], n. 2.

To Gertrude Stein and Alice Toklas, Bilignin, France

11 Sept[ember]. 1939   50 Deepwood Drive
                                                        New Haven, Conn[ecticut].

Dear dear Friends:
                    All the time I keep wondering what you are and will be doing?[1]

You will stay in Bilignin? You will put yourselves and your car into some activity for the Governments again?[2]

Here we read newspapers and listen to radios all day. We built dream-myths of hope and alarm.

I keep telling myself that Mr. Shoop is probably giving you the best attention in the world.[3]

In a few weeks I am going away to settle down to work in solitary confinement—in Washington, where I only know 3 people. Should you decide to return here I'll [i.e., I] can meet you in a few hours. I suppose Sam Stewart has been caught over there, and must wait his turn to get back to school.[4]

I have been sending out copies of The World is Round to my young friends. It's a very good-looking book—I think the illustrations are the best of all I'd seen.

I wish I were with you and could hear you talking everything over.

If there's anything in the world I can do let me know. The Kiddies and I are now in renewed lively rapport after our joyous meetings in Springfield and Stockbridge this Summer.

All my devoted love; ever
                    Thornton

1. On the morning of 1 September 1939, Germany invaded Poland. England and France, committed by treaty to the defense of Poland, declared war on Germany on 3 September. However, Germany did not invade France until May 1940, ending the *drôle de guerre*, the so-called phoney war.

2. In August 1914, at the outbreak of World War I, Stein and Toklas, in England to see the publisher John Lane, were staying with Alfred North Whitehead and his wife at their home in Lockeridge. They remained with the Whiteheads until 17/18 October 1914, when they returned to Paris. In March 1915, Stein and Toklas left Paris for Spain and eventually Palma de Majorca, where they stayed until mid-June 1916, when they returned to Paris. Stein and Toklas joined the American Fund for French Wounded in March 1917, remaining with the organization and driving a supply truck until mid-June 1919 (information from a chronology prepared by Rosalind Moad, "1914–16: Years of Innovation in Gertrude Stein's Writing" [Diss., University of York, England, 1993], chap. 1, 9–74, and Appendix to chap. 1, 397–417).

3. See Wilder to Stein, [?15 June 1939], n. 4.

4. Steward returned to Marseille from Algeria on 12 August. Arriving on 14 August, Steward visited Stein for several days before going to Paris and sailing, after delays caused by the war, on the S.S. *Harding* from Le Havre on 15 September (Steward to Stein, 29 August and 15 September, YCAL).

To Thornton Wilder, Atlantic City, New Jersey

[postmark: 18 September 1939]   [Bilignin par Belley
                                                                  Ain]

My dearest Thornton,

         I know you are being worried about us and a little about my having been [?away], well these things will happen and xcept for one or two moments of scare not about bombs but about our beloved France we are hopeful, Basket and Pepe have never taken it on, we are staying on here another month and then back to Paris,[1] after that we do not know, we have now settled down to go on, Alice is type-writing Ida[2] I am writing, Basket and Pepe are asleep the rain is raining and the fire is crackling, your friend Giraudout [i.e., Giraudoux] is very popular in his job,[3] Francis Rose is a stretcher bearer in London at a convent the Rops have gone back to Paris the family at Beon keep their courage up, Madame Pierlot says 3 wars in one life-time are too many, well so are two, are you coming over, we would like to see you, Betty Leyris who is here with her 3 months old baby said about the book The World is Round, I hope when Johnny is old enough to read it the world will still be round,[4]

       well we all hope so, Dear Thornton we love you very much
               always
               Gtrde and Alice.

1. Stein and Toklas obtained a pass to return to Paris sometime between this letter and 26 September (Stein to Goodspeed, postmark 26 September 1939, YCAL). Once there, they collected winter

clothing, arranged their finances, and stored household goods. Daniel-Henry Kahnweiler, the art dealer and historian, saw them during their visit: "Gertrude and Alice were at Bilignin when the second world war broke out. I was in Paris. One autumn day I received a telephone call from them. They had just arrived in Paris in order to take some pictures back to Bilignin and they wanted to return there as soon as possible. . . . I hurried there [the rue Christine]. Entering, I saw Alice with one foot on the frame of the portrait of Madame Cézanne, trying to remove the picture. I stopped her, and set myself to unframing this magnificent work in a less violent manner. They wanted to carry away with them only this picture and the portrait of Gertrude by Picasso, despite my protestations that they should take at least some small Picassos, which would be very easy to wrap and would take up very little room. A happy Providence justified their confidence. The pictures left in Paris survived" ("Introduction," *Painted Lace And Other Pieces* [1914–1937], xvii–xviii). Stein wrote of the outbreak of the war and her decision to remain in Bilignin in "The Winner Loses A Picture Of Occupied France," in *The Atlantic Monthly* 166, 5 (November 1940): 571–83.

2. There is no typescript of the novel in YCAL. Whether Stein was working on "Arthur and Jenny," the second version of *Ida A Novel*, or had begun the third and final version of the novel is not clear.

3. Giraudoux was appointed head of the central office of French wartime propaganda in the Daladier government on 29 July 1939. His radio announcements were published in newspapers and placed on billboards. When Daladier resigned on 20 March 1940, Giraudoux was replaced.

4. See Stein to Wilder [?25 August 1938], n. 3.

To Thornton Wilder, Atlantic City, New Jersey

[postmark: ?1 October 1939]   Bilignin par Belley
                                                                       Ain

My dear dear Thornton,
                    Well we are still here and thought we were settled down but they suggest that I go over for a flying trip to read my book and lecture, I suppose it would be about war-time,[1] and there is so little to do here xcept be a comfort to each other that is the village and us, thank heaven France and England seem to be this time so well organised that the rest of us can only sit and hope and we do, so perhaps I might [be] most useful over there for a bit, by the way, you know our favorite audience subject, well since the war I have heard the radio for the first time and that as the creation of a modern world as it is because of an entirely new audience [?existence], destroying even the present with which I was at one time in contact,[2] well if we come over we will talk about that and if we do not come over we will talk about that, and go to see if you are in New York [John] McCullough my editor 224 Eleventh Street and help him help me to decide
                              lots of love
                              Gtrde.

1. John McCullough wrote Stein on 16 September to congratulate her on the publication of *The World Is Round* and asked whether she would consider "leaving France at this moment for a flying

lecture tour" (YCAL). On 9 October he wrote that he had discussed his idea with Carl Van Vechten, who was negative about a lecture agent, and with Russell Potter of Columbia University. On 5 November McCullough acknowledged Stein's cable informing him that she thought it best to postpone plans until the following season (YCAL).

2. Stein had, of course, heard the radio, but she had never pondered its implications. The themes of "recognition" and "audience" are central to this correspondence and to their relationship, and here Stein meditates on how the perception of reality is being transformed by the radio. She felt that radio, by making her a captive audience, interfered with the immediate perception of the actual world, always the source of her writing.

To Gertrude Stein and Alice Toklas, Bilignin, France

20 Oct[ober] 1939   Atlantic City [New Jersey]

Dear Ones:

Both your letters arrived here together and you can imagine my joy.[1] I had already been in touch with Mr. Van Vechten and the Kiddies and we were all comparing our "thoughts" about you.

I think of you so often and your walks in the village and the shopping in Belley and what words you must exchange [with] the people there. In a few minutes—after being cooped up in this Atlantic City all day, "working"—I shall go out to get the afternoon papers and hope and dread in every muscle.

Next week I shall be in New York again apartment-hunting—I procrastinate the hunt week after week, but I must move from New Haven—I shall look up Mr. McCoullough and talk over the lecture tour possibility. I should say that a lot depended on the degree of interest shown in the answers from the clubs and schools he may already have approached on the matter. The practicability of the Second lecture-tour seems not to depend on merit, or previous response or anything. The Bigger the name often the quicker the vogue. Margo[t] Asquith, [Maurice] Maeterlinck, Admiral Byrd,—all seem to have been a One-Tour value. It all comes down to the fact that the American public doesn't attend large-scale lectures for "the words." However, we will "ransack" the subject over here on this side, and I hope Mr. McCoullough will feel that the responses have justified asking you to come over. And naturally, for that *dio mio* I have my own private reasons. If the war is to be long and terrible, should you be there with it around you—especially should you be in Paris?

Mme Pierlot's words gave me a start. Yes, she must have remembered the War of 1870 also. Hard to realize.

I have no news. Hesitation. Uncertainty. Distaste for most of the associations about me. I have been down here alone for a week. The luxury of not having to talk, and of not being talked to, talked at.

Under my window the waves are coming in per since creation. The sun's going down.[2]

Give my devoted regards to the Pierlot household. Think of me as you drive in the country; my head's full of European places all the time. I'm fretful not to be there,—there as place; I have no wish to be near it as war.

More soon,—and all my love.

Thornton.

P.S. Oh, I forgot to say that Poetry is bringing out 5 pages of the 200 Stanzas.[3] The editors are very pleased. The standards of the review have written [i.e., ?risen] very high these last few years. I forgot to ask the editors how much they were paying, but I'll report on that very soon. *Tendresses*.

T.

Do we get all one another's letters, I wonder. I hope soon. Have you heard of any gone astray?

1. Stein's letters postmarked 18 September and 1 October both arrived in New Haven on 17 October. Throughout this letter, Wilder misspells McCullough as McCoullough. In the next letter, he writes MacCullough.

2. Following the failure of *The Merchant of Yonkers*, his problems with Jed Harris, his visit to Europe on the brink of war, and his performances in *Our Town*, Wilder is frustrated and is casting about for ways to write his new play, *The Skin of Our Teeth*. He is in the location that will eventually be incorporated into the play.

3. *Poetry* published six stanzas numbered consecutively: I is part II, stanza 1; II is part IV, stanza IV; III is part III, stanza II; IV is part V, stanza LXXXI; V is part V, stanza LXXXII; VI is part V, stanza LXXXIII (see *Poetry, A Magazine of Verse* 55, 5 (February 1940): 229–35). Later Stein wrote to Ellen Du Poy that *Poetry* "paid nicely" (n.d., 1940, YCAL).

To Gertrude Stein and Alice Toklas, Bilignin, France

25 Oct[ober]. 1939   The Century Association
                                                     7 West Forty-Third Street
                                                     New York [New York]

Dear Kinder-Kinder:

I have just had a talk with Mr. MacCullough. He is very nice and loves you sight-unseen.

He says that the first soundings-out of committees and universities etc where you might be speaking are very favorable, and he is going to sound out some more. So my fears about the fickleness and superficiality of lecture-audiences and their directors were unjustified.

He thinks that a tour like this—assembled so late in the season—ought perhaps to be in the hands of a professional manager. Those managers are of the wolf-family, but they do save a lot of work, and Mr. MacCullough thinks that this one would accede to any condition you might make as to limitations of audiences, fees, etc.[1]

I tried to interest him in *Four in America* of which I am fonder and fonder. He wants to see it. I would love to see that in as attractive and appropriate a format as "The World is Round."

My nights and days are suddenly taken up with making a rapid adaptation of Farquhar's *The Beaux' Stratagem.*[2] Surely you read that curled up in the window of the Army Club Library on Sutter St?

Now I am going apartment-hunting—near Washington Square. I never pass "our house" there, without a glance at Alice's sewing-room on the Second Floor, and a vision of the dogs making the tour of the Square.[3]

MORE SOON AND that which makes THE WORLD GO ROUND
LOVE
Thornton

1. McCullough (Wilder's misspelling) had contacted the lecture agents Colston Leigh and Ford Hicks (see McCullough to Stein, 5 and 18 November 1939, 4 January 1940, YCAL).
2. The proposal came from Cheryl Crawford, who had become an independent producer. The production never materialized. Wilder and Crawford met in the late 1920s when she was an executive assistant at the Theatre Guild. She was a cofounder of several theaters—the Group Theatre with Harold Clurman and Lee Strasberg in 1931; the American Repertory Theatre with Eva Le Gallienne and Margaret Webster in 1946; and the Actor's Studio with Elia Kazan and Robert Lewis in 1947. Wilder's adaptation is in YCAL.
3. See Toklas to Wilder, 7 June 1935.

To Gertrude Stein and Alice Toklas, Bilignin, France

(18 Nov[ember]. 1939)   My new apartment is:
                                                          81 Irving Place
                                                          New York City[1]

Dear Ones:
          Probably you've already seen the enclosed, but I send it on the chance.[2]
          I've lived five days in my New York home and am already flooded with a new overwhelming feeling about New York.

I went to Clare Luce's play and all I can say is that it's dreadfully easy, emphatic and vulgar.[3]

Bob Ardrey's fourth play is so immediate a failure that it is being withdrawn after a week. He can't see that the propaganda he pours into it doesn't really mean a thing to him. I wish you were there to "lui laver la Tête" [straighten him out].[4]

Maybe you will be here soon.

I have a bad cold and am a mass of aches and stoppages, so I won't wheeze along any further,

> But send you
> all my
> love
> Thornty

1. The *New York Times* on 9 November 1939, 43, announced, "Thornton Wilder Signs for a Suite."

2. The enclosure has not remained with the letter.

3. *Margin for Error* by Clare Boothe [Luce] opened at the Plymouth Theatre, New York, on 3 November and ran for 264 performances. Staged by Otto Preminger, the play was an anti-Nazi comedy-melodrama.

4. Ardrey's *Thunder Rock*, presented by the Group Theatre and staged by Elia Kazan, opened at the Mansfield Theatre, New York, on 14 November and closed after twenty-three performances. The play is about Charleston (Luther Adler), a radical who goes to work as a lighthouse attendant at Thunder Rock, an island in northern Lake Michigan. Living in solitude, he creates a ghost world and brings back the passengers and crew of a ship that had foundered on Thunder Rock in 1849. Charleston lives through their crises and realizes that there has been great improvement in the human condition in the ninety years since the shipwreck. Charleston decides to come out of his solitude and take up the fight for liberty and democracy. In "Preface to the Plays" in *Plays*, Ardrey discusses its origin.

To Thornton Wilder, New York, New York

[postmark: ? November 1939]   [Bilignin par Belley
[received New Haven,   Ain, France]
27 November 1939]

My dearest Thorny,

Glad to get your letter, no I do not really believe that they go astray, they linger on the road the letters but they manage to arrive as far as I know all of them, I am sorry you are not with us, I don't know if there has to be a war, in spite of it all it does do something, it intensifies the concentration of isolation even though you converse more than ordinary and see more people and saw more wood and look at more animals,[1] I am doing a child's story about war-time, it interests me a lot I wish you were here, you would like it you know, particularly in the country, cities are not so good, we have been snowed under and Basket got run over but thank heaven nothing but a stiff neck and that is gone and Pepe sits by the Brulet fire, it is a lovely brulet fire and Alice is inordinately busy, and I am very active, and writing three books, the one about Paris, France all about what they say here, and it is kind of wonderful,[2] we do wish you were here, of course we won't go over at any rate until it is certain that we could get back, because we would not like not getting back, so don't trouble too much, and Alexander [Woollcott] is on the stage, Bennett [Cerf] writes me,[3] and thanks about the Stanzas, and be a good boy and look at the moon and remember us

Gtrde and Alice.

1. Stein is responding to Wilder's letter of 20 October and is continuing her reflections on her changed situation (see Stein to Wilder [?1] October 1939).

2. Stein is working on "Helen Button A Story Of War-Time," *Paris France*, and *Ida A Novel*. She incorporated "Helen Button" into *Paris France*, pages 80–92. Hélène Bouton, a seventeen-year-old girl from the village of Céyzérieu, not far from Bilignin, replied on 12 September 1939 (YCAL) to an offer of employment that Stein had placed in *Le Bugiste*, a local newspaper (see Burns, *Letters*, 2:652).

3. Cerf wrote Stein on 17 October (YCAL), the day after the George Kaufman and Moss Hart play *The Man Who Came to Dinner* opened at the Music Box Theatre in New York. In the play, Sheridan Whiteside, a character based on Alexander Woollcott, gets a Christmas Eve transatlantic call from Gertrude Stein in Paris. Whiteside explains that Stein telephones him, wherever he is in the world, so that he can hear the chimes of Notre Dame.

1940

Alexander Woollcott in a vest perhaps given to him by Stein. A portrait by John Decker painted in 1942 from this photograph by an unknown photographer hangs in the Castleton, Vermont, Free Public Library.

To Thornton Wilder, New York, New York

[postmark: 10 January 1940]   Bilignin par Belley
                                                                   Ain

My dearest Thornton,

        Oh where oh where are you, not a Christmas greeting not a New Years greeting, shall auld acquaintance be forgot in the glory of a New York residence or are you sick in bed, Thornton where are you. With us it is easy because we are here, we just are, we set before the fire[1] we brave the frosty air, we go in and we go out, we have the visits of all the permissionnaires,[2] we have lots of new friends some nice English among others,[3] and we have just finished our book Paris, France and everybody seems to like it and it will very soon be out[4] but we have no Thornton, where oh where is Thornton, are you on your way over, where is Thornton,

        lots of love
        Gtrde

    1. "Set," New England colloquialism.

    2. Soldiers on short leave. Stein and Toklas started a Foyer du Soldat, a rest and recreation center, in Bilignin and in Belley (see Stein to Goodspeed, postmark 29 December 1939, YCAL).

    3. The English painter John Selby-Bigge and his wife, Ruth, and their three daughters rented a house in Yenne, on the Rhone, in the summer of 1939, and through Gordon Onslow Ford, a painter who lived not far from Bilignin, they met Stein.

    4. In a letter to Van Vechten, also postmarked 10 January 1940, Stein wrote that she was sending a typescript of *Paris France* in a few days. In England it was published by B. T. Batsford in April 1940 and in America by Charles Scribner's Sons on 14 June 1940 (see Burns, *Letters*, 2:663).

To Gertrude Stein and Alice Toklas, Bilignin, France

28 Janu[uary]. 1940   50 Deepwood Drive
                                                         New Haven, Conn[ecticut].

Dear Ones:
                 Last year I lost my little black engagement-diary-address book.
    Is your address 5 or 15 or something else rue Christine? Would the
postman correct such a mistake? All my notions of France go into my doubt;
so I shall send this to the postladies of Belley; they too have a very low opinion
of all letters not addressed to themselves, but I think (some day) they will
forward this to you, just to get it out of their way.
    I have no news.
    Health, inertia, and a shocking busyness over trifles.
    I have a New York apartment until March 15, and I am all adazzle about
my new acquaintance, New York. Walks, walks, subway rides; then more
walks. To all proposals—dinners, committees, lectures,—I say no—not as formerly a defensive anxious apologetic no, but the easy no of the indifferent and
absent-minded. I don't go to the theatre,—this is the year that the movies have
finally risen and surpassed the stage.
    I like it.
    Just as that summer at Peterborough I laid everything aside and read The
Making of Americans, read, and reread, and made cross-references and went
about in a walking dream of complete immersion in it;[1] so I have been for
months engaged with Finnegans Wake, decoding that unbroken chain of
complicated erudite puzzles.[2] I've only skimmed the surface, but I know more
about it than any article on it yet published. Finally I stopped, and put it away
from me as one would liquor or gambling; I ceased tearing off to the public
library to verify Persian moon goddesses, and the astronomical conditions over
the British Isles in January, and the Danish word for goat.
    But it was wonderfully absorbing while it lasted.
    Mabel Luhan is in New York and has opened a salon.[3] The first Friday
night it was on Civil Liberties; the second: T.W. will elucidate eight pages of
Finnegans Wake; the third Psychoanalysis and Medicine; the fourth on Censorship. I had much hope that it would be a Something, but it wasn't. It takes a
will of iron, and Mabel hasn't that, so it's petering out.
    The movie magnate for "Our Town" confused because I would accept
no money for the interminable conferences over the script, gave me an automobile for Xmas. I don't like 'em, but there it is. So when my apartment-lease
is up I shall take it and drive far away.[4]
    I had some hours with Robert Haas and he has sent me his thesis which I
like very much; now I am eager to go back and reread The Geographical
History. I hope he goes on to do a very very good book about you.[5] I wish I

could hear Bob Davis's discussion of the Haas thesis. His *aperçus* would leap farther and brighter than Haas's, but his soul has gone murky like his English style. Clouds of smoke.[6]

A letter from Sir Francis [Rose] asking if I could see any kind of call or engagement for him in America.[7] The galleries and dealers; the glazed paper women's magazines;—he must have closer approaches to them than I have. I'm still deep in Austrian exiles[8] and in trying to establish Max Reinhardt in a dramatic school in New York or in a college near here, and I've had some success in finding teaching posts and pension grants etc, etc, for teachers and writers, but I wouldn't know where to turn for Sir Francis.[9]

The Hutchins were in New York for a few days during the holidays.

It would take the whole of a drive to Vienne and back to lay that situation before you.

I summarize it by saying that Maude's going crazy and in such a way that one is torn between pitying her for a desperately sick mind and hating her for a vulgar pretentious tiresome goose. Such dances as she leads Bob, with tantrums, caprices, changes of mind and talk, talk, talk.

And the effect of it on the two daughters!

The Wilders are fine. Isabel at last starts in this week on a job. She is to be assistant to the supervisor of the Connecticut branch of Federal Writers Project. Charlotte will have after many years a volume of prose ready this spring— Proust-like evocations of her childhood in Berkeley and China.[10] Janet rec'd her PHD from the University of Chicago and is teaching at Mt. Holyoke. Amos's Katharine is about to give us another baby.[11] Mother is fine.

Is it still possible you will be over this Spring. When I get back to New York I shall verify through Lee Keedick and Mr. McCullough how things are progressing.

(Tuesday—back in New York)

A letter came from you this morning. I deserve your reproaches, but shall mend my ways.

I called up Lee Keedick today. He is out of town but his secretary (an old friend of mine—that demon of personalizing everything always sets me to wooing secretaries—yes, yes, it's to take the curse off business transactions and to apologize for the exchange of moneys) tells me that some important decision on the matter of your tour is to be reached this week.

Now I'm reading another splendid book: The letters of Madame du Deffand to H. Walpole. The absurdity, the agony, the dazzling crystalline French—"les grandes passions sont celles de quatre-vingt ans" said Disraeli.[12]

How I wish, dear sister-stars, that I could rush into your dear sitting room (amid barking) and kiss you on both cheeks and read the MS of Paris, France.

Ever thine
Thornton

1. See Wilder to Stein, 22 June, and telegram and letter of 24 June 1937.

2. See Wilder to Stein [20 August 1939], n. 4.

3. Mabel Dodge Luhan, who lived in Taos, New Mexico, rented a tower apartment at One Fifth Avenue, New York, for the winter of 1939–40. On Friday evening, 12 January 1940, Wilder read and explicated eight pages from *Finnegans Wake*, repeating his talk the next evening for his sister Isabel's birthday party in New Haven. To Edmund Wilson, Wilder wrote, "It went off all right last night but 'they do these things better in France.' I passed out mimeographed sheets reprinting the first three paragraphs, the Nocturne on p. 244 and the close from 626. Overcrowded apartment; latecomers refused admission [. . .] The damndest thing in the whole business of the exposition of great books is to receive the flattering charge that one has read beauties into them. I used to get that often after the Dante hours at the U. of Chicago. One can take it from students; but last night from writers and critics. The notion that out of a deluded schwarmerei I had been kind enough to invest a poor nonsensical work of Joyce with merits it had no right to" (13 January 1940, YCAL).

Among those who spoke at Luhan's evenings were Roger N. Baldwin, an advocate of civil and humanitarian rights, on 4 January; A. A. Brill, a noted psychoanalyst—Luhan's own analyst—on 19 January; and John Collier, United States commissioner for Indian affairs, on 9 February. Despite Luhan's efforts, these evenings lacked the spontaneity of her pre–World War I salon at 23 Fifth Avenue, and they were abandoned. To Luhan, the morning after Brill spoke, Wilder wrote, "Dr. Brill—while inspiring every confidence as menschenkenner—gave us that extended parallel between an amoeba and a man and I was horrified—it did not rise above the level of midnight beer-discussions when we were sophomores at college. . . . I divined last night that the discussion would get nowhere if it remained in generalities and my apparently dull question to Dr. Hornay [i.e., Karen Horney] was an effort to bring her back to a discussion of the Aggression Instinct and its various expressions, but I did it badly and it misfired. . . . Anyway, it was very rewarding just to see the heads of those great workers" (n.d., YCAL).

4. The producer Sol Lesser proposed a film version of *Our Town* in September 1939. On 5 October, Lesser sent Wilder a "First Rough Draft," prepared by Frank Craven and Harry Chandlee. For the next six months, Lesser and Wilder saw each other frequently and exchanged letters about the script and the filming. When the film was finished, Wilder shared in the writing credit. Lesser telegraphed Isabel Wilder on 4 December, "WHAT MAKE OF CAR WOULD THORNTON LIKE FOR CHRISTMAS." She replied the next day, "THORNTON DOESN'T DRIVE ANY MORE BUT HAS ALWAYS SAID IF HE HAD CAR WANTED A CHRYSLER CONVERTIBLE WITH RUMBLE SEAT."

Wilder was consulted by Lesser about the film script. Their letters concern problems faced in transforming a play into a film. On the major change of the added happy ending, Wilder commented to Lesser on Easter Night 1940, "In the first place, I think Emily should live. I've always thought so. In a movie you see the people so *close to* that a different relation is established. In the theatre they are halfway abstractions in an allegory; in the movie they are very concrete. So insofar as the play is a generalized allegory, she dies—we die—they die; insofar as it's a concrete happening it's not important that she die; it's even disproportionately cruel that she die.

"Let her live—the idea will have been imparted anyway" (*Anthology*, 377–78). A selection of the Wilder-Lesser letters is published in "*Our Town*—From Stage to Screen: A Correspondence between Thornton Wilder and Sol Lesser," in *Theatre Arts* 24, no. 11 (November 1940): 815–23. A shortened version of the article is in *Theatre Arts Anthology: A Record and a Prophecy 1916–1948*, eds. Rosamond Gilder, Hermine Rich Isaacs, Robert M. MacGregor, and Edward Reed (New York: Theatre Arts Books: Robert M. MacGregor, 1950), 363–78.

The film version of *Our Town*, directed by Sam Wood, received Academy Award nominations as Best Picture of the Year, and Martha Scott, who recreated her Broadway role as Emily Webb, was nominated for Best Actress. The awards were won by Alfred Hitchcock's *Rebecca* and Ginger Rogers for her performance in *Kitty Foyle*. In the film, Frank Craven and Doro Merande also recreated their Broadway roles. Aaron Copland composed the music, which he later incorporated into *Music for Movies* (1942). He also adapted three excerpts for piano (1944) and arranged about ten minutes of the score into an orchestral suite (1945).

In 1951, Copland and Rudolf Bing, general manager of the Metropolitan Opera, discussed a commission for making *Our Town* into an opera. Wilder rejected the idea: "I'm convinced I write amusical plays: that my texts 'swear at' music; that they're after totally different effects; that they delight in the homeliest aspects of our daily life. . . . Music and particularly opera is for the unlocked throat; the outgoing expressive 'idea and essence' behind our daily life. I hope my plays don't lack that idea and essence, but they singularly shrink from an explicit use of it. They are homely and not one bit lyrical" (quoted in a letter from Vivian Perlis, Director, Oral History, American Music, School of Music, Yale University, New Haven, to the *New York Times*, Sunday, 31 January 1988, sec. H, 16. The ellipses are those of Perlis).

5. The master's thesis of Haas, "An Analysis of the Present as an Aesthetic Process in the Critical Writings of Gertrude Stein." When Haas was working on his chronology of Stein's writings at the Yale library for several days in early January, Wilder spent time with him (see Haas to Stein, 3 January 1940, YCAL).

6. Wilder is recalling the perceptive readings by Davis of Stein and Whitehead in 1935 (see Wilder to Stein, 9 July 1935).

7. Stein sent Wilder's address to Rose in a letter postmarked 5 January 1940 (Katz transcription, YCAL). Rose's letter to Wilder has not been located.

8. Wilder helped Ernst Waldinger, Frederick Lehner, Richard Beer-Hofmann, and Hermann Broch, among others (see Wilder to Stein, 2 March 1939, nn. 8, 9).

9. Queens College in New York City was one of several colleges unsuccessfully approached to establish a school for Reinhardt. In California, in addition to professional productions, Reinhardt established the Max Reinhardt Workshop, a training school, which lasted from August 1938 to October 1942. During these years, both in the workshop and in his Max Reinhardt Theatre productions, he and his wife, Helene Thimig, presented limited-run performances of Wilder's *Queens of France, The Long Christmas Dinner, Pullman Car Hiawatha*, and *The Happy Journey to Trenton and Camden*. On 19 February 1941, Reinhardt's theater presented a single performance of *The Merchant of Yonkers*. (See Huesmann, *Welttheater Reinhardt*.)

10. This book was never published. Her first volume of poetry was *Phases of the Moon* (1936), followed by *Mortal Sequence* (1939).

11. Amos Tappan Wilder was born in Boston on 6 February 1940.

12. *Horace Walpole's Correspondence with Madame du Deffand and Wiart*, edited by W. S. Lewis and Warren Hunting Smith, was published by Yale University Press in December 1939. The first two volumes in this six-volume series had been published in 1937. Wilder quotes or paraphrases Benjamin Disraeli, "The great passions are those of eighty years."

To Gertrude Stein and Alice Toklas, Bilignin, France

Middle of March [1940]   50 Deepwood Drive
                                                                  New Haven, Connecticut

Dear Bonnies over the Water:

How often I went down to the Battery at night and listened to the waves slapping the sea-wall and thought of you across the million waves.[1] It's awful, but it doesn't do any good to talk about it. I just send you some strong telepathic currents of love and longing. Now that I have become non-gregarious, my sociable self has become more and more intense towards the six people in the world I do care for, and there are two of them in Belley.

This is my news:

The Yale Library to show its pride in your MSS is going to have a show of Gertrude Stein material in the Fall. They're so pleased with [Robert] Haas's cataloguing, too, and with the many acquisitions they've made from purchase and gift, that they want a SHOW.[2] You can guess what dreams this sets going in my head: your presence here; a reception of honor; a lecture tour,—to which I don't hesitate to add a world-at-peace, and an uninfested ocean.

Reading the enclosed letter you can imagine the agony of indecision I've been going through: shall I lend or give to the library my *As a Wife has a Cow.* Pro, con. At last I have decided to give it. Their feeling of approaching a Complete Collection is more ultimately valuable than my joy of possession.[3]

¶ Edmund Wilson came to New York and we talked until four in the morning. I did what I could to share with him Audience, and the Present and so on. He was deeply interested, yes, and moved.[4]

¶. My New York residence is over. I got many fine things out of it and am glad it's over. Now I'm taking driving lessons. That movie producer gave me a beautiful car for Xmas and soon I shall be out on the road—sleeping in tourist-camps and drawing near to the first tumble-weeds and the desert,—"[']my[']
air and light and sky."

¶ Oh, how I look forward to reading Paris France.

¶ I have a nephew four weeks old, healthy and fine and with my dimple in his chin, Amos Tappan Wilder. Is it a disadvantage to be named after an abolitionist, quickly tell.[5]

¶ Maude Hutchins has become more so and if I were less vexed with her I would be more concerned about her.

Maybe I shall be on the road when I next write you, in and out of hundreds of American villages. All my regard to the friends at Béon, an extra bonne bouche [good tidbit] to the dogs in my name, and a world of devoted thoughts to yourselves.

                              love
                              Thornton

                    Later: Easter night

I've been down to the library again and seen the new cataloguing of your material.

It's exemplary library-technique.

About eight large black boxes, with neatly pasted labels.

And in each box a dozen handsome folders, each carefully labelled with the MS or fragment of MS by title and date (the date being [Robert] Haas's expert contribution.)

At present in the library there's a large Frank Stockton exhibition (!) and a Sinclair Lewis one.[6]

In the new Yale Review, a certain Jerome Mellquist reviews a group of six books on art and closes with: ". . . Miss Stein's discussion—which emphasizes and re-emphasizes that Picasso is primarily a Spaniard—gets so much said about the painter in such a small space that it ranks as an invaluable appreciation of the subject."[7]

Oh, Angels, I wish I could hear your reflections on the War. I don't like my own and I don't like anybody else's. Oh, to take a walk up and around Lolo's house,[8] and a good long drive in the country.

LOVE,

P.S. I had to take out the Librarian's letter because of overweight, but will send it in another envelope

Love,

T.

1. Wilder lived at 81 Irving Place from November 1939 until early March 1940 (see Wilder to Stein, 18 November 1939, n. 1).

2. An exhibition of Stein manuscripts and books, organized by Norman Holmes Pearson and Donald Gallup, was held at the Sterling Memorial Library from 22 February to 29 March 1941. Gallup, a Yale graduate, began working at the library in February 1940. The catalogue consists of Gallup's bibliography of the published works and revisions by Haas of the chronological bibliography that Stein had prepared for *transition* 15 (February 1929): 47–55.

3. A letter of 19 March (YCAL) from Donald G. Wing, head of the accessions department of the Yale library, listing works needed to complete the library's Stein collection. Wilder responded by giving his copy of *A Book Concluding With As A Wife Has A Cow A Love Story*, which Stein had inscribed,

> If Thornton by Thornton
> as Thornton for Thornton for
> Thornton is Thornton as Thornton
> us too
> for you
>
> Gtde.
> Paris and the nice Autumn 1935

4. Wilder and Wilson met in New York on 5 March and discussed Stein, Dickens, and Joyce (see Wilder to Wilson, 8 and 13 January and 23 February, YCAL).

5. Wilder's nephew was named after the abolitionist leader Arthur Tappan, his maternal grandmother's grandfather.

6. Both exhibitions were in the Sterling Memorial Library. Lewis, a graduate of Yale ('07), had recently donated the typewritten manuscript and the corrected galleys for his novel *Bethel Merriday* (1940).

7. Mellquist's review, "American Color Reproduction," in *The Yale Review* 29, 3 (March 1940): 632–36.

8. Louis "Lolo" Reynaud, a very young poet, playwright, and aspiring critic, became friendly with Stein in 1929/30 and appears in a number of Stein's texts. He lived in Hauteville, a short drive from Belley. We do not know if Wilder ever met him.

To Thornton Wilder, St. Augustine, Florida

[postmark: 25 March 1940][1]   Bilignin par Belley
                                                                Ain

My dearest Thornton,

Spring has come and a nice cheque from Poetry, Chi-
cago, you are a saint Thornton and thank you, and the spring my gracious
what a spring, all March we have been sitting out on the terrace without coats
and such masses of violets, primroses, jonquils and even birds, a sky lark the
beginning of March, don't you want to see the spring, and everybody is having
permission agricole, and the fields and the oxen and the sheep, only cows are
still confined, I begged the peasants to let them out to see the spring time but
they say they kick up their heels too much when they are first let out so they
don't let them out until the spring fever is past, such is the life of cows, and
Thornton, Bennett Cerf sounds as if he would very much like to do a book of
mine again, if the poems get attention you might ask him if he would like to
see the ms. if you would, but of course all that to your judgment,[2] we have had
a nice lot of chasseurs alpins and now we are to have the foreign legion so they
say, anyway the spring has come, and nothing can stop it now,

thanks and thanks again, always
all of us
Gtrde.

1. This letter arrived in New Haven on 14 April and was forwarded to Wilder in Florida.
2. Cerf had written to Stein, "I hope that you are going to let us see both your book about Paris
and the novel [*Ida A Novel*] you are working on" (11 January 1940, YCAL).

To Gertrude Stein and Alice Toklas, Bilignin, France

29 March 1940   50 Deepwood Drive
                                                 New Haven, Connecticut

Dear Ones:

Here are the clippings that were overweight in my last letter.[1]
Two days ago I passed my driver's licence-test and free of the roads. But I
don't think I'll ever like driving: you can't look about you enough.
But maybe I'll start out for San Francisco soon.[2] Alec [Woollcott] is breaking all theatre records playing in that play and offers me a tiny mute part in the
cast for a month on the road tour—up through the Sacramento Valley, Oregon
and Washington. I don't think I'll do that,—tempting though it is *for fun.*[3]

x   x

For the last week the American view of the Allied cause in the War has darkened: "they" are now saying that the ultimate situation is more precarious than we thought. However, these alternations of fright and talk are continual. *Speriamo* [Let's hope].

Devotedly
Thornton

1. The enclosures have not remained with the letter.

2. Wilder did not go to San Francisco. Instead, starting on 8 April, he drove to Florida, arriving on 15 April and remaining until early May. He reluctantly learned to drive, never became a good driver, and had numerous accidents (Isabel Wilder interviews).

3. George Kaufman's and Moss Hart's comedy *The Man Who Came to Dinner* opened in New York at the Music Box Theatre on 16 October 1939. It was an immediate hit, and when it closed on 12 July 1941, it had run 739 performances. In addition to the Broadway company, there were three road companies. Woollcott, playing the role of Sheridan Whiteside, a character based on himself, opened with a Pacific Coast touring company on 10 February at the Lobero Theatre, Santa Barbara, California.

To Thornton Wilder, St. Augustine, Florida

[postmark: 4 April 1940][1]   [Bilignin par Belley
                                                               Ain]

My dearest Thorny,

Perhaps after you read Paris, France, you will see how peaceful we are and you will come over to see us, my spring is lovely here, I had no idea it could be so lovely, so many primroses and violets and birds and sun-shine, March was a lovely month, April is showering a bit, but we hope for better things, and we garden passionately, as Alice says gardening with us means making the garden look lovely and empty, but then there are the box hedges and I am cutting them all by myself and they are beautifully green, and smell, well that is our pastoral and now so many thanks for the Yale Library, it pleases us a lot, might they not ask Carl Van Vechten to lend them the ms. of Four Saints which I gave him in a vellum container, I think if they asked him to present to them a complete set of the photos he made of us, I think he would be pleased and it would be a valuable contribution,[2] they are suggesting that I come over and do 15 lectures about France,[3] and I am suggesting that they might do Alice B. Toklas at Hollywood, and they seem to think it might be, that would be fun and in that way we could stay awhile,[4] well anyway and in every way we love Thorny always

Gtrde.

1. This letter arrived in New Haven on 23 April and was forwarded to him in Saint Augustine.

2. Stein recognized the importance and benefit of a Yale exhibition and wrote Van Vechten the same day without mentioning Wilder: "They have just written me that the Yale Library wants to make a show of all my mss. in the fall and I have suggested to them that you might lend them Four Saints and also might give them a complete set of our photos, I am telling you that I suggested it, it would please me a lot to have your photos of us kept with the mss" (Burns, *Letters*, 2:671). Van Vechten gave the library both the manuscript and a complete set of photographs on the occasion of the exhibition.

3. Three lecture agents were actively pursuing Stein for a second lecture tour. John McCullough, an editor at William R. Scott, the firm that had published Stein's *The World Is Round*, was working with Colston Leigh of the Leigh Lecture Bureau when he was contacted by Lee Keedick on 27 January 1940, who offered to match Leigh's offer to Stein. In Chicago, Samuel Steward was in touch with Ford Hicks of the National Lecture Bureau. On 15 December 1939 (YCAL) Hicks proposed to Toklas a tour before large audiences and offered Stein $375 per lecture—in 1934–35 her fee had been $100. On the verso of Hicks's letter, Toklas drafted a reply that set out Stein's conditions, one of which was that colleges unable to pay the fee would not be excluded. Stein's decision to remain in France after it fell to the Germans in June 1940 ended the negotiations.

4. In March–April 1935 Stein discussed with Lillian May Ehrman and Ivan Kahn, her brother and a Hollywood agent, turning "The Gentle Lena" and perhaps *The Autobiography Of Alice B. Toklas* into films. Nothing came of these discussions (see Stein to Wilder, postmark 2 April 1935, n. 1). The lure of Hollywood returned in September 1936, when she read of the large salary being paid to P. G. Wodehouse for doing very little work (see Stein to Wilder, letter 2, received 10 September 1936, n. 1). Perhaps thoughts of Hollywood offered an escape from the realities of war as well as a hope of making money.

To Van Vechten, Stein had written, "I dream that Hollywood might do the Autobiography of Alice Toklas, they could make a very good film out of that and then they would pay us large moneys to go out and sit and consult and that would be all new and I would like that and once over there I could lecture or not as I liked." Stein also asked Van Vechten to speak to Cerf about the idea: "[P]erhaps he could do something but I do not like to ask him, you can always make him do anything you think he ought to do so if you think he ought to do this then you make him, it is just a dream" ([15 February 1940], in Burns, *Letters*, 2:667–68).

Van Vechten reported on his meeting with Cerf on 19 March [1940]: "I talked to Bennett [Cerf] about the motion picture possibilities of The Autobiography which are ENORMOUS, but motion picture people are peculiar. You can't approach *them*. They must approach *you*. I think the time to take this up is when you are lecturing in Hollywood. . . Of course you both would have to appear in the picture. Even Greta Garbo and Lillian Gish couldn't be you and Alice" (Burns, *Letters*, 2:669–70).

To Gertrude Stein and Alice Toklas, Bilignin, France

3 May 1940   [Ormond Beach, Florida]

At a one-night stop fifteen miles South of St. Augustine where some millionaires have built a big dazzling new kind of aquarium where you damn near walk in and out among the sharks and porpoises and congereels.

Dear Ones:

Today's the day of the bad news from Norway, but it doesn't do any good my talking about it.[1] Looks like things'll get worse and worse. I can always bear the thought of my own death-day, but when I think of others dying by the thousands I get rattled.

Anyway, you keep out of harm's way.

I got a great joy out of *Paris France*. It's the same wonderful bolt of cloth. Didn't nobody write that but Gertrude. Like a high, singing, tight-drawn golden wire or electric current, Gertrude's style. I read long stretches of it aloud to some company at my house and their faces had that amazed look: all that wit and wisdom coming out so smooth together. Yes, it's from the same bolt of cloth.

I have sent it on to [Robert] Haas.[2]

I suppose its New York publication is arranged for, and when you suggested that I interest Bennett Cerf in another book you meant the Stanzas. I'll try. But since he turned down Four in America I despair of his bringing out "that side" of your work.[3]

Alec Woollcott had a heart-attack the other day. He had been playing the chief role in the second company of the play *The Man Who Came to Dinner*—a great New York success—a play written about him. So in the second company he was playing himself and in San Francisco the play broke all the house records. His illness cancelled the further tour, and he will soon be returning to the Vermont Island.[4]

I am now a driver, Alice, though I'm not yet able to "park" my car in city streets. I don't think I'll ever really like driving, but I'm grateful for its making me more the master of my comings and goings. If the War stops—ah, Iddio, Dio, di grazia, di grazia! [Lord, by your grace]—I'll bring it over and look at France more closely. The drives I took with you admitted me to more sense of France than all my previous lookings put together.

On this trip I've lived in Tourist Camps, elbow-close to my fellow-census-numbers among the 130 millions. Are they coming on and along the path of those qualities and possibilities that Gertrude brought out? I have the feeling that they've stopped somewhere.

Wish you were here. Florida sun on the cactus and palmetto; and the ocean under my window.—By June first I shall be back in the MacDowell Colony at Peterborough; in July I shall probably be acting in my play again up in Maine; August home.

The possibility that you will be lecturing here in the Fall gives me something to rejoice and smile over as I cover these endless miles.[5] May it all come true.

All my love like always

                    Thy
                    Thornton

1. Germany invaded Denmark and Norway on 9 April. Denmark surrendered after five hours but Norway continued fighting until 9 June.

2. Wilder received a copy of *Paris France* from William G. and Mildred Rogers and sent it on to Haas (see Haas to Stein, 25 April 1940, YCAL).

3. Wilder is responding to Stein's letter of 25 March, with an accurate estimate of the extent of Cerf's adventuresomeness. Cerf's interest was in the "public" books. His enthusiasm for *Ida A Novel* may have come from Stein's connecting it with the Duchess of Windsor.

4. Woollcott was stricken on 21 April with what was first thought to be an attack of indigestion, later diagnosed as a heart attack. The tour of *The Man Who Came to Dinner*, which had been booked until 1 June in Salt Lake City, was therefore canceled. Woollcott returned East by train on the evening of 4 May and stopped in Syracuse on 9 May to be examined by his personal physician and Hamilton College classmate, Dr. Albert Getman, before returning to his home on Neshobe Island, Vermont.

5. Wilder began his return to New Haven the morning of 15 May, spent the night of the eighteenth in New York and arrived the next morning in New Haven. For the next nine days, he commuted between New York and New Haven. On 29 May he drove to South Hadley, Massachusetts, for the evening and then spent two days with Woollcott on Neshobe Island before going to the MacDowell Colony. (See Wilder to Stein, 31 July 1940, n. 5.)

To Thornton Wilder, Saint Augustine, Florida

[? May 1940]   [Bilignin par Belley
                                                                Ain]

My dearest Thornton,
              I have a kind of a feeling that you need a bath of Europe, why don't you come over it can't be very difficult now but you do need a bath of Europe, you are one of the Americans that needs it more than most do come over and see our spring time, and will you let Donald G. Wing know that I have written to Bernard Fay asking him to send them Americains d'Amerique, and when we get back to Paris, I will try and find Descriptions of Literature Portrait of Mabel Dodge and Have they attacked Mary, for them, the recordings they can get from Columbia University, under whose auspices it was done, and then if you come over you can take another batch along. I will send them the Italian translation of Three Lives,[1] the sun is shining terrifically, even Pepe wants his coat off, Madame Roux has lost her son which has upset us all, he died of meningitis, in the army,[2] if you see Alexander the Bishop give him our love,[3] I told you several people are trying to make somebody make a movie of the Auto of Alice B, it might be fun to go over to help them do that if you see anybody who might want to ask to do it you might get them to want to ask, I understand Hollywood is never suggested to, they must have the idea themselves, I think I would rather do that than lectures, after a winter of radio, lecturing seems rather a dismal business,[4] Sammy Steward

sent Alice a Mixmaster to make cakes and spoon bread and mashed potatoes an electric mixer and Alice is fascinated, nothing but,[5] I sent Bennett Cerf the first half of Ida and he liked it, so I am finishing it for him,[6] we are still liking our country life, we have some pretty English girls in the neighborhood now, with a father and mother,[7] I think they might easily make a fuss of Thornton if he came, and I guess that is all xcept a lot of love and go easy on that driving,

Always
Gtrde.

1. Donald G. Wing had written to Wilder about books he needed for the Yale Stein Collection, and Wilder had forwarded the letter to Stein (see Wilder to Stein, Middle of March 1940, n. 3).

2. Services for Marcel Roux, son of Stein's housekeeper, were held on 20 April; announcements of his death appeared in the local *Journal de l'Ain* on 24 April and *Le Bugiste* on 27 April.

3. Alexander Woollcott.

4. See Stein to Wilder [4 April 1940], n. 4.

5. Steward first spoke of a Mixmaster on 14 December 1939 (YCAL); it was received on Easter Sunday 1940 (see Steward, *Dear Sammy*, 145–52).

6. The typescript had been sent to Cerf with an undated letter in March (Columbia-R.H.). He returned it on 2 April, urging Stein to "go over it very carefully" and to "get it finished . . . and we'll publish it in just as lovely a format as we can devise for it" (see Gallup, *Flowers*, 350–51).

7. Perhaps a reference to the Selby-Bigges and their daughters.

To Thornton Wilder, Peterborough, New Hampshire

[postmark: 18 May 1940][1]   [Bilignin par Belley Ain]

My dearest Thornton,

Bobby Haas has just written to me that they are planning to print his bibliography for the show at Yale, I can't tell you how much pleasure all that gives me, thanks and thanks again, and I am sending them practically everything I have down here, which are some magazines that might be interesting and some mss. and proofs, but I will wait for a quieter moment and then send them so that they will have them in plenty of time,[2] Bennett [Cerf] is doing Ida this fall, it has finally gotten itself done, and now I am xciting myself with a child's book called To Do[3] and all about alphabets and Birthdays, it makes Alice laugh and so I am pleased, and we do so want to see you, no I do not really think I could lecture again, no the sound of the human voice over the radio has forever stopped my interest in the problem of the human voice and its relation to the audience no not again,[4] but I am glad you liked Paris France and we would like to drive over America, it sounds all right, there is some idea of my doing a book about America like Paris France about France but I don't know, I think I would have to drive over it a bit first, to get it back again, so if we can't live together in Washington Square we might live together all over it over there, it would be fun,[5] Bobby Haas seems to be deep in a correspondence with your sister and they seem to be very happy together,[6] he has the measles just now so could not quite find out what it was all about, I am so sorry about Alexander Woollcott, do please give him our love and hoping he will get better, and do take your play-acting easy and not get tired too, otherwise Pepe and Basket have just had worm medicine, we are gardening Alice and Mme. Roux plant and care for the plants while I clean paths and it is summer but I did like winter,

　　　lots of love and so much love and always and always
　　　　　　　　Gtrde & Alice.[7]

　　1. This letter arrived in New Haven on 11 June and was forwarded to Wilder at the MacDowell Colony. Here there are more than thirty instances in which Wilder wrote above Stein's words what he thought she had written. We have printed this letter as written, not as Wilder transcribed it.
　　2. Haas reported to Stein that Norman Holmes Pearson, who was coordinating the Yale exhibition, asked if his bibliography could be used for the exhibition (25 April 1940, YCAL).
　　3. "To Do: A Book Of Alphabets And Birthdays" was posthumously published in 1950 in the collection *Alphabets And Birthdays* with an introduction by Donald Gallup. The book moves through the alphabet with four names for each letter. Wilder, Haas, Van Vechten as well as other friends and neighbors come into the book, which she began in early May and finished by 26 May. See Stein to Haas, postmark 4 June 1940 (YCAL).
　　4. See Stein to Wilder [?1 October 1939], n. 2.
　　5. See Wilder to Stein, 26 May 1935, n. 13, and Toklas to Wilder, 7 June 1935.
　　6. Haas wrote Stein on 25 April 1940 (YCAL) that Charlotte Wilder had sent him "a nice letter about the thesis, and we hope to go on corresponding to clear one or two matters up for ourselves." Haas, impressed with Charlotte Wilder's grasp of his ideas, wrote Stein, "I wish Thornton's sister would collaborate (magic word) with me on the anthology." (Charlotte Wilder to Haas, 14 April and ?May–June 1940, Collection Haas.)
　　7. Both signatures are Stein's.

——————

To Thornton Wilder, Gloucester, Massachusetts

[?6] July [1940]   Bilignin par Belley
[postmark: 8 July 1940][1]   (Ain)

My dearest Thornton,
　　　　　　Well come and we will tell you everything and as we sit on the terrace we will tell you so many stories, when will you come, there is so much to tell that you can see that all we can say is that we are here, and that Bilignin was beautiful through it all, my dearest Thornton love to you
　　　　　　　　Gtrde and Alice.[2]

　　1. This letter arrived in New Haven on 24 July and was forwarded to Wilder at the Bass Rocks Theatre in Gloucester, Massachusetts. On the front of the envelope, Wilder wrote, "Gertrude after

the invasion of France." The Germans invaded the Low Countries on 9 May and then proceeded into France. On 10 June the French government fled from Paris to Tours, and two days later Paris was declared an "open city." France capitulated to the Germans and signed an armistice on 22 June, and on 24 June an armistice was signed with the Italians.

2. Both signatures are Stein's.

To Gertrude Stein and Alice Toklas, Bilignin, France

31 July 1940   50 Deepwood Drive
                                                    New Haven, Conn[ecticut].

                                                    (Bass Rocks Theatre
                                                    Gloucester, Mass.)

Dear Friends:

At last news of you.

All your children—the Kiddies; [Samuel] Steward; [Robert] Haas,—Thorny—were writing one another for an address for you.[1]

Bravig Imb[s] has been spreading the story that he saw you in Washington Square and that you said you didn't want anybody to know that you were here (!).[2] That was told me by Janet Flanner the other day at [Alexander] Woollcott's Island, but she didn't believe it, and I didn't.[3]

Yes, angels, I wish I were there to hear what you had to tell—what am I saying—to be just there, and give you a good hug. And to see the Rhone, and Provence, to look at France & Alice, all my teasing quibbling about France has been removed. Her very defections have clarified my admiration.

Attitudes are stiffening very fast here. I expect to be in olive before the year's out.[4]

I'm acting in my play again. The world's weather has done something to the reception of the play—the last act always was sad—now it's convulsive—Lordy, I never meant that!

All August I shall be back in New Haven working on a new one. I've at last found a subject that "permits" perseverance.[5]

Letters from Sibyl [Colefax]—gallant as Chantecler [i.e., Chanticleer]: désespérant sans le savoir.[6]

Oh, for a good long talk with you about all these things. Tell yourselves Thorny loves you and needs you and scrutinizes events for the sign when he may rejoin you.

                    lots of love
                    Ever
                    Thornton

1. In letters to Haas on 9 July and to Steward on 12 July (YCAL), Wilder asked for news of Stein.

2. Why Imbs, who in February had written to Stein in Bilignin, would have spread such a story is not clear (see Gallup, *Flowers*, 347–48). Sherwood Anderson wrote Stein that he had heard she and Toklas had been seen in Topeka, Kansas. "And then I heard that you were both in New York, that you had come in secretly, disguised as someone else" (see White, *Sherwood Anderson/Gertrude Stein*, 110–11).

3. Janet Flanner, who settled in Paris in 1921 to pursue a career as a writer, met Stein and Toklas in the early 1920s. From October 1925 until shortly before her death in November 1978, she was a contributor to *The New Yorker*, writing profiles, reporter-at-large pieces, and her "Letter from Paris" signed Genêt. In January 1940, she left France for the United States, where she remained until she returned to Europe in October 1944.

4. Wilder is alluding to the continuing debate about aid to Britain and America's possible entry into the war.

5. After spending May 30 and 31 at Woollcott's home on Neshobe Island, Wilder settled in at the MacDowell Colony on 1 June for a month and a half to work on his new play, *The Skin of Our Teeth*, then called "The Ends of the Worlds." He wrote in his journal on 6 July, "Began my play on "The Ends of the Worlds," Monday, June 24, in the Veltin Studio.

"The difficulty of finding a subject. During the last year subject after subject has presented itself and crumbled away in my hand.

"Can this one hold out?

"The difficulty of finding the right tone" (Wilder, *The Journals*, ed. Gallup, 21).

Wilder again stopped at Woollcott's on 16 and 17 July on his way back to New Haven. By 21 July he was in Gloucester, Massachusetts, preparing for his role as the Stage Manager in *Our Town* at the Bass Rocks Theatre. After his performance on 4 August, he remained on Cape Cod until 13 August and then went to Amherst, Massachusetts, to repeat his role in a production he staged for the Amherst Drama Festival at the Kirby Memorial Theatre for one week beginning 19 August.

6. The letters from Sibyl Colefax to Wilder (YCAL) are described as "gallant as Chanticleer: desperate without knowing it."

To Gertrude Stein and Alice Toklas, Bilignin, France

3 Sept[ember] 1940   The Graduates Club
                                          One Hundred Fifty-Five Elm Street
                                                 New Haven, Connecticut

Dear Gertrude Dear Alice:
                         Your letter joyously received and broadcast throughout the company of disciples.

I had lunch with the Kiddies in Springfield and such affectionate talk of you.[1] We love you more and more every day. I can't wait for the times to permit me to come and see you and hear all about it.

A card came from Sir Francis [Rose] asking me to give you his address. He has joined the something or other. He adds: "Have just discovered our national dish of fish and chips and am mad about them." Dio mio![2]

Tomorrow I'm going to New York and I'm going to call on Mr. Perkins of

Scribner's and am going to "lui laver la tête"—seems to me that they sank your book into oblivion just as the book was cropping up in the week's Best Seller List. What was it? Some thought that people wouldn't want to read about the city these days. Dio mio![3]

Summer's over.

I'm hard at work on a "good one." A laugh and a tear in every word. ¶ I acted again throughout the Summer theatres; the new "Old Homestead."[4]

¶ There's an abrupt optimistic turn in the air about things. Happy meetings.[5] ¶ I see I've omitted to give F. Rose's address:

1300799 Rose, F.

c/o Guard Room No I E.F.T.S.

Hatfield Herts.

He's [i.e., He] sounds lonesome and dépaysé [lost] and would love to get a letter. ¶ Reread all your American lectures and the "Narration" the other day. Gertrude, you're a wonder; you're a seer; you're my Toasted ice-cream.[6] ¶ I've been ivory-towering with Flaubert's letters—astonishing how struggling through to light are so many of your positions about audience and recognition. LOTS OF LOVE

Thornie

1. On 20 August, the day after his opening in *Our Town* at Amherst, Wilder drove to Springfield for a radio broadcast and lunch with William and Mildred Rogers (see Wilder to Stein, 31 July 1940, nn. 1, 5).

2. Rose's card to Wilder has not been located. Stein wrote to Rose, "Thornton Wilder has just written me that he has heard from you and has your address. I am sending this to him to send to you, it seems the most sure way of reaching you, we have been so anxious to have news of you, and there you are eating fish and chips, and here we are eating what we always eat, we never did leave Bilignin and now we seem to be laying in wood for another winter" (15 September [1940], Leon Katz's transcription, YCAL).

3. Maxwell Perkins, the well-known editor at Scribner's, the American publisher of *Paris France*, to whom Wilder plans to give a piece of his mind.

4. *The Skin of Our Teeth*. Wilder is here connecting *Our Town* with one of the most popular plays of the American stage, Denman Thompson's and George W. Ryer's celebration of rural New England, *The Old Homestead*. Thompson himself created the part of Joshua Whitcomb and played it from 1887 until his death in 1911.

5. The "optimistic turn" may refer to President Roosevelt's decision on 2 September to transfer fifty overaged destroyers to Britain in exchange for ninety-nine-year leases on eight bases on British territory in the Western Hemisphere.

6. An echo of "Toasted susie is my ice-cream," the last line of Stein's "Preciosilla."

To Thornton Wilder, New Haven, Connecticut

15 Sept[ember]. [1940]¹   Bilignin par Belley
                                                          (Ain)

My dear Thornton,
                 Your letter came quickly, I am sorry you did not see To Do
which has I think a nice bit about you, but you will,² here we are laying in
wood for the winter, it is a fascinating life this, so completely different from
anything we xpected to live, and every day is stranger than the day before, we
have lots of new friends, and the last and most interesting is of all things in the
world, the president of the Tribunal of Belley, a man about 38, and a poet, a
real one,³ as Mme Pierlot says you never know what Belley is going to produce
for you, we walk to Belley all the time, and everybody turns up on foot on
bicycles, and even the D'Aiguys sometimes with an army horse, it does not
turn out to be at all a solitary life, so come along Thornton, start and somehow
some way you will get here, Belley has seen so many populations in a year, do
come along and si [i.e., ci] inclus is a letter from [i.e., for] Francis [Rose], will
you send it to him, we have not had a word from each other since June,⁴ and
thanks so much, and come Thornton come,
                              lots of love from us all,
                              Gtrde.

    1. This letter is preserved in the original but was also transcribed by Wilder (see Stein to Wilder,
(1) received 10 September 1936, n. 1-e). At the top of this letter Wilder, in blue pencil, wrote "For my
box/letter."
    2. The first and only mention to Wilder of "To Do" was on 18 May. For the letter "T," Stein
connects Wilder and her childhood friend Tillie Brown, whose family, like Wilder's, were mission-
aries and whose early childhood was spent in China (see "To Do: A Book Of Alphabets And Birthdays," in *Alphabets And Birthdays*, 53–56; see Stein to Wilder, 18 May 1940, n. 4).
    3. Pierre Van Der Meulen, a judge in Belley, published both poetry and fiction. He is briefly
alluded to in Stein's *Mrs. Reynolds*: "There was another judge who wrote poetry when he did not
judge and he had a wife and a little boy and the wife died and the little boy lived with her father and
her mother so that judge had no one" (16).
    4. A letter to Sir Francis Rose, serving with the Royal Air Force, was enclosed with this letter (see
Rose to Stein, 5 November 1940, YCAL).

To Gertrude Stein and Alice Toklas, Bilignin, France

30 Oct[ober] 1940   Chateau Frontenac
                                                     Quebec [Canada]¹

Dear Friends:
                 I thought it all over. About coming to see you. Get a journalists'
permit; tell the State Department that I was a polyglot; that I'd write fascinating reports for them and the New York papers about Portugal and Spain and

France. Then I go to Belley (where, the newspapers tell us, some are)[2] and call on you.

But it all blew away.

I wish I could. And I wish I could fortified with the convincing arguments to bring you home. But at least I won't go into that now; no doubt all your other correspondents from this side ring enough changes on that subject. I don't go in for prophecy, nor for attempts at argumentative coërcion.

Your letter has gone off to Sir Francis [Rose].

I have just received a new one from him with an amended address. It is so characteristic of him that no Balzac could have contrived it for him:

c/o Wireless Room No 1 E.F.T.S.
Hatfield Herts

Oct 6. [1940]

Dear Thornton Wilder. This is a very strange War. There is really no difference in rank but a strong class feeling, (but a pleasant one.) Although we all know each other and call each other by clever names it is not intimacy. . . . . . I have done lots of drawings and painted some scenery which was nearly blown up when 4 bombs fell. Everything collapsed leaving me and my work undamaged amidst shambles. It would have been amusing if 18 people had not been killed and 30 wounded. We bring down every plane that attacks us. The enemy send children of 18 (and even one of 16) as pilots. They have none of the chic of youth. Our morale is magnificent. . . . . . Cecil Beaton is doing magnificent work, hurrying all over the country for the Ministry of Information. Sir Kenneth Clark is trying to get me a commission."[3]

x   x

The election in America is dividing homes and giving all sorts of people the heroics. My mother is pro-Wil[l]kie; I'm not allowed to mention my affiliation without letting lo[o]se such a flood of moral superiority as drives me to Canada.[4]

The way the draft went through—the little anecdotes surrounding it— was extraordinary. The absence of cant. You couldn't believe your ears.[5]

x   x

I was in Chicago for a few days.[6]

Lunch with Alice Rouiller, a darlin'; tea with Bobbsie [Goodspeed], everything well in hand.

I signed up to go back and teach at the University next Summer Quarter. Why?

Only one reason:

Bob [Hutchins] asked me to in a way that admits no other answer. If you and I were in *le petit salon* I could a tale unfold of such agony. Oh! Oh!

Maude [Hutchins] is one of *les diaboliques*. Such ingenuity in torture. Bob just short of the breaking point. But I will say that—as far as my lights stretch—Maude seems to have done some remarkable paintings.

x   x

Quebec is very beautiful.

The color blue here explores all its resources. My window on this great rock looks over the prodigious St. Lawrence to the palisades of Lévis on the further bank.

Such dawns.

Alice, we must tell Gertrude about dawn. Dawn's best.[7]

x   x

Your non-community man is obeying his nature. Beyond ordering (atrocious) meals I haven't spoken to a soul for two weeks.

Quel luxe.

I hate talking. And since the War the talk in America has grown worse and worse. Everybody talks badly about the War, and this little Abou Ben Adhem led all the rest.[8]

x   x

I'm at work.

Yes, ma'am, this play'll them blow out of their chairs. Such theatric vitality hasn't been seen since Sardou. It's got everything: the violence of the ten-twent-thirts; the world-in-pieces of vaudeville clowns; the tirades of Monte-Cristo;—it's got everything except pathos.

Hot dog![9]

x   x

Quebec's a French-speaking city. Even my chambermaid doesn't understand English. The Breton-Norman obstinacy has gone on a two-century sit-down strike not to learn English.

Yet even my French is better than theirs.

Endlessly curious to see England and France through the distorting glass of Colonial and emigrée. Debased carbon-copies. French without esprit; English without "my-world-is-the-best."

x   x

I'm getting kind of fond of my car. Tender is the word. Every other day we go for a ride. To the frightening vulgarity and rapacity of Ste. Anne de Beaupré. On to the Falls of Montmorency—100 feet higher than Niagra, and Alice, such bedazzlements: effects in veils, and mists and parsley leaves and rainbows and ladders and climbing serpents, as you never saw. On over the country-side where the *habitants* have taken the nineteenth-twentieth century American house, porch and scroll-work and front fence, and done something with it through picking out mouldings and door-frames and alternate posts in fresh ox-blood paint or ochre yellow that makes all the difference. Mighty pretty.

In other words I'm very happy, impenitently happy. Silence; surroundings; work; and car.

Isn't that awful?

I have a deep confidence about the War. (Great luxury not to have to put that into words in New Haven, and hear the scandalized haranguing I'd receive in return.)

But how I wish that tomorrow we could walk the dogs over the great battlefield of the Plains of Abraham—here Wolfe fell, and here Montcalm.[10] That's all I lack—just to see you.

Lots of love,

Thorny

1. As he has done before, Wilder has sought out a place where he is not known and has no obligations to concentrate on writing.

2. German and Italian troops.

3. Wilder made minor changes in transcribing these excerpts from Rose's letter (YCAL).

4. In the presidential election of 1940 Franklin Delano Roosevelt ran against Wendell Willkie. Wilder, like Woollcott, was pro-Roosevelt, while many of his friends, including Robert Hutchins, were either anti-interventionists or isolationists.

5. After an acrimonious debate that began in June, the bill authorizing the first compulsory military service in peacetime was ratified by Congress on 14 September 1940.

6. At the end of September, Wilder spent several days with Woollcott on Neshobe Island, before leaving for Chicago on the evening of 3 October. When he arrived the next morning, he spent the day working on a lecture, "Religion and Literature," and the evening at a performance of *Life With Father*. The next day he traveled to Madison, Wisconsin, where he had been born, to speak at the Centennial Celebration of his family's church, the First Congregational Church on University Avenue. On Sunday evening, 6 October, he had dinner with Sinclair Lewis, who was then living and teaching in Madison. When he returned to Chicago on the seventh, Wilder had dinner with Carl Sandburg and Lillian Gish, who was appearing in *Life With Father*. The next day he participated in a convocation at the University of Chicago honoring its fiftieth anniversary. It was at this time that President Hutchins invited him to teach during the summer of 1941 (see Wilder to Isabella Wilder, 6 to 11 October, YCAL).

7. Stein was a late riser while Toklas typically rose at dawn to prepare meals and to organize their day (see also Wilder to Stein, 28 July 1941).

8. In James Henry Leigh Hunt's popular poem "Abou Ben Adhem and the Angel," Ben Adhem learns from the Angel that his name is not on the list of "those who love the Lord." When he asks that his name be listed as "one that loves his fellow men," the Angel writes something and then vanishes. When the Angel reappears the next night, he shows the list of the names "whom love of God had blessed, / And lo! Ben Adhem's name led all the rest."

9. Wilder returned to Neshobe Island on 12 October and stayed there until the fifteenth, when he drove to Montreal for the night and on the following morning on to Quebec. He remained in Canada working on *The Skin of Our Teeth* until 29 November, when he returned to Neshobe Island and then to New Haven. In his *Journals*, pages 21–33 and 37–38, and in his date book (YCAL), he records his progress. The following are the entries dealing with the play from his date book:

Monday, 21 October: (open Act II)
Friday, 25 October: Miss Atlantic City outburst—End of Act II—Address to Conveeners
Sunday, 3 November: (Finding a better approach to the opening of Act I)

Tuesday, 5 November: (Refugees scene)
Monday, 11 November: Finished the draft of Acts I and II
Thursday, 14 November: Began Act III
Saturday, 16 November: "Rehearsal Scene"
Friday, 22 November: Begin Act I again
Monday, 25 November: Act I Greek and Hebrew Broadcast opening

10. In the battle for Quebec, which established British supremacy in Canada, both the English general James Wolfe and the French general Louis Joseph de Montcalm-Gorzon were killed on 13 September 1759, on the Plains of Abraham. The classic account of the battle is in Francis Parkman's *Montcalm and Wolfe* (1884).

To Thornton Wilder, Alexandria, Virginia

November.   Bilignin par Belley
[postmark: 18 November 1940][1]   (Ain)

My dearest Thornton,

       Here is such a sweet letter from you written July 31 and all this time held in the occupied area and only now let out but very welcome, and in it you say you will come, come, it would be wonderful to see you and for you to see us so busy being country people, now so completely country people that we wonder what a city is like, and now because I am writing about France[2] the way it is they have given me permission to drive my car and the other day we crossed the Rhone on a flat-boat, a most xciting moment driving the car onto it, we have lots of friends around here, they seem to increase and multiply and one I want you to know the President of the Tribunal who judged the butchers of Belley,[3] and Thornton what is the latest news of Sibyl [Colefax] and has Francis [Rose] had my letter and what has happened to Janet Flanner, and whenever you feel like sending books or weeklies or monthlies, n'hesite pas, we would like them and so much love and come soon and come all the time all yours

    Alice and Gertrude and Basket II and Pepe (he has to have worms out to-morrow.[)]

1. This letter arrived in New Haven on 31 January 1941 and was forwarded to Wilder at the Hotel George Mason in Alexandria, Virginia.
2. "The Winner Loses: A Picture Of Occupied France," which tells of Stein's life in Bilignin from the outbreak of the war in September 1939 to the armistice in June 1940, was published in *The Atlantic Monthly* 166, 5 (November 1940): 571–83. Stein's original title was "Sundays And Tuesdays," reflecting on events that seemed to happen on those days. It was Edward Weeks, editor of *The Atlantic Monthly*, who changed the title: "I ask for only one small change—an editor's privilege to change the title. As a substitute for your original phrase, I have chosen three consecutive words which appear in

your final paragraph. What they are, I leave you and Alice Toklas to guess" (10 September 1940, YCAL). Weeks added to "the winner loses" the descriptive subtitle.

    3. The butchers protested the Vichy government's restrictions on hours and sales. Pierre Van Der Meulen, president of the local tribunal, was Stein's friend.

To Gertrude Stein and Alice Toklas, Bilignin, France

29 Nov[ember]. [1940]   Montreal, P.Q.[1]

                                                  Crossing the border in a few hours

Dear Friends:

          The good chapter and the Cure of Silence comes to a close.

    Last night I had dinner at the McGill chapter of my Fraternity.[2] A few men left. The rest flying overseas. A number dead already. In a few minutes I go out to lunch at the Mess Hall of The Black Watch.

    In the University Library I read your account in the Atlantic Monthly.[3] Seeing and telling. I feel it's like a letter to me and I must answer it. Give my love to Madame Pierlot and the d'Aiguys. I wish I knew your new friend—the Poet-Judge.

    I think of you so much. It's like hunger and thirst.

    Enclosed find an interesting clipping. V[irgil]. Thompson [i.e., Thomson] has been tearing the mélomane man world wide open. He claims that our esteemed musical monarchs around here have been wandering about without any clothes on. Agitations, glee and terror.[4]

    Alice, have you any errand for me to do. I'm jealous of Sam [Steward]'s Mixmaster.[5]

    Gertrude, Carl Van Vechten has given all your letters to the Yale Library, and there'll be a big show and a lecture about you.[6] I have been corresponding with the Librarian about you. His name is [Bernhard] Knollenberg and he's just published a book about George Washington which will require every preceding Life to be revised. I have directed him to *Four in America* for some lights he would not otherwise obtain.[7]

    I am going back to teach at the U. of Chicago this summer. From Jan[uary]—June I think I shall be in Washington.[8] Next Fall the War will be over and I shall be not where you are not; two negatives make a positive.

    I miss you.

    Love—turbid with human nature is what I send

          Thorny

1. Wilder was at the Mount Royal Hotel in Montreal but wrote on stationery of the Chateau Frontenac in Quebec.

2. Alpha Delta Phi.

3. "The Winner Loses."

4. The clipping has not remained with the letter. From his first review as chief music critic of the *New York Herald Tribune* on 11 October 1940, Thomson was outspoken and refused to tailor his criticism to the interests of the musical establishment. He remained with the paper until 1954. Some early reviews are collected in A *Virgil Thomson Reader*, pages 189–207.

5. See Stein to Wilder [? May 1940], n. 5.

6. See Wilder to Stein, Middle of March 1940, nn. 2, 3; see Stein to Wilder, 4 April 1940, n. 2.

7. Knollenberg's *Washington and the Revolution: A Reappraisal; Gates, Conway, and the Continental Congress* (New York: Macmillan, 1940).

8. Secretary of State Cordell Hull, at the suggestion of Archibald MacLeish, librarian of Congress, invited Wilder to make a good-will tour of South America from March to May 1941. To enable Wilder to prepare for his trip while continuing work on *The Skin of Our Teeth*, MacLeish made a small office at the Library of Congress available to Wilder. The official announcement of the mission was made in February 1941 (see the *New York Times*, 28 February 1941, 8).

To Thornton Wilder, Alexandria, Virginia

[postmark: 18 December 1940][1]   Bilignin par Belley
                                                              (Ain)

My dearest Thornton,

Thanks for telling me what Francis [Rose] said, it is always such a pleasure to know what is happening,[2] I had a letter from Cecil Beaton written about the same time and I do hope everything continues to go well,[3] here is another letter for him which will you send and please will you send him a copy of the Atlantic Monthly with my article in it so that he may know what did happen to us here in Bilignin in these days I know that will give him pleasure.[4] Helas that you did not come with a journalist permit, you would have liked it and we would have liked and they would have liked it, and now back to Chicago but there is a spring before there is a summer, and perhaps the spring will be ours before the summer belongs to Chicago. We have settled down for the winter, I like a country winter, Basket and I have gotten so we can walk 10 to 12 kilometres and not be tired, Pepe confines himself to xercise to barking at the postman, Alice sits by the fire and sews, we see a good many people, and I work quite a bit, I am on a new novel now, Mrs. Reynolds it is called, Ida you know is to be published in January, and now I wonder is this Mrs. Reynolds more a novel than Ida.[5] Sometimes I dream that I have found a way to write a novel and sometimes I dream that I only dream it, but I like novels bad novels, poor novels, detective novels, sentimental novels, these days I read all the wishy washy novels of the end of the last and the beginning of this century and I long oh how I long to write my novel like that but will I, well anyway Mrs. Reynolds is such a heroine even if it is all about Hitler and Stalin, bless you Thornton, do not suffer too much, they do in those novels I have been reading[6] but do not you suffer too much come to see us but do not suffer too much, and please forward this letter to Francis and lots and lots and lots of love to you from us all

Always
Gtrde.

1. This letter arrived in New Haven on 4 February 1941 and was forwarded to Wilder at the Hotel George Mason in Alexandria, Virginia.

2. See Wilder to Stein, 30 October 1940.

3. In an undated letter to Stein (YCAL), Beaton wrote of his wartime activities and gave Stein news of Sir Francis Rose, Lord Berners, and Daisy Fellowes. For Stein, in unoccupied France, it was easier and perhaps wiser to send mail for England via the United States.

4. Stein enclosed a letter dated 17 December for Sir Francis Rose (see Leon Katz's transcription, YCAL).

5. Stein was writing Mrs. Reynolds from 1940 until 1942; it was posthumously published in 1952. The daily life in war of Mr. and Mrs. Reynolds, Stein and Toklas, is developed through conversations but is overshadowed by Hitler and Stalin as Angel Harper and Joseph Lane. In an "Epilogue" Stein wrote, "This book is an effort to show the way anybody could feel these years. It is a perfectly ordinary couple living an ordinary life and having ordinary conversations and really not suffering personally from everything that is happening but over them, all over them is the shadow of two men, and then the shadow of one of the two men gets bigger and then blows away and there is no other. There is nothing historical about this book except the state of mind" (167). See also Stein to Wilder, postmarked 15 May 1941.

6. See Stein to Wilder, postmark 6 March 1941.

Thornton and Isabel Wilder in a photograph taken for the launching of her first novel,
Mother and Four, in 1933

Thornton Wilder and Armina Marshall as Mr. and Mrs. Antrobus in *The Skin of our Teeth*, Westport (Connecticut) Country Playhouse, 18 August 1948. Photograph by Carl Van Vechten, whose wife, Fania Marinoff, played the Fortune Teller.

To Thornton Wilder, Bogotá, Colombia

[postmark: 13 January 1941][1]

Bilignin par Belley
(Ain)

My dear Thornton,

Thanks for the telegram and do you want an errand, well we could do with a bit of literature, something to read, you might begin with the book about Washington that the librarian wrote, Alice says that when she was little she always thought that she would like to have lived in Washington's time, it would have been just right, and now she thinks perhaps Petain, first in peace and first in war and first in the hearts of his countrymen, might be like that,[2] books do come through Thornton, and you might send us a few any week, I know you always have a lot, you would like our life, it is very pioneer full. Alas Mme Pierlot died, the cold and the betises humains [human stupidities] was too much for her, we loved her very much and now it is all over,[3] our friend the poet judge is alas taken to promotion to near Saint Etiénne, we miss him very much, some day we will take you to see him,[4] had a letter to-day from Francis [Rose] straight away from London, England and it was a pleasure to have it[5] lots of love

Gtrde.

1. This letter was received in New Haven on 20 March and forwarded to Wilder in Bogotá, where it arrived sometime in April.

2. Wilder's telegram has not been located. Bernhard Knollenberg's *Washington and the Revolution* is mentioned in Wilder's letter of 29 November 1940. The passage about Toklas' wish to have lived in Washington's time, along with the children's rhyme, is almost literally reproduced in *Mrs. Reynolds*, pages 42–43.

3. The Baroness Pierlot died of pulmonary congestion on 1 January and was buried in the family vault in the Béon cemetery on 4 January. She was a presence in many of Stein's writings; in 1937 Stein had described her: "She is small and blue eyed and exciting, she is elegant and generous and compelling.

"She likes to stimulate things but not arrange them" ("La Baronne Pierlot," in *Painted Lace And Other Pieces* [1914–1937], 316).

4. Pierre Van Der Meulen moved to St. Étienne, eighty-five miles away (see Stein to Wilder, 15 September 1940, n. 3).

5. In a letter of 5 November 1940, postmarked in London and received in Belley on 9 January (YCAL), Rose wrote of life in the Royal Air Force, his painting, and mutual friends.

To Gertrude Stein and Alice Toklas, Bilignin, France

10 Feb[ruary] 1941   The George Mason [Hotel]
                                                        Alexandria, Virginia

Dear and very Dear Sisters:

I love you very much and that being said I shall go on to non-essentials. I think of you all the time and try to imagine your life there, and the old friends and the new friends, and the thoughts that go through your head. Two letters from you arrived within the week, one of them long delayed on route, and with word that one of mine had taken two months to reach you.[1] On the chance that others had gone astray I repeat the outlines of my plans: on the 28th of this month I sail for Colombia, Ecuador and Peru, a three months "goodwill tour" at the invitation of Secretary Hull. I have been a month in (i.e., 10 miles from) Washington, working every day in the Library of Congress learning Spanish and reading up the history and literature of the countries I am to visit.[2] On June first I return to New Haven to give my sister Janet away in marriage to a very nice (and well-to-do!) young man.[3] And then I go West to teach the whole Summer at the University of Chicago.

My dream is that if I do well in South America, the State Department will find some mission for me to do in Europe.

On Feb 22d (I like it's being Washington's birthday—that great novelist's) I am giving a speech on Gertrude Stein at the Yale University Library, on the occasion of the opening of the exhibition of her works and memorabilia.[4] In the hope of having some ideas and a moment or two of recognition I shall endeavor to exclude all thought of audience from my mind and merely say what I know at the moment of knowing it. But there will be one element of audience in it, for it will be the only moment in my life since I met you that I shall not be able to say: I wish you were here.

I have just sent on the letter to Sir Francis Rose,[5] and will send the copy of The Atlantic Monthly when I get home next week. Also I shall send a heterogeneous bundle of magazines and newspaper clippings.

We are all well.

Last Saturday I drove (in my beautiful car, with which I have now made my peace; we are now old friends; I drive with precision, musicality and dash) to Baltimore to see Alec [Woollcott] playing the rôle in *The Man Who Came to Dinner* which was based on his character. The play is a vast success; four companies have been presenting it over the country; the original cast is in its second year in New York. It is very funny, and Alec is excellent.[6]

My play is almost done and is almost as good as I hoped it would be. There are two spots in it that I cannot get quite right, so I shall not give it to Jed [Harris] for production this Spring, but hold it for just the right thoughts and have it produced next Fall. It will probably be called *The Skin of Our Teeth*; and it is very unlike *Têtes de Rechange* (remember?)[7]

Twice you adjure me not to suffer too much, but Lordy, I am often stuck with the fact that I do not suffer enough and am all too easily given to a blithe complacent absorption in the Trivia that interest me, like a sparrow enjoying himself in a dust-bath.

You ask after Sibyl [Colefax]. I receive frequent letters from her, and as I am distinguished by the fact that I can read her handwriting I serve as secretary for a group of friends and send out copies. Her house is still standing; she is busy distributing redcross material, and with her two maids sleeps in the cellar of the Office of Works.

After a long silence Bob Hutchins made a public utterance on the subject that is filling every one's mind. His view is the direct opposite of mine and of the majority opinion; it seems to me badly argued, and seems to me to be deeply sentimental though it follows the main lines of the school of thought that proudly claims itself to be free of humanitarian sentimentality. His trustees and the Chicago Gold Coasters are rapturous with delight, and everybody else I know is everywhere from appalled to contemptuous.[8]

Some very interesting months lie ahead of me, but I must say that I don't greatly want to go. I am no longer mixed up in my head as to whether I am gregarious or solitary; and I shall have to be damned gregarious in Bogotá, Quito and Lima, and in Spanish—but!—Voyages and Duty are the two most meretricious Temptations that can haunt the human mind from its only justifiable activity, and this Mission combines both.

Aïe, aïe, as you sit in the evening in that 'petit salon' that I love so tell yourself that 12,000 feet up the Andes there's someone who loves you more than tunkantell, and who thinks he is forging the links of a chain that will bring him over to see you.

Ever ever affectionately yours
Thornton

1. Stein's letters postmarked 18 November and 18 December 1940.

2. This is the first extant letter with details of the good-will mission undertaken at the invitation of Secretary of State Cordell Hull (see Wilder to Stein, 29 November 1940, n. 8).

3. Janet Wilder, who was teaching at Mount Holyoke College, married Winthrop ("Toby") Saltonstall Dakin, an attorney, at his home in Amherst, Massachusetts.

4. In *Four In America* Stein imagines Washington as a novelist. For an abstract of Wilder's talk, see Wilder to Stein, 1 April 1941, n. 1.

5. A letter to Rose enclosed in Stein's letter to Wilder of 18 December 1940.

6. In January Woollcott returned to a national road company of *The Man Who Came to Dinner* that took him to several East Coast cities and to Chicago. Wilder saw the play on 3 February at Ford's Theatre in Baltimore. During the play's two-week run in Washington, D.C., Woollcott stayed in the White House, and President and Mrs. Roosevelt attended a performance on 25 February (see letter to Lynn Fontanne, 21 February, in Kaufman and Hennessey, *Letters*, 269–72, and E. B. White's imaginary portrait of Woollcott in the White House in *The New Yorker*, 15 March 1941, 19).

7. Wilder continued work on *The Skin of Our Teeth* until shortly before its first performance at the Shubert Theatre in New Haven, Connecticut, on 15 October 1942. Despite the acrimony that developed during the production of *Our Town*, Wilder recognized the genius of Harris and wanted him to produce and direct his play. Wilder and Stein had seen a revival of Jean-Victor Pellerin's *Cris des coeurs* on 2 November 1937; his *Têtes de rechange* was not being performed during Wilder's stay in Paris in 1937. It may be that he and Stein read the play after seeing *Cris des coeurs*. *Têtes de rechange*, an expressionist drama in which the multiple personalities and daydreams of the restless and disillusioned Ixe appear on stage and interplay with Ixe and his uncle Opéku, was first presented in April 1926 by Gaston Baty. Wilder perhaps means to suggest that characters in his play, such as Dinosaur and Mammoth, are not projections of the unconscious of Mr. Antrobus. (See Stein to Wilder [3 November 1937], n. 1.)

8. Because censors opened letters, Wilder's language here and in other letters is deliberately vague when discussing the war. Hutchins, while never a member of the America First Committee, articulated his anti-interventionist views in a number of widely reported speeches including his University of Chicago convocation address of 11 June 1940. On 23 January 1941, Hutchins gave an address, "America and the War," on the NBC radio network in which he argued his views from a "humanitarian" point of view: "More than half our people are living below the minimum level of subsistence," he said. "More than half the army which will defend democracy will be drawn from those who have had this experience of the economic benefits of 'the American way of life.'" Hutchins argued that he could see no prospect that if the nation went to war the economic deficiencies afflicting "the sharecroppers, the Okies, the Negroes, the slumdwellers, [and] downtrodden" would be corrected (see Ashmore, *Unseasonable Truths*, chap. 20).

To Thornton Wilder, Lima, Peru

[postmark: 6 March 1941][1]   Bilignin par Belley
                                                               (Ain)

My dear Thornton

What is this, the Kiddy says that your sister is married, which sister and which married, do tell us, we are so xcited, of course Thornton married would be more xciting but that could not be not without his telling us,[2] and now there is Ida. Have you seen the book, it has just come and I am all xcited because it is a novel it really is, and it has characters just like a real novel, I am reading Mrs. Oliphant and Mrs Betham Edwards and East Lynne, and Mrs Braddon all from Aix[-les-Bains] and English friends and I am so xcited that to make una pittura, that I too have written a really truly novel tell me if you think it is one too,[3] and what is the news of Francis [Rose], I have not had a word about him for so long, do whenever you hear from him let me know right away because I do get anxious, and want to know as soon as you hear. Otherwise the spring is coming, we are getting ready to plant vegetables, we all go on being hopeful and xtremely busy, we xchange prophecies and we telephone to each other[4] and I am having my car changed to burn alchohol instead of essence, we can make alcohol, and the days and weeks go by so quickly, living when living is difficult is a very occupying occupation, and it keeps us good and busy, we are even thinking of planting sweet potatoes, and we have a wonderful sugar made of grapes,[5] and Alice thinks up new ways of making a little go very far, and lots of love

Gtrde.

1. This letter arrived in New Haven on 17 April and was forwarded to Wilder in Lima, Peru, where it arrived on 8 May.

2. Stein had not yet received Wilder's letter of 10 February about his sister's marriage, which would have clarified Rogers's letter of 9 January 1941 (YCAL). The wedding may have been rescheduled because of the groom's mother's illness. Stein's letters to Rogers have not been located. She must have replied immediately because Rogers wrote on 22 January (YCAL), "Well if she isn't Thornton's sister, she lives at his address and she looks like him, so if she isn't there's something very funny about it all."

3. See Stein to Wilder, 18 December 1940. Stein often bought books from the bookshop connected with the Anglican church in Aix-les-Bains. *East Lynne* (1861) is by Ellen (Mrs. Henry) Wood. *Ida A Novel* was published on 15 February.

4. With the Selby-Bigges Stein was able to talk about the difficulties and prospects of daily life under difficult conditions. In the spring of 1941 Stein was still able to lend them money, and they were most careful to make arrangements for repayment. The Selby-Bigges left France in mid-July 1941, and after several months in Portugal, they managed to return to England, where he began to work for the BBC (see Stein to Wilder, 10 January 1940, n. 3; the Selby-Bigges to Stein in YCAL. Portions of John Selby-Bigge's unpublished autobiography were made available to the editors by Andrew Murray of the Mayor Gallery, London).

5. The sweetness of grape sugar becomes associated with Sherwood Anderson's "sweetness" in Stein's tribute to Anderson, who died on 8 March while on a South American cruise with his wife, Eleanor. Wilder was on the same Grace liner, the *Santa Lucia*. "Sherwood's Sweetness" appeared in *Story* 19, 91 (September–October 1941): 63, a special Anderson Memorial Issue. Anderson, who met Stein in 1921, wrote "The Work of Gertrude Stein," as preface to *Geography And Plays* (1922).

To Gertrude Stein and Alice Toklas, Bilignin, France

1 April 1941
Hotel Europa
Medellin–Colombia

Dear Gertrude & Alice·
Love and Love.
You should have seen the beauty and wit and thoroughness and dignity of the Exhibition at Yale.

And forgive me if I say I spoke all right. The Librarian says it was the best speech he ever heard. Many said that you were in the room: wise, good, beautiful, earnest, playful and great.

Very curious for me: because for 5 years I had lost the purity of Public Address.[1]

x   —   x

I reread hundreds of your pages. With new power to understand. And with this new ability to read I shall spend the Summer entering into the new-acquired territory. Your loving son Thornton.

x   x

A month has passed in Bogotá. The Colombians with their passion for poetry—their ever renewed line of distinguished poets. Their insecure vanity without malice. Their melancholy (the Spanish & Indian & negro blood warring within them) their "absences"—but spontaneous and loveable.

x   x

Next week to Ecuador. The most beautiful country in the world.

x   x

From home, good and bad news. Janet got married and Charlotte had— long deferred—her nervous breakdown.[2]

x   x

From Ecuador I hope to write you—in peace and quiet, for *there* not everybody is a writer, so my days will not be so full—a letter about *Ida*.[3]

x   x

I try to imagine what your days are like. God bless you. The crescendo is so furious that I begin to hope for its resolution. Shall I see you before long; maybe if I do this work well I shall be sent abroad.

In the petit salon I love tell yourselves that I am
your loving
Thornton

1. There is no manuscript or typescript of Wilder's talk at the Yale University Library opening of the Gertrude Stein exhibition on 22 February; a single typed page is included with this letter. Although the text is in English, the heading reads, "Extrait de l'agenda de la femme d'un Professeur d'Histoire Contemporaine à l'Université de Yale" and may indicate a précis written by the wife of a history professor:

> Thornton Wilder talked about Gertrude Stein with such liveliness and penetration one wishes she could know about it.
> It was in the Yale Library a month ago. The big room was filled—people stood three deep around the sides of the room. He began with some of the earliest things and came all the way up to "Ida," reading parts from "Making of Americans," "As a wife has a Cow," "The Grammar," some of the single poems, some things from "Ida," etc., etc . . .
> He was moving and affectionate, and searching and apt and lively and real. The audience loved it all and afterward clapped and clapped—hoping he would go on for another hour.
> In the next room was a collection of photographs—mostly Carl van Vechten's, I think—

manuscripts and first editions; a fine and illuminating collection. For the weeks it was there, the room was full always of students and people who like to know and think about her and who follow what she does with excitement.

2. Wilder only later learned that after seeing him off for South America, his mother and sister hospitalized Charlotte in a clinic on Long Island. Except for brief periods, she remained hospitalized until her death in 1980.

3. If Wilder did write Stein about *Ida A Novel*, the letter has not been located.

To Gertrude Stein and Alice Toklas, Bilignin, France

8 May 1941   Gran Hotel Bolivar
                                                           Lima—Peru

                                                           January first just rec'd.[1]

Dear Friends:

How far away.

How I wish I were with you. What things I would ask. And what a lot to tell. A month in Colombia, the country of poets. The sweet land of Tears-in-the-Eyes. A month in Ecuador. Everywhere the noiseless scurry of the long-enduring Indian. Glittering baroque churches. And the peaks, Oh, my sisters, Cotopaxi and Chimborazo. "Higher each time than the eye is prepared for." And now my 3rd day in Peru. I wish the Incas had won.

June first I fly to Miami in a day and a half. Two weeks with my family, then back to the Summer Course (only) at University of Chicago.

You ask which sister got married? The youngest, Janet, the Doctor of Biology. She married Means, good looks and pur sang!![2] But my oldest sister Charlotte has had a nervous breakdown. Only after six weeks did the doctor permit the folks to call on her. Here pause a moment, to feuilleter [finger] the three volumes between the lines.

Angelines, at this distance I cannot manage to send you the volumes and magazines you wish. I cannot entrust it to my family who are "all wrought up," but I shall be back to attend to your commissions with[in] 3½ weeks.

No further word from Francis [Rose].

Dearies in my modest corner I have been fulfilling what I was sent for. The foremost Colombian novelist is dedicating a novel to me this week; and a favorite Brazilian novelist is dedicating a travel book. I have been made an honorary member of the chief "cultural" society in Quito, and am first names with all the poets and novelists in sight. I give lectures (but few!) in Spanish, and am the only Northamerican who has not a shade of condescension in his voice. But, oh, I'm tired.[3] I certainly am. And shall be very glad to get back to a Childs Restaurant again.

I see with what joy that Columbia University (N.Y.) has taken over the Exhibition of your MSS, Gertrude.[4]

Love and Kisses. Love and Kisses
                    Thorny

1. The context of this letter suggests that Wilder is responding to Stein's letter postmarked 13 January. "January first" may be an error in reading the postmark.

2. See Wilder to Stein 10 February 1941, n. 3, and Stein to Wilder [postmark 6 March 1941], n. 2.

3. During the three months he spent in South America, Wilder lectured, gave radio interviews, and met with students, writers, artists, and political figures. His engagement book for 1941 (YCAL) and an eight-page handwritten "Diary" (YCAL) detail his crowded days. About Fernando Gonzalez's *El maestro de escuela*, which is dedicated to him, Wilder wrote to his mother and sister, "Just today I heard that my favorite Colombian novelist has arrested the printing of his forthcoming novel so as to add that it is dedicated to me" (4 April 1941, YCAL). The Brazilian writer was Erico Verissimo; his *Gato Prêto em Campo de Neve*, a volume of impressions of the United States, was dedicated "To my North-American friends in the person of Thornton Wilder" when it was published in November 1941. A chapter on Wilder, "Os Wilders De New Haven," is included in the book (167–73), and an inscribed copy is in YCAL. The Sociedad Jurídico-Literaria ceremony was held on 15 April.

4. The Yale Stein exhibition was shown at the Columbia University library from 18 April to 17 May (see Van Vechten to Stein, 24 April [1941], in Burns, *Letters*, 2:716–18).

To Thornton Wilder, Chicago, Illinois

[postmark: 15 May 1941]   Bilignin par Belley
                                                           (Ain)

My dearest Thornton,

            Everybody says it was like that, just as good as you said it was and helas it was not recorded, it just bloomed like a flower, bless it and you.[1] I do envy you your South America, it must be wonderful, do you remember Diane D'Aiguy one of the daughter-in-laws at Beon, she came from Columbia, and she is like that.[2] When you come you will meet and have lots to tell and we will listen, Oh Thornton, conversations, every day there is some bit, of conversation that is as wonderful as the day before. I try and try again in my new novel Mrs. Reynolds, I am longing to talk to you about that, it takes a state of war, to do it, and Bennett [Cerf] says Ida is selling quite nicely and that is a pleasure,[3] come so I can tell you all about conversations,[4] most xciting subject, lots of love to lots

                    Always
                    Gtrde.

1. The letter, a response to Wilder's letter of 1 April describing the opening of the Yale Stein exhibition, arrived in New Haven on 3 July and was forwarded to Wilder in Chicago.

2. Diane d'Aiguy, born in Colombia (Stein's misspelling), was the wife of Count François d'Aiguy, one of the Baroness Pierlot's two sons from her first marriage. During the war, she lived in Monte Carlo looking after her aged father. Her husband remained in Béon.

3. On 19 and 25 March Cerf wrote Stein about reactions to *Ida A Novel*, published the month before (Columbia-R.H.).

4. See Stein to Wilder, postmarked 18 December 1940, n. 5.

Isabel Wilder: To Gertrude Stein, Bilignin, France

16 May 1941   50 Deepwood Drive
                                                        New Haven, Connecticut

Dear Gertrude,

This enclosed letter came to me from Sir Francis Rose, to send on.[1] I hope you receive it soon.

The exhibition of your MSS. in the Library here in Feb[ruary] and early March, was a lovely thing to see. And I do wish you & Alice might have heard Thornton's talk. He *never never* did better. It was wonderful in its simplicity, conviction, admiration & restraint. A huge roomful of people sat in thickest silence spellbound.

It seems a long time that he's been gone on this trip, although really only 3 months. He's due back June 5th. Good reports are coming in of how well he's done in meeting so many people & winning them. He's worked so hard. Yet he's found it rewarding beyond measure although so exacting & exhausting to live so long in a show case.

The Spring has been beautiful, although now a drought with the flowers already into Summer too soon.

I feel I know your charming house & garden from Thornton's descriptions & I think of you both there often.

I'm busy preparing a radio series based—but only based—on *Our Town*.[2]
With love to you both.

Affectionately
Isabel Wilder

1. In a letter to Isabel Wilder of 14 April Rose asked about Stein, "[L]et me know when you have any news as I am very worried about her." He enclosed what may be his "Easter" letter, which Isabel forwarded along with his letter to herself (both letters YCAL).

2. See Isabel Wilder to Stein, 7 July 1941, n. 4.

Isabel Wilder: To Gertrude Stein, Bilignin, France
[Typed]¹

7 July 1941   50 Deepwood Drive
                                               New Haven, Connecticut

Dear Gertrude,

Francis Rose has asked me to send you these recipes. I copied them off from his letter because they were in longhand on several pages and made too heavy an envelope.²

He asks me and sends messages to Thornton to beg you to come home. It would be wonderful to see you and have you near.

We are staggering out a series of too early and too continued a period of heat waves.

Thornton was with us a brief fortnight before going to Chicago to start his 10-weeks teaching course. He was in splendid shape in spite of the terrific fatigues of the trip. He writes with a kind of truly unChristian abandonment of the privacy and solitude he has found there—until he is discovered. The routine will get going faster and faster until, as he whirls, his feet will be indistinguishable from his head. However, at the moment he says, except when he is in class or a very occasional meal, he doesn't see a soul and have to talk and be talked at—a rest from the sound of his own voice.³

I'm still sitting on the edge of my chair waiting for the radio program of OUR TOWN to find a sponsor. For six weeks the sale was held up after I'd done my work as far as possible, for copyright laws etc. Now it is actually on the market—and a competitive, hardboiled market, too—the advertising world.⁴

My love and best wishes to you both. These recipes sound marvelous. I'm going to try them. I'm collecting some more for Alice. I should like to send the ingredients with the recipes—but I forward Francis' anyway in order to carry out his request.

Affectionately,
Isabel Wilder

1. Typographical errors are silently corrected.
2. Rose mentioned sending recipes to Isabel Wilder in his letter of 1 June 1941 (YCAL) to Stein. Neither Rose's letter nor Wilder's typed recipes have been located. In an interview, Isabel Wilder remembered that they included a salad with nasturtiums, which she found "ridiculous especially in troublesome times."
3. For her description of his life in Chicago, Isabel Wilder draws on letters to the family received in June and early July (YCAL). See Wilder to Stein, 28 July 1941.
4. A radio series based on *Our Town* did not find a sponsor in 1941. But Janet Cohn, an associate of Wilder's literary agent, Brandt & Brandt, reported to Isabel on 24 April and 8 May 1942 that the idea "looks pretty hot again." The series was to be a summer replacement for Dupont's *American Cavalcade*, and if successful it would become a permanent series in the fall. On 18 May Cohn wrote Isabel that "the deal seems to be off again." She did not, however, give up on the project; on 29 May Cohn

inquired if Isabel would consider trying "a new OUR TOWN script on your own which would be up-to-date." This project, too, was never realized. (Cohn letters in Brandt & Brandt files, YCAL.)

To Gertrude Stein and Alice Toklas, Bilignin, France

28 July 1941 [Port Washington, Wisc.]

Faculty Exchange, University of Chicago
until Sept[ember] first.
Then: 50 Deepwood Drive, New Haven,
Conn[ecticut]

Dearest Friends:

Friday night your ears burned and—as the Chinese put it—your eyelids twitched. You were being discussed.

There was a meeting of the JUNIOR SECTION of the CHICAGO CHAPTER of the SOCIETY OF THE FRIENDS OF GERTRUDE STEIN.

There were present:
Mr and Mrs Wendell Wilcox
Mr " Mrs Robert Livingstone (Gertrude Abercrombie)
Gladys Campbell
Samuel Stewart
and the *secrétaire perpetuel.*

It was held in my apartment that you know so well. Wendell made a delicious sauce for the spaghetti; Esther [Wilcox] made a *salade Lucy Amiably;* Gladys made a *consommé en gellée Ida;* and I provided the *Boissons Mrs. Reynolds.*

We retold the *twelve legends,* and meditated on the *nine precepts;* and after we had been very grave and moved and tender for a while we took good care to be very gay and impudent and gross for a while.

Norman Pierson [i.e., Pearson] was in town, but had an unbreakable engagement for the evening and was inconsolable about it.

All, all send their love and long thoughts.

The *secretaire perpetuel* remains the very foolish fellow you know.[1]

He should never have made the decision to come here this summer.

He loves Chicago more than ever, and prefers twelve Chicagoans to four million New Yorkers; but he teaches worse and worse and is being visibly *abruti, abêti* [annoyed], by doing—with very hard work and long hours—a very bad thing badly.

Jed Harris has begun casting the new play *The Skin of Our Teeth* even before the last act is finished. The last act is relucting. Its crystalization, I like to think, is much impeded by the weather. It is hard to sit in remote hotel rooms, the perspiration rolling down one's naked sides, and write pages of world-embracing gaiety. Acts One and Two are all right; the dance of the molecules have not released Act Three.[2]

The Government wants me to return to South America and woo some more Republics. It may have changed its mind, however, after reading the Report that I submitted ten days ago, in which I attacked the majority of the devices which they are employing as propaganda. It was from you I learned that no souls are won by flattery, argumentation or coërcion; that description paints no pictures and that purity is the only propaganda.[3]

Out of our differences we make our harmonies. Alice and I are ranged against Gertrude: we are chemically Early Risers. I try not to pretend that it is a moral virtue. I rise at six and make my breakfast. By seven I am at work.[4] From ten to one I teach. [Homer, Sophocles; *Inferno* and Don Quixote Part One—all in one summer. Vulgar, I call it.] Then at one I make my lunch. As I don't know how to cook lunch is just like breakfast. I am all worn out. For five hours I loathe the sight of a book or a pen. I take a nap. I am miserable. Then at seven I begin to come to life again. I tell myself I am a very fine fellow; that I lectured star-like on the Oedipus Rex; that I could have the Presidency of Ecuador for the asking; and that I have a fine head of long black hair. I drive downtown and get a good dinner and get the least bit drunk. Then I come home, a last hour of work and go to bed at 10:30. For half an hour I read something that has nothing to do with anything except excellence [I have just read 500 letters of Voltaire's old age.] Unfortunately two afternoons there are Office Hours, crowded with all Chicago's hall-bedroom poets, waiting their turn as in a dentist's waiting room, and there are various five-to-seven visits to make.[5] But I don't *eat* with anybody except the Hutchins.

So. . so. . so. . I have all the disadvantages of both Solitude and Gregariousness, and the rewards of neither. But I have found a Pattern for arranging the day which I can put to better advantage elsewhere.

Heigh-ho!

Mr. Knollenburgh was delighted when I told him that you would like to read his book on George Washington.[6] I talked over with him what periodicals I could send you and he said that there was not a one, no not one, that was worth your reading which was also not banned.

Think, Angèles, of all the things between the lines, and all the things I like to tell you about the Chicagoans and their notions of what ought to be done, and about how gnats and hornets do not prevent a young horse from arriving at his destination, and of all the love and longing that I should see you again before long. Ever your old devoted

Thornton

1. Except for Steward, then teaching at Loyola University of Chicago, Stein had met each of these people through Wilder in 1934–35. Stein had seen paintings by Gertrude Abercrombie, a member of her seminar, in Chicago. Her portrait of Wilder is now in YCAL. After a performance of Donald Vestal's marionette production of "Identity," she wrote Stein, "So now Wendell and I are so excited that we want to make a movie of Identity. I know one thing I am going to be in it. Wendell will be in it and direct it too. And I think we'll cast his little wife Esther. She said she would be the little dog but we'll find a real little dog. John Pratt will do the sets and Richard Gregg has the movie machine. It's a sound one but we may make it silent because Thornton has told me many times what you and Charlie Chaplin said about two mechanical devices. We'll make Thornton be in it too" (13 July 1936, YCAL). Nothing came of this project. Before her marriage, Abercrombie was romantically involved with Robert Davis. Gladys Campbell was a student of Wilder's at Chicago and became a writer and a teacher.

2. Wilder had left New Haven on 19 June to begin his summer teaching at the University of Chicago. Work on *The Skin of Our Teeth* proceeded slowly, and it was mainly on weekends, away from Chicago, that he could devote himself to his play. This letter is written from Port Washington, Wisconsin (Wilder's brackets), one of his weekend "work-studios." From another, in Holland, Michigan, he wrote his sister Isabel a week earlier, "Here working from Friday at six to (today) Monday at noon. Have got the plan of my Act III all straight at last. . . . This week-end of playwriting has given a sense to the whole summer which began, I thought, to need some" (21 July, YCAL).

Whether Harris had read acts I and II of *The Skin of Our Teeth* and discussed them with Wilder is not clear. Before leaving for South America he had worked intermittently on act III. It was proving particularly difficult, and it was not until his weekends outside of Chicago that he returned to it (see letter to his mother, Isabella Wilder, 17 January 1941, YCAL). In August he would write home, "These three week-ends I have taken to work on the play have been able to "warm it up" and I have found the right track for that difficult spot in Act III" (?25 August 1941, YCAL). Work on the play would again be delayed when Wilder attended the International P.E.N. Congress in London in September.

3. A copy of Wilder's report on his South American trip submitted to Charles Thomson, chief of the Division of Cultural Relations of the Department of State, is in YCAL. One of Wilder's conclusions was that "neither money, flattery, nor reason can persuade a South American in the vital international decision that approaches so quickly" (13).

4. See Wilder to Stein, 30 October 1940, n. 7.

5. During the summer, Wilder taught classes in classics in translation and in creative writing.

6. Wilder first mentioned Knollenberg's book (Wilder's misspelling) on 29 November [1940]; Stein replied that she would like to read it in her letter postmarked 13 January 1941. The book is again alluded to in Wilder's letter of 8 May 1941.

To Isabel Wilder, New Haven, Connecticut

[postmark: 31 July 1941][1]   Bilignin par Belley
                                                               (Ain)

My dear Isabel,

            Thanks so much for sending on Francis' [Rose] letter[2] and here is one in return and once more all thanks, everybody told us how wonderful Thornton was that day, and the only sadness is that it should have been recorded and would have been if the man had not gone away,[3] I do wish it had been, it would have been a great pleasure for us, no news of Thornton since he came back, but there will be of that we can always be certain, bless him. We are having a terrifically hot summer and vegetables grow and we are at them and then we eat them, they have even invaded the flower garden, we never ate our own potatoes before but we are doing it now and our own early potatoes are a pleasure, thanks again for writing and for being so efficient an intermediary with Francis, Alice wants to be remembered

Always
Gtrde.

1. There is no indication when this letter arrived in New Haven.

2. The Harry Ransom Humanities Research Center of the University of Texas at Austin has Rose's collection of more than two hundred letters from Stein. Most of these are undated, and the letter mentioned here may be among them. See Isabel Wilder to Stein, 16 May 1941, n. 1.

3. The man who could have recorded the opening ceremonies had enlisted in the army.

To Isabel Wilder, New Haven, Connecticut

[? August–September 1941][1]   [Bilignin par Belley
                                                       Ain]

My dear Isabel,

Thanks and thanks again for being our post office, it is a great relief to be able to hear directly from Francis [Rose] and know that all is well with him, we are very very fond of him, and so again and again thanks. His recipes do sound marvellous but in these days of what an American friend calls cooking with scissors, we cannot try them but you can and you can tell us, Thornton is faithless, not a letter not a word, nothing, but then he is that way, we know he loves us but he is that way, .

Always
Gtrde.

1. No envelope has been located for this letter, written in response to Isabel Wilder's letter of 7 July.

To Thornton Wilder, New Haven, Connecticut
[Postcard: BELLEY—Grande Rue]

[postmark: 19 August 1941]   [Bilignin par Belley
                                                              Ain]

My dear Thornton,

   The Washington book came from Knollenberg and I am
reading it with a great deal of pleasure,[1] but no books from you, perhaps you
sent too many in a package, send a few at a time and they come, and even if the
magazines are not all that you would want them to be they will be much appreciated not only by us but a considerable reading public English [?households],
vegetables grow and we eat them and we eat them and they grow, and we are at
this moment surrounded by real authors, a new one has just come who has
written a very bright book,[2] and so life goes on, lots of love so much love always
          Gtrde.

  1. Stein's inscribed copy of Bernhard Knollenberg's *Washington and the Revolution: A Reappraisal; Gates, Conway, and the Continental Congress* (1940) is in YCAL. She wrote to him, "Helas to
our great sorrow we have both finished the Washington and enjoyed every line of it, it has a singular
quality of intimacy and to-dayness partly I suppose because the situation here and now in this country
is so much like that" (postmark 7 October 1941, YCAL).
  2. Elena Genin, a native English speaker, with her French husband, Paul, and her daughter Joan
Clegg by her first husband had recently moved from Arcachon in the occupied zone to Chazey, near
Belley. Paul Genin's *Richesses réelles: A Propos d'un meilleur monde* had been recently published by
Recueil Sirey in Paris. A flyer and inventor, he had at the outbreak of the war joined his family's textile
business. Genin was interested in economics and philosophy.

To Thornton Wilder, New Haven, Connecticut
[Postcard: Environs de BELLEY—Vieux pont de Bognens]

[postmark: 21 August 1941]   [Bilignin par Belley
                                                              Ain]

My dear Thornton,

   I am sending you a book by a young frenchman and the
style of it interests me a lot, if it interests you let me know as he needs
encouragement,[1] the sun is getting autumnal but the garden is still spring-
like, lots of love

          Gtrde.

  1. Genin's *Richesses réelles.*

To Gertrude Stein and Alice Toklas, Bilignin, France

[7 September 1941]   [Bermuda, B.W.I.]

Dear Alice-Angel and Gertrude-Glory—

    The strangest thing has happened.

    In a few hours I am flying by Clipper to London. I have just spent four days in Washington and N[ew] Y[ork] wading through bolts of red-tape. I begged and hammered the S[tate]. Department to give me a Visa for France, but with no result. I shall be in Lisbon for days yearning to cross the Pyrenees to you.

    The stay in London is for three weeks only. Invited to attend the P.E.N. Congress[.][1]

    I cannot see you, but I've been with you much—rereading Everybody's Autobiography with bewitchment, as though for the First Time. (Is that because the Actor-Temperament suffers less than others from the deadening effects of repetitions; or because the Wilders aren't quite bright and are Dawned Upon Slowly?) And have been entering into the Mallorca plays; and have been understanding more about Romance and Money.[2]

    Thanks, eternal thanks to the great good Mind that tells us what she knows and enlarges our Listening.

    When I return here I shall write you with moderate distinctness of some of our friends.

    This is the third postponement to the completion of my play (South America and University of Chicago); but I shall be back here by the first week in October and presumably the play will go on in December.[3] Alec [Woollcott] will be in London, too, broadcasting to them and to us.[4] Wherever you are—pardlike spirits beautiful and swift you are loved by

Thornton

1. The invitation to participate in the Seventeenth International Congress of P.E.N. came late in August. Neither Wilder nor John Dos Passos, the other American delegate, had been selected by the American P.E.N. Center (see Chute, P.E.N., 36–37). Instead, they were personally invited by their British hosts. Wilder may have been a last-minute substitute for Archibald MacLeish, the librarian of Congress, who was about to be appointed director of the newly established Office of Facts and Figures. In a message to the P.E.N. Congress, MacLeish wrote, "My inability to attend the Congress is a matter of deep personal regret to me. No one can speak for American writers with more authority and understanding than Thornton Wilder" (see Ould, ed., Writers, 6).

    Wilder and John Dos Passos flew from New York to Bermuda on 6 September. After a delay of twenty-four hours, they flew to Lisbon and the next day to London, arriving just after the opening ceremonies of the congress on 10 September. Wilder spoke at the opening session on 11 September and was quoted in the New York Times the next day under the sub-banner headline, "Wilder Bids Authors 'Be Patient.' ": "In times of difficulty we writers must learn to curb our impatience. Since my arrival in London last night I have seen that hope and confidence can be transmitted by a glance.

    "My personal presence here has meant a great deal to me. I know that John Dos Passos and I can speak for thousands and millions at home who wish to express their gratitude and homage to you people of London" (12). His speech was taken down stenographically, but for publication, Wilder reshaped it. As he explained to E. M. Forster, "Might I ask the favor of yourself and Mr. Ould, and whoever else would be responsible in this case to submit to you also *not what I said*, but a reshaped and I hope more considered statement of it. On the journey here I had meditated a speech on a specific aspect of the Congress's proposed theme, but on the evening of the 10th hearing that I was to speak in the opening session, the following morning, I assembled as hastily as I could a number of themes that might be more appropriate for an opening session" (24 September 1941, Texas; see Wilder's "The Duty of the Writer," in Ould, ed., *Writers*, 36–37).

The main theme of the congress was "Literature and the World after the War," but the heart of the issue was the responsibility of the writer in time of war. Storm Jameson, president of the British P.E.N., insisted that members commit themselves exclusively to propaganda for the Allied cause. This stand was opposed by Wilder, Rebecca West, and Forster, a group that came to be called the humanists.

A controversial issue of the congress was the reaction to the *Seven Mysteries of Europe* of Jules Romains (1940). Romains, the international president of P.E.N., had emigrated to America and was not present at the congress. He had collected seven previously published essays revealing how he had dabbled in politics, meeting statesmen and politicians during the years preceding September 1939. His "megalomania" was denounced by the Austrian writer Robert Neumann, who attacked him for his visit to Berlin in 1934 and for his obvious pleasure at his reception by Goebbels and other Nazi leaders: "Did he ask to be shown the cellars of Columbia House? Dachau Concentration Camp, where there were scores of German writers; men crucified, starving, cleaning latrines, slowly beaten to death. There are among us to-day writers who have been to Dachau. Or did he ask to see Orianienburg?" ("When a Writer Goes into Politics," in Ould, ed., *Writers*, 102).

At the end of the congress, H. G. Wells was elected international president but promptly declined. A motion was made to elect Wilder, but Jameson thought the international president should live in or near London. Wells proposed a compromise, a presidential committee of four members and the international secretary, Hermon Ould. Wells, Wilder, Thomas Mann, and Jacques Maritain were elected. But when Mann and Maritain, neither of whom was at the congress, declined, Denis Saurat (France) and Hu Shih (China) were added to the committee, which served until 1946. Wilder agreed to serve one final year, 1947, together with Forster, François Mauriac, and Ignazio Silone until a new president was elected.

When the congress was over on 13 September, Wilder saw plays, met old friends, and visited his aunt, Charlotte Wilder, who worked for the YWCA in London. Robert Longman, his English publisher who had helped to defray his travel expenses, took him on his warden's rounds. Wilder learned "what it was like to live through the conditions that began last September." To his mother and his sister he wrote, "The central Post; turning on the lights in the shelters that no one has visited for months; then at last one shelter in which five people were already asleep, one old woman who had been bombed out of first home, and then successive homes, and at last, weary, weary, could only sleep underground." About Lady Colefax, he added, "[H]aving broken her back and wearing a steel corset [she] is still the pivot of many privileges. . . . . If the Ministry feels it can release petrol-rations to me I shall drive with Sibyl down to Max Beerbohm's and to Desmond MacCarthy's" (18 September, YCAL). He also managed to meet Sir Francis Rose, "Isabel's correspondent," attend a soldiers' concert, visit an R.A.F. headquarters, and watch bombers take off for the continent.

The weekend of 27 September he addressed meetings in Edinburgh and Glasgow, and when he returned to London on 1 October was honored at a luncheon by the English-Speaking Union, where Wells introduced him. The same abbreviated text of Wilder's talk was printed in two publications, "Mr Thornton Wilder Interprets," in *Time and Tide*, and "Thornton Wilder—E-S. U. Luncheon," in *The English-Speaking World* (see bibliography). Wilder also broadcast on the BBC to Europe. Wilder and Dos Passos left London on 12 October for four days in Bristol and three days in Lisbon and arrived in New York on 18 October. Wilder's "After a Visit to England" was published in *The Yale Review* 31, 2 (December 1941). 217–24.

2. From April 1915 to April 1916, Stein and Toklas lived in Mallorca. Work from this period was published in *Geography And Plays*. Romance and money are subjects in Stein's *Geographical History Of America, Narration,* and *What Are Masterpieces.*

3. *The Skin of Our Teeth* was completed on 1 January 1942 and, after tryouts in New Haven and Baltimore, opened in New York at the Plymouth Theatre on 18 November.

4. Woollcott arrived in England on 7 October to do a series of broadcasts for CBS Radio and the BBC. His first CBS broadcast was on 9 October; the *New York Times* printed a transcript of another broadcast on 26 October, sec. 9, p. 12, "Town Crier, Minus Bell." Woollcott returned to New York via Lisbon on 24 November.

To Gertrude Stein and Alice Toklas, Bilignin, France

12 Nov[ember]. 1941   50 Deepwood Drive
                                                 New Haven, Conn[ecticut].

Dear Friends:

Here's a letter I forward to you unread.[1]

I had a wonderful journey to that country and wish I could have obtained permission to see you, too. I saw Francis Rose who is just the same, is in the educational work, has built a theatre, and is very worried about what work he can obtain when the present preoccupations have ended. Saw the former Mrs von Hofmannsthal and Fred[erick] Ashton who send their love. Sibyl [Colefax] is energetic and devoted. [Alexander] Woollcott arrived just as I left; he is full of zip and go having long since been condemned by the doctors to bed and gruel.[2]

[Robert] Hutchins has come into a good deal of unpleasant notoriety over here as he does not agree with the rest of us on some very important matters.[3]

I have a few articles and lectures to do[4] and am finishing up Act III on my play.[5] It is hard to settle down after the wild tempo of South American travel, Chicago Summer-Teaching and this last excursion. I may go out to California to work with Charlie Chaplin on a short film in connection with some things that are on all our minds.[6] Everytime I pass a magazine stand I look for some periodicals that I could recommend to you, but can see nothing except the Crochet and "Knitting Guide" and "Filmplay." However a few days ago I sent you the new Van Doren book on the Benedict Arnold coterie which has received very favorable notices from all the historians.[7] In the last port I stopped in on the homeward journey I picked up a copy of a review called Patrie published in North Africa. It had an article (excellently bright as Ben Jonson said) on the French Language.[8] The biographical material said in it you were living on Long Island and I hurried home to embrace you, in vain, and with what redoubled extreme regret.

I am looking daily for the young Frenchman's book you have sent me.[9]

So much to ask you and so much to tell. When I can at last see you again brace yourself for the impetus of my jump.

lots of love

Thornton

1. An undated letter from Cecil Beaton (YCAL).

2. W. G. Rogers wrote Stein on 13 October of hearing a Woollcott broadcast: "The N.Y. announcer said that, among other speakers, there would be a report direct from London by Alexander Woollcott! Imagine. And sure enuf, there was, in his best radio voice telling how, planes being too small for him and his luggage, he crossed the ocean in a British battleship. And, says he, explaining that London still was a cosmopolitan place, just before I came to this studio, he said, whom should I see but Thornton Wilder getting onto a bus in Piccadilly!" (see Gallup, *Flowers*, 357).

3. Hutchins remained anti-interventionist until the attack on Pearl Harbor.

4. Among his activities were a talk at the Council for Democracy (21 October); a report on his trip to England on the council's radio series, "Speaking of Liberty," hosted by Rex Stout (30 October); a speech on the P.E.N. Congress to the New York P.E.N. at a dinner at the Ambassador Hotel (7 November); a "Memorandum of the Meeting of the New York (or 'American') Center" sent to the international secretary, Hermon Ould (letter of 21 November 1941, Texas); and his article "After a Visit to England" for *The Yale Review.*

5. Although he was still working on act III of *The Skin of Our Teeth*, Wilder gave a reading of the play at home on 6 November (date book). He spent Thanksgiving with his sister Janet and her husband in Amherst, and later in the month he drove to Neshobe Island to see Woollcott, who had returned from England. By 9 December Wilder was in the Viking Hotel in Newport, Rhode Island, continuing work on act III. He wrote home, "It is hard—what with the President's speech [Roosevelt's Declaration of War] last night, and the Boston papers!—to assemble my concentration for the Act III, but I have begun copying it onto new pages which is my way of Awakening the Fancy. . . . I'm hoping I can get that resistant corner of Act III ironed out soon,—the only part that requires Isolation to produce—and so return home to put the last alterations on the rest and carry to the typist's" (10 December 1941, YCAL).

6. From the time Chaplin finished *The Great Dictator*, in October 1940, until *Monsieur Verdoux*, March 1947, he produced no films. Although he worked on and abandoned several projects, there is nothing to suggest Wilder's participation. It is possible that in England a propaganda film for the British war effort had been discussed with Wilder as a possible project for Chaplin (see Robinson, *Chaplin*, 509–43).

7. Carl Van Doren's *Secret History of the American Revolution; an account of the conspiracies of Benedict Arnold and numerous others, drawn from the secret service papers of the British Headquarters in North America, now for the first time examined and made public* (New York: Viking, 1941).

8. Stein's "La Langue Française," in *Patrie: Revue Mensuelle illustrée de l'Empire*, 10 August 1941, 36–37. In a telegram of 28 May (YCAL), Stein had been approached by Richard de Rochemont of the American Red Cross in Marseille on behalf of *Patrie:* "Jean Masson editor of new magazine Patrie to appear shortly under patronage Marshal Petain asked me suggest prominent American writer who might do thousand word article on the importance or prestige of French language for inaugural number and I took liberty suggesting you Stop article non political and will be paid for Stop." Masson's counterpart in Algeria was Paul Bringuier. The article showed a photograph of Stein at Bilignin but identified her as "dans sa maison de Long-Island, près de New York," a caption perhaps meant to protect her. In Jonson's *Cynthia's Revels*, each stanza of Hesperus's song to Cynthia (V, vi) ends with the line "Goddess, excellently bright."

9. Paul Genin's *Richesses réelles* (see Stein to Wilder [19 August 1941], n. 2).

Isabel Wilder: To Gertrude Stein, Bilignin, France

1 December 1941[1]   50 Deepwood Drive
                                              New Haven, Connecticut

Dear Gertrude,

　　　　　Enclosed you will find the last letter which has come for you
from Francis [Rose].[2]

　　　We were so glad to have Thornton back with us. Such wonderful things
he saw & heard. Such courage & strength at work. ¶ Now he is finishing his
play, & lecturing.[3]

　　　The autumn has been so long & mild & beautiful. Today the tempera-
ture was over 60.

　　　My older sister has been very ill for many months, & we worry about her;
but looking above our own noses, that is a very little thing. Yet it is so close &
real that I find it hard to forget always. When it has gone on longer we may
grow accustomed to it.[4]

　　　We think & speak of you often; & people who do not know you but know
we do, ask us for good news of you & Alice. With the holiday Season so close
we think of you most fondly & send deep & wide & high best wishes for 1942.

　　　With love to you & Alice,

　　　　　　　　　affectionately,
　　　　　　　　　Isabel.

　　　1. On the top of the first page and at the bottom of the second page of this letter, Isabel Wilder
pasted decorative stars.
　　　2. Perhaps Rose's letter of 9 October in which he mentions meeting Wilder in London (YCAL).
　　　3. See Wilder to Stein, 12 November 1941, n. 4.
　　　4. Charlotte Wilder (see Wilder to Stein, 1 April 1941, n. 2). For a summary of the history of her
illness, see Harrison, *The Enthusiast*, 246–49.

―――――――――――

To Thornton Wilder, New Haven, Connecticut

[postmark: 4 December 1941][1]   Bilignin par Belley
                                              Ain

My dear Thornton,

　　　　　Thanks for sending us Cecil [Beaton]'s letter, and telling
all about Francis [Rose], they seem not to be too much bothered by the
situation, and indeed xcept for those for whom it is very bad it is not so bad. I
wish we might have seen you, and you will be pleased I know that we had a
thanksgiving dinner, we still remember it, thanks to our neighbors the young

man whose book I sent you and his wife half Scotch half Spanish and raised in Mexico, we had turkey and Alice made mince pie and ice cream, it was a real feast, and that is one of the nice things these days a feast is a feast. The young man has just written a new book Mon livre de Pourquoi that I think very good and I will send you the ms. I think it will interest you.[2] And now Thornton about my literature not that that I write but that I read. Could you instead of sending me books well thought of by historians could you go to a railway station or to the nearest drug store and send me every few weeks or once a month or once four or five of the mystery stories that the man in charge recommends as the best, everybody when they send me reading matter consult not my tastes but my education, I suppose even when I give you the detail of the method of pleasing me you won't because after all to a good American principles are more important than pleasure, and Alice would so love the knitting magazines and any picture magazine that gives any photographs of any American, but not a cinema star's but you won't, I plead and I plead but you don't, well we have to love you even so but it is hard, but we love you even so bless you

Gtrde and Alice.

1. A response to Wilder's letter of 12 November.

2. Stein and Toklas invited Paul and Elena Genin and their daughter Joan Clegg for Thanksgiving dinner. Paul Genin's new book, *Essai sur le chaos. mon livre de pourquoi*, was recommended by Stein to Max-Pol Fouchet and Albert Camus of Editions Charlot, who had published *Paris France*. The book, published in 1945, was in part inspired by conversations with Stein.

Stein and Toklas with local friends René Reuloz, Charlotte Chaboux, Doctor Gaston Chaboux, and Pierre Reuloz. On the back of this photograph Toklas wrote that the salon at Bilignin had Louis XVI mural paintings.

1942

Château le Colombier, Culoz, where Stein and Toklas lived from February 1943 to December 1944

To Gertrude Stein and Alice Toklas, Bilignin, France

25 March 1942[1]

50 Deepwood Drive
New Haven, Connecticut

Dearest Friends:

Yours postmarked December 4th just arrived, but no copy of the book by the author-friend. I am very eager to see it.[2]

Yes, after I sent you the Carl Van Doren history I heard that it was not very good. For a few weeks the reviewers were shrieking "definitive". . . . "revises all previous histories". . . and then the tumult died down and everybody was saying in their usual tone of voice, not very good.[3]

Yes, indeed, I will send you detective stories.

I have been very wicked you-wards. I have read you; talked about you; had a Quaker concern about you; but have not written you. I no longer believe in repentances, forgivenesses, nor explanations; so all I can ask you to do is accept me: inconsistent and wicked.

It is very probable that in a month or two I shall be in uniform and far away. Archie MacLeish heard of my efforts to get into something and asked me what I wanted to do. I almost risked losing his powerful advocacy by coming out, plump with the words, "not writing" and not "office-sitting." I think my first command will be to learn the Japanese language.[4]

The performance of my new play has been postponed until the Fall in order to obtain the services of the real right actor for it who until then is engaged in Hollywood.[5] I think you will like it. I tried to write a tragedy without tears, real *sec* knowing and telling, but I'm afraid a few Wilder tears got in, not many and not enough to sink the piece, dear.[6] And it is full of theatre, theatre, and full of the spirit of play. And there are many passages that for me are written under the sign of Gertrude Stein. Now I am hurriedly finishing another play.[7] They may both be running next Fall and sustaining my family in my absence. I have two dependents—a 69 year-old-mother (mighty alive still) and a sister—Charlotte—who has been a whole year in a hospital for mental diseases. These two play-subjects are all that I have in my knapsack and when they are written I temporarily close the door on the whole matter of writing and turn to other things. These last months I have been harrassingly engaged in broadcasts to South America and making motion-pictures for the government.[8] I have no sense of conviction about their efficacy and lay them aside with relief.

I never pass that house in Washington Square without longing that you were there.[9]

I don't have to tell you how interesting looking seeing and listening these days are,—the internal even more than the external. The basic American swinging into view. The industrial organization of the factories—vast without giantism; work, work, work, yet with the composure of a man picking his teeth with a grass-stem; the miraculous conducted as though it were the matter-of-course. Old America.

Literature and the fine arts have fallen down to the level of bathos and cute scraps, but it doesn't matter. "Mrs. Murray Crane requests the pleasure of your company on the Xth and Yth of March at 9:00. Mr. Frederic Prokosch will talk on Modern Poetry, and Mr. Glenway Wescott on Modern Novel respectively.[10] It is hoped that interesting discussion will follow." "Yale University announces that it will introduce a system of toughening up the students who have remained on the campus. It will consist of three hours a week, jumping over barrels, etc. . . . . .!!" But those Eastern Seabord jerks and fidgets don't matter. The dynamo is revolving elsewhere.

Yes, knitting magazines for Alice but where where can I find a magazine that shows pictures of Americans not movie stars and that does not contain controversial matter?

I do hope the young neighbor's book comes through and the manuscript of mon (can't read the next word) de Pourquoi. If I am here I will try and find a publisher for it.[11]

The important thing is that everything is electrically alive and I am breathing down to the bottom of my diaphragm. I have a new enthusiasm in my life it is the figure of Simon Bolivar. I read the thousands of letters by him and laugh all the time at the contemplation of such gifts, and I hope I get just that mixture that you and he have of complete despair and complete hope, and now I see where Freud and Joyce got it wrong, and have returned from my infidelities to your dear knees and shall go no more a-whoring by the light of the moon. I cannot wait to see your dear four eyes again and stand before you, wicked, impenitent, but loving

Thornton

1. This is Wilder's first letter to Stein since 12 November 1941. Absorbed with the completion and production of *The Skin of Our Teeth*, he allowed correspondence to lag, as he had done in the spring of 1938 when completing and staging *Our Town*.

2. See Stein to Wilder, postmark 4 December 1941, n. 2.

3. See Wilder to Stein, 12 November 1941, n. 7.

4. At the Century Club in New York, Wilder met with an FBI agent doing a background check on Frederic Prokosch for a job with William Donovan's Office of Strategic Services (see also Wilder to Leslie Glenn, 23 March 1942, YCAL). While there, he met Archibald MacLeish and discussed his desire to do active war service even though he would be forty-five in April. Wilder enlisted, and in May, through MacLeish's efforts, was accepted into the Army Air Intelligence School in Harrisburg, Pennsylvania. He began his basic training on 24 June 1942 in Miami Beach, Florida.

5. Fredric March. See Appendix VIII.

6. Wilder, anticipating charges of sentimentality, may be referring to the *Geographical History* and the concluding lines of "A portrait of Thornton Wilder":

> He has no fears
> At most he has no tears.
> For them very likely he is made of them. (73)

Commenting later on these lines he would write, " 'For them' means for a large part of the reading public—and for you—*The Bridge of San Luis Rey* and *Our Town* are tender, tear-drenched, and consoling. But they aren't, they're hard and even grimly challenging, for 'He has no fears' " (Wilder's copy of a letter to Richard Goldstone, 19 November 1968, YCAL).

7. *The Alcestiad*. Wilder's "tragedy without tears" is *The Skin of Our Teeth*.

8. Wilder did an NBC radio broadcast with Dorothy Massey on 15 February 1942, and on 7 April he would be interviewed by Frances Grant about eighteenth-century Lima and *The Bridge of San Luis Rey* in a series of broadcasts to Central and South America organized by the New York P.E.N. Center. A draft of his talk is in YCAL. For a summary of Wilder's activities from November to December 1941, see Wilder to Stein, 12 November 1941, n. 4.

9. See Wilder to Stein, 26 May 1935, nn. 13.

10. Frederic Prokosch spoke on 25 March and Glenway Westcott on 31 March. Their lectures, attended by more than thirty guests, were followed by a discussion and then supper. Although invited, Wilder attended neither lecture (see Wilder to Stein, 4 September 1937, nn. 1, 2; see Crane diaries, YCAL, for guest lists).

11. See Stein to Wilder, postmarked 4 December 1941.

To Thornton Wilder, New Haven, Connecticut

[postmark: Belley, Ain,   Bilignin par Belley (Ain)
7 July 1942][1]

My dearest Thornton,

It was the third of July and I was out walking in the evening and I suddenly thought that when I came in Alice would call out and say imagine who it is that is here, and I would say who, and she would answer Thornton, but alas when I got back it was not so, and the next day was the fourth of July and we forgot it until all our friends called us up to congratulate and the first one we said for what and they said it was the fourth of July and it was, well that is all our news xcept that it is hot, and how hot and the garden is all drying up and that is a sadness but otherwise everything is alright, lots of friends new and old but not much mail, and that we do miss most frightfully, any news recently of Francis [Rose], and where are you are you a real soldier, or on a mission, and perhaps well perhaps it was not true the third of July but it will be true in the sweet by and by, it would be nice if you came on a mission, I am working nicely not too much but nicely, May D'Aiguy has translated my First Reader and the ballad is to be printed shortly in a new review Confluences, that is all my literary news,[2] and lots of love, and write soon, and also make my dream come true, bless you all

Gtrde.

1. Wilder has supplied the postmark information. On 30 August, Isabel Wilder copied this letter with some minor errors and sent it to Sir Francis Rose (I. Wilder to Rose, Texas).

2. May d'Aiguy's translation of *The First Reader* was published on 30 April 1944 as *Petits poèmes pour un livre de lecture* in the Collection Fontaine, edited by Max-Pol Fouchet and published by Editions Edmond Charlot in Algiers, Algeria. This was the same publisher who in September 1941 published her translation of *Paris France*. René Tavernier was the editor of *Confluences*, which published "Ballade" in issue no. 12 (July 1942): 11–12. "Ballade" is "Lesson Eighteen" in *The Gertrude Stein First Reader & Three Plays*, 49–52.

To Thornton Wilder, Hamilton Field, California

[postmark: 21 September 1942]   Bilignin par Belley
                                                              (Ain)

My dearest Thornton,

We wonder and wonder where each and every one is, in your last you were on your way to study Japanese,[1] are you far far away or are you quite near, the letters come quite rapidly now, and the Kiddy frequently writes but it is some time since he has given us news of you, we have had a dry summer, not a drop of rain and the garden is consequently sad, and we have to use the well, but now the summer is over and the pleasures of autumn have begun. I work quite a lot and the book To Do which has you in China in it, is out, and I hope you like it.[2] May d'Aiguy has translated the poems of the First Reader and they are being printed here and there and seem very much liked,[3] there is everybody here as always, a nice youn[g] Canadian who had been in the University of Chicago long discussions of [Robert] Hutchins made me feel quite homesick.[4] And here is a letter of Daniel Rops which he asks me to send you,[5] no news of Francis [Rose] for a long time, the last from Cecil Beaton from Portugal but that some months back,[6] let us do let us know how you are and where you are and that you are always our own dear Thornton,

Always

Gtrde.[7]

1. See Wilder to Stein, 25 March 1942.

2. At this time Stein did not know that "To Do" had not been published. She had announced its completion to Carl Van Vechten on 26 May 1940 and sent it to him on 3 June to forward to John McCullough, an editor at William R. Scott. McCullough felt it lacked episode and had less appeal than *The World Is Round*, which he had published in August 1939 (see Burns, *Letters*, 2:675–76, and McCullough to Stein, 7 August 1940, YCAL). Van Vechten then sent the manuscript to Bennett Cerf, who replied on 19 November 1940 (YCAL) that Random House, which would publish *Ida A Novel* in February 1941, could not do more than one Stein book a year. After much prodding from Van Vechten, Cerf confessed that everyone at Random House was "as cold as a slab of alabaster" about "To Do" (9 January 1941, YCAL). Harcourt Brace and Charles Scribner's Sons also rejected the book. Meanwhile, McCullough suggested a book more clearly aimed at children, with the title "Gertrude Stein's First Reader." Stein immediately took up the idea. On 30 March 1941, Stein suggested that Van Vechten give the typescript of "To Do" to Margot Johnson, a literary agent with Ann Watkins, Inc. Throughout 1941 and 1942 a number of publishers and agents discussed "To Do" and the *Gertrude Stein First Reader*. By January 1942, Harrison Smith had agreed to publish "To Do," and although contracts had been signed, the book was postponed and eventually they did not. When, on 11 November 1942, complete occupation of France by German forces began, and Stein was cut off from communication with America, she still believed that "To Do" was about to be published by Harrison Smith. It was posthumously printed in the Yale Edition in *Alphabets And Birthdays* (1957).

3. Stein finished the *First Reader* by April 1941 and sent it to Van Vechten. Translated by May d'Alguy, it was published as *Petits Poèmes pour un livre de lecture* by Editions Charlot in Algeria on 30 April 1944. As *The Gertrude Stein First Reader & Three Plays*, illustrated by Francis Rose, it was published in London by Maurice Fridberg on 16 November 1946. (For the publishing history of each book, see Burns, *Letters*, 2:675–758.)

4. We have not succeeded in identifying this person.

5. Enclosed was a letter of 16 September from Daniel-Rops asking Wilder to contribute to an issue of *Présences* planned in homage to Charles Du Bos, the French writer who had died on 24 August 1939. Wilder did not contribute to the volume, which appeared in 1945. Wilder and Du Bos met through Samuel Steward in Chicago in 1938. Du Bos wanted to lecture in private homes, clubs, and at the university, and Wilder arranged introductions (Du Bos to Wilder, YCAL; Wilder to Du Bos, Doucet-Paris).

6. At the outbreak of the war, Beaton went to work for the British Ministry of Information photographing life in the military and the effects of war on civilian populations. Following a three-month tour of Royal Air Force bases in Africa and the Near East, he arrived in Lisbon on 9 July. He wrote Stein the next day (YCAL), expressing concern and reporting that he had last had direct news of her from Wilder when they met in London in September 1941. Wilder mentioned meeting Beaton to his family on 18 September 1941 (YCAL).

7. See Appendix IX.

Liberation, September 1944: Stein and Basket II in Culoz

1944

Lieutenant Colonel Thornton Wilder, Belgrade, Yugoslavia, February 1945

René and Hélène Tavernier with Captain William K. Mc Kown,
U.S. Army, after the liberation, September 1944

Isabel Wilder: To Gertrude Stein and Alice Toklas, Culoz, France

Friday [Nantucket, Massachusetts]
8 September 1944

Dear, dear Gertrude & dear, dear Alice,

The very day, the glorious day, we read in the Tribune (Herald, N.Y.) that you two had been found safe & sound by Eric Sevareid,[1] I received a letter from Thornton who, incidentally, has been worrying a great deal over you with the rest of your devoted friends. He said as of August 27th "It's highly probable that an armored American column will have pushed through Gertrude's vicinity by now. In the last war she made friends with G.I.'s like a duck to water. I hope she's made some new ones & got a good mess of K-rations in return."[2] I think he's always believed you would be safe somewhere so great is his faith in you!

Thornton joined up in June 1942, commissioned a Captain. He took basic Air Corps training at Miami Beach through the dreadful heat, then graduated later from the Air Intelligence School at Harrisburg. He was assigned to an Air Field in California, Hamilton Field on San Francisco Bay, above Richmond. He loved it there—the work he wanted, that is, in with the men. In mid-Nov[ember]. an important—self important—little Colonel wanting an author in tow, got the poor Capt. to Washington & there he was at a desk in the Pentagon until May. A punishment indeed for crimes unknown. But at times the work was rewarding—it was editing an Army Air Manual. This newer branch of the Services had not yet a "bible." It was hardly, however, work for which an author was suited or needed. Rather a field-day for editor or statis[ti]cian. Well, then, at last to N. Africa, as a Major. He has worked hard, & usually at a desk, but under the world's condition there's nowhere he'd rather be, except there doing what he's told. From various sources we've heard he's done & is doing a "magnificent" job. He can't tell us what it is, but his

languages & maturity & powers of concentration & his wonderful, unending
enthusiasm are valuable. He writes he may soon be going to England & that
could easily lead to France. You can be certain he will seek you out as soon as
possible. I've sent him immediate news of you Two.[3]

Mother and I have been keeping the home going. My older sister is still
in the Mental Hospital. Was much better at last, & then presto, in July a
relapse. Mid-June I was taken desperately ill—gallstones. The operation revealed complications. It's taking me so long to get over it. I write from Nantucket. Mother & I came 2 days ago for a fortnight. A unique little place—the
nearest thing to a foreign land these days. ¶ Would I were a nurse with the Red
+, & were over there. I've hopes of getting to London this winter with an "Our
Town" company which Jed Harris is organizing & probably getting permission to take.[4] ¶ So, in brief this is the Wilders' news. Please take temporarily
from me Thornton's devoted affection & gratitude that he'll be seeing you two
before too long. And mine. With love,

Isabel Wilder.

1. This must have been one of the earliest letters that Stein received after having been cut off
from America for nearly two years. Sevareid's article, "Gertrude Stein Safe in France with New Book,"
appeared in the *New York Herald Tribune* on 2 September, 5. The story was picked up and run by other
newspapers, e.g., the *New York Times*, 2 September, 9. On the morning of 1 September, Sevareid, a CBS
correspondent, invited some fellow journalists to join him in seeking out Stein, who he knew lived in
the region of Grenoble, where they were stationed with Gen. Alexander Patch's U.S. Seventh Army.
General Patch's army had landed on the beaches between Toulon and Cannes on 15 August and, after
liberating Marseille, proceeded up the valleys of the Rhone and the Isère to Grenoble. Sevareid, who
had known Stein in Paris in 1938, cabled CBS in New York to ask her publisher, Random House, for an
exact address and received the Bilignin address.

Sevareid arranged for an army jeep, driven by Sgt. William B. Druggan, and brought along Price
Day of the *Baltimore Sun*, Newbold Noyes of the *Washington Evening Star*, Carl Mydans, a *Time-Life*
photographer, and Frank Gervasi, a correspondent for *Collier's Weekly*, on the mission to "liberate"
Stein. Near Chambéry their jeep broke down, and when a passing jeep stopped to help them, Sevareid
learned that its occupants, Lt. Col. William Perry and his driver, PFC John Schmaltz, had just spent
the night with Stein and Toklas in Culoz. Sevareid and his fellow journalists proceeded to Culoz,
where they met Stein and later that day filed their stories. Price Day's appeared in the *Baltimore Sun*
on 3 September, 3, and Newbold Noyes's in the *Washington Evening Star* on 5 September, A 2. Carl
Mydan's photo-essay, "The Liberation of Gertrude Stein," appeared in *Life* on 2 October 1944, 83–84.
The book referred to in articles as "Wars I Remember," "All the Wars I Remember," and "All the Wars
I've Known" is Stein's *Wars I Have Seen*.

Stein asked Frank Gervasi, who was returning to the United States, to deliver the manuscript of
Wars I Have Seen, which Toklas was still typing, to Bennett Cerf. On Sunday, 3 September, Sevareid
and Gervasi drove to Culoz for lunch and then brought Stein back to Voiron, a town forty miles
from Culoz where the press was staying, to record a broadcast for CBS. The day before, when Gervasi came to Culoz to pick up the typescript, Stein gave him a sealed envelope containing a handwritten copy of "A Ballad," a poem incorporated into her *First Reader*. The gift commemorated their
meeting. Sevareid's account, with an abridged version of her broadcast at Voiron, is in his *Not
So Wild a Dream* (1946; rpt. New York: Atheneum, 1976, 457–62; see also Stein, *How Writing*,
133–34).

Gervasi recounted his experiences in "The Liberation of Gertrude Stein," in the *Saturday
Review of Literature* 54 (21 August 1971): 13–14, 57 (illustrated by Thérèse Bonney photographs, taken

in 1942). An expanded version, together with "A Ballad," is the concluding chapter of his *The Violent Decade. Collier's* published selections from *Wars I Have Seen*, illustrated in color by Harry Beckhoff, in the issues of 16 December and 23 December under the title "Liberation, Glory Be!" The *Collier's* editors standardized Stein's language. See Wilson, *A Bibliography*, C 167 and 168.

2. Quoted from a letter of 25 (not 27) August (YCAL).

3. Wilder entered the military with the rank of captain; he was promoted to major in April 1944, and to lieutenant colonel in August 1944. Writing home from Caserta, Italy, on 29–30 October 1944 (YCAL), Wilder told of his wartime activities following his flight from Maine to Scotland on 21 May 1943:

> Now after a year and a half have gone by I can tell you some of my movements in May 1943. The night of the day after I had visited Bobby Burns' birthplace we were descending at Casablanca; we spent two nights there. There had been three other Majors on the crossing since Maine, all three of whom I was to work with later when I joined plans, and all three of them have since returned to U.S. and are at the Pentagon as veterans of overseas experience in staff work!! Two nights at Casablanca; then up in the air eastward; descended for lunch at Oran and who should be standing in front of me at the snack bar qeue but Michel St. Denis, in Africa, to set up certain services in the Radio-Alger. Quick greetings. Then to Algiers for a day and get my orders and on to Constantine [Algeria]. There I put in a month's work in the Intellig[ence] section of the 12th Air Force, Gen. Spaatz commanding. The occupations of Panteleria [Italian island in the Mediterranean Sea] and Sicily are being prepared and whom should I meet but Dr. Buckermann become a great consultant in the statistics of bomb damage. Thereby hangs a story to tell later. During the month I am being groomed and oriented for the job on the planning staff, i.e. liaison between the Intellig[ence]. Section of Northwest Afric[an]. Air Forces and Plans. And soon report to Algiers. At once I am set to go on trips, sewing up last details on the Sicily matter. Oran on the West, to Sousse [Tunisia] and Bizerte [Tunisia] on the East. Unforgettable days.

Wilder served with the Planning Division of both the Advanced and the Rear Headquarters of the Northwest African Air Force from late May until 2 July in Constantine, Algeria; from 3 July to 19 August 1943 in Bouzareah, Algeria; from 20 August to 12 December 1943 in La Marsa, Algeria; and with the Headquarters of the Mediterranean Allied Armed Forces from 12 December 1943 to March 1944 in Bouzareah, Algeria; from 10 March to June 1944 in Algiers, Algeria; and from 8 July 1944 to 15 April 1945 in Caserta, Italy—while stationed in Caserta, Wilder made a trip to Belgrade, Yugoslavia, on 21–28 February 1945. Among the Wilder papers is a copy of a letter of 4 February 1945 from Wilder to Marshal Josip Broz (Tito) about a possible production of *Our Town* in Belgrade. An official itinerary for this visit suggests that Wilder's was a cultural mission but gives no indication of a production of *Our Town* at that time. In a letter of 3 April 1945 to the American Consul in Belgrade, Wilder authorizes translation and future productions of the play.

4. Jed Harris had directed a two-week revival of *Our Town* that opened in New York's City Center on 10 January 1944. Frank Craven was to have repeated his role as the Stage Manager, but at the last minute he could not rearrange his Hollywood schedule. On five days' notice, the playwright and director Marc Connelly was persuaded to learn the role. Martha Scott, Evelyn Varden, and Doro Merande from the original cast returned to repeat their roles. George Gibbs was played by Montgomery Clift, who had played Henry Antrobus in *The Skin of Our Teeth*. Because of wartime problems, Harris was not able to bring his production to London until 1 May 1946. In it Marc Connelly again played the Stage Manager. (See Connelly's "Notes on a Possible Retirement," in the *New York Times*, 16 January 1944, II, 1.)

In June 1944, a noncommercial version by members of the American Armed Forces was presented in London and in Edinburgh with Joan Young, an English actress, as Emily Webb.

Wilder prepared a production of *Our Town* for the Allied Force Headquarters Theatre Club in Caserta, which played for twelve nights beginning 27 November 1944. He worked with the company for five weeks and then turned over the direction to M.Sgt. Lester Martin Kuehl, who had been in Jed Harris's Pacific Coast production, "for two more weeks of final polishing and knitting-together" (237). Sgt. John Hobart, who before the war had been a drama critic for the *San Francisco Chronicle*, played the Stage Manager and later wrote about the production, "Grover's Corners, Italy," in *Theatre Arts*, April 1945, 234–39.

To Gertrude Stein and Alice Toklas, Culoz, France

[?16–30 September 1944]   Lt. Col. Thornton Wilder
                                                              A C HQ MAAF
                                                              APO 650
                                                              U.S. Army

Dearest Gertrude and Alice:

                        Perhaps this will reach you in a few days.

    I hope I may follow it before long.

    Love, lots of love.

    I read *Wars I Remember*—by a kind of miraculous chance a fellow officer had a copy for a few hours in his tent.[1]

    Wonderful "To hear again that well-remembered voice."[2]

    Joe Still who may be putting these lines in your hands is my very good friend,—scold him and spoil him as you've always done me.[3]

                  Love, lots of love
                    Thornton[4]

1. Frank Gervasi, on his way back to the United States, passed through Caserta, Italy, where the manuscript was examined by the field censor, possibly the fellow officer Wilder mentions. Wilder read the manuscript, on which someone had written, "Liberation of Gertrude Stein by Gertrude Stein c/o Colliers Weekly—New York" and wrote on the title page, "To Whom it may concern: Miss Stein's original title 'WARS I REMEMBER' is far more appropriate to this work than the title placed here by the P.R. Officers. I have read every word and submit that there is nothing to which a censor could object.   Thornton Wilder, Lt Col./Hq. MAAF Sept. 16." The manuscript is stamped "Passed Field Press Censor" on page 1 (see typescript in NYPL-Special Collections).

2. Here Wilder perhaps echoes the letter of 18–22 July 1818 from Keats to Benjamin Bailey. As so often, he unconsciously paraphrases and varies the passage, which he himself marks, in a quotation. Writing home on 30 September about *Wars*, whose speedy publication he anticipated, Wilder added an astute comment: "It's very charming and very interesting to see that at intervals the sufferings of the war wrung a dismayed exclamation from her; great voluntarist that she is, she has never accorded to invidual suffering the recognition it deserves in the 'picture' of life. It is there to 'surprise' her."

3. Dr. Joseph Still, attached to the same command headquarters as Wilder, was undertaking a mission into France that required changing trains in Culoz.

4. The awkwardness and stiffness of this first letter since 25 March 1942 cannot be explained by the fact that Wilder was under the constraint of his military position. His next letter, nearly a year later, 20 July 1945, is different in tone but equally awkward. At the end of the war and after he returned home, Wilder found it difficult to resume contact with some close friends, though he did not abandon all correspondence. Sibyl Colefax was concerned about him, and Isabel Wilder kept in touch with her, describing his condition in several letters. One acknowledged the ear infection and continued, "[A] fatigue so great that he will be many more months overcoming that. . . . He is weary to some inner

core of being . . . not functioning like a normal person; not even able to delegate work . . . a terrible restlessness" (carbon, 23 July 1946, YCAL). The irregular flow of letters at the end of the war is in large part a result of difficulties given by the war situation rather than by personal relationships. Stein answered both Isabel's and Thornton's letters but then perhaps waited to hear from him. Some letters may have gone astray. The longer the silence lasted, the more Stein and Toklas felt confused and hurt. Two months after Stein's death, in his condolence letter to Toklas of 8 October 1946, he made an attempt to bridge the silence.

To Thornton Wilder, Caserta, Italy

[? October 1944][1]   Culoz, Ain, France

My dear dear darling Thorny, to think it is a lieutenant colonel, and an authority on aviation, well did I ever, no I never did, bless you Thornton, we can't believe it, Alice and I kept saying over and over again, I can't believe it, and we can't we just can't, our own little Thorny, a lieutenant colonel, in the great american army, bless him, well here we are and there was lots of it, and [Joseph] Still is awfully nice and he will tell you all about it, how we have talked and talked, wonderful days we have had and such a lot to tell, do you know whether the ms. got over to America and is there any way I can have news from Bennett Cerf, they all know about us but there seems no way of our hearing from them,[2] and the Kiddy, well you write to him and tell him, oh bless you Thornton dear Thornton come over to us soon, we are a mission a really mission do come over to us soon, bless you and bless you again

always
Gtrde.

[Alice Toklas]

We are so happy so overjoyed to know that you are so near and you just must come—not hope but come at once—because we must see you here and then in Paris.[3] Just one question does being a Lt. Col. make a difference—or are you just more than ever our boy dear Thornie. Well any way we are yours. Your friend is so nice but he won't remember all the messages so here's one

all my love
Alice

1. This letter was delivered by Still to Wilder, in an envelope addressed by Stein "Lieutenant Colonel Thornton Wilder/United States Army." At the top Wilder later identified it "Gertrude Stein" but did not date it. We know that on 29 November 1944, Wilder wrote home, "Joe Still is back not having got to that capital after all" (YCAL), and in a letter to Stein and Toklas dated 10 October 1944 (YCAL), Joe Still had written, "Henry and I enjoyed recalling the stories you & the mayor [Justin Rey, mayor of Culoz] told us and later had the pleasure of recounting some of them to Thornton apparently several we heard in your house were not included in 'Wars I Remember.'"

"Your order to Thornton concerning his 'mission' has been transmitted & he promises to carry it out if only he can get his right hand to forget what" (the conclusion of this letter has not been located).

2. Stein on 2 September gave Frank Gervasi the typescript of "Wars I Remember," published as *Wars I Have Seen*. Believing that he was returning directly to the United States, she cabled Bennett Cerf from Voiron on 3 September that she was sending the manuscript. Not knowing Gervasi's itinerary and not hearing from Cerf, she contacted Capt. Peter Rhodes, a U.S. information officer in Lyon whose Paris office cabled Cerf. On 12 November 1944 (YCAL) a reply came to William R. Tyler, deputy director of the Office of War Information in Paris, which was forwarded to Stein in care of René Tavernier, Delegation d'Information in Lyon: "Peter Rhodes asked me to cable New York to find out what was being done by Bennett Cerf about 'Wars I Have Seen.'

"I am happy to bring you the answer received by cable as follows:

" 'Please notify Gertrude Stein that manuscript of book *Wars I Have Seen* is in hand and will be published in a few months. Furthermore Collier's have bought two instalments for two thousand dollars.' " On 17 November, in a tone that suggests she had not yet received his cable of 12 November, Stein wrote to Cerf that she expected to be back in Paris in three weeks and asked for his publishing plans. On 23 November she again cabled. Cerf replied on 27 November that he was publishing the book and had thought the Office of War Information had given her the details (Cerf to Stein, Columbia-R.H.; Stein to Cerf, YCAL).

3. The precise day of Stein's return to Paris in mid-December is difficult to determine. In her letter of 17 November to Cerf she speaks of returning to Paris in "three weeks." Toklas wrote to Katherine Dudley, an old friend in Paris, on 13 November 1944, "For with—as I commenced to say—with all you are doing, we'll be coming back as soon as we can get things in order, in less than a month I hope" (Leon Katz's transcription, YCAL). A letter of 14 November from Dudley details the Gestapo's entry into the apartment and repairs in anticipation of their return (see Gallup, *Flowers*, 370–71).

In an article titled "We Are Back In Paris," published in 1945 in *Transformation Three*, Stein wrote of their return, "And so we made up our minds to come, to come back the middle of December. It was cold, and there were floods, and we had to have a camion and a taxi, a wood burning one, and we had to pack, and we did not know whether to bring up everything we had accumulated in those five years or to give them away, and finally we decided to bring up almost everything, and we did, luckily we did.

"We in the taxi were to start earlier, that is to say at midnight, and the camion later, that is to say at day-break, and we started" (see Schimanski, in bibliography). Lewis Gannett in "Gertrude Stein Returns to Paris; Nazis Looted Home but Left Art" (*New York Herald Tribune*, 29 December 1944, 1, 5) is also vague about when Stein returned. In her letter of support of Bernard Faÿ, addressed to Maître Chresteil on 14 March 1946, Stein writes that she returned to Paris on 15 December 1944 (YCAL).

1945

Stein after her return to the Rue Christine apartment, with copies of *Confluences* and *Fontaine*, two of the journals in which she published during the war

Isabel Wilder: To Gertrude Stein, Paris, France

10 May [19]45   [50 Deepwood Drive
New Haven, Connecticut]

Dear Gertrude,

Thank you so much for your note.[1] I think you must have heard from Thornton by now. We have not seen him but he is in this country, in Miami. He telephoned Sunday evening. For 4 weeks we expected him. Then it was all off, then on. The last week it was on again. So we waited every day. Now he is here, many states away; held at the air base by medical exams etc. It will be a fortnight in all before he darkens our door. So many people will have seen him first. He will have seen lots of faces, friends & strangers, shaken hands, kissed cheeks, laughed & told his best stories. He will not be a brand new soldier straight from Wars with that awe-inspiring & even frightening aura around him. But of course, to us, he will be new & strange & although he will have seen so many & told so much, we will have to inspire him to think & feel he has just landed, & has arrived at last at home. I've cleaned the house so many times & then it stubbornly got dirty again. We've put off eating this & that dish "until Thornton comes,"—we've remade a pretty hat for mamma, & sewed fine seams, & he stays amid the sun beams & oranges & heaven knows what else of the charms of Florida. I thought of you especially on the 8th,[2] tried to think what it would feel like to be there, on the soil of France on the day of peace in Europe.

Thornton must have written you he will soon be there near you. It is not a job he should be doing. It is a job he can do, & do very well, but he will not be an expert doing it on technique & so thus having a part of himself safe & inviolate within. He does it like the amateur actor or craftsman, from the toes up, with the [?fixed] breath, the extra hearty gesture, the too loud cordiality to cover up the self consciousness of feeling his inadequacies. So you & Alice must take great & good care of him. Don't let him hurt & strain himself. He can say no or neglect a friend, but to the stranger, the pushing mercilessly stranger he is vulnerable. As a private person & in his public office he is exposed to the 2nd & 3rd & 4th class persons. So please you & Alice take care of him.[3]

I am reading your new book. It is wonderful & your voice speaking so clear makes you seem not so far away although at the same time you speak of things & events from a background of war that is so very unknown.[4]

May we soon be having one more day of final victory. And then let's us exchange recipes again.

Mother joins me in warm greetings to you & Alice.

With affection, too,

Isabel (Wilder)

1. We have not located Stein's note.
2. VE Day.
3. Writing from Caserta, Italy, on 3 March, Wilder had alerted his family, "The State Department has found a job and requested my services" (YCAL). The official letter appointing him cultural relations attaché in the American Foreign Service at the American embassy in Paris was received in Caserta on 11 April. It was a post for which he had been recommended by Assistant Secretary of State Archibald MacLeish. Wilder expected that when he finished his service with the Mediterranean Allied Armed Forces he would take up his new assignment. Confusion between the War Department and the State Department delayed the orders for almost a month. Having trained his replacement, Wilder was at liberty for the first time since May 1943. On 16 April he left for a brief stay on Capri and wrote home on 20 April 1945, "In the meantime waiting could not be more attractively passed than on Capri in Spring. It's an air force rest camp and the combat crews in rotation come here for about a week in rotation and talking with them is the best part of my stay here." On 24 April he cabled home, "ORDERS DELAYED AM WELL LOVE." On 30 April, he wrote about the confusion in his orders: "You must be mighty surprised. There's a long story that I'll tell you some day if I won't have forgotten it, about a cable that was sent requesting my orders to be issued by the War Dept; weeks later it was found that the cable had never been sent but was lying in the cable section through someone's oversight—that mishap got mixed up with another as to whether because of my illness I should go by boat or by air, which produced further contradictions and misunderstandings; the whole probably further complicated by the fact that the State Dept doesn't want me to go home at all, but to hurry on to Paris—with the result that I'm hurrying nowhere.

"In the meantime I am the recipient of more goodbye parties until I blush to show my face. Delayed orders, however, are frequent in this world. My official appointment to Paris has arrived and I'm eager to set at the work." Wilder finally arrived in Miami Beach, Florida, on 6 May, but because of formalities he did not leave for New Haven until 23 May. For the next several weeks his letters home speak about his eagerness to assume the State Department assignment.

By the summer, however, Wilder seemed less eager to accept the appointment. On 18 August 1945, while on a trip from New Haven to Miami Beach, Florida, where he thought his final orders of separation would be issued, he would write in a postscript to a letter to his family, "On V-J + II [16 August] I called at the State Dept. which was all but empty and happened to find Archie Macl[eish]. in his office. Very cordial. He begged me to go to Paris—could find no one else—but I told him I was a shattered man, as you well know." In her "Foreword" to *The Alcestiad*, Isabel Wilder wrote, "[L]ike millions of other soldiers, he had returned home not only a disoriented and exhausted man but a changed one" (xii). (Wilder's letters to his family are in YCAL.)

4. Random House published *Wars I Have Seen* on 6 March 1945. The "Epilogue," not part of the original manuscript, was brought to New York by Capt. Peter Rhodes of the Office of War Information

in either October or November 1944. Following the completion of *Wars I Have Seen*, Stein began work on a play about France during the occupation. *In Savoy* (the title was changed to *Yes Is For A Very Young Man* at the suggestion of Norma Chambers, an actress traveling with a USO company who had read the play). According to Donald Gallup, "The play in its original form was either already complete when Gertrude and Alice returned to Paris on December 15, 1944, or finished very shortly afterwards, for I remember that Gertrude mentioned it when I first went to see her on January 5, 1945, and I know that I read it in its then complete form in the manuscript notebook which is now at Yale when I went to rue Christine for the second time on January 12, 1945" (Stein, *Last Operas*, xiv). The last scene of the play, in "preview" form, was published in the *Saturday Review of Literature*, 5 May 1945, 5–7. Plans for a production of the play at the American Army University at Biarritz were canceled when Stein learned that it was to be a workshop production without scenery and performed before a specially invited audience (see Toklas to Van Vechten, 12 November 1946, YCAL). Stein entrusted the play to Lamont Johnson, an actor who was touring with a USO company of *Kind Lady*. Johnson worked with Stein on revising the play for production. *Yes Is For A Very Young Man* was produced for the first time at the Pasadena (California) Playhouse on 13 March 1946 (see Stein, *Last Operas*, xii–xiii).

From the time of her return to Paris in December 1944 until her death in July 1946, Stein wrote very little. She wrote essays describing her return to Paris, her encounters with new painters, her flying trip to Germany, her observations on American soldiers, her thoughts on fashion, her opinion on the painter Raul Dufy, and a series of meditations and reflections, including "Reflection On The Atomic Bomb." The two full-length works from this period are *Brewsie And Willie* and the libretto *The Mother Of Us All*. *Brewsie And Willie*, a record of her encounters and conversations with American soldiers and nurses, was begun in August 1945 (see C. L. Sulzberger, *New York Times*, 25 August 1945, 13). The book was published by Random House on 22 July 1946. Stein's last full-length work was *The Mother Of Us All*, a libretto for Virgil Thomson, who had been commissioned by the Alice M. Ditson Fund of Columbia University to write an opera. Stein and Thomson met in Paris in October 1945 and worked out details of the libretto based on the life and struggles of Susan B. Anthony. Stein completed the libretto by March 1946; the opera had its world premiere at Brander Matthews Hall, Columbia University, on 7 May 1947.

To Gertrude Stein and Alice Toklas, Paris, France

20 July 1945   50 Deepwood Drive
                                                                     Hamden 14, Connecticut

Angels ever Bright and Fair:
                    Greetings, Selah, and Mizpah.
    It may have been reported to you that I was arriving in Paris momently to be Attaché at the Embassy. It's all off. The doctors say I must take 6 months' to a year's rest. My picture of the job consisted mostly of hugging, kissing, and question-asking in the rue Christine. So that's all postponed.
    What's my sickness? I don't know. Everything and nothing. It's like the ol' hoss shay.[1] Anyway, let's not talk about it for more than an hour at a stretch. There's nothing organic the matter. There's nothing that a revolver can't cure. So as soon as I get out of the Army I'm going to Colorado to write a mess of plays.

You may have wondered, dears, why all this silence from me.

Have I given up letter-writing?

Oh, no, I write 'em east, west, south, and north.

Have I forgotten Gertralicitude?

No, no, they're the fixed love in my heart.

Then why?

Dears, those *others* are located in time and place. They must be answered. They must be provoked to answers. They must be dealt with, they must be propaganda-ized.

But my loved Algertrudicé is always there, wise, sweet, and unhurried. If I should die or if she should die I would be vexed but not frustrated. She's always there and I'm always here.

My next play will make a lot of money. About the hundredth performance I'm publishing *Four in America* at my own expense. Beautiful printing, beautiful margins. Gertrude may have other *inédits* she prefers, but that's the one *I've caught up to* and I think it's wonderful. Such law (I said: law) such wit and grace, such beauty, such plummet lines to such fathoms, such cha-a-a-rm. For a while I thought of doing a foreword to lend a hand to Bennett Cerf and Bobbsy [Goodspeed] and the Joneses; but no! damn the public: it must be my fair copy, all gold. I almost forgot to say that *you* could have copies, too. The reason that I forgot was—as I've just said—that you are like Constellations, always there. Do Constellations read their own works? do they care what becomes of their radiant works?

So: you see how little I have to say: and how that little gets in the way of what I have to convey:

love and dreams

Thorny

1. Wilder compares himself to the sturdily built one-horse chaise—the Deacon's masterpiece in the poem of the same name by Oliver Wendell Holmes. It lasted exactly one hundred years and then in one spill totally disintegrated. We have found no precise medical information regarding Wilder's health at this time. When he began the required medical examinations at various redistribution stations prior to his discharge, Wilder was forty-eight years old. The only time that he had been hospitalized during his military service was for an abscessed eardrum following his return from Yugoslavia in February 1945. Wilder, in letters written at this time, spoke only in vague terms about psychic and physical exhaustion.

Isabel Wilder: To Gertrude Stein, Paris, France

31 July [19]45   [50 Deepwood Drive
                                                        Hamden 14, Connecticut]

Dear Gertrude,

We read in the paper that you were on a most exciting trip, the cargo of a C-47 & the delightful travelling companion of a group of GI's. Thornton was green with envy. Me too.[1]

T. has written you all his news. I can only add that it is for the best that he is not going to Paris. He is still far from well, though his improvement is notic[e]able. Now if he can only get discharged from the Army & have 3 months or 6 to write his play, he will be a whole man again. To do his own work for a year on end will cure him, nothing else.[2]

We, mother & I, have had glorious weeks with Thornton here, the first real sight of him in 3 whole years. Such laughings, & arguments, & eatings, & loungings around. It's been wonderful & it means having a home again. If there is a man in the family you have to have him around once in a while to make your home a home and as you know Thornton is much more than an ornament where his shadow falls. He's the bones & flesh of the walls he inhabits. So for many weeks now we've been privileged characters. Oh, I wrote for a *special purpose* & here's the last page! I have 2 little food parcels packed for you & Alice. I was about to mail them, when T. said, "no, they may be in Paris, they may be in Culoz, write & ask where to send the packages."[3] A line in a letter to T. or a post card with an address to any of us will do.

    With love to you & Alice.
                                    Isabel

1. At the invitation of *Life*, Stein and Toklas left Paris on 19 June for a five-day tour of Germany and Austria. Stein wrote of the trip in "Off We All Went To See Germany," *Life* 19, 6 (6 August 1945): 54–58. The article comments on Germans and Germany and, like her article of 3 June 1945, "The New Hope In Our 'Sad Young Men,'" *New York Times Magazine* (5, 38), gives her observations on the servicemen she met.

2. Like many returning soldiers, Wilder learned the meaning of "Hurry up and wait." When his orders did come, they were to return to the United States for discharge and then to assume his State Department assignment. Wilder arrived in Miami Beach, Florida, on 6 May. For the next four months he traveled between New Haven, New York, Washington, D.C., and Miami Beach until he was officially discharged from the military at Camp Devens, near Ayer, Massachusetts, on 19 September 1945, having begun his service on 24 June 1942.

The play is *The Alcestiad*. Wilder began making notes for a play about Alcestis in the summer of 1938 while waiting for Max Reinhardt to begin his production of *The Merchant of Yonkers*. He worked on it intermittently in 1939, at the same time that he was beginning *The Skin of Our Teeth*, eventually laying it aside. He tried to return to it in 1942, but complications with the production and casting of *The Skin of Our Teeth* and his decision to work with Alfred Hitchcock on *Shadow of a Doubt* forced him to abandon his plans. In her "Foreword" to the play, Isabel Wilder writes, "The morning that Mother and I said goodbye to him he patted his bulging duffle bag. 'I have the manuscript of *The*

Alcestiad in my kit. I've been thinking how I could make it into a good one-act. It's very possible by using just the big second act scene.'" (xi–xii).

The play occupied him between June 1942 and May 1943, but once he left for active duty in North Africa, it was put aside. Almost immediately upon his return to the United States, in May 1945, he began working on *The Alcestiad* and on his novel *The Ides of March*. From Miami Beach, Florida, he wrote home on 12 May, "My thoughts are getting very civilian—I've thought up lots on that Julius Caesar novel and I go down to the Public Library here and read up on my dramatis personae." On 20 May, again from Miami Beach, he wrote about *The Alcestiad*: "All I can say for myself is that I've begun writing the Second Act of The Alcestiad, but it's not coming along very well."

Over the next few months, while he awaited his discharge, Wilder alternated between the play and the novel. In an undated letter from Florida, probably written in either June or July, he announced to his family that a "Horrible thing happened today. My play went dead on me. Tripe. Let's not talk about it."

According to Isabel Wilder, in September while he was waiting to be separated from the military at Camp Devens, his notebooks for the play were lost: "The commanding officer of the post offered a three-day pass. Thornton went straight from the Back Bay station to the Boston Public Library on Copley Square, where he drowned himself once more in the Golden Age of Greece" (*The Alcestiad*, xii). From Ponte Vedra, Florida, on 8 November 1945, having rewritten early sections from memory, he reported, "I'm sitting here in my kitchenette (sic) which has a table just suitable for my needs and where I put in many hours work yesterday and today. I've finished the second act and the scene between Hercules and Admetus is some scene believe you me, and of course the act's ending will leave an audience weak. They'd better smoke a cigarette and pull themselves together because Act III opens with a scene that does not allow the attention to wander or the eye to dry."

A few days later, on 11 November, he reported, "The cast of Alcestiad is getting bigger and bigger—!! like Ben Hur. I can't help it." But on 17 November, from Brunswick, Georgia, where he had stopped for a few days on his way back to New Haven, he wrote his sister, "I was galloping through my Act III when I suddenly had a revulsion. I knew I was writing straight melodrama and not maintaining the air of mystery that's got to hang over every minute of the play." On 20 November, still in Brunswick, all he could report to his family was that, "Monotony's horrible. But the play is profiting by it and that's all that matters." However, the next day he wrote to his sister Isabel; "Now a funny thing has happened.

"I was writing The Alcestiad too fast. I'm not a fast writer. It dictates itself to me, in little spurts of its own choosing, and my pushing and pushing doesn't do any good. It merely means I rewrite and rewrite.

"But The Alcestiad is all right. It's *there* and will be finished in its own time. But it won't be ready to submit to anyone until the late Spring for Fall showing." Wilder continued, "So just for fun, I began the Caesar-Clodia-Catullus-Cicero novel in letters. There's quite a lot of it already. Part of it is sheer fun; parts of it are, of course, the hardest writing I've ever done—the letters between Caesar and 'Ned Sheldon' on poetry, love, religion, politics etc. To be sure I pilfer all the greatest things that have been written by anybody and stir them up with Gertrude Stein,—but they're not easy.

"Of course it's dangerous to interrupt The Alcestiad with another work. It's a thing I've never done before, but for the present I take the sign of my enjoyment as a sign that all's well.

"The letter-form is intensely readable. The pages crackle with diversity: Clodia directing her steward on the preparation of a banquet; dowagers exchanging gossip; frantic love letters; meditative essays; Cicero being elegant; Caesar's wife being a little goose."

The Ides of March, dedicated to two friends, Lauro De Bosis and Edward Sheldon, was published by Harper and Brothers in March 1948. Wilder did not return to *The Alcestiad* until 18 September 1953. The play was first performed, with the title *A Life in the Sun*, at the Church of Scotland Assembly Hall, The Mound, Edinburgh, on 22 August 1955 as part of the Edinburgh Festival. Tyrone Guthrie directed, and the roles of Alcestis and Admetus were played by Irene Worth and Robert Hardy. (Isabel Wilder discusses the composition of the play in her "Foreword" to *The Alcestiad*, ix to xxi; see also Wilder, *Journals*, 186–88. Wilder's letters to his family are in YCAL.)

3. Stein was in Paris.

1946

Alice Toklas at Chartres, 8 October 1949, photographed by Carl Van Vechten

Gertrude Stein in the studio at Rue de Fleurus, 1920

To Alice Toklas, Paris, France

8 October 1946
50 Deepwood Drive
Hamden 14, Connecticut

Dear Alice:

These last weeks, in whatever company I've been in, I've silenced the aimless talk that goes on in order to tell them about Gertrude, about the several Gertrudes, the Gertrude who with zest and vitality could make so much out of every moment of the daily life, the Gertrude who listened to each new person with such attention and could make out of her listening such rich reinforcing friendship, the Gertrude of intellectual combat who couldn't let any nonsense or sentimentality or easy generalization go by unpunished, and finally the greatest Gertrude of all, the inspired giant-Gertrude who *knew*, and who *discovered* and who broke the milestones behind her.[1]

Oh, miserable me, I lost my mother this summer.[2] I haven't a right sense of time. I've lived as though I assumed that we'd have these infinitely treasurable people always with us. I never foresee their not being there. It may be that this makes my losses twice as cutting, but I think it has one consolation: while they were alive I had them really as a possession, *I didn't feel them as temporary.* My Gertrude is always there, as she was there before I knew her. Which is to say: always here.

My poignant self-reproach at not having written her is acute. It doesn't help that I remember that she taught me how all those audience-activities—"articles," letter-writing, and conversation itself are impure at the source,—but oh! that I had at least sent her signs and signals of my ever-deeper love and indebtedness.

At the time of her death, so soon after my mother's, I was booked up with engagements acting in my plays in the summer theatres.[3] I was unable in that stupefying work to write an adequate a half-adequate article for one of the weekly reviews,—revolted though I was at the incomprehension of their papers about her. Again, this unmarked sense of time came into play—that *someday* when I had realized fully her loss and had penetrated still further into the greatness of her achievement I should write what I remembered and what I had come to grasp.

During the War I was not exposed to any particular danger or even tension; I have no right, compared to my friends in combat, to claim any long slow and difficult readjustment; but nevertheless that's what I've been undergoing. I seem only now to be emerging from a long torpor and misanthropy and paralysis of the will. My outward health soon recovered—the disabilities that prevented my fulfilling the appointment to the Embassy in Paris—but the psychological effects have dragged on for a long time.

I do not know whether this silence and "absence" led Gertrude to believe that the literary executorship of her work would better be transferred to another person. If she felt so, I would very well understand it. If, however, she wished me to assume it I am as eager as ever and I hope as efficient. I mention it because I have interested the editors of the Yale University Press in a possible publication of *Four in America* which seems to me one of her most significant as well as her most charming works. It is the one I dreamed of publishing myself "the next time I made some money." My money-making capabilities have slowed down, along with the rest of me, and if this turns out to be a real offer of publication I think it should be accepted. In whose hands would you like to place the negotiations?[4]

I have not said anything, dearest Alice, about the loneliness you must be feeling. All I can say is: WASN'T IT WONDERFUL TO HAVE KNOWN AND LOVED HER? What glory! What fun! What goodness! What loveableness!

Everything one can say falls short of it. Some day before long I shall try to put all that down in words as carefully chosen as I can choose them—in the meantime she grows in my mind and heart and realization. Her greatness in the larger world has scarcely begun yet; long after you and I are dead she will be becoming clearer and clearer as the great thinker and the great soul of our time.

With much love, dear Alice
much love
Thornton

1. On 19 July 1946, Stein and Toklas, in a car driven by Joseph Barry, a young GI they had met in Paris who had stayed on, left rue Christine for Le Prieure St. Martin, the country home of Bernard Faÿ in Luceaux (Sarthe). Barry stayed with them a day or two and, before returning to Paris, took them on a drive to Azay-le-Rideau, "where [they] had once considered buying a home. The lovely house had been sold and the château no longer had its park of woods about it" (Toklas, *What Is Remembered*, 172). Stein became so ill that they spent the night at a local inn, where she was examined by a doctor. The next day she, Toklas, and Barry returned by train to Paris, where they were met by an ambulance,

arranged for by Stein's nephew Allan Stein. Stein was taken to the American Hospital in Neuilly, and on 23 July she made out her will. In the afternoon of Saturday, 27 July, she underwent surgery for cancer and during the operation lapsed into a coma and died. In her will she named Toklas and Allan Stein as executors and instructed them to provide Carl Van Vechten, her literary executor, "[S]uch sum of money as . . . [he] shall, in his own absolute discretion deem necessary for the publication of my unpublished manuscripts."

2. Isabella Niven Wilder had died of cancer on the morning of 29 June 1946 in Nantucket, Massachusetts, where she was vacationing.

3. Wilder appeared as the Stage Manager in *Our Town* at the Westport (Connecticut) Country Playhouse from 5 to 10 August. He played Mr. Antrobus in *The Skin of Our Teeth* with the South Shore Players in Cohasset, Massachusetts, from 19 to 24 August and then played the Stage Manager in *Our Town* at the John Drew Memorial Theatre, East Hampton, Long Island, from 26 to 31 August.

4. With an introduction by Thornton Wilder that was the condition for publication and a "Note on the Manuscript" by Donald Gallup, *Four In America* was published by Yale University Press on 21 October 1947.

William G. Rogers on his first visit to Stein after reading the *Autobiography* and discovering himself in it as one of the doughboys of the Great War, Bilignin, May 1934

Appendix I.

Gertrude Stein's American Lecture Tour
Introduction by William Rice

By July of 1934 when Gertrude Stein had decided to undertake her tour, she was already a celebrity in America. Beginning with the serial publication of *The Autobiography Of Alice B. Toklas* in *The Atlantic Monthly*, from May to July of 1933, through *Time* magazine's cover-story review of the book in September of that year and the production of *Four Saints In Three Acts* in February 1934, scarcely a month went by without comment in the literary or the popular press. As she writes in *Everybody's Autobiography*, her first reaction to fame was one of shock and disbelief: "Nothing inside me needed to be written" (66), and she was unable to write for nearly a year. What short pieces she did write, including *Blood On The Dining Room Floor*, did not satisfy her.

Her agent, William A. Bradley, had successfully negotiated with Harcourt Brace the sale of the *Autobiography* and, by the spring of 1934, was pressing her to lecture in America. Stein was resistant and, when Bradley went so far as to book a tour without her consent with the Colston Leigh Agency, she dismissed him as her agent and canceled the tour.

William G. Rogers, whom she had met as a doughboy in France during World War I, had renewed his friendship with Stein in April 1934, after reading the *Autobiography* and seeing the Hartford premiere of *Four Saints*. Meeting him again after many years, Stein was impressed with him as a serious journalist and consulted him about what she might expect if she were to tour. As a newspaper man, Stein felt, Rogers was more in touch with American popular sentiment and could gauge reactions better than other friends, for example, Sherwood Anderson and Carl Van Vechten, who were also encouraging her to visit. By July, she not only decided to tour but began writing the lectures.

Stein enlisted Marvin Chauncey Ross, an art historian and a friend of Faÿ, to plan with Rogers the preliminary arrangements for the tour. Faÿ had also advised Stein to get in touch with Bobsy Goodspeed in Chicago as a connection to President Robert Hutchins of the University of Chicago. That summer Stein met Goodspeed through Fanny Butcher, a Chicago journalist who had visited Stein in 1931. Butcher wrote Stein on 9 July about the possibilities for lecturing in Chicago.

Bennett Cerf had become Stein's publisher in 1934 when *Three Lives* was printed in his new Modern Library series in September of that year. On the strength of its popularity—it was for a time the Modern Library's best-seller—he encouraged Stein to tour, offered to do advance publicity and proposed a collection of portraits, eventually entitled *Portraits And Prayers*, to coincide with her visit. Harcourt Brace, publishers of the *Autobiography*, had issued the short version of *The Making Of Americans* with an introduction by Bernard Faÿ that spring.

Throughout the tour Stein and Cerf were in touch, and Cerf, concerned that she was getting only local publicity, organized her coast-to-coast broadcast of 12 November. He also undoubtedly helped arrange her appearance on Pathé News, shown in movie theaters across the country. The hastily written notes for "Pathé," filmed on her first day in New York City, give an overview of her lectures and emphasize Stein's confidence in a reader's ability to understand her work. Never before published, "Pathé" is included in this appendix. In the summer of 1934, Stein had enlisted James Laughlin to make synopses of the lectures for publicity, and William Rogers also scripted abbreviated versions to pass out to the media. "Pathé" may have been based on these versions, which have apparently not survived. On the surviving film clip, it is reduced to one minute and ten seconds of playing time.

Prior to her first big lecture at the Colony Club on 1 November—to the members of the Museum of Modern Art—Stein, uneasy about facing a large, formal New York audience, asked Carl Van Vechten whether she might ease herself into lecturing by addressing a small group. Van Vechten asked Prentiss Taylor, a young artist friend, to arrange for an appropriate audience. Taylor spoke to Mrs. John W. Alexander, the well-connected widow of the painter, and with her planned an evening at her apartment at 170 East 78th Street, on Tuesday, 30 October at 9 P.M., for invited guests selected with "discrimination and tact" to hear Stein's lecture, "Plays."

A detailed account of that appearance survives in a letter from Taylor and a note to Taylor from Alexander. On 1 November, Taylor wrote to his mother,

> We had only fifty seats & by Wednesday of last week were refusing right & left. By Tuesday evening I was both fed up and delighted. The delight won completely after that. Carl [Van Vechten] brought Miss Stein and Miss Toklas. Miss Stein in a plain coat and the hat that a gangplank reporter described as out of Robin Hood's forest & Miss Toklas in something that was gathered about her

& that billowed. Mrs. Alexander took them to her room until things were ready & I was called in to meet them (I was ushering people in as I knew who most of them were & being a sort of host to the business. Mrs. Alexander was lurking near her door to keep people from going near it.) Miss Stein was drinking water and talking to Mrs. Alexander & she put out her hand to me without stopping either & then thanked me warmly for all I'd done. There is a first shock on finding her smaller than you expected. She has a perfect ruddy skin & her close cropped hair, her amplifying placidity, & her brown robe? dress give her a cloister air. Miss Toklas is small, with sharply modeled features, kind grey eyes & a marionette crispness. She is eager & thoughtful, very happy & anxious about all that is happening & as she stands bulwarked in a black taffeta dress she shakes a finger across her mouth to ward off anything that might deny what she wants most to do or say. I've seldom met anyone as considerate & charmingly spontaneous. First she wanted me to put the reference books on the table & then she decided she must do it, that Miss Stein must enter first, uninterrupted, alone, "Miss Stein must be all courage." However, by the time we got down the hall, Miss Stein asked me to lead her into the room, to show the way & give moral support, she said.

She read the lecture & it was not always easy to follow. Some of it was in her nearly vague style & always she uses simple words with fresh emphases that are difficult to catch as they go quickly by. She reads well & much more meaning comes out of her reading. She had much to say of her early theatre going in San Francisco & how through those observations she thought of her approach in maturity. There was considerable complicated and subtle development I couldn't begin to give you here, but most of us came away with a sympathetic approach, much more understanding. Not Mrs. Colby, she groaned I'm told & afterward was quietly scathing, but she always gauges her reactions to claim an audience for herself.

I forgot to say that on our entering the room Miss Toklas was heard by a friend of mine to say, "O she has stage fright." Other than a witty reference to nervousness & a few deep breaths there was no indication of it.

After the lecture they stayed about and talked for nearly an hour & everything had gone perfectly.

Since writing this last I've been to the first official Stein lecture. The one on pictures, for the Museum of Modern Art, at the Colony Club. I suppose because I didn't worry about how I was going to get in, it was for members only, I finally had four invitations. Miss Toklas gave me one of Miss Stein's tickets. I didn't like it in any way as well as Tuesday night. First I hate ballrooms as lecture halls. The chairs are always packed in & fussy old ladies put chairs in the already scanty aisles. The light & angle are never sympathetic. She had quite a little that was provocative and amusing to say about pictures, what constituted an oil painting, but she had less to give in it and sometimes the style seemed needlessly difficult. The audience was the maximum of course, 500, & that naturally included many who were neither sympathetic nor really interested. That is what she will come up against all along now. A man, in the question period afterward, asked her if there wasn't a similarity between her repetition & that in the RAVEN, & wasn't it the repetition in the RAVEN that made it a great poem. She laughed off the similarity & said the RAVEN was great for what it did not for its repetition.

Her charm will win her audiences and certainly many more will be convinced of her sincerity. She enjoys what she does. I think there is every reason to believe she will "go out" before a great while. Anyone as markedly of his age is bound to be a fashion, but like a family that has importantly occupied a church pew for years & then died, she will leave her memorial window. She will surely never go out completely.

In a note to Taylor of 1 November, Alexander also commented, "I think the Stein evening went off very well and I must say I am delighted to know Miss Stein and feel much more able to understand what she is trying to do since I heard her speak. I do not see, however, that she has the power to become a very popular lecturer, she will succeed this winter as a curiosity." Alexander, who was an astute observer, did not realize that Stein would indeed become a popular lecturer who drew crowds. Stein herself, limiting her audiences to five hundred or fewer, did not wish to reach larger groups.

Within a week of her arrival, problems with lecture bookings developed. Owing to a misunderstanding between Marvin Ross and Russell Potter of the Columbia University Institute of Arts and Sciences, Stein's first Columbia lecture of 2 November was oversold. Potter made new arrangements and the Columbia lectures went forward. At the Chicago premiere of *Four Saints* on 7 November Stein and Toklas discovered that Rousseau Voorhies, whom Stein had met through Bernard Faÿ in the summer of 1932, had been writing and lecturing about her in Chicago, capitalizing on their meetings. He had encouraged the university student organization to overbook and to charge for two lectures. Fanny Butcher and Bobsy Goodspeed, who in September had arranged for engagements in Chicago before the Renaissance Society and the Arts Club, helped Stein rearrange her Chicago lectures.

In his memoir, *Les Précieux*, Faÿ discusses Voorhies without naming him and acknowledges his own unwitting role in the affair. The only evidence from Stein of her reaction to the difficulties in Chicago is in a letter to Faÿ written on the flight back to New York after the *Four Saints* premiere. She dissociates herself from Voorhies and his misrepresentations, expressing anger over his having reproduced without her permission her letter to him of March 1934. On the back of the envelope Faÿ noted that he saw her the evening of her return in an uncomfortable session in her rooms at the Algonquin.

The University of Chicago student newspaper, the *Daily Maroon*, chronicled the publicity campaign organized by Voorhies and *Comment*, the student literary magazine. The magazine had sponsored a contest in which prizes would be awarded for the best composition in emulation of Stein's style. The two sold-out lectures of 27 and 28 November were canceled, but the three lectures scheduled by Fanny Butcher went ahead as planned. Later, in two articles in *Real America* of

January and February 1936, Lucille Hecht presented the Voorhies side of the story in interviews with him, a much-distorted account of his relationship with Stein and Faÿ, showing how badly he had mismanaged the Chicago lecture plans.

Voorhies was not Stein's only problem. In the summer of 1934, when she had agreed to let Marvin Ross handle the tour, she had spelled out her conditions: audiences of no more than five hundred, lectures not oftener than three times a week; a schedule allowing free time when not lecturing; no introductions; no luncheons or dinners in her honor; no tickets to benefit funds or causes; $100 fee for schools, $250 fee for clubs; mixed groups rather than women's clubs preferred. By the third week in November, when Alice Toklas had taken over management of the tour from Ross, she found correspondence in disorder, confusion over dates, and Stein's expressed wishes disregarded. In reviewing the Ross letters, Stein realized that she had been right to ask Rogers to work with him and to orchestrate press coverage for the East and the New England tour, which was a great success. When Stein immediately became first-page copy, Rogers was concerned that the often silly and belittling headlines might reinforce public misconceptions. However, he found the accounts themselves in almost all cases to be careful and accurate reporting (Rogers, *When This You See*, 96ff.).

The tours of the Midwest and the South went smoothly, and by 24 February 1935, Stein was back in Chicago, beginning to draft the *Narration* lectures. On 5 March Alice Toklas wrote Samuel Steward that Stein had written four new lectures with titles that do not appear in the published book: "The American Language and How It Is Made," "Narrative In Prose and Poetry," "Is History Narrative," and "Is History Literature." Including the Choate School lecture, "How Writing Is Written," Toklas wrote, "These five are what she will give for Texas and California, and let us hope Oregon, Washington, and Montana. I have always so much wanted Miss Stein to see the Northwest where I spent four happy years" (see Steward, *Dear Sammy*, 125). A Northwest tour did not materialize because of booking difficulties, and Stein did not follow the plan described in the Toklas letter.

Writing to Bernard Faÿ in Paris on 2 April from Pasadena, California, Stein described what would have been another lecture that she hoped to write before returning to New York later that month: "[A]bout Utopias on the one and the European situation on the other and its [?relation] to time sense and audience, that will nicely complete my series." She does not appear to have written this lecture but recalls its ideas in *Everybody's Autobiography* (88).

It is, of course, impossible to recreate the lectures themselves as they were delivered. We do know that Stein departed from her texts and often improvised at some length. Some accounts have her speaking for two hours, much longer than any given lecture as written. Carl Van Vechten, who attended her William and Mary lecture, was surprised on reading her text at how it differed from what he remembered hearing. And Toklas, in a letter to Van Vechten of 25 February 1935, said about Stein's Tulane lecture, "What Is English Literature," that the text "was discarded and hotly said" (Burns, *Letters*, 1:398).

A front-page account of her Radcliffe lecture, "Portraits And Repetition," in the *Boston Herald* of 20 November 1934 by Donald Fessenden gives a hint of how she may have departed from her written texts. Although Fessenden probably relied on hastily written or shorthand notes, he could have verified her many quotations in *Portraits And Prayers*, published on 7 November, but it is not clear that he did. He quotes in the present tense sentences written in the past. He also gives different examples of early portraits from those that are in the printed text of the lecture. "Four Dishonest Ones" is the first printed example but "Matisse" is the one Fessenden quotes as the first. In the lecture she writes, "A great many so-called intelligent people . . . mix up remembering with talking and listening." But he quotes her as saying, "The essence of intelligence is that you know it before you know it." Reading from the second Picasso portrait, Fessenden notes, "[S]he said, 'And so shutters shut, and so, and also.' She looked up and remarked coolly, 'Now you see in some mysterious way, that is more exciting than if you told what he did.' "

For the preparation of this chronology I have relied on the Stein Collection at the Beinecke library at Yale University for letters from William Rogers, Bernard Faÿ, Marvin Ross, Fanny Butcher, Elizabeth (Bobsy) Goodspeed, and Bennett Cerf. A particularly valuable source has been the William Rogers memoir, *When This You See Remember Me*. Bennett Cerf's date books in the Columbia University library were also important sources of information, as were archives of institutions where Stein spoke.

The order of the lectures in *Lectures In America* approximates the order of their composition. In a letter to Rogers of July 1934, Stein writes that she has finished "pictures" and "theatre" and is working on "English literature," then will do three about her work designed to reflect her development as a writer.

Lecture titles have been standardized to conform with the printed texts in *Lectures In America*. The titles would often vary from location to location. We have an indication of how Stein modified them when we compare the published titles with the titles Voorhies announced in the *Chicago Tribune* of 29 August 1934. Here are the lectures with some variant titles: "Portraits And Repetition" is often titled "The Conception Of Personality And Its Expression In Portraits, Poetry And *Tender Buttons*" or "Insistence And Repetition." "Poetry And Grammar," the lecture most often given on the tour, becomes "The Question Of Tenses, Grammar And Their Relation To Telling A Story." To "The Gradual Making Of *The Making Of Americans*" she added the phrase "And Its Gradual Change Into Something Else." "Pictures" was also announced as "Pictures, That Is, Paintings, And What They Mean To Me." "What Is English Literature" also appears as "The History Of English Literature As I Understand It" or "As I See It." "Plays," the lecture the least often given, sometimes became "Plays And What They Are."

In *What Is Remembered* (143) Toklas notes that when the reporters on the S.S. *Champlain* asked Stein if she had come to instruct America, she said, "Never, no, I have come to see and hear as well as to talk." The American lecture tour left Stein with an experience of success and acceptance more profound than anything she had dared hope for. It confirmed that she mattered in ways she had never known when in isolation she wrote the great texts of early literary modernism; this new popularity was not incompatible with writing that was perfectly clear to her, though many failed to comprehend it. To Rogers in August 1934 she wrote, "Lectures are for a pretty intelligent audience and though they are clear very clear, they are not too easy."

Of the many newspaper clippings she kept, only one has notations in Stein's hand. In an interview with no byline in the *Springfield Union* (Massachusetts) of 16 January 1935, the journalist noted that Stein had bought some paintings of snow scenes by a Vermont artist and misquoted the number as fourteen. Stein carefully corrected it to four. She was reportedly asked if there were any contemporary American painters equal to European painters of the past; Stein changed the word "past" to "present."

Stein and Toklas preserved not only memories but mementos of the tour; these remain in the Stein Collection. Their later letters to many friends returned to the American tour again and again with recollection never dulled by the years.

CHRONOLOGY

OCTOBER 1934

Wednesday 24   Stein arrives in New York on the S.S. *Champlain*. Greeted by W. G. Rogers, Carl Van Vechten, Bennett Cerf, and Alan Blackburn of the Museum of Modern Art. Joseph Alsop interview for the *New York Herald Tribune* published unsigned on 25 October.

Evening: Filmed by Pathé News in her suite at the Algonquin Hotel. Dinner with Fania Marinoff and Carl Van Vechten at their apartment, 150 West 55 Street.

Thursday 25   Visit to publishers Harcourt Brace and Random House. Lunch with Carl Van Vechten at the Algonquin.

Friday 26   Lunch at the Van Vechtens.

Evening: See Fania Marinoff performing in Elmer Rice's *Judgment Day*.

Saturday 27   Pathé film released to theaters.

Tuesday 30   "Plays," before an invited audience at the home of Mrs. John W. Alexander, 170 East 78th Street, 9 P.M.

Wednesday 31   Party for Stein at Random House given by Cerf.

NOVEMBER 1934

Thursday 1   Accounts differ about their stopping at the Gotham Book Mart and meeting Frances Steloff.

"Pictures," to members of the Museum of Modern Art, ballroom of the Colony Club, 9 P.M.

Friday 2   Meets Alexander Woollcott at luncheon given by Cerf.

"The Gradual Making Of *The Making Of Americans*," to members of the Institute of Arts and Sciences, Columbia University, McMillin Academic Theatre, 8:30 P.M.

Saturday 3   Photo session with Carl Van Vechten in his apartment which continues into the next day.

Interview with Laurie Eglington published in *Art News*.

Sunday 4   Stein and Toklas dine at the Van Vechtens and listen to Woollcott's broadcast, which mentions Stein.

Monday 5   Evening: "The Gradual Making," McCosh Auditorium, Princeton University, sponsored by the Spencer Trask Fund.

Tuesday 6   "Poetry And Grammar," New School for Social Research.

Wednesday 7   *Portraits And Prayers* published by Random House.

An abbreviated version of "The Gradual Making," to the Committee on Literature and Art, the Colony Club, 11:30 A.M., followed by a lecture in French by Bernard Faÿ on Stein's importance for twentieth-century literature and their friendship. The only documented Stein lecture of three proposed for 7, 14, and 21 November.

Afternoon flight to Chicago with Carl Van Vechten.

Four Saints In Three Acts, Chicago premiere, Auditorium Theatre, conducted by Virgil Thomson, benefit for the Vocational Society for Shut-Ins, first of five performances. Wilder, who has a speaking engagement in Minneapolis, is not at the performance and does not meet Stein until 25 November. Postperformance party at Bobsy Goodspeed's Lakeview Avenue apartment, where Stein spends the night.

Thursday 8   Afternoon flight to New York. Meets with Bernard Faÿ at the Algonquin Hotel, late evening.

Friday 9   Sir Francis Rose exhibition opens at The Arts Club of Chicago, with a catalogue introduction by Stein, who lent thirteen works.

"Portraits And Repetition," second Columbia University Institute of Arts and Sciences lecture, McMillin Academic Theatre, 8:30 P.M.

Following lecture, Stein auctions off autographed copies of *Portraits And Prayers* ($22), *Four Saints In Three Acts* ($8), and *Three Lives* ($9) at a benefit auction for "needy authors and painters" under the auspices of the Artists' and Writers' Dinner Club at the Barbizon Plaza Hotel.

Saturday 10   "Portraits And Repetition," Avery Hall, Vassar College, Poughkeepsie, New York.

Sunday 11   Dinner given by Bennett Cerf, with Miriam Hopkins, Donald Klopfer, and other guests.

Monday 12   Book signing, Brentano's.

Interview with William Lundell broadcast over NBC radio network, 8 P.M., introduced to studio audience by Bennett Cerf. Published in *Paris Review* (Fall 1990): 85–97.

Tuesday 13   Alice Toklas writes to Mark Lutz that she is taking over tour arrangements from Marvin Ross.

"What Is English Literature," Cosmopolitan Club, 122 East 68th Street, sponsored by the Artists' Interests Committee, Mrs. F. Lewis Slade, chairwoman, 3:30 P.M. Carl Van Vechten in audience.

"The Gradual Making," to the Brooklyn Institute of Arts and Sciences, Brooklyn Academy of Music, 8:15 P.M.

Wednesday 14   "Poetry And Grammar," Goodhart Hall, Bryn Mawr College, Bryn Mawr, Pennsylvania. Stein stays at the Deanery, Bryn Mawr, until 16 November.

Thursday 15   "Portraits And Repetition," to the Philadelphia Art Alliance, Barclay Ballroom, 8:30 P.M.

Announcement in the *New York Herald Tribune* that Stein's lecture at the New Jersey College for Women (Douglass College) is canceled because it exceeds Stein's audience limit of five hundred.

Friday 16   Announcement in the *Chicago Tribune* (21): "Miss Stein cancels two lectures at the University of Chicago [27 and 28 November] because sponsors allowed more than 500."

Returns to New York one hour late for a New York Christmas Fund benefit luncheon and musicale at the Ritz Towers Hotel. Arriving after excerpts from *Four Saints* and the Stein-Thomson "cantata" *Capital Capitals*, conducted by Virgil Thomson, she speaks briefly about the opera, quoting from "Plays."

Afternoon: "Poetry And Grammar," to the extension course in contemporary literature, given by Professor John H. Lyons, McMillin Academic Theatre, Columbia University.

Evening: "Poetry And Grammar," to the Institute of Arts and Sciences, Casa Italiana, Columbia University.

Saturday 17   Dinner with Bernard Faÿ at the home of Helen and William Simpson.

Sunday 18   Evening: Supper party for Stein at the Van Vechtens, with forty guests, including the principals of *Four Saints*.

Monday 19   Afternoon: "Portraits And Repetition," Radcliffe College, Agassiz Theatre. President Ada L. Comstock accompanies Stein to her evening lecture at Harvard.

Evening: "Portraits And Repetition," sponsored by the Signet Club of Harvard University at their clubhouse. The lecture, arranged by Professor Theodore Spenser and John J. Slocum, the club's president, is followed by a reception at the *Harvard Advocate* and a formal dinner at the Harvard Club. Returns to New York on midnight train.

Tuesday 20   At the Dutch Treat Club, a weekly Manhattan luncheon club meeting at the Hotel McAlpin, for artists and writers. Stein's remarks respond to suggested questions.

Evening: "What Is English Literature," Stein's fourth and final lecture to the Columbia University Institute of Arts and Sciences, McMillin Academic Theatre.

Wednesday 21   "Portraits And Repetition," to the Brooklyn Institute of Arts and Sciences, Brooklyn Academy of Music, 3:30 P.M.

Thursday 22   Dinner at the Van Vechtens.

Friday 23   "Poetry And Grammar," to the Brooklyn Institute of Arts and Sciences, Brooklyn Academy of Music, 8:15 P.M. Stein's lecture was the sixth in a course of sixteen lectures entitled "The Enjoyment of Literature," sponsored by the Department of Philology, Dr. Houston Peterson, chairman. Meeting with Marianne Moore.

Saturday 24   Flight to Chicago. Stays with Bobsy Goodspeed until the twenty-eighth, when she moves to the Drake Hotel.

Sunday 25   Wilder meets Stein for the first time at a luncheon, where they talk until four.

Evening: "What Is English Literature," to the Arts Club of Chicago at their Wrigley Building clubhouse following a dinner in her honor. Wilder attends the lecture and the party at the Goodspeeds' apartment.

Monday 26   Evening: Dinner with Bobsy Goodspeed. With her and Wilder attends performance of *Lohengrin* by the Chicago Grand Opera Company; Elsa sung by Maria Jeritza.

Tuesday 27   Evening: Dinner with Wilder and the Goodspeeds at the home of Robert and Maude Hutchins. Heated discussion with President Hutchins and Mortimer Adler after dinner. Police take Stein on tour of duty arranged by Fanny Butcher. Hutchins and Adler invite Stein to lead their Great Books class on 4 December.

Wednesday 28   Moves to the Drake Hotel.

Afternoon: "Pictures," to the Chicago Woman's Club.

Evening: "Poetry And Grammar," sponsored by the English Department of the University of Chicago, introduced by Professor Charles R. Baskerville, chairman, International House, 8:30 P.M.

Thursday 29   Lunch with Bobsy Goodspeed.

Evening: Wilder accompanies Stein to a P.E.N. dinner in her honor.

Friday 30   "Portraits And Repetition," to the Friday Club at their luncheon given in her honor.

Late afternoon: Wilder and Stein meet with Alice Roullier.

DECEMBER 1934

Saturday 1   Book signing, Marshall Field Department Store.

Sunday 2   Evening: "Pictures," to the Renaissance Society, Ida Noyes Hall,

University of Chicago, following a supper in her honor that she did not attend, though she was present at an informal reception afterward.

Monday 3 Attends performance of *Salome* by the Chicago Grand Opera Company with Maria Jeritza in the title role.

Tuesday 4 Leads the Hutchins and Adler General Honors 100 class. The two-hour class includes discussions of Aristophanes and epic poetry.

Wednesday 5 Stein's dinner party for Chicago friends.

Thursday 6 Morning flight to Madison.

Afternoon: "What Is English Literature," Memorial Union, University of Wisconsin at Madison.

Evening: "What Is English Literature," to students and faculty, University of Wisconsin.

Friday 7 Flight to St. Paul, 10 A.M.

Saturday 8 Evening: "What Is English Literature," to the Women's Club of St. Paul.

First of two reunions with Sherwood Anderson, who is visiting family in Stillwater, Minnesota.

Sunday 9 Lunch with Van Vechten's friend Mahala Douglas at her home in Wayzata, Minnesota. Scheduled to fly from St. Paul to Chicago and connect to a flight to Iowa City, where Stein is to give "The Gradual Making" before a Gertrude Stein Club organized by the painter Grant Wood, but inclement weather diverts flight to Milwaukee. From there takes a tram car to Chicago.

Tuesday 11 Afternoon flight from Chicago to Detroit.

Wednesday 12 "The Gradual Making," to the Detroit Women's City Club in their auditorium.

Book signing, J. L. Hudson and Company, department store.

Thursday 13 Joseph Brewer, president of Olivet College, with a "cavalcade" of students and faculty drives Stein and Toklas to the campus. Stein meets informally with students and faculty.

Friday 14 After lunch at Olivet College, Brewer drives Stein and Toklas to Ann Arbor.

"Portraits And Repetition," the University of Michigan at Ann Arbor, 4:30 P.M., sponsored by the Avery Hopwood Award Committee.

Saturday 15 Evening: "The Gradual Making," to the Contemporary Club of Indianapolis at the John Herron Art Institute.

Monday 17 Morning: Arrives Columbus.

Afternoon: "Poetry And Grammar," to the Chi Delta Phi Honorary Literary Society of Ohio State University at Columbus, University Hall Chapel, organized by Jean Reeder.

Late afternoon flight to Toledo.

Tuesday 18   "Poetry And Grammar," Ohio State University at Toledo. Remains in Toledo until the twentieth.

Thursday 20   "Pictures," Cleveland Museum.

Sunday 23   Morning: Flight from Cleveland to Washington, D.C. Julian and Rosellen Stein drive Stein and Toklas to Rosehill, their Pikesville, Maryland, home, where they stay as guests.

Monday 24   Visits F. Scott Fitzgerald in Baltimore.

Tuesday 25   With the Julian Steins.

Friday 28   "Pictures," Baltimore Museum.

Saturday 29   Morning: Emily Chadbourne drives Stein from Pikesville to Washington. Stein stays with Ann Archbold.
"Pictures," Phillips Collection, Washington (see Marjorie Phillips, *Duncan Phillips and His Collection* [New York: W. W. Norton, 1970], 184–87).

Sunday 30   Tea at the White House with Eleanor Roosevelt.
"What Is English Literature," to the American Association of University Women, Ballroom, Willard Hotel, Washington.

Monday 31   New Year's Eve at the home of Mr. and Mrs. Richard Crane, Westover, Virginia. Among the guests are Emily Chadbourne, Crane's sister, Ellen La Motte, both old friends, and Mark Lutz.

JANUARY 1935

Tuesday 1   Spends night with Ann Archbold in Washington.

Wednesday 2   Lunch with Princess Cantacuzene, granddaughter of President U. S. Grant. Afternoon train to New York.

Thursday 3   Sees Bennett Cerf, 4 P.M.

Friday 4   Photo session with Carl Van Vechten in his apartment. Dinner with Van Vechten at the Algonquin Hotel, followed by a visit to Florine Stettheimer's studio, where Stein sees her paintings and the maquettes for *Four Saints*.

Sunday 6   Lunch at Cerf's home, Alexander Woollcott among the guests.

Monday 7   Noon: Leaves New York by train for Springfield, Massachusetts.
Evening: "The Gradual Making," to the Century Club at the home of Dr. and Mrs. William Kirkham, where she spends the night.

Wednesday 9   "Poetry And Grammar," Johnson Chapel, Amherst College, Amherst, Massachusetts. Stays with President and Mrs. Stanley King.

Thursday 10   "The Gradual Making," Sage Hall, Smith College, Northampton, Massachusetts.

Friday 11   "Pictures," Berkshire Museum, Pittsfield, Massachusetts.

Saturday 12   Afternoon: Dudley Fitts, teacher of English who arranged the lecture at the suggestion of James Laughlin, a Choate alumnus, drives Stein from Pittsfield to the Choate School, Wallingford, Connecticut.

Dinner with the headmaster, Dr. St. John, and his wife.

"How Writing Is Written," under the auspices of the *Choate Literary Magazine*, 8 P.M. Lecture composed for this occasion.

Sunday 13   Late afternoon, returns to Springfield, Massachusetts.

Tuesday 15   "Plays," Wesleyan University, Middletown, Connecticut.

Wednesday 16   "Plays," Chapin Auditorium, Mount Holyoke College, South Hadley, Massachusetts, under the auspices of Play and Poetry Shop Talk, Department of English and Drama, Jeannette Marks, chair, 8:00 P.M.

Friday 18   "Pictures," Avery Memorial Theatre, Wadsworth Atheneum, Hartford, Connecticut, 8:30 P.M. Spends night in Hartford and then returns to Springfield.

Monday 21   Travels in a snowstorm from Springfield to Providence, where she lectures at Brown University.

Wednesday 23   Evening: "Pictures," Kimball Museum of Fine Arts, Springfield.

Thursday 24   "What Is English Literature" and "The Gradual Making," Springfield College Extension Program, Springfield High School gymnasium.

Friday 25   Returns to New York by train.

Saturday 26   Lunch with Carl Van Vechten, Fania Marinoff, and Joseph Brewer at Henri Charpentier.

Sees Bennett Cerf, Algonquin Hotel, 5 P.M.

Monday 28   After dinner with Van Vechten, attends performance of Katharine Cornell's *Romeo and Juliet.* Supper afterward at Cornell's home.

Tuesday 29   Lunch with Bennett Cerf.

Wednesday 30   Signs contract with Herald Tribune Syndicate for series of articles entitled "The American Scene" (see Stein to Wilder, 23 January, n. 1).

Records excerpts from *The Making Of Americans, Madame Recamier: An Opera,* "A Valentine To Sherwood Anderson," "If I Told Him: A Completed Portrait Of Picasso," and "Matisse." A recording on aluminum discs is made in Milbank Hall, Columbia University, for their collection of speech records; the same pieces are recorded for the National Council of Teachers of English at the Erpi Studios, in the Aeolian Hall Building, 250 West 57th Street.

Thursday 31   Dinner party at the Van Vechtens. Mary and Louis Bromfield and Lillian May Ehrman are among the guests.

FEBRUARY 1935

Friday 1   Lunch with Bennett Cerf.

Sunday 3   Arrives Charlottesville, Virginia, with Van Vechten at 7:45 P.M., greeted at the train station by Dr. John Lloyd Newcomb, president of the University of Virginia and the Raven Society, sponsors of her lecture. Stays at the Monticello Hotel. Van Vechten remains until after her lecture of 10 February.

Monday 4   10 A.M.: Driven to university.

Luncheon with students and faculty at the Farmington Country Club. Visits Jefferson's home at Monticello, James Monroe's estate, Ash Lawn, and Amelie Rives Troubetzkoy's home at Castle Hill. Photographed by Van Vechten. Stein works on two of her syndicated articles before lectures.

Evening: "Poetry And Grammar," Cabell Hall, University of Virginia at Charlottesville to the Raven Society. After lecture and question period with members, dinner in her honor.

Tuesday 5   Morning: Dr. Newcomb gives Stein key to Poe's room at the university.

2 P.M.: Stein, Toklas, and Van Vechten driven to Richmond, Virginia, by String-fellow Barr of the University at Charlottesville. Stays at the Hotel Jefferson until 11 February.

Dinner at the home of Ellen Glasgow. Van Vechten, Mark Lutz, Hunter Stagg, the James Branch Cabells among the dinner guests. After dinner, thirty-five additional guests arrive to meet Stein.

Wednesday 6   "What Is English Literature," Cannon Memorial Chapel, University of Richmond, sponsored by the Student Government, 8:30 P.M.

Thursday 7   Afternoon: Stein, Toklas, and Van Vechten visit the Poe Shrine and attend tea given by the board of directors of the Poe Foundation in her honor.

Photographed by Van Vechten.

"Pictures," in the Woman's Club Auditorium, Richmond Academy of Arts, under their auspices, 8:30 P.M.

Friday 8   Luncheon at the President's House, College of William and Mary, Williamsburg, Virginia.

Photographed by Van Vechten.

Afternoon: "Portraits And Repetition," sponsored by the Phi Beta Kappa Society of the college.

Visit to Yorktown, followed by a tea in her honor at Carter's Grove, Mrs. Archibald McCrae, hostess.

Sunday 10   "The Gradual Making," in the chapel of Sweet Briar College, Sweet Briar, Virginia.

Monday 11   12:30 P.M.: Van Vechten returns to New York City.

Tuesday 12   Arrives in Chapel Hill, North Carolina.

Meets DuBose Heyward, author of *Porgy*.

Wednesday 13   "Poetry And Grammar," South Carolina Hall, Charleston, sponsored by the Poetry Society of South Carolina, Josephine Pinckney, president.

Flies from Charleston to Atlanta and then on to Birmingham.

Thursday 14   Invited to lecture at Black Mountain College in North Carolina, which Stein's schedule does not permit (see Wilder to Stein, 13 February).

Saturday 16   "What Is English Literature," to students from Birmingham-Southern College, at the Tutwiler Hotel, Birmingham, 8:30 P.M.

Sunday 17   In Birmingham, en route by plane to New Orleans.

Monday 18   Second meeting with Sherwood Anderson, New Orleans, lunch at Antoine's.
"What Is English Literature," E. B. Dixon Hall, Tulane University, New Orleans.

Tuesday 19   "Pictures," sponsored by the Gallery of Arts and Crafts Societies, New Orleans.

Wednesday 20   Lunch at Galatoires with Mr. and Mrs. Frederick Hand.

Thursday 21   "Miss King Discusses Gertrude Stein and Art," by Georgiana King, professor of art at Bryn Mawr College and an old friend of Stein's, in *Bryn Mawr College News*, 1, 4.

Friday 22   Morning: New Orleans to Chicago flight diverted to Memphis, because of a snowstorm. Takes train to St. Louis.

Saturday 23   In St. Louis at Hotel Park Plaza. Stein and Toklas visit U. S. Grant's cabin.

Sunday 24   Arrives Chicago, 2:30 P.M., takes up residence in Thornton Wilder's apartment for her two-week stay.
Evening: With Wilder attends a dinner meeting of the University of Chicago chapter of Kappa Alpha, an honor society, at the home of Professor Robert Morss Lovett. The discussion topic is propaganda and literature.

Monday 25   Stein begins writing the first *Narration* lecture, plans reading list, and makes arrangements for student conferences. Four lectures are scheduled to be given before audiences of five hundred, and six two-hour conferences with thirty students selected by Wilder are arranged.
Afternoon: Mrs. Harold McCormick gives a tea for Stein, with Wilder among the guests.

Tuesday 26   Writing *Narration* lectures.

Wednesday 27   Continues writing *Narration* lectures. Meets with Wilder at 3 P.M.

Thursday 28   First two lectures completed.

MARCH 1935

Friday 1   First *Narration* lecture, International House Theatre, 4 to 6 P.M.
Toklas prepares dinner in Wilder's apartment. After dinner, Wilder returns to the university for his classes and to interview students for Stein's conference groups.

Saturday 2   Afternoon: Attends the "Mirror Show" at the University of Chicago.
Dinner at Hull House with Robert Morss Lovett. (Wilder attends a dinner party given by Helen Harvey for David Adler.)

Sunday 3   "American Newspapers" [I], the first of Stein's Herald Tribune Syndicate articles is published.
Late afternoon: Meets with Wilder.

Monday 4   First of Stein's conferences with students, Cobb Hall, 2 to 4 P.M.
Alexander Woollcott arrives in Chicago.

Tuesday 5   Second student conference, 2 to 4 P.M.
Dinner with Woollcott and Wilder.

Wednesday 6   Second *Narration* lecture, 4 P.M.
Evening: With Lloyd Lewis and Wilder to a performance of *H.M.S. Pinafore* by the D'Oyly Carte Company.

Thursday 7   Third student conference, 2 to 4 P.M.
At 4:15 P.M. Stein chairs a debate on international munitions control between the University of Chicago and Willamette (Oregon) University at the Oriental Institute Assembly, sponsored by the University Debate Union. An announcement in the university's student newspaper, the *Daily Maroon*, 6 March, 4, says, "During the course of her first attempt at chairmanizing, Gertrude Stein will express her views on war and peace."
Dinner with Wilder, 6:15 P.M., followed by student conferences at 7:30 P.M.

Friday 8   Third *Narration* lecture, 4 to 6 P.M.
Evening: D'Oyly Carte Company performance of *Iolanthe* with Bobsy Goodspeed, followed by a supper at her apartment.

Saturday 9   "The Capital Capitals of the United States of America," Herald Tribune Syndicate.
Works on the last *Narration* lecture.
Isabel Wilder, on a tour to promote her novel *Heart Be Still*, arrives in Chicago. Lunch in Wilder's apartment for the Wilders, Fanny Butcher, and her husband, Richard Bokum.
Evening: Party for Stein given by Wilder, with a mixture of colleagues and students.

Sunday 10   Dinner meeting of the University of Chicago chapter of Kappa Alpha at the home of student member Noel B. Gerson. Philip Allen of the German Department leads discussion on the topic of succession in poetry.

Monday 11   With Wilder to the Quadrangle Club, 6 P.M. Student conferences, 7:30 P.M.

Tuesday 12   Student conferences, 7:30 P.M.

Wednesday 13   Final *Narration* lecture, 8 P.M.

Thursday 14   *Lectures In America* published by Random House.
Lunch with Thornton and Isabel Wilder.
Final student conferences, 4:30 P.M.

Friday 15   Tea with Wilder, followed by a talk at International House, University of Chicago, before an audience of approximately 150 students. Stein speaks for thirty minutes and then answers questions.

Saturday 16 "American Education And Colleges," Herald Tribune Syndicate. Dinner with Wilder and Woollcott, 7 P.M.

Sunday 17 Flight to Dallas. Stays until the twentieth at the Hockaday School.

Monday 18 Lecture at the Hockaday School, the first event in the new College Building.

Tuesday 19 Afternoon: "Pictures," to the Fort Worth Woman's Club.

Wednesday 20 Hockaday School, Dallas.

Thursday 21 Evening: Arrives in Austin, stays until the twenty-third. Interviewed for the *Daily Texan*, the University of Texas at Austin's student newspaper, by Mildred Cooke and Walter Cronkite, students at the university. Interviews published the following day.

Friday 22 Evening: "Poetry And Grammar," Hogg Memorial Auditorium, University of Texas at Austin. Reception at Littlefield Dormitory follows. A report of this lecture, datelined 27 March, ran in the *California Daily Bruin*, the student newspaper of the University of California, Los Angeles, on 28 March.

Saturday 23 "American Newspapers" [II], Herald Tribune Syndicate. First *Narration* lecture to the Houston Junior League, sponsored by the Arts and Interests Committee. Spends the night at the Warwick Hotel, Houston.

Sunday 24 Driven from Houston back to Austin for flight to Oklahoma City. Stays at Huckins Hotel until the twenty-sixth. At the suggestion of Alexander Woollcott she visits the Stephen Foster Museum.

Tuesday 26 "The Gradual Making," to the Town Club, Harding Hall, Oklahoma City, 11 A.M. Returns to Fort Worth. Evening: Dinner with "a Princeton man" who had started an all-Black Little Theatre company and Franklin D. Roosevelt, Jr. Sees the company's production of *Porgy* (*Everybody's Autobiography* [Random House], 241; [Vintage], 278).

Thursday 28 Lunch in Fort Worth with students from the Hockaday School, including Sarah Basima Trent, who noted it on her bookplate of an inscribed copy of *Three Lives*. Flight to Pasadena, California, where she stays at the Hotel Vista Del Arroyo until 2 April. Interview with Kenneth O'Hara is published in the *Los Angeles Times* 30 March, 1–2.

Saturday 30 "American Crimes and How They Matter," Herald Tribune Syndicate.

Sunday 31 "What Is English Literature," at the Pasadena Community Playhouse.

APRIL 1935

Monday 1 Evening: Party for Stein given by Lillian May Ehrman, a friend of Van Vechten, at her Beverly Hills home. At the party Stein meets Charles

Chaplin, Paulette Goddard, Lillian Hellman, Dashiell Hammett, and Anita Loos, among others (see Stein to Wilder, 2 April).

Tuesday 2   Speaks at the Writer's Clubhouse luncheon in Pasadena.
Rents a car and drives to San Francisco, stopping along the way.

Saturday 6   "American States and Cities and How They Differ from Each Other," Herald Tribune Syndicate.

Sunday 7   Arrives in Del Monte, California. Evening: Party at the home of Noël Sullivan in nearby Carmel, Lincoln Steffens among the guests. Reads from *Lectures In America*.

Monday 8   Arrives in San Francisco.

Tuesday 9   P.E.N. dinner at the San Francisco Bohemian Club as the guest of Gertrude Atherton.

Wednesday 10   Scheduled to give "How Writing Is Written," she instead gives the first *Narration* lecture to the English Club of Stanford University in the Women's Gymnasium.

Thursday 11   "What Is English Literature," to the San Francisco Women's City Club, City Club Auditorium, 8:30 P.M.

Friday 12   "Pictures," to the San Francisco Women's City Club, City Club Auditorium, 2:30 P.M.
Meets Angelo J. Rossi, mayor of San Francisco, who gives her a key to the city.

Saturday 13   "American Food and American Houses," Herald Tribune Syndicate.
"Poetry And Grammar," Mills College, Oakland, sponsored by the English Club.
Visits her old neighborhood in Oakland.

Monday 15   Lunch for members of the Phi Beta Kappa Honor Society, University of California at Berkeley, where Stein answers questions.
First *Narration* lecture at International House, University of California at Berkeley.

Tuesday 16   Lunch at the home of Mr. and Mrs. William H. Crocker, owners of nJ. F. Millet's *Man with a Hoe*, mentioned in "Pictures." Mary Garden is among the guests.

Wednesday 17   "Pictures," second Stanford lecture.

Friday 19   Night flight to Chicago by way of Omaha.

Saturday 20   Bobsy Goodspeed dinner for Stein, Wilder among the guests. Spends night in Goodspeed's apartment.

Sunday 21   Returns to New York.

Monday 22   Lunch with the Van Vechtens at the Algonquin Hotel.

Tuesday 23   Dinner at the Van Vechtens. Photo session. Stein gives Marinoff one of her waistcoats.

Wednesday 24 A "listening" (Stein's phrase) to her recordings made for the National Council of Teachers of English, Erpi Studio. Among the guests are Van Vechten, Mabel Foote Weeks, an old friend and professor at Barnard College, and Michael Strange, the former Mrs. John Barrymore.

Friday 26 Dinner with the Van Vechtens at the Algonquin Hotel.

Monday 29 Stein cancels her final American lecture, to have been given to the American Arbitration Association at the French Institute of New York, because the sponsors charged an admission. As part of the gala evening, Stein was to have given her first *Narration* lecture and Virgil Thomson would have conducted members of the original cast in selections from *Four Saints In Three Acts.*

Dinner with the Van Vechtens at the Algonquin Hotel.

Tuesday 30 Cerf gives dinner and party for Stein, which lasts until 4 A.M., including Carl Van Vechten, Miriam Hopkins, Edna Ferber. George Gershwin plays music from *Porgy and Bess.*

MAY 1935

Thursday 2 Dinner with the Van Vechtens and photo session.

Friday 3 Farewell dinner with Wilder.

Saturday 4 Van Vechten sees them off on the S. S. *Champlain.* Stein's review of Sherwood Anderson's *Puzzled America* published in the *Chicago Daily Tribune.*

"PATHÉ"

[The manuscript of this text is headed "Pathe 1934." Our transcription is that of the typed text with additions in Stein's hand, which we have placed in brackets. Eds.]

My lectures are to be a simple way to say that if you understand a thing you enjoy it and if you enjoy a thing you understand it.

And in these lectures I want to tell so simply that anybody will know it and know it very very well that you can enjoy the things I have been writing. And since you can enjoy them you can understand them. I always say in my lectures, knowledge is what you know, and I do want you to have knowledge and to know this that understanding and enjoying is the same thing.

My first lecture is about my book called MAKING OF AMERICANS, and I tried to tell in this book all about every kind there is of men and women, now I will read you some of it so that you know what I mean.

(Quote) [Page 232]

And I tried to tell not only what every one does and what every one says and what every one knows but also what every one is.

[deleted by Stein: (Quote)]

If you try to do all this you have to write a very long book and THE MAKING OF AMERICANS is a long book, but it does try to tell what every one what every kind there is of men and women is.

My second lecture is called PORTRAITS AND REPETITION. In that I tell about how I came to write the portraits of people that I have written. How I learned what they were, and how I said it. In order really to do this everybody that one meets must be wonderful to you that is full of wonder for you, and you have to be ready to learn all they are over and over again until you are full of it and then you know it all of a sudden and then you have to get it down, not as you learned it but as you know it when you know it altogether. That is what I call doing a portrait and all the Portraits I have done I have put together and they are called PORTRAITS AND PRAYERS. Now listen to some of the, [in MS them,]

This is a portrait [deleted: of] (Quote)

    [A valentine to Sherwood Anderson

    Page 151]

Then I wrote a lecture called POETRY AND GRAMMAR and in this and for me it is the most exciting thing I have ever done, I have found out really found out what poetry is and what prose is and why, and I have been able to tell it so simply tell it, and it is really very exciting to know it and to be able to simply tell it, and I found out that grammar and punctuation are really at the bottom of it. And it all comes from the fact that sentences have not any emotion in them but that paragraphs have, and anybody looking at anything in a newspaper will see what I mean. Head lines have emotion because they are not a whole sentence. They are poetry, and paragraphs have emotion, but sentences just sentences have not. Now you may not know why this is so exciting but it is, it just explains everything and that is why this lecture is [xciting] it is this explanation.

I will quote some sentences and paragraphs that I have made and some poetry I have made that will show all that.

(Quote)

[These are the sentences

Page 27 Page 28 How to Write

Poetry in Tender Buttons Pg 54 (? three words)]

Then I have written a lecture about PLAYS and of course that means operas too. and in this I explain what plays I have seen and what I felt about them, then when I saw them and now when I remember them.

And I explain how FOUR SAINTS is what I think plays really ought to be a stable thing, a thing that cannot go away, which is what a landscape is and FOUR SAINTS is a landscape, things happen in a landscape but the landscape is always there and that is what a play ought to be and so I made FOUR SAINTS a landscape a Spanish landscape which is what a play called FOUR SAINTS ought to be and if you enjoyed it and a lot of people did enjoy it then they did understand it because if you do understand it you do enjoy it. Now here is some of the landscape, which is always there, and this is what happened in it as the women were washing their linen in the cold river and they brought their warm water with them, and the river water was cold very very cold.

(Quote) Page 15

STEIN'S NARRATION LECTURES:
SUGGESTED SUPPLEMENTARY READING AND OUTLINE OF THE LECTURES

On 25 February 1935, the day after Stein and Toklas arrived in Chicago, Toklas wrote to Carl Van Vechten, "All to-day has been taken up with arranging the hours of the lectures, the hours of the classes, the subjects of the lectures and the subjects of the classes, writing the first lecture and arranging the reading for the students in the classes in preparation" (Burns, *Letters*, 1: 398). Three days later, on 28 February, Stein wrote to Van Vechten, "Here we are here we really are and pretty soon I will be sending you the mimeographed copy of what I am doing, golly. . . . I am terribly frightfully busy because I have 4 lectures to write about narrative, I have just finished 2 in three days and now I have to do two more, I have found some interesting things to say to Thornton and Alice and I think well anyway and then I have 10 conferences with small bodies of students and then two hours consultations a time with anybody who wants to talk to me" (Burns, *Letters*, 1: 401–02). What Stein sent to Van Vechten was a mimeographed sheet with a reading list for each of the four lectures. On the sheet she wrote, "End up third one with not having finished or really begun the question of history but it will be oh yes it will be both finished and begun." She concluded her third *Narration* lecture by writing, "Next time I am going to write more history for you, auto-biography I have already done, biography I have already done I will tell you about that one, and so slowly yes slowly I will come to some knowing what it is that makes anything what it is what it was and what it has become. But really and truly all about history and biography and autobiography will be both finished and begun oh yes it will it really will be both finished and begun in the next one" (*Narration*, 45).

SUGGESTED SUPPLEMENTARY READING

I   The Contrast between the English Daily Life and the American Lack of a Daily Life

Carlyle	:	Emerson
Jane Eyre	:	The Scarlet Letter
Coleridge	:	Edgar Allan Poe
Wordsworth	:	Walt Whitman
Walter Scott	:	Fenimore Cooper
George Meredith	:	Henry James
Dickens	:	Mark Twain

II   Narrative in Prose and Narrative in Poetry
     Robinson Crusoe and Paradise Lost
     The Vicar of Wakefield and Ballad Poetry
     Henry Esmond and St. Agnes' Eve

III History as Narrative and the Newspaper as Narrative
     Caesar's Gallic War
     Green's Shorter English History
     Gibbon
     The Hauptmann Trial

IV   Narrative, The Novel and the Mystery Story
     The Mysteries of Udolpho
     Poe
     Dashiel[l] Hammett

OUTLINE OF THE LECTURES

[Among Stein's papers is a one-page outline of her Chicago lectures. The mimeographed sheet has handwritten insertions by Stein and Toklas, which are here enclosed in brackets. Eds.]

[How writing is written]
NARRATION (Miss Gertrude Stein)
Four Lectures and Classes
Lecture I
[The American Language & How It Is Made]

The relation of the literature that is narrative that is how is anything told to the habit of doing anything and living which that country has.

The comparison between English literature and American literature, the complete difference in their habits although they use the same language, and its connection with their narrative.

Lecture II

The difference between poetry and prose and the relation of that difference to the stating of events or what happens. Knowing thoroughly the difference between poetry and prose and its connection with vocabulary and grammar, what is the inevitable effect of this upon narrative in prose and narrative in poetry and how can either of them be done now.

Lecture III

History and is history narrative, and why does it generally speaking fail as a method of literary expression. Is it due to its connection with past present and future. The newspaper and its effort to create narrative and the connection of that with the writing of history. What is the connection of all this with repetition the inevitable repetition which connects itself with daily life and with war. Is it also because it is not sufficiently understood that war and catastrophe are merely the publicising of repetition of success and failure which as common knowledge everybody already knows.

Lecture IV
[Is History Literature]

Narrative and its relation to physical qualities of a country, difficulty of separating people from the country when the consciousness of the people has not yet made the two things one, its effect upon novels that is narrative, and the slow relation to the time sense of the people in its relation to the country. Ordinary novels mystery stories what is the degree of consciousness of time sense that changes writing from being exciting to being soothing, has this not a great deal to do with the present becoming past and the future becoming past although it is at the same time present. Analysis of the difference of relating action to completion or to relief.

Appendix II.

The University of Chicago
Production of Handel's *Xerxes*

The University of Chicago Chorus and Orchesis, the university dance group, and the university symphony orchestra presented the first Chicago performances of George Frederick Handel's only comic opera, *Xerxes*, at Mandel Hall on Saturday and Sunday evenings, 16 and 17 February 1935 at 8:15 P.M. According to a press release, "The production of *Xerxes* will mark the debut of Thornton Wilder as a stage director. Working together with John Pratt, the Chicago artist who designed the settings, Mr. Wilder is planning a performance which will combine an authentic knowledge of the baroque style of Handel's time with whimsical 1935 comment upon some of the amusing features of that style" (Chicago). These performances of *Xerxes* coincided with the celebration of Handel's 250th birthday.

The libretto used for the performance was the standard translation by Bayard Quincy Morgan, though Cecil Michener Smith, music director, points out, "Mr. Wilder, for reasons which became apparent with a close study of the Morgan translation, re-worked at least one complete aria, and a number of the recitatives" (copy, letter to Roosevelt Walker, 27 February 1935, Chicago).

Adapting the libretto and serving as stage manager were not Wilder's only contributions. A *Time* magazine article (25 February 1935, 50) prints a photograph of Wilder in costume and reports, "He not only [reworked the Morgan libretto and directed the performance] but also put himself in the chorus to sing a few notes. Wilder's part came in the second act for which he discarded his spectacles, donned baggy blue trousers, black top boots, a silver-trimmed cape and a pancake hat. Thus disguised as a soldier, he proved himself an able baritone with his one big line: 'Do you expect to find him here in some puddle?'"

356

Under the headline "Wilder Comments on 'Xerxes,'" the *Daily Maroon* (1, 4), the University of Chicago student newspaper, published a background essay on the opera's history and details of the Chicago production. Wilder's article has never been reprinted and is not listed in bibliographies of his work:

Handel's only comic opera "Xerxes" was written during a time when the composer was weighed down by a load of cares, was about to be hauled into court as a bankrupt, and was in so low a state of health that in a few months he was to suffer a stroke of paralysis. Like his other great works it was written in an incredibly short time. It was begun on Christmas day, 1737, (two days after the completion of his previous opera) and it was finished as far as the melodic line was concerned on February 6 of the next year. The details of orchestration were completed on February 14. His greatest work, "The Messiah" was even more swiftly turned out; it was sketched and scored in twenty-one days. His bankruptcy was not due to any lack of appreciation on the part of the people of London. It resulted partly from the fact that he had undertaken the duties of the theatre-management and partly from the animosity of his rival impresarios and composers. Among other efforts to ruin him his enemies had taken to seeing that important balls and banquets were given on the nights that Handel's opera company was launching a new production. Fortunately Handel survived this low ebb in his health and fortunes by twenty-one years of unremitted work and finally gained sufficient private fortune to endow a Foundlings Hospital with a new organ, an occasion which he celebrated by offering for the first performance in the world his latest oratorio "The Messiah."

Like Mozart, Handel's most joyous works appeared when external circumstances were darkest. Although the term "comic opera" appears in the announcements and on the title page of "Xerxes" and although there are farcical and clowning passages during the action, the greater part of the work is romantic and even noble. No one knows who composed the libretto. It appears to be based upon some French or Spanish drama of intrigue to which at the last moment a classical Persian series of proper names has been appended. Throughout the whole of the original score only one allusion has been injected to identify it with the Near East. At the wedding ceremony at the close, the stage direction says there shall be an altar in front of an image of the sun with golden rays darting out from it. The librettist had heard of the Zoroastrian sun-worship and threw it in. The action of the opera abounds in disguises, kings incognito, letters falling into the wrong hands, princesses who go to the wars dressed as soldiers and attempted abductions.

The complicated and preposterous plot is only a few degrees worse however than most plots in opera. Only in this case the activity of the characters is supported by great and sincere music, as though the plot made sense, as though the action was adequately motivated, as though the characters were flesh and blood. "Xerxes" is full of arias and duets of love and suffering and rage and revenge, music of a vitality and truth that would do justice to a Shakespearean play. And between these serious passages there are long stretches in which the comic servant and the playful mischief-making lady of the court continue their activities in dialogue none too freshly written but supported by music that breathes wit and charm. All these contradictions, however, are unified by the great Eighteenth Century manner, the high Baroque Style. It will be the effort of the production on February 16, to find a manner that will both reproduce the conditions of the original London production of 1738 and will yet contain a twentieth century amused comment on the often absurd conventions of that age. The audiences will have an opportunity to see something of the life behind the scenes during the Golden Age of operatic activity. The curtain of Mandel Hall will never be lowered and however early the audience arrives it will not be too early to see something going on upon the stage.

Those who in rehearsal had the privilege of learning by endless repetition the splendid music of the score, feel more and more the desire to add one more gesture of homage to the great man who was born two hundred and fifty years ago on February the twenty-third; and when the curtain falls on the beautiful closing chorus, with the horns at the end of each phrase faintly blowing a surprising series of repeated notes, with Miss Van Tuyl's dancers marking the measures, and with the full strength of the soloists and chorus and orchestra lifting the great melody to the last corners of our dingy but cherished Mandel Hall, we hope that one more tribute of appreciation will have been paid to the composer of the most loved melody in the world, Handel's Largo, which by a coincidence, has been lifted by the world from this very work, the "Xerxes."

Other articles in the *Daily Maroon* were written by Cecil Michener Smith, 29 January, 1, 4; Marian Van Tuyl, 5 February, 1; and John Pratt, 14 February, 1, 3. Lawrence Goodnow did a general article on the production on 15 February, 1.

Appendix III.

Wilder on John Pratt

John Pratt graduated from the University of Chicago in 1933. While still a student, he did the decorations for the Tap Room of the Alpha Delta Phi fraternity house (see Wilder to Woollcott, n.d. 1933, Harvard-Theatre). He was a talented painter, costumer, and commercial fabric designer who, as a young man, worked for the Federal Theatre Project. In 1939 Pratt met Katherine Dunham and began designing sets and costumes for her dance company. They were married in July 1941.

Wilder contributed a "Foreword" to the brochure for Pratt's exhibition of thirty-one watercolors at the Increase Robinson Gallery at 540 North Michigan Avenue in Chicago from 23 September to 14 October [n.y. ?1935]. It has not been reprinted since.

Foreword

The first generation of American artists born during this century in the Middle West,—born into a world of Methodist Episcopal Sunday Schools, Greek candy stores and the paintings on grocer's calendars,—went mad, or became trivial, or applied their gifts cynically to commercial uses; or went to Paris, where they wrote poems about absinthe and painted bloodless imitations of the impressionists.

The next generation, however, was able, redefining beauty, to draw from that very scene which had filled their predecessors with horror, effects of grace, energy and tenderness. John Pratt's drawings, even when they seem to be adventuring in cosmic fantasy, still contain an allusion to the modes of thought in a small Indiana town,—even the Assyrian bulls in redbuttoned vests and the angels who are preparing to abandon Heaven or who are lugging with such difficulty a reluctant newcomer into Paradise.

But it is not the literary content of this artist's work, witty and trenchant though it is, that most commands our attention; it is the purely artistic endowment. He has in composition a great fertility of invention and an unerring hand through the most intricate patterns. Above all, he has a rare felicity in color,— colors often unusual but discreet, and always original.

There are then, several kinds of pleasure to be derived from this work, and the sum of them introduces us to an artist, brilliantly American, already mature, and of a complete distinction.

Thornton Wilder.

Appendix IV.

Stein-Vestal: The Puppet Play
(Including Wilder's
"Introduction to Miss Stein's Puppet Play")

Donald Vestal, a puppeteer, had introduced himself to Stein while she was walking on Michigan Avenue in Chicago in 1934. Vestal was with the Works Progress Administration and promoting his work with marionettes wherever he could. Stein wrote to him in a letter postmarked 5 December 1934 that she had spoken to Alice Roullier about this and, "she would like to see you, so the best of good luck to you both" (Harvard-Theatre).

Vestal wrote to Stein on 13 August 1935 (YCAL) reminding her of their meeting on 30 November 1934 and asked if she would write a play for marionettes. She replied, "I am very pleased that you have come to be the marionette end of an alphabet, and I have by no means forgotten you, and I am interested to be sure actually all I know about marionettes is punch and judy, which when I first came to Paris I used to stand and watch and partly because I had seen it there when I was a child, otherwise I have never seen a marionette, but I am quite sure that that does not make any difference."

Vestal's was not the first proposal to use marionettes for a Stein play. She went on,

> At Olivet College they did a very successful marionette with one of the things in Portraits and Prayers, called Playing [i.e., *Play*], they had two very cubist marionettes and they made them dance to the rythm of the piece read aloud. I am asking Random House to send you a copy of Portraits and Prayers, and Joseph Brewer or the head of the English dept at Olivet College, Mich. can tell you more about it. I did not myself see it but they told me it was the only thing encored at the marionette show they gave there. I am writing at present a long book which concerns itself with the relation of human nature to the human

mind and one of my illustrations for this is a little play based upon I am I because my little dog knows me. I am not sure that it could not be made into a marionette play, I will think about it, it would be rather amusing, as it deals with a dog and identity, tell me what you think about it, I did enjoy enormously being in America and I certainly do xpect to be there again, I am full of meditations these days but I find I must know about the relation [of] human nature and geography to the human mind, but you see it does connect itself with possibly a marionette. (Stein to Vestal, postmarked 29 August 1935, Harvard-Theatre)

Stein stitched together a play for Vestal from plays she was writing into *The Geographical History Of America Or The Relation Of Human Nature To The Human Mind.* (The play was first printed in *What Are Masterpieces*, 71–79; see *A Stein Reader*, 588–94). Vestal responded to Stein, " 'I am I because my little dog knows me' is a consummated story in nine words and it sounds like delightful marionette material" (9 September 1935, YCAL). After receiving the play, he wrote of his progress and reported that Owen Haynes, a young Chicago composer, was writing the music for it. (See Vestal to Stein, 12 November 1935, YCAL.)

Identity was performed for a private audience in Chicago in early June 1936. By this time, Vestal had met Wilder and asked him to write an introduction for the program of the first official performance of the piece at the National Puppetry Conference in Detroit on 9 July 1936. Wilder's "Introduction to Miss Stein's Puppet Play" was finished by 7 July 1936, but the illness of Wilder's father delayed his getting the text to Vestal in time for inclusion.

Introduction to Miss Stein's Puppet Play

In this puppet-play and in several of her recent works Miss Gertrude Stein has been developing a theory about the relation between Human Nature and the Human Mind.

Human Nature, she says, is based on identity. That is: it insists on its self, on self-assertion and the protection and the survival of its identity. Consequently in Human Nature and from Human Nature are wars, propaganda, politics, crime, jealousy, sex. Human Nature in order to be sure that it exists must employ memory and audience. Memory informs it that it was itself in the past; and audience reassures it that it is itself in the present. As the play here will say: "*I am I*" said the little old lady, "*because my little dog knows me.*" [Wilder's emphasis]

But the Human Mind does not know TIME or IDENTITY or AUDIENCE. It gazes at Pure Existing. Every moment it knows what it knows when it knows it. Its highest activity is to write, because in writing there is no audience but itself—in oratory, in conversation, the audience is present and deflects the HUMAN MIND into persuasion or into pleasing or flattering and those are in the Realm of Human Nature.

There is a great deal about dogs in this play. Miss Stein is continually using her dogs as illustrations of Human Nature. Everybody says that Human Nature is interesting (she says) but it is not. It is occupying, but it is not interesting. If people were only truly honest with themselves they would realize that they are no longer really interested in the manifestations of Human Nature—in crimes, and in the assertion of nationalism, in the I-I-I aspect of most conversation. The dogs can do most of the things that Human Nature used to think its dignity reposed upon. They can yearn, and long; they can weep; but there is one thing they cannot do and that is WRITE. The Human Mind can write, and its record in literary masterpieces is the most important subject of Miss Stein's new book to appear in the autumn.

Her discussion of the Human Nature and the Human Mind is very serious to her; but everything she does is also done in the spirit of gaiety. The reward of difficult thinking is an inner exhilaration. Miss Stein is never tired of emphasizing the spirit of play in the artist's work. Her use of repetition is part emphasis, part musicality, and part fun. This play should make you think and should make you laugh. The thinking, and the poetry and the gaiety make a very original mixture which it is your pleasure to accept. As Miss Stein always says of her work: "Be natural and you will understand it."

The manuscript of the introduction is in the Harvard-Theatre Collection. The "Introduction" was first published in *Twentieth Century Literature, Gertrude Stein Issue*, ed. Edward Burns, 24, 1 (Spring 1978): 94–95.

The participants in Vestal's performances were Owen Haynes, piano; Rita Smith, soprano; Carl Harms, reader and manipulator; Burr Tilstrom, reader and manipulator, later famous for "Kukla, Fran and Ollie"; and Donald Vestal, who in addition to being a reader and manipulator designed and constructed the sets. Vestal wrote Stein about the performances in a letter, 13 July 1936 (YCAL), and later sent her photographs of the production which Stein acknowledged in a letter [? November 1936] (Harvard-Theatre).

Appendix V.

Gertrude Stein to
Alexander Woollcott

[MS Harvard-Houghton]

[? December 1935]   27 rue de Fleurus
                                                                      Paris. [France]

My dear friend

I want to tell you all about Basket, but first how touched I was by your story, it was a lovely story, and a beautiful to me finish to the war story of the Lonesome Pine, one's biography by song is interesting, when young adolescence dreamed in A Spanish cavalier stood on his retreat and on his guitar played a tune love, and my medical school was accompanied by And the moon was shining bright upon the Wabash and the moon was shining bright upon the sea, the men used to croon that while we worked, and in the public schools it used to be come with thy lute to the fountain sing me a song of the mountain, and I have no idea who wrote any of them either words or music, but you will know, and that too is a most enormous pleasure, but I want to tell you about Basket, Basket did one thing that was lovely when we came back from the country he had no basket in which to sleep, he has one in the country and he had one here but when we left him and his basket when we were in America he was so miserable that he tore his basket all up, so when we got to Paris I put down a blanket and he slept on it not too unhappily and then after a couple of days one day while I happened to look at him he deliberately tried to fit himself into the little Mexican dog's basket, he solemnly tried he protruded first one side and then the other never looking at me but solemnly trying to fit himself into the tiny basket, it was one of the most comical and one of the most reproachful things I have ever seen, of course I immediately took him out and bought him a basket, the matter has never again been mentioned between us, I think I told you that once when Basket was playing with his ball, by the way Basket's vocabulary all goes with b. he has bed and basket, and beg and bone and ball, he only talks in bs well the little Mexican got Basket's ball and sat on it and I looked up and there was Basket making the beau sitting up and begging for the ball, the little Mexican looked up at him as if he had gone mad and went on chasing the ball, for the first time in his life Basket had sat up and begged and not gotten what he asked he was disillusioned and there were tears in his eyes he has never been quite the same trusting dog since, he is a darling and I do hope someday you and he will meet, he is perhaps too friendly he errs on that side, and even when another dog bites him, he is convinced that it was an accident, he cannot accept it as intentional, he keeps his spirit pure and even when the little lambs in the village follow him because they think he is a sheep and the mother sheep butts him because she thinks he is leading off her babies to destroy them, he is just surprised. He only barks when the little Mexican tells him to, and he also only chases chickens when the little one leads the way, in short he is a happy fool, and a great comfort, and some day you will meet, there have I written you a lovely letter about Basket, there he is all white on the rug and sends you his best, merriest of merry Christmases as you are giving every one

Always and always
Gtde Stein.

Appendix VI.

Wilder's Notes on
Conversations about *Ida A Novel*

Ah, how fast this story is going already. There's Ida and already you're talking about her and quarreling about her. Later the whole world was to talk about her and quarrel about her, and here are the elements in Ida starting their action already.

Does it make you angry or pleased or puzzled to know that she had a dog born blind, that she hesitated before eating, that she didn't know what she had to have until she had it? But after all, it doesn't matter how it affects you: Ida will never give a thought to what she arouses in you. You must never forget that Ida was never strange to herself. Even when the whole world was looking at her, she was not interested in that.

The trouble with this book is that it has too many interesting characters. There are too many.

Woodward's another. To know that he never sighed is bad enough but to hear that he never listened when everybody was talking about Ida,—that is the last straw. He thought about Ida, of course, but it was about another Ida than the one the world was talking about. Does that mean that only Woodward was, in a way, like Ida?

Do you feel that you look like the people you have admired?

There is a limit to which novels should be interesting and I think this novel is exceeding the limits.

And now, like everybody in the world, we are eager to know more about Ida and we are already terrified lest we may never really know, really know the last last word about Ida.

But wait a moment. It's perfectly clear that if Ida was on the front page of the newspapers Ida was idle. The people who get in the headlines may appear to be doing something—escaping from five prisons and shooting ten policemen, or flying across oceans, or all those other things—but we know [?we] watchers, that inside them is a terrible great calm absence. Of course, there is. So different from our busy active lives. That's why we love them: they are so idle. their idleness makes us active and then maybe our activity makes them a little bit active. At least that's what we're here to find out. And it's terribly important. As I said before— novels must not, should not be too interesting and I'm very much afraid that this novel is too interesting.

CHAPTER SIX	Is.
CHAPTER SEVEN	Bayshore
CHAPTE[R] Eight	The dog Iris

Things happen to Ida that never happen to other people however hard they try. If you want to state Ida in one word all you have to say is that she never tried.

A viper bit her.

The whole world goes about longing to be bit by vipers, but it only happens to Ida.

And wouldn't Ida live at a place called Bayshore where there was practically no water.

You must read carefully if you want to watch Ida very closely (and who doesn't). Did you notice that Tuesday is two days. For a minute Ida is a little like the rest of us in that.

When our grandmothers said, "I'll spend Sunday with you," they meant Sunday. But today we're all a little confused about that. Sunday is a sort of extensible day; it begins Saturday and it's hard to say when it ends Monday. Ida's a little like us in that; we read in Chapter One that she had to have her Tuesday and we know that feeling all too well, and now we know that for her a day you had to have was two days.

Now what we want to know is who first looked at Ida, who was the first of all those millions and millions.

[x'd out: CHAPTER EIGHT   The dog Iris]

CHAPTER NINE   Money isn't Money.

[This in pencil? at end of sheet—repeated again in pen]

CHAPTER NINE   Money isn't money.

Should a novel be taxing? Novels used to be taxing, but this is the first novel in a long time that's really taxing.

Apparently it's going to discuss money,—money, that subject which everybody both longs to discuss and dreads to discuss.

But what has that to do with Ida?

Why, everything.

No, not in the sense you mean: neither Ida nor any of those others ever did anything "for money." How could they?

No, money in the other sense.

There's air and there's fire and there's water and there's money. In that sense.

When two people are married, really married, where's the money then? When a government gives money to everybody in the country and everybody in the country gives money to the government where's the money then? When William Shakespeare dead, gets three million dollars royalties, are they William Shakespeare's money? When it costs three million marks to ride on a German street car in one year and fifty pfennigs two years later where did all those marks go.

It's terribly hard to think about money and you won't be happy until you've looked in the mirror and asked yourself earnestly whether money is money; just as you ask yourself whether life is long or short, or what is it?

Appendix VII.

Wilder, Jed Harris, and *Our Town*

When Thornton Wilder sailed for Europe on 3 July 1937, his plans included participation in the Institut International de Coopération Intellectuelle conference in Paris, a trip to the Salzburg Festival, and a visit with Gertrude Stein. Wilder then hoped to devote three months to writing—the first long period without commitments since he had resigned from the University of Chicago at the end of the summer of 1936. Perhaps at the suggestion of the Arnold Wolfers, a Swiss couple then living in New Haven, Wilder selected Zurich as his writing haven.

Wilder had with him drafts and notes for several plays he had been working on since 1935: *The Merchant of Yonkers*, then called "Stranger Things Have Happened," *Our Town*, "The Hell of the Vizier Kabäar," a play about Haroun al-Raschid, and "Homage to P. G. Wodehouse." Within five months of arriving in Europe, however, his plans for an extensive period of writing came to an end. After a flurry of telegrams and telephone calls from the producer-director Jed Harris, a hastily arranged meeting in Paris, and a visit to London Wilder returned to the United States. *Our Town* ushered in a period of tumultuous activity for Wilder that continued almost unabated until he entered the armed forces in June 1942.

A crucial element of this period, alluded to only in these letters, is Wilder's relationship with Jed Harris. Their professional relationship began in 1937, with Ibsen's *A Doll's House*, which Wilder adapted, Harris produced and directed, and Ruth Gordon—a close friend of Wilder's and the lover of Harris—starred in. The roller-coaster ride of admiration and animosity that begins with this production and continued throughout with the production of *Our Town* is an important element in Wilder's career. In spite of the tensions Harris created, Wilder regarded him as a genius, and he remained his director of choice. Even after Harris rejected *The Skin of Our Teeth*, Wilder continued to seek out his advice about other projects, including the unfinished play "The Emporium" and *The Alcestiad*.

The background of their first meeting is important because it gives some insight into their relationship. Although Harris and Wilder were at Yale at the same time, they seem to have had only a passing acquaintance. Wilder was comfortable at Yale and was easily accepted into its society. His father and brother, both named Amos, were Yale men. His father was warmly remembered as a public speaker, and his brother, destined for the ministry, was also remembered as an outstanding tennis player. Although the Wilders were poor, their Congregationalist background and their cultural aspirations made them acceptable in New Haven society.

Harris, who was born Jacob Horowitz in Vienna in 1900, had come to America in 1901. When he entered Yale in 1917, he was an outsider, a Jew in a university in which chapel was mandatory and anti-Semitism was openly expressed. Even among the few Jews at Yale, Harris, who came from a poor family, felt himself an outsider. More than sixty years after he was expelled for failure to attend classes, Harris bitterly remembered the anti-Semitic treatment he suffered at Yale (see Harris, *A Dance*).

According to both Harris and Wilder, their first real encounter was on a train going from Miami to New York during Christmas week in 1927. As Wilder wrote to a family friend, Mrs. Harold H. Mudgett, "I was mistaken for him [i.e., his brother Amos] by someone on a train in Florida who turned out to be Jed Harris the new theatrical wizard of Broadway. Yale ex '17 and with him was Maxwell Anderson of What Price Glory?" (11 January 1928, YCAL). In interviews after *Our Town* opened, both Wilder and Harris recalled this meeting and Wilder's promise to give Harris first refusal when he wrote a full-length play. Wilder recalled, "In 1927 in a club car coming north from Florida Wilder ran into Harris and Maxwell Anderson and voiced his desire to turn from novels to plays. Harris encouraged him to the extent of asking to see a script" (interview with Wilder, *New York Herald Tribune*, 13 February 1938, NYPL-Lincoln Center; see interview of Harris by Malcolm Johnson in the *New York Sun*, 5 May 1938, NYPL- Lincoln Center).

At the time they met, Harris was a leading Broadway producer—"destiny's tot," as he was dubbed by Noel Coward. From September 1926 until August 1928, Harris produced four of Broadway's most successful plays: Philip Dunning's and George Abbott's *Broadway*, Abbott's and Ann Preston Bridgers's *Coquette*, George S. Kaufman's and Edna Ferber's *The Royal Family*, and Ben Hecht's and Charles MacArthur's *The Front Page*. On 3 September 1928, Harris was on the cover of *Time* and prominently featured in the article on the coming Broadway season.

After their meeting on the train, Wilder and Harris continued to see each other, in New York or in Chicago, where after 1930, Wilder was teaching at the

University of Chicago. The friendship was no doubt useful to each in different ways. Wilder was flattered that someone like Harris had taken an interest in him, and he used this connection to recommend his protégé Robert Ardrey to Harris (see Wilder to Stein, 6 April 1935, n. 4). For Harris, Wilder was the intellectual and well-connected friend he never made at Yale. In many of the articles that appeared in connection with *Our Town*, the Harris-Wilder-Yale connection figures prominently. The repetition of the information suggests it came from Harris's publicity assistant. Another element connecting Harris and Wilder was Ruth Gordon. Gordon and Harris had been introduced in 1927, and their son, Jones Kelley Harris, was born on 16 October 1929. Wilder had met Gordon in early 1929, probably through Alexander Woollcott, and he remained passionately attached to her until his death.

Throughout the early 1930s Wilder and Harris met and discussed the theater and Wilder's playwriting plans. In *Heaven's My Destination*, Wilder draws on Harris for the character of George Burkin, the movie director "with a thin, sardonic face," who goes on trial with George Brush. Burkin, perhaps echoing Harris, says of himself, "I'm the best that ever was or will be. I'm the greatest artist America ever had in any line. See?" (218–19).

Harris lost most of his money in the stock market crash of 1929, and he temporarily retired from the theater. He returned to produce several plays, including *Serena Blandish, Uncle Vanya, Wonder Boy, The Green Bay Tree*, and *The Lake*, but none rivaled his previous successes. In early April 1937, Harris asked Wilder to prepare a new acting version of Ibsen's *A Doll's House*: "Although my wonderful long-awaited Free Time had begun it was suddenly interrupted by an S.O.S. from Jed Harris commanding me to revise an acting-version of the Doll's House for Ruth Gordon. Rehearsals were to have begun yesterday and I sat down and from German and English versions began a completely new 'translation' of the play. I worked like a madman only to find that production has been postponed" (Wilder to Joe Etta Lee Clarke, 9 April 1937, YCAL).

A Doll's House played at the Central City Opera House in Denver from 17 July to 7 August 1937. Wilder was already in Europe when the production opened, but Ruth Gordon's letters provided a running account of the performances and information about Harris. From Woollcott's home on Neshobe Island Gordon wrote,

> You know we went up and did the play for Ned [i.e., Edward Sheldon]. The whole cast and pianist with the exception of Dennis King. Jed read his part. Ned was simply wonderful. He said it was the best performance Ibsen had ever had, that your work was positively magnificent and that I must immediately start work on Lady Macbeth. . . . I'm a little mad at Jed. I'm mad at him because I saw him succumbing to the temptation I spend my life in fighting. There is a stage in the creative act where one rises up to destroy the work in creation. The same mind that is intelligent enough to create something is also at every moment intelligent enough to see every fault in the work and to turn and destroy it. That impulse

must remain in the subconscious as corrective power. On the Friday before I left, at that rehearsal Jed had opened the trapdoor to the destructive impulse and was tearing his work to pieces. (Gordon to Wilder, 18 August [1937], transcribed by Wilder. This and subsequent mentions of transcribed letters in this note are described in Stein to Wilder, received 10 September 1936 (1), n. 1-d)

Gordon's description reinforced what Wilder already knew about the character of Harris and may have played a role in Wilder's reaction to his telegrams and telephone calls a month later.

On 11 October, after a vacation and some cast changes, the production of *A Doll's House* went on a three-month tour prior to its Broadway opening on 27 December. Everywhere it played the production was enthusiastically greeted, and Harris, perhaps to revitalize his reputation and to prove that the wunderkind of 1926–28 still had the ability to be provocative, began to pressure Wilder for the promised play.

Harris wired Wilder in Zurich three days after *A Doll's House* opened in Toronto: "Dear Thornie Toronto hails you critically and editorially as greatest living adapter of classics rave notices for show Ruth and all of us[.] sailing tomorrow morning aboard Normandie arriving London Wednesday please if possible let us meet briefly in Paris have much to tell you and am most anxious to see you otherwise shall phone you from London affectionately Jed" (New York, 14 October, transcribed by Wilder). Wilder did not answer this telegram, but must have mentioned it in a letter to Lady Colefax, who responded, "The cable very Jed. I'm glad you feel so fine and independent of Jed. You know I think he is only good if treated as more or less a means to an end. (Of course I think him fascinating too)" (postmarked 21 October, transcribed by Wilder). From London, Harris cabled Wilder: "Dear Thornie did you get my cable I am most anxious to see you or speak to you on the telephone can you come to Paris for a few days what is your phone number and address please wire me immediately Savoy much love Jed" (22 October, transcribed by Wilder). On 25 October he again cabled: "Dear Thornie don't understand your forwarding your telephone number by letter may have to leave here immediately please wire me number will phone tonight Jed" (transcribed by Wilder). And again on the 28 October he cabled Wilder: "Dear Thornie i would like to meet you in paris either monday or tuesday morning whichever you prefer i am very anxious to get on with our town and if i could have the script monday morning i would have it typed in paris before going back to america if you prefer to make it sunday that will be ok seeing sybil tonight affectionately Jed" (transcribed by Wilder, time noted: 10:52 A.M.). Following this cable, Harris telephoned Wilder, and it is that conversation that is mentioned in Wilder's letter to Stein of 28 October.

Wilder's uneasiness about Harris was based on personal experience over several years and on what he knew of his relationship with Ruth Gordon. A letter received from Lynn Fontanne may have reinforced his anxiety about Harris:

Now about your plays, which should really have been first, except that I know your interest in Amphitryon. The description of them in your letter makes me very angry. They sound so wonderful that I am jealous that anybody else should have them but us, and wonder furiously what Jed has got, in your opinion that we have not, that makes you give him the refusal of . . . . [Wilder's dots] is it ALL your plays, for God's sake? This is in no sense, of course, a criticism of Jed, as we have had no business experience with him and our personal experience with him has been most delightful. What charm! What a really darling little person he is. But of course, everybody prophesies some dire debacle always with Jed. However, should it be true; I can imagine nobody more capable of meeting it, so perhaps everything is all right. (National Theatre, Washington, D.C., 21 October, transcribed by Wilder; Wilder's letter to Fontanne is not in the Lunt-Fontanne papers at the State Historical Society-Wisconsin and has not been located)

Wilder had, for some time, been writing his friends about his works in progress. From Salzburg he wrote his family, "I write every morning in my room. 'Stranger Things have Happened' has taken a whole new turn and it's picking up vitality every day. Shall I expose it to Reinhardt before I go?" (n.d., ?August 1937, YCAL—this letter, and other family letters quoted here from 1937 are from transcriptions made by Janet Wilder and made available to us by Isabel Wilder; the original letters are now in YCAL.) From Innsbruck he wrote them, "I read Sibyl [Colefax] all the fragments of my plays. She's delighted with them all, and especially loves the outlined but still unwritten one about Haroun-Al Raschid. . . . The Second Act of Our Town will be radiant, and of course the Third Act in the cemetery will be awe-some" (3 September 1937, YCAL) and a few days later, from Zurich, he concluded a letter to them, "Did I tell you that both Frau Tal and Sibyl loved the Nestroy play and Our Town, but nobody liked the Wodehouse. The Prince of Baghdad will be best however" (8 September 1937, YCAL). The next day he wrote his sister Isabel, "Worked fine this A.M. Second Act of Our Town is rolling up. And the Third will be easier still. The Second is no longer any Long Xmas Dinner; that is discarded. It is now the wedding of the Doctor's son and the Editor's daughter" (9 September 1937, YCAL).

The letters that Wilder transcribed from Fontanne, Gordon, and Lady Colefax make clear that he wrote his friends about his works in progress. Lady Colefax's letters suggest that Wilder may have read to her from both *The Merchant of Yonkers* and *Our Town* during their six days together in Salzburg (see transcribed letter, postmarked 3 September 1937). It was probably at this time that Wilder either read or outlined *The Merchant of Yonkers* to Reinhardt, who expressed interest in the play. There is nothing, however, to suggest that Wilder read his plays to Stein during his visit in August. We know that they discussed the deposit of her papers in the Yale University library and her problems writing *Ida A Novel*. Wilder, who had recently finished reading the complete version of *The Making Of Americans*, spent long hours in discussion with Stein—discussions that find their way into *Our Town*—in particular into Act III. Wilder, who years later would refer to Stein as his Diotima, was perhaps uneasy about presenting his teacher with an unfinished work that employed her ideas. It is interesting to note that except for Stein's anxiety about the opening of *Our Town*, and a mention of seeing an article about it, she never comments on the play.

From Zurich, before leaving for Sils-Maria and Sils-Baselgia, he wrote to his family, "I've finished the Second Act of Our Town and it's just lovely, as is the opening of Act III. . . . Seems like I'll finish Our Town by Friday and then I'll polish up Nestroy-Moliere for Reinhardt. (If Jed hears about that, he'll be terrific.) Then I do the Prince of Baghdad which is the best of 'em all" (15 September 1937, YCAL). Reports on his progress continued. On 18 September he wrote his mother that he was "working every day on Act II of 'Our Town' & going fine" (YCAL). On 22 September, from Sils-Baselgia, he wrote his mother and sister Isabel, "Soon 'Our Town' will be finished, and then I attack the Nestroy-Moliere which will glitter like the Kohinoor. Then the Prince of Baghdad and I can come home" (YCAL).

Wilder continued to work on both *The Merchant of Yonkers* and *Our Town* during the next several weeks. To his mother he wrote on 22 October from Zurich, "I finished Act Four of the Nestroy-Moliere-cum Wilder today; and Act II last week. Act III is half-done and there's a Big Unsolved Block ho[l]ding me up. Act I has to be completely rewritten. The Other Play's all done and put away in the cupboard to cool off. Jed's in London and wants to see me in Paris, but I don't budge" (YCAL). Following his telephone conversation with Harris on 28 October he wrote his family, "He wants to know if 'Our Town' would be a good play for the Xmas season in New York. Would it?!! And guess who might act the lanky tooth-picking Stagemanager? Sinclair Lewis! He's been plaguing Jed to let him act for a long time; and there's a part for his famous New England parlor-trick mono-logues." He wrote to his family the morning of 30 October telling of his plans to leave for Paris and his meeting with Harris: "Yes, I'll have to tell Jed that Play #2 is for Reinhardt. Disappointment; cold anger; scenes. Then the going away to read it to him and ask advice on some cruces" (YCAL).

Wilder and Harris each arrived in Paris the morning of 31 October. That evening, after a dinner at the Brasserie Lipp, they went to see Stein, where *Our Town* may have been read informally.

The next day Harris and Wilder met to read the play and to discuss the production. Sinclair Lewis was not selected to play the Stage Manager on Broad-way, although he did perform the role in summer stock theaters. Harris left the morning of 2 November for Southampton where, before he left for New York, he cabled Wilder, "My dear Thorny you have made me very happy you ought to hear me read Our Town all you can do is write Jed" (3 November, transcribed by Wilder).

If Stein was the intellectual underpinning for many of Wilder's ideas, Lady Colefax was the practical friend whom Wilder used as a sounding board. Probably based on what Wilder had told her she concluded about Harris, "He is a bully and for a bully you just keep quiet and quite firm . . . [Wilder's dots] he'll have to come for the plays and have to make up his mind and you decide how long he has to do that in. Remember he is *never never never* to be trusted for one moment unless you have the upper hand" (3 October, transcribed by Wilder; Lady Colefax refers to Harris as Joe, which Wilder transcribes as "[i.e., Jed]").

Knowing that Wilder planned on coming to London for a few days to see Lady Colefax, whom Wilder would call the "God-mother of *Our Town*," Harris cabled her, "Dear Mother thanks for everything now do your duty and make Wilder go home end of next week your loving chit Jed" (New York, 8 November, transcribed by Wilder).

Wilder arrived in London on 6 November and then returned directly to Zurich and by 18 November was again in Paris (see Stein to Wilder, 11 November, n. 1, and Wilder to Stein, 24 November, n. 1). Just before leaving Zurich, he received another urgent cable from Harris: "DEAR THORNIE PLEASE IF YOU POSSIBLY CAN DO SAIL THIS WEEK AS I NEED YOU VERY BADLY FOR ABOUT TWO WEEKS BEFORE WE GO INTO REHEARSAL CASTING PROVISIONALLY UNDER WAY CABLE OPINION OF FRANK CRAVEN FOR STAGE MANAGER AFFECTIONATELY=JED" (New York, 17 November, YCAL).

When Wilder left Cherbourg on 25 November, he carried with him several packages of Stein's manuscripts destined for the Yale University library and the nearly completed script of *Our Town*. It would be two months before he found the time to sort through Stein's manuscripts and take them to the library. Almost immediately upon his arrival he was sequestered by Harris; as one headline announced, "Wilder Locked Up Till He Finishes That Play of His" (*New York World-Telegram*, 7 December 1937, NYPL-Lincoln Center). Harris, in a desire to revitalize his career and wanting to capitalize on the success of *A Doll's House*, worked feverishly to bring *Our Town* to Broadway.

On the morning of 22 January 1938, a few hours before the world premiere of *Our Town* at the McCarter Theatre in Princeton, New Jersey, Wilder wrote a note detailing his apprehensions about Harris' direction and then sealed it.

> The Following Elements in the Production of
> "Our Town" are likely to harm and perhaps
> shipwreck its effectiveness

(1) The First Act—and in large measure the play—is in danger of falling into trivial episodes, through failure to build up the two great idea-pillars of the Stage-Manager's interruptions. The Professor's speech has been reduced to pleasant fooling, instead of being made forceful and informative, as I have often requested; the Passage on the future has been watered down, and the actor has not been vigorously directed.

(2) The element of the Concrete Localization of the town has been neglected; in fact, the Director has an astonishingly weak sense of visual reconstruction. Characters talk to one another from Mrs Webb's back door to Main Street; and from

one end of Main Street to another in the same tone of voice they use when they are in the same "room." They stroll practically in and out of Main Street when they are in a house; Emily's grave is one minute here and soon after *there*.

(3) In spite of express promises to remove them a series of interpolations in the First Act remain; each one of these has the character of amiable dribbling, robbing the text of its nervous compression from which alone can spring the sense of Significance in the trivial Acts of Life which is the subject of the play.

(4) The recent alteration to the closing words of Mrs Gibbs and Emily in Act III are soft, and bathetic.

(5) There seems every likelihood that a pseudo-artistic inclination to dim lights will further devitalize the Stage-Manager's long speeches; and the last Act. The eternal principle that the Ear does not choose to hear, if the eye is not completely satisfied particularly applies in this play.

After opening at the McCarter Theatre, Princeton, New Jersey, on 22 January 1938, the play traveled to Boston before opening in New York at the Henry Miller Theatre on 4 February.

Appendix VIII.

Thornton Wilder: January 1942 to May 1943

The period from January 1942, when Wilder finished *The Skin of Our Teeth*, until May 1943, when he left for active military duty in North Africa, was one of the most active in Wilder's life.

When he returned from England on 18 October 1941, he took up this play, which had been continually postponed during most of that year (see Wilder to Stein [September 1941]). Wilder had sent Jed Harris acts I and II during the summer. On finishing act III he sent it immediately to Harris, hoping he would produce the play and, if he finished *The Alcestiad*, that play as well, before Wilder enlisted in active military service prior to his forty-fifth birthday in April 1942.

As it turned out, Jed Harris refused to produce and direct *The Skin of Our Teeth*, and from the end of January until mid-May, Wilder was consumed with the details of finding a director, getting the play cast, and raising money for its production. During this time, Wilder wrote the scripts for two army training films: *Manuelito Becomes an Air Cadet* and *Your Community and the War Effort*. This assignment for the Office of War Information had been arranged by Wilder's friend Archibald MacLeish, who was assistant director.

In mid-May, just when he thought he could return to *The Alcestiad*, he received a telegram from Alfred Hitchcock inviting him to Hollywood to write the screenplay for his new film, *Shadow of a Doubt*. Concerned for the financial security of his family, Wilder accepted the offer. In June, almost immediately after returning from Hollywood, he went to Miami Beach to begin military training. There is no evidence that Wilder wrote to Stein from March 1942 until his undated letter of September 1944 following news that she was safe in France. His military activities are summarized in Isabel Wilder's letter to Stein of 8 September 1944.

What follows is, in large part, the production history of *The Skin of Our Teeth*, from the difficulties in choosing a director and in casting the play to the tumultuous and acrimonious rehearsals and performances that have become part of theater legend. Wilder's biographers, as well as two of the principals, Tallulah Bankhead and Elia Kazan, have contributed to this history.

In spite of the difficult personal and professional relationship with Jed Harris, Wilder had offered him the new play. By midsummer or early fall 1941 Wilder had given Harris acts I and II; there is nothing in the Wilder papers to indicate the reaction of Harris to them. Wilder finished act III on New Year's Day and on 7 January mailed it to Harris in California, where he and his new wife, the actress June Platt, were living. Edward Goodnow, who had been the stage manager for *Our Town* and was now an assistant to Harris, asked Wilder to send new copies of acts I and II because the originals had been lost. Wilder sent them on 9 January (Goodnow letter unlocated, see Wilder to family, 14 January 1942, YCAL. Unless otherwise noted, all subsequently quoted letters are in YCAL) and on the same day wrote to Alexander Woollcott,

> It shows how that fine American family Mr. and Mrs. George Antrobus, their children Henry and Gladys, and their girl, Sabina, of Excelsior, New Jersey, go through the Ice Age, the Flood and a War, with a lot of screaming, absurdity and a few shreds of dignity. . . . Probably I shall go to Hollywood in a few weeks to look narrowly at Jed Harris. Rumor says that he is not at liberty to occupy himself with the play. I can embrace that eventuality without despair, but with some trepidation and have a plan all made. (Harvard-Theatre)

Wilder knew his play needed more work, and as he waited for word from Harris, he wrote home on 14 January, from Philadelphia, where he had gone to hear Woollcott lecture,

> On the play, I've decided to be a good deal more forthright. To begin with the announcement of the sunrise and the wedding ring.
> And there'll be other changes.
>
>   x
>
> If I don't hear from Jed by Friday, I'll write him in the tone of assuming that his hesitation is final rejection, and start bestirring myself with the other copies. [The "other copies" with covering letters were to be sent to Alfred Lunt, Dudley Digges, and Orson Welles.]

On 22 January, from Baltimore, where he was attending a P.E.N. dinner and working on the script for one of the Army Air Corps training films, he wrote home, "Isa: I'm telegraphing Jed (the Baltimore address being an advantage!) [']Assume through your silence you find decision difficult. I do not wish to hurry your decision but I should like to hear your discussion of the problems. Cordially' " (the original of the telegram to Harris has not been located).

Harris replied on 27 January. He had thought a great deal about the play and questioned whether he should "speak about it with the utmost frankness." He found the first act "noble, not merely in statement, in conception, in theme, but in sheer comic aptitude" but found the whole second act, "a comparatively faulty and a confused restatement of theme." About the third act, Harris wrote,

> [A]fter all that had gone before, [it] seemed to me utterly trivial. . . . If I were a religious man I would go to church and pray: Pray that you don't give this play to some foolish producer or director who will be so carried away with it that you will be persuaded to let it go into production. I think that such an event would be at least a minor disaster for you and the play and for me. (see Harrison, *The Enthusiast*, 218–19; we have been unable to locate the original letter to verify the transcription)

Wilder's reply of 29 January has not been located, but he kept a "sketch of letter sent":

Dear Jed:

Many thanks for your letter.

Sure, you know that that way of talking is what I like best.

Rê Acts II and III.

Act II.

Yes sir, that concept's very hard to swing.

First, because of the break in tone from Act One. And second, because of all the new kind of things that have to be coordinated in it.

All I can say is that since I sent it to you, I think I've found the way of: from laying down the Sabina menace-to-the-home much earlier; and from building up the motif that the World is a Convener's riot-and-orgy 'enjoying itself.' Since you're on the point of praying for me, pray for me on that.

Act Three:

Yes, I'm very uneasy about the philosophers-as-hours, and will continue to grope about that, but Act III has its core which is stronger than anything in Act II and equal to Act One: The conflict of Father and Son and the statement of War as the anguish of the 'emptinesses.'

And it's very mean of you, old sour-puss to brush away Act III so high handedly and not accord me a B-boutonnière on the dramatic interest of the two women living under the stage for seven years.

Oh, Jed, Jed, with Dorothy Heyward's play and this—you should have rolled up your sleeves and returned to the old battlefield.

You'll hear from me again.

To your knees—rosary forwarded under separate cover.

The next day, 30 January, an announcement appeared in the New York papers that *The Skin of Our Teeth*, which Wilder recently submitted to Jed Harris, would be produced by Michael Myerberg: "Rehearsals are expected to start in mid-February, with a Broadway opening promised for late April after an out-of-town engagement" (*New York Times*, 22). The suddenness of the announcement and Wilder's previous statement to Woollcott on 9 January that he "had a plan all made" suggest that Wilder and Myerberg had been discussing the possible rejection of the play by Harris and at dinner on 27 January had finalized their agreement and the announcement.

From 1929 to 1935 Myerberg had worked in various capacities on Broadway productions, and beginning in 1936 he had been the business manager for Leopold Stokowski. When he and Wilder met at Mabel Luhan's Taos home in 1938, he had expressed an interest in working with Wilder. That opportunity arose in January 1941, when Wilder sent Max Reinhardt notes for a performance planned by his workshop of *The Merchant of Yonkers*. Reinhardt replied that in addition he was planning a production of Pirandello's *Six Characters in Search of an Author* in New York, to be produced by Myerberg and asked Wilder to revise the translation. Wilder's play opened in Hollywood on 19 February. Nothing came of the Pirandello project, and it is not listed in Heusmann's *Welt Theater Reinhardt*. (See Reinhardt to Wilder, 23 January and 12 February 1941.)

With Harris out of the project, Wilder and Myerberg began the search for a director and a cast. From New York, on 2 February 1942, Wilder wrote home,

> Lunch with M[ichael]. M[yerberg].
> Ilka Chase is crazy about the play. "I was born to play Sabina."
> Dudley Digges thinks it's defeatest. Wants to keep it a few more days, though. Says he hasn't been well and may have read it too cursorily . . . . . .
> [Wilder's ellipses]
> Have made some short but deep-going emendations in Act II and shall now find some for III.

Wilder and Harris had discussed casting Alfred Lunt and Lynn Fontanne as Mr. and Mrs. Antrobus, and a completed script had been sent to them in January. Even without Harris, Wilder hoped they would do the play. Wilder received a telegram from Lunt on 3 February that is undoubtedly the text quoted in his letter to Edward Sheldon of [? February 1942]:

> We sent it to X [a distinguished actor-director] for his direction and we hoped, his performance, and he telegraphed back, "The play is brilliant, original, profound, and very funny too, but it troubles me. Am writing." Five days have gone by and no letter has come. (Quoted in Barnes, *The Man Who Lived Twice*, 221–22. We have been unable to locate either Lunt's telegram or Wilder's letter to Sheldon. It is probable that the "X [a distinguished actor-director]" is Lunt, but whether Wilder or Barnes characterizes him as "X" remains unclear.)

On 4 February, Lunt had written to Woollcott that he found the title of the play "most unattractive at the moment," but recognized that "it's very funny, profound and most original—easy to act and should be exciting to look at. . . . But when all's said and done," Lunt continued, "I'm sure an audience would go from the theatre in a complete state of bewilderment & slightly resentful" (Harvard-Theatre).

Wilder wrote the Lunts on 5 February,

Dear Friends:

I didn't answer Lynn's lovely letter, because I knew that I soon would have another matter to write you on. Jed with the manuscript was being silent week after week and I foresaw I would have the text back and be released of the promise to give it into his hands first.

Then I didn't write you with the sending of the script because such letters—half deprecation—are so unnecessary.

But now with Alfred's telegram, of which—whatever happens—I shall always be proud, I shall write a letter about the play even before receiving Alfred's letter.

x

Lately, my eyes have been opened with a shock to one aspect of it.

It's struck some people as 'defeatest.' I have only read it to a few friends, mostly in our academic group in New Haven. One distinguished doctor said that it haunted him for days but that "the government ought to prevent it's being shown"; others variously said it was "anti-war" or "pacifistic." And I suddenly remember that Sibyl [Colefax], who heard the first two acts in London, said that the Second Act was "so cruel."

And three or four days ago my eyes were opened, and I could see with amazement how I had given so wrong an impression of what I had meant.

It's that old thing again. that New England shame-facedness and shyness of the didactic, the dread of moralizing, the assumption that the aspirational side of life can be taken for granted.

I had omitted (though thinking it self evident!) any scene of conjugal love and trust between Mr. and Mrs. Antrobus; and any speech that would give open voice to her and to his confidence, through discouragement, in the unshakable sense that work and home and society move on towards great good things.

Now with a sort of eagerness I have set to rendering more explicit all things which for me were always there and which I now feel to be urgent for expression. With what mortification I now see that the Second Act—vindication of the unit of the family—exhibits only the exasperating side of children and the "nagging" side of Mrs. Antrobus; and how especially I shirked Mr. Antrobus's broadcast to the Natural World; and how the positive affirmative elements of Act Three are muted and evaded to the point of spiritual thinness.

x

Jed's objections which he says apply only to the Second and Third Acts have to do with theatrical contrivances and "tricks." He doesn't specify which ones he objects to; but the ones I have resolved to modify are in the last act.

I have tried writing the Third Act straight through, without the interruption of the Rehearsal of the Hours-as-Philosophers, and am preparing some less obtrusive way of giving the impression of the overarching world of time, weather and natural history that surrounds the Antrobus family.—But the chief thing is to inform all that with the tone of warmth and courage and confidence about the human adventure which I had too much "taken for granted."

x

I don't have to tell you what hopes I keep in relation to you both.

But it's enough for the present that Alfred's telegram tells me of his warm interest in the text itself. And any suggestions from that comprehensive God-given understanding of what the theatre is in heights and depths are reward enough for me.

With devoted affection
Thornton

Post-Script:

This Michael Myerberg whose association with the play was published as manager is an old friend who is really serving in the capacity of what Brandt and Brandt never really has done. He is not a member of the Manager's Association; there is no contract between us; and his enthusiasm led him to "do something about it" as inspirator and friend.

T.

On 19 February Wilder did respond to Lunt's 3 February telegram:

Dear Alfred:

Many thanks for your telegram. Yes, you are right to reserve your comments on a script which is undergoing so many alterations.

And so have our plans. The director whom we want and who wishes to do the play has another commitment for the Spring; so we will probably have to wait until Fall.

In the meantime I have begun writing another [i.e., *The Alcestiad*], and the work on the government movies goes on. Of those I think the next one will be good. All my best to you both.

Cordially ever
Thornton
(Wilder's letters to Lunt and Fontanne are in SHS-
Wisconsin)

Lunt's letter explaining his feelings about the play is dated 20 February, but the postmark from Waukesha, Wisconsin, is 3 March:

Dear Thornton:

I still think that "Skin of Our Teeth" is original, profound & witty, but for the life of me, I don't quite know what you are trying to get at, and this feeling, I am sure, will be shared by an audience if the play is produced as now written. It is very obscure and before presentation I think should be clarified.

Both Mr. and Mrs. Antrobus are clear enough, and so is Sabina (a wonderful part) but Henry in the first two acts is pretty mysterious. And may I suggest that at the end of Act I instead of having ushers ripping up chairs it be done by the orchestra. Asking an audience to tear up their seats might not have the effect intended. (It would embarrass me to death.) But if the orchestra handed up first their music, then their racks, then their chairs, and finally their instruments—during the latter part of which goings on, the sound of the ushers doing their damndest to demolish the theatre, might possibly prove pretty exciting. A vaude-ville act named "The Britons" used to smash up every instrument in the band as the finale, and it was very funny indeed.

And the very end of the play distresses me. The announcers—I just don't get it. I know, dear Thornton, I am not over-bright, but I think I am pretty representa-tive of a theatre going public, and so I presume to write you. You are a very great and brilliant writer, and I should hate to have your play misunderstood, which I am afraid it will be by people like me. [A]nd unfortunately there are so many of us—

Too bad there are no Russian artists in this country to do the scenery. Someone, for instance, who worked at the Kamerny Theatre.
Our love to you,
Alfred

Clearly by 19 February, Wilder was no longer thinking of Lunt as director. Among the other directors Wilder and Myerberg had considered were Dudley Digges, the Irish-born actor and director, Orson Welles, whom Wilder had known since the early 1930s, and Elia Kazan. Digges did not respond enthusiastically to the play, and Welles, who had released *Citizen Kane* in 1941, was working on *The Magnificent Ambersons*.

The director ultimately chosen was Elia Kazan. Kazan himself does not discuss how Wilder and Myerberg came to select him. Both Goldstone (*An Intimate Portrait*, 165) and Simon (*His World*, 165) suggest he was recommended by Robert Ardrey. Kazan, a member of the Group Theatre, had done some directing with the Theatre of Action before he directed Ardrey's *Casey Jones* (1938) and *Thunder Rock* (1939) for the Group Theatre. While Ardrey may have suggested Kazan, it was probably after seeing his direction of *Cafe Crown*, H. S. Kraft's play about the Yiddish Theatre which had opened on 23 January, that Wilder and Myerberg were convinced of Kazan's abilities.

On 18 February, Wilder, who had met with Fredric March and Florence Eldridge in the afternoon and had spoken by phone with Kazan, wrote to Woollcott, "Fredric March wants to play in my play and he's changed his mind about Mrs. March not necessarily being in his company. He thinks she'd be a wonderful Mrs Antrobus. . . . . I think I can come up and see you sooner than I thought. Depends on whether Kazan will be free to direct our play" (Harvard-Theatre).

This letter shows that Wilder is no longer thinking of the Lunts as possible actors. In his autobiography Kazan gives a detailed account of meeting with March and Eldridge, who, having agreed to play Mr. and Mrs. Antrobus, had a clause in their contract giving them approval of the director (Kazan, *A Life*, 192–

97). Wilder and Myerberg had hoped to go into rehearsal immediately, but March's commitment to René Clair's film *I Married a Witch* forced postponement of rehearsals until September to be followed by out-of-town tryouts beginning in New Haven on 15 October and an opening in New York on 18 November.

At the time Wilder and Myerberg approached him, Kazan was negotiating with the producers Edward Choate and Alexander Kirkland to direct Paul Vincent Carroll's play *The Strings, My Lord, Are False*. With that play scheduled for a mid-May opening, and with March in Hollywood, *The Skin of Our Teeth* was postponed until fall. Wilder had announced in a letter to Woollcott on 27 March, "Now that 'The Skin of Our Teeth' . . . is on the shelf until August, I have begun another, *The Alcestiad*" (Harvard-Theatre).

On 14 April, a *New York Times* article on the coming theater season announced Ruth Gordon's engagement for *The Strings, My Lord, Are False*, to be directed by Kazan. The same article mentions that Myerberg had seen the new Walter Kerr play, *Art and Prudence*, at the Catholic University in Washington, D.C., and planned to bring it to Broadway in the autumn. "This will not interfere," the article went on to say, "with his plans to bring Thornton Wilder's 'Skin of Our Teeth' to Broadway in November, with Fredric March and Florence Eldridge in the leading roles" (17). It is interesting that Kazan is not named as the director in this article.

Wilder, who attended a rehearsal and later a preview performance of Carroll's play on 16 May, wrote to Woollcott the next day, "Kazan is a fine director and Ruth is a great actress, but plays should be written by dramatists" (Harvard-Theatre). Ruth Gordon in *My Side* (437) writes that Wilder said after seeing the Carroll play that "he was going to ask Elia to direct *The Skin of Our Teeth*." Gordon's recollection is faulty; the decision to engage Kazan had been made in February.

The search for an actress to play Sabina proved difficult. It is generally assumed that Wilder had Ruth Gordon in mind when he wrote the role. Yet in her undated letter of [?March–April 1942] to Woollcott, Gordon wrote of a planned meeting between herself, Kazan, and Wilder:

> I am having dinner with Thornton and the Kazans tomorrow because K. wants to meet me. I take it naturally to be sex but Thornton implies it is part business and it may be K. thinks I would be good for a part in Thornton's play which I still have never read but which all the columns imply I am going to appear in as that seems to the columnists the only possible reason that I could be giving Thornton such a rush at the Stork Club for. Winchell wanted to print that we were going to be married but Leonard Lyons talked him out of it. (Harvard-Theatre)

Given Wilder's friendship with Gordon, it seems odd that she had not seen the finished script, which was already in circulation to potential actors and directors. Myerberg, for his part, felt that she was not right for the role. There is no indication that Wilder wished Gordon to play Sabina—a role, incidentally, that she never played on the stage.

When Helen Hayes was sent the script, she at first thought she was being offered the role of Mrs. Antrobus (a role she would later play on the stage). In her memoir, *A Gift of Joy*, she writes,

> *The Skin of Our Teeth* was hot off the typewriter when Thornton Wilder telephoned me and said, "I have a new play that I want you to do." . . . He sent me the script, and, when I finished reading it, I went into Charlie's study and said, "It isn't possible. It just can't happen twice to an actress, but this role, this Mrs. Antrobus, is even greater than Victoria". . . . I phoned Thornton and went on and on blabbing to him about how I loved the play and the role, and finally after a good deal of conversation—the two of us almost breathless—I said, "And who's going to play my husband?" There was a deathly moment of silence and then Thornton said, "I didn't mean for you to play Mrs. Antrobus. I meant you to play Sabina." (146–47)

While Hayes considered the role of Sabina, she wrote to Woollcott on 2 July 1942,

> I'm very fogged at this point in my career and I want help. Have you read Thornton's play, 'Skin of Our Teeth'? I think it is one of the great plays of our time. His mysterious producer, Mr. Myerberg, sent it to me with the suggestion that I play Sabina. Of course there's only one person to play that part—the person for whom I suspect it was written—Ruth. I won't dare attempt it since I'd be haunted by the thought of the way she'd speak every line. It's very distracting, though, to have to turn down a good play. (Harvard-Theatre; Woollcott quotes this in his letter to Wilder, 20 July 1942, published in Kaufman and Hennessey, *Letters*, 345–46)

Hayes eventually said no to the role of Sabina but suggested Tallulah Bankhead.

Apparently at some point Gordon had been offered the role of Sabina because in his autobiography, Kazan writes that he received a call from Myerberg telling him that she "had given him his 'out,' and he'd been able to get the person he wanted for Sabina. Tallulah Bankhead" (201). The out was probably Gordon's decision to appear in Katharine Cornell's revival of Chekhov's *The Three Sisters*, directed by Guthrie McClintic and scheduled to open in New York on 21 December 1942. Gordon, who wanted to establish herself in the "classics," agreed to play the role of Natasha, opposite Judith Anderson's Olga and Cornell's Masha.

Also, Gordon's reaction to Kazan changed radically after the failure of the Carroll play. Initially, after reading it she wrote Woollcott, "Elia Kazan is going to direct it. He has turned into a great director" (undated letter [?March–April 1942], Harvard-Theatre). But the play was not well received, and it closed on 30 May after fifteen performances. In a denunciation of Kazan she wrote to Wilder on 9 June [1942],

> Right off I must say you must not have Elia do it. Not because of the show he just did but he never for years to come, if ever could direct it. He hasn't the personal

self discipline. He hasn't the practicality. He hasn't the true theatrical imagination. He cannot do it. The play must stand or fall by the director. It is *True True True*. Just as if Gertrude Stein said it. It is the truest thing in the whole world. My typewriter blanches to think I could compare anything I have to say to anything Gertrude Stein might have to say but it nonetheless remains TRUE. When you wrote that play you said only Jed could direct it and I think only JED can. But anyway Elia can't. He really can't. He must learn a whole lot more.

On 12 August Wilder would write to Woollcott from his army intelligence training school in Harrisburg, Pennsylvania, "Phone calls from that other world reach me to the effect that Tallulah is eager to play the character of Sabina. I must say that March & Florence Reed [who played the Fortune Teller] & Tallulah would make crackle on the stage" (Harvard-Theatre). A few days later he wrote Woollcott, "Yesterday Michael Myerberg came down to report to me on the play. Tallulah is signed up for the obstreperous daughter of nature, Sabina. She not only loves the part, but knows every corner of the play. Already she's asking that such-and-such a line be transferred to her rôle. That's right. Sabina's greedy—to thrust herself forward, and she can scream and protest and interfere and raise hell as much as she wants" (16 August 1942, Harvard-Theatre). Wilder telephoned his pleasure to Bankhead, who responded by a telegram: "IT WAS SO SWEET OF YOU TO PHONE ME I WAS SO PROUD TO BE IN YOUR WONDERFUL PLAY AND SO HAPPY THAT YOU SEEM PLEASED ABOUT IT AND HOW I HOPE THAT YOU WILL BE ABLE TO BE WITH US DURING REHEARSALS TO GUIDE US LOVE==TALLULAH" (?17 August 1942).

On 4 February Wilder and Gordon had gone to see Bankhead starring in *Clash By Night* by Clifford Odets. At that time he might have thought of using her in the role. The character of Sabina gave him immense difficulties. He drafted the following memorandum during the three days, 6–8 March, that he spent in Atlantic City, New Jersey, with Kazan working on the play (see Wilder to Woollcott, 8 March [1942], Harvard-Theatre):

MEMO: rê Sabina as a beauty.
Atlantic City, March 1942

Something's the matter with the Second Act.

Trying to get at the root of it I seem to see this: Gradually it's getting too realistic and pathetic and superficially credible.

My God!—an Act that begins with a Six-Thousandth Annual Convention of Mankind and ends with an Imaginary Kangaroo carr[y]ing a turtle down the central aisle of the theatre cannot dare to be realistic-pathetic for ten minutes.

The greatest sin in a play (and the explanation of 90% of all failures there) is the failure to preserve homogeneity of imaginative tone in an imaginative thing.

My mistake begins in Act One. The Broadway-Panhandler Refugees inevitably bring pathos, mutes suffering, etc. And from then in Mr. Antrobus's apoplectic stroke reduce the tone to almost-recognizable domestic anguish.

Oh! Oh!—if I could only write that also as though it Giant-Comic-Grotesque.

Nevertheless—with Act One we can *get by*. The shift to human-heart trouble is gradual.

Act Two with the opening broadcasts shifts back to large-scale comic brave absurdity.

Then the Family Scenes on the Boardwalk begin to get dangerous. But not too dangerous.

The Big Danger—the loss of the Act—takes place in the Seduction Scene. The wheedling of Mr. Antrobus.

If Sabina is a beautiful girl the whole scene settles down, slackens, becomes easy,—Farce Situation 89, Musical Comedy convention—satire easily grasped—and there is no support for the next surprise: Sabina's announcement to the audience that she refuses to play the scene.

All this is Correctible, if we return to my first idea Sabina is LIVELY-SHRILL and pretty UGLY. Almost the COMIC VALENTINE ugly servant-girl with a lot of straw blond hair in a series of psyche-knots.

Then the preposterousness of her being a siren and a peril to Mr. Antrobus keeps the high wind of absurdity blowing through the Act. It joins together Fortune-teller excitement, and conveener craziness, and broadcast to the whole world, and the children-play-by-adults.

By 27 March rehearsals for *The Skin of Our Teeth* were postponed until September, and Wilder hoped to use the spring and summer to work on the play and to finish *The Alcestiad*. Two things were to interfere with his plans: a telephone call from Archibald MacLeish and a telegram from Alfred Hitchcock.

On Wednesday 6 May, MacLeish telephoned Wilder and asked him to come to Washington the following week to discuss Wilder's military service. Through MacLeish's influence it was arranged that Wilder, after passing his physical examinations, would enter the Military Intelligence Training School at Harrisburg, Pennsylvania, on 1 July. After meeting with Maj. Richard Harris on 11 May, Wilder wrote to MacLeish that afternoon, "A very exciting day in my life. . . . I hope I pass my examination. And I hope I prove a credit to your sponsorship" (Library of Congress, M.D.).

When he returned to New Haven, Wilder found a thousand-word telegram from Alfred Hitchcock inviting him to come to Hollywood and write the screenplay for his new film, *Shadow of a Doubt*, based on a story idea of Gordon McDonnell's. On 12 May Wilder wrote Woollcott,

> Mr. Hitchcock of the thriller movies wants me to come out to California for six weeks and write the screen treatment of a movie. He recounts the plot. It's about American small-town life and big-city murderer. I'm a consultant on small-town life to the tune of fifteen thousand dollars and murder has no secrets from him.
>
> The plot he recounts is corny.

> I very much doubt whether I can supply one convincing small-town speech.
> And I haven't got six weeks.
>
> But I'm going to compromise with time, art and money. And go for five
> weeks for ten thousand dollars. (Harvard-Theatre)

Wilder did not have six weeks because he was scheduled to enter a newly
instituted basic training program beginning 27 June and running through 8 August, when he would be ready to enter intelligence school. From Hollywood on
10 June he concluded a letter to Woollcott, "Anyway, I should think the picture of
me at bayonet practice (muttering 'Jed Harris' and leading the class in ferocity)
would be so tonic that no one could wish me anywhere else" (Harvard-Theatre).

Rosalie Stewart, Wilder's Hollywood agent, wired him on 13 May 1942 that
she had closed the deal with Hitchcock and his producer Jack Skirball guarantee-
ing Wilder fifteen thousand dollars for the first draft of the screenplay. So anxious
was Hitchcock to begin working with Wilder before 23 May, Stewart continued in
her telegram, that he was willing to fly to New York and then return with Wilder.
Because of a change in his physical examinations, Wilder did not leave for California until Tuesday, 19 May, and after a stopover in Dallas arrived on Wednesday
evening, 20 May, in Hollywood.

Wilder's work with Hitchcock began the next day. If his initial reaction to the
idea for the film was less than enthusiastic, meeting and working with Hitchcock
changed his mind. On Saturday afternoon, 23 May, he wrote to Woollcott, "But
the only news I have for you is this: that I am deeply interested in the movie we're
doing, that Mr. Hitchcock and I get on fine together. In long story conferences we
think up new twists to the plot and gaze at one another in appalled silence: as
much as to say 'Do you think an audience can *bear* it' " (Harvard-Theatre).

Shadow of a Doubt was Hitchcock's sixth American film, but his first to focus
on a small town in America. When François Truffaut asked Hitchcock, "Did you
select Thornton Wilder or did someone suggest him to you?" Hitchcock replied,
"I wanted him." After recounting for Truffaut how he came to the original story
idea, Hitchcock continued, "We worked together in the morning, and he would
work on his own in the afternoon, writing by hand in a school notebook. He never
worked consecutively, but jumped about from one scene to another according to
his fancy. I might add that the reason I wanted Wilder is that he had written a
wonderful play called *Our Town*."

Wilder finished his work on the screenplay on 23 June, and that night he and
Hitchcock took a train to New York to continue fine-tuning the script. Hitchcock
thought the screenplay needed some "comedy highlights," and Wilder recommended Robert Ardrey but Hitchcock thought "he was more inclined toward
serious drama, so Sally Benson was brought in."

The screenwriting credit for *Shadow of a Doubt* was given to Thornton
Wilder, Sally Benson, and Alma Reville, Hitchcock's wife and long-time collaborator. In addition, Hitchcock took the unusual step of including a special screen
credit just before his own: "We wish to acknowledge the contribution of Mr.

Thornton Wilder to the preparation of this production." When Truffaut asked about it, Hitchcock said, "It was an emotional gesture; I was touched by his qualities" (Truffaut, *Hitchcock*, 151–55).

After his return from California, Wilder briefly saw his family and then left for Miami Beach, Florida, for six weeks of basic training from 27 June to 8 August. His intelligence training at the army school in Harrisburg, Pennsylvania, began on 10 August, and when he finished, he was ordered to join the Fourth Air Force, 328th Fighter group at Hamilton Field, California, effective 19 September.

On Sunday, 24 August, Myerberg and Kazan went to Harrisburg to see Wilder, who reported to Isabel, "[T]hey were down here today and we 'did' Acts I and II. No, there is to be no circus ballyhoo in the lobby." He also wrote of his plans to come to New York the following weekend and meet with Myerberg and Gadget (Kazan's nickname) to run through details of act III. Aware of tensions between Bankhead and Myerberg, Wilder continued, "I want you to be there, if you can. Then Michael wants to give us dinner *and* Tallulah! I'm very fond of M's cook but not for her cooking. How can we upset this plan for Tallulah's sake? I must invent an 8:00 o'clock date. So DISCUSSION 5–7:30 then you and I disappear and I hope, Tallulah. Then resume at Sardi's—I want to meet Montgomery Clift and I *want to be in Sardi's*. All of us chewing rag at Sardi's. Then you and I home to New Haven on the 11 or 12 train." Another reason for coming to New York, he wrote Woollcott, was "to induce Tallulah to wear an atrocious blonde wig in Act One and play it for a zaney" (undated letter, Harvard-Theatre).

Rehearsals for *The Skin of Our Teeth* began in New York on 23 September. The cast now included Montgomery Clift as Henry Antrobus, Frances Heflin as Gladys Antrobus, and Florence Reed as the Fortune Teller. Once in California, Wilder depended on letters from his sister Isabel for news of the rehearsals. Trained in the theater, she represented her brother and sought to calm the tensions that quickly developed between members of the cast, Kazan, and Myerberg. Wilder's days were taken up with his training, and he was also assigned to work on three courts-martial. As he adjusted to the routine of army life, he found some time for his own work, as he wrote to his mother:

> I get up at 6:15 by bugle call and go to bed at 9:45, but the time after dinner is free. I feel the need of literature; but (a) I'm in no position to get it and (b) I wouldn't even like to read if I had it. (I was surprised at how less good "Bella" [a novel by Jean Giraudoux] seemed.) so—as simply as falling off a log I found a solution: I started making my own. I began the Alcestiad. I wrote only about 10 speeches an evening. If I find that it moves into the center of my interest, or keeps me awake at night, I'll have to give it up. But so far it contributes its fragment tranquilly every night. And on Sundays I can do a larger portion.—As I see it now it's very Helen Hayes. Anyway, so far it's still a secret. (7 October 1942)

Letters from Isabel told of the tensions at rehearsals and on the road after the New Haven opening on 15 October. "Two of our stars," he wrote his mother on 20 October, "are in a distraught state. Tallulah & Florence Reed. Got telegrams from them high pitch asking me to correct a matter: 3 actors had been discharged. Which sabotaged the play, etc. I've written placating letters in all directions." The following day he wrote Isabel,

> Isn't it damnable!—that Michael [Myerberg] turns out to be Destroyer, too.
> I got frantic telegrams from Florence Reed and Tallulah (Tallulah quotes: Every good and excellent thing . . . . . . razor edge of danger . . . . . . wants a home or a play—isn't she a fascinating being between times!) I wrote them both. I first telegraphed Michael and enclose the letter to him.
> Oh, Isabel, what I do here is tiny but I can't ask for a leave (a) Everything I can do here depends on the fact that I never allude to the fact that I'm a well known author; and (b) the Army's not made that way.
> If its still on the razor edge of danger on the eve of entering New York, I may try.
> But let's hope that I won't have to.
> I'm very curious to know how old theatre centers like Baltimore take to it.
> But I'm horrified at Michael's removing "He's only 5,000 years old." That's as bad as Jed's removing "That ain't the whole truth Simon Stimson and you know it."

Wilder enclosed a copy of the letter he had sent to Myerberg. At the top of the letter he wrote, "Isabel: Here's the letter I wrote Michael: show it to Tallulah and Freddie and the two Florences and Gadget [Elia Kazan] if you think fit."

> Dear Michael:
> Certainly something must be the matter.
> And I don't want to hear the story from other people but from you.
> What lines have been removed from the play that I or others would regard as integral?
> What actors have been removed that would seem to so many people as essential?
> And why couldn't these things have been done without so much sincere alarm and regret?
> Remember that no actor or co-worker ever worked with Reinhardt who didn't long to work with him again.
> Remember the same of Charles Frohman.
> Remember that no actor or co-worker ever worked with Sam Harris who wasn't crazy to work with him again.
> And remember that no one (except Ruth) ever worked with Jed without loathing the thought of ever working with him again.
> The great manager is also the peak of consideration and tact, even when business considerations or decisions as to entertainment values require his doing difficult things.
> And they deeply value actors and actors' peace of mind and find ways to secure their undistracted concentration on the play.

Do, Michael, drop me a letter about all this and do everything to establish so fine a company into the harmonious working unit they have a right to be.

I want them to admire you and long to work for you in many future great productions.

Ever your old
Thornton

The animosity can be seen in Bankhead's letter to Myerberg of 28 October 1942, a copy of which she sent to Wilder:

Dear Mr. Myerberg:

Because of your ignorance of the ethics and behavior of a producer towards the ARTIST participating in a production, I am compelled to write you this letter. Your lack of courtesy and consideration toward every member of this company has been so shocking and unprofessional that it beggars description; your idea of authority is sadly dated; authority is not snapping your fingers at waiters, or in this case, actors . . . [Bankhead's ellipses throughout] it is something innate . . . something that springs from inner dignity; true knowledge, tolerance and simplicity. In your obviously frustrated desire to be at long last respected, your utter disregard for human relationships have succeeded only in making of yourself a figure of ridicule; for this sad state of affairs I am deeply sorry for you. However, these are minor details in comparison to the issue at stake . . . which concerns my JOB . . . . my professional integrity toward myself and most important toward the public; and here I can best clarify that for you by quoting an excerpt from a letter I have received from Captain Wilder, to wit:

"Oh I wish I were there and could try to be useful in anything that distresses you; your mind should be free to do nothing but project your wonderful force and wit. I hate to think of you worried and annoyed. It's so necessary for the play that each of your changes of mood and especially the 'break throughs' to the audience come with such spontaneous inner reality that they don't seem to the audience to be author's contrivances, but pure SABINA-NATURE; and for that you need your undistracted mind."

"Anyway, Tallula-Walkyrie, you are not only the great artist of nerves, fire, hatred-of-the-almost, fierce susceptibility, but you are a great woman of a great House. It's in your carriage and the superb modelling of your head. Draw on all those resources of patience and poise in whatever storms may arise. I dream of submitting a text to you some day . . . Royal, that's what it'll be. And in the meantime, I strain to do everything I can do to make the situation such that you can be all yourself . . . that's why I asked so urgently the other night whether you enjoyed yourself during the performance."

I have not asked permission of Captain Wilder to include any part of his letter to me; and if by doing so I have offended or disappointed him, I will regret it all the days of my life. I do not profess to have a gift of words but if Captain Wilder can call upon Aristotle, Spinoza, Plato and the Bible, who am I not to call upon the Master Wilder?

I detect in you a curiously sinister respect for the letter of the Law. Could this be a guilty conscience? Equity is not only a tribunal of Law, its Council and Executives are made up of fellow artists, sensitive and human folk, who have always leaned over backwards to be fair to the Managers; but, as in all status quo, including Equity, there is an unwritten law . . . the human element . . . the law of nature. Just because I do not have specified in my Equity contract that I do not have to be submitted to Spanish inquisition tortures during the performance of a play, it does not mean they will condone the Gestapo methods that have been forced on me in this production. Comedy is a creative thing of the moment, subject to all the ills that flesh is heir to; I cannot emerge from an iron lung suffering from claustrophobia, as I do, and gaily trip the light fantastic without it jeopardizing my performance and also seriously undermining my health, which is the only gilt-edged security I possess. Period. It is at your suggestion that I have written this letter which has been most painful and distasteful to me but it's too late now to pull punches! I *do* know how to say it; *You are Henry—Henry is YOU*!!

This letter up to this point was written on Sunday and this is the first opportunity I have had to continue it, largely due to the slipshod manner in which this production has been allowed to get on by the skin of its teeth. To point out just a few of the glaring blunders or deliberate negligence of duty to the Company:

There were no drawing rooms, which is a breach of contract. The alibi of priorities does not hold water as the hotels and stations informed me they were available if they had been engaged within a reasonable time.

There is no legitimate Company Manager. Only by the grace of God did the production arrive in time for performance, due to the above-mentioned lack of foresight, thereby putting the actors under additional uncalled-for distress.

There have been no hotels posted on the call board for the benefit of the general actors. This situation has been appalling in towns like Baltimore and will be more so in Washington; both of which are boom towns where hotel accommodations are at a premium of cost and are almost impossible to obtain without advance notification.

There is no excuse for this, as I pointed out to you and Mr. Kazan the first week of rehearsals this inconvenience would arise and it was only fair the Company should be warned. The consequence was that in Baltimore quite a few of the actors spent half the day and night searching for some place to live, thereby missing a rehearsal.

Most important of all, you specifically promised and boasted of carrying a fly man with the production. This is as important a factor to the play as the actors. However, last night you again reiterated this promise that said fly man would be with the production before the opening in Washington and continue with us into New York. I can only hope this will prove to be the tangible truth. My sincere doubt in this matter is understandable after many cries of "Wolf" we have endured. The slides have always been bad and not sufficient in number; this being agreed upon by all concerned, including yourself, and yet after nearly three weeks of playing these essential things have not been rectified.

Last but most important, and I hesitate to say this for fear that it will forever jeopardize certain portions of the play because of your almost pathological reaction to any profound suggestion coming from professional people of real experience but I feel so strongly about this that I must take a chance and I also feel that the author and his representatives agree with me: the mechanical device used in the first act for the so-called effect of wind is infantile and in complete contradiction of the author's avowed intention of leaving those things to the imagination of the audience's chance of understanding the refugees. This mechanical situation also applies more drastically to the absurd effect at the end of the second act when the storm before the flood drowns out all the important lines of the play. The audience haven't the faintest idea that Mr. Antrobus is referring to the animals when he says 'Jump up on my back, here, take the turtles in your pouch, etc.' They can't hear him; they can't see him; and the impression is given that he is asking the audience to come with him. The fortune-teller's lines which are vitally important, are completely blurred and the whole end of the second act is complete chaos; a dreadful let-down for the audience; making it an up-hill fight in the third act.

All these things I know from professional experience of 23 years of active participation and knowledge of an audience's reaction. Producers of vaster knowledge and experience would recognize these obvious faults at once or at least when they were pointed out by someone who has the sincere interest of the play at heart and is personally concerned with its outcome as I am, give it earnest consideration.

Exchanges with his sister, Bankhead's letter, and other sources led Wilder to painful conclusions about what was happening to his play. To Woollcott he wrote on 2 November from Hamilton Field, California,

I suspect that the three things have happened that would most embarrass me.

(1) they're not spontaneous—improvising—unliteral enough (2) the quiet scenes are under-lit,—I hate sentimental darkness on the stage; & (3) that at the end of Act II there's so much noise that the audience can't hear the words.

Play after play of mine may succeed or fail, but finally I'll have taught them the style: words, gestures and personalities on a platform evoking its scene and its passions by magic, commanding time and place and idea,—and then after the style has been disseminated by imitators, the plays will be put on again and no one, actor or audience, will have any difficulty with them. ¶ Naturally there are divers passages of Skin of Our Teeth that I'm not proud of, but look what I bit off to chew! (Harvard-Theatre)

Wilder was far more direct and bitter in a reply to Isabel's letter of 26 October: "Another furiously interesting letter from you—rê Tallulah's blow-up.

"My only hope is that the others will get something of a Doctor-to-Patient attitude towards her goings-on and suffer for her as well as for themselves. But how

rotten that she should try to instruct Florence Eldridge in her part—how ex-
cruciatingly obtuse!" ([?2 November 1942]. We have not been able to locate Isabel
Wilder's letter.)

After seeing the play in Philadelphia, Woollcott telegraphed Wilder about
his "exciting and fascinating play" and urged him to go there and fix parts of it.
But in recounting this to his mother on 2 November, Wilder wrote, "[B]ut he
guessed I couldn't. And I can't." Writing from New York on 4 November, Woollcott laid out what he thought of the play; his letter must have added to the sense of
chaos and impending doom:

> Having seen *The Skin of Our Teeth* and thought about it and read it, I know
> what I think about it. I think no American play has ever come anywhere near it. I
> think it might have been written by Plato and Lewis Carroll in collaboration, or
> better still by any noble pedagogue with a little poltergeist blood in him. I had not
> foreseen that you could write a play that would be both topical and timeless,
> though I might have remembered from *The Trojan Women* that it could be done.
> What I do not now and will not know until I have seen it again, which I am both
> eager and determined to do, is how completely the present production realizes
> the script.
>
> One thing I *am* sure of. Tallulah does not know how to play Sabina and
> cannot be taught to. She has some assets as an actress but she is without any
> comic gift. Kit [Cornell] is not a comedienne and is ruefully aware of the fact.
> Tallulah is not a comedienne and thinks she's a wonderful one. When she comes
> to a line which she thinks should be read amusingly she manages it with a throaty
> vocal trick suitable for inferior wisecracks tossed around Sardi's in 1924. It's the
> vocal equivalent of a flirt of the fanny. She's like the little daughter of the hostess
> who feels an obligation to be entertaining. One can describe the product only as
> embarrassing. In the first act I found her afflicting. In the second and third acts I
> was quite reconciled to her. It was not until I read the play that I saw how in every
> scene and every line it aches for Ruth Gordon. It will be played many times and
> by many women. It will never be really played until Ruth plays it. March is good.
> Florence Reed is surprisingly good. Florence Eldridge is simply superb. Tallulah
> is, I think, a misfortune—how great a misfortune only those can say who know the
> play. (see Kaufman and Hennessey, *Letters*, 4 November 1942, 373–75)

In spite of his criticism of Bankhead, Woollcott believed in the play, and on
his return to New York he telephoned Brooks Atkinson, the *New York Times*
theater critic, and urged him to go to Philadelphia to see the play so that he would
not have to write a one-hour review of it after the New York opening.

Bankhead and Woollcott had never liked each other, and when she learned
that Myerberg was thinking of having him play the offstage role of the announcer
during the News Events of the World sequence that opens the play, she flew
into a rage, sending Wilder a special delivery letter from Washington, D.C., on
10 November:

Darling, precious Thornton:-

The likes of Alec Woollcott have never gotten me down! I have never been one of his admiring little clique—and visa versa—we have only one thing in common—that is, a morbid curiosity about murder stories. I hope this doesn't sound bitter; I respect constructive criticism, and have often been helped by suggestions from the average theatre-goers; and God knows if you were here, a whole World of enlightenment would unfold. My personality has always been such that it antagonizes, as well as attracts. Alec once wrote of me in a performance he had never seen me in, referring to the American production-quote-"This part was played in London by our own Tallulah Bankhead-said not boastfully, but as a fact." All this has nothing to do with the real reason for this letter, but I am afraid it will make you think I am slightly prejudiced; I promise you that is not the case, and you believe me! Alec has offered to be the Announcer for the first week in New York; this absolutely appalls me-not because of any personal feeling, but I think it's an affront to this play and assembled cast to have such a cheap circus stunt for one week in New York. He made a record of it, which I suffered through for two performances, and nearly died, because it's impossible to gauge the audience's reactions; they vary at every performance; and the Saturday night in Philadelphia, the bloody record just didn't play, so I had to start the play without the audience hearing a word of "The News Events of the World," and when a faint glimmer of the voice did come through, the reaction of the audience was a surprised confusion as to whose voice it was, thereby losing the content of the author's lines. This could be the case whether Alec, Bob Benchley, whom I adore, Groucho Marx, or any other well known voice played the Announcer. Soooooo!! if Mr W. plays the part for the first week only, it sets a false premise, and certain Helen Hokinson characters of the New Yorker would feel they had been cheated of something they would never have missed. I have tried repeatedly to get you on the phone-to discuss this with you long before I received your letter, and knew nothing of its contents. I have in my contract the approval of the cast, in conjunction with the Author. *Please* bear me out in this-I speak for all of us-it isn't only me. I know Alec is an old-and probably dear-friend of yours, and I know that he thinks 'The Skin of Our Teeth' is a great play-and I love him for that; I know you wouldn't hurt your worst enemy, if you had one, which you haven't! (and I don't mean the Nazis and Japs) I want so to enjoy this play, because you want me to—anything you want me to do I would do; but every day something arises that torments me so that I am almost ready to give up the ghost; however—and I hope this pleases you-the general impression is that I am having a wonderful time in the part, and there is no reason in God's World why I shouldn't, except for that MONSTER Myerberg—his attitude is that of a Gestapo agent in a conquered Country, and his ignorance of everything is dementing.

You know I am the queen of non-sequitur, but what I am driving at is that I really do enjoy myself once I am before the audience, but due to said Myerberg's conflicting and confusing 'orders,' I have a feeling of dreadful suspense up until the play begins; one is *never* told if something that directly concerns me is going to be changed; also he is a pathological liar. I am sending you a copy of a letter that I was forced to write him because he refused to contact me. It shocks me to think that I had to say such vitriolic things to another human being, and that you, after reading it, may never love me again, or find my noble head no longer noble, but just bloody; but whatever my poor head is, it is still unbowed!!

Bankhead added a handwritten postscript to the typed letter:

> I love and treasure every word you have written me. Your letters are always close at hand and in my heart. Isabel and I are Ruth and Naomi. I don't know what I would have done without [her.] She has saved my life and her sole reward is being kept up until four of a morning. But she is holding her own better than any one else. God Bless her— (postmark 10 November 1942)

During the New York performances, Morton Da Costa played the Announcer and the Broadcast Official.

As letters, telephone calls, and telegrams kept him informed of the back-stabbing and bickering that infested the rehearsals and the tryouts, Wilder prepared the text for publication. On 26 October, he had written his sister,

> ¶ Note: the text cannot be published by Harpers until I've submitted it to them, i.e. "prepared a final printed version." At present I have no such text. I didn't retain copies of the various rewrites. MM is sending me the present text of Act I page 20—the end of the Act. But I have no copy of Antrobus' speech ("razor edge") in Act III nor the close of Act II. All the rest I have, I think. My publisher's text will not vary from the acted text as much as "Our Town's" does; but I shall go on making "a" version without regard to what's being acted. And I want to write in more stage directions to aid the readers' imagination.
>
> So with this shipping of MSS across the country I doubt whether Harpers could meet a publication date of Nov 30. But I'll be as quick as I can for the Xmas trade. They can make up a travelling salesman dummy of the 1st 20 pages, if they wish.

On 10 November, he wrote her that the script had been sent off:

> The script! Every time I've prepared one for the Publisher (which is after all the script that really counts) I've had to do it hugger-mugger from battered texts and frayed memory. Whereas it's the one I should be able to "concentrate" on as in the days at Quebec when I was "concentrating" on Acts I and II.
>
> However, it's in.
>
> There are a number of places where I disagree with the acted text. I prefer Sabina's taunt to the Conveeners "I suppose you must have girls but where you find them and what you do with them is not of interest to me"—(really High Comedy—from an uppity slut!). I've left out the Ancestors. Restored the platform at the back of the stage for the Hours. I left out the singing of the planets. But someday that'll go back.

Now I've left for Gene Saxton to find Greek and Hebrew type for the Home and Moses. Yes. I've resolved that *that* is the needed crown of the Refugee Scene and will propose no other. Woollcott thinks the scene needs something and so does M. M. and that should be there. Let the audiences laugh or not, I like it.

On 12 November he was temporarily reassigned for sixty days to Army Air Corps Headquarters in Washington, D.C., and a tour of air force bases brought him to New York on Monday, 17 November, the day before the play opened. From Chicago, on the twenty-first, he wrote a card to his mother and his sister, again focusing on *The Skin of Our Teeth*: "Isa; Sat with the Marches until late after the Thursday performance; I think all is well now. Pretty fair audience and performance. Talked with Arthur Hopkins and Spencer Tracy. Arthur says 'they' didn't have faith in the play's effect: all that hurry-hurry in the direction is always a sign of lack of faith."

When he returned to San Francisco, he wrote to Woollcott,

> Through no connection with the play I was in New York from Monday to Friday. I caught parts of several performances, though not the *Opening Night*.
>
> A very funny feeling.
>
> It's all right. Nobody's blame.
>
> But it's astonishing that anyone could escape the self-evident character, to me, of this reading and of that. *Here* slower, *there* faster. Self-evident.
>
> Fortunately the Third Act came off best of all, but I was shocked at the undifferentiated hurry-hurry of Act One—so many carefully calculated points ignored.
>
> Oh, well, Ishkablbble. (24 November 1942, Harvard-Theatre)

After generally favorable reviews, cast tensions died down. But if Wilder thought the problems could now be put into the background while he enjoyed the pleasure of a well-received production, he was mistaken. On 19 December, the *Saturday Review of Literature* published the first of a two-part article titled "The Skin of Whose Teeth?" by Joseph Campbell and Henry Morton Robinson (see bibliography). Without directly accusing Wilder of plagiarism, they charged that the play was "not an entirely original creation, but an Americanized re-creation, thinly disguised, of James Joyce's 'Finnegans Wake.'" They accused Wilder of knowingly "quoting from and actually naming some of his characters after the main figures of Joyce's masterpiece." They charged that "Important plot elements, characters, devices of presentation, as well as major themes and many of the speeches, are directly and frankly imitated, with but the flimsiest veneer to lend an American touch to the original features" (part I, p. 3).

Henry Seidel Canby, associate editor of the *Saturday Review of Literature*, a Yale professor, and a friend of the Wilders, had written Isabel Wilder on 14 December about the article: "It is already in this issue, and indeed, has to be run this week or not at all. I read it very carefully myself and, of course, there is no suggestion even of plagiarism. We had our lawyer go over it so as to be sure of that." In an interview Isabel Wilder remembered that Canby wanted to create a furor to increase circulation. For Campbell and Robinson Wilder's failure to acknowledge Joyce as a source for his play's origins became a cause. In interviews they demanded that Wilder give Mrs. Joyce part of his author's royalties from the play (*Variety*, 23 December 1942, Lincoln Center).

In a letter of 18 December to his mother from Washington, D.C. (dated by Isabel Wilder 13 December), he repeated his response to journalists and gave instructions about his reply to Campbell and Robinson:

> "All I can say is that those who are interested should read Finnegans Wake and make up their own minds on the matter."
>
> X   X
>
> I now feel about the letter that I sent you (the letter to the Editor of the Sat Review): let's hold it up a week or two and make them wait for their reply. The waves will lash about and die down and people will be able to read it more attentively.

No reply by Wilder was printed in the *Saturday Review of Literature*, and the letter he left with his mother has not been located.

Time, concluding an unsigned article on the controversy, added the following to Wilder's press statement: "The few initiated stalwarts who had both read *Finnegans Wake* and seen the play, were of the opinion that Campbell & Robinson were trying to make headlines out of what should have been footnotes, were confusing influences with imitation" (*Time*, 28 December 1942, 62).

Campbell, then beginning his career as a professor at Sarah Lawrence College, and Robinson, a senior editor at Reader's Digest, were admirers of Joyce and since the publication of *Finnegans Wake* in 1939 had been tracing the allusions in the novel. Although newspapers and magazines picked up the story, the accusations failed to create a firestorm, perhaps because so few readers were familiar with *Finnegans Wake* and did not feel adequate to engage in discussion.

The few letters the *Saturday Review* did print tended to support Wilder. Carl Balliett, Jr., wrote that Wilder was "an unabashed borrower, who felt, it would seem, that for intelligent readers no explanations or guidebooks were necessary." Esther Willard Bates wrote that Campbell and Robinson ignored the fact that the device of "having the Hours pass across the stage, intoning sublime instructions," had been used by Wilder in his play *Pullman Car Hiawatha* in 1931 (see *Saturday Review of Literature*, 2 January 1943, 11, and 9 January, 11). On the other hand, Karen Barrett charged Wilder with violating André Obey's play *Le Viol de Lucrèce* in his translation for Katharine Cornell in 1932 (27 March, 15). Finally Julian Sawyer extended the charges against Wilder to his indebtedness to Stein in *Our Town* (17 April 1943, 27). Sawyer's letter is discussed in Wilder to Stein, 13 September 1937, n. 1.

Edmund Wilson, as he had a dozen years earlier when Michael Gold attacked Wilder's *The Woman of Andros* (1930) as an example of bourgeois escapism that ignored the tragedy of an unemployed working class, came to Wilder's defense. In "The Antrobuses and the Earwickers" (*Nation*, 30 January 1943, 167–68), Wilson acknowledges that Wilder's "general indebtedness to Joyce in the conception and plan of the play is as plain as anything of the kind can be; it must have been conscious on Wilder's part." Wilson acknowledges that Wilder has "written and lectured on *Finnegans Wake*; is evidently one of the persons who has most felt its fascination and most patiently explored the text." Wilson continues, "This derivation would not necessarily affect one way or the other the merits of Wilder's play. Joyce is a great quarry, like Flaubert, out of which a variety of writers have been getting and will continue to get a variety of different things; and Wilder is a genuine poet with a form and imagination of his own who may find his themes where he pleases without incurring the charge of imitation" (83; see "The Antrobuses and the Earwickers," in Wilson's *Classics and Commercials*, 81–86).

At the end of his "Preface" to *Three Plays* (Harper, 1957, xiv) Wilder wrote, "The play [i.e., *The Skin of Our Teeth*] is deeply indebted to James Joyce's *Finnegans Wake*. I should be very happy if, in the future, some author should feel similarly indebted to any work of mine. Literature has always more resembled a torch race than a furious dispute among heirs."

Some good news came to Wilder in *Theatre Arts* for January 1943, which published a favorable review of *The Skin of Our Teeth* by Rosamond Gilder (9–11) and a profile by Edith J. R. Isaacs, "Thornton Wilder in Person," in the same issue (21–30). However, January also brought the death of his mentor, friend, and confidant, Alexander Woollcott. On 23 January, Woollcott suffered a heart attack while appearing on a radio program, "The People's Forum," and died later that night. In March, the *Atlantic Monthly* posthumously published his article, "Mr. Wilder Urges Us On," a tribute to *The Skin of Our Teeth* (see Woollcott, *Long, Long Ago*, 244–47).

The Drama Critics Circle passed over Wilder's play, awarding their prize to Sidney Kingsley's *The Patriots*. Campbell and Robinson must have felt some triumph. When the Pulitzer Prize Committee gave its award to *The Skin of Our Teeth*, Campbell and Robinson protested in a sharply worded telegram, part of which was published in *PM* (New York) on 5 May (22), which repeated the allegations made in their original article. Their anger continued to surface over the years. In an article, "The Curious Case of Thornton Wilder," Robinson sustained his attack on Wilder, this time dissecting *The Matchmaker* in relationship to its sources in Nestroy's *Einen Jux Will Er Sich Machen* and John Oxenford's *A Day Well Spent*, trying to locate "Mr. Wilder's handsome acknowledgment to his literary predecessors" (*Esquire*, March 1957, 70–71, 124–26). Robinson also reviewed the charges made earlier against Wilder. Campbell took pains in an interview with Donald Newlove in 1977 to refer to the controversy: "Then the war came and Wilder went from captain to major to colonel almost, and we were just a pair of micks and Joyce wasn't the civilization we were fighting for and they came down like a pack of wolves on us" (*Esquire*, "The Professor with a Thousand Faces," September 1977, 99–103, 132, 134–36).

The measure of Wilder's "crime" and the ferocity with which Campbell and

Robinson pursued him seem at odds. Perhaps a source for the animosity can be found in Wilder's letters to the publisher Benjamin W. Huebsch, the first American publisher of Joyce's *A Portrait of the Artist as a Young Man*. In a letter to Huebsch on 28 June 1940, Wilder wrote, "Edmund Wilson and I are still corresponding about the knottier problems of *Finnegans Wake*. I've found out a thousand new things—many of them mighty dirty." Huebsch replied on 12 July, discussing their common concern for European exiles then living in the United States and discussing a role for Wilder as editor of a new edition of *The Golden Legend*. Huebsch also mentioned a Joyce project:

> That you have been kept busy there can be no doubt, for "Finnegans Wake" would seem to offer material for endless conjecture and study. I think I told you about the intention of H. M. Robinson and Joseph (?) to write a short book, a sort of key to "Finnegans Wake." The preliminary material which they submitted was good but we finally decided against it. This, however, does not represent a final attitude on the subject and if you alone, or with Edmund Wilson, should ever decide to commit your discoveries (even including the "mighty dirty" ones) to paper, you will find me responsive.

Wilder replied on 25 August, "I have put away *Finnegans Wake*, too time devouring, but what a book!" (Wilder-Huebsch correspondence, Library of Congress-M.D.)

We do not know whether Huebsch, in 1940, at the time he turned down the Campbell and Robinson manuscript, mentioned to them that Wilder and Wilson might be interested in doing such a study. But if he did, then Campbell's statement that "we were just a pair of micks" might contain the source of his and Robinson's resentment. Selections from their *A Skeleton Key to Finnegans Wake* were published in the *Saturday Review of Literature* of 19 June 1943 under the title "Unlocking the Door to Joyce" (4–6, 28). In a brief introductory note the editors refer to the controversy: "In these pages recently Mr. Robinson and Mr. Campbell published two articles pointing out numerous similarities between Thornton Wilder's 'The Skin of Our Teeth,' and James Joyce's 'Finnegans Wake.' Their findings were based on a skeleton key to Joyce on which they had been working for three years. In the following article, they present a cross-section of the results of their study." *A Skeleton Key to Finnegans Wake* was published by Harcourt, Brace in July 1944.

During the whole controversy, desk duty in Washington kept Wilder busy through long days and nights. After completing a dreary assignment to write a chapter for an air force manual, the kind of work he detested, he was finally given his active duty assignment. At a stop on Presque Isle, Maine, on 21 May 1943, en route to North Africa, he ended a postcard home, "It's enough to know that I'm happily proceeding to do what I want to do."

Appendix IX.

Gertrude Stein: September 1942 to September 1944

At the beginning of the war, on 18 September 1939, Stein described to Wilder their forty-eight-hour "run to Paris to get our winter clothing and arrange our affairs and then we were back for the winter." They had ignored a notice given on 24 August 1939 by the American ambassador, William C. Bullitt, urging American citizens to return to the United States, and they would ignore a second advisement on 14 May 1940 to proceed home by way of Bordeaux.

In "The Winner Loses: A Picture Of Occupied France," which tells of life during the "phony war," from September 1939 to June 1940, Stein writes of a trip to Lyon, where they consulted the American consul, who advised them to return home: "[W]e were stopped every few minutes by the military; they were preparing to blow up bridges and were placing anti-aircraft guns and it all seemed very near and less than ever did I want to go on the road" (*Selected Writings*, 624). Returning to Bilignin, they met their friends Doctor Gaston and Madame Charlotte Chaboux. After a discussion, Doctor Chaboux advised them:

> "I had friends who in the last war stayed in their homes all through the German occupation, and they saved their homes and those who left lost theirs. No. . . . I think unless your house is actually destroyed by a bombardment, I always think the best thing to do is to stay. . . . Everybody knows you here; everybody likes you; we all would help you in every way. Why risk yourself among strangers?"
>
> "Thank you," we said, "that is all we need. We stay." (*Selected Writings*, 624)

Stein had finished *Paris France* in December 1939 and completed *Ida A Novel* in May–June 1940. On 16 May she wrote to Robert Bartlett Haas, who was preparing part of the catalogue for the Yale University library exhibition of her books and manuscripts, "I have just begun and almost done a children's book 'To Do. A Book of Alphabets and Birthdays'" (see Stein to Wilder, 21 September 1942, n. 2). On 11 July, she advised William Rogers that she was beginning a "short thing that I call Sundays and Tuesdays, do you think some magazine would like to pay me a thousand dollars." Under the title, "The Winner Loses," it was published in the *Atlantic Monthly* in November.

On the same day that she wrote Rogers, she replied to bibliographical questions from Haas. His letter is not among her papers, and he did not keep a copy. His inquiry about description led her to one of her rare commentaries on her work and on the situation she faced in the war:

My dear Bobolink,

Yours was the very first letter that came through after everything and with it the photos of you, was that after measles, the toile is lovely and what is that other background, the chintz the sitting one, and you look a little thin, are you a little thin, but they'll soon fatten you up, and you did have the measles not the whooping cough in To Do but that you probably have seen now, and now the questions. Yes Carl has all the ms. and you ask him and he will probably arrange something for you, he has everything xcept a few things that were printed as soon as written. I think his collection is practically complete xcept for a few small latest things, by the way I have begun a new novel called Mrs. Reynolds, and a short thing about our xperiences here called Sundays and Tuesdays. Now the other questions, about the description, yes it is funny about that, I am always wondering about it myself, in a way it is always direct description and yet the description the more you describe the more it is at once outside and inside, description is awfully bothersome, you see just at present I am awfully interested in predictions, wars do make you interested in predictions and that throws a whole lot of light upon the question of description, in a way a prediction, astrological or otherwise is a description, but, and really since my Acquaintance with Description, I have not read that in years does it say anything about description, and Phenomena of Nature and How to Write, seemed to me to say something about Description, but all that you know better than I do as your acquaintance with all that is much more recent, that is the reason I cannot really advise you about what to choose to illustrate you know all that better than I do now, you see in these two things I am doing now I am very much interested in the relation of predictions to descriptions, I have attacked that subject from so many angles, I think To Do has another thing to say about Description, the relation of Description to Imagination, there is no real separation of course not, even in dreams of course not, and war is very interesting from the stand point of description, that is one of the things I want to do in the novel, it is all very clear and confused, but you know and lots of love

Always
Gtde.

The war dominated the news and conversation. It entered her writing as it entered her life. In October 1939 she had spoken to Wilder of her aversion to the radio, which threatened her perception of reality. Yet now it became a necessary part of everyone's daily routine throughout the war: General de Gaulle's speeches from London, which began on 18 June 1940; the German-controlled Radio-Paris; Swiss radio from Geneva and Berne; occasional wireless broadcasts from America, and beginning in November 1942 the BBC French Service. These nightly fifteen-minute broadcasts, *The French Speak to the French*, gave hope to the French during the darkest days of World War II. The programs, directed by Maurice Schumann, a journalist and spokesman for de Gaulle's Free French Forces headquartered in London, faded in and out as the Germans tried to jam them, gave important war news and through codes information to the Resistance (see *Wars I Have Seen*, 121–22, 125, 141, 145, 155–56).

Under the stress of war, Stein returned to writing the daily life in *Mrs. Reynolds*, a narrative of "a perfectly ordinary couple living an ordinary life and having ordinary conversations and really not suffering personally from everything that is happening." But "all over them is the shadow of two men," Angel Harper and Joseph Lane—Hitler and Stalin. The "Epilogue" to the novel concludes, "then the shadow of one of the two men gets bigger and then blows away and there is no other. There is nothing historical about this book except the state of mind" (267). However, throughout the novel there are echoes of conversations with friends, the interest in prophecies, and the worry about food in a time of privation. Toklas in her cookbook speaks of the hopeless monotony of their diet.

Thérèse Bonney, an American freelance photojournalist covering the war, except for fleeting trips back to America, visited Stein in May 1941. "Gertrude Stein in France," her article about that visit with photographs of Stein and Toklas at their house, was not published until 1 July 1942 in *Vogue* (60–61, 70). In her report Bonney quotes briefly from a Stein letter of January 1942 about the importance of mail and work as a part of the daily life.

Throughout 1941 Stein worked steadily on *Mrs. Reynolds*. Efforts to publish and produce other books also continued. Her correspondence with Carl Van Vechten shows her persistent attempts to publish "To Do" even though they were unsuccessful. John McCullough, her editor for *The World Is Round*, suggested a book more directly written for children, and Van Vechten enthusiastically supported the idea, offering the title *The Gertrude Stein First Reader*. Stein began the book in March 1941 and finished it in less than two months. That summer, Stein wrote "La langue française" for *Patrie*, which was published in August (see Wilder to Stein, 12 November 1941, n. 8) and in September May d'Aiguy's translation of *Paris France* was published in Algeria by Éditions Charlot.

In the summer of 1942, *Mrs. Reynolds* was completed and arrangements were somehow made with Thérèse Bonney to receive the typescript. A letter from Stockholm dated only "Le 18," probably written in August 1942, speaks of her having received a letter from Stein and asks Stein to let her know if there is anything she can do for her, as letters get to Sweden in three to four days. On 16 December, still in Stockholm, Bonney wrote Stein, "Miracle des Miracles, Mme. Reynolds est arrivée sans aucune difficulté." We do not know how Stein, with the Germans occupying all of France since 11 November 1942, managed to get the typescript to Bonney.

Time magazine on 3 May 1943 (55) reported that the typescript had reached Bennett Cerf via Sweden, but that Cerf "could make nothing of it" and felt it "could probably be read from either end." However, he had "decided to publish it." Cerf, whose enthusiasm for Stein extended only to her public works, never did, and it was not printed until 1952 in the Yale Edition.

The saga of *Mrs. Reynolds* continued, however. By the following year, in the unsigned "Talk of the Town" for the 19 February issue of *The New Yorker* appeared a report produced by two staff writers, Russell Maloney and Mendez Marks, Jr. The piece indicated that because of wartime paper shortage Cerf did not plan to publish *Mrs. Reynolds* until after the war, as is confirmed in Cerf's *Try and Stop Me* (New York: Simon and Schuster, 1944, 130–31). It is likely that Harold Ross obtained the typescript of *Mrs. Reynolds* from Cerf, his close friend, and assigned it for coverage in the "Talk of the Town":

> There are four people in New York who have read the manuscript of Gertrude Stein's new novel. Three of the people do not matter at all well hardly at all but the fourth is us and that is a good thing because we can tell you all about Gertrude's new novel. The name of the novel is Mrs. Reynolds but it would do you no good to go into Brentano's and ask for Mrs. Reynolds until after the war. While the war is going on Random House wants to print Quentin Reynolds, alas. Bennett B. Toklas the editor of Random House may not know much but he knows that much. He knows that Quentin Reynolds will sell better than Mrs. Reynolds not Mrs. Quentin Reynolds but Gertrude's Mrs. Reynolds. Paper is scarce but there are still plenty of pigeons.
>
> Mrs. Reynolds is not all about roses, it is more about Tuesdays than about roses. Mrs. Reynolds had many kinds of Tuesdays. That's what Gertrude says in her book, and she also says, "Mrs. Reynolds was very well-born. She was born on Tuesday. And the next day was Wednesday." Quentin Reynolds looked three days old last Wednesday, probably something he ate in the Stork Club but Gertrude does not say that at least not in Mrs. Reynolds. She tells about a lot of people named Roger and Joseph Lane and Lydia and Eph Ell, and especially about Angel Harper. Angel Harper is a character who will make the critics sit up and take notice when Mrs. Reynolds is published alas. "When a little dog sticks himself on a needle on the floor he cries right away. When a little child falls down he does not cry until he is picked up. This has a great deal to do with Angel Harper. A great deal." That's what Gertrude says about Angel Harper. She also says that Mrs. Reynolds' brother could not remember what Angel Harper looked like, and that Claudia thought she was married to Angel Harper but that she was mistaken because Angel Harper was never married he did not even have a brother.
>
> Gertrude filled up two hundred and sixty-nine pages of typewriter paper writing Mrs. Reynolds. She wrote it in France so it had to be smuggled out, it

could have gone by pigeon if it hadn't been so heavy, alas. A friend of hers smuggled it out in the front of her dress. She had trouble getting it through the customs because the customs men thought it was in code but she told them no, it was a novel by Gertrude Stein and they all said oh. (18–19)

When she visited Paris in September 1939, Stein almost certainly entrusted her art collection to Bernard Faÿ, who may have been her single most important French friend of the last fifteen years. On 22 December 1941, Stein wrote to William Rogers that after not seeing Faÿ for two years, she had just spent an evening with him in Lyon (Faÿ, *Les Précieux*, 162). Faÿ was in Lyon to lecture, possibly on the same topic as the one for his talk in Clermont-Ferrand of 15 December, "Qu'est-ce que la Franc-Maçonnerie" [What Is Freemasonry?]. It was a question of central importance for the political events in Vichy-France and for Faÿ.

Freemasons, where not prohibited, form the largest, most powerful secret organization in the world, with decentralized, autonomous, national grand lodges that observe elaborate rituals and degrees. Originating in the apprenticeship system of early stonemasons, Freemasons subscribe to liberal, democratic principles with allegiance to a local but not central authority, hold to a belief in a Supreme Being, and rely on secret ceremonies. The Catholic Church always opposed Masonic anticlericalism, forbidding Catholics to join lodges. Fearful of religious toleration, political compromise, loyalty to local authority, and the power of secrecy, totalitarian states—from Nazi Germany and Austria, Fascist Italy, Spain, and Portugal to the Soviet Union and Communist China—banned Freemasonry. In France, many, including Pétain, held Freemasonry in part responsible for the Dreyfus Affair and blamed it for the Third Republic, the decline of France under Léon Blum, and the defeat in 1940. Many wealthy and powerful men were Masons and came to be seen as a danger to the state, as were Jews. Both were thought to open the danger of Bolshevism. By an edict of 13 August 1940, Pétain outlawed all secret societies and revoked their membership privileges. To execute his order, he appointed Faÿ, who had done extensive research on Freemasonry going back to the Revolutionary War and beyond as director of the Bibliothèque Nationale. Faÿ gave the Germans documentation on Freemasons. He edited the monthly *Les Documents maçonniques* (October 1941–June 1944). From July 1940 until June 1944, Faÿ was also an editor of the only journal financed by the Germans, the anti-Jewish *La Gerbe*.

It is possible that at the meeting in Lyon Faÿ proposed that Stein translate for Americans the speeches of Marshall Pétain, *Paroles aux Français. Messages et écrits, 1934–1941*, published by Librairie H. Lardanchet in Lyon on 30 September 1941 with an introduction by Gabriel-Louis Jaray, the executive director of the Comité France-Amérique, under whose auspices the volume appeared. Pétain had been president of the comité, an organization going back to World War I, until his appointment as ambassador to Spain (1939), a post from which he was recalled in 1940 to back French morale.

Vichy-France at this time still maintained diplomatic relations with the

United States, whose support Faÿ wished to secure for the marshall; his approval of the project and the translator appeared likely. Stein apparently went to work and between Christmas 1941 and late January 1942 drafted an introduction to the speeches for an American audience. Her copy of the book, her handwritten introduction, a typed transcription of it and a typed carbon copy of a translation into French by Paul Genin, "Projet d'introduction à un edition américaine des 'Paroles Aux Français,'" are among her papers. Transcribed from the manuscript, her introduction reads,

Introduction to Pétain's Paroles aux français

  I want to present to my compatriots the words that Maréchal Pétain has spoken directly to the french people, Maréchal Pétain who in the last war saved France by a great victory and in this war has saved them throughout their great defeat.

  I am well aware that until just now it would have been quite impossible to interest my fellow country men in these words which tell so convincing and so moving a story.

  We in the United States until just now have been spoiled children. Since the civil war until today, when the action of Japan has made us realize the misery the grief and the terror of war all this time we have tender hearts we have always felt for others and helped them all we could, but we did not understand defeat enough to sympathize with the french people and with their Maréchal Pétain, who like George Washington, and he is very like George Washington because he too is first in war first in peace and first in the hearts of his countrymen, who like George Washington has given them courage in their darkest moment held them together through their times of desperation and has always told them the truth and in telling them the truth has made them realise that the truth would set them free.

  We have not all of us and I too have been of that number over here in France always had faith in the Maréchal but in the end we have all come to have faith, and now I will tell a little more what he has done and how he has done it and why I want everybody in America to realise it.

  In the last war we waited day after day and Verdun did not fall, that was when we first knew about Pétain, and Verdun did not fall. Then for a long time there was nothing about him, and then he was sent to Spain as ambassador after the Spanish civil war, and then everybody remembered about him and everybody said that it was interesting. Then there was this war and week by week things were getting more and more terrible, and then they said Pétain was to be at the head of the army and we felt a little hope. To be sure there was the old prediction that when the enemy had gotten to Lyons the country that is France would be saved by an old man on a white horse and Pétain had always ridden a white horse, his name was Monastir, and as a matter of fact he did make the armistice in front of Lyons.

  And now he had to defend his armistice as he had defended Verdun, and he did. In the days immediately following the armistice when the Germans had left the Zone Libre, and in the other zone the french were accepting their life as it was everybody began to talk again and the thing they talked about most at first was the age of the Maréchal. He had become not Pétain not Maréchal Pétain but the Maréchal.

Everybody worried about his age, was he too old to last and they realized that being as old as he was and not having a family, he had no future, he had only the future of France, and as french people without people who have a future they could just then trust in the Maréchal because he being as old as he was and without a family had only France's future and so they did pretty well all of them did trust him. Longevity is always respected in France and this longevity of the Maréchal was a very special thing and so they did trust him and when he told them anything he told them the truth and very often he did not tell them anything.

Then came the time when the french people practically came to feel what they did feel, what they always do feel that they do not at all think alike all of them about anything. As a frenchman explained it to me it is not only that they do not think alike with their neighbors but they do not think alike within themselves. As he said, You take any one french one, that one french one has quite logically perhaps four points of view. Supposing he has a son a prisoner, well he wants the war over as quickly as possible so that his son will come home, so he wants the german to win as that would finish the quickest, at the same time he is a business man and he wants business to go on, and that would only happen if the Germans were defeated and England won, then he wants the maréchal and as the English are opposed to him they would insist on bringing back into France all the people who helped to ruin France so they do not want England to win and then there is Russia, and that is even more complicating. You see, said this Frenchman no frenchman can feel simple about this thing.

And then gradually the Maréchal either did what any one and every one thought he ought to do or he did not, and whether he did or whether he did not and really nobody really knew there was one thing that was certain and that was that like Benjamin Franklin he never defended himself, he never explained himself, in short his character did not need any defense.

And so there came this considerable period when everybody had feelings about the Maréchal about one thing they were all agreed and that is that he had achieved a miracle, without arms without any means of defense, he had succeeded in making the Germans more or less keep their word with him. Gradually this miracle impressed itself upon every one.

Always there were rumors and more rumors and sometimes everybody believed them, that the Maréchal had yielded this or he had yielded that to the germans, and gradually in spite of all the feeling of bitterness that was around everybody in their hearts knew that it was not true, [?word] that he had not. Nice stories began to be told. The germans wanted to take something in the zone libre which they had no right to take, the percentage of material. The Maréchal said, I do not wish it. The germans and the people around the Maréchal said what can you do about it. I can do nothing about it said the Maréchal but I do not wish it. And it ended in their not doing it.

We used to all sit and on the country roads and discuss, this time the Maréchal has given in, and we almost were sure that he had given in, but actually he never has given in. Gradually they began to tell that when he was asked who was going to win the English or the germans, he did not answer and when he was pressed he touched his breast and answered Moi.

I cannot tell you how many times in this long difficult year we thought many of us thought that he had gone under, under one thing or under another, and we all talked and talked but no, the miracle which is a miracle, and his defense of his armistice has been a miracle, and here it still is.

A nice story was told me the other day about him which has nothing to do with this but which is a story that I like. He was at that time a colonel it was before the last war and he belonged to a military club. All the young officers were talking about the possible coming war and they were excited and laughing and shouting and slowly there was a silence and Colonel Pétain said and so you think war is always funny, toujours drôle.

And so we in France having seen France governed, having seen everybody pretty well fed having seen everybody slowly regain their health and strength, felt every one gradually recovering their liberty and their activity, and having seen every time that all being lost actually everything was being held together, I must say little by little the most critical and the most violent of us have come gradually to do what the Maréchal asks all french people to do, to have faith in him and in the fact that France will live. And this is to introduce the actual words said by the Maréchal when it was necessary for him to say something and it is a convincing and moving story.

By 7 February 1942, Faÿ wrote her about the marshall's response to the plan, "Pour la traduction je n'ai point encore eu l'occasion d'en parler en détail avec le Maréchal, mais en gros, l'idée lui plaît." The next day, 8 February, he acknowledged receipt of her introduction. Some of her analogies and stories for American readers appear also in *Wars I Have Seen* (80–87). Faÿ thought the text should be published but wanted to make sure of Pétain's approval, "[j]e crois que ce serait très bien de la publier mais peut-être vaudrait-il mieux . . . que je parle au Maréchal." Faÿ not only hoped that Stein's name would add to American support of Pétain but also expected that a translation by a distinguished writer and long-time resident in France might for Americans add luster to the marshall's book and personality. No doubt Faÿ hoped in turn it would help to assure Stein's safety in wartime France—the Germans had not yet occupied the free zone. Both Faÿ and Stein appear to have entered the project of the translation in good faith.

In a letter of 7 August 1942 to Paul Genin, a Monsieur Cusset of the Comité France-Amérique refers to an earlier letter of 20 February from Genin (not preserved) announcing his interest in cooperating with Stein and him on the project and asks why he has heard nothing for six months. This letter also informs Genin that a second volume with 1942 Pétain speeches is in preparation. Genin's draft for an answer, dated 20 August, acknowledges the information and confirms their readiness to work on the project. It also indicates that Stein, working with American editors, would select speeches of particular interest to an American readership, emphasizing that her great literary and philosophical authority among her compatriots would facilitate the selection if she was in principle given the liberty to choose. We do not know whether this letter was further revised or when it was sent (Genin correspondence courtesy of Paul Genin and Joan Chapman).

On 1 September 1942, Stein wrote to Rogers that it was almost decided that she was to do the translation. The next document is a brief note dated 14 September from Jaray to Stein, who had apparently invited him when he was traveling and could not respond. On 23 October Jaray answered a 19 October letter from Stein and a 15 October letter from Genin (neither preserved) enclosing a contract, with copy to Genin, to be signed by Stein and forwarded by registered mail. Though no copy of the contract is preserved, it appears that Stein signed it, for the correspondence continues with a letter of 8 December from Jaray to Genin about proofs for the second volume to be sent for a brief period for her examination and possibly selection.

We do not know exactly when Stein began or stopped the translations, but she may have prepared some of them even before she wrote to Rogers, between February and September. Her notebooks give evidence of immense labor, with extensive revisions and editorial participation of Toklas, especially in rendering French political terminology and idiom. Not all the speeches are translated, but nothing is known about whether those translated are a selection and whether it is hers or was made in consultation with others. Only a few typed leaves are among the papers; they do not tell us whether a typescript was completed or submitted. The last text translated, a routine speech for Christmas 1940, stops at the end of her manuscript notebook in midspeech, midsentence, a procedure quite unlike Stein, who was orderly and finished what she started: was there another notebook, not preserved, which might have gone beyond and revealed what happened to make her stop? The texts and letters preserved do not give us enough facts for interpretation.

In November 1942 the Germans occupied all of France, but by that fall they had also begun to lose ground. The Allies had taken North Africa in September and November, and the Russian victory of 2 February 1943 at Stalingrad became a forecast of German defeat. Pétain himself had gradually lost power and prestige even earlier in 1942.

On 30 December 1942 Cusset asked Stein to confirm arrangements for the proofs, and on 15 January 1943, he sent the 164 pages for volume 2 of *Paroles aux Français* for Stein to review within two weeks. On 15 January 1943, Faÿ wrote that he hoped to see her about the translations. By February Stein moved to Culoz. At some point, Maurice Sivan, the Sous-préfet, a local official, and Paul Genin supposedly prevailed upon her to abandon the project because it drew excessive attention to her in an already risky situation under the occupation. By the time she stopped, she had translated approximately three-fifths of the French printed text. (In *Wars I Have Seen* Stein misspells Sivan as Sivain, corrected to Sivan by Joan Chapman.)

Stein had known Bernard Faÿ, a specialist in American intellectual history, since the early twenties, and from 1927 on a warm personal friendship had developed. Faÿ came from a family of bankers and lawyers with Royalist and Catholic ties and was well connected in the world of power and the world of the arts. He had known Pétain since World War I, when, as a polio victim with a limp, he had worked for the French ambulance service (Faÿ, *Les Précieux*, 38–42). He had written a dissertation on the American Revolution in the French press and in 1927 published *The Revolutionary Spirit in France and America*, followed by biographies of Franklin (1929) and Washington (1932), a study of American novelists, as well as essays, lectures, and further books on a great variety of subjects, including Freemasonry. Stein introduced him to Bravig Imbs, who translated the biographies into English; she herself had critically read them and checked the translations. Faÿ said he learned from Stein to think in English.

His first academic appointment was at the University of Clermont-Ferrand. He did research and published widely in France and the United States and lectured regularly at major American universities. By 1932, competing against the senior economist André Siegfried, he won an appointment to a professorship at the Collège de France in Paris. Stein shared his interest in the working of power and supported him through years of efforts cultivating ministers and people of influence to obtain the coveted position. The appointment gave him access to further power, for example, as consultant on American publications for Éditions Stock, publisher of the French translation of an abbreviated version of *The Making Of Americans*. His academic position was important to Stein, who respected universities, responded to prestige, and had faith in students as makers of the new. During her American lecture tour, Faÿ, experienced in lecturing on the college circuit, helped pave her way, arranged talks, wrote and spoke about her, and planned his lectures to coincide with hers in New York and Chicago. He advised her through all phases of the tour.

In 1930, with the poet Grace-Ives de Longevialle, Faÿ translated "Melanctha" and in 1933 the *Autobiography*. He wrote about Stein in French and lectured about her in France and in America. In 1932 and 1933, with Louis Bromfield, he planned articles and publicity promoting her. He supervised the translation by Renée de Seillère of the short *The Making Of Americans* published by Éditions Stock in 1933. The same selection, which Faÿ had helped prepare, was published in English by Harcourt Brace with a preface by him even though Stein had always insisted that prefaces were redundant; *Lectures In America* also was dedicated to Faÿ, whose experience with speaking had sustained her during their writing. The only other friend to receive such devoted dedication was Carl Van Vechten.

From early years in their relationship, Faÿ helped Stein with practical problems in France, as did Georges Maratier, another friend experienced in French ways. She consulted both on working permits for foreign servants and problems with the country house. Faÿ, who came from a family of lawyers, helped her, through a local solicitor in Belley whom he knew, obtain a lease for the house she wanted once the officer who occupied it was transferred to a post elsewhere. As a result, his friendship was always associated with the house in Bilignin.

In 1937, he negotiated with Jean Paulhan for publication in *La Nouvelle Revue Française* of his translation of "What Are Masterpieces." In 1937–38, the war in sight, he was looking for safe passage to the United States with guarantee of speedy reentry into France for Stein and Toklas.

The key to Faÿ's activities in the war was his relationship with Pétain, whose eyes and ears he became and who in turn protected him. He had admired Pétain, the hero of Verdun, since World War I and offered his services to him when on 16 June 1940 he succeeded Paul Reynaud as premier. When Pierre Laval offered him a ministry in the late summer, he declined but accepted instead the directorship of the Bibliothèque Nationale. A year later, on 18 August 1941, he wrote to Fanny Butcher of the *Chicago Tribune*, "I am very happy as a historian because we are living in a very historical time and it is very stimulating to dream of our time while living it. . . . The Marshall is very nice to me and they say he will appoint me as a minister soon. I know they are wrong, the Marshall would not like to dismiss me and he always dismisses ALL his ministers, so there is no danger in fact for me" (Texas). Through the Vichy years, he was stationed in Paris but spent a week every month in Vichy as advisor to Pétain. Early in the war, he saw to it that Stein received driving privileges; throughout the months he also sent her extra rations. More important, under his initiative, the marshall authorized a direct telephone contact number to his office from the office of Maurice Sivan, in case Stein needed protection or ran short of essential supplies (Faÿ, *Les Précieux*, 162; interview Burns, 1969).

Early in the war, Stein apparently executed a document empowering Faÿ to watch over and preserve her art collection. Notes for a power of attorney, dated 10 September 1940, are scribbled on an envelope. Periodically Faÿ reported to Stein on the safety of her collection. He apparently also discussed legal problems about the document with Georges Maratier.

When the Germans entered her Paris apartment in the last days of the occupation, Faÿ was alerted by Picasso. Through Count Metternich, with whom he had collaborated documenting monuments, he managed to stop the Germans from removing paintings, apparently by reclassifying the collection and creating confusion among German bureaucrats (see also Katherine Dudley to Stein, 14 November 1944). Stein had reason to feel that she owed to him the preservation of her collection and probably her life.

Faÿ was arrested at the Bibliothèque Nationale on 19 August 1944 and held in various prisons until his trial as a collaborator, from 29–30 November to 6 December 1946. Stein and, after her death, Toklas made efforts to lend support to his defense though as foreigners they could not testify in court. Among her papers is a typed letter of 14 March 1946 from Stein to Maître Chresteil, Avocat de la Cour, identified by Toklas as her testimony in support of Faÿ. She cites his saving her collection, witnessed by Picasso; his devotion to French-American relations; his pride in his former American research assistant, who joined the U.S. Army; his wish for Allied victory, voiced upon a two-day visit to Stein, September 1943; his care for the Bibliothèque Nationale; his dislike of Germans. It is not a powerful testimony.

Faÿ was sentenced to hard labor for life, a sentence later reduced to twenty years in prison. On 30 September 1951, with the help of friends, he escaped from prison, first to Spain and then to Fribourg, Switzerland, where he lived and worked under an assumed name, Philippe Conaint. By means of the sale of one or more works on paper by Picasso, Toklas helped to finance the escape. In 1958 Faÿ was pardoned by the then minister of justice, François Mitterrand, and allowed to return to France.

This account of Faÿ goes well beyond Stein's daily life in the war. It supersedes the information given in our letter to *The Nation* (5 December 1987, 666), in response to the article by Natalie Robins, "The Defiling of Writers: The F.B.I. and American Lit" (10 October 1987, 367–72). The very full details are necessary for an understanding of Stein's situation, her survival, her trust, and her loyalty.

On 25 October 1946 Toklas wrote to Bobsy Goodspeed in Chicago to ask for her help in alleviating Faÿ's suffering. It had become a sacred trust of friendship for Toklas, as it had for Stein, to work for his liberation. She carefully describes the relationship: "You know that Gertrude had a long and intimate friendship—it had its moments of more or less intensity but since we came back from the U.S. in '35 it never varied. Gertrude completely disagreed with his political ideas—fairly left for U.S. and royalist for France—she didn't agree with a number of other ideas of his. I tell you this to show you she knew—understood—appreciated and finally became very fond of him—and she never had any doubt of his complete loyalty to his friends and his two countries. He made many enemies—he once said he collected them" (*Staying on Alone*, 24–26).

It is not difficult to understand that in 1941, after Pearl Harbor, of which she speaks in her introduction, Stein began the translation project in support of Pétain, as Faÿ had suggested. Like many French people going back to World War I, she had faith in Pétain as a savior of France. Even in the late play *Yes Is For A Very Young Man* echoes of his voice return: "France is a country that can be beaten but not conquered" (*Last Operas*, 15). One can also understand her wish at that time to gain American support for France by publishing the translations in America. In her biography, *Everybody Who Was Anybody* (1975), Janet Hobhouse claims, without documentation, that Stein attempted to interest the *Atlantic Monthly* in publishing her versions of Pétain (218), a step for which we have been unable to find evidence.

What is difficult to understand, however, is how Stein continued with the project once edicts against Jews were issued and deportations begun, and how she persisted into January 1943, even after Pétain by November 1942 had lost control. It is as if in 1942–43 she was insulated from understanding what was happening. She had always been conservative, reactionary, and fearful of communism, and in the Spanish Civil War she had been anti-Loyalist. We do not know to what extent she continued to rely on Faÿ's judgment and what she understood of his political activities, his active anti-Semitism, his hatred of Bolshevism, his collaboration. Even her own conservatism might have kept her from examining the implications of what was happening. When warned about the Pétain project by William Rogers, who in his book quotes extensively from her letters and his responses, she aggressively defended the translation and her political views, perhaps to mask her uneasiness. In *Wars I Have Seen,* filled with astute observation of daily life, a reactionary tone sometimes creates discomfort. What she understood about Faÿ and how she saw the situation remains a troublesome puzzle.

An astonishing conclusion to the Pétain project appears in the Random House/Bennett Cerf Papers at Columbia University in one more undated letter of Stein to Cerf, her publisher, from Bilignin, written almost certainly at the beginning of 1942. For Christmas 1941, at her request, Cerf had sent her a number of books, including *The Decline and Fall of the Roman Empire:*

> My dear Bennett,
>
>   We are reading every day a chapter of the Decline and Fall. I can't tell you how exciting it is to hear that everything is as it is, I like it to be and that is one thing. Now another. I am giving a letter of introduction to Robert Alkan, Hotel Seville, 29th Street and Madison Avenue, that is to say I am giving him a letter to you. He is a very interesting man, an inventor, a co-[?word] [?word], a frenchman and he will make you understand things as they are which I think you over there do not quite see, I am beginning at the same time the translation of the Petain to his people, I found the book convincing and moving to an extraordinary degree and my idea was to write an introduction telling how my feelings have changed about him, I have had strong ups and downs and I think it would all do a lot of good, we all now over here can begin to understand that life with its reverses, are not what they were when all went alright. Now please Bennett if this idea interests you let me know as soon as possible because I would naturally prefer you but if not someone else but please do see Alkan as soon as possible, I know you will find him extremely interesting, so much love, always Gtde.

Cerf did not receive this letter at his office until early February 1946. Not realizing when it had been written, he answered right away, on 7 February, with a firm no, describing Pétain as an "appeaser, collaborator, Fascist." "Don't go upsetting the apple cart [i.e., of new, profitable, and promising publications—*Wars I Have Seen* and *Brewsie And Willie*] with that Pétain idea of yours." Of course Robert Alkan, a brilliant engineer, inventor, and friend of Paul Genin, who worked for the United States armaments through the war but returned to France after the war, no longer needed to be contacted. On 23 February 1946 Gertrude cabled Cerf,

"KEEP YOUR SHIRT ON BENNETT DEAR LETTER RE PETAIN WAS WRITTEN IN
1941."

About Stein's politics many questions have been raised, especially since World
War II. In her thinking about political, social, and economic matters, she was a
conservative Republican with what William Rogers called the mentality of a
"rentier," a person of property. She opposed Roosevelt and the New Deal and was
more afraid of communism than of fascism. In 1937, during the Spanish Civil
War, she did not oppose the dictatorship of General Franco, "for the majority
does want a dictator," as she wrote to Rogers (217).

Stein's habit of making provocative statements, which always came out of
the context of her thought, has led to many interpretations and misinterpreta-
tions. An example is an interview with Lansing Warren conducted in Paris and
published in the *New York Times Magazine* (6 May 1934, 9, 23). It begins with a
sampling of outrageous "sibylline" Stein statements taken out of context. Then
follows a description of her studio as a place of "order and sanity," and of Stein
herself as "striking, self-possessed and energetic" with an "impish expression."
One of the initial shocking utterances is then amplified: "I say that Hitler ought to
have the peace prize, because he is removing all elements of contest and of
struggle from Germany. By driving out the Jews and the democratic and Left
elements, he is driving out everything that conduces to activity. That means
peace."

Later, however, she is quoted as asserting that what matters in a country is
"competition, struggle, interest, activity that keep the people alive and excited"—
the very opposition that Hitler wishes to remove. The proposal about the peace
prize, then, is ironic, a point of black humor. Taken literally and out of context,
the statement about Hitler is easily misread. See, for example, the accusation that
Stein in 1938, with other intellectuals, proposed Hitler for the Nobel Peace Prize,
used in 1995 to underscore Jews' failing to support their own interests, in *Nativ*, an
Israeli journal of politics and the arts for September 1995, 67–68, and quoted in
the English language edition of the *Forward*, 2 February 1996, 1, 4. This information has been denied by the office of the Nobel Peace Prize Committee in Oslo.
Also, on 31 January 1937, Hitler had decreed that no German could ever receive
the Nobel Prize in any category.

By November 1942, with the free zone of France occupied by the Germans,
correspondence with friends abroad virtually ceased, and Stein and Toklas were
increasingly cut off from the world and at the same time more exposed. In *Wars I
Have Seen*, Stein asks whether it is worse to be scared than to be bored (81). Toklas
speaks about more than cooking when she comments on "the hopeless monotony
of the menus" (*Cook Book*, 227). Their days became drab. War narrowed the
world. What new writing she did—much of her work was preparing older pieces
for translation into French or recasting earlier writing—focused on a restricted
and tense life, but her writer's discipline endured, keeping her perceptions sharp

and her mind open. René Tavernier, writing from Lyon, described life in war-time, without pungent anecdotes or charming diversions, with not even a laugh at a publisher or editor, and without a chance to restore himself as often as he wished in conversation with Stein in the beautiful Bugey: "Ce temps est triste-ment dépourvu de piquantes anecdotes, de charmantes escroqueries, de diver-tissements, . . . On n'a pas tous les jours un Sorlot pour s'indigner et un Bou-telleau pour rire. Pas tous les jours surtout, ce ravissant Bugey, votre terrasse si admirablement encadrée de verdure, et votre conversation qui est tonique pour l'esprit" (Tavernier to Stein, 23 June 1943; his ellipsis).

Because Monsieur and Madame Putz, the owners of the house in Bilignin that they had leased since 1929, wanted it for their own use, Stein and Toklas were forced to move. In February 1943 they rented Le Colombier, also referred to as Propriété Poncet, a well-equipped house with servants just outside of Culoz, a railroad junction some ten kilometers from Bilignin. Though a railroad junction appears more exposed than their former remote hamlet, it offered some protec-tion because the Germans, who depended on cooperative local labor for a func-tioning railroad, behaved well (Rogers, *When This You See*, 199). Stein recounts events that led to the move in *Wars I Have Seen* (48–49), begun soon after they settled in the new house.

Just before the move, they went to see their lawyer in Belley, who at the behest of Maurice Sivan urged them to flee immediately to Switzerland, "tomor-row if possible otherwise they will be put into a concentration camp" (*Wars I Have Seen*, 50–51). Stein recounts the exchanges about what to do: cross the Swiss border illegally, to which she claimed to object though she surely knew it was going on, hide in a safe house they were offered high in the mountains, or stick to the planned move to Culoz, their final choice. Echoes of the decision return in *Yes Is For A Very Young Man*: "in time of danger stay where you are, there if you are killed . . . there where you are. Trying to get away from danger is useless . . . I stayed" (*Last Operas*, 13). In *Wars I Have Seen*, these and other debates are largely conducted by Stein alone, with Toklas only as the faithful listener. While this method keeps the narrator's voice steady and confident, it sometimes sounds engaged in denial of danger that was real indeed.

In her writing, Stein often makes broad statements about national charac-ter—American, English, Italian, German, and French. She rarely, however, cate-gorized people by group or class, and she did not identify herself and Toklas as Jews. In a letter to Rogers, who took her to task for her reactionary politics, she quoted herself speaking to students: "For me gens [people] were just gens, and really they arouse a different kind of interest if you like one class or another class, like dull or not dull but really otherwise they were just what they were that is people" (Rogers, *When This You See*, 219). Perception of people is central to the power and freedom of her writing. Stein herself, however, coming from a bour-geois background and living on a fixed income, had become increasingly class-conscious as she became famous. The chateau at Culoz must have seemed more appropriate than a remote house in the mountains. She liked contact with members of the upper classes—Elisabeth de Gramont, the Duchesse de Clermont-Tonnerre, who had translated her lectures, Sir Robert and Lady Diana Abdy, and Lord Berners in England. She was devoted to the Baroness Pierlot and the d'Aiguys in Béon, some of whom were members of the conservative, pro-Vichy Croix de Feu.

The two women were accepted by the local community and not considered outsiders. A good listener, Stein was a friend to farmers and their families as well as to those who had permanent summer residences. Toklas shared the interests of people in the village. Both were helpful to others. They were lucky not to be counted when local officials, under orders to report foreign residents, looked the other way and disregarded the presence of the two Americans. Eric Sevareid, who saw Stein on 1 September 1944, reported in his memoir that Justin Rey, the mayor of Culoz, always protected her secret from the Germans as had all the people of the village.

Stein was also close to some members of the *maquis*, especially Romain Godet, a neighbor who later was posted to the United Nations. He reported that he and his friends were aware of her and had plans to protect her if need arose (Burns, Interview, 1969). She wrote about "the mountain boys" in *Wars I Have Seen*.

But even the good will of friends could not fully protect them. According to a list of events in Culoz under the occupation, written in a French hand and preserved among the Stein papers, twice enemy soldiers were billeted to Le Colombier—Germans from 7 to 14 August and Italians from 18 to 29 August 1943. The list documents what Toklas remembered:

> Suddenly we had Germans billeted upon us, two officers and their order-lies. Hastily rooms were prepared for them in a wing of the house far removed from our bedrooms. Provisions were hidden, but there was not enough time to gather together and put away the many English books scattered throughout the rooms. In the best guest room there was a charming coloured English engraving of Benjamin Franklin demonstrating one of his discoveries on a lake in an English park. The Germans did not notice it but one of the Italian officers billeted upon us later spoke of it appreciatively.
>
> . . .
>
> Just when the communiqués were getting almost unbearably exciting, two officers and thirty soldiers of the Italian army were billeted upon us, the officers in the house naturally and the soldiers in the garages and chauffeur's quarters—worrisomely near the vegetable garden and fruit trees. Would they respect what was missing from their army rations? Their captain said they would and surprisingly they did. . . . Presently the soldiers were selling me on the black market such cigarettes as they could spare, a most welcome relief from my tobaccoless state. (*Cook Book*, 212, 217)

With local children, Stein read Shakespeare plays filled with crisis, war, ghosts, and ominous predictions that recalled readings of her youth after the Civil War (*Wars I Have Seen*, 13–14). Of the three plays she had written for children, two, *In A Garden A Tragedy In One Act* and *Look And Long, A Play In Three Acts*, were performed in the grand salon of the Château de Béon on 29 August 1943 with local children, including Rose d'Aiguy, Mark and Moki (Maurice) Godet, Marie Madeleine Dolfus from the village of Tallissieu, and Coryse de Ravignan, a cousin of Rose. Numerous local friends came, as well as the couturier-to-be Pierre Balmain, who did the children's costumes. With minimal means the performance provided diversion in a dull and fearful time. Instead of a curtain, a large screen was used, which toppled over. The children were bored and Rose d'Aiguy sulked about her costume (interview with Joan Chapman, Burns, Dydo, 6 May 1994).

Wars I Have Seen is a continuation of the lives and events that became *Mrs. Reynolds*. Its autobiographical voice ranges from early events and stories told Stein in childhood at home to books significant for the experience of war. As she began, she seems to have thought of the book as a second reader, a war book, or another autobiography. "I am really writing my autobiography," she says on the inside cover of the first notebook, and plays with titles, "Gertrude Stein War Autobiography," "Foreign, Domestic and Civil Wars," "My Emotional Autobiography." The book becomes a record of the daily life from the move to Culoz until the liberation. Related events appear in Toklas' *Cook Book* and in her memoir, *What Is Remembered*. Stein considered it safe to write the new book because her handwriting would have been indecipherable even if the manuscript had been confiscated; however, Alice Toklas delayed typing until August 1944, when the danger was over (*Wars I Have Seen*, 229).

By the time she moved to Culoz, Stein was cut off from America, England, and new writing in English as she was also cut off from publication in English. Except for the aborted Pétain project, during the later years of the war she published mainly French translations by May d'Aiguy of work written earlier. But writing in English also continued with *Wars I Have Seen*. Daily life was tight and gray and required physical effort—growing crops, chopping wood, obtaining supplies. Long meditative walks kept her observing people, the land, wartime activities. The habit of daily writing that she had followed for all the years kept her alive, for the act of writing held the mind steady and kept helplessness at bay. With astonishing accuracy she recorded in local, personal stories what was happening, with few comments on the larger political scene. Only indirectly did she hint at the deep personal anxiety of the time. Here and there, however, she lost control of her voice, indulging in a tone of excessive self-assurance or demonstrative honesty, and including anecdotes that are not amusing even when told by outsiders. At the same time, the low, sober stringing together of events and details creates a haunting, monotonous order from which rises gradually the desire for lively disorder.

Out of touch with America, she no longer had access to funds. Stein had always lived carefully on income from investments administered by Julian Stein, her banker cousin in Baltimore, and on royalties she received from writing. In a letter to William Rogers, dated by him about 15 September 1941 and quoted in his book, she contrasts Hemingway's success with *For Whom the Bell Tolls* and her own scant income from writing: "Paris France brought me less than a thousand and [T]he Winner Loses $250 and yet it was read all over the world and Ida which seems much loved only $350, it is sad" (Rogers, *When This You See*, 227). In July 1941 she was still able to lend some six thousand French francs to John and Ruth Selby-Bigge before they left for England. Their letters detail the difficulties of repayment. After November 1942, when the Germans occupied the free zone, Stein and Toklas could no longer draw on American funds and were left with insufficient means. Paul Genin, who as a businessman was able to shift funds, offered to tide her over with a monthly allowance in the amount she required and with no immediate obligation to repay. Stein speaks of his offer as that of "a young man interested in literature" (*Wars I Have Seen*, 112; see also Rogers, *When This You See*, 189); she had supported his efforts at publication by sending his book to Thornton Wilder in America and to Jean Denoël, coeditor with Max-Pol Fouchet of *Fontaine* and Éditions Charlot in Algiers. After six months of drawing on the loan from Genin, Stein apparently decided that she could not continue to become indebted. She made the only decision open to her: "I sold a picture I had with me quite quietly to someone who came to see me and so I thanked Paul Genin and paid him back" (*Wars I Have Seen*, 112). On 1 January 1944, the dealer César M. de Hauke, whom Stein had met in 1941 when he returned to Paris from New York, wrote her from Paris: "Serieuse, éclatante Madame Cezanne sur mon mur. . . . " [Solemn, dazzling, Madame Cezanne on my wall. . . .] In 1952 the painting was sold, presumably by de Hauke, to Emile Bührle, the Czech industrialist in Zurich, in whose collection it remains. Stein retained the other painting she had with her, the Picasso portrait of herself. The note about the sale of the Cézanne that follows the letter from Toklas of 25 December 1946 to Carl and Fania Van Vechten (*Staying on Alone*, 40–43) was based on word-of-mouth information by a friend of Toklas that has since proved to be in error.

The journal that regularly published her in the second half of the war was *Confluences*, edited at first, numbers 1–3, July–September 1941, by Jacques Aubénique, then by René Tavernier. How Stein and Tavernier met is unclear, though it may have been through Bernard Faÿ. As a young man, in October 1936, in Grenoble, Tavernier had introduced Stein for the lecture "La France Est Mon Chez-Moi" ("An American And France") (see Stein to Wilder, 10 October 1936, n. 3). There is no evidence that this early contact continued.

By December 1942, when the preserved correspondence with Tavernier begins, the July issue (no. 12) of *Confluences* had already published her "Ballade," an eerie poem that can be read with political overtones, about big birds threatening little birds; it is section 18 of the *Gertrude Stein First Reader*, in a French translation by May d'Aiguy, who may have been the contact for publication. Tavernier's letters show an admiring, gifted poet, who submitted his work to Stein for critical review, dedicated a poem to her ("Les Arbres/A Gertrude Stein,"

Signes [Lyon: Confluences, 1943]: 13–14), and gave her inscribed volumes of his earlier poems *De Vous La Merveille* (Éditions Denoël, 1937) and *Sens de la Solitude* (Librairies Vega, 1938); he was also an editor of intelligence and wide interests and a friend who with his wife, mother, and children shared a warm family relationship with her and Toklas and watched out for them.

As editor, Tavernier was in a difficult position. Censorship put constraints upon publishing, and paper shortage was a constant worry. He did not distribute *Confluences* in the north so as not to run into trouble with the occupying power. Even in the free zone *Confluences* was watched by the Vichy censors, who knew that some work appeared under pseudonyms and some political pieces were called reprints but were not. The journal was suspended on 16 August 1942 for publishing Louis Aragon's poem "Nymphées." In March 1943, threatened with arrest, Tavernier went into hiding for some weeks. Yet throughout these years he planned new issues and wrote reviews and cultural reports for each number.

Under the title "Autobiographies," starting with the February 1943 issue (no. 17) and continuing in March (no. 18), Tavernier published in French two sections (from chapters 1 and 2) of *Everybody's Autobiography*, preceded by a brief introduction made up of passages from the lecture "Poetry And Grammar" (Stein, *Lectures*, 214–17), rewritten in the third person and signed by the translator May (La Baronne) d'Aiguy; in no. 25, for September–October 1943, and no. 27, December 1943, he added two further installments (from chapter 3 to page 124). These sections are edited perhaps by Stein and Toklas or Stein and May d'Aiguy. Isolated single sentences are left out. Also omitted are some stories about living local people and some American references, such as the one to e.e. cummings, confined to a French camp in World War I. Comments on the Germans as a warlike nation are deleted with care. We do not know whether she consulted with Faÿ regarding the deletions.

The fact that Tavernier twice published selections from *Everybody's Autobiography*, in both cases marking the second "fin," suggests that he may already have planned to issue *Everybody's Autobiography* as a book, a project not realized until after the war, when his firm, renamed Éditions Confluences, moved to Paris and began issuing books. Tavernier signed his dedication to Stein of *Signes*, his volume of poems (1943), as "son futur editeur," her publisher-to-be, suggesting perhaps that he planned to print books of hers. If books were in his mind in 1943, the project was stopped by May, when the third list of proscriptions, List "OTTO," went into effect. The first list had been published in October 1940, the second on 8 July 1942. These two lists had included German emigrés opposed to the Nazis and French and other translated writers that were unacceptable. The third list, issued by French publishers in response to the demand of the Germans, targeted Jewish writers by particular works published in France. Stein was on the list for *Picasso*, published in 1938 by Librairie Floury, the only work that had been issued recently in Paris by a French publisher and was in print, as the French *The Making Of Americans* (1933) presumably no longer was. Authors of works published in Algeria, which was not occupied, were not on the list.

On 7 August 1943, Tavernier informed Stein that her work had been included on the German list OTTO of proscription, which also prevented him from
publishing her. He wondered whether the list was instigated by Fernand Sorlot,
the collaborating publisher, and whether Bernard Faÿ might intercede: "En vous
remerciant de votre mot, je vous annonce hélas! une mauvaise nouvelle: j'ap-
prends que vos ouvrages viennent d'être mis sur la récente liste OTTO qui est une
liste allemande de proscription. Cette honneur m'empêche malheureusement
de vous publier. Faut-il voir là un manoeuvre de Sorlot. En signalant immediate-
ment le fait à M. Faÿ, peut-être pourra-t-il obtenir votre grâce." [Thank you for
your letter. Alas, I must give you bad news. I hear that your works have been put
on the recent list OTTO, a German list of proscription. This honor prevents me
unfortunately from publishing you. Are we to consider it a maneuver on the part
of Sorlot? If you inform Mr. Faÿ right away, perhaps he may be able to do
something.] The phrasing suggests that Tavernier had received word of the list but
had not seen it. Her name on the list implied total proscription. We do not know
whether she contacted Faÿ, though it appears likely; nor do we know whether Faÿ
undertook anything, or what he could do—what "grâce" might have meant. We
do know that even after the list appeared, *Confluences* in September–October
and December printed further sections of *Everybody's Autobiography*. Being on
the list constituted an interdict against sale and translation of any and all books by
the authors named. It is not clear whether it left open the possibility of magazine
publication, especially reprints of old work. Perhaps Tavernier's comment that he
could not publish her implied that *Everybody's Autobiography* could not be
printed as planned. (It finally appeared in 1946 with a preface by Léonie Villard of
the University of Lyon; other volumes were devoted to St. Exupéry [1947], the
Jews [1947], Communism [1947].)

When Tavernier on 23 May 1943 asked Stein to contribute to the special issue
on the novel, she apparently responded immediately; a postcard of 11 June 1943
thanked her for the "roman" text. She wrote "Realism In The Novel," not published complete in English until it was included in *Gertrude Stein and the Making of Modernism*, edited by Shirley Neuman and Ira Nadel (1988). Contrary to
Neuman's assertion, however, it was translated into French by May d'Aiguy as "Le
réalisme dans les romans," printed in the special issue of *Confluences*, nos. 21–24
(July–August 1943): 304–05, and reprinted in *Problèmes du roman*, edited by Jean
Prevost (Lyon and Brussels: Le Carrefour, 1945), 262–63.

In *Wars I Have Seen*, Stein speaks of "prisoners prisoners every where" and
"you would imagine that with all that I would no longer want to read mystery
stories and spy stories and all that but not at all I want to read them more than
ever, to change one reality for another" (46). By the next page, in May or June
1943, she began drafting "Realism in Novels":

"Realism.

"After all there has to be realism realism in romance and in novels and the
reason why is this. Novels have to resemble something and in order that they do
there must be realism" (48).

The context of Culoz in 1943 places the issue of realism perfectly between the terrible reality of daily life and the need to exchange that reality for relief with another. Tavernier also asked her to contribute to a number on painting, and she again responded, sending him by March 1944 "Tableaux," a translation of her lecture, "Pictures," omitting the quotations from *Portraits And Prayers* that were in the original lecture. This piece also appeared later in book form in *Les Problèmes de la Peinture*, edited by Gaston Diehl (Paris: Éditions Confluences, 1945), 443–62. (Stein's letters to Tavernier are in the collection of the Institut Mémoires de l'Édition Contemporaine, Paris.)

In a section for February 1944 in *Wars I Have Seen* (153), Stein speaks repeatedly of frightening things that were happening: "everything is a little frightening, enough said, they are a little frightening, especially if the dog stays with them, well they really are, they have just given us a passport of protection." The "Passeport de Protection," preserved among the Stein papers, was issued to Stein with the indication "réside temporairement en France" [resides temporarily in France] and with the date 12 February 1944, by the Swiss Legation in Vichy through François Lachenal, who was also a friend of René Tavernier.

After the liberation in August 1944, Stein finished *Wars I Have Seen*, and Toklas typed it as quickly as possible for forwarding to Bennett Cerf. The typescript was entrusted to the journalist Frank Gervasi, who was returning to the United States, and while in Caserta, Italy, by a "miraculous chance" Wilder read it, certified its authenticity and saw to it that it was not held up by censors (see Isabel Wilder to Stein, 8 September 1944, n. 1; Wilder to Stein [?16–30 September 1944], n. 1).

Once the Allied journalists had reached her and she had given her broadcast at Voiron (*Wars I Have Seen*, 246), Stein was no longer cut off but could speak and be heard. Letters also could at last be written and received. One of the very first must have been Isabel Wilder's letter of 8 September 1944, from Nantucket, responding to the newspaper announcement of 2 September of Stein's liberation. That letter was followed by countless others that opened the world. Except for Wilder's brief note of September 1944, it would be ten months before she would receive a letter from him.

A month before Stein returned to Paris on 15 December, at René Tavernier's invitation she spoke at Lyon on 3 November, repeating her lecture of 1936, "La France Est Mon Chez-Moi" at the Centre de Documentation de la Delegation Régionale de l'Information. Soon thereafter Tavernier moved to Paris. So did Stein, never to return to the Bugey.

Appendix X.

Principal Works of Gertrude Stein

[Note: Citations in the notes are to the first printed edition or to specific collections unless otherwise noted. This bibliography includes reprints only for works difficult to find or published with significant introductions.]

Alphabets And Birthdays. New Haven: Yale University Press, 1957. Introduction by Donald Gallup. Yale Edition of the Unpublished Writings of Gertrude Stein, volume 7. Rpt., Freeport, N.Y.: Books for Libraries Press, 1969.

An Acquaintance With Description. London: Seizin Press, 1929. In *A Stein Reader.*

As Fine As Melanctha (1914–1930). New Haven: Yale University Press, 1954. Foreword by Natalie Clifford Barney. Yale Edition of the Unpublished Writings of Gertrude Stein, volume 4. Rpt., Freeport, N.Y.: Books for Libraries Press, 1969.

The Autobiography Of Alice B. Toklas. New York: Harcourt, Brace, 1933. London: John Lane, The Bodley Head, 1933. In *Selected Writings.* Rpt., New York: Vintage Books, 1960; rpt., New York: Modern Library, 1993.

Bee Time Vine And Other Pieces (1913–1927). New Haven: Yale University Press, 1953. Preface and notes by Virgil Thomson. Yale Edition of the Unpublished Writings of Gertrude Stein, volume 3. Rpt., Freeport, N.Y.: Books for Libraries Press, 1969.

Before The Flowers Of Friendship Faded Friendship Faded. Paris: Plain Edition, 1931. In *Look at Me Now.* Rpt. with Georges Hugnet's poem *Enfances* on facing pages in *Exact Change Yearbook 1995, No. 1,* Boston: Exact Change, 1995, with an introduction by Juliana Spahr.

Blood On The Dining-Room Floor. Pawlet, Vt.: Banyan Press, 1948. Foreword by

Donald Gallup. Rpt. Berkeley: Creative Arts Book Co., 1982, introduction by John Herbert Gill; rpt., London: Virago Press, 1985, with an introduction by Janet Hobhouse.

A Book Concluding With As A Wife Has A Cow A Love Story. Paris: Galerie Simon (Daniel-Henry Kahnweiler), 1926. Lithographs by Juan Gris. Facsimile edition: West Glover, Vt.: Something Else Press, 1973. In *A Stein Reader.*

Brewsie And Willie. New York: Random House, 1946.

Composition As Explanation. London: Hogarth Press, 1926. The essay, "Composition as Explanation," is in *Selected Writings; Look At Me Now; A Stein Reader.*

Descriptions Of Literature. Englewood, N.J.: As Stable Pamphlets [George Platt Lynes and Adlai Harbeck], 1926. Cover drawing by Pavel Tchelitchew. In *A Stein Reader.*

Dix Portraits. Paris: Editions de la Montagne, 1930. English text with French translation.

An Elucidation. Paris: Transition, 1927. In *A Stein Reader.*

Everybody's Autobiography. New York: Random House, 1937. London: William Heinemann, 1938. Rpt., New York: Vintage Books, 1973 (contains an index); rpt., London: Virago Press, 1985, with an introduction by Janet Hobhouse; rpt., Cambridge, Mass.: Exact Change, 1993.

Fernhurst, Q.E.D., And Other Early Writings. New York: Liveright, 1971. Includes "A Note on the Texts" by Donald Gallup, "Introduction" by Leon Katz, and "The Making of *The Making of Americans*," by Donald Gallup. Rpt., London: Virago Press, 1995, with an introduction by Alison Hennegan.

Four In America. New Haven: Yale University Press, 1947. Introduction by Thornton Wilder. Rpt., Freeport, N.Y.: Books for Libraries Press, 1969.

Four Saints In Three Acts. New York: Random House, 1934. Introduction by Carl Van Vechten. In *Selected Writings; Last Operas and Plays.*

——. Vocal Score, words by Gertrude Stein, music by Virgil Thomson, and scenario by Maurice Grosser. New York: Music Press, 1948.

——. Abridged Recording. RCA Victor, 1947, reissued 1965. Conducted by Virgil Thomson.

——. Complete recording. Elektra/Nonesuch Records, 1982. Joel Thome, conductor, Orchestra of Our Time.

The Geographical History Of America Or The Relation of Human Nature To The Human Mind. New York: Random House, 1936. Introduction by Thornton Wilder. Rpt., New York: Vintage Books, 1973 (includes Wilder introduction and an introduction by William H. Gass); rpt., Baltimore: Johns Hopkins University Press, 1995 (this edition reprints only the Gass essay).

Geography And Plays. Boston: Four Seas, 1922. Preface, "The Work of Gertrude Stein," by Sherwood Anderson. Rpt., New York: Something Else Press, 1968; rpt., Madison: University of Wisconsin Press, 1993. Introduction and notes by Cyrena N. Pondrom.

The Gertrude Stein First Reader & Three Plays. Dublin and London: Maurice

Fridberg, 1946. Decorated by Sir Francis Rose. Boston: Houghton Mifflin, 1948 (with decorations by Rose).

Gertrude Stein On Picasso. New York: Liveright, 1970. Edited by Edward Burns with an afterword by Leon Katz and Edward Burns. Reprinted as *Picasso: The Complete Writings,* Boston: Beacon Press, 1985 (illustrations differ from those in the Liveright edition).

Have They Attacked Mary. He Giggled. New York: Privately printed by Henry McBride, 1917. In *Selected Writings.*

How To Write. Paris: Plain Edition, 1931; rpt., West Glover, Vt.: Something Else Press, 1973; rpt., New York: Dover Editions, 1975, with an introduction by Patricia Meyerowitz.

How Writing Is Written. Volume 2, Previously Uncollected Writings Of Gertrude Stein. Los Angeles: Black Sparrow Press, 1974. Edited with a preface by Robert Bartlett Haas.

Ida A Novel. New York: Random House, 1941. Rpt., New York: Vintage Books, 1971. In *Look at Me Now.*

In Savoy Or Yes Is for A Very Young Man (A Play of the Resistance in France). London: Pushkin Press, 1946. In *Last Operas and Plays.*

Last Operas And Plays. New York and Toronto: Rinehart & Co., 1949. Edited and with an introduction by Carl Van Vechten. Rpt., New York: Vintage Books, 1975; rpt., Baltimore: Johns Hopkins University Press, 1995. This edition does not reprint the Van Vechten introduction; it includes a new introduction by Bonnie Marranca and reprints Stein's lecture "Plays."

Lectures In America. New York: Random House, 1935. Rpt., Boston: Beacon Press, 1957; rpt., New York: Vintage Books, 1975; rpt., Boston: Beacon Press, 1985, with an introduction by Wendy Steiner (same as London: Virago Press, 1988).

Look at Me Now and Here I Am: Writings and Lectures 1909–45. New York and London: Penguin Books, 1971. Edited by Patricia Meyerowitz, with an introduction by Elizabeth Sprigge.

Lucy Church Amiably. Paris: Plain Edition, 1931. Rpt., New York: Something Else Press, 1969.

The Making Of Americans Being A History Of A Family's Progress. Paris: Contact Editions, 1925. Abridged edition, New York: Harcourt, Brace, 1934, preface by Bernard Faÿ. Rpt. of 1925 edition, New York: Something Else Press, 1966. Selections with headnotes by Leon Katz in *A Stein Reader.* Rpt. 1925 edition, Normal, Ill.: Dalkey Archive Press, 1995, with a foreword by William H. Gass and an introduction by Steven Meyer.

Matisse Picasso And Gertrude Stein, With Two Shorter Stories. Paris: Plain Edition, 1933. Also known as *GMP,* the book includes "A Long Gay Book," "Many Many Women," and "G.M.P." Rpt., Millerton, N.Y.: Something Else Press, 1972. "A Long Gay Book" is in *A Stein Reader.*

The Mother Of Us All. Vocal Score: libretto by Gertrude Stein, music by Virgil Thomson, scenario by Maurice Grosser. New York: Music Press, 1947.

——. Complete recording. New World Records, 1977. Raymond Leppard conductor, Santa Fe Opera.

Motor Automatism. New York: Phoenix Book Shop, 1969. Includes "Normal Motor Automatism" by Leon M. Solomons and Gertrude Stein, and "Cultivated Motor Automatism: A Study of Character in its Relation to Attention," by Gertrude Stein. Reprinted from *Psychological Review* 3, 5 (September 1896): 492–512; 5, 3 (May 1898): 295–306.

Mrs. Reynolds And Five Earlier Novelettes. New Haven: Yale University Press, 1952. Foreword by Lloyd Frankenberg. Yale Edition of the Unpublished Writings of Gertrude Stein, volume 2. Rpt., Freeport, N.Y.: Books for Libraries Press, 1969. Rpt., *Mrs. Reynolds* alone, Los Angeles: Sun & Moon Press, 1989.

Narration. Chicago: University of Chicago Press, 1935 [rpt. 1969]. Introduction by Thornton Wilder. Rpt., New York: Greenwood Press, 1969; rpt., Folcroft, Penn.: Folcroft Library Editions, 1977.

A Novel Of Thank You. New Haven: Yale University Press, 1958. Introduction by Carl Van Vechten. Yale Edition of the Unpublished Writings of Gertrude Stein, volume 8. Rpt., Freeport, N.Y.: Books for Libraries Press, 1969. Rpt. *A Novel Of Thank You* alone, Normal, Ill.: Dalkey Archive Press, 1994, with an introduction by Steven Meyer.

Operas And Plays. Paris: Plain Edition, 1932; rpt., Barrytown, N.Y.: Station Hill Press, 1987, with a foreword by James R. Mellow.

Painted Lace And Other Pieces [1914–1937]. New Haven: Yale University Press, 1955. Introduction by Daniel-Henry Kahnweiler. Yale Edition of the Unpublished Writings of Gertrude Stein, volume 5. Rpt., Freeport, N.Y.: Books for Libraries Press, 1969.

Paris France. London: B. T. Batsford, 1940; New York: Charles Scribner's Sons, 1940; rpt., New York: Liveright, 1970.

Picasso. Paris: Librairie Floury, 1938 (in French).

Picasso. London: B. T. Batsford, 1938; New York: Charles Scribner's Sons, 1939. Rpt. with different illustrations, Boston: Beacon Press, 1959; rpt. with different illustrations, New York: Dover Publications, 1984. In *Gertrude Stein On Picasso.*

Portrait Of Mabel Dodge At The Villa Curonia. Florence: Privately printed for Dodge, 1912. In *Selected Writings.*

Portraits And Prayers. New York: Random House, 1934.

A Primer For the Gradual Understanding Of Gertrude Stein. Los Angeles: Black Sparrow Press, 1971. Edited by Robert Bartlett Haas.

Reflection On the Atomic Bomb. Volume 1 of the Previously Uncollected Writings of Gertrude Stein. Los Angeles: Black Sparrow Press, 1973. Edited and with a preface by Robert Bartlett Haas.

Selected Writings Of Gertrude Stein. New York: Random House, 1946. Edited, introduction, and notes by Carl Van Vechten. Rpt., New York: Modern Library, 1962, with a general introduction by F. W. Dupee.

Stanzas In Meditation And Other Poems [1929–1933]. New Haven: Yale University Press, 1956. With a Preface by Donald Sutherland. Yale Edition of the Unpublished Writings of Gertrude Stein, volume 6. Rpt., Freeport, N.Y.: Books for Libraries Press, 1969. Rpt. of the poem *Stanzas In Meditation,* Los Angeles: Sun & Moon Press, 1994, with a preface by Douglas Messerli. Selections in *A Stein Reader.*

A Stein Reader. Evanston, Ill.: Northwestern University Press, 1993. Edited and with an introduction by Ulla E. Dydo. The texts in this edition have been checked against the manuscripts, typescripts, and first printed editions and are presented complete (except selections from *The Making Of Americans* and *Stanzas In Meditation*).

Tender Buttons. New York: Claire Marie, 1914. Rpt., Los Angeles: Sun & Moon Press, 1990. In *Selected Writings; Look at Me Now.*

Things As They Are. Pawlet, Vt.: Banyan Press, 1950. A corrected text, with the original title *Q.E.D.,* is in *Fernhurst, Q.E.D., And Other Early Writings.*

Three Lives. New York: Grafton Press, 1909. Rpt., New York: Modern Library, 1933, with an introduction by Carl Van Vechten. In *Selected Writings.* Numerous current reprints.

Two (Gertrude Stein And Her Brother) And Other Early Portraits (1908–1912). New Haven: Yale University Press, 1951. Foreword by Janet Flanner. Yale Edition of the Unpublished Writings of Gertrude Stein, volume 1. Rpt., Freeport, N.Y.: Books for Libraries, 1969.

Useful Knowledge. New York: Payson & Clarke, 1928. Rpt, Barrytown, N.Y.: Station Hill Press, 1988. Foreword by Edward Burns and introduction by Keith Waldrop.

A Village Are You Ready Yet Not Yet A Play In Four Acts. Paris: Galerie Simon (Daniel-Henry Kahnweiler), 1928. Lithographs by Elie Lascaux.

Wars I Have Seen. New York: Random House, 1945.

A Wedding Bouquet. London: J. & W. Chester, 1938. Ballet with chorus: music by Gerald Hugh Tyrwhitt-Wilson, Lord Berners, words by Gertrude Stein.

What Are Masterpieces. Los Angeles: Conference Press, 1940, with a foreword by Robert Bartlett Haas. Rpt., New York: Pitman Publishing, 1970, with an afterword by Robert Bartlett Haas.

The World Is Round. New York: William R. Scott, 1939, with pictures by Clement Hurd; new edition, New York: Young Scott Books, 1967; rpt., San Francisco: North Point Press, 1988, with an afterword by Edith Thatcher Hurd.

——. London: B. T. Batsford, 1939, with illustrations by Sir Francis Rose. Rpt., New York: Haskell House, 1965.

Appendix XI.

Principal Works of Thornton Wilder

[Note: Citations in the notes are to the first printed edition or to specific collections. This bibliography does not include all reprints or list all periodical publications.]

The Alcestiad, or A Life in the Sun. A Play in Three Acts with A Satyr Play The Drunken Sisters. New York: Harper & Row, 1977. Foreword by Isabel Wilder.
——. New York: Samuel French, 1979. Foreword by Isabel Wilder (different from foreword in Harper & Row edition).
The Alcestiad: An Opera in Three Acts. New York: C. Fischer, 1978. Libretto by Wilder, music by Louise Talma. The premiere of the opera was at Frankfurt am Main, Germany, 2 March 1962.
American Characteristics and Other Essays. New York: Harper & Row, 1979. Edited by Donald Gallup with a foreword by Isabel Wilder. Included are Wilder's introductions to Stein's *Narration* (1935), *The Geographical History Of America* (1936), and *Four In America* (1947).
The Angel That Troubled the Waters and Other Plays. New York: Coward-McCann, 1928.
The Bridge of San Luis Rey. New York: A. & C. Boni, 1927. Illustrated by Amy Drevenstedt; 1929 reprint illustrated by Rockwell Kent. Rpt., New York: Heritage Press, 1962, with an introduction by Granville Hicks and illustrations by Jean Charlot. Numerous reprints.
The Cabala. New York: A. & C. Boni, 1926. Rpt., New York: Modern Library, 1929, with an introduction by Herbert Gorman; rpt., New York: Washington Square Press, 1954. Numerous reprints.

Childhood: A Comedy in One Act. New York: Samuel French, 1960.

The Eighth Day. New York: Harper & Row, 1967.

Heaven's My Destination. New York: Harper & Bros., 1935. Rpt., Garden City,
    N.Y.: Doubleday (Anchor Books), 1960, introduction by John Henry Raleigh.

The Ides of March. New York: Harper & Bros., 1948; rpt., 1950 with an introduc-
    tion by Brooks Atkinson; rpt., New York: Perennial Library, 1987.

Infancy: A Comedy in One Act. New York: Samuel French, 1961.

*The Journals of Thornton Wilder, 1939–1961, with two scenes of an uncompleted
    play "The Emporium."* New Haven: Yale University Press, 1985. Selected and
    edited by Donald Gallup, foreword by Isabel Wilder.

The Long Christmas Dinner and Other Plays in One Act. New Haven: Yale
    University Press, 1931; New York: Coward-McCann, 1931. Collected in this
    edition are *The Long Christmas Dinner, Queens of France, Pullman Car Hia-
    watha, Love and How to Cure It, Such Things Only Happen In Books, The
    Happy Journey to Trenton and Camden.* Rpt., New York: Avon Books, 1980,
    with an introduction by John Gassner. This edition, with no explanation, omits
    Such Things Only Happen in Books. Each of these plays except *Such Things* is
    available in a Samuel French acting edition.

The Long Christmas Dinner; An Opera in One Act. Mainz: B. Schott's Sohne;
    New York: Schott Music Corp. (Associated Music Publishers), 1961. Libretto by
    Wilder, music and German version by Paul Hindemith. The premiere of the
    opera was at Mannheim, Germany, 20 December 1961.

Lucrèce. Boston: Houghton Mifflin, 1933. Wilder's translation of André Obey's
    play *Le Viol de Lucrèce.*

The Matchmaker. London: Longmans, 1957. In *Three Plays.*

The Merchant of Yonkers. New York: Harper and Bros., 1939.

Our Century: A Play in Three Scenes. New York: Century Association, 1947.

Our Town. New York: Coward-McCann, 1938. Numerous editions. In *Three Plays.*

——. Avon, Conn.: Limited Editions Club, 1974. Introduction by Brooks Atkin-
    son and illustrated by Robert J. Lee.

——. New York: Samuel French, 1939 (includes Wilder's notes).

——. United Artists [1940], Hollywood Home Theatre, 1980. Screenplay by
    Thornton Wilder, Frank Craven, and Harry Chandler. Directed by Sam
    Wood, music by Aaron Copland.

Shadow of a Doubt. Universal Pictures [1942], MCA Home Video, 1988. Screen-
    play by Thornton Wilder, Sally Benson, and Alma Reville. From an original
    story by Gordon McDonell. Directed by Alfred Hitchcock.

The Skin of Our Teeth. New York: Harper & Bros., 1942. In *Three Plays.*

Someone from Assisi. New York: Samuel French, n.d. (photocopy of typescript).

Theophilus North. New York: Harper & Row, 1973. Rpt. as *Mr. North*, New York:
    Carroll & Graff, 1988.

*Three Novels: A Thornton Wilder Trio: The Cabala, The Bridge of San Luis Rey,
    The Woman of Andros.* New York: Criterion Books, 1956. Introduction by Mal-
    colm Cowley.

Three Plays: Our Town, The Skin of Our Teeth, The Matchmaker. New York: Harper & Bros., 1957. With a preface by Wilder. Rpt., New York: Bantam Books, 1958, with illustrations by Alex Tsao; rpt., New York: Avon Books, 1976; rpt., New York: Perennial Library, 1985.

The Woman of Andros. New York: A. & C. Boni, 1930.

The Wreck on the Five-Twenty-Five. Yale Review 82, 1 (October 1991): 17–41. Introductory note by Donald Gallup.

ESSAYS AND LECTURES

[Periodical publications are fully cited in the notes except for the following.]

Wilder, Thornton. In *Le Destin Prochain des Lettres.* Paris: Société des Nations, Institut International de Coopération Intellectuelle, 1938. See 30–32, 80–81, and 267–70.

——. "*Our Town*—From Stage to Screen: A Correspondence between Thornton Wilder and Sol Lesser," in *Theatre Arts* 24, 11 (November 1940): 815–23. A shortened version is reprinted in *Theatre Arts Anthology: A Record and a Prophecy 1916–1948,* edited by Rosamond Gilder, Hermine Rich Isaacs, Robert M. MacGregor, and Edward Reed. New York: Theatre Arts Books: Robert M. MacGregor, 1950, 363–78.

——. "Mr. Thornton Wilder Interprets," in *Time and Tide* 22, 41 (11 October 1941), 863. Extracts from Wilder's speech of 1 October 1941 before the English-Speaking Union, London, England.

——. "Thornton Wilder—E. S. U. Luncheon," in *The English Speaking World,* 23, 11 (November 1941): 274–76. Same as above, extracts from Wilder's speech of 1 October 1941 before the English-Speaking Union, London, England.

——. "The Duty of the Writer," in *Writers in Freedom, A Symposium Based on the XVII International Congress of P.E.N. Club Held in London September, 1941,* ed. Hermon Ould, 36 37. London: Hutchinson, 1942.

Bibliography

[Note: Works fully documented in a note are not repeated here.]

Abdy, Jane, and Charlotte Gere. *The Souls: An Elite in English Society, 1885–1930*. London: Sidgwick & Jackson, 1984.

Adler, Mortimer J. *Philosopher at Large: An Intellectual Autobiography*. New York: Macmillan, 1977.

Aldrich, Mildred. *A Hilltop on the Marne; being letters written June 3–September 8, 1914*. Boston & New York: Houghton Mifflin, 1915.

———. *Told in a French Garden; August 1914*. Boston: Small, Maynard, 1916.

———. *On the Edge of the War Zone; From the Battle of the Marne to the Entrance of the Stars and Stripes*. Boston: Small, Maynard, 1917.

———. *Peak of the Lead; the waiting months on the hilltop from the entrance of the Stars and Stripes to the second victory of the Marne*. Boston: Small, Maynard, 1918.

———. *When Johnny Comes Marching Home*. Boston: Small, Maynard, 1919.

———. "Confessions of a Breadwinner." Unpublished autobiography, Schlesinger Library, Radcliffe College.

Ardrey, Robert. *Plays of Three Decades*. New York: Atheneum, 1963.

———. "The Education of Robert Ardrey: An Autobiography." Unpublished manuscript (1979), Department of Special Collections, Rutgers University, New Brunswick, New Jersey.

Ashmore, Harry S. *Unseasonable Truths: The Life of Robert Maynard Hutchins*. Boston: Little, Brown, 1989.

Atkinson, Brooks. *Broadway Scrapbook*. New York: Theatre Arts, 1947.

Bankhead, Tallulah. *Tallulah: My Autobiography*. New York: Harper and Brothers, 1952.

Barnes, Eric Wollencott. *The Man Who Lived Twice: The Biography of Edward Sheldon.* New York: Charles Scribner's Sons, 1956.

Barney, Natalie Clifford, ed. *In Memory of Dorothy Ierne Wilde "Oscaria."* Privately printed, 1951.

Bennett, Melba Berry. *The Stone Mason of Tor House: The Life and Work of Robinson Jeffers.* Los Angeles: Ward Ritchie Press, 1966.

Bibliothèque Nationale, Paris. *Jouvet, Dullin, Baty, Pitoëff: Le Cartel.* Exhibition Catalogue. Paris: Bibliothèque Nationale, 1987.

Blank, Martin. "Thornton Wilder: A Broadway Production History," in *Theatre History Studies* 5 (1985): 57–71.

Bridgman, Richard. *Gertrude Stein in Pieces.* New York: Oxford University Press, 1970.

Bryer, Jackson R., ed. *Conversations with Thornton Wilder.* Jackson: University of Mississippi Press, 1992.

Burns, Edward, ed. *The Letters of Gertrude Stein and Carl Van Vechten: 1913–1946.* 2 vols. New York: Columbia University Press, 1986.

Butcher, Fanny. *Many Lives—One Love.* New York: Harper & Row, 1972.

Camfield, William A. *Francis Picabia: His Art, Life, and Times.* Princeton: Princeton University Press, 1979.

Campbell, Joseph, and Henry Morton Robinson. "The Skin of Whose Teeth?" in *Saturday Review of Literature.* Part I, "The Strange Case of Mr. Wilder's New Play and 'Finnegans Wake,'" 19 December 1942, 3–4; Part II, "The Intention Behind the Deed," 13 February 1943, 16, 18–19.

Chute, Marchette. *P.E.N. American Center: A History of the First Fifty Years.* New York: P.E.N American Center, 1972.

Clurman, Harold. *The Fervent Years: The Group Theatre and the Thirties.* New York: Alfred A. Knopf, 1975.

Coley, Thomas. *"Our Town" Remembered.* New York: Hudson Rudd, 1982.

Cooper, Douglas. *Juan Gris: Catalogue raisonné de l'oeuvre peint.* Etabli avec la collaboration de Margaret Potter, 2 vols. Paris: Berggruen Editeur, 1977.

Edelstein, J. M., comp. *A Bibliographic Checklist of the Writings of Thornton Wilder.* New Haven: Yale University Library, 1959.

Faÿ, Bernard. *De la prison de ce monde. Journal, prières et pensées, 1944–1952.* 1952; Rev. ed., Paris: Plon, 1974.

——. *Les Précieux.* Paris: Librairie Académique Perrin, 1966.

Fouché, Pascal. *L' Édition Française sous l'Occupation; 1940–1944.* 2 vols. Paris: Bibliothèque de Littérature française contemporaine de l'Université Paris 7, 1987.

Freud, Sigmund. *The Diary of Sigmund Freud, 1929–1939: A Record of the Final Decade.* Translated, annotated, with an introduction by Michael Molnar. New York: Scribner's, 1992.

Gallup, Donald. "The Gertrude Stein Collection," in *Yale University Library Gazette,* 22, 2 (October 1947): 21–32.

——, ed. *The Flowers of Friendship. Letters Written to Gertrude Stein*. New York: Alfred A. Knopf, 1953.

——. "Gertrude Stein and 'The Atlantic,'" in *Yale University Library Gazette*, 28, 3 (January 1954): 109–28.

——. *Pigeons on the Granite: Memories of a Yale Librarian*. New Haven: Beinecke Rare Book and Manuscript Library, Yale University, 1988.

Gallup, Donald C., and Robert Bartlett Haas. *A Catalogue of the Published and Unpublished Writings of Gertrude Stein*. New Haven: Yale University Library, 1941.

Genin, Paul. *Les Richesse réelles*. Paris: Sirey, 1941.

——. *Essai sur le chaos: mon livre de pourquoi*. Algiers, Algeria: Éditions Charlot, 1945.

Gervasi, Frank. "The Liberation of Gertrude Stein." *Saturday Review* 54 (21 August 1971): 13–14, 57.

——. *The Violent Decade*. New York and London: W. W. Norton, 1989.

Goldstone, Richard H. *Thornton Wilder: An Intimate Portrait*. New York: Saturday Review Press/E. P. Dutton, 1975.

——, and Gary Anderson. *Thornton Wilder: An Annotated Bibliography of Works by and about Thornton Wilder*. New York: AMS Press, 1982.

Gordon, Ruth. *Myself among Others*. New York: Atheneum, 1971.

——. *My Side: The Autobiography of Ruth Gordon*. New York: Harper & Row, 1976.

Gottfried, Martin, *Jed Harris, The Curse of Genius*. Boston: Little, Brown, 1984.

Green, Martin. *Mountain of Truth: The Counterculture Begins, Ascona, 1900–1920*. Hanover and London: Tufts University, University Press of New England, 1986.

Harris, Jed. *Watchman, What of the Night? An Episode Out of a Fabulous Broadway Career*. Garden City, N.Y.: Doubleday, 1963.

——. *A Dance on the High Wire. Recollections of a Time and Temperament*. New York: Crown, 1979.

Harrison, Gilbert. *The Enthusiast: A Life of Thornton Wilder*. New Haven and New York: Ticknor & Fields, 1983.

Hause, Steven C., with Anne R. Kenney. *Women's Suffrage and Social Politics in the French Third Republic*. Princeton: Princeton University Press, 1984.

Hayes, Helen, with Lewis Funke. *A Gift of Joy*. New York: M. Evans, 1965.

Hort, Jean. *La Vie Hérpïque des Pitoëff*. Geneva: Éditions Pierre Cailler, 1966.

Huesmann, Heinrich. *Welttheater Reinhardt*. Munich: Prestel-Verlag, 1983.

Hutchins, Robert Maynard. *No Friendly Voice*. Chicago: University of Chicago Press, 1936.

Imbs, Bravig. *Confessions of Another Young Man*. New York: Henkle-Yewdale House, 1936.

Kaufman, Beatrice, and Joseph Hennessey, eds. *The Letters of Alexander Woollcott*. New York: Viking, 1944.

Kazan, Elia. *Elia Kazan: A Life*. New York: Alfred A. Knopf, 1988.

Kellner, Bruce, ed. *Letters of Carl Van Vechten*. New Haven: Yale University Press, 1987.

——. *A Gertrude Stein Companion: Content with the Example*. New York: Greenwood Press, 1988.

Lachenal, François. *Editions des Trois Collines: Genève—Paris*. Paris: IMEC Éditions, 1995.

Leider, Emily Wortis. *California's Daughter: Gertrude Atherton and Her Times*. Stanford: Stanford University Press, 1991.

Lifton, Paul. *"Vast Encyclopedia": The Theatre of Thornton Wilder*. Westport, Conn.: Greenwood Press, 1995.

Lochner, Louis P. *Fritz Kreisler*. New York: Macmillan, 1952.

Lowe, Victor. *Alfred North Whitehead: The Man and His Work*. 2 vols. Baltimore: Johns Hopkins University Press, vol. I, 1985; vol. 2, edited by J. B. Schneewiind, 1990.

Luhan, Mabel Dodge. *Intimate Memories*. 4 vols. New York: Harcourt, Brace, 1933–37. Vol. 1: *Background* (1933); Vol. 2: *European Experiences* (1935); Vol. 3: *Movers and Shakers* (1936); Vol. 4: *Edge of the Taos Desert* (1937).

MacKenzie, Jeanne. *The Children of the Souls: A Tragedy of the First World War*. London: Chatto & Windus, 1986.

McLeod, Kirsty. *A Passion for Friendship: Sibyl Colefax and Her Circle*. London: Michael Joseph, 1991.

Moad, Rosalind. *"1914–1916: Years of Innovation in Gertrude Stein's Writing."* Dissertation, University of York, England, 1993.

Neuman, Shirley, and Ira B. Nadel, eds. *Gertrude Stein and the Making of Literature*. London: Macmillan Press, 1988.

Ould, Hermon, ed. *Writers in Freedom: A Symposium Based on the XVII International Congress of P.E.N. Club Held in London, September 1941*. London: Hutchinson, 1942.

Pearson, Norman Holmes. *"The Gertrude Stein Collection," Yale University Library Gazette* 1b, 3 (January 1942): 45–47.

Pétain, Philippe. *Paroles aux Français: messages et écrits, 1934–1941*. Lyon: H. Lardanchet, 1941.

Picasso, Pablo. *Picasso écrits*. Préface de Michel Leiris; textes établies, présentés et annotés par Marie-Laure Bernadac et Christine Piot; texts en espagnol traduits par Albert Benoussan. Paris: Réunion des musées nationaux; Gallimard, 1989.

Preminger, Marion Mill. *All I Want Is Everything*. New York: Funk & Wagnalls, 1957.

Prokosch, Frederick. *Voices, A Memoir*. New York: Farrar, Straus, Giroux, 1983.

Puche, Michel. *Edmond Charlot, éditeur*. Préface de Jules Roy. Pézenas, France: Domens Éditions, 1995.

Rather, Lois. *Gertrude Stein and California*. Oakland: Rather Press, 1974.

Reinhardt, Gottfried. *The Genius: A Memoir of Max Reinhardt by His Son.* New York: Alfred A. Knopf, 1979.

Robinson, David. *Chaplin: His Life and Art.* New York: McGraw-Hill, 1985.

Rogers, William Garland. *When This You See Remember Me: Gertrude Stein in Person.* 1948. Rpt., New York: Discus Books/Avon, 1973.

———. *Wise Men Fish Here: The Story of Frances Steloff and The Gotham Book Mart.* New York: Harcourt, Brace & World, 1968.

———. *Ladies Bountiful.* New York: Harcourt, Brace & World, 1968.

———.*Gertrude Stein Is Gertrude Stein Is Gertrude Stein: Her Life and Work.* Children's biography. New York: Crowell, 1973.

Rudnick, Lois Palken. *Mabel Dodge Luhan: New Woman, New Worlds.* Albuquerque: University of New Mexico Press, 1984.

Schimanski, Stefan, and Henry Treece, eds. *Transformation Three.* London: Lindsay Drummon, 1945.

Schorer, Mark. *Sinclair Lewis: An American Life.* New York: McGraw-Hill, 1961.

Sevarcid, Eric. *Not So Wild A Dream.* 1946; Rpt., New York: Atheneum, 1976.

Simon, Linda. *Thornton Wilder: His World.* Garden City, N.Y.: Doubleday, 1979.

Steward, Samuel. *Angels on the Bough.* Caldwell, Idaho: Caxton Printers, 1936.

———, ed. *Dear Sammy: Letters from Gertrude Stein and Alice B. Toklas.* Edited with a Memoir by Samuel M. Steward. Boston: Houghton Mifflin, 1977.

Thomson, Virgil. *Virgil Thomson* New York: Alfred A. Knopf, 1966.

———. *A Virgil Thomson Reader.* With an introduction by John Rockwell. Boston: Houghton Mifflin, 1981.

Toklas, Alice B. *The Alice B. Toklas Cook Book.* 1954. Rpt., New York: Harper & Row, 1984, with a foreword by M. F. K. Fisher and a publisher's note by Simon Michael Bessie.

———. *What Is Remembered.* 1963. Rpt., Berkeley, Calif.: North Point Press, 1985.

———. *Staying On Alone: Letters of Alice B. Toklas.* New York: Liveright, 1973. Edited by Edward Burns with an introduction by Gilbert Harrison.

Truffaut, François. *Hitchcock.* Rev. ed., New York: Touchstone Book, Simon & Schuster, 1985.

Ulrich, Conrad. *Der Lesezirkel Hottingen.* Zurich: Buchverlag Berichthaus, 1981.

Ulrich, Dorothy. "Thornton Wilder, A Classic of Tomorrow." *Avocations* 1, 3 (December 1937): 248–255; "Thornton Wilder Bibliography," 289–91.

———. "Thornton Wilder; Professor and Playwright." *University of Chicago Magazine* 30, 6 (April 1938): 7–9.

———. "SOLD, A Classic of the Future?" *Avocations* 2, 2 (May 1938): 158–61.

———. "Take Your Avocations on a Trip." *Avocations* 3, 4 (January 1939): 250–54.

———. "Gertrude Stein in Summer." *Avocations* 3, 5 (February 1939): 309–15.

Walsh, Claudette, comp. *Thornton Wilder: A Reference Guide, 1926–1990.* New York: G. K. Hall, 1993.

Weiss, Louise. *Combats Pour Les Femmes: 1934–1939. Mémoires d'une Européenne.* Vol. 3. Paris: Albin Michel, 1990.

White, Eric Walter. *Stravinsky: The Composer and His Works.* 2d ed., Berkeley and Los Angeles: University of California Press, 1979.

White, Ray Lewis, ed. *Sherwood Anderson/Gertrude Stein: Correspondence and Personal Essays.* Chapel Hill: University of North Carolina Press, 1972.

——, comp. *Gertrude Stein and Alice B. Toklas: A Reference Guide.* Boston: G. K. Hall, 1984.

Whitehead, Alfred North. *Process and Reality: An Essay in Cosmology.* New York: Macmillan, and Cambridge: University of Cambridge Press, 1929. Corrected edition, ed. by David Ray Griffin and Donald W. Sherburne, New York: Free Press, 1978.

Wilcox, Wendell. "A Note on Stein and Abstraction." *Poetry,* 55, 5 (February 1940): 254–57. Reprinted in *Gertrude Stein Advanced: An Anthology of Criticism,* ed. Richard Kostelanetz, 105–07. Jefferson, N.C.: McFarland, 1990.

——. *Everything Is Quite All Right.* New York: Bernard Ackerman, 1945.

——. "La Véritable Stein (Excerpts 1938)." In *Gertrude Stein Advanced: An Anthology of Criticism,* ed. Richard Kostelanetz, 190–203. Jefferson, N.C.: McFarland, 1990.

Wilder, Charlotte. *Phases of the Moon.* New York: Coward-McCann, 1936.

——. *Mortal Sequence.* New York: Coward-McCann, 1939.

Wilder, Isabel. *Mother and Four.* New York: Coward-McCann, 1933.

——. *Heart Be Still.* New York: Coward-McCann, 1934.

——. *Let Winter Go.* New York: Coward-McCann, 1937.

Wilson, Edmund. *Classics and Commercials.* 1950. Rpt., New York: Vintage Books, 1962.

Wilson, Robert A., comp. *Gertrude Stein: A Bibliography.* New York: Phoenix Bookshop, 1974. References in the notes are to this edition.

——, assisted by Arthur Uphill. *Gertrude Stein: A Bibliography.* Rockville, Md.: Quill & Brush, 1994. Revised and expanded version of the 1974 bibliography.

Woollcott, Alexander. *Long, Long Ago.* New York: Viking Press, 1943.

Zaller, Robert. *The Cliffs of Solitude: A Reading of Robinson Jeffers.* Cambridge: Cambridge University Press, 1983.

Index of Names and Works by
Gertrude Stein and Thornton Wilder

Guinsburg, Harold, 10*n*
Guthrie, Tyrone (1900–1971), 326*n*

Haas, Robert Bartlett (b. 1916), xxiii, 145*n*, 172,
    173*n*, 182, 183*n*, 218, 231*n*, 254, 255, 257*n*, 259*n*,
    263, 264*n*, 265–67, 268*n*, 401
Halleck, Fitz-Greene (1790–1867), 128*n*
Hamilton, John, 189*n*, 238
Hammett, Dashiell (1894–1961), 20*n*, 349, 354
Hand, Mr. & Mrs. Frederick, 347
Handel, George Frederick (1685–1759), xxv, 9,
    16, 50*n*, 356
The Happy Journey to Trenton and Camden
    (Wilder, in *The Long Christmas Dinner*), 15,
    165*n*, 257*n*
Harcourt, Alfred (1881–1954), 69, 82
Harden, Elmer, 194, 195*n*
Hardwicke, Cedric (1893–1964), 132
Hardy, Robert, 326*n*
Harms, Carl, 363
Harper, Paul, 85*n*
Harris, Jed (1900–1979), xxiv, xxvi, 23*n*, 35*n*, 89,
    111*n*, 113*n*, 132*n*, 135*n*, 141, 143*n*, 191, 192*n*–
    194*n*, 197, 198, 206–08, 210, 217*n*, 291, 293*n*,
    314, 315*n*, 369–75, 377–81, 386, 388, 390
Harris, Jones Kelly (b. 1929), 89, 371
Harris, Maj. Richard, 387
Harris, Sam H. (1872–1941), 390
Harrison Smith, 309*n*
Hart, Moss (1904–1961), 250*n*, 261*n*
Harvey, Helen, 347
Hatcliffe, William, 207*n*
Hauke, César Mange de (1900–1965), 418
Hauptmann, Gerhard (1862–1946), 354
Hawthorne, Nathaniel (1804–1864), 129*n*
Hayes, Helen (1900–1993), 34, 35*n*, 121*n*, 385,
    389
Haynes, Owen, 362
Healy, John Vincent, 235*n*
Heaven's My Destination (Wilder), xvi, xx, 7*n*,
    10*n*, 11*n*, 18*n*, 70*n*, 96, 371
Hecht, Ben (1894–1964), 370
Hecht, Lucille, 337
Heflin, Frances, 389
Hegel, Friedrich (1770–1831), 53*n*
"Helen Button A Story Of Wartime" (Stein, in
    Paris France), 250*n*
"The Hell of the Vizier Kabaar" (Wilder, un-
    finished play in YCAL), 369, 373
Hellman, Lillian (1906–1964), 20*n*, 349
Helpman, Robert Murray (1908–1986), 144*n*
Hemingway, Ernest (1899–1961), xvi, 122, 128,
    129*n*, 173, 418
"Henry James" (Stein, in *Four In America*), 217*n*

Henry VIII (1491–1547), 232*n*
Hepburn, Katharine (b. 1909), 105*n*
Herriot, Edouard (1872–1957), 158
Heyward, Dorothy (1890–1961), 379
Heyward, Du Bose (1885–1940), 346
Hickes, Ford, 247*n*, 262*n*
Hitchcock, Alfred (1899–1980), 256*n*, 325*n*, 377,
    378, 388, 389
Hitler, Adolf (1889–1945), 84, 85*n*, 117*n*, 140*n*,
    277, 403, 414
Hobart, John, 315*n*
Hobhouse, Janet (d. 1991), 412
Hocking, William Ernest (1873–1966), 84, 86*n*,
    87
Hofmannsthal, Alice von (1902–1956), 298
Hofmannsthal, Hugo von (1874–1929), 166*n*,
    175*n*
Hofmannsthal, Raimund von (1906–1974), 166
Hokinson, Helen (1894–1949), 395
Holmes, Oliver Wendell (1809–1894), 324*n*
"Homage to P. G. Wodehouse" (Wilder, un-
    finished play in YCAL), 142*n*, 147*n*, 369, 373
Homer, 122, 292
Hopkins, Arthur (1878–1950), 23*n*, 397
Hopkins, Miriam (1902–1972), 340, 351
Horner, Frances Graham Lady (1858–1940),
    230, 231*n*, 232*n*, 236
Horner, Jack, 230, 232*n*
Horney, Dr. Karen (1885–1952), 256*n*
Horowitz, Vladimir (1904–1989), 103
Hotson, John Leslie (1887–1992), 206, 207*n*
How To Write (Stein), 83, 209, 352, 402
"How Writing Is Written" (Stein), 344, 350
How Writing Is Written (Stein), 13*n*, 105*n*, 107*n*,
    129*n*, 314*n*
Howells, William Dean (1837–1920), 131*n*
Hoyt, Charles, 228*n*
Hoyt, Edwin P., 209*n*
Hu Shih (1891–1962), 297*n*
Huebsch, Benjamin W. (1876–1964), 400
Hughes, Thomas (1822–1896), 113*n*
Hugnet, Georges (1906–1974), 54*n*, 214*n*, 240*n*
Hugo, Victor (1802–1885), 240*n*
Hull, Cordell (1871–1955), 276*n*, 282, 283*n*
Hunt, James Henry Leigh (1784–1859), 273*n*
Hurd, Clement, 232*n*
Hurley, Prof. L. B., 82*n*
Hutchins, Anna Laura Murch (mother), 122,
    123*n*
Hutchins, Frances (b. 1926), 9, 92
Hutchins, Joanna Blessings (b. 1936), 92, 93*n*,
    122, 213
Hutchins, Maude (1889–?), 92, 113*n*, 182, 255,
    258, 272, 342

INDEX

450 INDEX

Sterossebsky, Maj., 120
Stettheimer, Florine (1871–1944), 344
Steward, Samuel Morris (1909–1993), 168–172, 173*n*, 175, 176*n*, 177, 178, 185, 194, 211, 212*n*, 221, 222*n*, 223*n*, 239, 241–243, 244*n*, 262*n*, 264, 265*n*, 267, 268*n*, 275, 291, 293*n*, 309*n*, 337
Stewart, Rosalie, 388
Stickels, W. L., 94*n*
Still, Dr. Joseph, 316, 317
Stock, Frederick (1872–1942), 22*n*
Stockton, Frank R. (1834–1902), 258
Stokowski, Leopold (1887–1977), 380
Stout, Rex (1886–1975), 299*n*
Strange, Michael (1890–1950), 350
"Stranger Things Have Happened." See *The Merchant of Yonkers*
Strasberg, Lee (1901–1982), 248*n*
Stratemeyer, Edward (pseud. Arthur M. Winfield, 1863–1930), 40*n*
Strauss, Johann (1825–1899), 220*n*
Stravinsky, Igor (1882–1971), 9, 10*n*, 103
Strömgen, Bengt, 105*n*
Sturges, Preston (1898–1959), 105*n*
Sullivan, Noel, 350
Sulzberger, Cyrus Leo (b. 1912), 323*n*
"Sundays And Tuesdays." See "The Winner Loses"
"Superstitions" (Stein, in *Ida A Novel*), 240*n*
Swift, Jonathan (1667–1745), 86*n*

Tal, E. P., 167*n*
Tal, Lucy (1887–?), 163, 373
Talmadge, Gov. Eugene, 87*n*
Tanner, Allan (1898–1989), 214*n*
Tappan, Arthur (1786–1865), 259*n*
Tarski, Alfred, 135*n*
Tavernier, René (1915–1989), 117*n*, 308*n*, 318*n* 415, 418, 419, 420, 421
Taylor, Prentiss (1907–1991), 134*n*, 135*n*, 334, 336
Tchelitchew, Pavel ("Pavlik," 1898–1957), 214*n*
Tender Buttons (Stein, in *Selected Writings, Look At Me Now*), 83, 184*n*
Tessan, François de, 158*n*
Testimony Against Gertrude Stein (pamphlet), 234
Thackeray, William Makepeace (1811–1863), 217
Thalberg, Irving G. (1899–1936), 115, 116*n*
Theophilus North (Wilder), xviii
Thimig, Helene (1889–1974), 257*n*
Thompson, Daniel, 213, 214*n*
Thompson, Denman (1833–1911), 269*n*
Thomson, Charles, 293*n*

Thomson, Virgil (1896–1989), xv, 43, 181, 214*n*, 240*n*, 275, 276*n*, 323*n*, 340, 341, 351
Three Lives (Stein), 83, 114*n*, 209, 334, 340, 349
Tilstrom, Burr (1917–1985), 363
Tito, Marshall Josip Broz (1892–1980), 315*n*
"To Do: A Book Of Alphabets And Birthdays" (Stein, in *Alphabets And Birthdays*), xx, 265, 266*n*, 270*n*, 309*n*, 402, 403
Tolstoy, Leo (1828–1910), 34*n*
Tonny, Kristians (1906/07–?), 214*n*
"Top of the World." See *The Ides of March*
Toscanini, Arturo (1867–1957), 44, 46, 47*n*, 49, 50*n*, 149, 175*n*, 229, 231*n*
Toulouse, Roger, 194
"Tourty Or Tortebatte. A Story Of The Great War" (Stein, in *Geography And Plays, A Stein Reader*), 211*n*
Trac, Nugyen, 130*n*
Tracy, Spencer (1900–1967), 397
Trollope, Anthony (1815–1882), 213, 217
Troubetzkoy, Amelie Rives, 345
Troxell, Gilbert McCoy (1893–1967), 165*n*
Truffaut, François (1932–1984), 388, 389
Tunney, James Joseph (Gene, 1898–1978), 9, 11*n*, 39*n*
Tura, Cosimo (1430–1510), 32
Tyler, William R., 318*n*
Tzara, Tristan (1896–1963), 234*n*

Ulrich, Conrad, 183*n*
Ulrich, Dorothy Livingston, 223, 224
Useful Knowledge (Stein), 13*n*, 83
Utrillo, Maurice (1883–1953), 157*n*

Valéry, Paul (1871–1945), 145, 148, 149*n*, 156, 158, 201
Van der Meulen, Pierre, 270*n*, 275*n*, 282*n*
Van Dongen, Kees (1877–1968), 132, 135*n*
Van Doren, Carl (1885–1950), 298, 299*n*, 305
Van Tuyl, Marian, 358
Van Vechten, Carl (1880–1964), xv, xxi, xxiv, 12*n*, 20*n*, 22*n*, 23*n*, 25, 29*n*, 34*n*, 39*n*, 47*n*, 51, 54*n*, 65*n*, 67, 68*n*, 69, 71*n*, 73, 74*n*, 79, 96, 106*n*, 114*n*, 134*n*, 136*n*, 140*n*, 168*n*, 176*n*, 181, 229, 231*n*, 232*n*, 246, 253, 261, 262*n*, 266*n*, 275, 286*n*, 288*n*, 309*n*, 323*n*, 331*n*, 333, 334, 337, 339–346, 349–351, 353, 402, 403, 410, 418
Van Vechten, Fania. See Marinoff, Fania
Varden, Evelyn, 315*n*
Vega, Lope de (1562–1635), 57*n*, 175
Verdi, Giuseppe (1813–1901), 46, 47*n*, 50*n*, 149
Verissimo, Erico (1905–1975), 288*n*
Vermeer, Jan (1632–1675), 57

JAN 1997

DATE DUE